The Hamlyn A-Z of British
FOOTBALL RECORDS

COMPLETELY REVISED SECOND EDITION

Phil Soar

HAMLYN

ACKNOWLEDGEMENTS

I should like to acknowledge the help and assistance of the following in compiling this material: Forrest Robertson, author of *Mackinlay's A–Z of Scottish Football*, who was responsible for researching and authenticating the Scottish League tables, and for authenticating other Scottish material in the book; Ian Laschke, author of *Rothmans Book of Football League Records 1888–1979*, who kindly provided dates and venues for Third Division games and whose book is essential for any football statistician; Adrian Titcombe of the Football Association for providing the dates and results of numerous FA Cup matches; Norman Epps for invaluable information on Corinthian-Casuals; Cyril George and Patrick Woods, on Celtic's prewar results and, in particular, on that club's record undefeated run; George Peat, secretary of Airdrieonians FC; Grant Cullen, programme editor for Albion Rovers; J. Sneddon of Dundee FC; Andrew Wilkie for information on East Fife FC; Robert McCutcheon for vital information on some early Scottish Cup incidents; G. Allison for providing detailed information on Kilmarnock FC; Robert McElroy for detailing

Rangers prewar match records; Brian Weir for keeping me informed of all records established in Northern Ireland; and I should also like to mention Peter Corrigan and Malcolm Brodie for their invaluable histories of (respectively) Welsh and Irish football. I must also mention Lionel Francis, for access to his magnificent library, and Martin Tyler, for use of his personal collection of early material. Others who have contributed vital corrections and additional facts are Tim Carder, David Marshall, Lars-Olof Wendler, A.E. Beagley, Gordon Smailes of the A.F.S and, via his excellent club histories, Norman Lovett. I would like to thank several members of the Association of Football Statisticians, an organisation devoted to the long overdue codification of the game's history, and the authors, editors and publishers of the four titles that are essential features on the desk of any statistician, viz: Jack Rollin's annual *Rothmans Football Yearbook* (Queen Anne Press/Macdonald Futura), Ian Laschke's *Rothmans Book of Football League Records* (Queen Anne Press/Macdonald Futura), Maurice Golesworthy's *The Encyclopedia of Association Football* (Robert Hale) and Forrest Robertson's *Mackinlay's A–Z of Scottish Football* (Macdonald Publishers, Lonehead).

Editor: Richard Widdows
Art Editor: Phil Bush
Tables compiled by Forrest Robertson and Richard Widdows

First published in 1981
Revised edition published in 1984 by
The Hamlyn Group Limited
London ● New York ● Sydney ● Toronto
Astronaut House, Feltham, Middlesex, England
Copyright © Hastings Hilton Publishers Limited
  1981, 1982, 1983, 1984
ISBN 0 600 34728 1

Printed and bound by Graficromo s.a., Cordoba, Spain

Introduction to Second Edition

Welcome to the revised and updated second edition of the Hamlyn A–Z of British Football Records. With over 1000 new, additional or updated references, the A–Z can again claim to be *the* authoritative guide to all of the records established in the first 120 years of organised football in the countries that gave the world its favourite sport.

Inevitably the compilation of a book of this sort presents special problems, not the least being that of space. It has been necessary in many instances to abbreviate seasons, from 1921–22 to 1922 as an example. Any researcher finds that there are numerous discrepancies in the recording of international matches over the years – their dates, results and, on occasions, whether they were played at all – and many of these discrepancies arise from wrongly dated newspaper reports of the period. Classification of what is or is not an official international remains a constant problem, one which we have tried to solve with different gradations of international in the tables. For instance, in our view the first England v Scotland and Scotland v Wales games cannot really be viewed as 'official' internationals. There are numerous unanswerable disputes about the status of FA Select XIs, or 'Commonwealth' teams; even in very recent times the FA decided to award full caps to England teams in Australia and Iceland when they were clearly 'B' squads.

There is the perennial problem of record wins and defeats – is 10-3 better than 9-1, for instance? In general, we have taken wins to reflect attacking performance, and have hence gone for the highest number of goals, no matter how many were conceded. Similarly, a defeat is a record of defensive frailty. Substitutes have lately become a major source of dispute. Our guide has been that substitutes should usually be recorded if they play in a game, but not if they don't. Many records, of course, are only correct up to the date of going to press. We have indicated these with an appropriate date at which the record was accurate.

We have always tried to use contemporary names in specific instances, and in the tabular sections have used the name a club was playing under at that time. In the League tables we have *not* included a club's suffix (e.g. Norwich *City*, Derby *County*) where that town has only one first – class club and there is no danger of any confusion. We have included suffixes where a town has now, or has had, more than one club, and have tried to indicate when a club was using a different suffix (e.g. Millwall Athletic, Chesterfield Town). Lastly, we have tried to use popular names rather than formal names or initials (e.g. Bill rather than William, Rangers rather than Glasgow Rangers).

The other major clarification should be on what constitutes a senior game. By and large these records refer only to Football and Scottish League fixtures, FA Cup and Scottish Cup ties from the first round proper, Football League Cup and Scottish League Cup games, the Charity Shield, the three major European tournaments and the European Super Cup. Where there are exceptions, these are made clear.

We have also attempted, we believe for the first time, to put exact dates on all incidents recorded. With very few exceptions we have rejected all records, suppositions and assumptions, even if previously published, where we cannot put an exact date on an incident or a sequence. We have given days of the week for almost all games, except where the date is obvious (Cup finals are always played on a Saturday) or where repetition would be tedious. The reader can assume that any date for which the day is not given is a Saturday. In the first edition of the A–Z I asked readers to write in with any corrections that they noticed, or any additions they could suggest. Well over one hundred did so and I extend the same invitation again. It has been calculated that there are in excess of 150,000 separate items and facts in the following pages and it would be naive to suggest that none can be questioned. Many of the obvious errors have been corrected, but I would still welcome any comments or suggestions.

TITLE PAGE: *The team which established the world record win in a first-class football match — Arbroath, who defeated Bon Accord 36-0 in the first round of the Scottish Cup on Saturday 12 September 1885. John Petrie, who also established the record number of goals for a single player in a single match (13), is seated on the left. It has emerged in recent years that opponents Bon Accord were probably a cricket club called Orion who received the match details by mistake.*

THIS PAGE: *The time is 3pm on Saturday 28 April 1923 and the very first Wembley FA Cup final, between Bolton and West Ham, should be about to kick-off. The counted attendance was eventually 126,047 but the actual crowd was probably in excess of 150,000, making it the largest ever at a football match in Britain, and possibly in excess of 200,000, which would make it the largest for a single sporting event anywhere in the world.*

ENDPAPERS: *Glenn Hoddle's penalty wins the 1982 FA Cup final replay against QPR. It was a remarkable final for several reasons; this was Hoddle's third scoring shot in the four games which made up the 1981 and 1982 finals (though one was deflected), it was the first final since 1938 to be won by a single penalty and was the only Wembley final not to attract a capacity crowd.*

Contents

David Johnson, Jimmy Case, Terry McDermott and Graeme Souness mob Kenny Dalglish after the Liverpool forward had scored against Manchester United during Liverpool's remarkable 1978–79 season. That year they established the effective defensive record for any English League team by conceding only 16 goals. McDermott and Dalglish went on to become the only two players to be awarded both the Sportswriters' Footballer of the Year Award and its PFA equivalent in the same season, while Liverpool went on in the first four seasons of the 1980s to become the first club this century to win four consecutive Cup finals, the first ever to appear in four consecutive Cup finals (in both cases the Milk Cup/Football League Cup) and the first club for half a century to win a hat-trick of League Championships.

Eric Bell heads home Bolton's third goal in the 1953 Cup final. The game resulted in the highest Cup final aggregate (4-3) and is the only time the losers have scored 3.

Aggregates

Overall record: 36 – Arbroath 36 Bon Accord 0, Scottish Cup first round, Saturday 12 September 1885.

English record: 26 – Preston North End 26 Hyde 0, FA Cup first round, Saturday 15 October 1887.

Any League game: 17 – Tranmere 13 Oldham 4, Division 3N, Wednesday 26 December 1934. The only other occasion that a first-class game played under the auspices of the Football League finished with 17 goals was a Third Division South Cup match at Exeter on Wednesday 24 January 1934, when Exeter City beat Crystal Palace 11-6. At this time the Third Divisions organised their own cup competitions in addition to the normal League programme.

Division 1: 14 – Aston Villa 12 Accrington 2 on Saturday 12 March 1892 & Tottenham 10 Everton 4 on Saturday 11 October 1958.

Division 2: 14 – Manchester City 11 Lincoln City 3 on Saturday 23 March 1895.

Division 4: 11 – recorded on six occasions: Hartlepools United 10 Barrow 1 on Saturday 4 April 1959;
Crystal Palace 9 Accrington Stanley 2 on Thursday 20 April 1961;
Wrexham 10 Hartlepools United 1 on Saturday 3 March 1962;
Oldham Athletic 11 Southport 0 on Wednesday 26 December 1962;
Torquay United 8 Newport County 3 on Saturday 19 October 1963;
Shrewsbury Town 7 Doncaster Rovers 4 on Saturday 1 February 1975.

League Cup: 11 – Leyton Orient 9 Chester 2 in the third round on Wednesday 17 Oct 1962.

Scottish League: 16 – Airdrie 15 Dundee Wanderers 1 in Div 2 on 1 December 1894.

Scottish Division 1/Premier: 13 – Heart of Midlothian 10 Queen's Park 3 on Saturday 24 August 1912.

FA Cup final: 7 – Blackburn Rovers 6 The Wednesday 1 in 1890 & Blackpool 4 Bolton Wanderers 3 in 1953.

Scottish Cup final: 7 – Renton 6 Cambuslang 1 in 1888, Celtic 4 Queen's Park 3 in 1900, Hearts 4 Celtic 3 in 1901 & Celtic 6 Hibernian 1 in 1972.

Season: In 1957–58 Manchester City scored 104 goals and conceded 100 in Division 1, the only occasion that a club has both scored and conceded 100 goals in a League season. The record aggregate in a season by one club is 224 (78 for, 146 against) by Edinburgh City in Scottish Division 2 in 1931-32.

Explanations from the Kettering Town attack after an injury to the Stafford Rangers keeper in the 1979 FA Challenge Trophy final at Wembley. Stafford won 2-0 with two Alf Wood goals but later that year, in October 1979, did even better in setting up the Alliance League's record away win with a 6-3 success at Kettering.

The English record is 212 (76 for, 136 against) by Nelson in Division 3N in 1927-28.

Whole League: The most goals scored in a whole season is 6985, recorded by the 92 Football League clubs in 1960-61. Most goals in a single division is obviously confused by the number of clubs in the division etc, but the record is probably the Scottish Second Division in 1956-57 when the 19 teams averaged over 90 goals each. In strict terms, the most goals scored in a single League is the 1855 in Division 2 in 1962-63.
See also: DEFEATS, GOALSCORING, VICTORIES.

Alliance Premier League

Founded in season 1979–80 by the leading clubs in the Southern and Northern Premier Leagues, its primary object was to obtain entry to the Football League for the better non-League sides. It was agreed that the new League would put only one candidate forward for election in any year and so avoid split voting, which had prevented the election of many deserving sides in the past. The name was derived from the Football Alliance set up in 1889 by northern clubs denied entry to the Football League (and won in its 3 seasons before becoming the Second Division by The Wednesday, Stoke and Nottingham Forest). The winners have been as follows;

- 1979-80 Altrincham
- 1980-81 Altrincham
- 1981-82 Runcorn
- 1982-83 Enfield

FA AMATEUR CUP FINALS

Year	Venue	Winners		Runners-up	
1894	Richmond	Old Carthusians	2	Casuals	1
1895	Leeds	Middlesbrough	2	Old Carthusians	1
1896	Leicester	Bishop Auckland	1	R. A. (Portsmouth)	0
1897	Tufnell Park	Old Carthusians	*1	Stockton	1
(R)	Darlington	Old Carthusians	4	Stockton	1
1898	Crystal Palace	Middlesbrough	2	Uxbridge	1
1899	Middlesbrough	Stockton	1	Harwich & Parkeston	0
1900	Leicester	Bishop Auckland	5	Lowestoft Town	1
1901	Harwich	Crook Town	*1	King's Lynn	1
(R)	Ipswich	Crook Town	3	King's Lynn	0
1902	Leeds	Old Malvernians	5	Bishop Auckland	1
1903	Reading	Stockton	*0	Oxford City	0
(R)	Darlington	Stockton	1	Oxford City	0
1904	Bradford	Sheffield	3	Ealing	1
1905	Shepherd's B.	West Hartlepool	3	Clapton	2
1906	Stockton	Oxford City	3	Bishop Auckland	0
1907	Stamford Bridge	Clapton	2	Stockton	1
1908	Bishop Auckland	Royal Engineers (Depot)	2	Stockton	1
1909	Ilford	Clapton	6	Eston United	0
1910	Bishop Auckland	R.M.L.I. (Gosport)	2	South Bank	1
1911	Herne Hill	Bromley	1	Bishop Auckland	0
1912	Middlesbrough	Stockton	*0	Eston United	0
(R)	Middlesbrough	Stockton	1	Eston United	0
1913	Reading	South Bank	*1	Oxford City	1
(R)	Bishop Auckland	South Bank	1	Oxford City	0
1914	Leeds	Bishop Auckland	1	Northern Nomads	0
1915	Millwall	Clapton	1	Bishop Auckland	0
1916–19	Not contested				
1920	Millwall	Dulwich Hamlet	*1	Tufnell Park	0
1921	Middlesbrough	Bishop Auckland	4	Swindon Victoria	2
1922	Middlesbrough	Bishop Auckland	*5	South Bank	2
1923	Crystal Palace	London Caledonians	2	Evesham Town	1
1924	Millwall	Clapton	3	Erith & Belvedere	0
1925	Millwall	Clapton	3	Southall	1
1926	Sunderland	Northern Nomads	7	Stockton	1
1927	Millwall	Leyton	3	Barking Town	1
1928	Middlesbrough	Leyton	3	Cockfield	2
1929	Highbury	Ilford	3	Leyton	1
1930	Upton Park	Ilford	5	Bournemouth Gswks A.	1
1931	Highbury	Wycombe W.	1	Hayes	0
1932	Upton Park	Dulwich Hamlet	7	Marine (Liverpool)	1
1933	Dulwich	Kingstonian	*1	Stockton	1
(R)	Darlington	Kingstonian	4	Stockton	1

Year	Venue	Winners		Runners-up	
1934	Upton Park	Dulwich Hamlet	2	Leyton	1
1935	Middlesbrough	Bishop Auckland	*0	Wimbledon	0
(R)	Stamford Bridge	Bishop Auckland	2	Wimbledon	1
1936	Selhurst Park	Casuals	*1	Ilford	1
(R)	Upton Park	Casuals	2	Ilford	0
1937	Upton Park	Dulwich Hamlet	2	Leyton	0
1938	Millwall	Bromley	1	Erith & Belvedere	0
1939	Sunderland	Bishop Auckland	*3	Willington	0
1940–45	Not contested				
1946	Stamford Bridge	Barnet	3	Bishop Auckland	2
1947	Highbury	Leytonstone	2	Wimbledon	1
1948	Stamford Bridge	Leytonstone	1	Barnet	0
1949	Wembley	Bromley	1	Romford	0
1950	Wembley	Willington	4	Bishop Auckland	0
1951	Wembley	Pegasus	2	Bishop Auckland	1
1952	Wembley	Walthamstow A.	*2	Leyton	1
1953	Wembley	Pegasus	6	Harwich & Parkeston	0
1954	Wembley	Crook Town	*2	Bishop Auckland	2
(R)	Newcastle	Crook Town	*2	Bishop Auckland	2
(SR)	Middlesbro	Crook Town	1	Bishop Auckland	0
1955	Wembley	Bishop Auckland	2	Hendon	0
1956	Wembley	Bishop Auckland	*1	Corinthian Casuals	1
(R)	Middlesbrough	Bishop Auckland	4	Corinthian Casuals	1
1957	Wembley	Bishop Auckland	3	Wycombe Wanderers	1
1958	Wembley	Woking	3	Ilford	0
1959	Wembley	Crook Town	3	Barnet	2
1960	Wembley	Hendon	2	Kingstonian	1
1961	Wembley	Walthamstow A.	2	West Auckland Town	1
1962	Wembley	Crook Town	*1	Hounslow Town	1
(R)	Middlesbrough	Crook Town	4	Hounslow Town	0
1963	Wembley	Wimbledon	4	Sutton United	2
1964	Wembley	Crook Town	2	Enfield	1
1965	Wembley	Hendon	3	Whitby Town	1
1966	Wembley	Wealdstone	3	Hendon	1
1967	Wembley	Enfield	*0	Skelmersdale United	0
(R)	Maine Road	Enfield	3	Skelmersdale United	0
1968	Wembley	Leytonstone	1	Chesham United	0
1969	Wembley	North Shields	2	Sutton United	1
1970	Wembley	Enfield	5	Dagenham	1
1971	Wembley	Skelmersdale U.	4	Dagenham	1
1972	Wembley	Hendon	2	Enfield	1
1973	Wembley	Walton & Hersham	1	Slough Town	0
1974	Wembley	Bishops Stortford	4	Ilford	1

*after extra time

Altrincham applied for election to the League in 1980 and failed by just one vote to displace Rochdale in Division 4. The senior clubs in this League also provide the players for occasional semi-professional internationals. The first and second of these tournaments, organised between England, Scotland, Holland and Italy, were won by England, the fourth, played in Aberdeen in 1982, was won by Scotland.

See also: SOUTHERN LEAGUE, RE-ELECTION & RESIGNATION.

Amateurs

AMATEUR CUP

Founded in 1893–94, the Amateur Cup (strictly named the Football Association Amateur Challenge Cup) finally went out of existence in 1974 when the FA decided that the designation 'amateur' had no significant meaning. From this point on, the United Kingdom ceased to submit entries for the sham-amateur Olympic Games.

Most wins: Bishop Auckland of the Northern League won the Amateur Cup on 10 occasions. This was exactly twice as many times as their nearest rivals, Clapton and Crook Town.

Hat-tricks: Bishop Auckland were also the only team to win the Amateur Cup on three consecutive occasions – 1955, 1956 and 1957.

Football League winners: Both Middlesbrough (1895 and 1898, when in the Northern League) and Wimbledon (1963, Isthmian League) have won the Amateur Cup. Neither side has won the FA Cup and Middlesbrough, despite a long senior history, have yet to even reach a semi-final.

Attendances: 100,000 people were present at 5 of the postwar Amateur Cup finals, all played at Wembley: 1951, 1952, 1953, 1954 and 1955. The 1954 final went to 3 games and drew a record aggregate crowd of 192,735.

INTERNATIONALS

Last amateur international: Bernard Joy of Arsenal played for England v Belgium in Brussels on Saturday 9 May 1936, when England lost 3-2. He later appeared in a wartime international, against Scotland, on Saturday 14 October 1944, but this is not an officially recognised game. The last amateurs to play for Scotland were Bob Gillespie and Jimmy Crawford, both of Queen's Park, who played against England on Saturday 1 April 1933. Scotland won 2-1.

Last for England from an amateur club: Edgar Kail of Dulwich Hamlet played in England's games on their European tour of 1929, including the 4-3 defeat by Spain in Madrid on Wednesday 15 May, which was England's first on foreign soil.

Last amateur England captain: A.G. Bower of Corinthians, who captained the side against Wales on Saturday 12 February 1927 in Wrexham. He played right-back in a 3-3 draw.

Last full amateur side: England last fielded a fully amateur international side against Wales at Queen's Club, Kensington, on 18 March 1895. The team, which had been picked by the Corinthians, drew 1-1. G.O. Smith scored the goal and Charles Wreford-Brown, who coined the term 'soccer', played centre-back. Scotland technically only played amateurs until professionalism was legalised in 1893.

FOOTBALL LEAGUE AND FA CUP

Leading scorers: George Bromilow scored 22 goals for Southport in 1955–56 to lead their scoring list. From 1908 to 1912 Harold Stapley led Glossop's scorers for 4 consecutive seasons and recorded a total of 67 goals. Most of Bromilow's career was spent with Northern Nomads, the Merseyside equivalent of the Corinthians.

Most appearances: J.C. Burns of QPR and Brentford made 263 League appearances as an amateur between 1927 and 1936.

Cup winners medals: Three amateurs have won Cup winners medals with professional sides since professionalism was legalised in 1885:

S.B. Ashworth, Manchester City, 1904;

H.P. Hardman, Everton, 1906 (plus a runners-up medal in 1907). He later became Chairman of Manchester United;

Rev. K.R.G. Hunt, Wolves, 1908.

Bill Slater won a runners-up medal as an amateur with Blackpool in 1951 and a winners medal as a professional with Wolves in 1960.

Bob Paisley won an Amateur Cup winners medal with Bishop Auckland in 1939, but was left out of the 1950 FA Cup final side by Liverpool, despite having played in all of the previous rounds at left-half and scoring in the semi-final.

FA Cup winners: Old Etonians were the last amateur side to win the FA Cup, beating Blackburn Rovers 1-0 in 1882.

FA Cup final appearances: Queen's Park (Glasgow) were the last amateur side to appear in an FA Cup final, when beaten 2-0 by Blackburn Rovers in 1885. Old Etonians were the last English amateur side to appear in a Cup final, when they lost 2-1 to Blackburn Olympic in 1883.

Amateur Cup and FA Cup: Two sides have won both trophies. Old Carthusians (from Charterhouse School, one of the founding

members of the FA) won the FA Cup by beating Old Etonians 3-0 in 1881, and the first ever Amateur Cup, beating Casuals 2-1 in 1894. Royal Engineers won the FA Cup in 1875, also beating Old Etonians by 2-0 in a replay, and the Amateur Cup in 1908. In the latter case, they were officially known as Depot Battalion, Royal Engineers, but they were based at Chatham and were effectively the same organisation.

Anglo-Italian Competitions

These tournaments grew out of the need to give Swindon Town some reward for winning the League Cup in 1969 (as a Division 3 side they could not be admitted to the Fairs Cup) and also as part of the search for additional revenue for major, and later minor, clubs who had no other European engagements. The Anglo-Italian Cup was later renamed the Anglo-Italian Tournament, though its official name has become the Anglo-Italian Semi-Professional Inter-League Cup and it is now contested by the leading non-League sides who are not professional. The only record of note set up during these rather superfluous events was Blackpool's biggest

first-class win – 10-0 v Lanerossi Vicenza on Saturday 10 June 1972.

The Royal Engineers side before the first FA Cup final on 16 March 1872. In the middle standing is Major Francis Marindin, who took the field in a record 10 finals. As well as winning the FA Cup in 1875, the Engineers went on to win the Amateur Cup in 1908.

Lord Arthur Fitzgerald Kinnaird, who played in more FA Cup finals than any other man – five on the winning side and four on the losing. Kinnaird was the first man to have appeared in consecutive finals for different teams (Wanderers in 1878 and Old Etonians in 1879). Later President of the FA, with Charles Alcock and Francis Marindin he must be regarded as one of the three founding fathers of organised football.

Anglo-Scottish Cup

Born out of the remains of the Texaco Cup, the Anglo-Scottish Cup was originally an early season contest for those sides who had not reached Europe. At various other stages items such as aggregate goals scored were taken into account for qualification and it gradually became a Second Division preserve. The Scottish clubs withdrew in 1981, when it became the Group Cup, and in 1982 it was further renamed the Football League Trophy. Newcastle were disqualified in the quarter-finals in 1977 for fielding an unnecessarily weak team in their first leg at Ayr, which Ayr won 3-0.

Finals were as follows (up to 1980-81 played over two legs):

1976	Middlesbrough	1	Fulham	0
1977	Nottingham F.	5	Orient	1
1978	Bristol City	3	St Mirren	2
1979	Burnley	4	Oldham Athletic	1
1980	St Mirren	5	Bristol City	1
1981	Chesterfield	2	Notts County	1
1982	Grimsby Town	3	Wimbledon	2
1983	Lincoln	2	Millwall	3

See also: SPONSORED TOURNAMENTS.

Appearances

MOST IN CAREER

Most individual, League only: 824 – Terry Paine for Southampton and Hereford United, 1957-77. In addition, John Trollope (with 770 for Swindon, holder of the record of most appearances for one club), Jimmy Dickinson, Roy Sproson, Alan Oakes, Martin Peters, Mike Summerbee, Ian Callaghan, Stanley Matthews, Pat Jennings and Alan Ball all recorded more than 700 League appearances.

Scottish League only: The record for Scottish League appearances is held by Englishman Bob Ferrier of Motherwell, with 626 between 1918 and 1937.

All games: Pat Jennings is the only player from the British Isles to have appeared in over 1000 first-class games. He reached this mark at the Hawthorns on 26 February 1983, playing in goal during a 0-0 draw for Arsenal against WBA. The 1000 games are made up as follows:

Football League	695
Full internationals	95
Other internationals (U23)	3
FA Cup	81
League/Milk Cup	65
European competitions	55
Charity Shield	2
Texaco Cup	2
Anglo-Italian Cup	2

OTHER INDIVIDUAL RECORDS

Consecutive appearances: Harold Bell of Tranmere did not miss a League match from the opening game of the 1946-47 season in Division 3N (a 4-1 home defeat by Rotherham on Saturday 31 August 1946) to Saturday 27 August 1955, when Tranmere also lost at home, 1-0 to Carlisle. That was the last of 401 consecutive League appearances. With FA Cup and other competitions added in, he appeared in 459 consecutive senior games. The First Division record is 265 consecutive League games by Bobby McKinlay of Nottingham Forest from April 1959 to October 1965.

All six divisions: Ray Straw of Derby and Coventry is thought to be the only player to have appeared in all 6 divisions of the Football League, which he did between 1952 and 1960.

Most in season: Dick Habbin played a record 48 Football League games in 1974-75. He appeared 27 times for Reading and, after being transferred, a further 21 times for Rotherham.

INCOMPLETE SIDES

Fewest players used: The fewest number of players used by any side throughout a complete first-class game is thought to be 7, by Kilmarnock at Port Glasgow Athletic on Saturday 4 January 1908. The other 4 failed to turn up and Kilmarnock lost 4-1.

Fewest players finishing game: Apart from the Burnley v Blackburn incident mentioned under UNFINISHED, the least number of players a team has ended a game with is thought to be 5. Notts County had only that number on the field after 90 minutes at Preston on Saturday 12 December 1891. One man had been sent off and the rest had gone off due to the weather conditions. Preston won 6-0. Leicester Fosse are also thought to have ended their Division 2 game at Grimsby on Saturday 6 January 1912 with just 5 players, the rest having left the field because of the appalling weather. Leicester lost 4-0.

Less than full side: It was not particularly uncommon for teams to mislay players in the nineteenth century. The most bizarre incident was on 26 December 1896 when Walsall Town Swifts lost 4 players on the way to Darwen for a Division 2 fixture and played with 7 men and a committee member. Darwen, near the bottom of the Division, won 12-0, thus scoring one fifth of their season's goals in a single afternoon. The most recent instance of a team failing to start a match with a full side was on 25 April 1981 when Stockport began their match at Bury with only 8 of their selected team plus the substitute after bad weather held up the others.

Spectators playing: The only instance where there is proof that this happened was a Wartime League South game between Norwich and Brighton on Wednesday 25 December 1940. Brighton arrived with only 5 players and asked some spectators to make up the numbers. They lost 18-0.

Refused to play: The Welsh club Druids, of Ruabon, arrived with only 10 men before their fourth round FA Cup tie at West Bromwich in 1884–85 and refused to kick-off. West Bromwich did and scored within 5 seconds, at which Druids decided to take to the field. Albion scored again but the result is usually given as 1-0 rather than 2-0.

Weather conditions: On Saturday 1 September 1906 Manchester City finished their Division 1 home game against Arsenal with just 6 men; the other 5 had gone off with heat exhaustion. City lost the game 4-1 on what is thought to be the hottest day a League programme has ever been completed – the temperature was over 90°F (32°C).

12 players on field: The only occasion when one side is known to have fielded 12 players in a first-class match happened on 11 November 1952. France were playing Northern Ireland at Stade Colombes and one of their players, Bonifaci, was injured. A substitute took his place, but Bonifaci came back after treatment and the French played with 12 men for the rest of the first half, scoring their first goal in that period. France won 3-1.

TEAM RECORDS

Fewest players used in season: Liverpool used just 14 players in season 1965–66, one of whom made just one appearance, when they won the League Championship. Aston Villa equalled this record in 1980–81. In Scotland Dundee used just 15 players in season 1961–62, and also won the Championship.

Most players used in season: Queen's Park used 50 players in their 38 Scottish Division I matches in 1914–15, of which they won only 4 and finished bottom. Coventry used 44 in Division 2, 1919–20, scored only 35 goals but avoided relegation. It was during this season that Coventry went 11 games without scoring a goal.

Championship side, most players: Arsenal used 30 players in winning the Championship in 1938, more than twice as many as Liverpool in 1966.

See also: FOOTBALL LEAGUE, INTERNATIONALS (for international appearances), OLDEST PLAYERS, YOUNGEST PLAYERS.

Attendances

LARGEST

Overall record: 200,000 plus at the 1923 FA Cup final between Bolton Wanderers and West Ham United at Wembley Stadium. The recorded attendance was 126,047, but the gates were broken down and it is impossible to assess the total who saw the game.

International: 160,000 plus at Scotland v England, played at Hampden Park on 17 April 1937. The official attendance was given as 149,415 (sometimes recorded as 149,547) but at least 10,000 people broke in and saw the game without paying. Scotland won 3-1. This game also produced the highest *official* attendance at any game played inside the British Isles.

Any club game: 144,303 (sometimes given as 147,365) at the Scottish Cup final between Aberdeen and Celtic on 24 April 1937 (one week after the Scotland v England game above) also at Hampden. Celtic won 2-1.

Any game other than an International or Cup final: 143,570 at the Scottish Cup semi-final between Rangers and Hibernian at Hampden Park on 27 March 1948. Rangers won 1-0.

LEFT: The very first programme issued by Aston Villa, on 1 September 1906. This was the hottest day that League football has ever been played and numerous games ended without a full complement of players. Villa beat Blackburn 4–2.
BELOW: Terry Paine, holder of the League record of 824 appearances.

European club game: 136,505 at the European Cup semi-final second leg between Celtic and Leeds at Hampden Park on Wednesday 15 April 1970. This attendance, sometimes given as 135,826, is also a record for *any* European Cup tie (including finals) played anywhere in Europe and is also the highest attendance ever in the British Isles for a game *not* played on a Saturday.

Any League game: 118,567 at Ibrox Park, Glasgow, on 2 January 1939 for Scottish Division 1 game between Rangers and Celtic.

English club game: 105,000 saw Everton play Liverpool at Goodison Park on 11 March 1967; 65,000 watched the game live in the ground and another 40,000 saw it on closed circuit television at Anfield on the other side of Stanley Park. Everton won 1-0. Apart from the 1923 Cup final, only three other games in England have attracted crowds of more than 100,000. They were:

1901 FA Cup final – Tottenham Hotspur v Sheffield United, 114,815;
1905 FA Cup final – Aston Villa v Newcastle United, 101,117;
1913 FA Cup final – Aston Villa v Sunderland, 120,081.

All of the last three games were played at the old Crystal Palace ground.

Normal English club game: 84,569 saw Manchester City defeat Stoke City 1-0 in the quarter-final of the FA Cup at Maine Road on 3 March 1934. This is the highest single attendance for any club game (excluding a Cup final) played in England.

Football League: 83,260 at Maine Road for the Division 1 game between Manchester United and Arsenal on 17 January 1948, when Old Trafford was unusable because of

bomb damage. The final score was 1-1.

Division 2: 68,029 at Villa Park for Aston Villa v Coventry City, 30 October 1937. The final score was 1-1.

Division 3: 51,621 at Ninian Park for Cardiff City v Bristol City, 7 April 1947. The final score was 1-1 with Cardiff promoted as Division 3S champions and Bristol City finishing third. Since reorganisation the record Division 3 crowd was one of 49,309 at Hillsborough for Sheffield Wednesday v Sheffield United on the morning of Wednesday 26 December 1979.

Division 4: 37,774 at Selhurst Park for Crystal Palace v Millwall on 31 March 1961. Millwall won 2-0.

Scottish Premier: 69,594 at Ibrox Park for Rangers v Celtic on 30 August 1975. This was the very first day of the first season of the Scottish Premier League.

Scottish non-Division 1/Premier: 27,205 for Queen's Park v Kilmarnock in Division 2 on 14 January 1950.

Football League Cup: 63,418 for the semi-final second leg game between Manchester United and Manchester City at Old Trafford on 17 December 1969 (apart from finals).

Scottish League Cup: 107,647 for the final at Hampden Park between Celtic and Rangers on 23 October 1965. Celtic won 2-1.

English midweek game: 80,407 at Maine Road, Manchester, for the FA Cup semi-final replay between Derby County and Birmingham City on Thursday 28 March 1946. Derby won 4-0.

Friendly: 104,493 at Hampden Park, Glasgow, on 17 October 1961 to see Rangers play Eintracht Frankfurt.

English friendly: 90,000 plus who saw Chelsea v Moscow Dynamo on 10 November 1945 at Stamford Bridge; 74,000 are known to

The Valley, the largest club ground in England and the only one never to have been filled; 75,031 attended the FA Cup 1-1 draw with Aston Villa on 12 Feb 1938 but space remained.

have paid but at least 16,000 entered when the gates were broken down and the total attendance may well have exceeded 100,000. The biggest attendance at a friendly between English sides is 92,500 for the Charity Shield at Wembley between Tottenham and Aston Villa on 22 August 1981. Excluding this traditional fixture, the largest friendly attendance was on 18 September 1972 when 60,538 attended Bobby Charlton's testimonial match against Celtic at Old Trafford.

SMALLEST

Overall first-class record: 0 – the official attendance at the Bradford City v Norwich City FA Cup second round second replay played at Lincoln in 1915 was nil. The FA had responded to a debate in the House of Commons about shells failing to explode in a First World War battle at Neuve Chapelle by refusing to allow games to be played near munitions factories during working hours. As there were munitions factories in Lincoln, the game was played behind closed doors, though a couple of hundred people did apparently climb into the ground to see the game. The paying entry, however, was definitely nil. There are two other instances of official paying attendances of zero. Both were European games where fans had been banned because of previous crowd trouble. The first was West Ham v Castilla (Madrid) on 1 October 1980 in the Cup Winners Cup. The counted non-paying attendance that night, including players, press, ground staff etc was 118. The second instance was Aston Villa v Besiktas at Villa Park in Sept 1982 in the European Cup after the notorious crowd behaviour at Anderlecht the previous season. The counted attendance was around 200 and Villa won 3-1.

Lowest under normal circumstances: 32- East Stirlingshire v Leith Athletic in Scottish Division 2 on 15 April 1939. There are several other instances of Scottish Second Division crowds of under 100, most recently at Meadowbank Thistle in Edinburgh. On 12 April 1978 their game against Stranraer had an official attendance of 49, while on 22

December 1979 they and Stenhousemuir were watched by just 80 people.

Football League, lowest known: 405 at West Bromwich v Derby County in the Football League on 29 November 1890. Although this figure is thought to be accurate, it is very unlikely to have been the lowest attendance in the nineteenth century and West Brom receive the accolade only because they are the best documented of the major clubs. The lowest First Division crowd since the First World War is almost certainly the 4554 who turned out to see Leeds beat Arsenal 3-0 at Highbury on Thursday 5 May 1966. The Cup Winners Cup final between Liverpool and Dortmund was shown live on television the same night but, surprisingly, Leeds were second in the division at the time.

Lowest at normal League match: 450 who watched Cambridge United defeat Rochdale 2-0 away at Spotland in Division 3 on 5 February 1974. Because of power cuts, the game was played on a Tuesday afternoon. The lowest attendance for a Football League match played at a normal scheduled time is believed to be the 469 who saw Thames defeat Luton 1-0 on Saturday 6 December 1930 in Division 3S. The oft-quoted attendance of 13 at Old Trafford for Stockport v Leicester City in Division 2 on 7 May 1921 has since been discredited. Contemporary newspaper reports indicate a crowd of approximately 2000.

Home International Championship: 600 to watch Scotland play Wales at Tynecastle, Edinburgh, on 26 March 1892. This is also thought to be the lowest attendance at any official international involving any of the home countries. In recent years the record is easily held by the Wales v Northern Ireland game at Wrexham on 27 May 1982 which Wales won 3-0. The FA Cup final replay between Spurs and QPR was televised at the same time and the attendance was just 2315.

Major final: The Scottish League Cup final of 1981 at Dens Park had an attendance of 24,456 but as only 25,000 tickets were

The unique programme issued by West Ham prior to their Cup Winners Cup tie against Castilla in 1980. The uniqueness was due to the fact that spectators were banned and the attendance was therefore nil.

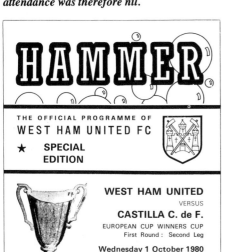

HAMMER

THE OFFICIAL PROGRAMME OF
WEST HAM UNITED FC

★ SPECIAL
EDITION

WEST HAM UNITED
VERSUS
CASTILLA C. de F.
EUROPEAN CUP WINNERS CUP
First Round : Second Leg

Wednesday 1 October 1980

KICK-OFF AT 7.30 pm

Boleyn Ground - Green Street
Upton Park - London E13

PRICE : 50 PENCE

RECORD ATTENDANCES OF CURRENT LEAGUE CLUBS

FOOTBALL LEAGUE

Aldershot	19,138 v Carlisle United, FA Cup 4th rd. replay, 28.1.10
Arsenal	73,295 v Sunderland, Division 1, 9.3.35
Aston Villa	76,588 v Derby County, FA Cup quarter-final, 2.3.46
Barnsley	40,255 v Stoke City, FA Cup 5th round, 15.2.36
Birmingham City	66,844 v Everton, FA Cup 5th round, 11.2.39
Blackburn Rovers	61,783 v Bolton Wanderers, FA Cup quarter-final, 2.3.29
Blackpool	39,118 v Manchester United, Division 1, 19.4.32
Bolton Wanderers	69,912 v Manchester City, FA Cup 5th round, 18.2.33
Bournemouth	28,799 v Manchester United, FA Cup quarter-final, 2.3.57
Bradford City	39,146 v Burnley, FA Cup 4th round, 11.3.11
Brentford	39,626 v Preston North End, FA Cup quarter-final, 5.3.38
Brighton	36,747 v Fulham, Division 2, 27.12.58
Bristol City	43,335 v Preston North End, FA Cup 5th round, 16.2.35
Bristol Rovers	38,472 v Preston North End, FA Cup 4th round, 30.1.60
Burnley	54,755 v Huddersfield Town, FA Cup 3rd round, 23.2.24
Bury	35,000 v Bolton Wanderers, FA Cup 3rd round, 9.1.60
Cambridge United*	12,140 v Aston Villa, FA Cup 4th round, 26.1.80
Cardiff City†	57,800 v Arsenal, Division 1, 22.4.53
Carlisle United	27,500 v Birmingham City, FA Cup 3rd round, 5.1.57
Charlton Athletic	75,031 v Aston Villa, FA Cup 5th round, 12.2.38
Chelsea‡	82,905 v Arsenal, Division 1, 12.10.35
Chester	20,500 v Chelsea, FA Cup 3rd round replay, 16.1.52
Chesterfield	30,968 v Newcastle United, Division 2, 7.4.39
Colchester United	19,072 v Reading, FA Cup 1st round, 27.11.48
Coventry City	51,457 v Wolverhampton W., Division 2, 29.4.67
Crewe Alexandra	20,000 v Tottenham Hotspur, FA Cup 4th round, 30.1.60
Crystal Palace	51,801 v Burnley, Division 2, 11.5.79
Darlington	21,023 v Bolton W., League Cup 3rd round, 14.11.60
Derby County	41,826 v Tottenham Hotspur, Division 1, 20.9.69
Doncaster Rovers	37,149 v Hull City, Division 3N, 2.10.48
Everton	78,299 v Liverpool, Division 1, 18.8.48
Exeter City	20,984 v Sunderland, FA Cup quarter-final replay, 4.3.31
Fulham	49,335 v Millwall, Division 2, 8.10.38
Gillingham	23,002 v QPR, FA Cup 3rd round, 10.1.48
Grimsby Town	31,657 v Wolverhampton W., FA Cup 5th round, 20.2.37
Halifax Town	36,885 v Tottenham Hotspur, FA Cup 5th round, 14.2.53
Hartlepool United	17,426 v Manchester United, FA Cup 3rd round, 5.1.57
Hereford United	18,114 v Sheffield Wednesday, FA Cup 3rd round, 4.1.58
Huddersfield Town	67,037 v Arsenal, FA Cup quarter-final, 27.2.32
Hull City	55,019 v Manchester U., FA Cup quarter-final, 26.2.49
Ipswich Town	38,010 v Leeds United, FA Cup quarter-final, 8.3.75
Leeds United	57,892 v Sunderland, FA Cup 5th round, 15.3.67
Leicester City	47,298 v Tottenham Hotspur, FA Cup 5th round, 18.2.28
Lincoln City	23,196 v Derby County, League Cup 4th round, 15.11.67
Liverpool	61,905 v Wolverhampton W., FA Cup 4th round, 2.2.52
Luton Town	30,069 v Blackpool, FA Cup quarter-final replay, 4.3.59
Manchester City	84,569 v Stoke City, FA Cup quarter-final, 3.3.34
Manchester United§	70,504 v Aston Villa, Division 1, 27.12.20
Mansfield Town	24,467 v Nottingham Forest, FA Cup 3rd round, 10.1.53
Middlesbrough	53,596 v Newcastle United, Division 1, 27.12.49
Millwall	48,672 v Derby County, FA Cup 5th round, 20.2.37
Newcastle United	68,386 v Chelsea, Division 1, 3.9.30
Newport County	24,268 v Cardiff City, Division 3S, 16.10.37
Northampton Town	24,523 v Fulham, Division 1, 23.4.66
Norwich City	43,984 v Leicester City, FA Cup quarter-final, 30.3.63
Nottingham Forest	49,946 v Manchester United, Division 1, 28.10.67
Notts County	47,301 v York City, FA Cup quarter-final, 12.3.55
Oldham Athletic	47,671 v Sheffield Wednesday, FA Cup 4th rd., 25.1.30
Orient	34,345 v West Ham United, FA Cup 4th round, 25.1.64
Oxford United	22,730 v Preston, FA Cup quater-final, 29.2.64
Peterborough United	30,096 v Swansea Town, FA Cup 5th round, 20.2.65
Plymouth Argyle	43,596 v Aston Villa, Division 2, 10.10.36
Portsmouth	51,385 v Derby County, FA Cup quarter-final, 26.2.49
Port Vale	50,000 v Aston Villa, FA Cup 5th round, 20.2.60
Preston North End	42,684 v Arsenal, Division 1, 23.4.38
Queen's Park R.	41,000 v Leeds U., FA Cup 3rd rd., 9.1.32 (at W. City)
Reading	33,042 v Brentford, FA Cup 5th round, 19.2.27
Rochdale	24,231 v Notts County, FA Cup 2nd round, 10.12.49
Rotherham United	25,000 v Sheffield Wednesday, Division 2, 26.1.52 & Sheffield United, Division 2, 13.12.52
Scunthorpe United	23,935 v Portsmouth, FA Cup 4th round, 30.1.54
Sheffield United	68,287 v Leeds United, FA Cup 5th round, 15.2.36
Sheffield Wednesday	72,841 v Manchester City, FA Cup 5th round, 17.2.34
Shrewsbury Town	18,917 v Walsall, Division 3, 26.4.61
Southampton	31,044 v Manchester United, Division 1, 8.10.69
Southend United	28,059 v Birmingham City, FA Cup 4th round, 26.1.57
Stockport County	27,833 v Liverpool, FA Cup 5th round, 11.2.50
Stoke City	51,380 v Arsenal, Division 1, 29.3.37
Sunderland	75,118 v Derby County, FA Cup q-final replay, 8.3.33
Swansea City	32,796 v Arsenal, FA Cup 4th round, 17.2.68
Swindon Town	32,000 v Arsenal, FA Cup 3rd round, 15.1.72
Torquay United	21,908 v Huddersfield Town, FA Cup 4th round, 29.1.55
Tottenham Hotspur	75,038 v Sunderland, FA Cup quarter-final, 5.3.38

FOOTBALL LEAGUE

Tranmere Rovers	24,424 v Stoke City, FA Cup 4th round, 5.2.72
Walsall	25,453 v Newcastle United, Division 2, 29.8.61
Watford	34,099 v Manchester United, FA Cup 4th round, 3.2.69
West Bromwich A.	64,815 v Arsenal, FA Cup quarter-final, 6.3.37
West Ham United	42,322 v Tottenham Hotspur, Division 1, 17.10.70
Wigan Athletic	27,500 v Hereford, FA Cup 2nd round, 12.12.53
Wimbledon	18,000 v HMS Victory, Amateur Cup, 3rd rd., 23.2.35
Wolverhampton W.	61,315 v Liverpool, FA Cup 5th round, 11.2.39
Wrexham	34,445 v Manchester United, FA Cup 4th round, 26.1.57
York City	28,123 v Huddersfield Town, FA Cup 5th round, 5.3.38

*ground record is 14,000 for friendly v Chelsea, 1.5.70 †ground record is 61,566 for Wales v England, 14.10.61 ‡ground record is an estimated 90,000 for friendly v Dynamo Moscow, 10.11.45 §ground record is 76,962 for Wolverhampton Wanderers v Grimsby Town, FA Cup semi-final, 25.3.39

SCOTTISH LEAGUE

Aberdeen	45,061 v Hearts, Scottish Cup 4th round, 13.3.54
Airdrieonians	24,000 v Hearts, Scottish Cup 4th round, 8.3.52
Albion Rovers	27,381 v Rangers, Scottish Cup 2nd round, 8.2.36
Alloa Athletic	13,000 v Dunfermline, Scottish Cup 3rd rd rply, 22.2.39
Arbroath	13,510 v Rangers, Scottish Cup 3rd round, 23.2.52
Ayr United	25,225 v Rangers, Division 1, 13.9.69
Berwick Rangers	13,365 v Rangers, Scottish Cup 1st round, 28.1.67
Brechin City	8,123 v Aberdeen, Scottish Cup 3rd round, 3.2.73
Celtic	83,500 v Rangers, Division 1, 1.1.38
Clyde	48,500 v Celtic, Scottish Cup 2nd round replay, 7.12.14
Clydebank	14,900 v Hibernian, Scottish Cup 1st round, 10.2.65
Cowdenbeath	25,586 v Rangers, League Cup quarter-final, 21.9.49
Dumbarton	18,000 v Raith Rovers, Scottish Cup quarter-final, 2.3.57
Dundee	43,024 v Rangers, Scottish Cup 4th round, 7.2.53
Dundee United	28,000 v Barcelona, Fairs Cup 2nd round, 16.11.66
Dunfermline Athletic	27,816 v Celtic, Division 1, 30.4.68
East Fife	22,515 v Raith Rovers, Division 1, 2.1.50
East Stirlingshire	11,500 v Hibernian, Scottish Cup 2nd round, 10.2.60
Falkirk	23,100 v Celtic, Scottish Cup 3rd round, 21.2.53
Forfar Athletic	10,800 v Rangers, Scottish Cup 2nd round, 7.2.70
Hamilton A.	28,281 v Hearts, Scottish Cup 3rd round, 3.3.37
Heart of Midlothian	53,496 v Rangers, Scottish Cup 2nd round, 13.2.32
Hibernian	65,840 v Heart of Midlothian, Division 1, 2.1.50
Kilmarnock	34,246 v Rangers, League Cup, 20.8.63
Meadowbank Thistle	4,000 v Albion Rovers, League Cup, 9.8.74
Montrose	8,983 v Dundee, Scottish Cup quarter-final, 17.3.73
Morton	23,500 v Celtic, Scottish Cup 3rd round, 21.2.53
Motherwell	35,632 v Rangers, Scottish Cup 4th round replay, 12.3.52
Partick Thistle*	49,838 v Rangers, Division 1, 18.2.22
Queen of the South	25,000 v Hearts, Scottish Cup 3rd round, 23.2.52
Queen's Park†	95,722 v Rangers, Scottish Cup 1st round, 18.1.1930
Raith Rovers	32,000 v Hearts, Scottish Cup 2nd round, 7.2.53
Rangers	118,567 v Celtic, Division 1, 2.1.39
St Johnstone	29,972 v Dundee, Scottish Cup 2nd round, 10.2.52
St Mirren	47,428 v Celtic, Scottish Cup 4th round, 7.3.25
Stenhousemuir	13,000 v East Fife, Scottish Cup 4th round, 11.3.50
Stirling Albion	26,400 v Celtic, Scottish Cup 4th round, 14.3.59
Stranraer	6,500 v Rangers, Scottish Cup 1st round, 24.1.48

*ground record is 54,728 for Scotland v N. Ireland, 25.2.28 †ground record is 149,415 for Scotland v England, 17.4.37

The Chelsea team lines up before the biggest crowd ever seen at a club game in England – 90,000 plus v Moscow Dynamo late in 1945.

issued this could not be said to count. The realistic lowest attendance for a major single-leg Cup final (some early Football League Cup finals attracted less) was the 27,173 who attended the Scottish League Cup final between Aberdeen and Dundee United on 8 December 1979. The game ended 0-0. The lowest attendance at a major final this century was the 20,740 who attended the 1901 FA Cup final replay between Spurs and Sheffield United at Burnden Park, Bolton, on Saturday 27 April 1901. Spurs also featured in the only Wembley Cup final (since 1923) for which tickets were available at the gate. This was the 1982 FA Cup final replay against QPR on 27 May 1982, which Spurs won 1-0. The official attendance was later given as 90,000 but the actual figure is though to have been rather less.

AGGREGATE

Single season: The highest number ever to watch Football League matches in a season was 41,271,414 in 1948–49, when 1,848 games were played. The lowest number in a season since the Second World War was 24,540,627 in 1978–79, when there were 2,028 games. In 30 years, the average attendance had therefore fallen by nearly 50% — from 22,333 to 12,100.

Single day: The highest number of people thought to have watched a Football League programme on a single day is 1,253,570 on Monday 26 December 1949. Most games played that day were local derbies.

Single club: Manchester United averaged 57,758 for their Division 1 home games in 1967–68 – a total of 1,212,900. Previously the record had been held by Newcastle United with an average of 56,351 in Division 2 in 1947–48 (when they finished second). Tottenham averaged 55,486 in 1950–51 when they won the Championship.

Single tie: 265,199 watched the two matches between Rangers and Morton in the 1948 Scottish Cup final, both at Hampden Park. In England, the record aggregate for any tie is 209,749 in the three games it took to conclude the 1977 League Cup final between Aston Villa and Everton. The highest aggregate for a game other than a final is 169,163 for the four-game FA Cup semi-final between Liverpool and Arsenal in 1980 – the only time the semi-final has needed four full matches in the FA Cup.

ALL-TICKET

First: The first all-ticket game is thought to have been Scotland v England at the First Cathkin Park on 15 March 1884, when 10,000 tickets were sold.

Most tickets sold: 150,000 tickets were sold for Scotland v England at Hampden Park in both April 1937 and April 1939.

Cup final: The FA Cup final was made all-ticket in 1924 and has remained so ever since. The figure of 100,000 (all ticket or not) has been published for internationals on several occasions since, for most FA and League Cup finals, and for five Amateur Cup finals, all at Wembley. In actual fact, the Empire Stadium's records show that, apart from the

ABOVE: The first crowd ever to exceed 100,000 – at Crystal Palace for the 1901 Cup final. BELOW: Closed gates at Hampden on 17 April 1937 where 149,415 watch Scotland win 3-1.

1923 Cup final, none of these games was actually attended by as many as 100,000 people.

Receipts: The first game in Britain to have receipts of more than £1,000,000 was the West Ham v Arsenal FA Cup final in 1980; £700,000 came from those attending the match and £300,000 plus from TV fees, programme sales etc. As a comparison the first Wembley final 57 years before took £27,000 – with a somewhat larger crowd.

Away from Home

SINGLE MATCH VICTORIES

Overall record: Redding Athletic 0 Came-lon 17, Scottish Cup 2nd round, Saturday 24 September 1887.

English record: Clapton 0 Nottingham Forest 14 in the FA Cup first round on Saturday 17 January 1891. Clapton were an amateur side and Forest were in the Football Alliance at the time.

League game: Airdrie 1 Hibernian 11 in Scottish Division 1 on Saturday 24 October 1959.

Football League game: Burslem Port Vale 0 Sheffield United 10 in Division 2 on Saturday 10 December 1892. This is the only occasion on which the away side in a Football League game has reached double figures. A contemporary report noted that the Port Vale keeper had 'lost his spectacles in the mud'.

Division 1: Cardiff 1 Wolves 9 on Saturday 3 September 1955, (Cardiff won away 2-0 at Wolves that same season) & Newcastle

United 1 Sunderland 9 on Saturday 5 December 1908. Newcastle, undisputably the best team of the period, won the League that season, but it was Sunderland's 8th win in 11 visits to St James' Park.

Division 2: Burslem Port Vale 0 Sheffield United 10 (*see above*).

Division 3: Accrington Stanley 0 Barnsley 9 in Division 3N on Saturday 3 February 1934.

Division 4: Crewe Alexandra 1 Rotherham United 8 on Saturday 8 September 1973.

Scottish Division 1/Premier: Airdrie 1 Hibernian 11 (*see above*).

Scottish non-Division 1/Premier: Alloa 0 Dundee 10 on Saturday 8 March 1947.

Football League Cup: Coventry City 1 Leicester City 8 on Tuesday 1 December 1964.

Scottish League Cup: Alloa 0 Third Lanark 10 on Saturday 8 August 1953.

10 goals away: Apart from the four games mentioned above, there is only one other instance of a side scoring 10 goals away against first class opposition: Patrick Thistle 2 Hibernian 10 in Scottish Division 1 on Saturday 19 December 1959.

SEASON'S RECORDS
Complete season: Rangers are the only club to have won every away League game in a season, winning all 9 in Scottish Division 1 in 1898–99.

Undefeated: On eight other occasions, a side has remained undefeated away from home throughout a whole season:
- Preston in Football League in 1888–89
- Liverpool in Division 2 in 1893–94
- Celtic in Division 1 in 1897–98
- Kilmarnock in Division 2 in 1898–99
- Celtic in Scottish League in 1916–17
- Rangers in Scottish League in 1920–21
- Rangers in Division 1 in 1967–68
- Raith Rovers in Division 2 in 1975–76

Most wins: Doncaster Rovers won 18 games out of 21 away from home in Division 3N in 1946–47. The Scottish record is held by Rangers with 16 out of 21 in 1920–21.

Goals conceded: Darwen conceded 109 goals in 17 away games in 1898–99, easily an English record with an average of nearly 6½ per game. Vale of Leven conceded 73 in 11 games in the Scottish League in 1891–92, an even worse average of 6.6 goals per game.

RADIO
First game broadcast: Arsenal v Sheffield United at Highbury on Saturday 22 January 1927. The game ended 1-1.

First Cup final broadcast: Cardiff v Arsenal on Saturday 23 April 1927. This was the first game which was heard live throughout the country. Cardiff won 1-0.

First ban: The first ban on live broadcasting was initiated by the Football League on Monday 1 June 1931, but it did not last for any length of time.

TELEVISION
First game shown: The first match from which any parts were shown either live or in recorded form was probably a practice game between Arsenal and Arsenal Reserves on Thursday 16 September 1937. The use of Highbury for these early broadcasts is explained by its proximity to the first BBC studios and transmitter at Alexandra Palace.

First Cup final: Parts of the 1937 final between Sunderland and Preston were televised, but the first game shown live in its entirety was the 1938 final on 30 April, in which Preston beat Huddersfield with a penalty in the last minute of extra time. While nearly 100,000 saw the game live, no more than 10,000 saw it on television. The BBC have shown all finals since with the sole exception of 1952, when permission was refused by the FA.

First game other than a final: The fifth round FA Cup tie between Charlton and Blackburn at The Valley on Saturday 8 February 1947 was shown live. Charlton won 1-0. Live transmission of Football League matches was reintroduced in the 1983–84 season, the first being Tottenham v Nottingham Forest from White Hart Lane on Sunday 2

TOP: Leeds striker Allan Clarke hits the bar with Chelsea keeper Peter Bonetti stranded during the drawn out 1970 Cup final, the only one played at Wembley that has ended in a draw and the only one ever that has gone to 240 minutes. The first game generated enormous interest and was watched, on both channels, by 32 million people, the highest TV audience ever for a football match. It was also the biggest audience for any programme in the 1970s.
RIGHT: Arsenal players, including George Male, Ted Drake and Herbie Roberts, gather round a BBC television camera at Highbury on 16 September 1937, after an Arsenal practice game had become the first match ever to be televised.

Arsenal's Brian Talbot shields the ball from Liverpool's Alan Kennedy during the 1979 Charity Shield game at Wembley. The match created a record attendance (90,000) for any non-competitive game in England. These two clubs have been the most successful in this annual game – Liverpool having won the trophy on 10 occasions, Arsenal on 7.

October. Spurs won 2-1.

Football League game: The first League game to be shown live was between Blackpool and Bolton on the evening of Friday 9 September 1960. Bolton won 1-0 but the game was a poor one and the idea of televising one game live on a Friday night (which was to start a few weeks later) was immediately dropped.

'Match of the Day': The first BBC 'Match of the Day' was between Liverpool and Arsenal on Saturday 22 August 1964. The BBC2 audience for the game was 75,000, only a few more than saw the game live at Anfield. Liverpool won 3-2.

Colour: Anfield was also the venue for the first ever colour transmission of a football match when Liverpool beat West Ham 2-0 on Saturday 15 November 1969 (BBC).

First ITV game: The first game put out by a member station of the Independent Television network was a third round FA Cup replay between Bedford Town and Arsenal on Thursday 12 January 1956. Having only drawn 2-2 at home, Arsenal won 2-1.

First Scottish game: The first game shown live in Scotland was the 1955 Cup final between Clyde and Celtic on 23 April. Kenneth Wolstenholme was the commentator. The first League game shown live in Scotland was Clyde v Aberdeen on 3 September 1955.

Charity Shield

This competition, which traditionally starts the season, has generally been held between the two strongest clubs in the country – though sometimes there have been deviations from that rule. Since the game was transferred to Wembley in 1975, it has always been between the winners of the Football League and FA Cup, though in previous years it had been between Select XIs, or the winners of the Football League and Southern League. It was preceded by the Sheriff of London's Charity Shield, which was between

a team chosen to be the best amateur side and the best professional team. The record for appearances in Charity Shield games is held jointly by Ray Clemence and Phil Thompson who (on 1 January 1984) had each played 7 times in the fixture.

First game: The first of the recognised charity

CHARITY SHIELD

Year	Home	Score	Away	Score
1898†	Corinthians*	2:2	Sheffield U.*	2:2
1899†	Aston Villa*	1	Queen's Park*	1
1900†	Corinthians	2	Aston Villa	1
1901†	Aston Villa	1	Corinthians	0
1902†	Tottenham H.	5	Corinthians	2
1903†	Sunderland	3	Corinthians	0
1904†	Corinthians	10	Bury	3
1905†	The Wednesday	2	Corinthians	1
1906†	Liverpool	5	Corinthians	1
1907†	Newcastle U.	5	Corinthians	2
1908	Manchester U.	1:4	QPR	1:0
1909	Newcastle U.	2	Northampton T.	0
1910	Brighton	1	Aston Villa	0
1911	Manchester U.	8	Swindon Town	4
1912	Blackburn R.	2	QPR	1
1913	Professionals	7	Amateurs	2
1914–19	Not contested			
1920	WBA	2	Tottenham H.	0
1921	Tottenham H.	2	Burnley	0
1922	Huddersfield T.	1	Liverpool	0
1923	Professionals	2	Amateurs	0
1924	Professionals	3	Amateurs	1
1925	Amateurs	6	Professionals	1
1926	Amateurs	6	Professionals	3
1927	Cardiff City	2	Corinthians	1
1928	Everton	2	Blackburn R.	1
1929	Professionals	3	Amateurs	0
1930	Arsenal	2	Sheffield W.	1
1931	Arsenal	1	WBA	0
1932	Everton	5	Newcastle U.	3
1933	Arsenal	3	Everton	0
1934	Arsenal	4	Manchester C.	0
1935	Sheffield W.	1	Arsenal	0
1936	Sunderland	2	Arsenal	1
1937	Manchester C.	2	Sunderland	0
1938	Arsenal	2	Preston N.E.	1
1939–47	Not contested			
1948	Arsenal	4	Manchester U.	3
1949	Portsmouth*	1	Wolves*	1
1950	England XI	4	Canadian XI	2
1951	Tottenham H.	2	Newcastle U.	1
1952	Manchester U.	4	Newcastle U.	2
1953	Arsenal	3	Blackpool	1
1954	WBA*	4	Wolves*	4
1955	Chelsea	3	Newcastle U.	0
1956	Manchester U.	1	Manchester C.	0
1957	Manchester U.	4	Aston Villa	0
1958	Bolton Wanderers	4	Wolves	1
1959	Wolves	3	Nottingham F.	1
1960	Burnley*	2	Wolves*	2
1961	Tottenham H.	3	FA XI	2
1962	Tottenham H.	5	Ipswich Town	1
1963	Everton	4	Manchester U.	0
1964	Liverpool*	2	West Ham*	2
1965	Liverpool*	2	Manchester U.*	2
1966	Liverpool	1	Everton	0
1967	Manchester U.*	3	Tottenham H.*	3
1968	Manchester C.	6	WBA	1
1969	Leeds United	2	Manchester C.	1
1970	Everton	2	Chelsea	1
1971	Leicester C.	1	Liverpool	0
1972	Manchester C.	1	Aston Villa	0
1973	Burnley	1	Manchester C.	0
1974	Liverpool‡	1	Leeds United	1
1975	Derby County	2	West Ham	0
1976	Liverpool	1	Southampton	0
1977	Liverpool*	0	Manchester U.*	0
1978	Nottingham F.	5	Ipswich Town	0
1979	Liverpool	3	Arsenal	1
1980	Liverpool	1	West Ham	0
1981	Aston Villa*	2	Tottenham H.*	2
1982	Liverpool	1	Tottenham H.	0
1983	Manchester U.	2	Liverpool	0

*each club retained shield for six months †Sheriff of London's Charity Shield ‡Liverpool won 6-5 on penalties

15

matches was for the Sheriff of London's Shield on Saturday 19 March 1898, when Corinthians and Sheffield United drew 2-2 before a crowd of 20,000 at Crystal Palace. After another drawn game, United refused to play extra-time because of disagreements with some of the referee's decisions.

Sheriff's Shield revival: In 1931, games for the Sheriff of London's Shield were briefly revived. In that year Arsenal beat Corinthians 5-3, in 1933 Arsenal won the same fixture 9-2 and in 1934 Tottenham beat the Corinthians 7-4 at White Hart Lane. Thirty years later there was a second revival, with Arsenal beating the now named Corinthian Casuals 7-0 in 1965 and 5-2 in 1966. The Shield was again revived at Watford to celebrate Corinthians centenary in 1983.

Consecutive Sequences

WINS

Consecutive first-class wins: 31 – Belfast Celtic won 31 consecutive matches in the Irish League, Belfast City Cup and Irish Cup in season 1947–48. In 1949 they resigned from the Irish League and have never played since. In their last ever competitive game, on Sunday 29 May 1949, they defeated the touring Scottish national side 2-0 in New York. There is some reasonable doubt about whether their 31-game run can be regarded as a first-class record, being Irish games only.

Consecutive wins, British first class: 23 – Celtic won 23 consecutive matches between a 2-0 win at Morton on 30 April 1966 and a 7-3 defeat of Stirling Albion on 2 November 1966. Their next game was a 1-1 home draw with St Mirren on 5 November. Of the 23 games, 11 were League, 10 were League Cup and 2 were European Cup ties against FC Zurich. Celtic also won 2 Glasgow Cup games (4-0 v Rangers, 4-0 v Queen's Park) in this period, making 25 games in all if these matches are counted as first-class.

Consecutive League wins, overall: 24 – Morton won their last game of the 1962–63 Scottish Division 2 season and their first 23 of the 1963–64 season before losing 3-1 to East Fife at Methil on Saturday 1 February 1964. Rangers won 22 consecutive League games in seasons 1898–99 and 1899–1900.

Consecutive wins, England: 14 – by Bristol City in Division 2 between their 5-1 defeat at Manchester United on Saturday 2 September 1905 and their 1-1 draw at Leeds City on Saturday 9 December 1905. All were League games and this is also a League record. This was also achieved by Manchester United in Division 2 between drawing 1-1 at Bradford City on 8 October 1904 and drawing 1-1 at Bristol City on 7 January 1905. It was later matched by Preston North End in 1950–51, also in Division 2, between drawing 1-1 at home with Coventry on 23 December 1950 and

drawing 3-3 at Southampton on 31 March 1951.

Consecutive home wins, overall: 23 – Rotherham won their first 20 Division 3N games in 1946–47 plus two home FA Cup matches (2-0 v Crewe and 2-1 v Scunthorpe) to make 22 wins in all. They then spoilt the record with a 3-3 draw against Rochdale on 7 June, their very last home game of the season. As they had won their last home Cup game of the 1945–46 season (2-1 v Barnsley) the total sequence is 23.

Consecutive home League wins: 22 – Rotherham won the last two home games of their 1938–39 Division 3N season and the first 20 of the 1946–47 season, making 22 in all. They did not lose or draw a recognised League fixture between Saturday 1 April 1939 (0-2 to Hull City) and Saturday 7 June 1947 (3-3 v Rochdale) but did, however, draw a League game 2-2 with Darlington on Saturday 2 September 1939 (the day before war was declared). The few games played before the 1939–40 season was abandoned were withdrawn from all official records, but if they are taken into account for these purposes, then the record belongs to Brentford rather than Rotherham. The Londoners won all 21 of their home games in Division 3S in 1929–30, the only time that this has happened in a full season of 42 games or more. Oddly, they lost their last home game of the 1928–29 season, 2-0 to Plymouth, and their first game of the 1930–31 season, 4-0 to Northampton, so their run is confined to the single season. In 1929–30 Brentford lost their first round FA Cup tie 1-0 away at Southend. Between 21 November 1931 and 4 November 1933, Brentford Reserves surpassed their seniors by winning 44 consecutive home London Combination fixtures, a record for any major league of that level or above.

Consecutive away wins, overall: 18 – Rangers won 17 consecutive away games in the 1927–28 and 1928–29 seasons, 16 League and one Scottish Cup. If their win in the 1928 Cup final at Hampden against Celtic (4-0) is also counted, this makes a run of 18 consecutive away wins.

Consecutive away League wins: 16 – Rangers

won 16 consecutive games in Scottish Division 1 in 1928 and 1929 before losing 3-1 at Douglas Park, Hamilton, on Wednesday 27 March 1929. That game was also the end of Rangers' run of 38 consecutive League games without defeat that had lasted for 1 year and 10 days. The English record is held by Spurs with 8 consecutive away Division 1 wins in 1960–61, their double season. They won their first 8 games of the season, until defeated by Sheffield Wednesday at Hillsborough 2-1 on 12 November 1960.

Consecutive wins against same opposition: Cardiff defeated Arsenal on three consecutive Saturdays in three consecutive matches in 1924, the first two in the League:
19 January 1924 Arsenal 1 Cardiff 2;
26 January 1924 Cardiff 4 Arsenal 0;
2 February 1924 Cardiff 1 Arsenal 0 (second round FA Cup).

Consecutive wins from start of season: 23 – by Morton in Scottish Division 2, 1963–64. This covers League games only. The English record is 11 by Spurs in Division 1, 1960–61, their first point being dropped at home in a 1-1 draw with Manchester City on Monday 10 October.

WITHOUT A DEFEAT

British overall record: 62 – Celtic were undefeated from their 2-0 reverse by Hearts at Tynecastle on Saturday 13 November 1915 to Saturday 21 April 1917, when Kilmarnock beat them in their final home game at Celtic Park. Of the 62 games, 49 were won and 13 drawn. All were Scottish League games, the Scottish Cup having been suspended for the duration of the war. In peace-time, Rangers hold the Scottish record with 45 games from Saturday 17 March 1928 to Wednesday 27 March 1929 in both the Scottish League and Cup.

English first-class record: 40 – Nottingham Forest were undefeated in first-class matches after their FA Cup defeat at The Hawthorns on Saturday 11 March 1978 until Liverpool beat them 2-0 at Anfield on Saturday 9 December 1978. The run involved League, League Cup, European Cup and Charity Shield games, though Forest did lose 2 close-season friendlies during this period. They

1912	Lincoln City *	1948	Newcastle U.
1913	Manchester U.	1949	Burnley
1914	Everton	1950	Blackpool
1915	Huddersfield T.	1951	Wolves
1916	*Not contested*	1952	Wolves
1917	*Not contested*	1953	Wolves
1918	*Not contested*	1954	Everton
1919	*Not contested*	1955	Bolton W.
1920	Blackpool	1956	Manchester U.
1921	Manchester U.	1957	Liverpool
1922	Sheffield U.	1958	Wolves
1923	WBA	1959	Wolves
1924	WBA	1960	Manchester U.
1925	Huddersfield T.	1961	Sheffield W.
1926	Huddersfield T.	1962	Burnley
1927	WBA	1963	Burnley
1928	Stoke City	1964	Aston Villa
1929	The Wednesday	1965	Blackburn R.
1930	Aston Villa	1966	Sheffield U.
1931	Huddersfield T.	1967	Blackburn R.
1932	Wolves	1968	Everton
1933	WBA	1969	Liverpool
1934	WBA	1970	Liverpool
1935	WBA	1971	Liverpool
1936	Derby County	1972	Derby County
1937	Leeds United	1973	Liverpool
1938	Everton	1974	Liverpool
1939	Manchester U.	1975	Liverpool
1940	*Not contested*	1976	Liverpool
1941	*Not contested*	1977	Liverpool
1942	*Not contested*	1978	Manchester C.
1943	*Not contested*	1979	Liverpool
1944	*Not contested*	1980	Liverpool
1945	*Not contested*	1981	Liverpool
1946	Sheffield W.	1982	Liverpool
1947	Manchester U.	1983	WBA

*first team (all others reserve teams)

ABOVE: The Central League is for Northern and Midland reserve sides.
LEFT ABOVE: Arsenal goalkeeper Jack Kelsey collects the ball from Bedford forward Steel during an FA Cup third round replay which Arsenal won 2-1 on 12 January 1956. The significant point about the picture, however, can be seen behind Kelsey for the match was the first ever to be covered by the Independent Television Network and their cameras can be observed underneath the tarpaulins.

thus beat a record which had stood for nearly a century – Blackburn Rovers' run of 35 competitive games (31 wins, 4 draws) in 1881–82 which was brought to an end by their FA Cup final defeat at the hands of Old Etonians on 25 March 1882.

League matches only: 62 – Celtic's record (*see above*) involved League matches only, including the occasion (Saturday 15 April 1916) on which they beat Raith and Motherwell on the same day.

Football League matches only: 42 – Nottingham Forest became the only club in modern times to go a whole year of games without a defeat when, on 25 November 1978, they beat Bolton Wanderers 1-0 at Burnden Park. Their previous defeat had been on 19 November 1977 when they lost 1-0 to a Ray Hankin goal for Leeds at Elland Road. Liverpool broke the run when they won 2-0 at Anfield on Saturday 9 December 1978.

All home games: 85 – Liverpool between their 3-2 defeat by Birmingham on Saturday 21 January 1978 and the 2-1 win by Leicester, then bottom of Division 1, on Saturday 31

January 1981. The total comprised 63 League, 9 League Cup, 6 FA Cup, 6 European Cup and 1 Super Cup. Liverpool won 69 of the matches, scoring 213 goals and conceding only 35. The previous English record was held by Gillingham, who from 9 April 1965 played 48 League and 4 Cup games without defeat.

Home League games: 63 – Liverpool, between the fixtures mentioned above, both of which were in Division 1. The previous record was 61 by Airdrie, between 23 September 1922 and 5 December 1925.

Home Scottish games: 67 – Airdrieonians played 67 home League and Cup games between 23 September 1922 and 5 December 1925 without defeat.

All away games: 36 – Celtic were undefeated in 36 consecutive away games (all in the Scottish League) between Saturday 13 November 1915 and Saturday 3 November 1917. This is also the record for consecutive away League games without defeat.

All away games, England: 23 – Nottingham Forest played 23 away games without defeat during their run of 40 consecutive games (*see above*). If their 5-0 Charity Shield victory over Ipswich at Wembley and their two League Cup finals against Liverpool are not taken as away matches, then the run of 20 is still a record. It lasted from 11 March 1978 to 9 December 1978.

Away League games, England: 22 – Nottingham Forest from 19 November 1977 to 9 December 1978.

All Cup matches: 25 – Spurs were undefeated in 25 consecutive cup matches between their 0-1 League Cup defeat by West Ham on 2 December 1980 and their 1-3 League Cup final defeat by Liverpool on 13 March 1982. Of these 13 were in the FA Cup, 7 in the League Cup and 5 in the Cup Winners Cup. From their FA Cup game at Swindon on 26 January 1980 to their FA Cup final replay victory over QPR on 27 May 1982, Spurs were clearly assisted by never being drawn to play outside London in a one-legged match. This run of 41 games did include 6 that were played elsewhere as one-half of two-legged ties and 2 FA Cup semi-finals but it also included 9 consecutive home FA Cup draws.

FA Cup games only: 24 – Blackburn Rovers went 24 FA Cup matches without defeat between 18 November 1882 and 30 October 1886 and won the trophy three times in the period.

Football League Cup ties: 17 – Nottingham Forest were undefeated in a League Cup tie (comprising 25 games in all) between 20 Sept. 1976 when Coventry

Tinsley Lindley, who scored in 9 consecutive internationals for England between 13 March 1886 (v Ireland in Belfast) and 31 March 1888 (also v Ireland in Belfast). Lindley failed to score in just 2 of his 13 internationals, recording 15 goals in all. He also entered the record books after Notts County had a point deducted for playing him unregistered (see POINTS).

City beat them 3-0 and Saturday 15 March 1980 when Wolves won the 1980 final 1-0.

Scottish Cup ties: 25 – Queen's Park won 25 consecutive ties from the start of the 1879–80 competition to the quarter-finals of the 1882–83 series, when Dumbarton beat them 3-1, comprising 29 games in all.

Scottish League Cup games: 39 – Celtic were undefeated in 39 Scottish League Cup games (the earlier rounds were then played as groups) between Saturday 21 August 1965, when Dundee beat them 2-0 at Celtic Park, and Wednesday 13 August 1969, when Rangers won 2-1 at Ibrox. They won 37 and drew 2.

Home FA Cup ties: 26 – Huddersfield did not lose a home FA Cup tie between 1913 and 1932.

Away FA Cup ties: 11 – Arsenal were undefeated despite 11 consecutive away draws (calling semi-finals and finals away games) from the third round at Yeovil in 1970–71 to the 1972 final, when they lost 1-0 to Leeds. They actually played 14 games on grounds other than Highbury during this run. Technically Wanderers surpassed this record in playing 15 games undefeated in seasons 1875–76, 1876–77 and 1877–78. As they had no ground of their own, all the games were played at 'away' venues, usually Kennington Oval – which had effectively become their 'home' ground as a result.

Consecutive League games in single season: 30 – Burnley in 1920–21 between a 2-0 defeat at Bradford City on Saturday 4 September 1920 and a 3-0 defeat by Manchester City (who came second in the League) at Hyde Road on Saturday 26 March 1921. This was a run of 30 League games in a single season, but Burnley had been knocked out of the FA Cup in the interim by Hull City of Division 2.

Consecutive League games from start of season: 29 – Leeds were not defeated until the 30th game of their 1973–74 Division 1 season, when Stoke City beat them 3-2 on Saturday 23 February 1974 at the Victoria Ground. Liverpool also completed 29 games undefeated from the start of their first ever Football League season, in Division 2 in 1893–94. They played 28 games in the division undefeated, plus one test match, to complete 29 in that season, and then drew their first two games of the next season, making 31 in all. In this sense, their record is better than that of Leeds, as is Celtic's, who were not defeated in the first 36 games of their 1916–17 Scottish League season. This, however, was part of a much longer run of undefeated games and was conducted in the rather different conditions of wartime football.

DEFEATS

Consecutive first-class matches: 18 – Rochdale lost 18 consecutive matches after beating New Brighton 3-2 on Saturday 7 November 1931 through to Wednesday 9 March 1932, when they drew 1-1 with the same team. This includes the record for consecutive League defeats, 17 of those games, plus a 2-1 defeat by Scunthorpe in the first round of the Cup.

Away defeats: 25 – Nelson drew 1-1 at Halifax on Saturday 29 March 1930 and then proceeded to lose every subsequent away game they ever played as a first-class club. By the time they failed to gain re-election at the end of the 1930–31 season, they had lost 24 consecutive away *League* games – a first-class British record, which, of course, might

have been extended had they been re-elected. In addition they lost a replayed second round FA Cup tie 3-0 at York after having a previous game abandoned when they were losing 2-0. This made 25 consecutive games.

Home defeats: 14 – Rochdale lost 14 consecutive home games in Division 3N. After beating New Brighton 3-2 on 7 November 1931, they lost their 13 remaining home games and also their first in the 1932–33 season (0-1 to Carlisle). They drew their next game, 0-0 with Barrow on Tuesday 6 September 1932, and their 14 game record is an overall first-class home record as well as the League record. In the FA Cup, they lost 2-1 away to non-League Scunthorpe.

From start of season: 12 – Manchester United lost their first 12 Division 1 fixtures in 1930–31. Their first point was in a 2-0 win over Birmingham at Old Trafford on Saturday 1 November 1930. Among their defeats were two big ones at home – 0-6 to Huddersfield and 4-7 to Newcastle – within the space of three days. Clydebank lost the first 10 of their Scottish Division 2 games in 1930–31.

WITHOUT A WIN

Overall record: 36 – Forfar Athletic did not win a single first-class game between 25 September 1974 (when they beat Raith 2-0) and 4 October 1975 (when they beat Stenhousemuir 3-1). This was a run of 36 games, of which 27 were lost and 9 drawn.

English record: 32 – shared by Crewe Alexandra, who did not win a game between Wednesday 19 September 1956 and Saturday 13 April 1957, and Cambridge United, who

broke a Division 2 duck with a 1-0 home defeat of Newcastle on 28 April 1984. As two of Crewe's matches were in the FA Cup (draw and defeat) while Cambridge lost their only FA Cup match during the run, Cambridge hold the League games only record with 31.

Away games: 63 – Merthyr Town did not win a first-class away game between Saturday 30 September 1922, when they beat Charlton 1-0 at The Valley, and Saturday 19 September 1925, when they won 2-0 at Swindon. Their run of 61 away *League* games without a win also constitutes a record, and they did not win a Cup game during the four seasons that this remarkably unsuccessful spell covered. Norwich City beat West Ham 3-1 at Upton Park on the first day of the 1977–78 season (Saturday 20 August) and did not win away again until their first game of the 1979–80 season, at Everton on 18 August 1979. This run of 41 matches is thought to represent a record sequence of unbroken Division 1 away games without success.

At home: 16 – Rochdale did not win a home game between 7 November 1931, when they beat New Brighton 3-2 and 1 October 1932, when they beat Mansfield 2-1. These were all League matches.

FA Cup: 13 – Leeds United did not win one of 13 games between 1952 and 1963, and hence did not pass the third round once. Only two years later they reached their first FA Cup final.

From start of season: 31 – Ayr United, in 1966–67, did not win a game until their 32nd, when they defeated St Johnstone on 8 April 1967. That was their 29th Scottish

ABOVE LEFT: Wilfred Milne, the Swansea full-back who played exactly 500 League games before scoring a goal. He broke his duck on Monday 2 April 1934 with a penalty against Lincoln City – the game's only goal.

ABOVE: Terry Cooper attacks the Stoke defence but is powerless to save Leeds' record of 29 consecutive games undefeated from the beginning of the Division 1 1973–74 season. Stoke were the first side to defeat Leeds that season, winning 3-2 at the Victoria Ground on 23 February 1974.

Division 1 game. They had drawn with Rangers and then lost to them in the League Cup, and also lost a Scottish Cup tie at Elgin City, making 31 games in all. In the Football League, the record is held by Newport County who did not win a game in Division 4 until 15 January 1971, when they beat Southend 3-0. This was their 26th game of the season in Division 4 (though they did win a League Cup tie) and they lost the first 10 outright. Newport won half their remaining fixtures and finished third from bottom.

DRAWS
Overall record: Torquay United drew 8 consecutive Division 3 games between Saturday 25 October 1969 and Saturday 13 December 1969. This is thought to be a record for consecutive drawn League games. Four games ended 1-1, two 0-0 and two 2-2. This spell was broken by a 2-1 defeat at Tamworth in the FA Cup on 15 November 1969.

DEFENSIVE SEQUENCES
Without conceding a goal, League: 12 – Aberdeen played 12 consecutive games in Scottish Division 1 without conceding a goal between 31 October 1970 and 16 January 1971. Hibernian broke this sequence with a 2-1 win. Scottish international keeper Bobby Clark was in goal for Aberdeen at the time.
Without conceding a goal, England: 12 – York City from 1 October 1973, when they drew 0-0 at home to Chesterfield in Division 3, to 8 December 1973, when they beat Southport 4-0. The run consisted of 11 League games and one FA Cup tie and was broken by a 5-3 defeat at Mansfield in an FA Cup first round replay on 10 December 1973.
FA Cup games without conceding a goal: 12 – Bradford City played 12 consecutive games between the second round of 1910–11 and the quarter-finals in 1911–12 without conceding a goal. This run came to an end after 3 consecutive goalless draws with Barnsley when Barnsley won the fourth game 3-2. The run encompassed 8 consecutive rounds. Queen's Park did not concede a goal in 11 Scottish Cup games (11 rounds) between 1873 and 1876.
Consecutive games without scoring a goal: 11 – Coventry did not score a goal in 11 Division 2 games between Saturday 4 October 1919, when they lost 2-1 at home to Leicester, and Thursday 25 December 1919, when they beat Stoke 3-2 at the Victoria Ground.
Away games without scoring a goal: 15 – after losing 3-1 at Merthyr on Thursday 12 April 1923, Exeter City did not score away from home again in first-class matches until winning 1-0 at Swindon on Saturday 16 February 1924. In the 1923–24 Division 3S season Exeter scored only 4 goals away from home; 14 of these games were in the League and the 15th was a second round Cup replay at Watford, which Exeter lost 1-0.

GOALSCORING
Internationals: 9 – Tinsley Lindley, who played for Cambridge University, Notts County and Nottingham Forest, scored for England in nine consecutive internationals between 13 March 1886 and 31 March 1888 (12 goals in all).
League games: 15 – Finn Dossing, a Danish international, scored in 15 consecutive games for Dundee United in Scottish Division 1 in 1964–65.
FA Cup ties: 12 – Stan Mortensen scored in 12 consecutive rounds that Blackpool played between the 1945–46 and 1949–50 competitions (including the 1948 final). He did not score in every game played (missing out on some replays) but did get on the scoresheet in 9 consecutive games.
Penalties: Peter Noble converted 27 consecutive penalties for Burnley between 1974 and 1979.
Games without scoring: 500 – Wilfred Milne, a Swansea Town full-back, played exactly 500 Football League games after his debut in 1919 before scoring his first goal – a penalty against Lincoln on Monday 2 April 1934 to give Swansea a 1-0 victory.

APPEARANCES
Individual: 401 – Harold Bell made 401 consecutive League appearances for Tranmere between August 1946 and August 1955.
Unchanged team: 28 – Tranmere Rovers played the same team for 28 Division 3 games in 1977–78.
Finals: 14 – Celtic appeared in 14 consecutive Scottish League Cup finals between 1964–65 and 1977–78, a world record in any major competition.
See also: APPEARANCES, DEFEATS, FA CUP, FOOTBALL LEAGUE, SCOTTISH CUP, SCOTTISH LEAGUE, WINS, VICTORIES.

Corners

Corners were first introduced by the FA in 1872. It became legal to score direct from a corner-kick after the meeting of the International Board in 1924.
First goal: The first goal to be scored direct from a corner-kick was by a St Bernard's winger named Alston against Albion Rovers in Scottish Division 2 on Thursday 21 August 1924.
First English goal: The first goal scored in a Football League game direct from a corner was by Billy Smith for Huddersfield v Arsenal on Saturday 11 October 1924. Huddersfield won 4-0.
First FA Cup goal: Cardiff's Willie Davies won a quarter-final tie against Leicester on 7 March 1925 with the last kick of the game direct from a corner. Cardiff won 2-1 as a result and Davies apparently did not know that he had scored until the crowd invaded the pitch. Cardiff reached Wembley that season.
First international goal: Alex Cheyne of Aberdeen scored the only goal of the Scotland v England international at Hampden in the 88th minute on 13 April 1929 direct from a corner. Cheyne had been selected for the team only 48 hours before kick-off and the Scots played most of the game with 10 men. This was obviously a Cheyne speciality, for he is also the only player to score two goals direct from corners in a single game. This was for Aberdeen v Nithsdale Wanderers in the second round of the Scottish Cup at Pittodrie on 1 February 1930. Aberdeen won 5-1.
Consecutive kicks: Charlie Tully of Celtic scored direct from the corner flag from successive kicks against Falkirk at Brockville Park on 28 February 1953, but the first goal was disallowed because the referee said the ball had been placed outside the quarter. Celtic won the tie 3-2.
Dribbled into net: When Everton played Spurs at Goodison on Saturday 17 January 1925 the Everton winger Sam Chedgzoy dribbled the ball from the corner flag direct into the net, as the new law did not specify that the player taking the corner could not play it twice. Everton won 1-0. The law was changed at the end of the 1924–25 season to prevent this happening again. In fact, Eddie Baily of Spurs did make a goal for Len Duquemin by playing the ball twice at a

Club	Score	Opponent/Details
Aldershot	0-9	v Bristol City, Division 3S, 28.12.46
Arsenal	0-8	v Loughborough Town, Division 2, 12.12.96
Aston Villa	1-8	v Blackburn Rovers, FA Cup 3rd round, 16.2.89
Barnsley	0-9	v Notts County, Division 2, 19.11.27
Birmingham City	1-9	v Sheffield Wednesday, Division 1, 13.12.30
Blackburn Rovers	0-8	v Arsenal, Division 1, 25.2.33
Blackpool	1-10	v Small Heath, Division 2, 2.3.01 & v Huddersfield Town, Division 1, 13.12.30
Bolton Wanderers	0-7	v Manchester City, Division 1, 21.3.36
Bournemouth	0-9	v Lincoln City, Division 3, 18.12.82
Bradford City	1-9	v Colchester United, Division 4, 30.12.61
Brentford	0-7	v Swansea Town, Division 3S, 8.11.24 & v Walsall, Division 3S, 19.1.57
Brighton	0-9	v Middlesbrough, Division 2, 23.8.58
Bristol City	0-9	v Coventry City, Division 3S, 28.4.34
Bristol Rovers	0-12	v Luton City, Division 3S, 13.4.36
Burnley	0-10	v Aston Villa, Division 1, 29.8.25 & v Sheffield United, Division 1, 19.1.29
Bury	0-10	v Blackburn Rovers, FA Cup pr. round, 1.10.87
Cambridge United	0-6	v Aldershot, Division 3, 13.4.74 & v Darlington, Division 4, 28.9.74
Cardiff City	2-11	v Sheffield United, Division 1, 1.1.26
Carlisle United	1-11	v Hull City, Division 3N, 14.1.39
Charlton Athletic	1-11	v Aston Villa, Division 1, 14.11.59
Chelsea	1-8	v Wolverhampton W., Division 1, 26.9.53
Chester	2-11	v Oldham Athletic, Division 3N, 19.1.52
Chesterfield	1-9	v Port Vale, Division 2, 24.9.32
Colchester United	0-7	v Leyton Orient, Division 3S, 5.1.52 & v Reading, Division 3S, 18.9.57
Coventry City	2-10	v Norwich City, Division 3S, 15.3.30
Crewe Alexandra	2-13	v Tottenham H., FA Cup 4th round replay, 3.2.60
Crystal Palace	4-11	v Manchester City FA Cup 5th round, 20.2.26
Darlington	0-10	v Doncaster Rovers, Division 4, 25.1.64
Derby County	2-11	v Everton, FA Cup 1st round, 18.1.90
Doncaster Rovers	0-12	v Small Heath, Division 2, 11.4.03
Everton	4-10	v Tottenham Hotspur, Division 1, 11.10.58
Exeter City	0-9	v Notts County, Division 3S, 16.10.48 & v Northampton Town, Division 3S, 12.4.58
Fulham	0-9	v Wolverhampton W., Division 1, 16.9.59
Gillingham	2-9	v Nottingham Forest, Division 3S, 18.11.50
Grimsby Town	1-9	v Arsenal, Division 1, 28.1.31
Halifax Town	0-13	v Stockport County, Division 3N, 6.1.34
Hartlepool United	1-10	v Wrexham, Division 4, 3.3.62
Hereford United	1-6	v Tranmere Rovers, Division 3, 29.11.74 & v *Wolverhampton W., Division 2, 2.10.76
Huddersfield Town	0-8	v Middlesbrough, Division 1, 30.9.50
Hull City	0-8	v Wolverhampton W., Division 2, 4.11.11
Ipswich Town	1-10	v Fulham, Division 1, 26.12.63
Leeds United	1-8	v Stoke City, Division 1, 27.8.34
Leicester City	0-12	v Nottingham Forest, Division 1, 21.4.09
Lincoln City	3-11	v Manchester City, Division 2, 23.3.95
Liverpool	1-9	v Birmingham City, Division 2, 11.12.54
Luton Town	1-9	v Swindon Town, Division 3S, 28.8.20
Manchester City	1-9	v Everton, Division 1, 3.9.06
Manchester United	0-7	v Aston Villa, Division 1, 27.12.30
	2-8	v Nottingham F., Football Alliance, 22.11.1890

Club	Score	Opponent/Details
Mansfield Town	1-8	v Walsall, Division 3N, 19.1.33
Middlesbrough	0-9	v Blackburn Rovers, Division 2, 6.11.54
Millwall	1-9	v Aston Villa, FA Cup 4th round, 28.1.46
Newcastle United	0-9	v Burton Wanderers, Division 2, 15.4.95
Newport County	0-13	v Newcastle United, Division 2, 5.10.46
Northampton Town	0-11	v Southampton, Southern League, 28.12.01
Norwich City	2-10	v Swindon Town, Southern League, 5.9.08
Nottingham Forest	1-9	v Blackburn Rovers, Division 1, 10.4.37
	0-12	v Small Heath A, Football Alliance, 8.3.1890
Notts County	1-9	v Aston Villa, Division 1, 29.9.88 & v Blackburn Rovers, Division 1, 16.11.89 & v Portsmouth, Division 2, 9.4.27
Oldham Athletic	4-13	v Tranmere Rovers, Division 3N, 26.12.35
Orient	0-8	v Aston Villa, FA Cup 4th round, 30.1.29
Oxford United	0-5	v *Nottingham F., Lge Cup 3rd rd., 4.10.78
Peterborough United	1-8	v Northampton, FA Cup 2nd rd. 2nd replay, 18.12.46
Plymouth Argyle	0-9	v Stoke City, Division 2, 17.12.60
Portsmouth	0-10	v Leicester City, Division 1, 20.10.28
Port Vale	0-10	v Sheffield United, Division 2, 10.12.92 & v Notts County, Division 2, 26.2.95
Preston North End	0-7	v Blackpool, Division 1, 1.5.48
Queen's Park R.	1-8	v Mansfield Town, Division 3, 15.3.65 & v Manchester United, Division 1, 19.3.69
Reading	0-18	v Preston, FA Cup 1st round, 27.1.94
Rochdale	1-9	v Tranmere Rovers, Division 3N, 25.12.31
Rotherham United	1-11	v Bradford City, Division 3N, 25.8.28
Scunthorpe United	0-8	v Carlisle United, Division 3N, 25.12.52
Sheffield United	0-13	v Bolton W., FA Cup 2nd round, 1.2.90
Sheffield Wednesday	0-10	v Aston Villa, Division 1, 5.10.12
Shrewsbury Town	1-8	v *Norwich City, Division 3S, 13.9.52 & v Coventry City, Division 3, 22.10.63
Southampton	0-8	v Tottenham Hotspur, Division 2, 28.3.36 & v Everton, Division 1, 20.11.71
Southend United	1-11	v Northampton T., Southern League, 30.12.09
Stockport County	1-8	v Chesterfield, Division 2, 19.4.02
Stoke City	0-10	v Preston North End, Division 1, 14.9.89
Sunderland	0-8	v West Ham United, Division 1, 19.10.68 & v Watford, Division 1, 25.9.82
Swansea City	1-8	v Fulham, Division 2, 22.1.38
Swindon Town	1-10	v Manchester C., FA Cup 4th round replay, 29.1.30
Torquay United	2-10	v Fulham, Division 3S, 9.9.31 & v Luton Town, Division 3S, 2.9.33
Tottenham Hotspur	0-7	v Liverpool, Division 1, 2.9.78
Tranmere Rovers	1-9	v Tottenham H., FA Cup 3rd round replay, 14.1.53
Walsall	0-12	v Small Heath, Division 2, 17.12.92 & v Darwen, Division 2, 26.12.96
Watford	0-10	v Wolves, FA Cup 1st round replay, 13.1.12
West Bromwich A.	3-10	v Stoke City, Division 1, 4.2.37
West Ham United	2-8	v Blackburn Rovers, Division 1, 26.12.63
Wigan Athletic	2-5	v *York City, Division 4, 15.9.79
Wimbledon	0-8	v Everton, League Cup 2nd round, 29.8.78
Wolverhampton W.	1-10	v Newton Heath, Division 1, 15.10.92
Wrexham	0-9	v Brentford, Division 3, 15.10.63
York City	0-12	v Chester, Division 3N, 1.2.36

corner against Huddersfield on 2 April 1952. His first kick hit the referee, knocked him to the ground, and Baily centred the rebound for Duquemin to head home. Spurs won 1-0 and Huddersfield protested, but the referee claimed that he thought another player had touched the ball after it had hit him.

Without a corner: Only one League game is recorded as having been completed without a corner – Newcastle v Portsmouth in Division 1 on Saturday 5 December 1931. Not surprisingly, it ended 0-0.

First game decided by corners: Rangers were deemed to have won the Scottish Southern League Cup at Hampden Park on 8 May 1943 by virtue of the fact that they had been awarded 11 corner-kicks to Falkirk's 3. The teams had drawn the final 1-1. After a 0-0 draw the following season, Hibs 'beat' Rangers 6-5 on corners. These two matches are the only instances of first-class games in Britain being decided by the number of corners won.

Debuts

GOALSCORING

Most goals: Jim Dyet, in his first ever first-class game, scored 8 goals for King's Park v Forfar in the Scottish Division 2 on Thursday 2 January 1930. The game was played at Forthbank, Stirling, a ground no longer used for first-class football, and King's Park won the match 12-2.

Most goals in English game: George Hilsdon scored 5 goals on his debut for Chelsea v Glossop North End on the opening day of the Division 2 season in 1906–07. That was the day, Saturday 1 September 1906, on which the temperature at every League ground was over 90°F, the hottest ever on which a full League programme has been played. Chelsea won the game 9-2. Ted Harston scored 3 goals in the first 7 minutes of his debut for Mansfield at Southport in Division 3N on 19 October 1935. The game ended 3-3. Several players have scored 4 goals on their debuts, the most recent being on Saturday 5 January 1957 – I. Lawson for Burnley v Chesterfield in the FA Cup third round (Burnley won 7-0).

Quickest goal: Barry Jones of Notts County scored after only six seconds of his first ever first-class game, against Torquay United at Meadow Lane, Division 3, Saturday 31 March 1962. County won 2-0. This is also usually taken to be the fastest goal after the kick-off ever scored in English football, sharing the distinction with two others. Bill Nicholson recorded the fastest ever debut goal in an international career when he scored for England against Portugal after just 19 seconds at Goodison Park on 19 May 1951. England won 5-2 and Nicholson, who had scored just five League goals in the five seasons since the War, never played for England again. There are two known instances of a player scoring with his first touch

Aberdeen	0-8	v Celtic, Division 1, 30.1.65	East Stirlingshire	1-12 v Dundee United, Division 2, 13.4.36
Airdrieonians	1-11	v *Hibernian, Division 1, 24.10.59	Falkirk	1-11 v Airdrieonians, Division 1, 28.4.51
Albion Rovers	1-9	v Motherwell, Division 1, 2.1.37	Forfar Athletic	2-12 v King's Park, Division 2, 2.1.30
Alloa Athletic	2-11	v Hibernian, League Cup quarter-final, 26.9.65	Hamilton Acad.	1-11 v Hibernian, Division 1, 6.11.65
Arbroath	0-8	v Kilmarnock, Division 2, 3.1.49	Heart of Midlothian	1-8 v *Vale of Leven, Scottish Cup 3rd round, 30.12.1882
Ayr United	0-9	v Rangers, Division 1, 16.11.29 &	Hibernian	0-10 v Rangers, Division 1, 24.12.98
		v Heart of Midlothian, Division 1, 28.2.31	Kilmarnock	1-9 v Celtic, Division 1, 13.8.38
		v Third Lanark, Division 2, 4.12.54	Meadowbank Thistle	0-8 v Hamilton Academicals, Division 2, 14.12.74
Berwick Rangers	1-9	v Dundee United, Division 2, 21.4.56	Montrose	0-13 v Aberdeen Reserves, Division C, 17.3.51
		v Hamilton Academicals, Division 1, 9.8.80	Morton	1-10 v Port Glasgow Athletic, Division 2, 5.5.94
Brechin City	0-10	v Cowdenbeath, Division 2, 20.11.37		v St Bernard's, Division 2, 14.10.33
		v Albion Rovers, Division 2, 15.1.38	Motherwell	0-8 v Aberdeen, Division 1, 26.3.79
		v Airdrieonians, Division 2, 12.2.38	Partick Thistle	0-10 v Queen's Park, S. Cup 5th round, 3.12.1881
Celtic	0-8	v Motherwell, Division 1, 30.4.37	Queen of the South	2-10 v Dundee, Division 1, 1.12.62
Clyde	0-11	v Dumbarton, Scottish Cup 4th round, 22.11.1879 &	Queen's Park	3-10 v Heart of Midlothian, Division 1, 24.8.12
		v Rangers, Scottish Cup 4th round, 13.11.1880	Raith Rovers	2-11 v Morton, Division 2, 18.3.36
Clydebank	1-9	v Gala Fairydean, S. Cup qualifying round, 15.9.65	Rangers	1-7 v Celtic, Scottish League Cup final, 19.10.57
Cowdenbeath	1-11	v Clyde, Division 2, 6.10.51	St Johnstone	1-10 v *Third Lanark, S. Cup 1st round, 24.1.03
Dumbarton	1-11	v Albion Rovers, Division 2, 30.1.26 &	St Mirren	0-9 v Rangers, Division 1, 4.12.1897
		v Ayr United, League Cup qualifying rd., 13.8.52	Stenhousemuir	2-11 v Dunfermline Athletic, Division 2, 27.9.1930
Dundee	0-11	v Celtic, Division 1, 26.10.95	Stirling Albion	0-9 v Dundee United, Division 1, 30.12.67
Dundee United	1-12	v Motherwell, Division 2, 23.1.54	Stranraer	1-11 v Queen of the South, S. Cup 1st round, 16.1.32
Dunfermline Athletic	0-10	v Dundee, Division 2, 22.3.47	*away team	
East Fife	0-9	v Heart of Midlothian, Division 1, 5.10.57		

Frank Haffey's despairing dive can do nothing to stop Bryan Douglas's shot entering the net for England's fourth goal against Scotland at Wembley on Saturday 15 April 1961. The Scots' 9-3 reverse that day is that country's largest ever defeat.

in his first international. Billy Foulkes, Wales right-winger, scored with his first kick against England on 20 October 1951 at Cardiff. The game ended 1-1. He is the only player known to have scored with his first international kick.

Without a kick: Joe Craig of Scotland scored his first international goal without even kicking the ball. Coming on as substitute v Sweden at Hampden on Wednesday 27 April 1977, his international debut, his first touch was a goalscoring header. Scotland won 3-1.

Unlikely goals: Tosh Chamberlain of Fulham scored with his first ever kick in League football – against Lincoln on 20 November 1954. This is not unique, but its distance probably is – a shot from just inside the halfway line. Fulham eventually won this Division 2 game 3-2.

OTHER DEBUTANTS

Unhappiest: Stan Milton, Halifax Town's reserve keeper, let in 13 goals against Stock-

port on his first team debut in Division 3N on Saturday 6 January 1934. Stockport won 13-0, one of only 3 occasions on which a Football League goalkeeper has let in as many as 13 goals.

Managers: On Bill Nicholson's first game as Tottenham manager, Saturday 11 October 1958, his side defeated Everton 10-4.

Most: When Rochdale played Carlisle at Spotland on 27 August 1932, only one of their 11 players had ever appeared for the first team before. They lost 1-0.

Leagues: Grimsby Town were founder members of Division 2, Division 3S and Division 3N.

Defeats

FEWEST IN A SEASON

Undefeated: The only English or Scottish

League club to go through a whole season without a single defeat is Preston North End in the inaugural season of 1888–89, playing 22 League games and 5 FA Cup games and winning 23 with 4 drawn. All of the other sides who have enjoyed an undefeated League season (Liverpool, Rangers, Celtic and Kilmarnock) were beaten in the Cup.

The records of the five clubs with undefeated League records are:

Preston North End, 1888–89 in Division 1, 18 wins from 22 games;

Liverpool, 1893–94 in Division 2, 22 from 28 games;

Celtic, 1897–98 in Scottish Division 1, 15 from 18 games;

Rangers, 1898–99 in Scottish Division 1, 18 from 18 games;

Kilmarnock, 1898–99 in Scottish Division 2, 14 from 18 games.

Southampton also completed the 1896–97 Southern League season without losing a game.

Two League defeats: No Football League club has ever gone through a full season and lost only one match, though this has happened 14 times in Scotland. Three League clubs have suffered only 2 League defeats in a season and one, Leeds United, hold the record for the fewest defeats in a full 42-game Football League season (Division 1, 1968–69). The other examples are Burnley in Division 2 in 1897–98 (30 games) and Bristol City in Division 2 in 1905–06 (38 games). There are many examples of Scottish clubs ending a season with only 2 league defeats.

Three League defeats: Seven clubs have suffered only 3 defeats in a Football League season:
Liverpool, 1904–05, Division 2 (38 games);
Wolves, 1923–24, Division 3N (42 games);
Doncaster, 1946–47, Division 3N (42 games);
Port Vale, 1953–54, Division 3N (46 games);
Leeds United, 1963–64, Division 2 (42);
Nottingham F., 1977–78, Division 1 (42);
Nottingham F., 1978–79, Division 1 (42).
Division 4: The record is held by Lincoln City with 4 defeats out of 46 games in 1975–76.

MOST IN A SEASON

Overall record: 33 – Rochdale lost 33 out of 40 Division 3N matches in 1931–32, which is easily the worst ever record by first-class club in a full-length season. Statistically, Abercorn in Scottish Division 1 in 1896–97 and Clyde in the same division in 1899–1900 had even worse records, each with 16 defeats out of 18 games. After 7 November 1931 Rochdale played 27 games (including an FA Cup tie) over the rest of the season, losing 26 and drawing the other.
Division 1: 30 – Leeds United in 1946–47 & Blackburn in 1965–66.
Division 2: 31 – Tranmere in 1938–39.
Division 3: 33 – Rochdale (see above).
Division 4: 32 – Workington (out of 46) in 1975–76.
Scottish Division 1/Premier: 31 – St Mirren (out of 42 games) in 1920–21. St Johnstone had a worse statistical average with 28 defeats out of 36 games in 1975–76, as did Clyde and Abercorn (see above).
Scottish non-Division 1/Premier Division: 30 – Brechin (out of 36) in 1962–63. Lochgelly United also lost 30 out of 38 games in 1923–24 and Forfar Athletic lost 30 out of 38 in 1974–75 in Division 1.
At home: 15 – Barrow in Division 3N in 1925–26 and Blackpool in Division 1 in 1966–67.
Away from home: 21 – Nelson in Division 3N in 1930–31, Bradford PA in Division 4 in 1968–69 and Rochdale in Division 4 in 1977–78.
Consecutive: Newport County lost 2-7 at home and 0-13 away in consecutive Second Division games in 1946–47, easily a record.

SINGLE GAMES

Three double-figure defeats: Two clubs have suffered three double-figure defeats in a single season. Darwen lost three games 10-0 in the 1898–99 season, during which they

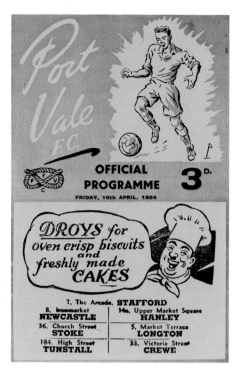

DROYS for oven crisp biscuits and freshly made CAKES

conceded 141 goals in 34 matches. They were: Saturday 18 February 1899 Manchester City 10 Darwen 0; Saturday 4 March 1899 Walsall 10 Darwen 0; Saturday 1 April 1899 Loughborough Town 10 Darwen 0. Remarkably, these three Division 2 defeats came within the space of six weeks.
Brechin City lost three games 10-0 in Scottish Division 2 in 1937–38. They were: Saturday 20 November 1937 Cowdenbeath 10 Brechin 0; Saturday 15 January 1938 Albion Rovers 10 Brechin 0; Saturday 12 February 1938 Airdrieonians 10 Brechin 0.
Most goals by defeated club: 6 by Huddersfield on Saturday 21 December 1957 when Charlton Athletic beat them 7-6 in a Division 2 game at The Valley. Huddersfield were

winning 2-0 at half-time and winning 5-1 after 55 minutes. Charlton won the match with the last kick of the game, by John Ryan. Stenhousemuir also beat Dunfermline 7-6 in Scottish Division B on 15 April 1950. Manchester City were leading Luton Town 6-2 in a third round FA Cup tie on 20 January 1961 when the game was abandoned after 69 minutes. Luton won the replay 3-1, so City scored seven goals and still lost the tie.

INTERNATIONALS
England's biggest defeat: 1-7 v Hungary in Budapest on Sunday 23 May 1954.
Scotland's biggest defeat: 3-9 v England at Wembley on Saturday 15 April 1961.
Wales' biggest defeat: 0-9 v Scotland at the First Hampden Park on Saturday 23 March 1878.
Ireland/Northern Ireland's biggest defeat: 0-13 v England at Belfast on Saturday 18 February 1882.
Eire's biggest defeat: 0-7 v Brazil, Uberlandia Stadium, Belo Horizonte, 27 May 1982.
See also: VICTORIES.

ABOVE LEFT: The programme from Port Vale's Div 3N game against Southport on Friday 16 April 1954. This match ended 0 – 0 and was the 26th time that season Vale had prevented their opponents from scoring. In all, Port Vale kept a clean sheet in 30 of their 46 games in the 1953-54 season and conceded just 21 goals. These performances were both records, though the 21 goals was finally beaten by Liverpool in 1978–79, who conceded just 16 goals. Liverpool's own 85th and last goal of that season was scored by David Johnson at Leeds (the Liverpool players are seen celebrating it below) and gave them a record difference for League Champions of 69. They conceded only 4 goals at Anfield, another record.

Defensive Records

FEWEST GOALS CONCEDED

Overall record: 12 – by Dundee in Scottish Division 1 in 1902–03, out of 22 games. Statistically this is considerably 'worse' than the records of Celtic and Liverpool below.

English record: 15 – Preston conceded just 15 goals in 22 games in the League's first ever season, 1888–89. However, the effective record must be taken to be 16, which Liverpool conceded in winning the League Championship in 1978–79, with only 7 coming in their last 21 games. Their goal difference, 69, was also an English First Division record and this performance is unarguably the best defensive season by any British club when contemporary circumstances are taken into account.

Division 2: 22 – by The Wednesday in 1899–1900 and Woolwich Arsenal in 1903–04 (both from 34 games). In a 42-game season, the record is 23 by Manchester United in 1924–25.

Division 3: 21 – Port Vale in Division 3N in 1953–54 (46 games), Southampton in Division 3S in 1921–22 (42 games) and Stockport in Division 3N in 1921–22 (38 games).

Division 4: 25 – Lincoln City in 1980–81 (46 games).

Scottish Division 1/Premier: 14 (apart from Dundee, *above*) – Celtic conceded only 14 goals in 38 games in 1913–14. Statistically this is better than Liverpool or Dundee, representing only one goal every three games.

Scottish non-Division 1/Premier: 13 – Clydebank in 1975–76 in Scottish Division 2 (out of 26 games). In a fuller season, prior to reorganisation, Morton conceded only 20 goals in 38 Division 2 games, but the wide variation in the number of games played in the Scottish divisions over the years makes direct comparisons both difficult and a little pointless.

At home: Celtic conceded only 3 goals at home in Scottish Division 1 in 1910–11. In England three clubs have conceded only 4 in a League season: Lincoln City in Division 2 in 1901–02 (17 games), Plymouth Argyle in Division 3S in 1921–22 (21 games) and Liverpool in Division 1 in 1978–79 (21 games).

Away from home: Preston conceded only 8 goals in Division 1 in 1888–89 (11 games) but Liverpool's record of conceding 10 in 21 away games in Division 1 in 1975–76 is superior on every reasonable basis.

Clean sheets: 30 – Port Vale did not concede a goal in 30 of their 46 Division 3N matches in 1953–54. In Scotland, Celtic kept a clean sheet in 26 of their 38 Division 1 games in 1913–14. They conceded two goals on only two occasions that season.

Time spans: Queen's Park did not have a goal scored against them from their foundation in July 1867 until 16 January 1875, when Vale of Leven broke the record. However, they played questionably few games of a high-class nature in that spell.

Unrewarded: Cardiff had the best defensive record in Division 1 in 1928–29 (59 goals conceded) but were still relegated.

FA Cup: Only two sides have won the FA Cup without conceding a goal. Preston in 1888–89 scored 11 goals in 5 games, while Bury in 1902–03 scored 12 in 5 games.

MOST GOALS CONCEDED

Overall record: 146 – Edinburgh City in 38 games in Scottish Division 2 in 1931–32.

English record: 141 – Darwen in 34 Division 2 games in 1898–99. Statistically this is considerably worse than Edinburgh City's performance.

Division 1: 125 – Blackpool in 1930–31. Surprisingly, they were not relegated.

Division 3: 136 – Nelson in 42 Division 3N games in 1927–28. Statistically Rochdale had an even worse record with 135 in 40 Division 3N games in 1931–32. Merthyr Town also conceded 135 in 42 Division 3S games in 1929–30.

Division 4: 109 – Hartlepools United from 46 games in 1959–60.

Scottish Division 1/Premier: 137 – Leith from 38 Division 1 games in 1931–32.

Scottish non-Division 1/Premier: 146 – Edinburgh City (*see above*). Interestingly, 5 of the 8 clubs which established these records were no longer in first-class leagues in 1980.

Away from home: 109 – Darwen in 17 Division 2 games in 1898–99.

At home: 63 – Rochdale in 20 Division 3N games in 1931–32.

Any League: Woodard Wanderers, of the West Bromwich Youth League, are thought to hold the domestic record after conceding 422 goals in 18 games in 1981–82. They scored just 4.

See also: DEFEATS

Colin Stein equalises for Rangers in the final seconds of the game v Celtic at Ibrox on 2 January 1971. As fans tried to get back to see what had happened, 66 died in the crush.

Disasters

There have been three major disasters at British football grounds, two of them at Ibrox Park in Glasgow, which was also the scene of two deaths in 1961:

Saturday 5 April 1902: Part of a temporary wooden stand collapsed at Ibrox Park during the Scotland v England international. It is said to have happened when Bob Templeton, the Scotland and Aston Villa right-winger, went on one of his dazzling runs and the crowd strained to follow his progress. 25 people were killed but many in the ground did not know the accident had happened and the game was completed as a 1-1 draw.

Saturday 9 March 1946: A massive crowd had come to see the FA Cup quarter-final between Bolton Wanderers and Stoke City and, though the gates had been closed, thousands pushed their way in. In the resulting crush a wall and several barriers collapsed and 33 people died.

Saturday 2 January 1971: By far the worst of the three accidents happened at the end of a traditional Rangers v Celtic New Year derby at Ibrox. Celtic were leading 1-0 towards the end of the game and Rangers fans were leaving the ground when, with 2 minutes left, Rangers' forward Colin Stein equalised and many of the crowd on Stairway 13, hearing the cheers, turned back to see what had happened. They met those who then decided to leave and the result was 66 persons suffocated in the chaos that followed. It was after this accident that the government, acting on the Wheatley Commission Report, introduced stringent new safety regulations for all major sports grounds, which have considerably reduced accommodation and accelerated a trend towards more seats.

Divisions

North v South: Formal competitions were organized between Division 3S and Division 3N representative teams in the 1950s. Results of the six games were as follows:
Wednesday 16 March 1955, Reading, South 2 North 0;
Thursday 13 October 1955, Accrington, North 3 South 3;
Monday 8 October 1956, Coventry, South 2 North 1;
Tuesday 2 April 1957, Stockport, North 2 South 1;
Wednesday 30 October 1957, Selhurst Park, South 2 North 2;
Tuesday 18 March 1958, Carlisle, North 0 South 1.

Division 3 Cups: To make up for the lack of competitive fixtures (and the fact that only one team from each division was promoted) Cup competitions were organised in the 1930s, with Division 3N and Division 3S declaring their own winners:

Division 3 South:
1933–34 Exeter City 1 Torquay 0
1934–35 Bristol Rovers 3 Watford 2
1935–36 Coventry City 5 Swindon 2 (agg)
1936–37 Millwall 1 Watford 1 (shared)
1937–38 Reading 6 Bristol City 1
1938–39 Competition uncompleted

Division 3 North:
1933–34 Darlington 4 Stockport 3
1934–35 Stockport 2 Walsall 0
1935–36 Chester 2 Darlington 1
1936–37 Chester 3 Southport 1
1937–38 Southport 4 Bradford City 1
1938–39 Bradford City winners

Played in all divisions: Coventry City are the only club to have played in all 6 divisions of the Football League (1, 2, 3, 4, 3N and 3S). Grimsby claim the same thing, but their appearance in Division 3S in 1920–21 is arguable because, although the division was essentially made up of the old Southern League, Division 3N was not created until a year later. For that year alone, therefore, the division was designated Division 3. Grimsby were transferred to the new Division 3N at the end of the 1920–21 season. Queen of the South played in the old Scottish Divisions 1, 2 and 3 and have played in the new Divisions 1 and 2, but never in the Premier.

Ups and downs: There are four instances of a club being promoted or relegated in five consecutive seasons. The old Clydebank club moved between Scottish Division 1 and 2 from 1921 to 1926; Stirling Albion moved between the same divisions from 1948 to 1953; Hearts between the Premier and Division 1 from 1976 to 1981 and Wimbledon between Division 4 and Division 3 from 1978 to 1983. Stirling's was the most remarkable record as they continued the yo-yo act with five more moves between 1955 and 1962, making 10 in all in just 14 seasons. In a way Wimbledon's record was as odd as they joined the League in 1977 and failed to be promoted or relegated in only

the first of their initial six seasons.

Longest promotion run-in: Plymouth Argyle were runners-up in Division 3S for 6 consecutive season, 1921–22 to 1926–27. No club has ever come close to matching this record run of near misses. In the next three years they were 3rd, 4th and, finally, 1st – meaning that they had been constantly in the running for promotion for 9 years. Their most remarkable season was the first of that run – 1921–22. On the penultimate Saturday of the season they led the League by 4 points from Southampton, who had two games to play against Plymouth's one. Southampton won 1-0 at Merthyr on Monday 1 May and then beat Newport 5-0 at home on Saturday 6 May, the last day of the season. This should not have stopped Plymouth – but they lost 2-0 at QPR on 6 May and Southampton went up on goal average. This is the biggest gap ever closed by a club to win a divisional championship in the final week of a season.

League Champions: Only two clubs who began their League careers in the Third or Fourth Divisions have ever gone on to win the League Championship – Portsmouth in 1949 and 1950 and Ipswich Town in 1962 – though 10 other clubs who have won the Championship have appeared in Division 3 at some time in their careers – Aston Villa, Blackburn, Burnley, Derby, Huddersfield, Nottingham Forest, Preston, Sheffield United, Sheffield Wednesday and Wolves. Huddersfield, Sheffield United and Portsmouth are the only Championship winning sides to have dropped as far as Division 4.

Cup finals: Only one Division 4 club has ever reached a major Cup final – Rochdale, who were beaten 4-0 in the 1961–62 League Cup final by Norwich. On the way there Rochdale had beaten Blackburn of Division 1 and Southampton and Charlton of Division 2. Two Division 3 sides – Queen's Park Rangers (1967) and Swindon Town (1969) – have won the League Cup, but no Division 3 or 4 side has ever appeared in an FA Cup final.

Lancashire round-up: Lancashire clubs won all four divisional championships in 1972–73 – Liverpool, Burnley, Bolton and Southport. No other county or city has ever achieved this on any other occasion.

Three division winners: Aston Villa, Blackburn, Derby, Ipswich, Nottingham Forest, Portsmouth, Preston and Wolves have all won the Championships of Divisions 1, 2 and one of the various Division 3s.

See also: ATTENDANCES, DEFEATS, FIXTURES, POINTS, VICTORIES, WINS.

Doubles

LEAGUE AND CUP

England: Four teams have won the League and Cup double – Preston in 1888–89, Aston Villa in 1896–97, Spurs in 1960–61 and Arsenal in 1970–71.

Scotland: By 1980 Rangers had won the League and Scottish Cup double on 11 occasions (1928, 1930, 1934, 1935, 1949,

1950, 1953, 1963, 1964, 1976 & 1978) and Celtic on 10 occasions (1907, 1908, 1914, 1954, 1967, 1969, 1971, 1972, 1974 & 1977).

OTHER DOUBLES

Near misses: The following teams have won one of the major trophies and been runners-up in the other. The trophy they won is given:
1904 Manchester City (Cup)
1905 Newcastle United (League)
1913 Aston Villa (Cup)
1913 Sunderland (League)
1948 Manchester United (Cup)
1954 West Bromwich Albion (Cup)
1957 Manchester United (League)
1960 Wolverhampton Wanderers (Cup)
1972 Leeds United (Cup)
1974 Liverpool (Cup)
1977 Liverpool (League)
Of the Cup winners who just missed out on the League, Leeds came closest in 1972. Having beaten Arsenal 1-0 in the Cup final on 6 May, they went to Wolverhampton two days later needing just one point to take the Championship from Derby. They lost 2-1.

Runners-up in League and Cup: This has happened on six occasions: Huddersfield in 1928, Arsenal in 1932, Wolves in 1939, Burnley in 1962 and Leeds in both 1965 and 1970. Leeds' string of runners-up positions in the decade 1965 to 1975 is remarkable – five in the League, three in the FA Cup, one in the European Cup, one in the European Cup Winners Cup and one in the Fairs Cup.

League and League Cup: Nottingham Forest won the League Championship and the League Cup in 1977–78, the first time that the League Cup had been paired with one of the two major domestic trophies. Liverpool emulated this feat by winning both in 1982 and 1983.

Welsh Cup: Cardiff created a unique double by winning the FA Cup and Welsh Cup in the same season, 1926–27.

Consecutive FA Cup wins: Four teams have won the FA Cup on consecutive occasions. Wanderers won it in 1872 and 1873 (as well as their treble in 1876–78), Blackburn won in 1890 and 1891 (as well as their treble in 1884-86), Newcastle United won in 1951 and 1952, and Tottenham Hotspur won in 1961 and 1962 and again in 1981 and 1982.

See also: FA CUP, FOOTBALL LEAGUE, SCOTTISH CUP, SCOTTISH LEAGUE.

Draws

MOST

Season: 23 – Norwich City drew 23 out of 42 Division 1 matches in 1978–79, 10 at home and 13 away. They won only 7 games.

Scottish season: 18 – Hibernian drew 18 of their 36 Scottish Premier Division games in 1976–77. This is the only occasion on which a Scottish club has drawn half or more of its League games.

FA Cup: 15 – there were 15 draws (out of 32 games) in the third round of the FA Cup on Saturday 9 January 1954.

At home: 14 – Southport in Division 3 in 1973–74.

Away: 14 – Chester in Division 3 in 1977–78 and Plymouth in Division 3 in 1920–21.

Most in season: 1252 in the Football League in 1977–78.

LEAST

Season: There have been 19 occasions on which a first-class side has completed a season without a draw. The highest number of games played in a League season by these teams is 30 – by both Lincoln City and Walsall Town Swifts in Division 2 in 1894–95, by Stoke in Division 1 in 1895–96, and by Darwen in Division 2 in 1896–97. The last time it happened was in 1907–08, when Ayr Parkhouse won 11 and lost 11 of their 22 Scottish Div 2 games. They scored 38 goals and conceded the same number. It has not happened in England since Darwen in season 1896–97.

SINGLE GAMES

Highest known draw: 7-7, in a Scottish Cup first round tie played at Nunholm, Dumfries, on 8 September 1883. The contestants were Queen of the South Wanderers and South Kircubrightshire Rifle Volunteers.

Highest League game: There are four recorded occasions on which a League match has ended in a 6-6 draw. They are:
Leicester City 6 Arsenal 6 in Division 1 on Monday 21 April 1930 (the following season Arsenal won the same fixture 7-2 away);
Queen of the South 6 Falkirk 6 in Scottish Division 1 on Saturday 20 September 1947;
Motherwell 6 Dumbarton 6 in Scottish Division 2 on Saturday 10 April 1954;
Charlton 6 Middlesbrough 6 in Division 2 on Saturday 22 October 1960. No Cup game has ended as a 6-6 draw.

Comeback to draw: The most remarkable of all the 5-5 draws recorded in the Football League occurred at Owlerton, Sheffield, on Saturday 12 November 1904. Everton, away from home, went 5-0 up by half-time, but early in the second half their goalkeeper was injured and The Wednesday came back for the game to end 5-5. The last 5-5 draw was Bristol Rovers v Charlton in Division 2 on 18 November 1978.

Cup progress: In the early days of the FA and Scottish Cups, several clubs were allowed to progress to the next round having only drawn their tie. In the first ever FA Cup competition, 1871–72, Crystal Palace and Hitchin drew 0-0 in the first round and both went through to the second round, and the Wanderers and Crystal Palace also drew in the third round and both went through. In fact Wanderers won only one game before the final – their first round opponents Harrow Chequers scratched, they beat Clapham Rovers 3-1 in the second, they drew with Crystal Palace in the third and then drew with Queen's Park in the semi-final. Queen's Park could not afford to travel to London for the replay, so Wanderers went through to the final, which they won 1-0. As they only had to play in the final the next year, 1873 (this being the only time the 'Challenge' principle was applied), they took the FA Cup twice in a row by winning a total of just 3 games.

LEFT: Derek Dougan scores the goal that robbed Leeds of the double on 8 May 1972; Leeds needed a point for the Championship – but Wolves beat them 2-1.
BELOW: George Robledo's header wins the 1952 FA Cup final and makes Newcastle the first team this century to retain the FA Cup.

European Football

Note that these records apply only to clubs from the British Isles competing in Europe and are not necessarily European records.

WINNERS

Most trophies: Liverpool have won 5 European trophies – the European Cup in 1977, 1978 and 1981 and the UEFA Cup in 1973 and 1976. They beat Borussia Monchengladbach and Bruges twice each in their finals, and completed an unprecedented (for British clubs) hat-trick of European successes in 1976–78. No other British club has won more than 2 trophies – Nottingham Forest have won two European Cups, Leeds two Fairs Cups and Tottenham the Cup Winners Cup and the UEFA Cup.

Trophies retained: Only Liverpool in 1978 and Nottingham Forest in 1980 have retained a trophy they won the previous season. Leeds lost the 1967 Fairs Cup final and came back to win the trophy the following year.

Trophies won undefeated: Leeds in the Fairs Cup in 1967–68, Tottenham in the UEFA Cup in 1971–72, Nottingham Forest in the European Cup in 1978–79 and Liverpool in the European Cup in 1980–81 all won the trophy without losing a single game. Arsenal also set up a unique European record by not losing a game in the Cup Winners Cup in 1979–80 but still not winning the trophy – they drew 0-0 with Valencia after extra-time in the final and then lost the first final tie ever to be decided on penalties. Strangely, this was the only European tie in the whole season that had to be decided on penalties. Other clubs have, of course, gone out of competitions in earlier rounds without losing a game (on the away goals rule).

Most games in Europe: Liverpool have played more European games than any other British club – up to 1 January 1984 a total of 130 matches. In the European Cup alone, Liverpool had played 65 by that date, compared with 70 by Celtic.

Most wins in Europe: Of the 126 games played by Liverpool up to August 1983, they had won 73, drawn 25 and lost 28.

VICTORIES

Biggest in single game: Chelsea 13 Jeunesse Hautcharage (Luxembourg) 0 at Stamford Bridge in the Cup Winners Cup on Wednesday 29 September 1971. The biggest win in the European Cup by a British club is 10-0, which has occurred on 3 occasions. Manchester United beat Anderlecht by that score at Maine Road on Wednesday 26 September

John McGovern lifts the European Cup in Munich to bring it back to England for the third consecutive year.

1956 in United's first ever European tie at home, played at City's ground because Old Trafford did not have floodlights. Ipswich beat Floriana (Malta) at Portman Road on Tuesday 25 September 1962 and Leeds beat Lyn Oslo at Elland Road on Wednesday 17 September 1969 to equal United's record. The record victory in a Fairs/UEFA Cup match is 12-0 by Derby County over Finn Harps (Ballybofey, Eire) on Wednesday 15 September 1976 at the Baseball Ground. As many of the minor European nations cannot provide first-class opposition, it is perhaps more sensible to suggest that United's win over the Belgian champions is effectively the biggest in serious competition in Europe.

Biggest aggregate: Chelsea 21 Jeunesse Hautcharage 0 (8-0, 13-0) in the Cup Winners Cup in September 1971. Leeds United hold the record for both the European Cup and the Fairs/UEFA Cup, in both cases with a 16-0 aggregate. In the European Cup they defeated Lyn Oslo in September/October 1969 (10-0, 6-0) and in the Fairs Cup defeated Spora Luxembourg in October 1967 (9-0, 7-0).

Consecutive wins: Three British sides have won 6 consecutive European matches. Manchester United won their first 6 games in the 1965–66 European Cup with an aggregate of 22-6 before going out to Partizan Belgrade in the semi-final. Leeds also won their first 6 games in the 1969–70 European Cup before losing both their semi-final legs to Celtic. Their goalscoring and defensive run of 24-0 in those six games remains unsurpassed by a British club in Europe. Their victims were Lyn Oslo, Ferencvaros of Budapest and Standard Liège. Wolves also won the first six games of the UEFA Cup in 1971–72, beating Academica Coimbra of Portugal, Den Haag of Holland and Carl Zeiss Jena of East Germany with an aggregate of 18-2. They then drew away at Juventus but did not lose a game until the final, which they lost 3-2 on aggregate to Spurs.

Consecutive games undefeated: Leeds went

Terry McDermott scored the opening goal of the 1977 European Cup final against Borussia Moenchengladbach in Rome's Olympic Stadium. For Liverpool it was the end of a journey that had encompassed 12 years of effort. In the premier competition they had not, up to that point, progressed beyond an abortive and suspiciously refereed semi-final with Inter-Milan in the Merseysiders' first ever season. This time things were different as Tommy Smith and Phil Neal made the game safe following an Allan Simonsen equaliser.

EUROPEAN CUP—BRITISH WINNERS

CELTIC 1966–67

Pr.	FC Zurich (*Switzerland*)	(H2–0, A3–0) 5–0
1	Nantes (*France*)	(A3–1, H3–1) 6–2
Q–F	Vojvodina (*Yugoslavia*)	(A0–1, H2–0) 2–1
S–F	Dukla Prague (*Czech.*)	(H3–1, A0–0) 3–1

Final

Celtic 2 Inter-Milan (*Italy*) **1**
(Lisbon, 25.5.67, 45,000)

Celtic: Simpson, Craig, Gemmell, Murdoch, McNeill, Clark, Johnstone, Wallace, Chalmers, Auld, Lennox
Inter: Sarti, Burgnich, Facchetti, Bedin, Guarneri, Picchi, Domenghini, Mazzola, Cappellini, Bicicli, Corso
Scorers: Gemmell; Mazzola (pen)

MANCHESTER UNITED 1967–68

1	Hibernians (*Malta*)	(H4–0, A0–0) 4–0
2	Sarajevo (*Yugoslavia*)	(A0–0, H2–1) 2–1
Q–F	Gornik Zabrze (*Poland*)	(H2–0, A0–1) 2–1
S–F	Real Madrid (*Spain*)	(H1–0, A3–3) 4–3

Final

Manchester U. 4 Benfica (*Portugal*) **1** [aet]
(Wembley, 29.5.68, 100,000)

United: Stepney, Brennan, Dunne, Crerand, Foulkes, Stiles, Best, Kidd, Charlton, Sadler, Aston
Benfica: Henrique, Adolfo, Humberto, Jacinto, Cruz, Graca, Coluna, Augusto, Eusebio, Torres, Simoes
Scorers: Charlton, Best, Kidd; Graca

LIVERPOOL 1976–77

1	Crusaders (*N. Ireland*)	(H2–0, A5–0) 7–0
2	Trabzonspor (*Turkey*)	(A0–1, H3–0) 3–1
Q–F	St Etienne (*France*)	(A0–1, H3–1) 3–2
S–F	FC Zurich (*Switzerland*)	(A3–1, H3–0) 6–1

Final

Liverpool 3 Borussia M'gladbach (*W. G.*) **1**
(Rome, 25.5.77, 52,078)

Liverpool: Clemence, Neal, Jones, Smith, R. Kennedy, Hughes, Keegan, Case, Heighway, Callaghan, McDermott
Borussia: Kneib, Vogts, Klinkhammer, Wittkamp, Bonhof, Wohlers (Hannes), Wimmer (Kulik), Stielike, Simonsen, Schafer, Heynckes
Scorers: McDermott, Smith, Neal (pen); Simonsen

LIVERPOOL 1977–78

1	Bye	
2	D. Dresden (*E. G.*)	(H5–1, A1–2) 6–3
Q–F	Benfica (*Portugal*)	(A2–1, H4–1) 6–2
S–F	B. M'gladbach (*W. G.*)	(A1–2, H3–0) 4–2

Final

Liverpool 1 Bruges (*Belgium*) **0**
(Wembley, 10.5.78, 92,000)

Liverpool: Clemence, Neal, Hansen, Thompson, R. Kennedy, Hughes, Dalglish, Case (Heighway), Fairclough, McDermott, Souness
Bruges: Jensen, Krieger, Leekens, Maes (Volders), Cools, De Cubber, Vandereycken, Ku (Sanders), Simoen, Sorensen
Scorer: Dalglish

NOTTINGHAM FOREST 1978–79

1	Liverpool (*England*)	(H2–0, A0–0) 2–0
2	AEK Athens (*Greece*)	(A2–1, H5–1) 7–2
Q–F	Grasshoppers (*Switz.*)	(H4–1, A1–1) 5–2
S–F	1 FC Cologne (*W. G.*)	(H3–3, A1–0) 4–3

Final

Nottingham Forest 1 Malmö FF (*Sweden*) **0**
(Munich, 30.6.79, 57,500)

Forest: Shilton, Anderson, Clark, McGovern, Lloyd, Burns, Francis, Bowyer, Birtles, Woodcock, Robertson
Malmo: Moller, R. Andersson, Jonsson, M. Andersson, Erlandsson, Tapper (Malmberg), Lungberg, Prytz, Kinnvall, Hansson (T. Andersson), Cervin
Scorer: Francis

NOTTINGHAM FOREST 1979–80

1	Oesters Vaxjo (*Sweden*)	(H2–0, A1–1) 3–1
2	Arges Pitesti (*Rumania*)	(H2–0, A2–1) 4–1
Q–F	Dynamo Berlin (*E. G.*)	(H0–1, A3–1) 3–2
S–F	Ajax (*Holland*)	(H2–0, A0–1) 2–1

Final

Nottingham Forest 1 SV Hamburg (*W. G.*) **0**
(Madrid, 28.5.80, 50,000)

Forest: Shilton, Anderson, Gray (Gunn), McGovern, Lloyd, Burns, O'Neill, Bowyer, Birtles, Mills (O'Hare), Robertson
Hamburg: Kargus, Kaltz, Nogly, Jakobs, Buljan, Memering, Keegan, Hieronymous (Hrubesch), Milewski, Magath, Reimann
Scorer: Robertson

LIVERPOOL 1980–81

1	Oulun Palloseura (*SF*)	(A1–1, H10–1) 12–2
2	Aberdeen	(A1–0, H4–0) 5–0
Q–F	CSKA Sofia (*Bulgaria*)	(H5–1, A1–0) 6–1
S–F	Bayern Munich	(H0–0, A1–1)* 1–1

Final

Liverpool 1 Real Madrid (*Spain*) **0**
(Paris, 27.5.81, 48,360)

Liverpool: Clemence, Neal, A. Kennedy, Thompson, R. Kennedy, Hansen, Dalglish (sub Case), Lee, Johnson, McDermott, Souness
Real Madrid: Rodriguez, Garcia Cortes, Camacho, Stielike, Sabido (sub Pineda), Del Bosque, Juanito, De Los Santos, Santillana, Navajas, Cunningham
Scorer: Alan Kennedy

ASTON VILLA 1981–82

1	Valur (*Iceland*)	(H5–0, A2–0) 7–0
2	Dynamo Berlin (*EG*)	(A2–1, H0–1)*2–2
Q–F	Dynamo Kiev (*USSR*)	(A0–0, H2–0) 2–0
S–F	Anderlecht (*Belgium*)	(H1–0, A0–0) 1–0

Final

Aston Villa 1 Bayern Munich 0
(Rotterdam, 26.5.82, 46,000)

Aston Villa: Rimmer (sub Spink), Swain, Williams, Evans, McNaught, Mortimer, Bremner, Shaw, Withe, Cowans, Morley **Scorer:** Withe
Bayern Munich: Muller, Dremmler, Horsmann, Weiner, Augenthaler, Kraus (sub Niedermayer), Durnberger, Breitner, Hoeness, Mathy (sub Guttler), Rummenigge

* on away goals

Peter Taylor (left) and Brian Clough relax at the end of their remarkable triumph in Munich. In an admittedly poor game, Forest had beaten Malmö of Sweden 1-0 with Trevor Francis scoring the only goal in his first European game. Forest's success was nonetheless astonishing – just 25 months before the final they had been playing Second Division football.

16 consecutive European games without a defeat from 6 September 1967 when they drew 0-0 at home with Dynamo Zagreb in the Fairs Cup final (but lost the trophy as Dynamo had already won the first leg 2-0) through to 27 November 1968, when they lost 2-0 in Naples. All 16 games were in the Fairs Cup, which Leeds won in 1967–68 (the 1966–67 final with Dynamo Zagreb had been delayed to the following season).

In the premier competition, Nottingham Forest went 15 games from their first ever European Cup appearance against Liverpool on 13 September 1978 to 5 March 1980 (when Dynamo Berlin won 1-0 at the City Ground) before losing a game. This run includes two Super Cup matches against Barcelona. Both Chelsea and West Ham have gone 9 consecutive Cup Winners Cup games without a defeat, Chelsea in 1971 and West Ham in 1966. Chelsea's record may yet be extended, however, for on 3 November 1971 they left the competition undefeated on the away goals rule to Atvidaberg of Sweden and have not appeared in it since.

Consecutive ties undefeated: Liverpool went 16 consecutive *ties* without an aggregate defeat between losing to Ferencvaros in the second round of the Cup Winners Cup in November 1974 and losing to Nottingham Forest in the first round of the European Cup in September 1978. One of these ties was the European Super Cup defeat of SV Hamburg in 1977. The run consisted of 30 games, of which 21 were won, 4 drawn and 5 lost.

DEFEATS

Biggest in single game: The biggest defeat suffered by a side from the British Isles in a European tie is 0-12 on 15 September 1976 when Finn Harps lost in the UEFA Cup to Derby County. The biggest loss by a recognised first-class club is 6-0: Hibernian lost by that score against AS Roma in the Fairs Cup on Saturday 27 May 1961 and Rangers also lost by the same score to Real Madrid in the preliminary round of the European Cup on Wednesday 9 October 1963. The biggest loss by a Football League club is the 1-6 defeat of Coventry City by Bayern Munich on Tuesday 20 October 1970 in the Fairs Cup. Coventry won the return leg 2-1, and this remains the only season they have entered European competition.

Biggest aggregate: 1-16 defeat of Finn Harps by Derby County in the UEFA Cup in September 1976. The biggest aggregate defeat of a recognised first-class club is 4-12 by Eintracht Frankfurt over Rangers in the semi-final of the European Cup, in April/May 1960. Rangers lost 1-6 in Germany and 3-6 in Glasgow.

Consecutive defeats: Limerick lost the first 9 games they played in Europe, from a European Cup defeat by Young Boys Berne on 31 August 1960 to a UEFA Cup defeat at home by Southampton on 16 September 1981. Surprisingly, they broke the duck with a 1-1 draw at The Dell on 29 September 1981. They have so far lost 10 and drawn 2 of 12 games. The most consecutive

David Needham rises above the Grasshoppers defence during Forest's 4-1 home win in 1978-79. Forest won club football's greatest prize at the first attempt without a defeat.

defeats by a recognised first-class club is 5 by Rangers. They lost 2-0 to Seville in the Cup Winners Cup on Wednesday 26 September 1962, then lost their two games in the next round to Tottenham Hotspur. In the next season's European Cup, they lost home and away in the preliminary round to Real Madrid.

Without a win: Of the 43 major British clubs who have entered European competition, only Morton, who were twice defeated by Chelsea in 1968–69, have failed to secure a win. However nine Irish clubs, Cork Celtic, Finn Harps, Home Farm, Limerick, St Patrick's Athletic, Cliftonville, Crusaders, Distillery and Glenavon, have never won a match. Interestingly, both Welsh non-League teams (Bangor City and Borough United) who entered the Cup Winners Cup won a game.

Worst record: Excluding Limerick (*see above*) Glentoran arguably have the worst record of all UK clubs. They have entered European competitions on 17 occasions and have progressed past the first pair of games three times. They played their first game in the Fairs Cup v Real Zaragoza on Wednesday 26 September 1962 and competed every year for 10 seasons without winning a tie. In that time they won only one of 20 games – 1-0 v Arsenal on Monday 29 September 1969. They finally won a tie in September/

October 1973, knocking Chimia Romnicu (Rumania) out of the Cup Winners Cup 4-2 on aggregate. Of the first-class clubs, Everton probably have the worst record. In their 9 excursions into Europe they have been knocked out in the first round on 4 occasions, in the second round on 3 occasions and have never once got past the last 8.

GOALSCORING

Most in one game: Three British players have scored 5 goals in a single game: Ray Crawford for Ipswich v Floriana (Malta) on Tuesday 25 September 1962 in the European Cup (Ipswich won 10-0), Peter Osgood for Chelsea v Jeunesse Hautcharage on Wednesday 29 September 1971 in the Cup Winners Cup (Chelsea won 13-0) and Kevin Hector for Derby v Finn Harps on Wednesday 15 September 1976 in the UEFA Cup (Derby won 12-0).

Most in one tie: Peter Osgood scored 8 goals in the two Cup Winners Cup games for Chelsea v Jeunesse Hautcharage in September/October 1971.

In consecutive games: Tommy Taylor of Manchester United scored in 5 consecutive European Cup games between 16 January 1957 and 25 September 1957. He was later to die in the Munich air crash. Stan Bowles matched this feat in the 1976–77 UEFA Cup when he scored in QPR's first five games –

EUROPEAN CUP WINNERS CUP—BRITISH WINNERS

TOTTENHAM HOTSPUR 1962–63

Pr.	Bye		
1	Rangers (*Scotland*)	(H5–2, A3–2)	8–4
Q–F	S. Bratislava (*Czech.*)	(A0–2, H6–0)	6–2
S–F	OFK Belgrade (*Yugo.*)	(A2–1, H3–1)	5–2

Final

Tottenham H. 5 Atletico Madrid (*Spain*) **1**
(Rotterdam, 15.5.63, 49,143)

Spurs: Brown, Baker, Henry, Blanchflower, Norman, Marchi, Jones, White, Smith, Greaves, Dyson
Atletico: Madinabeytia, Rivilla, Rodrigues, Ramiro, Griffa, Glaria, Jones, Adelardo, Mendonca, Collar, Chuzo
Scorers: Greaves 2, White, Dyson 2; Collar (pen)

WEST HAM UNITED 1964–65

Pr.	La Gantoise (*Belgium*)	(A1–0, H1–1)	2–1
1	Sparta Prague (*Czech.*)	(H2–0, A1–2)	3–2
Q–F	Lausanne (*Switzerland*)	(A2–1, H4–3)	6–4
S–F	Real Zaragoza (*Spain*)	(H2–1, A1–1)	3–2

Final

West Ham United 2 TSV Munich 1860 (*W. G.*) **0**
(Wembley, 19.5.65, 97,974)

West Ham: Standen, Kirkup, Burkett, Peters, Brown, Moore, Sealey, Boyce, Hurst, Dear, Sissons
Munich: Radenkovic, Wagner, Kohlars, Bena, Reich, Luttrop, Heiss, Kuppers, Brunnenmaier, Grosser, Rebele
Scorer: Sealey 2

MANCHESTER CITY 1969–70

1	Atletico Bilbao (*Spain*)	(A3–3, H3–0)	6–3
2	Lierse SK (*Belgium*)	(A3–0, H5–0)	8–0
Q–F	Acad. Coimbra (*Port.*)	(A0–0, H1–0)	1–0
S–F	Schalke 04 (*W. G.*)	(A0–1, H5–1)	5–2

Final

Manchester City 2 Gornik Zabrze (*Poland*) **1**
(Vienna, 29.4.70, 7,968)

City: Corrigan, Book, Pardoe, Doyle (Bowyer), Booth, Oakes, Heslop, Bell, Lee, Young, Towers
Gornik: Kostka, Oslizlo, Florenski (Deja), Gorgon, Olek, Latogha, Szoltysik, Wilczek (Skowronek), Szarinski, Banas, Lubanski
Scorers: Young, Lee (pen); Oslizlo

CHELSEA 1970–71

1	Aris Salonika (*Greece*)	(A1–1, H5–1)	6–2
2	CSKA Sofia (*Bulgaria*)	(A1–0, H1–0)	2–0
Q–F	Bruges (*Belgium*)	(A0–2, H4–0)	4–2
S–F	Manchester City (*England*)	(H1–0, A1–0)	2–0

Final

Chelsea 1 Real Madrid (*Spain*) **1** [aet]
(Athens, 19.5.71, 43,000)
Scorers: Osgood; Zoco

Replay (Athens, 21.5.71, 35,000)
Chelsea 2 Real Madrid 1

Chelsea: Bonetti, Boyle, Harris, Cooke, Dempsey, Webb, Weller, Baldwin, Osgood (Smethurst), Hudson, Houseman
Real: Borja, Luis, Zunzunegui, Pirri, Benito, Zoco, Fleitas, Amancio, Grosso, Velasquez (Gento), Bueno (Grande)
Scorers: Dempsey, Osgood; Fleitas

RANGERS 1971–72

1	Stade Rennes (*France*)	(A1–1, H1–0)	2–1
2	Sporting Lisbon (*Port.*)	(H3–2, A3–4)*	6–6
Q–F	Torino (*Italy*)	(A1–1, H1–0)	2–1
S–F	Bayern Munich (*W. G.*)	(A1–1, H2–0)	3–1

Final

Rangers 3 Dynamo Moscow (*USSR*) **2**
(Barcelona, 24.5.72, 24,701)

Rangers: McCloy, Jardine, Mathieson, Greig, Johnstone, Smith, McLean, Conn, Stein, MacDonald, Johnston
Dynamo: Pilgui, Bassaliev, Dolmatov, Dolbonosov (Djerochkovich), Zhukov, Baidatchini, Yakubik, (Eshtrekov), Sabo, Makovikov, Evryuzhkin
Scorers: Stein, Johnston 2; Eshtrekov, Makovikov

*Rangers won on away goals rule

ABERDEEN 1982–83

Pr	Sion (*Switzerland*)	(H7–0, A4–1)	11–1
1	Dynamo Tirana	(H1–0, A0–0)	1–0
2	Lech Poznan (*Poland*)	(H2–0, A1–0)	3–0
Q–F	Bayern Munich	(A0–0, H3–2)	3–2
S–F	Waterschei (*Belgium*)	(H5–1, A0–1)	5–2

Final

Aberdeen 2 Real Madrid 1 (aet)
(Gothenburg, 11.5.83, 17,804)

Aberdeen: Leighton, Rougvie, McMaster, Cooper, McLeish, Miller, Strachan, Simpson, McGhee, Black (sub Hewitt), Weir
Real Madrid: Augustin, Jean Jose, Camacho, (sub San Jose), Metgod, Bonet, Gallego, Juanito, Angel, Santillana, Stielike, Isidro (sub Salguero)
Scorers: Black, Hewitt; Juanito (pen)

A despondent Graham Rix at the end of Arsenal's ill-fated 1979-80 season during which they played a record 70 first-class matches. Rix's penalty miss which ended the Cup Winners Cup final with Valencia left Arsenal with an undefeated record but no trophy to show for it.

the first they had ever played in Europe.

In one season: John Wark scored 14 goals for Ipswich in their UEFA Cup success of 1981, beating Jose Altafini's record aggregate of 13 in the 1972–73 European Cup, which was achieved in two fewer matches. In the European Cup Dennis Viollet in 1956–57 and Denis Law in 1968–69 both scored 9 goals for Manchester United and lead the European Cup goalscoring lists in those seasons. Alan Gilzean matched this feat with 9 for Dundee in 1962–63, when his side were knocked out by eventual winners AC Milan in the semi-finals.

Aggregate: Peter Lorimer scored 30 goals for Leeds in European competition between 24 November 1965 and 24 April 1975, when he scored in the European Cup semi-final in Barcelona.

Most players scoring: Nine Liverpool players scored in the club's 11-0 defeat of Stromsgodset (Norway) in the Cup Winners Cup on Tuesday 17 September 1974 – Boersma, Callaghan, Cormack, Heighway, Hughes, Ray Kennedy, Lindsay, Smith and Peter Thompson. Only Ray Clemence and Brian Hall failed to score – a record for any team in a European tie.

MISCELLANEOUS RECORDS

Most appearances: Ian Callaghan made 96 appearances in European competition for Liverpool between 1964 and 1977. Kenny Dalglish had made 55 European Cup appearances by 1 January 1984.

Biggest attendance: 136,505 for the Celtic v Leeds European Cup semi-final second leg at Hampden Park on Wednesday 15 April 1970. This is also the largest attendance for any European competitive game ever played.

Entries: Qualification for entry has varied enormously over the years and has often depended on whether or not other English/Scottish clubs won tournaments the previous year. In 1968 Newcastle qualified for the Fairs Cup after finishing only 10th in the League (and then proceeded to win the trophy) while Arsenal finished 4th in 1980 and did not obtain a place in Europe the following season.

Super Cup: Most successful British clubs in Europe have participated in the Super Cup, played between the winners of the Champions Cup and the winners of the Cup Winners Cup, since it began following Ajax's refusal to participate in the bruising World Club Championship – a contest in which both Celtic (1967) and Manchester United (1968) were beaten after games best forgotten.

1972 Ajax beat *Rangers 3-1, 3-2
1977 Liverpool beat *SV Hamburg 1-1, 6-0
1978 Anderlecht* beat Liverpool 3-1, 1-2
1979 Nottm. F.* beat Barcelona 1-0, 1-1
1980 Valencia beat *Nottm. F. 1-2, 1-0
1981 Liverpool did not compete
1982 Villa beat Barcelona* 0-1, 3-0
1983 Aberdeen beat Hamburg* 0-0, 2-0
[* home team in first leg]

Peter Osgood heads his third and Chelsea's eighth goal against Jeunesse Hautcharage at Stamford Bridge on 29 September 1971. Chelsea won 13-0 to establish several records. The aggregate score of 21-0 is the biggest in any European tie, Chelsea's 13-0 is the highest in a single game, and Osgood's 8 goals in the tie and 5 in the game are records for a British club.

LONDON*		1955–58
G† Basel *(Switzerland)*	(A5-0, H1-0)	6-0
G† Frankfurt* *(W. Germany)*	(H3-2, A0-1)	3-3
S–F Lausanne *(Switzerland)*	(A1-2, H2-0)	3-2

Final

London 2 Barcelona* *(Spain)* 2
(Stamford Bridge, 5.3.58, 45,466)

London: Kelsey *(Arsenal)*, P. Sillett *(Chelsea)*, Langley *(Fulham)*, Blanchflower, Norman *(Spurs)*, Coote *(Brentford)*, Groves *(Arsenal)*, Greaves *(Chelsea)*, Smith *(Spurs)*, Haynes *(Fulham)*, Robb *(Spurs)*
Barcelona: Estrems, Olivella, Segarra, Gracia, Gensana, Ribelles, Vasora, Evaristo, Martinez, Villaverde, Tejada
Scorers: Greaves, Langley (pen); Tejada, Martinez

Barcelona 6 London 0
(Barcelona, 1.5.58, 62,000)

Barcelona: Ramallets, Olivella, Segarra, Verges, Brugue, Gensana, Tejada, Evaristo, Martinez, Suarez, Vasora
London: Kelsey *(Arsenal)*, Wright, Cantwell *(West Ham)*, Blanchflower *(Spurs)*, Brown *(West Ham)*, Bowen *(Arsenal)*, Medwin *(Spurs)*, Groves *(Arsenal)*, Smith *(Spurs)*, Bloomfield *(Arsenal)*, Lewis *(Chelsea)*
Scorers: Suarez 2, Evaristo 2, Martinez, Verges

*composite side (all but one of the Barcelona players were from CF Barcelona) †group matches

BIRMINGHAM*		1958–60
1 1FC Cologne *(W. G.)*	(A2-2, H2-0)	4-2
Q–F Zagreb* *(Yugoslavia)*	(H1-0, A3-3)	4-3
S–F St Gilloise *(Belgium)*	(A4-2, H4-2)	8-4

Final

Birmingham City 0 Barcelona *(Spain)* 0
(St Andrews, 29.3.60, 40,500)

Birmingham: Schofield, Farmer, Allen, Watts, Smith, Neal, Astall, Gordon, Weston, Orritt, Hooper
Barcelona: Ramallets, Olivella, Gracia, Segarra, Rodri, Gensana, Coll, Kocsis, Martinez, Ribelles, Villaverde

Barcelona 4 Birmingham City 1
(Barcelona, 4.5.60, 70,000)

Barcelona: Verges for Gensana, Kubala for Kocsis, Czibor for Villaverde
Birmingham: Murphy for Orritt
Scorers: Martinez, Czibor 2, Coll; Hooper

*Composite side

LEEDS UNITED		1967–68
1 Spora *(Luxembourg)*	(A9-0, H7-0)	16-0
2 P. Belgrade *(Yugoslavia)*	(A2-1, H1-1)	3-2
3 Hibernian *(Scotland)*	(H1-0, A1-1)	2-1
Q–F Rangers *(Scotland)*	(A0-0, H2-0)	2-0
S–F Dundee *(Scotland)*	(A1-1, H1-0)	2-1

Final

Leeds United 1 Ferencvaros *(Hungary)* 0
(Elland Road, 7.8.68, 25,268)

Leeds: Sprake, Reaney, Cooper, Bremner, Charlton, Hunter, Lorimer, Madeley, Jones (Belfitt), Giles (Greenhoff), E. Gray
Ferencvaros: Geczi, Novak, Pancsics, Havasi, Juhasz, Szucs, Szoke, Varga, Albert, Rakosi, Fenyvesi (Balint)
Scorer: Jones

Ferencvaros 0 Leeds United 0
(Budapest, 11.9.68, 76,000)

Ferencvaros: Katona for Fenyvesi; Karaba substituted for Szoke
Leeds: Hibbitt (Bates) for Giles, O'Grady for Gray

NEWCASTLE UNITED   1968-69

1	Feyenoord (Holland)	(H4-0, A0-2)	4-2
2	Sporting Lisbon (Port.)	(A1-1, H1-0)	2-1
3	Real Zaragoza (Spain)	(A2-3, H2-1)	*4-4
Q-F	Vitoria Setubal (Port.)	(H5-1, A1-3)	6-4
S-F	Rangers (Scotland)	(A0-0, H2-0)	2-0

Final

Newcastle U. 3 Ujpest Dozsa (Hungary) 0
(St James' Park, 29.5.69, 60,000)

Newcastle: McFaul, Craig, Clark, Gibb, Burton, Moncur, Scott, Robson, Davies, Arentoft, Sinclair (Foggon)
Ujpest: Szentimihalyi, Kaposza, Solymosi, Bankuti, Nosko, E. Dunai, Fazekas, Gorocs, Bene, A. Dunai, Zambo
Scorers: Moncur 2, Scott

Ujpest Dozsa 2 Newcastle United 3
(Budapest, 11.6.69, 37,000)

Ujpest: Unchanged
Newcastle: Unchanged; Foggon substituted for Scott
Scorers: Bene, Gorocs; Moncur, Arentoft, Foggon

*Newcastle won on the away goals rule

ARSENAL   1969-70

1	Glentoran (N. Ireland)	(H3-0, A0-1)	3-1
2	Sporting Lisbon (Port.)	(A0-0, H3-0)	3-0
3	Rouen (France)	(A0-0, H1-0)	1-0
Q-F	Dyn. Bacau (Rumania)	(A2-0, H7-1)	9-1
S-F	Ajax (Holland)	(H3-0, A0-1)	3-1

Final

Anderlecht (Belgium) 3 Arsenal 1
(Brussels, 22.4.70, 37,000)

Anderlecht: Trappaniers, Heylens, Velkeneers, Nordahl, Kialunda, Cornelis (Peeters), Desanghere, Devrindt, Mulder, Van Himst, Puis
Arsenal: Wilson, Storey, McNab, Kelly, McLintock, Simpson, Armstrong, Sammels, Radford, George (Kennedy), Graham
Scorers: Devrindt, Mulder 2; Kennedy

Arsenal 3 Anderlecht 0
(Highbury, 28.4.70, 51,612)

Arsenal: Unchanged
Anderlecht: Maartens for Cornelis
Scorers: Kelly, Radford, Sammels

LEEDS UNITED   1970-71

1	Sarpsborg (Norway)	(A1-0, H5-0)	6-0
2	Dynamo Dresden (E. G.)	(H1-0, A1-2)	*2-2
3	Sparta Prague (Czech.)	(H6-0, A3-2)	9-2
Q-F	Vitoria Setubal (Port.)	(H2-1, A1-1)	3-2
S-F	Liverpool (England)	(A1-0, H0-0)	1-0

Final

Juventus (Italy) 2 Leeds United 2†
(Turin, 29.5.71, 45,000)

Juventus: Piloni, Spinosi, Marchetti, Furino, Morini, Salvadore, Haller, Causio, Anastasi (Novellini), Capello, Bettega
Leeds: Sprake, Reaney, Cooper, Bremner, Charlton, Hunter, Lorimer, Clarke, Jones (Bates), Giles, Madeley
Scorers: Bettega, Capello; Madeley, Bates

Leeds United* 1 Juventus 1
(Elland Road, 2.6.71, 42,483)

Leeds: Unchanged; Bates substituted for Madeley
Juventus: Tancredi for Piloni
Scorers: Clarke; Anastasi

*Leeds won on the away goals rule

†replayed first leg; the initial game was abandoned after 60 minutes because of a waterlogged pitch with the score at 0-0

TOTTENHAM HOTSPUR & WOLVERHAMPTON W.   1971-72

1	IB Keflavik (Iceland)	(A6-1, H9-0)	15-1
2	Nantes (France)	(A0-0, H1-0)	1-0
3	R. Bucharest (Rumania)	(H3-0, A2-0)	5-0
Q-F	UT Arad (Rumania)	(A2-0, H1-1)	3-1
S-F	AC Milan (Italy)	(H2-1, A1-1)	3-2

1	Acad. Coimbra (Port.)	(H3-0, A4-1)	7-1
2	Den Haag (Holland)	(A3-1, H4-0)	7-1
3	Carl Zeiss Jena (E. G.)	(A1-0, H3-0)	4-0
Q-F	Juventus (Italy)	(A1-1, H2-1)	3-2
S-F	Ferencvaros (Hungary)	(A2-2, H2-1)	4-3

Final

Wolverhampton W. 1 Tottenham Hotspur 2
(Molineux, 3.5.72, 45,000)

Wolves: Parkes, Shaw, Taylor, Hegan, Munro, McAlle, McCalliog, Hibbitt, Richards, Dougan, Wagstaffe
Spurs: Jennings, Kinnear, Knowles, Mullery, England, Beal, Gilzean, Perryman, Chivers, Peters, Coates (Pratt)
Scorers: McCalliog; Chivers 2

Tottenham Hotspur 1 Wolverhampton W. 1
(White Hart Lane, 17.5.72, 54,303)

Spurs: Unchanged
Wolves: Unchanged; Bailey substituted for Hibbitt, Curran substituted for Dougan
Scorers: Mullery; Wagstaffe

LIVERPOOL   1972-73

1	E. Frankfurt (W. G.)	(H2-0, A0-0)	2-0
2	AEK Athens (Greece)	(H3-0, A3-1)	6-1
3	Dynamo Berlin (E. G.)	(A0-0, H3-1)	3-1
Q-F	Dynamo Dresden (E. G.)	(H2-0, A1-0)	3-0
S-F	Tottenham H. (England)	(H1-0, A1-2)	*2-2

Final

Liverpool 3 Borussia M'gladbach (W. G.) 0
(Anfield, 10.5.73, 41,169)

Liverpool: Clemence, Lawler, Lindsay, Smith, Lloyd, Hughes, Keegan, Cormack, Toshack, Heighway (Hall), Callaghan
Borussia: Kleff, Vogts, Michalik, Danner, Bonhof, Kulik, Jensen, Wimmer, Rupp (Simonsen), Netzer, Heynckes
Scorers: Keegan 2, Lloyd

Borussia Moenchengladbach 2 Liverpool 0
(Moenchengladbach, 23.5.73, 35,000)

Borussia: Surau for Michalik
Liverpool: Unchanged; Boersma substituted for Heighway
Scorers: Heynckes 2

*Leeds won on the away goals rule †replayed first leg; the initial game was abandoned after 60 minutes because of a waterlogged pitch with the score at 0-0

LIVERPOOL   1975-76

1	Hibernian (Scotland)	(A0-1, H3-1)	3-2
2	Real Sociedad (Spain)	(A3-1, H6-0)	9-1
3	Slask Wroclaw (Poland)	(A2-1, H3-0)	5-1
Q-F	Dynamo Dresden (E. G.)	(A0-0, H2-1)	2-1
S-F	Barcelona (Spain)	(A1-0, H1-1)	2-1

Final

Liverpool 3 Bruges (Belgium) 2
(Anfield, 28.4.76, 56,000)

Liverpool: Clemence, Smith, Neal, Thompson, R. Kennedy, Hughes, Keegan, Fairclough, Heighway, Toshack (Case), Callaghan
Bruges: Jensen, Bastyns, Krieger, Leekens, Volders, Cools, Vandereycken, De Cubber, Van Gool, Lambert, Le Fevre
Scorers: Kennedy, Case, Keegan (pen); Lambert, Cools

Bruges 1 Liverpool 1
(Bruges, 19.5.76, 32,000)

Bruges: Unchanged; Sanders substituted for Lambert, Hinderyckx substituted for De Cubber
Liverpool: Case for Fairclough; Fairclough substituted for Toshack
Scorers: Lambert (pen); Keegan

IPSWICH TOWN   1980-81

1	Aris Salonika	(H5-1, A1-3)	6-4
2	Bohemians (Czech)	(H3-0, A0-2)	3-2
3	Widzew Lodz (Poland)	(H5-0, A0-1)	5-1
Q-F	St Etienne (France)	(A4-1, H3-1)	7-2
S-F	IFC Koln	(H1-0, A1-0)	2-0

Final

Ipswich Town 3 AZ 67 Alkmaar 0
(Ipswich, 6.5.1981, 27,532)
Ipswich: Cooper, Mills, McCall, Thijssen, Osman, Butcher, Wark, Muhren, Mariner, Brazil, Gates
Alkmaar: Treytel, Van der Meer, Spelbos, Metgod, Hovenkamp, Peters, Jonker, Arntz, Nygaard (Welzl), Kist, Tol
Scorers: Wark(pen), Thijssen, Mariner

AZ 67 Alkmaar 4 Ipswich Town 2
(Amsterdam, 20.5.81, 28,500)
Ipswich: Cooper, Mills, McCall, Thijssen, Osman, Butcher, Wark, Muhren, Mariner, Brazil, Gates
Alkmaar: Treytel, Reynders, Spelbos, Metgod, Hovenkamp, Peters, Welzl (Kist), Arntz, Jonker, Nygaard, Tol
Scorers: Welzl, Metgod, Tol, Jonker; Thijssen, Wark

Families

INTERNATIONALS

Three brothers: Three Bambridge brothers, A.L., F.C., and E.H., all played for Swifts and England between 1876 and 1887, though never all in the same international side. The closest a UK international team has ever been to having three brothers play in the same game was for Northern Ireland v Wales in Belfast on 4 November 1933 when the Jones brothers John 'Soldier' (of Linfield) and Sam (of Distillery) made up the half-back line with their brother-in-law, Billy Mitchell.

Pairs of brothers: Ivor and Len Allchurch and John and Mel Charles all played together in the Welsh side on three occasions – against Northern Ireland in Belfast on 20 April 1955 (3-2), against Israel in Tel Aviv on 15 January 1958 (2-0), and against Brazil in Rio on 12 May 1962 (1-3).

Two brothers: Brothers appearing together in the same international side was a common feature in the early days of the game. In recent years the most celebrated example is that of Bobby and Jack Charlton for England in the 1966 World Cup final (and on 27 other occasions). It has only happened twice, however, in Scotland's international history. The first time was in the very first international, against England on 30 November 1872, when James and Robert Smith, then playing for South Norwood in London but previously with Queen's Park, both appeared. On 25 March 1876 Harold (Queen's Park) and Moses (Rangers) McNeil both played against Wales at Hampden.

Club and country: The only instance of brothers from the same professional club playing for England together at the same time is that of Frank and Fred Forman of Nottingham Forest, who appeared in all the home internationals in 1898–99. Their nephew, goalkeeper Harry Linacre, also played for both Forest and England, winning two caps in 1905. Frank and Fred Forman also established an English record by both scoring in the 13-2 victory over Ireland at Sunderland on 18 February 1899.

Different countries: Brothers are known to have appeared for different countries on three occasions. Dave Hollins, born in Bangor, played in goal for Wales on 11 occasions between 1962 and 1966 while brother John, born in Guildford, played for England against Spain at Wembley on Wednesday 24 May 1967. More remarkable, however, is the case of the Scots brothers Goodall, both of whom were brought up in Kilmarnock. John, of Preston and Derby, happened to have been born in the south of England and, as a result, played 14 times for England between 1888 and 1898. His brother Archie, of Derby and Glossop, happened to have been born while the family was living in Ireland, and therefore played for the Irish on 10 occasions. A similar case was that of Joe and Gerry Baker, who were bought up by Scots parents in Edinburgh. Joe became the first man to be picked for England while playing outside it, while his brother Gerry later took American nationality and played for the USA.

FATHERS AND SONS

Football League side: There have been many instances of fathers and sons playing for the same club and several of both winning FA Cup medals, but the only occasion on which a father and son played *together* in the same Football League side was on Saturday 5 May 1951 when Alec Herd and his son David both appeared for Stockport v Hartlepools. Stockport won 2-0. Both won FA Cup winners and League Championship medals – the father with Manchester City, the son with Manchester United.

BROTHERS

Most in same side: On Saturday 16 November 1878 Notts County included three Cursham brothers and three Greenhalgh brothers against Nottingham Forest in the first round of the FA Cup. County (usually known as plain Nottingham at the time) lost 3-1.

Frank Forman, who joined Nottingham Forest from Derby in 1895 and was a member of the Cup winning team of 1898. A Forest committee member for over 50 years, he also saw Forest's next FA Cup success – in 1959. He and his brother Fred remain the only brothers to play together both for the same professional club and England. They played in all 3 internationals in 1898-99, and both scored in England's 13-2 defeat of Ireland at Sunderland on 8 February 1899.

One family, one side: The most brothers thought to have appeared in a single team at a reasonably senior level is 4, when William, Harold, Moses and Peter McNeil all played for Rangers in several first-class games in 1874. Harold and Moses both later played for Scotland, while Moses and William both played in Rangers' 1877 Scottish Cup final team.

Signed professional forms: The amazing number of 9 Keetley brothers (Albert, Arthur, Bill, Charlie, Frank, Harold, Joe, John and Tom) were all signed at some time by professional clubs. Four – Frank, Harold, Joe and Tom – played for Doncaster, though no more than three ever played in the same League side. The family came from Derby.

Three brothers in same side: Apart from the Keetley's (*see above*), three Carr brothers (George, John and William) appeared together in a League game, for Middlesbrough in Division 1 in 1919–20.

Players and managers: Willie and Tom Maley both played in Celtic's losing Cup final team of 1889 and then went on to manage Cup winning sides in the same year – 1904. Tom was at Manchester City, who beat Bolton 1-0 with a Billy Meredith goal, while Willie was managing Scottish Cup winners Celtic. While Bill and Bob Shankly never played together, they both managed Championship sides – Bob with Dundee in 1962 and Bill with Liverpool in 1964, 1966 and 1973. When Bob moved to Stirling Albion in 1970, both were managing clubs with grounds called Anfield

John Goodall towards the end of his career. He played 14 times for England while his brother Archie played 10 times for Ireland.

(though Stirling's is actually spelt Annfield).

Twins: Twins playing for the same side are not uncommon (for example the Futchers for Luton and Manchester City) but it is rare for them both to score in the same game. This happened most recently from both wings on several occasions when Ian and Roger Morgan were playing for QPR in the 1960s.

Scoring brothers: The most number of goals scored by a pair of brothers in an international (and easily the record) is 7 by Jack and Roger Doughty of Druids (Ruabon) for Wales against Ireland at Wrexham on 3 March 1888. Wales won 11-0.

Fines

Worst: In April 1970 Derby County were fined £10,000 and banned from Europe for a year for irregularities found in their books by a League commission. As they qualified for the Fairs Cup that year, it was certainly the most expensive fine ever imposed. The worst punishments, however, were the expulsions from the League of Leeds City in October 1919 (Port Vale took over their fixtures) and, ironically, Port Vale in 1968, in both cases for financial irregularities and unauthorised payments. Leeds City were immediately disbanded but Port Vale were able to obtain re-election. Coincidentally, the two clubs were under the management of two of football's most famous names at the time of their expulsions – Herbert Chapman was at Leeds and Port Vale were managed by Stanley Matthews.

The only comparable punishment was the deduction of 19 points from Peterborough United in November 1967 (plus a £500 fine) to ensure that they were relegated from Division 3 to Division 4. The number of points deducted was to vary according to the number needed to see them relegated. Apart from Leeds City (*see above*) the most severe penalty which was ultimately imposed on a club was against Manchester City in

John Charles, Mel Charles, Len Allchurch and Ivor Allchurch, two pairs of brothers who played for Wales v N. Ireland in Belfast on 20 April 1955. John scored a hat-trick.

1906. City players, including Billy Meredith, were accused of offering inducements to an Aston Villa player to throw a game on 29 April 1905. Villa eventually won that game 3-2. At the time City were running neck-and-neck with Newcastle for the Championship. The City team had been offered a £100 bonus (a massive sum at the time) to win the game and the club had been consistently in breach of the 1901 rules on maximum bonuses that could be offered to players. City were fined £250 but that was irrelevant compared with the other penalties. The secretary and chairman were suspended for life and the other directors were ordered to resign; 17 players were suspended until 1 January 1907, forbidden to ever play for City again and were auctioned off. Meredith was probably lucky to get away with such lenient treatment, particularly as he was later reported for trying to obtain wages and bonuses from

City while under suspension. He eventually moved to Manchester United.

Weakened teams: The most common reason for teams to be fined over the years has been for fielding weakened teams before vital Cup matches. Taking inflation into account, the biggest fine was slapped on Newcastle United just before the 1924 Cup final when they rested 9 men for a League game against Aston Villa, their Wembley opponents, a week before the final. They lost the League game 6-1, were fined £750, but still won the one that counted 2-0. Of the two men who had played, one, keeper Sandy Mutch, was injured and missed the final. Newcastle had made something of a habit of this offence – being fined £50 before the 1906 final and £100 before the 1910 game. Other teams that have been fined in similar circumstances are: **Everton**, who were also fined £50 before the 1906 final with Newcastle.

The crowd invasion at Elland Road on 17 April 1971 after the referee had failed to give Colin Suggett offside and WBA scored a goal which effectively cost Leeds the League Championship. The FA closed Elland Road at the start of the next season and Leeds had to play elsewhere.

Ken Hibbitt of Wolves scores against Pat Jennings and Arsenal on 29 September 1979. Wolves won 3-2. Hibbitt is one member of the League's most enduring pair of brothers – Terry played for Newcastle United.

West Brom were fined £150 for fielding a reserve side on 22 April 1912, midway between the cup final and a replay.

Arsenal were fined £250 for not playing their full team before the 1936 final against Sheffield United.

Burnley were fined £1,000 by the Football League for fielding 10 reserves on Saturday 11 March 1961 against Chelsea before their semi-final with Spurs. They drew with Chelsea 4-4 but lost the semi-final.

Everton were fined £2,000 in 1966 for not fielding a full side before the Cup final – and won at Wembley through two goals by a reserve forward, Mike Trebilcock.

Leeds were fined £5,000 for fielding reserves in League fixtures towards the end of the 1969–70 season. This was widely regarded as unfair, as Leeds were contesting the League, the FA Cup and the European Cup at the time, had massive fixture congestion, and, in the event, won no major trophy.

Liverpool were fined £7,000 for fielding a number of reserves against Manchester City on Monday 26 April 1971 before the 1971 Cup final. They drew 2-2 with City but lost the final 2-1 to Arsenal.

Points deducted: Apart from Peterborough (*see above*), Sunderland (in 1890), Stockport (in 1927), Preston (1974), Newport (1974) and Aldershot (1975) have all had points deducted for fielding ineligible players. This happened as recently as 1981–82 when both Bristol Rovers (Division 3) and Mansfield Town (Division 4) had two points deducted by the Football League.

Vale of Leven charged 6d (2½p) entrance fee to a Scottish Division 3 game against Galston in 1924 rather than the requisite one shilling (5p). The Scottish FA fined Vale of Leven the difference between the two prices.

Fixtures

GAMES PLAYED

Most: Notts County had played 3,384 Football League games by the beginning of the 1984–85 season, more than any other League club. As befits the oldest club in the League, they were the first to reach 3,000 fixtures when they drew 2-2 with neighbours Forest on Tuesday 25 March 1975.

Least: Bootle played only 22 games in their League career, finishing 8th in Division 2 in 1892–93.

In a season: Arsenal played 70 first-class games in season 1979-80 (in the League, FA Cup, League Cup, Cup Winners Cup and Charity Shield) appeared in two finals and won nothing. In 1932 Arsenal came close to winning the double and played only 48 games.

Congestion: West Bromwich played 7 games between 20 and 29 April 1912, including a Cup final and a Cup final replay against Barnsley. They did not win a single one. Celtic played 8 matches in 12 days at the end of the 1908–09 season, winning 6 and drawing 2.

Repeat meetings: Bury played Stoke City 7 times in 1954–55 and didn't beat them once. This is thought to be the record number of first-class meetings between the same clubs in a single season. Shrewsbury met Swindon 6 times in 1960–61 (League, League Cup and FA Cup) and did not lose once. Huddersfield and Plymouth also met 6 times in 1963–64 in League, FA Cup and League Cup. Nottingham Forest and Liverpool met 13 times in the three seasons after Forest's promotion to Division 1 in 1977 (6 League, 4 League Cup, 2 European Cup, 1 FA Cup). Forest won 4, Liverpool 3 and 6 were drawn.

Played all other clubs: At the beginning of the 1984–85 season, only six clubs had met all other 91 sides then in the Football League – Barnsley, Bury, Grimsby, Lincoln, Northampton and Portsmouth.

FA Cup coincidences: Leeds United drew Cardiff City at Elland Road in the third round of the FA Cup in 1955–56, 1956–57 and 1957–58. Cardiff won each of the games 2-1.

Length of season: The season was extended into August and May (the last Saturday of August to the first Saturday of May) as early as June 1919. In 1882 Darwen had scandalised the FA by arranging to play a friendly in Glasgow on Saturday 23 September. For many years the season was strictly

John Hollins pulls away from Willie Carr in the same game. Hollins is one of only three sets of brothers who have played for different countries (see FAMILIES).

limited to the winter 6 months, October to March.

Championship of the world: Two games between English and Scottish Cup finalists were billed as such in 1887 and 1888. Hibernian beat Preston in 1887 and Renton defeated West Bromwich 4-1 in a snowstorm in 1888 to be declared the last 'Champions of the World' – until Uruguay in 1930. Refereeing that Renton v WBA game was Frank Watt, who became secretary of Newcastle in 1895 and ran the club for 30 years.

Leagues competed in: Between 1960 and 1972 Gateshead played in the Football League, the Northern Counties League, the North-Eastern League, the Northern Regional League, the Northern Premier League, the Midland Counties League and had even applied to join the Scottish League.

Colour clashes: In three consecutive Cup finals – 1933, 1934 and 1935 – there were colour clashes and the teams had to change. In 1935 Sheffield Wednesday wore white shirts and blue shorts while West Bromwich wore blue shirts and white shorts. It was not until the 1979–80 season that teams were forced to change shirts, shorts and socks if there was any colour clash, which rendered many of the traditional strips irrelevant.

No colours at all: The only occasion when a team is known to have played a first-class match without a recognised uniform strip was on 29 December 1888 when Preston appeared at Leamington Road, Blackburn. They deliberately wore different jerseys of various colours and were described in the local paper the following day as '... like a troup of male mannequins ...'. Preston won 1-0 with a John Goodall goal.

Smallest League in Britain is the Scilly Isles League which has only two teams – St Mary's Rovers and St Mary's Rangers, who play each other up to 20 times a year. Until 1959 there were 4 teams but in a game between St Martin's and Tresco one St Martin's player broke a leg and another his neck and both sides subsequently withdrew from the league.

SUNDAY FOOTBALL

Ban lifted: In 1955 the FA lifted their ban on teams under their jurisdiction playing official matches on Sundays.

First professional match: Wisbech v Dunstable in the Southern League on 19 March 1967. Dunstable won 2-1 and the very first Sunday goal was scored by their forward Alan Clarke (no relation).

First-class matches: The first Sunday games played by first-class clubs were during the power crisis of 1973–74. The first game ever was a third round FA Cup tie at Cambridge on the morning of 6 January 1974 when 8,479 people saw Cambridge draw 2-2 with Oldham. That afternoon 39,138 saw Bolton beat Stoke 3-2, 13,062 saw Bradford City beat Alvechurch 4-2 and 23,456 saw Nottingham Forest beat Bristol Rovers 4-3.

First Football League game: Millwall v Fulham on the morning of 20 January 1974. Millwall won 1-0, Brian Clark scoring in the first minute with the first ever League goal on a Sunday. From 1981 the League allowed six games each Sunday, the first being Darlington v Mansfield on 15 February.

Scottish matches: The first Sunday games played in Scotland were Scottish Cup ties on 27 January 1974. The first scorer was Celtic's Dixie Deans in a 6-1 defeat of Clydebank.

FA COMPETITIONS

FA CHALLENGE TROPHY FINALS

Year	Venue	Attendance	Winners		Runners-up	
1970	Wembley	28,000	Macclesfield Town	2	Telford United	0
1971	Wembley	29,500	Telford United	3	Hillingdon Borough	2
1972	Wembley	24,000	Stafford Rangers	3	Barnet	0
1973	Wembley	23,000	Scarborough	2	Wigan Athletic	1
1974	Wembley	19,000	Morecambe	2	Dartford	1
1975	Wembley	21,000	Matlock Town	4	Scarborough	0
1976	Wembley	21,000	Scarborough	*3	Stafford Rangers	2
1977	Wembley	20,000	Scarborough	2	Dagenham	1
1978	Wembley	20,000	Altrincham	3	Leatherhead	1
1979	Wembley	32,000	Stafford Rangers	2	Kettering Town	0
1980	Wembley	26,000	Dagenham	2	Mossley	1
1981	Wembley	22,578	Bishop's Stortford	1	Sutton United	0
1982	Wembley	20,000	Enfield	*1	Altrincham	0
1983	Wembley	22,000	Telford United	2	Northwich Victoria	1

FA CHALLENGE VASE FINALS

1975	Wembley	10,000	Hoddesdon Town	2	Epsom	1
1976	Wembley	12,000	Billericay Town	1	Stamford	0
1977	Wembley	15,000	Billericay Town	1	Sheffield	1
	(R) City Ground	3,500	*Billericay Town*	*2*	*Sheffield*	*1*
1978	Wembley	16,000	Blue Star	2	Barton Rovers	1
1979	Wembley	18,000	Billericay Town	4	Almondsbury Greenway	1
1980	Wembley	11,500	Stamford	2	Guisborough Town	0
1981	Wembley	12,000	Whickham	*3	Willenhall Town	2
1982	Wembley	12,500	Forest Green Rovers	3	Rainworth Miners' Welfare	0
1983	Wembley	13,700	VS Rugby	1	Halesowen Town	0

FA SUNDAY CUP FINALS

1965	—		London	†6	Staffordshire	†2
1966	Dudley		Ubique United	1	Aldridge Fabrications	0
1967	Hendon		Carlton United	2	Stoke Works	0
1968	Cambridge		Drovers	2	Brook United	0
1969	Romford		Leigh Park	3	Loke United	1
1970	Corby		Vention United	1	Ubique United	0
1971	Leamington		Becontree Rovers	2	Saltley United	0
1972	Dudley		Newtown Unity	4	Springfield Colts	0
1973	Spennymoor		Carlton United	*2	Wear Valley	1
1974	Birmingham		Newtown Unity	3	Brentford East	0
1975	High Wycombe		Fareham Town Centipedes	1	Players Athletic Engineers	0
1976	Spennymoor		Brandon United	2	Evergreen	1
1977	Spennymoor		Langley Park	2	Newtown Unity	0
1978	Nuneaton		Arras	*2	Lion Rangers	*2
	(R) Bishops Stortford		*Arras*	*2*	*Lion Rangers*	*1*
1979	Southport		Lobster	3	Carlton United	2
1980	Letchworth		Tantail	1	Twin Foxes	0
1981	Birkenhead		Fantail	1	Mackintosh	0
1982	Hitchin		Dingle Rail	2	Twin Foxes	1
1983	Runcorn		Eagle	*1	Lee Chapel North	1
	(R) Walthamstow		*Eagle*	*2*	*Lee Chapel North*	*1*

*after extra time †aggregate score in two-legged final

FA Challenge Trophy

Organised by the Football Association in 1969, this competition is for the major professional and semi-professional sides who are not members of the Football League. It has usually been won by a member of the Northern Premier or Alliance. The final is played at Wembley where Scarborough, with 3 wins, are the most successful club. The FA Challenge Vase was introduced in 1974 to replace the Amateur Cup and is contested by sides from those Leagues which were previously amateur, plus other reasonably senior clubs around the country. Clubs cannot enter both the Challenge Trophy and the Challenge Vase. The FA Sunday Cup is for minor league teams.

FA Cup

HISTORY

The Football Association Challenge Cup (to give it its full title) was first suggested by the secretary of the FA, Charles W. Alcock, at a meeting on Thursday 20 July 1871. The first meeting of clubs to discuss the proposal was held on Monday 16 October 1871 and the members present were Barnes, Chequers, Civil Service, Clapham Rovers, Crystal Palace, Hampstead Heathens, Harrow School, Lausanne, Royal Engineers, Upton Park, Wanderers and Windsor Home Park, who all agreed to enter the first competition. Other clubs, such as Great Marlow, Maidenhead, Queen's Park and Donington School, Spalding, entered the competition within the next few weeks but Windsor Home Park and Lausanne dropped out before the first draw.

Cup final venues: Up to and including the 1984 game, the final has been held at the following venues: Wembley (56 times), Crystal Palace (20), Kennington Oval (20), Stamford Bridge (3), Lillie Bridge (1), Goodison Park (1), Fallowfield (1) and Old Trafford (1). Only three games – at Goodison, Fallowfield (ground of the Manchester Athletic Club) and Old Trafford – have been played outside London.

Replays: FA Cup final replays have been held at the following venues: Kennington Oval (1875 & 1876), Old Trafford (1911 & 1970), The Racecourse, Derby (1886), Burnden Park (1901), Crystal Palace (1902), Goodison Park (1910) and Bramall Lane (1912). Four Wembley finals, in 1970, 1981, 1982 and 1983 have had to be replayed.

Extra time: The FA Council decided on 20 July 1912 that extra time must be played in the final if scores were level at full time. This was after 3 consecutive replayed games. The next game to need extra time was Aston Villa v Huddersfield at Stamford Bridge on 24 April 1920. After 90 minutes the players shook hands and left the field, thinking the game was over. Extra time had been introduced for all replayed ties in the 1896–97 season. Extra time was introduced for the first semi-final tie from the 1980–81 season.

Trophies: There have been 3 separate Cups. The first was made in 1872 by Martin, Hall & Co. for £20 and was stolen from the window of W. Shillcock, a Birmingham shoe and boot manufacturer, in 1895. The second was identical to the first and was made by Messrs. Vaughtons Limited of Birmingham. This trophy was withdrawn in 1910 when duplicates were found to be in use for competitions in Manchester. It was presented to Lord Kinnaird, who appeared in more FA Cup finals than any other player, on Monday 6 February 1911 to commemorate his 21 years as President of the FA. The third and current Cup was made by Fattorini & Sons of Bradford in 1911 for £52.50 and was first won by Bradford City that year when they beat Newcastle 1-0 in a replay at Old Trafford. No Bradford club before or since has ever reached even the semi-finals of the FA Cup.

LEFT: Spurs' Alex Brown turns away after scoring for the Southern League side in the 1901 Cup final at Crystal Palace. The game ended 2-2 but Spurs won the replay against Sheffield United 3-1 and are the only non-League side to have won the FA Cup. Brown's 15 goals remain a record for a single season in the competition. Opposition keeper Billy Foulke was, at 20 stone plus, the largest man ever in first-class football.

BELOW: The oldest known picture of a football match; a Bayliss header for WBA against Villa during the 1887 Cup final at The Oval. It was the first of Aston Villa's record 7 wins as well as the second of WBA's 3 consecutive appearances. No other team appeared in 3 consecutive finals for 100 years.

FA CUP   1871-72

First round

Wanderers w.o. Harrow Chequers*
Clapham Rovers v Upton Park   3-0
Crystal Palace v Hitchin   §0-0
Maidenhead v Great Marlow   2-0
Barnes v Civil Service   2-0
Royal Engineers w.o. Reigate Priory*
[Donington School, Hampstead Heathens &
Queen's Park received byes]

Second round

Wanderers v Clapham Rovers   3-1
Crystal Palace v Maidenhead   3-0
Hampstead Heathens v Barnes   2-0
Queen's Park w.o. Donington School*
Royal Engineers v Hitchin   3-1

Quarter-finals

Wanderers v Crystal Palace   §†
Royal Engineers v Hampstead Heathens   2-0
[Queen's Park received bye]

Semi-finals

Wanderers v Queen's Park‡   0-0
Royal Engineers v Crystal Palace   3-0

Final

Wanderers 1 Royal Engineers 0
(Kennington Oval, 16.3.72, 2,000)

Wanderers: Welch, Bowen, A. Thompson,
E. Lubbock, Crake, Wollaston, Alcock, Hooman,
Betts, Vidal, Bonsor
Engineers: Merriman, Marindin, Addison,
Creswell, Mitchell, Renny-Tailyour, Rich,
Goodwyn, Muirhead, Cotter, Bogle
Scorer: Matthew Betts

*scratched   †drawn; score not available   ‡Queen's Park
could not afford to travel to replay in London   § both sides
went through after draw. Cup not actually presented to
Wanderers until 11 April at Pall Mall Restaurant.

FA CUP   1872-73

Second round

Maidenhead v 1st Surrey Rifles   3-1
Windsor Home Park v South Norwood   3-0
Oxford University v Clapham Rovers   3-0
[Queen's Park, Royal Engineers & Wanderers
received byes]

Third round

Maidenhead v Windsor Home Park   1-0
Oxford University v Royal Engineers   1-0
[Queen's Park & Wanderers received byes]

Quarter-finals

Oxford University v Maidenhead   4-0
[Queen's Park & Wanderers received byes]

Semi-finals

Queen's Park v Oxford University   ‡
[Wanderers received bye]

Final

Wanderers 2 Oxford University 0
(Lillie Bridge, 29.3.73, 3,000)

Wanderers: Welch, Bowen, Kinnaird,
Howell, Wollaston, Sturgis, Stewart, Kenyon-
Slaney, Kingsford, Bonsor, C. Thompson
Oxford: Leach, Kirke-Smith, Mackarness, Birley,
Longman, Maddison, Dixon, W. Paton,
Sumner, Vidal, Ottaway
Scorers: Kinnaird, Wollaston

‡after playing Oxford, Queen's Park (exempt until the
semi-final) scratched from the final because they could
not afford to travel to London

FA CUP   1873-74

Second round

Oxford University v Barnes   2-1
Clapham Rovers v Cambridge University   4-1
Sheffield v Pilgrims   1-0
Maidenhead v High Wycombe   1-0
Swifts v Woodford Wells   2-1
Wanderers w.o. Trojans*
Royal Engineers v Uxbridge   2-1

Quarter-finals

Oxford University v Wanderers   1-0
Clapham Rovers v Sheffield   2-1
Royal Engineers v Maidenhead   7-0
[Swifts received bye]

Semi-finals

Oxford University v Clapham Rovers   1-0
Royal Engineers v Swifts   2-0

Final

Oxford University 2 Royal Engineers 0
(Kennington Oval, 14.3.74, 2,500)

Oxford: Nepean, Benson, Mackarness, Birley,
Johnson, Maddison, Green, F. Patton,
W. Rawson, Vidal, Ottaway
Engineers: Merriman, Marindin, Addison,
Onslow, Oliver, Digby, Renny-Tailyour,
H. Rawson, Von Donop, Blackburn, Wood
Scorers: Mackarness, Patton

*scratched

FA CUP   1874-75

Second round

Royal Engineers v Cambridge University   5-0
Clapham Rovers v Pilgrims   2-0
Wanderers v Barnes   4-0
Maidenhead v Reigate Priory   2-1
Woodford Wells v Southall   3-0
Oxford University w.o. Windsor Home Park*
Shropshire Wanderers w.o. Civil Service*
[Old Etonians received bye]

Quarter-finals

Royal Engineers v Clapham Rovers   3-2
Oxford University v Wanderers   2-1
Shropshire Wanderers v Woodford Wells   †2-0
Old Etonians v Maidenhead   1-0

Semi-finals

Royal Engineers v Oxford University   †1-0
Old Etonians v Shropshire Wanderers   1-0

Final

Royal Engineers 1 Old Etonians 1 [aet]
(Kennington Oval, 13.3.75, 3,000)

Royal Engineers: Merriman, Sim, Onslow,
R. Ruck, Von Donop, Wood, H. Rawson,
Stafford, Renny-Tailyour, Wingfield-Stratford,
Mein
Etonians: A. Thompson, Benson, E. Lubbock,
Wilson, Kinnaird, Stronge, E. Patton, Farmer,
Bonsor, Ottaway, Kenyon-Slaney
Scorers: Engineers' scorer not known; Bonsor

Replay
Royal Engineers 2 Old Etonians 0
(Kennington Oval, 16.3.75, 3,000)

Royal Engineers: Unchanged
Etonians: Drummond-Moray, Farrer, E. Lubbock,
Wilson, Kinnaird, Stronge, Patton, Farmer,
Bonsor, A. Lubbock, Hammond
Scorers: Renny-Tailyour, Stafford

*scratched   †after draws for which scores are not recorded
The rule that teams change ends after each goal was
changed after the drawn final. Old Etonians, playing with
a gale, scored after 40 minutes but Royal Engineers
scored a minute later. Engineers then had to play out the
rest of the game facing the gale again

FA CUP   1875-76

Second round

Wanderers v Crystal Palace   3-0
Swifts v South Norwood   5-0
Reigate Priory v Cambridge University   0-8
Oxford University v Hertfordshire Rangers   8-2
Clapham Rovers v Leyton   12-0
Sheffield w.o. Upton Park*
Royal Engineers w.o. Panthers*
Old Etonians v Maidenhead   8-0

Quarter-finals

Wanderers v Sheffield   2-0
Swifts v Royal Engineers   3-1
Cambridge University v Oxford University   0-4
Old Etonians v Clapham Rovers   1-0

Semi-finals

Wanderers v Swifts   2-1
Oxford University v Old Etonians   0-1

Final

Wanderers 1 Old Etonians 1
(Kennington Oval, 11.3.76, 3,000)

Wanderers: Greig, Stratford, W. Lindsay,
Maddison, Birley, Wollaston, H. Heron, Hughes,
F. Heron, Edwards, Kenrick
Old Etonians: Kinnaird, Hogg, Welldon,
E. Lyttleton, A. Thompson, Meysey, Kenyon-
Slaney, A. Lyttleton, Sturgis, Bonsor, Allene
Scorers: Edwards; Bonsor

Replay
Wanderers 3 Old Etonians 0
(Kennington Oval, 18.3.76, 3,500)

Wanderers: unchanged
Etonians: Kinnaird, E. Lubbock, E. Lyttleton,
M. Farrer, Hogg, Stronge, Kenyon-Slaney,
A. Lyttleton, Sturgis, Bonsor, Allene
Scorers: Hughes 2, Wollaston

*scratched

FA CUP   1876-77

Third round

Wanderers v Pilgrims   3-0
Cambridge University v Rochester   4-0
Royal Engineers v Sheffield   1-0
Upton Park v Great Marlow   †1-0
Oxford University w.o. Queen's Park*

Quarter-finals

Cambridge University v Royal Engineers   1-0
Oxford University v Upton Park   †1-0
[Wanderers received bye]

Semi-finals

Wanderers v Cambridge University   1-0
[Oxford University received bye]

Final

Wanderers 2 Oxford University 1 [aet]
(Kennington Oval, 24.3.77, 3,000)

Wanderers: Kinnaird, Stratford, W. Lindsay,
Green, Birley, Wollaston, H. Heron, Hughes,
Wace, Denton, Kenrick
Oxford: Alington, Bain, Donnell, Savory, Tod,
Waddington, Fernandez, Hills, Otter, Parry,
W. Rawson
Scorers: Heron, Kenrick; Kinnaird (og)

*scratched   †after drawn match for which no score is
recorded

37

FA CUP 1877-78

Third round

Wanderers v Barnes	4–1
Oxford University v Clapham Rovers	3–2
Old Harrovians v Cambridge University	2–0
Upton Park v Remnants	3–0
Royal Engineers v Druids	8–0

[Sheffield received bye]

Quarter-finals

Wanderers v Sheffield	3–0
Royal Engineers v Oxford University	4–2
Old Harrovians v Upton Park	3–1

Semi-finals

Royal Engineers v Old Harrovians	2–1

[Wanderers received bye]

Final

Wanderers 3 Royal Engineers 1
(Kennington Oval, 23.3.78, 4,500)

Wanderers: Kinnaird, Stratford, W. Lindsay, Kirkpatrick, Green, Wollaston, H. Heron, Wylie, Wace, Denton, Kenrick

Engineers: Friend, Cowan, Morris, Mayne, Heath, Haynes, M. Lindsay, Hedley, Bond, Barnet, O. Ruck
Scorers: Kenrick (2), Kinnaird (RE unknown)

FA President Francis Marindin, who appeared in 2 finals and refereed a further 8, the last in 1890.

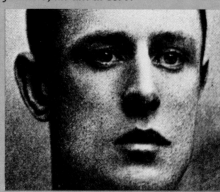

Winger Fred Spiksley, who scored both The Wednesday's goals in the 1896 final against Wolves on 18 April that year.

FA CUP 1878-79

Second round

Old Etonians v Reading	1–0
Minerva v Grey Friars	3–0
Darwen v Eagley	4–1
Remnants v Pilgrims	6–2
Nottingham Forest v Sheffield	2–0
Old Harrovians v Panthers	3–0
Oxford University v Royal Engineers	4–0
Barnes v Upton Park	3–2
Cambridge University v South Norwood	3–0
Swifts v Romford	3–1
Clapham Rovers v Forest School	10–1

Third round

Old Etonians v Minerva	5–2
Darwen v Remnants	3–2
Nottingham Forest v Old Harrovians	2–0
Oxford University v Barnes	2–1
Clapham Rovers v Cambridge University	1–0

[Swifts received bye]

Quarter-finals

Old Etonians v Darwen	5–5, 2–2, 6–2
Nottingham Forest v Oxford University	2–1
Clapham Rovers v Swifts	8–1

Semi-finals

Old Etonians v Nottingham Forest	2–1

[Clapham Rovers received bye]

Final

Old Etonians 1 Clapham Rovers 0
(Kennington Oval, 29.3.79, 5,000)

Etonians: Kinnaird, Hawtrey, Christian, Bury, E. Lubbock, Clarke, Pares, Goodhart, Whitfield, Chevallier, Beaufoy
Clapham: Birkett, Ogilvie, Field, Bailey, Prinsep, F. Rawson, Stanley, Scott, Bevington, Growse, Falconer
Scorer: Clarke

FA CUP 1879-80

Third round

Clapham Rovers v Pilgrims	7–0
Old Etonians v Wanderers	3–1
Royal Engineers v Old Harrovians	2–0
Nottingham Forest v Blackburn Rovers	6–0
Oxford University w.o. Aston Villa*	

[Grey Friars, Hendon, Maidenhead, Sheffield & West End received byes]

Fourth round

Clapham Rovers v Hendon	2–0
Old Etonians v West End	5–1
Royal Engineers v Grey Friars	1–0
Nottingham Forest v Sheffield	‡2–2
Oxford University v Maidenhead	1–0

Quarter-finals

Clapham Rovers v Old Etonians	1–0
Oxford University v Royal Engineers	†1–0

[Nottingham Forest received bye]

Semi-finals

Oxford University v Nottingham Forest	1–0

[Clapham Rovers received bye]

Final

Clapham Rovers 1 Oxford University 0
(Kennington Oval, 10.4.80, 6,000)

Clapham: Birkett, Ogilvie, Field, Weston, Bailey, Brougham, Stanley, Lloyd-Jones, Ram, Barry, Sparks
Oxford: Parr, Wilson, King, Phillips, Rogers, Heygate, Childs, Eyre, Crowdy, Hill, J. Lubbock
Scorer: Lloyd-Jones

*scratched †after draw for which no score recorded
‡Sheffield disqualified for refusing to play extra time

FA CUP 1880-81

Third round

Royal Engineers v Rangers	6–0
Clapham Rovers v Swifts	2–1
The Wednesday v Turton	2–0
Romford v Reading Abbey	2–0
Aston Villa v Notts County	3–1
Old Etonians v Hertfordshire Rangers	3–0

[Darwen, Great Marlow, Grey Friars, Old Carthusians, Stafford Road Works & Upton Park received byes]

Fourth round

Old Carthusians v Royal Engineers	2–1
Clapham Rovers v Upton Park	5–4
Darwen v The Wednesday	5–1
Romford v Great Marlow	2–1
Stafford Road Works v Aston Villa	3–2
Old Etonians v Grey Friars	4–0

Quarter-finals

Old Carthusians v Clapham Rovers	4–1
Darwen v Romford	15–0
Old Etonians v Stafford Road Works	2–1

Semi-finals

Old Carthusians v Darwen	4–1

[Old Etonians received bye]

Final

Old Carthusians 3 Old Etonians 0
(Kennington Oval, 9.4.81, 4,500)

Carthusians: Gillett, Norris, Colvin, Prinsep, Vincent, Hansell, Richards, Page, Wynyard, Parry, Tod
Etonians: Kinnaird, Foley, French, Rawlinson, R. Farrer, Chevallier, Anderson, Goodhart, Macaulay, Whitfield, Novelli
Scorers: Page, Wynyard, Parry

FA CUP 1881-82

Fourth round

Old Etonians v Maidenhead	6–3
Wednesbury Old Alliance v Aston Villa	4–2
The Wednesday v Heeley	3–1
Upton Park v Hotspur	5–0
Great Marlow w.o. Reading*	
Old Foresters v Royal Engineers	2–1
Blackburn Rovers v Darwen	5–1

Quarter-finals

The Wednesday v Upton Park	6–0
Great Marlow v Old Foresters	†1–0
Blackburn Rovers v Wednesbury Old Alliance	3–1

[Old Etonians received bye]

Semi-finals

Old Etonians v Great Marlow	5–0
Blackburn Rovers v The Wednesday	0–0, 5–1

Final

Old Etonians 1 Blackburn Rovers 0
(Kennington Oval, 25.3.82, 6,500)

Etonians: Kinnaird, French, De Paravicini, Rawlinson, Foley, Chevallier, Dunn, Macaulay, Goodhart, Anderson, Novelli
Blackburn: Howarth, McIntyre, Suter, Sharples, F. Hargreaves, Duckworth, Douglas, Strachan, Brown, Avery, J. Hargreaves
Scorer: Anderson

*scratched †after draw for which no score recorded

38

FA CUP 1882-83

Fourth round

Blackburn Olympic v Church	2–0
Druids v Eagley	2–1
Old Carthusians v Royal Engineers	6–2
Hendon v Great Marlow	3–0
Notts County v The Wednesday	4–1
Aston Villa v Walsall Town	2–1
Old Etonians v Swifts	2–0

[Clapham Rovers received bye]

Quarter-finals

Blackburn Olympic v Druids	4–0
Old Carthusians v Clapham Rovers	5–3
Notts County v Aston Villa	4–3
Old Etonians v Hendon	4–2

Semi-finals

Blackburn Olympic v Old Carthusians	4–0
Old Etonians v Notts County	2–1

Final

Blackburn Olympic 2 Old Etonians 1 [aet]
(Kennington Oval, 31.3.83, 8,000)

Blackburn Olympic: Hacking, Ward, Warburton, Gibson, Astley, Hunter, Dewhurst, Matthews, Wilson, Crossley, Yates
Etonians: Kinnaird, French, De Paravicini, Rawlinson, Foley, Chevallier, Anderson, Macaulay, Goodhart, Dunn, Bainbridge
Scorers: Matthews, Crossley; Goodhart

*first season where team drawn first played at home; previously teams tossed a coin for home advantage

FA CUP 1883-84

Fourth round

Blackburn Rovers v Staveley	5–0
Upton Park v Preston North End*	1–1
Swifts v Old Foresters	2–1
Notts County v Bolton Wanderers	2–2, 2–1
Old Westminsters v Wednesbury Town	5–1
Blackburn Olympic v Old Wykehamists	9–1
Brentwood v Northwich Victoria	1–3
Queen's Park v Aston Villa	6–1

Quarter-finals

Blackburn Rovers v Upton Park	3–0
Swifts v Notts County	1–1, 0–1
Blackburn Olympic v Northwich Victoria	9–1
Queen's Park v Old Westminsters	1–0

Semi-finals

Blackburn Rovers v Notts County	1–0
Queen's Park v Blackburn Olympic	4–1

Final

Blackburn Rovers 2 Queen's Park (Glasgow) **1**
(Kennington Oval, 29.3.84, 4,000)

Blackburn: Arthur, Beverley, Suter, McIntyre, J. Hargreaves, Forrest, Lofthouse, Douglas, Sowerbutts, Inglis, Brown
Queen's Park: Gillespie, Arnott, MacDonald, Campbell, Gow, Anderson, Watt, Smith, Harrower, Allan, Christie
Scorers: Brown, Forrest; Christie

*disqualified for paying players

FA CUP 1884-85

Fourth round

Blackburn Rovers v Romford	8–0
West Bromwich Albion v Druids	1–0
Old Carthusians v Grimsby Town	3–0
Chatham v Lower Darwen	1–0
Church v Darwen	3–0
Notts County v Walsall Swifts	4–1
Nottingham Forest v Swifts	1–0
Old Etonians v Middlesbrough	5–2
Queen's Park v Old Wykehamists	7–0

Fifth round

Old Carthusians v Chatham	3–0

[Blackburn Rovers, Church, Nottingham Forest, Notts County, Old Etonians, Queen's Park and WBA received byes]

Quarter-finals

Blackburn Rovers v West Bromwich Albion	2–0
Old Carthusians v Church	1–0
Nottingham Forest v Old Etonians	2–0
Queen's Park v Notts County	2–2, 2–1

Semi-finals

Blackburn Rovers v Old Carthusians	5–0
Queen's Park v Nottingham Forest	1–1, 3–0

Final

Blackburn Rovers 2 Queen's Park 0
(Kennington Oval, 4.4.85, 12,500)

Blackburn: Arthur, Turner, Suter, McIntyre, Haworth, Forrest, Lofthouse, Douglas, Brown, Fecitt, Sowerbutts
Queen's Park: Gillespie, Arnott, MacLeod, Campbell, MacDonald, Hamilton, Anderson, Sellar, Gray, McWhannel, Allan
Scorers: Forrest, Brown

FA CUP 1885-86

Fifth round

Blackburn Rovers v Staveley	7–1
Brentwood w.o. Burslem Port Vale*	
Swifts v Church	6–2
South Shore v Notts County	2–1
Old Westminsters v Bolton Wanderers†	
Small Heath Alliance v Davenham	2–1
Redcar v Middlesbrough	2–1
West Bromwich Albion v Old Carthusians	1–0

Quarter-finals

Blackburn Rovers v Brentwood	3–1
Swifts v South Shore	2–1
Small Heath Alliance v Redcar	2–0
West Bromwich Albion v Old Westminsters	6–0

Semi-finals

Blackburn Rovers v Swifts	2–1
West Bromwich v Small Heath Alliance	4–0

Final

Blackburn R. 0 West Bromwich Albion 0
(Kennington Oval, 3.4.86, 15,000)

Blackburn: Arthur, Turner, Suter, Douglas, Forrest, McIntyre, Heyes, Strachan, Brown, Fecitt, Sowerbutts
WBA: Roberts, H. Green, H. Bell, Horton, Perry, Timmins, Woodhall, T. Green, Bayliss, Loach, G. Bell

Replay
Blackburn R. 2 West Bromwich Albion 0
(Racecourse Ground, Derby, 10.4.86, 12,000)

Blackburn: Walton for Heyes
WBA: Unchanged
Scorers: Brown, Sowerbutts

*scratched after draw for which no score recorded
†Bolton disqualified for professionalism

FA CUP 1886-87

Fifth round

Aston Villa v Horncastle	5–0
Darwen v Chirk	3–1
Glasgow Rangers v Lincoln City	3–0
Old Westminsters v Partick Thistle	1–0
Notts County v Great Marlow	5–2
Preston North End v Old Foresters	3–0
Old Carthusians v Leek	2–0
West Bromwich v Lockwood Brothers	*2–1

Quarter-finals

Aston Villa v Darwen	3–2
Glasgow Rangers v Old Westminsters	5–1
Preston North End v Old Carthusians	2–1
West Bromwich Albion v Notts County	4–1

Semi-finals

Aston Villa v Glasgow Rangers	3–1
West Bromwich Albion v Preston North End	3–1

Final

Aston Villa 2 West Bromwich Albion 0
(Kennington Oval, 2.4.87, 15,500)

Villa: Warner, Coulton, Simmonds, Yates, Dawson, Burton, Davis, Brown, Hunter, Vaughton, Hodgetts
WBA: Roberts, H. Green, Aldridge, Horton, Perry, Timmins, Woodhall, T. Green, Bayliss, Paddock, Pearson
Scorers: Hunter, Hodgetts

*after disputed game for which no score recorded

FA CUP 1887-88

Fifth round

West Bromwich Albion v Stoke	4–1
Old Carthusians v Bootle	2–0
Derby Junction v Chirk	1–0
Darwen v Blackburn Rovers	0–3
Nottingham Forest v The Wednesday	2–4
Middlesbrough v Old Foresters	4–0
Crewe Alexandra v Derby County	1–0
Aston Villa v Preston North End	1–3

Quarter-finals

West Bromwich Albion v Old Carthusians	4–2
Derby Junction v Blackburn Rovers	2–1
Middlesbrough v Crewe Alexandra	0–2
The Wednesday v Preston North End	1–3

Semi-finals

West Bromwich Albion v Derby Junction	3–0
Preston North End v Crewe Alexandra	4–0

Final

West Bromwich Albion 2 Preston N. E. 1
(Kennington Oval, 24.3.88, 19,000)

WBA: Roberts, Aldridge, H. Green, Horton, Perry, Timmins, Bassett, Woodhall, Bayliss, Wilson, Pearson
Preston: Mills-Roberts, Howarth, N. Ross, Holmes, Russell, Graham, Gordon, J. Ross, J. Goodall, Dewhurst, Drummond
Scorers: Woodhall, Bayliss; Dewhurst

FA CUP 1888-89

Second round

Grimsby Town v Preston North End	0–2
Halliwell v Birmingham St George's	2–3
Chatham v Nottingham Forest	1–1, 2–2, 3–2
West Bromwich Albion v Burnley	5–1
The Wednesday v Notts County	3–2
Blackburn Rovers w.o. Swifts (scratched)	
Aston Villa v Derby County	5–3
Wolverhampton W v Walsall Town Swifts	6–1

Quarter-finals

Preston N.E. v Birmingham St George's	2–0
Chatham v West Bromwich Albion	1–10
Blackburn Rovers v Aston Villa	8–1
Wolverhampton W. v The Wednesday	5–0

Semi-finals

Preston North End v West Bromwich Albion	1–0
Wolverhampton W. v Blackburn Rovers	1–1, 3–1

Final

Preston North End 3 Wolverhampton W. 0
(Kennington Oval, 30.3.89, 22,000)

Preston: Mills-Roberts, Howarth, Holmes, Drummond, Russell, Graham, Gordon, J. Ross, J. Goodall, Dewhurst, Thompson
Wolves: Baynton, Baugh, Mason, Fletcher, Allen, Lowder, Hunter, Wykes, Brodie, Wood, Knight
Scorers: Gordon, Goodall, Thompson

FA CUP 1889-90

Second round

Blackburn Rovers v Grimsby Town	3–0
Preston North End v Lincoln City	4–0
Bolton Wanderers v Sheffield United	13–0
Notts County v Aston Villa	4–1
Bootle v Derby Midland	2–1
Wolverhampton Wanderers v Small Heath	2–1
Stoke v Everton	4–2
The Wednesday v Accrington	2–1

Quarter-finals

Bootle v Blackburn Rovers	0–7
Preston North End v Bolton Wanderers	2–3
Wolverhampton Wanderers v Stoke	3–2
The Wednesday v Notts C.	5–0*, 2–3*, 2–1

Semi-finals

Blackburn Rovers v Wolverhampton W.	1–0
Bolton Wanderers v The Wednesday	1–2

Final

Blackburn Rovers 6 The Wednesday 1
(Kennington Oval, 29.3.90, 20,000)

Blackburn: Horne, James Southworth, Forbes, Barton, Dewar, Forrest, Lofthouse, Campbell, John Southworth, Walton, Townley
Wednesday: Smith, Brayshaw, Morley, Dungworth, Betts, Waller, Ingram, Woodhouse, Bennett, Mumford, Cawley
Scorers: Townley 3, Lofthouse, John Southworth, Walton; Bennett
*replayed after protest

FA CUP 1890-91

Second round

Blackburn Rovers v Chester	7–0
Accrington v Wolverhampton Wanderers	2–3
Derby County v The Wednesday	2–3
Birmingham St George's v WBA	0–3
Darwen v Sunderland	0–2
Nottingham F. v Sunderland Alb.	1–1, 0–0, 5–0
Stoke v Aston Villa	3–0
Notts County v Burnley	2–1

Quarter-finals

Blackburn Rovers v Wolverhampton W.	2–0
The Wednesday v West Bromwich Albion	0–2
Sunderland v Nottingham Forest	4–0
Notts County v Stoke	1–0

Semi-finals

Blackburn Rovers v West Bromwich Albion	3–2
Sunderland v Notts County	3–3 0–2

Final

Blackburn Rovers 3 Notts County 1
(Kennington Oval, 21.3.91, 23,000)

Blackburn: Pennington, Brandon, Forbes, Barton, Dewar, Forrest, Lofthouse, Walton, John Southworth, Hall, Townley
County: Thraves, Ferguson, Hendry, Osborne, Calderhead, Shelton, McGregor, McInnes, Oswald, Locker, Daft
Scorers: Southworth, Dewar, Townley; Oswald

FA CUP 1891-92

Second round

West Bromwich Albion v Blackburn Rovers	3–1
The Wednesday v Small Heath	2–0
Sunderland Albion v Nottingham Forest	0–1
Middlesbrough v Preston North End	1–2
Wolverhampton W. v Sheffield United	3–1
Accrington v Sunderland	1–3
Burnley v Stoke	1–3
Aston Villa v Darwen	2–0

Quarter-finals

West Bromwich Albion v The Wednesday	2–1
Nottingham Forest v Preston North End	2–0
Wolverhampton Wanderers v Aston Villa	1–3
Sunderland v Stoke	2–2, 4–0

Semi-finals

West Bromwich v Nottingham F.	1–1, 1–1, 6–2
Aston Villa v Sunderland	4–1

Final

West Bromwich Albion 3 Aston Villa 0
(Kennington Oval, 12.3.92, 25,000)

WBA: Reader; Nicholson, McCulloch, Reynolds, Perry, Groves, Bassett, McLeod, Nicholls, Pearson, Geddes
Villa: Warner, Evans, Cox, H. Devey, James Cowan, Baird, Athersmith, J. Devey, Dickson, Campbell, Hodgetts
Scorers: Nicholls, Geddes, Reynolds

FA CUP 1892-93

Second round

Wolverhampton Wanderers v Middlesbrough	2–1
The Wednesday v Burnley	1–0
Accrington v Preston North End	1–4
Middlesbrough Ironopolis v Notts County	3–2
Darwen v Grimsby Town	2–0
Blackburn Rovers v Northwich Victoria	4–1
Sheffield United v Sunderland	1–3
Everton v Nottingham Forest	4–2

Quarter-finals

Wolverhampton Wanderers v Darwen	5–0
Preston v Middlesbrough Ironopolis	*2–2, 7–0
Blackburn Rovers v Sunderland	3–0
Everton v The Wednesday	3–0

Semi-finals

Wolverhampton W. v Blackburn Rovers	2–1
Everton v Preston North End	2–2, 0–0, 2–1

Final

Wolverhampton Wanderers 1 Everton 0
(Fallowfield, Manchester, 25.3.93, 45,000)

Wolves: Rose, Baugh, Swift, Malpass, Allen, Kinsey, Topham, Wykes, Butcher, Wood, Griffin
Everton: Williams, Howarth, Kelso, Stewart, Holt, Boyle, Latta, Gordon, Maxwell, Chadwick, Milward
Scorer: Allen

FA CUP 1893-94

Second round

Notts County v Burton Wanderers	2–0
Middlesbrough Ironopolis v Nottingham F.	0–2
Leicester Fosse v Derby County	0–0, 0–3
Newton Heath v Blackburn Rovers	0–0, 1–5
Liverpool v Preston North End	3–2
The Wednesday v Stoke	1–0
Sunderland v Aston Villa	2–2, 1–3
Newcastle United v Bolton Wanderers	1–2

Quarter-finals

Nottingham Forest v Notts County	1–1, 1–4
Derby County v Blackburn Rovers	1–4
The Wednesday v Aston Villa	3–2
Bolton Wanderers v Liverpool	3–0

Semi-finals

Notts County v Blackburn Rovers	1–0
Bolton Wanderers v The Wednesday	2–1

Final

Notts County 4 Bolton Wanderers 1
(Goodison Park, 31.3.94, 37,000)

County: Toone, Harper, Hendry, Bramley, Calderhead, Shelton, Watson, Donnelly, Logan, Bruce, Daft
Bolton: Sutcliffe, Somerville, Jones, Gardiner, Paton, Hughes, Dickinson, Wilson, Tannahill, Bentley, Cassidy
Scorers: Logan 3, Watson; Cassidy

WINNERS AND FINALS

Most wins: Aston Villa and Tottenham Hotspur have each won the FA Challenge Cup 7 times (by 1 January 1984).

Undefeated in finals: Tottenham Hotspur have won all 7 finals in which they have appeared; Wanderers have won all 5. Wanderers also hold the unique record of having won more finals than semi-finals (because of the challenge round in 1873, they appeared in only 3 semi-finals).

Final appearances: Newcastle and Arsenal have both appeared in 11 finals, WBA in 10. All of Arsenal's appearances have been since 1927 and therefore at Wembley.

Losing finalists: Arsenal have lost 6 Cup finals in all. Preston North End won only 2 out of the 7 finals in which they appeared. Leicester have lost all their 4 finals, – in 1949, 1961, 1963 and 1969.

Last English amateurs: Old Etonians in 1883 were the last of the FA's founding ex-public schoolboy amateur sides to appear in the final in 1883 (though amateurs Queen's Park did appear the following two years). Their game against Blackburn Olympic was tied 1-1 at full-time and Old Etonians agreed to play extra time (though they were not forced to do so) so that Olympic would not have to make the long journey again. They did this despite having only 10 men left and two of those being injured; Olympic won 2-1. The last significant amateur performance was Walthamstow Avenue's 1-1 draw with Manchester United at Old Trafford in 1953, though Tooting and Mitcham came within

FA CUP 1894-95

Second round
Aston Villa V Newcastle United	7–1
Liverpool v Nottingham Forest	0–2
Sunderland v Preston North End	2–0
Bolton Wanderers v Bury	1–0
Wolverhampton Wanderers v Stoke	2–0
The Wednesday v Middlesbrough	6–1
Everton v Blackburn Rovers	1–1, 3–2
Sheffield United v West Bromwich A.	1–1, 1–2

Quarter-finals
Aston Villa v Nottingham Forest	6–2
Sunderland v Bolton Wanderers	2–1
The Wednesday v Everton	2–0
West Bromwich Albion v Wolverhampton W.	1–0

Semi-finals
Aston Villa v Sunderland	2–1
West Bromwich Albion v The Wednesday	2–0

Final

Aston Villa 1 West Bromwich Albion 0
(Crystal Palace, 20.4.95, 42,560)

Villa: Wilkes, Spencer, Welford, Reynolds, James Cowan, Russell, Athersmith, Chatt, J. Devey, Hodgetts, Smith
WBA: Reader, Williams, Horton, Taggart, Higgins, Perry, Bassett, McLeod, Richards, Hutchinson, Banks
Scorer: Devey

FA CUP 1896-97

Second round
Aston Villa v Notts County	2–1
Preston North End v Stoke	2–1
Sunderland v Nottingham Forest	1–3
West Bromwich Albion v Liverpool	1–2
Blackburn Rovers v Wolverhampton W.	2–1
Derby County v Bolton Wanderers	4–1
Southampton St Mary's v Newton H.	1–1, 1–3
Everton v Bury	3–0

Quarter-finals
Aston Villa v Preston North End	1–1, 0–0, 3–2
Nottingham Forest v Liverpool	1–1, 0–1
Derby County v Newton Heath	2–0
Everton v Blackburn Rovers	2–0

Semi-finals
Aston Villa v Liverpool	3–0
Everton v Derby County	3–2

Final

Aston Villa 3 Everton 2
(Crystal Palace, 10.4.97, 65,891)

Villa: Whitehouse, Spencer, Evans, Reynolds, James Cowan, Crabtree, Athersmith, J. Devey, Campbell, Wheldon, John Cowan
Everton: Menham, Meechem, Storrier, Boyle, Holt, Stewart, Taylor, Bell, Hartley, Chadwick, Milward
Scorers: Devey, Campbell, Crabtree; Bell, Hartley

FA CUP 1898-99

Second round
Sheffield United v Preston North End	2–2, 2–1
Everton v Nottingham Forest	0–1
West Bromwich Albion v Bury	2–1
Liverpool v Newcastle United	3–1
Notts County v Southampton	0–1
Small Heath v Stoke	2–2, 1–2
Tottenham Hotspur v Sunderland	2–1
Derby County v Wolverhampton Wanderers	2–1

Quarter-finals
Nottingham Forest v Sheffield United	0–1
West Bromwich Albion v Liverpool	0–2
Stoke v Tottenham Hotspur	4–1
Southampton v Derby County	1–2

Semi-finals
Sheffield United v Liverpool	2–2, 4–4, 0–1*, 1–0
Derby County v Stoke	3–1

Final

Sheffield United 4 Derby County 1
(Crystal Palace, 15.4.99, 73,833)

United: Foulke, Thickett, Boyle, Johnson, Morren, Needham, Bennett, Beers, Hedley, Almond, Priest
Derby: Fryer, Methven, Staley, Cox, Paterson, May, Arkesden, Bloomer, Boag, McDonald, Allen
Scorers: Bennett, Priest, Beers, Almond; Boag

*abandoned

FA CUP 1895-96

Second round
The Wednesday v Sunderland	2–1
Burnley v Stoke	1–1, 1–7
Derby County v Newton Heath	1–1, 5–1
Grimsby T. v West Bromwich Albion	1–1, 0–3
Everton v Sheffield United	3–0
Blackpool v Bolton Wanderers	0–2
Newcastle United v Bury	1–3
Wolverhampton Wanderers v Liverpool	2–0

Quarter-finals
The Wednesday v Everton	4–0
Derby County v West Bromwich Albion	1–0
Bolton Wanderers v Bury	2–0
Wolverhampton Wanderers v Stoke	3–0

Semi-finals
The Wednesday v Bolton Wanderers	1–1, 3–1
Wolverhampton Wanderers v Derby County	2–1

Final

The Wednesday 2 Wolverhampton W. 1
(Crystal Palace, 18.4.96, 48,836)

Wednesday: Massey, Earp, Langley, Brandon, Crawshaw, Petrie, Brash, Brady, Bell, Davis, Spiksley
Wolves: Tennant, Baugh, Dunn, Owen, Malpass, Griffiths, Tonks, Henderson, Beats, Wood, Black
Scorers: Spiksley 2; Black

FA CUP 1897-98

Second round
Nottingham Forest v Gainsborough Trinity	4–0
Southampton St Mary's v Newcastle United	1–0
Bolton Wanderers v Manchester City	1–0
West Bromwich Albion v The Wednesday	1–0
Liverpool v Newton Heath	0–0, 2–1
Burnley v Burslem Port Vale	3–0
Everton v Stoke	0–0, 5–1
Wolverhampton Wanderers v Derby County	0–1

Quarter-finals
West Bromwich Albion v Nottingham Forest	2–3
Southampton St Mary's v Bolton W.	0–0, 4–0
Burnley v Everton	1–3
Liverpool v Derby County	1–1, 1–5

Semi-finals
Southampton v Nottingham F.	1–1, 0–2
Derby County v Everton	3–1

Final

Nottingham Forest 3 Derby County 1
(Crystal Palace, 16.4.98, 62,017)

Forest: Allsop, Ritchie, Scott, Frank Forman, McPherson, Wragg, McInnes, Richards, Benbow, Capes, Spouncer
Derby: Fryer, Methven, Leiper, Cox, A. Goodall, Turner, J. Goodall, Bloomer, Boag, Stevenson, McQueen
Scorers: Capes 2, McPherson; Bloomer

FA CUP 1899-1900

Second round
Notts County v Bury	0–0, 0–2
Preston North End v Blackburn Rovers	1–0
Nottingham Forest v Sunderland	3–0
The Wednesday v Sheffield United	1–1, 0–2
West Bromwich Albion v Liverpool	1–1, 2–1
Queen's Park Rangers v Millwall Athletic	0–2
Aston Villa v Bristol City	5–1
Southampton v Newcastle United	4–1

Quarter-final
Sheffield United v Bury	2–2, 0–2
Preston North End v Nottingham F.	0–0, 0–1
Millwall Athletic v Aston Villa	1–1, 0–0, 2–1
Southampton v West Bromwich Albion	2–1

Semi-final
Nottingham Forest v Bury	1–1, 2–3
Southampton v Millwall Athletic	0–0, 3–0

Final

Bury 4 Southampton 0
(Crystal Palace, 21.4.1900, 68,945)

Bury: Thompson, Darrock, Davidson, Pray, Leeming, Ross, Richards, Wood, McLuckie, Sagar, Plant
Southampton: Robinson, Meehan, Durber, Meston, Chadwick, Petrie, Turner, Yates, Farrell, Wood, Milward
Scorers: McLuckie 2, Wood, Plant

a ludicrous own goal and a penalty kick of defeating First Division Nottingham Forest in 1959 after taking a 2-0 lead. Forest won the Cup that year.

Consecutive final teams: The only times that the same clubs have contested consecutive finals was Blackburn Rovers v Queen's Park (Glasgow) in 1884 and 1885.

Repeat finals: The only sides to have met each other in 3 finals are Aston Villa and West Bromwich – in 1887, 1892 and 1895.

Professional final: The 1886 final between

Blackburn Rovers and West Bromwich was not only the first between professional clubs but also the first to be decided outside London – the replay was contested at The Racecourse, Derby.

Leading sides: The only occasion that the two sides topping the Football League have also contested the Cup final was in 1912–13 when Sunderland won the League (4 points clear of Aston Villa) and Villa won the Cup (1-0). The meetings between Blackburn Rovers and Queen's Park in 1884 and 1885

could also arguably be described as the Championship of Britain in their time.

Finalists return: The following sides were beaten one year but came back to win the trophy the next: Oxford University, 1873/1874; Royal Engineers, 1874/1875; Clapham Rovers, 1879/1880; Old Etonians, 1881/1882; West Bromwich Albion, 1887/1888; Preston North End, 1888/1889; Sheffield United, 1901/1902; Manchester City, 1933/1934; Preston North End, 1937/1938; Charlton Athletic, 1946/1947; Manchester City,

FA CUP   1900-01

Second round

Tottenham Hotspur v Bury	2–1
Bolton Wanderers v Reading	0–1
Middlesbrough v Kettering Town	5–0
Woolwich Arsenal v West Bromwich Albion	0–1
Notts County v Wolverhampton Wanderers	2–3
Small Heath v Burnley	1–0
Aston Villa v Nottingham Forest	0–0, 3–1
Sheffield United v Everton	2–0

Quarter-finals

Reading v Tottenham Hotspur	1–1, 0–3
Middlesbrough v West Bromwich Albion	0–1
Small Heath v Aston Villa	0–0, 0–1
Wolverhampton W. v Sheffield United	0–4

Semi-finals

Tottenham Hotspur v West Bromwich Albion	4–0
Sheffield United v Aston Villa	2–2, 3–0

Final

Tottenham Hotspur 2 Sheffield United 2
(Crystal Palace, 20.4.01, 114,815)

Tottenham: Clawley, Erentz, Tait, Norris, Hughes, Jones, Smith, Cameron, Brown, Copeland, Kirwan
United: Foulke, Thickett, Boyle, Johnson, Morren, Needham, Bennett, Field, Hedley, Priest, Lipsham
Scorers: Brown 2; Bennett, Priest

Replay
Tottenham Hotspur 3 Sheffield United 1
(Burnden Park, Bolton, 27.4.01, 20,740)

Tottenham: Unchanged
Sheffield United: Unchanged
Scorers: Cameron, Smith, Brown; Priest

FA CUP   1901-02

Second round

Sheffield United v Bolton Wanderers	2–1
Walsall v Bury	0–5
Manchester City v Nottingham Forest	0–2
Bristol Rovers v Stoke	0–1
Newcastle United v Sunderland	1–0
Lincoln City v Derby County	1–3
Reading v Portsmouth	0–1
Southampton v Liverpool	4–1

Quarter-finals

Newcastle United v Sheffield United	1–1, 1–2
Nottingham Forest v Stoke	2–0
Derby County v Portsmouth	0–0, 6–3
Bury v Southampton	2–3

Semi-finals

Sheffield United v Derby County	1–1, 1–1, 1–0
Southampton v Nottingham Forest	3–1

Final

Sheffield United 1 Southampton 1
(Crystal Palace, 19.4.02, 76,914)

United: Foulke, Thickett, Boyle, Needham, Wilkinson, Johnson, Bennett, Common, Hedley, Priest, Lipsham

Southampton: Robinson, Fry, Molyneux, Meston, Bowman, Lee, A. Turner, Wood, Brown, Chadwick, J. Turner
Scorers: Common; Wood

Replay
Sheffield United 2 Southampton 1
(Crystal Palace, 26.4.02, 33,068)

Sheffield United: Barnes for Bennett
Southampton: Unchanged
Scorers: Hedley, Barnes; Brown

FA CUP   1902-03

Second round

Sheffield United v Bury	0–1
Tottenham Hotspur v Bristol City	1–0
Aston Villa v Barnsley	4–1
Grimsby Town v Notts County	0–2
Nottingham Forest v Stoke	0–0, 0–2
Millwall Athletic v Preston North End	4–1
Everton v Manchester United	3–1
Derby County v Blackburn Rovers	2–0

Quarter-finals

Bury v Notts County	1–0
Tottenham Hotspur v Aston Villa	2–3
Millwall Athletic v Everton	1–0
Derby County v Stoke	3–0

Semi-final

Aston Villa v Bury	0–3
Derby County v Millwall Athletic	3–0

Final

Bury 6 Derby County 0
(Crystal Palace, 18.4.03, 63,102)

Bury: Monteith, Lindsey, McEwen, Johnson, Thorpe, Ross, Richards, Wood, Sagar, Leeming, Plant

Derby: Fryer, Methven, Morris, Warren, A. Goodall, May, Warrington, York, Boag, Richards, Davis
Scorers: Leeming 2, Ross, Sagar, Plant, Wood

FA CUP   1903-04

Second round

Woolwich Arsenal v Manchester City	0–2
Preston North End v Middlesbrough	0–3
The Wednesday v Manchester United	6–0
Tottenham Hotspur v Aston Villa	0–1†, 1–0
Bury v Sheffield United	1–2
Derby Co. v Wolverhampton W.	2–2, 2–2, 1–0
Blackburn Rovers v Nottingham Forest	3–1
Bolton Wanderers v Southampton	4–1

Quarter-finals

Manchester City v Middlesbrough	0–0, 3–1
Tottenham Hotspur v The Wednesday	1–1, 0–2
Derby County v Blackburn Rovers	2–1
Sheffield United v Bolton Wanderers	0–2

Semi-finals

Manchester City v The Wednesday	3–0
Bolton Wanderers v Derby County	1–0

Final

Manchester City 1 Bolton Wanderers 0
(Crystal Palace, 23.4.04, 61,374)

City: Hillman, McMahon, Burgess, Frost, Hynds, Ashworth, Meredith, Livingstone, Gillespie, A. Turnbull, Booth
Bolton: Davies, Brown, Struthers, Clifford, Greenhaigh, Freebairn, Stokes, Marsh, Yenson, White, Taylor
Scorer: Meredith

†abandoned after crowd invasion; replay at Villa Park

FA CUP   1904-05

Second round

Aston Villa v Bury	3–2
Manchester City v Bolton Wanderers	1–2
Bristol City v Preston North End	0–0, 0–1
The Wednesday v Portsmouth	2–1
Stoke v Everton	0–4
Wolverhampton Wanderers v Southampton	2–3
Fulham v Nottingham Forest	1–0
Tottenham Hotspur v Newcastle U.	1–1, 0–4

Quarter-final

Aston Villa v Fulham	5–0
Preston North End v The Wednesday	1–1, 0–3
Everton v Southampton	4–0
Bolton Wanderers v Newcastle United	0–2

Semi-finals

Everton v Aston Villa	1–1, 1–2
Newcastle United v The Wednesday	1–0

Final

Aston Villa 2 Newcastle United 0
(Crystal Palace, 15.4.05, 101,117)

Villa: George, Spencer, Miles, Pearson, Leake, Windmill, Brawn, Garratty, Hampton, Bache, Hall
Newcastle: Lawrence, McCombie, Carr, Gardner, Aitken, McWilliam, Rutherford, Howie, Appleyard, Veitch, Gosnell
Scorer: Hampton 2

FA CUP   1905-06

Third round

Everton v Bradford City	1–0
Woolwich Arsenal v Sunderland	5–0
Manchester United v Aston Villa	5–1
Tottenham Hotspur v Birmingham	1–1, 0–2
The Wednesday v Nottingham Forest	4–1
Liverpool v Brentford	2–0
Southampton v Middlesbrough	6–1
Newcastle United v Blackpool	5–0

Quarter-finals

Everton v The Wednesday	4–3
Manchester United v Woolwich Arsenal	2–3
Liverpool v Southampton	3–0
Birmingham v Newcastle United	2–2, 0–3

Semi-finals

Everton v Liverpool	2–0
Woolwich Arsenal v Newcastle United	0–2

Final

Everton 1 Newcastle United 0
(Crystal Palace, 21.4.06, 75,609)

Everton: Scott; W. Balmer, Crelly, Makepeace, Taylor, Abbott; Sharp, Bolton, Young, Settle, Hardman
Newcastle: Lawrence, McCombie, Carr, Gardner, Aitken, McWilliam, Rutherford, Howie, Veitch, Orr, Gosnell
Scorer: Young

FA CUP — 1906-07

Third round

The Wednesday v Sunderland	0–0, 1–0
West Bromwich Albion v Derby County	2–0
Crystal Palace v Brentford	1–1, 1–0
Woolwich Arsenal v Bristol Rovers	1–0
Barnsley v Bury	1–0
Liverpool v Bradford City	1–0
Everton v Bolton Wanderers	0–0, 3–0

Quarter-finals

The Wednesday v Liverpool	1–0
West Bromwich Albion v Notts County	3–1
Barnsley v Woolwich Arsenal	1–2
Crystal Palace v Everton	1–1, 0–4

Semi-finals

Woolwich Arsenal v The Wednesday	1–3
West Bromwich Albion v Everton	1–2

Final

The Wednesday 2 Everton 1
(Crystal Palace, 20.4.07, 84,584)

Wednesday: Lyall, Layton, Burton, Brittleton, Crawshaw, Bartlett, Chapman, Bradshaw, Wilson, Stewart, Simpson
Everton: Scott, W. Balmer, R. Balmer, Makepeace, Tallor, Abbott; Sharp, Bolton, Young, Settle, Hardman
Scorers: Stewart, Simpson; Sharp

FA CUP — 1907-08

Third round

Wolverhampton W. v Swindon Town	2–0
Portsmouth v Stoke	0–1
Bolton Wanderers v Everton	3–3, 1–3
Southampton v Bristol Rovers	2–0
Grimsby Town v Crystal Palace	1–0
Manchester City v Fulham	1–1, 1–3
Aston Villa v Manchester United	0–2
Newcastle United v Liverpool	3–1

Quarter-finals

Stoke v Wolverhampton Wanderers	0–1
Everton v Southampton	0–0, 2–3
Fulham v Manchester United	2–1
Newcastle United v Grimsby Town	5–1

Semi-finals

Wolverhampton Wanderers v Southampton	2–0
Newcastle United v Fulham	6–0

Final

Wolverhampton W. 3 Newcastle United 1
(Crystal Palace, 25.4.08, 74,967)

Wolves: Lunn, Jones, Collins, Hunt, Wooldridge, Bishop, Harrison, Shelton, Hedley, Radford, Pedley
Newcastle: Lawrence, McCracken, Pudan, Gardner, Veitch, McWilliam, Rutherford, Howie, Appleyard, Speedie, Wilson
Scorers: Hunt, Hedley, Harrison; Howie

"Happy" Harry Hampton (at near post) scores his second goal in the 1905 final for Aston Villa against Newcastle. This was the first of the Geordies' 4 final defeats in the space of 7 seasons (a quite unsurpassed record of failure) and they never won any of their 5 games at Crystal Palace. The crowd for this game, 101,117, is one of only 4 ever to exceed 6 figures at a single venue for an English game. Out of interest, compare the pitch markings with those of the final 4 years before (on p36).

FA CUP — 1908-09

Third round

Manchester United v Blackburn Rovers	6–1
Tottenham Hotspur v Burnley	0–0, 1–3
West Ham United v Newcastle United	0–0, 1–2
Bradford City v Sunderland	0–1
The Wednesday v Glossop North End	0–1
Derby County v Plymouth Argyle	1–0
Nottingham Forest v Millwall Athletic	3–1
Bristol City v Norwich City	2–0

Quarter-finals

Burnley v Manchester United	1–0*, 2–3
Newcastle United v Sunderland	2–2, 3–0
Derby County v Nottingham Forest	3–0
Glossop North End v Bristol City	0–0, 0–1

Semi-finals

Manchester United v Newcastle United	1–0
Bristol City v Derby County	1–1, 2–1

Final

Manchester United 1 Bristol City 0
(Crystal Palace, 24.4.09, 71,401)

United: Moger, Stacey, Hayes, Duckworth, Roberts, Bell, Meredith, Halse, J. Turnbull, A. Turnbull, Wall
City: Clay, Annan, Cottle, Hanlin, Wedlock, Spear, Staniforth, Hardy, Gilligan, Burton, Hilton
Scorer: A. Turnbull

*abandoned

FA CUP — 1909-10

Third round

Newcastle United v Blackburn Rovers	3–1
Leicester Fosse v Leyton	1–0
Swindon Town v Tottenham Hotspur	3–2
Aston Villa v Manchester City	1–2
Everton v Sunderland	2–0
Coventry City v Nottingham Forest	3–1
Queen's Park Rangers v West Ham	1–1, 1–0
Barnsley v West Bromwich Albion	1–0

Quarter-finals

Newcastle United v Leicester Fosse	3–0
Swindon Town v Manchester City	2–0
Coventry City v Everton	0–2
Barnsley v Queen's Park Rangers	1–0

Semi-finals

Newcastle United v Swindon Town	2–0
Barnsley v Everton	0–0, 3–0

Final

Newcastle United 1 Barnsley 1
(Crystal Palace, 23.4.10, 77,747)

Newcastle: Lawrence, Whitson, Veitch, Low, McWilliam, Rutherford, Howie, Shepherd, Higgins, Wilson
Barnsley: Mearns, Downs, Ness, Glendinning, Boyle, Utley, Bartrop, Gadsby, Lilycrop, Tufnell, Forman
Scorers: Rutherford; Tufnell

Replay
Newcastle United 2 Barnsley 0
(Goodison Park, 28.4.10, 69,000)

Newcastle: Carr for Whitson
Barnsley: Unchanged
Scorer: Shepherd 2 (1 pen)

FA CUP — 1910-11

Third round

Bradford City v Grimsby Town	1–0
Burnley v Coventry City	5–0
Middlesbrough v Blackburn Rovers	0–3
West Ham United v Manchester United	2–1
Derby County v Everton	5–0
Wolverhampton Wanderers v Chelsea	0–2
Darlington v Swindon Town	0–3
Newcastle United v Hull City	3–2

Quarter-finals

Bradford City v Burnley	1–0
West Ham United v Blackburn Rovers	2–3
Chelsea v Swindon Town	3–1
Newcastle United v Derby County	4–0

Semi-finals

Bradford City v Blackburn Rovers	3–0
Newcastle United v Chelsea	3–0

Final

Bradford City 0 Newcastle United 0
(Crystal Palace, 22.4.11, 69,098)

Bradford: Mellors, Campbell, Taylor, Robinson, Gildea, McDonald, Logan, Spiers, O'Rourke, Devine, Thompson
Newcastle: Lawrence, McCracken, Whitson, Veitch, Low, Willis, Rutherford, Jobey, Stewart, Higgins, Wilson

Replay
Bradford City 1 Newcastle United 0
(Old Trafford, 26.4.11, 58,000)

Bradford City: Torrance for Gildea
Newcastle United: Unchanged
Scorer: Spiers

FA CUP — 1911-12

Third round

Bolton Wanderers v Barnsley	1–2
Reading v Manchester United	1–1, 0–3
Blackburn Rovers v Wolverhampton W.	3–2
Fulham v Northampton Town	2–1
West Ham United v Swindon Town	1–1, 0–4
Oldham Athletic v Everton	0–2
Bradford Park Avenue v Bradford City	0–1
Sunderland v West Bromwich Albion	1–2

Quarter-finals

Barnsley v Bradford City	0–0, 0–0, 0–0, 3–2
Manchester United v Blackburn Rovers	1–1, 2–4
Swindon Town v Everton	2–1
West Bromwich Albion v Fulham	3–0

Semi-finals

Swindon Town v Barnsley	0–0, 0–1
Blackburn R. v West Bromwich Albion	0–0, 0–1

Final

Barnsley 0 West Bromwich Albion 0
(Crystal Palace, 20.4.12, 54,556)

Barnsley: Cooper, Downs, Taylor, Glendinning, Bratley, Utley, Bartrop, Tufnell, Lillycrop, Travers, Moore
WBA: Pearson, Cook, Pennington, Baddeley, Buck, McNeal, Jephcott, Wright, Pailor, Bowser, Shearman

Replay
Barnsley 1 West Bromwich Albion 0 [aet]
(Bramall Lane, 24.4.12, 38,555)

Barnsley: Unchanged
WBA: Unchanged
Scorer: Tufnell

FA CUP 1912-13

Third round

Aston Villa v Crystal Palace	5–0
Bradford Park Avenue v The Wednesday	2–1
Oldham Athletic v Manchester United	0–0, 2–1
Bristol Rovers v Everton	0–4
Liverpool v Newcastle United	1–1, 0–1
Burnley v Middlesbrough	3–1
Reading v Blackburn Rovers	1–2
Sunderland v Swindon Town	4–2

Quarter-finals

Bradford Park Avenue v Aston Villa	0–5
Everton v Oldham Athletic	0–1
Blackburn Rovers v Burnley	0–1
Sunderland v Newcastle United	0–0, 2–2, 3–0

Semi-finals

Aston Villa v Oldham Athletic	1–0
Sunderland v Burnley	0–0, 3–2

Final

Aston Villa 1 Sunderland 0
(Crystal Palace, 19.4.13, 120,081)

Villa: Hardy, Lyons, Weston, Barber, Harrop, Leach, Wallace, Halse, Hampton, Stephenson, Bache
Sunderland: Butler, Gladwin, Ness, Cuggy, Thompson, Low, Mordue, Buchan, Richardson, Holley, Martin
Scorer: Barber

FA CUP 1914-15

Third round

Sheffield United v Bradford Park Avenue	1–0
Birmingham v Oldham Athletic	2–3
Bolton Wanderers v Burnley	2–1
Southampton v Hull City	2–2, 0–4
The Wednesday v Newcastle United	1–2
Queen's Park Rangers v Everton	1–2
Bradford City v Norwich City	1–1, 0–0, 2–0
Manchester City v Chelsea	0–1

Quarter-finals

Oldham Athletic v Sheffield United	0–0, 0–3
Bolton Wanderers v Hull City	4–2
Bradford City v Everton	0–2
Chelsea v Newcastle United	1–1, 1–0

Semi-finals

Sheffield United v Bolton Wanderers	2–1
Chelsea v Everton	2–0

Final

Sheffield United 3 Chelsea 0
(Old Trafford, 24.4.15, 49,557)

United: Gough, Cook, English, Sturgess, Brelsford, Utley, Simmons, Fazackerley, Kitchen, Masterman, Evans
Chelsea: Molyneux, Bettridge, Harrow, Taylor, Logan, Walker, Ford, Halse, Thompson, Croal, McNeil
Scorers: Simmons, Kitchen, Fazackerley

FA CUP 1920-21

Third round

Southend United v Tottenham Hotspur	1–4
Aston Villa v Huddersfield Town	2–0
Hull City v Burnley	3–0
Luton Town v Preston North End	2–3
Everton v Newcastle United	3–0
Southampton v Cardiff City	0–1
Plymouth Argyle v Chelsea	0–0, 0–0, 1–2
Fulham v Wolverhampton Wanderers	0–1

Quarter-finals

Tottenham Hotspur v Aston Villa	1–0
Hull City v Preston North End	0–0, 0–1
Cardiff City v Chelsea	1–0
Everton v Wolverhampton Wanderers	0–1

Semi-finals

Tottenham Hotspur v Preston North End	2–1
Wolverhampton Wanderers v Cardiff C.	0–0, 3–1

Final

Tottenham Hotspur 1 Wolverhampton W. 0
(Stamford Bridge, 23.4.21, 72,805)

Tottenham: Hunter, Clay, McDonald, Smith, Walters, Grimsdell, Banks, Seed, Cantrell, Bliss, Dimmock
Wolves: George, Woodward, Marshall, Gregory, Hodnett, Riley, Lea, Burrill, Edmonds, Potts, Brooks
Scorer: Dimmock

FA CUP 1913-14

Third round

Burnley v Bolton Wanderers	3–0
Millwall Athletic v Sheffield United	0–4
Blackburn Rovers v Manchester City	1–2
Sunderland v Preston North End	2–0
Aston Villa v West Bromwich Albion	2–1
The Wednesday v Brighton	3–0
Birmingham v Queen's Park Rangers	1–2
West Ham United v Liverpool	1–1, 1–5

Quarter-finals

Sunderland v Burnley	0–0, 1–2
Manchester City v Sheffield U.	0–0, 0–0, 0–1
The Wednesday v Aston Villa	0–1
Liverpool v Queen's Park Rangers	2–1

Semi-finals

Sheffield United v Burnley	0–0, 0–1
Aston Villa v Liverpool	0–2

Final

Burnley 1 Liverpool 0
(Crystal Palace, 25.4.14, 72,778)

Burnley: Sewell, Bamford, Taylor, Halley, Boyle, Watson, Nesbit, Lindley, Freeman, Hodgson, Mosscrop
Liverpool: Campbell, Longworth, Pursell, Fairfoul, Ferguson, McKinlay, Sheldon, Metcalf, Miller, Lacey, Nicholl
Scorer: Freeman

FA CUP 1919-20

Third round

Aston Villa v Sunderland	1–0
Tottenham Hotspur v West Ham United	3–0
Chelsea v Leicester City	3–0
Notts County v Bradford Park Avenue	3–4
Bristol City v Cardiff City	2–1
Preston North End v Bradford City	0–3
Liverpool v Birmingham	2–0
Huddersfield Town v Plymouth Argyle	3–1

Quarter-finals

Tottenham Hotspur v Aston Villa	0–1
Chelsea v Bradford Park Avenue	4–1
Bristol City v Bradford City	2–0
Huddersfield Town v Liverpool	2–1

Semi-finals

Aston Villa v Chelsea	3–1
Huddersfield Town v Bristol City	2–1

Final

Aston Villa 1 Huddersfield Town 0 [aet]
(Stamford Bridge, 24.4.20, 50,018)

Villa: Hardy, Smart, Weston, Ducat, Barson, Moss, Wallace, Kirton, Walker, Stephenson, Dorrell
Huddersfield: Mutch, Wood, Bullock, Slade, Wilson, Watson, Richardson, Mann, Taylor, Swan, Islip
Scorer: Kirton

1955/1956; Manchester United, 1976/1977; and Arsenal, 1978/1979.

Surprisingly, only four sides have ever won the Cup in consecutive seasons: Wanderers, 1872/1873 & 1876/1877/1878; Blackburn Rovers 1884/1885/1886 & 1890/1891; Newcastle United 1950/1951; and Tottenham Hotspur 1961/1962 and 1981/1982.

Only five holders have returned to the final to lose the trophy the following year: Old Etonians 1882/1883; Everton 1906/1907; Newcastle United 1910/1911 (replays both years); Arsenal 1971/1972 & 1979/1980;

Leeds United, 1972/1973.

Three finals: The following sides appeared in 3 consecutive finals: Wanderers, 1876–78; Old Etonians, 1881–83; Blackburn Rovers, 1884–86; West Bromwich Albion, 1886–88; and Arsenal, 1978–80.

Met in two finals: Apart from Aston Villa v West Bromwich Albion and Blackburn Rovers v Queen's Park (*see above*), the following 9 pairs of sides have met in two finals. The number in brackets is the number of wins in the two games:

Wanderers (2) v Royal Engineers 1872, 1878;

FA CUP 1921-22

Third round

Blackburn Rovers v Huddersfield Town	1-1, 0-5
Millwall Athletic v Swansea Town	4-0
Stoke v Aston Villa	0-0, 0-4
West Bromwich Albion v Notts County	1-1, 0-2
Arsenal v Leicester City	3-0
Cardiff City v Nottingham Forest	4-1
Tottenham Hotspur v Manchester City	2-1
Barnsley v Preston North End	1-1, 0-3

Quarter-finals

Huddersfield Town v Millwall Athletic	3-0
Notts County v Aston Villa	2-2, 4-3
Cardiff City v Tottenham Hotspur	1-1, 1-2
Arsenal v Preston North End	1-1, 1-2

Semi-finals

Huddersfield Town v Notts County	3-1
Preston North End v Tottenham Hotspur	2-1

Final

Huddersfield Town 1 Preston North End 0
(Stamford Bridge, 29.4.22, 53,000)

Huddersfield: Mutch, Wood, Wadsworth, Slade, Wilson, Watson, Richardson, Mann, Islip, Stephenson, W. H. Smith
Preston: Mitchell, Hamilton, Doolan, Duxbury, McCall, Williamson, Rawlings, Jefferis, Roberts, Woodhouse, Quinn
Scorer: Smith (pen)

FA CUP 1922-23

Third round

Huddersfield Town v Bolton Wanderers	1-1, 0-1
Charlton Athletic v West Bromwich Albion	1-0
Liverpool v Sheffield United	1-2
Queen's Park Rangers v South Shields	3-0
Bury v Southampton	0-0, 0-1
Derby County v The Wednesday	1-0
Cardiff City v Tottenham Hotspur	2-3
West Ham United v Plymouth Argyle	2-0

Quarter-finals

Charlton Athletic v Bolton Wanderers	0-1
Queen's Park Rangers v Sheffield United	0-1
Tottenham Hotspur v Derby County	0-1
Southampton v West Ham United	1-1, 1-1, 0-1

Semi-finals

Bolton Wanderers v Sheffield United	1-0
West Ham United v Derby County	5-2

Final

Bolton Wanderers 2 West Ham United 0
(Wembley, 28.4.23, *126,047)

Bolton: Pym, Haworth, Finney, Nuttall, Seddon, Jennings, Butler, Jack, J. R. Smith, J. Smith, Vizard
West Ham: Hufton, Henderson, Young, Bishop, Kay, Tresadern, Richards, Brown, Watson, Moore, Ruffell
Scorers: Jack, J. R. Smith

*official figure; actual attendance could have been as high as 200,000

The great Billy Meredith, who played his last FA Cup game at St Andrew's on 29 March 1924, aged nearly 50, for Manchester City v Newcastle in a semi-final. His first FA Cup game was back in 1894.

FA CUP 1923-24

Third round

Watford v Newcastle United	0-1
Southampton v Liverpool	0-0, 0-2
Brighton v Manchester City	1-5
Cardiff City v Bristol City	3-0
West Bromwich Albion v Wolves	1-1, 2-0
Crystal Palace v Swindon Town	1-2
Burnley v Huddersfield Town	1-0
Aston Villa v Leeds United	3-0

Quarter-finals

Newcastle United v Liverpool	1-0
Manchester City v Cardiff City	0-0, 1-0
Swindon Town v Burnley	1-1, 1-3
WBA v Aston Villa	0-2

Semi-finals

Newcastle United v Manchester City	2-0
Aston Villa v Burnley	3-0

Final

Newcastle United 2 Aston Villa 0
(Wembley, 26.4.24, 91,695)

Newcastle: Bradley, Hampson, Hudspeth, Mooney, Spencer, Gibson, Low, Cowan, Harris, McDonald, Seymour
Villa: Jackson, Smart, Mort, Moss, Milne, Blackburn, York, Kirton, Capewell, Walker, Dorrell
Scorers: Harris, Seymour

FA CUP 1924-25

Third round

Sheffield United v Everton	1-0
Hull City v Leicester City	1-1, 1-3
West Ham United v Blackpool	1-1, 0-3
Tottenham Hotspur v Blackburn Rovers	2-2, 1-3
Southampton v Bradford City	2-0
Liverpool v Birmingham	2-1
West Bromwich Albion v Aston Villa	1-1, 2-1
Notts County v Cardiff City	0-2

Quarter-finals

Sheffield United v West Bromwich Albion	2-0
Blackburn Rovers v Blackpool	1-0
Southampton v Liverpool	1-0
Cardiff City v Leicester City	2-1

Semi-finals

Sheffield United v Southampton	2-0
Cardiff City v Blackburn Rovers	3-1

Final

Sheffield United 1 Cardiff City 0
(Wembley, 25.4.25, 91,763)

United: Sutcliffe, Cook, Milton, Pantling, King, Green, Mercer, Boyle, Johnson, Gillespie, Tunstall
Cardiff: Farquharson, Nelson, Blair, Wake, Keenor, Hardy, W. Davies, Gill, Nicholson, Beadles, J. Evans
Scorer: Tunstall

FA CUP 1925-26

Fifth round

Bolton Wanderers v South Shields	3-0
Southend United v Nottingham Forest	0-1
Millwall v Swansea Town	0-1
Aston Villa v Arsenal	1-1, 0-2
Clapton Orient v Newcastle United	2-0
Sunderland v Manchester United	3-3, 1-2
Notts County v Fulham	0-1
Manchester City v Crystal Palace	11-4

Quarter-finals

Nottingham F. v Bolton Wanderers	2-2, 0-0, 0-1
Swansea Town v Arsenal	2-1
Fulham v Manchester United	1-2
Clapton Orient v Manchester City	1-6

Semi-finals

Bolton Wanderers v Swansea Town	3-0
Manchester City v Manchester United	3-0

Final

Bolton Wanderers 1 Manchester City 0
(Wembley, 24.4.26, 91,447)

Bolton: Pym, Haworth, Greenhalgh, Nuttall, Seddon, Jennings, Butler, Jack, J. R. Smith, J. Smith, Vizard
City: Goodchild, Cookson, McCloy, Pringle, Cowan, McMullan, Austin, Browell, Roberts, Johnson, Hicks
Scorer: Jack

FA CUP 1926-27

Fifth round

Bolton Wanderers v Cardiff City	0-2
Chelsea v Burnley	2-1
South Shields v Swansea Town	2-2, 1-2
Reading v Brentford	1-0
Wolverhampton Wanderers v Hull City	1-0
Millwall v Middlesbrough	3-2
Southampton v Newcastle United	2-1
Arsenal v Liverpool	2-0

Quarter-finals

Chelsea v Cardiff City	0-0, 2-3
Swansea Town v Reading	1-3
Millwall v Southampton	0-0, 0-2
Arsenal v Wolverhampton Wanderers	2-1

Semi-finals

Cardiff City v Reading	3-0
Arsenal v Southampton	2-1

Final

Cardiff City 1 Arsenal 0
(Wembley, 23.4.27, 91,206)

Cardiff: Farquharson, Nelson, Watson, Keenor, Sloan, Hardy, Curtis, Irving, Ferguson, L. Davies, McLachlan
Arsenal: Lewis, Parker, Kennedy, Baker, Butler, John, Hulme, Buchan, Brain, Blyth, Hoar
Scorer: Ferguson

Wanderers (2) v Oxford University 1873, 1877 (in the first 14 years of the FA Cup only 10 different sides reached the final); WBA (2) v Preston North End 1888, 1954; Manchester C. (1) v Bolton (1) 1904, 1926; Aston Villa (1) v Newcastle U. (1) 1905, 1924; Sheffield W. (1) v Everton (1) 1907, 1966; Huddersfield T. (1) v Preston (1) 1922, 1938; Newcastle U. (2) v Arsenal 1932, 1952; Arsenal (2) v Liverpool 1950, 1971.
Non-Division 1 finalists: Since the League was founded in 1888, 22 clubs which were not in Division 1 have reached the FA Cup final

and a surprisingly high number (8) have won the trophy; 18 of these sides were in Division 2. Those teams are as follows, with an indication of whether they were also promoted that season:

1889–90	The Wednesday (Alliance)
1893–94	Notts County (winners)
1899–1900	Southampton (Southern League)
1900–01	Tottenham Hotspur (winners, Southern League club)
1901–02	Southampton (Southern League)
1903–04	Bolton Wanderers
1907–08	Wolverhampton W. (winners)

FA CUP 1927-28

Fifth round

Blackburn Rovers v Port Vale	2–1
Manchester United v Birmingham	1–0
Arsenal v Aston Villa	4–1
Manchester City v Stoke City	0–1
Leicester City v Tottenham Hotspur	0–3
The Wednesday v Sheffield United	1–1, 1–4
Nottingham Forest v Cardiff City	2–1
Huddersfield Town v Middlesbrough	4–0

Quarter-finals

Blackburn Rovers v Manchester United	2–0
Arsenal v Stoke City	4–1
Sheffield United v Nottingham Forest	3–0
Huddersfield Town v Tottenham Hotspur	6–1

Semi-finals

Blackburn Rovers v Arsenal	1–0
Huddersfield v Sheffield United	2–2, 0–0, 1–0

Final

Blackburn Rovers 3 Huddersfield Town 1
(Wembley, 21.4.28, 92,041)

Blackburn: Crawford, Hutton, Jones, Healless, Rankin, Campbell, Thornewell, Puddefoot, Roscamp, McLean, Rigby
Huddersfield: Mercer, Goodall, Barkas, Redfern, Wilson, Steele, Jackson, Kelly, Brown, Stephenson, W. H. Smith
Scorers: Roscamp 2, McLean; Jackson

FA CUP 1928-29

Fifth round

Leicester City v Bolton Wanderers	1–2
Blackburn Rovers v Bury	1–0
West Bromwich Albion v Bradford P. A.	6–0
Huddersfield Town v Crystal Palace	5–2
Bournemouth v West Ham United	1–1, 1–3
Reading v Aston Villa	1–3
Swindon Town v Arsenal	0–0, 0–1
Chelsea v Portsmouth	1–1, 0–1

Quarter-finals

Blackburn Rovers v Bolton Wanderers	1–1, 1–2
WBA v Huddersfield Town	1–1, 1–2
Aston Villa v Arsenal	1–0
Portsmouth v West Ham United	3–2

Semi-finals

Bolton Wanderers v Huddersfield Town	3–1
Portsmouth v Aston Villa	1–0

Final

Bolton Wanderers 2 Portsmouth 0
(Wembley, 27.4.29, 92,576)

Bolton: Pym, Haworth, Finney, Kean, Seddon, Nuttall, Butler, McClelland, Blackmore, Gibson, W. Cook
Portsmouth: Gilfillan, Mackie, Bell, Nichol, McIlwaine, Thackeray, Forward, J. Smith, Weddle, Watson, F. Cook
Scorers: Butler, Blackmore

FA CUP 1929-30

Fifth round

Middlesbrough v Arsenal	0–2
West Ham United v Millwall	4–1
Manchester City v Hull City	1–2
Newcastle United v Brighton	3–0
Aston Villa v Blackburn Rovers	4–1
Sunderland v Nottingham Forest	2–2, 1–3
Sheffield Wednesday v Bradford P. A.	5–1
Huddersfield Town v Bradford City	2–1

Quarter-finals

West Ham United v Arsenal	0–3
Newcastle United v Hull City	1–1, 0–1
Nottingham Forest v Sheffield Wednesday	2–2, 1–3
Aston Villa v Huddersfield Town	1–2

Semi-finals

Arsenal v Hull City	2–2, 1–0
Huddersfield Town v Sheffield Wednesday	2–1

Final

Arsenal 2 Huddersfield Town 0
(Wembley, 26.4.30, 92,448)

Arsenal: Preedy, Parker, Hapgood, Baker, Seddon, John, Hulme, Jack, Lambert, James, Bastin
Huddersfield: Turner, Goodall, Spence, Naylor, Wilson, Campbell; Jackson, Kelly, Davies, Raw, W. H. Smith
Scorers: James, Lambert

FA CUP 1930-31

Fifth round

Portsmouth v West Bromwich Albion	0–1
Chelsea v Blackburn Rovers	3–0
Sunderland v Sheffield United	2–1
Exeter City v Leeds United	3–1
Everton v Grimsby Town	5–3
Southport v Bradford Park Avenue	1–0
Barnsley v Wolverhampton Wanderers	1–3
Birmingham v Watford	3–0

Quarter-finals

WBA v Wolverhampton W.	1–1, 2–1
Sunderland v Exeter City	1–1, 4–2
Everton v Southport	9–1
Birmingham v Chelsea	2–2, 3–0

Semi-finals

Everton v West Bromwich Albion	0–1
Birmingham v Sunderland	2–0

Final

West Bromwich Albion 2 Birmingham 1
(Wembley, 25.4.31, 92,406)

WBA: Pearson, Shaw, Trentham, Magee, W. Richardson, Edwards, Glidden, Carter, W. G. Richardson, Sandford, Wood
Birmingham: Hibbs, Liddell, Barkas, Cringan, Morrall, Leslie, Briggs, Crosbie, Bradford, Gregg, Curtis
Scorers: W. G. Richardson 2; Bradford

FA CUP 1931-32

Fifth round

Newcastle United v Leicester City	3–1
Huddersfield Town v Preston North End	4–0
Bury v Stoke City	3–0
Manchester City v Derby County	3–0
Liverpool v Grimsby Town	1–0
Sheffield Wednesday v Chelsea	1–1, 0–2
Watford v Bradford Park Avenue	1–0
Portsmouth v Arsenal	0–2

Quarter-finals

Newcastle United v Watford	5–0
Bury v Manchester City	3–4
Liverpool v Chelsea	0–2
Huddersfield Town v Arsenal	0–1

Semi-finals

Chelsea v Newcastle United	1–2
Arsenal v Manchester City	1–0

Final

Newcastle United 2 Arsenal 1
(Wembley, 23.4.32, 92,298)

Newcastle: McInroy, Nelson, Fairhurst, McKenzie, Davidson, Weaver, Boyd, Richardson, Allen, McMenemy, Lang
Arsenal: Moss, Parker, Hapgood, C. Jones, Roberts, Male, Hulme, Jack, Lambert, Bastin, John
Scorers: Allen 2; John

FA CUP 1932-33

Fifth round

Everton v Leeds United	2–0
Burnley v Chesterfield	1–0
Derby County v Aldershot	2–0
Sunderland v Blackpool	1–0
Halifax Town v Luton Town	0–2
Brighton v West Ham United	2–2, 0–1
Middlesbrough v Birmingham	0–0, 0–3
Bolton Wanderers v Manchester City	2–4

Quarter-finals

Everton v Luton Town	6–0
Derby County v Sunderland	4–4, 1–0
West Ham United v Birmingham	4–0
Burnley v Manchester City	0–1

Semi-finals

Everton v West Ham United	2–1
Manchester City v Derby County	3–2

Final

Everton 3 Manchester City 0
(Wembley, 29.4.33, 92,950)

Everton: Sagar, Cook, Cresswell, Britton, White, Thomson, Geldard, Dunn, Dean, Johnson, Stein
City: Langford, Cann, Dale, Busby, Cowan, Bray, Toseland, Marshall, Herd, McMullan, Brook
Scorers: Stein, Dean, Dunn

1909–10	Barnsley
1911–12	Barnsley (winners)
1919–20	Huddersfield (promoted)
1920–21	Wolverhampton Wanderers
1922–23	West Ham United (promoted)
1930–31	WBA (winners, promoted)
1935–36	Sheffield United
1946–47	Burnley (promoted)
1948–49	Leicester City
1963–64	Preston North End
1972–73	Sunderland (winners)
1974–75	Fulham

1975–76	Southampton (winners)
1979–80	West Ham United (winners)
1981–82	QPR

There has been a Division 2 club in each of the 4 finals West Ham have reached – in 1923 and 1980 they were in the Second Division themselves, and in 1964 and 1975 they beat Division 2 clubs, Preston North End and Fulham respectively.

Relegated finalists: Four sides have been relegated the year they reached the final:
1915 Chelsea (lost 3-0)

1926	Manchester City (lost 1-0)
1969	Leicester City (lost 1-0)
1983	Brighton (lost 2-2, 4-0)

Though Chelsea were technically relegated, they were re-elected to Division 1 when it was extended in 1919–20. Barnsley were a Second Division side when they appeared in the 1910 and 1912 Cup finals and, in the intervening season, had to apply for re-election.

Extra time in final: Extra time has been played in the following finals:
1875 Royal Engineers 1 Old Etonians 1

FA CUP 1933-34

Fifth round
Sheffield Wednesday v Manchester C.	2–2, 0–2
Liverpool v Bolton Wanderers	0–3
Preston North End v Northampton Town	4–0
Birmingham v Leicester City	1–2
Tottenham Hotspur v Aston Villa	0–1
Arsenal v Derby County	1–0
Stoke City v Chelsea	3–1
Swansea Town v Portsmouth	0–1

Quarter-finals
Manchester City v Stoke City	1–0
Preston North End v Leicester City	0–1
Arsenal v Aston Villa	1–2
Bolton Wanderers v Portsmouth	0–3

Semi-finals
Manchester City v Aston Villa	6–1
Portsmouth v Leicester City	4–1

Final
Manchester City 2 Portsmouth 1
(Wembley, 28.4.34, 93,258)

City: Swift, Barnett, Dale, Busby, Cowan, Bray, Toseland, Marshall, Tilson, Herd, Brook
Portsmouth: Gilfillan, Mackie, W. Smith, Nichol, Allen, Thackeray, Worral, J. Smith, Weddle, Easson, Rutherford
Scorers: Tilson 2; Rutherford

FA CUP 1934-35

Fifth round
Norwich City v Sheffield Wednesday	0–1
Reading v Arsenal	0–1
Blackburn Rovers v Birmingham	1–2
Nottingham Forest v Burnley	0–0, 0–3
Tottenham Hotspur v Bolton W.	1–1, 1–1, 1–2
Everton v Derby County	3–1
Bristol City v Preston North End	0–0, 0–5
Stockport County v West Bromwich Albion	0–5

Quarter-finals
Sheffield Wednesday v Arsenal	2–1
Burnley v Birmingham	3–2
Everton v Bolton Wanderers	1–2
West Bromwich Albion v Preston North End	1–0

Semi-finals
Sheffield Wednesday v Burnley	3–0
Bolton W. v West Bromwich Albion	1–1, 0–2

Final
Sheffield W. 4 West Bromwich Albion 2
(Wembley, 27.4.35, 93,204)

Wednesday: Brown, Nibloe, Catlin, Sharp, Millership, Burrows, Hooper, Surtees, Palethorpe, Starling, Rimmer
WBA: Pearson, Shaw, Trentham, Murphy, W. Richardson, Edwards, Glidden, Carter, W. G. Richardson, Sandford, Boyes
Scorers: Rimmer 2, Palethorpe, Hooper; Boyes, Sandford

FA CUP 1935-36

Fifth round
Newcastle United v Arsenal	3–3, 0–3
Barnsley v Stoke City	2–1
Grimsby Town v Manchester City	3–2
Middlesbrough v Leicester City	2–1
Chelsea v Fulham	0–0, 2–3
Bradford City v Derby County	0–1
Bradford Park Avenue v Tottenham H.	0–0, 1–2
Sheffield United v Leeds United	3–1

Quarter-finals
Arsenal v Barnsley	4–1
Grimsby Town v Middlesbrough	3–1
Fulham v Derby County	3–0
Sheffield United v Tottenham Hotspur	3–1

Semi-finals
Arsenal v Grimsby Town	1–0
Fulham v Sheffield United	1–2

Final
Arsenal 1 Sheffield United 0
(Wembley, 25.4.36, 93,384)

Arsenal: Wilson, Male, Hapgood, Crayston, Roberts, Copping, Hulme, Bowden, Drake, James, Bastin
United: Smith, Hooper, Wilkinson, Jackson, Johnson, McPherson, Barton, Barclay, Dodds, Pickering, Williams
Scorer: Drake

FA CUP 1936-37

Fifth round
Sunderland v Swansea Town	3–0
Grimsby Town v Wolverhampton W.	1–1, 2–6
Millwall v Derby County	2–1
Bolton Wanderers v Manchester City	0–5
Everton v Tottenham Hotspur	1–1, 3–4
Coventry City v West Bromwich Albion	2–3
Burnley v Arsenal	1–7
Preston North End v Exeter City	5–3

Quarter-finals
Wolverhampton W. v Sunderland	1–1, 2–2, 0–4
Millwall v Manchester City	2–0
West Bromwich Albion v Arsenal	3–1
Tottenham Hotspur v Preston North End	1–3

Semi-finals
Sunderland v Millwall	2–1
Preston North End v West Bromwich Albion	4–1

Final
Sunderland 3 Preston North End 1
(Wembley, 1.5.37, 93,495)

Sunderland: Mapson, Gorman, Hall, Thomson, Johnson, McNab, Duns, Carter, Gurney, Gallacher, Burbanks
Preston: Burns, Gallimore, A. Beattie, Shankly, Tremelling, Milne, Dougal, Beresford, F. O'Donnell, Fagan, H. O'Donnell
Scorers: Gurney, Carter, Burbanks; F. O'Donnell

FA CUP 1937-38

Fifth round
Arsenal v Preston North End	0–1
Brentford v Manchester United	2–0
Luton Town v Manchester City	1–3
Charlton Athletic v Aston Villa	1–1, 2–2, 1–4
Sunderland v Bradford Park Avenue	1–0
Chesterfield v Tottenham Hotspur	2–2, 1–2
York City v Middlesbrough	1–0
Liverpool v Huddersfield Town	0–1

Quarter-finals
Brentford v Preston North End	0–3
Aston Villa v Manchester City	3–2
Tottenham Hotspur v Sunderland	0–1
York City v Huddersfield Town	0–0, 1–2

Semi-finals
Preston North End v Aston Villa	2–1
Sunderland v Huddersfield Town	1–3

Final
Preston North End 1 Huddersfield T. 0 [aet]
(Wembley, 30.4.38, 93,497)

Preston: Holdcroft, Gallimore, A. Beattie, Shankly, Smith, Batey, Watmough, Mutch, Maxwell, R. Beattie, H. O'Donnell
Huddersfield: Hesford, Craig, Mountford, Willingham, Young, Boot, Hulme, Isaac, McFadyen, Barclay, Beasley
Scorer: Mutch (pen)

FA CUP 1938-39

Fifth round
Portsmouth v West Ham United	2–0
Newcastle United v Preston North End	1–2
Huddersfield Town v Walsall	3–0
Sunderland v Blackburn Rovers	1–1, 0–0, 0–1
Wolverhampton Wanderers v Liverpool	4–1
Birmingham v Everton	2–2, 1–2
Chelsea v Sheffield Wednesday	1–1, 0–0, 3–1
Sheffield United v Grimsby Town	0–0, 0–1

Quarter-finals
Portsmouth v Preston North End	1–0
Huddersfield Town v Blackburn Rovers	1–1, 2–1
Wolverhampton Wanderers v Everton	2–0
Chelsea v Grimsby Town	0–1

Semi-finals
Portsmouth v Huddersfield Town	2–1
Wolverhampton Wanderers v Grimsby Town	5–0

Final
Portsmouth 4 Wolverhampton Wanderers 1
(Wembley, 29.4.39, 99,370)

Portsmouth: Walker, Morgan, Rochford, Guthrie, Rowe, Wharton, Worrall, McAlinden, Anderson, Barlow, Parker
Wolves: Scott, Morris, Taylor, Galley, Cullis, Gardiner, Burton, McIntosh, Westcott, Dorsett, Maguire
Scorers: Parker 2, Barlow, Anderson; Dorsett

1877	Wanderers 2 Oxford University 1
1883	Blackburn Olympic 2 Old Etonians 1
1912	Barnsley 1 WBA 0 (in replay)
1920	Aston Villa 1 Huddersfield T. 0
1938	Preston N.E. 1 Huddersfield T. 0
1946	Derby County 4 Charlton Athletic 1
1947	Charlton Athletic 1 Burnley 0
1965	Liverpool 2 Leeds United 1
1968	WBA 1 Everton 0
1970	Chelsea 2 Leeds U. 2 (first game)
	Chelsea 2 Leeds U. 1 (replay)
1971	Arsenal 2 Liverpool 1
1981	Spurs 1 Man City 1 (first game)
1982	Spurs 1 QPR 1 (first game)
1983	Man U. 2 Brighton 2 (first game)

Close finishes: The most dramatic finish to any final was in the last four minutes of the 1979 game when Manchester United pulled back from 2-0 down against Arsenal to equalise, only for Arsenal to win the game 3-2 before the final whistle. In the 1910 final Jock Rutherford scored for Newcastle in the last minute against Second Division Barnsley to square it at 1-1. Newcastle won the replay 2-0 and Rutherford's was the latest goal ever scored to save a final for the winning team. Had he not scored, it would have been Newcastle's fourth Cup final defeat in the space of six years. A better remembered dramatic finish to a Cup final was in 1953, when Blackpool were 3-1 down to Bolton after 68 minutes. Then Stan Mortensen scored and got another from a free-kick in the 90th minute of the game. Bill Perry won the match with Blackpool's fourth goal in injury time.

FA CUP 1945-46

Fifth round*

Brighton v Derby County (1–4, 0–6)	1–10
Stoke v Sheffield Wednesday (2–0, 0–0)	2–0
Bolton v Middlesbrough (1–0, 1–1)	2–1
Queen's Park R. v Brentford (1–3, 0–0)	1–3
Chelsea v Aston Villa (0–1, 0–1)	0–2
Barnsley v Bradford Park Avenue (0–1, 1–1)	1–2
Sunderland v Birmingham City (1–0, 1–3)	2–3
Preston N. End v Charlton Athletic (1–1, 0–6)	1–7

Quarter-finals*

Aston Villa v Derby County (3–4, 1–1)	4–5
Stoke City v Bolton Wanderers (0–2, 0–0)	0–2
Bradford P. A. v Birmingham C. (2–2, 0–6)	2–8
Charlton Athletic v Brentford (6–3, 3–1)	9–4

Semi-finals

Bolton Wanderers v Charlton Athletic	0–2
Derby County v Birmingham City	1–1, 4–0

Final

Derby County 4 Charlton Athletic 1 [aet]
(Wembley, 27.4.46, 98,000)

Derby: Woodley, Nicholas, Howe, Bullions, Leuty, Musson, Harrison, Carter, Stamps, Doherty, Duncan
Charlton: Bartram, Phipps, Shreeve, H. Turner, Oakes, Johnson, Fell, Brown, A Turner, Welsh, Duffy
Scorers: H. Turner (og), Doherty, Stamps 2; H. Turner

*two legs until semi-final

FA CUP 1946-47

Fifth round

Charlton Athletic v Blackburn Rovers	1–0
Sheffield Wednesday v Preston North End	0–2
Newcastle United v Leicester City	1–1, 2–1
Stoke City v Sheffield United	0–1
Nottingham Forest v Middlesbrough	2–2, 2–6
Liverpool v Derby County	1–0
Birmingham City v Manchester City	5–0
Luton Town v Burnley	0–0, 0–3

Quarter-finals

Charlton Athletic v Preston North End	2–1
Sheffield United v Newcastle United	0–2
Liverpool v Birmingham City	4–1
Middlesbrough v Burnley	1–1, 0–1

Semi-finals

Charlton Athletic v Newcastle United	4–0
Burnley v Liverpool	0–0, 1–0

Final

Charlton Athletic 1 Burnley 0 [aet]
(Wembley, 26.4.47, 99,000)

Charlton: Bartram, Croker, Shreeve, Johnson, Phipps, Whittaker, Hurst, Dawson, Robinson, Welsh, Duffy
Burnley: Strong, Woodruff, Mather, Attwell, Brown, Bray, Chew, Morris, Harrison, Potts, Kippax
Scorer: Duffy

FA CUP 1947-48

Fifth round

Manchester United v Charlton Athletic	2–0
Queen's Park Rangers v Luton Town	3–1
Middlesbrough v Derby County	1–2
Manchester City v Preston North End	0–1
Fulham v Everton	1–1, 1–0
Southampton v Swindon Town	3–0
Tottenham Hotspur v Leicester City	5–2
Blackpool v Colchester United	5–0

Quarter-finals

Manchester United v Preston North End	4–1
Queen's Park Rangers v Derby County	1–1, 0–5
Southampton v Tottenham Hotspur	0–1
Fulham v Blackpool	0–2

Semi-finals

Derby County v Manchester United	1–3
Blackpool v Tottenham Hotspur	3–1

Final

Manchester United 4 Blackpool 2
(Wembley, 24.4.48, 99,000)

United: Crompton, Carey, Aston, Anderson, Chilton, Cockburn, Delaney, Morris, Rowley, Pearson, Mitten
Blackpool: Robinson, Shimwell, Crosland, Johnston, Hayward, Kelly, Matthews, Munro, Mortensen, Dick, Rickett
Scorers: Rowley 2, Pearson, Anderson; Shimwell (pen), Mortensen

FA CUP 1948-49

Fifth round

Wolverhampton Wanderers v Liverpool	3–1
Manchester United v Yeovil Town	8–0
Hull City v Stoke City	2–0
West Bromwich Albion v Chelsea	3–0
Brentford v Burnley	4–2
Portsmouth v Newport County	3–2
Derby County v Cardiff City	2–1
Leicester City v Luton Town	5–5, 5–3

Quarter-finals

Wolverhampton W. v WBA	1–0
Hull City v Manchester United	0–1
Portsmouth v Derby County	2–1
Brentford v Leicester City	0–2

Semi-finals

Manchester U. v Wolverhampton W.	1–1, 0–1
Leicester City v Portsmouth	3–1

Final

Wolverhampton W. 3 Leicester City 1
(Wembley, 30.4.49, 99,500)

Wolves: Williams, Pritchard, Springthorpe, Crook, Shorthouse, Wright; Hancocks, Smyth, Pye, Dunn, Mullen
Leicester: Bradley, Jelly, Scott, W. Harrison, Plummer, King, Griffiths, Lee, J. Harrison, Chisholm, Adam
Scorers: Pye 2, Smyth; Griffiths

FA CUP 1949-50

Fifth round

Arsenal v Burnley	2–0
Leeds United v Cardiff City	3–1
Chesterfield v Chelsea	1–1, 0–3
Manchester United v Portsmouth	3–3, 3–1
Wolverhampton W. v Blackpool	0–0, 0–1
Everton v Tottenham Hotspur	1–0
Derby County v Northampton Town	4–2
Stockport County v Liverpool	1–2

Quarter-finals

Arsenal v Leeds United	1–0
Chelsea v Manchester United	2–0
Derby County v Everton	1–2
Liverpool v Blackpool	2–1

Semi-finals

Arsenal v Chelsea	2–2, 1–0
Liverpool v Everton	2–0

Final

Arsenal 2 Liverpool 0
(Wembley, 29.4.50, 100,000)

Arsenal: Swindin, Scott, Barnes, Forbes, L. Compton, Mercer, Cox, Logie, Goring, Lewis, D. Compton
Liverpool: Sidlow, Lambert, Spicer, Taylor, Hughes, Jones, Payne, Baron, Stubbins, Fagan, Liddell
Scorer: Lewis 2

FA CUP 1950-51

Fifth round

Stoke City v Newcastle United	2–4
Bristol Rovers v Hull City	3–0
Wolverhampton W. v Huddersfield Town	2–0
Sunderland v Norwich City	3–1
Chelsea v Fulham	1–1, 0–3
Birmingham City v Bristol City	2–0
Manchester United v Arsenal	1–0
Blackpool v Mansfield Town	2–0

Quarter-finals

Newcastle United v Bristol Rovers	0–0, 3–1
Sunderland v Wolverhampton W.	1–1, 1–3
Birmingham City v Manchester United	1–0
Blackpool v Fulham	1–0

Semi-finals

Newcastle U. v Wolverhampton W.	0–0, 2–1
Blackpool v Birmingham City	0–0, 2–1

Final

Newcastle United 2 Blackpool 0
(Wembley, 28.4.51, 100,000)

Newcastle: Fairbrother, Cowell, Corbett, Harvey, Brennan, Crowe, Walker, Taylor, Milburn, G. Robledo, Mitchell
Blackpool: Farm, Shimwell, Garrett, Johnston, Hayward, Kelly, Matthews, Mudie, Mortensen, Slater, Perry
Scorer: Milburn 2

Appearances: Major Marindin appeared in 10 finals – 2 as a player and 8 as a referee (including 7 in succession). He played for Royal Engineers in the first final of 1872 and refereed his last in 1890. Lord Kinnaird played in more finals than any other player (9), winning 5 winners medals.

All-English: The West Bromwich Cup winning side of 1888 were all local players, as were the 1893 Wolverhampton side. Conversely, the Cardiff City side that remains the only one to take the Cup outside England (in 1927) contained only one Englishman, Bill Hardy.

Man of the Match: An award given by journalists/BBC after the Cup final to the player with most popular votes. Allan Clarke, who played in 3 games in 4 years (1969, 1970 and 1972) won the award twice;
1969 Allan Clarke (*Leicester City*)
1970 Eddie Gray (*Leeds United*)
1971 George Graham (*Arsenal*)
1972 Allan Clarke (*Leeds United*)
1973 Jim Montgomery (*Sunderland*)

1981 Joe Corrigan (Man City)
1982 Peter Hucker (QPR)
1983 Gary Stevens (Brighton)

Third place play-off: A short-lived imitation of the World Cup idea between the two losing semi-finalists, played on the eve of the final:

1970 Manchester United 2 Watford 0
1971 Stoke City 3 Everton 2
1972 Not contested
1973 Wolverhampton W. 3 Arsenal 1
1974 Burnley 1 Leicester City 0

FA CUP 1951-52

Fifth round

Swansea Town v Newcastle United	0–1
Portsmouth v Doncaster Rovers	4–0
Blackburn Rovers v West Bromwich Albion	1–0
Burnley v Liverpool	2–0
Luton Town v Swindon Town	3–1
Leeds United v Chelsea	1–1, 1–1, 1–5
Southend United v Sheffield United	1–2
Leyton Orient v Arsenal	0–3

Quarter-finals

Portsmouth v Newcastle United	2–4
Blackburn Rovers v Burnley	3–1
Sheffield United v Chelsea	0–1
Luton Town v Arsenal	2–3

Semi-finals

Newcastle United v Blackburn Rovers	0–0, 2–1
Arsenal v Chelsea	1–1, 3–0

Final

Newcastle United 1 Arsenal 0
(Wembley, 3.5.52, 100,000)

Newcastle: Simpson, Cowell, McMichael, Harvey, Brennan, E. Robledo, Walker, Foulkes, Milburn, G. Robledo, Mitchell
Arsenal: Swindin, Barnes, L. Smith, Forbes, Daniel, Mercer, Cox, Logie, Holton, Lishman, Roper
Scorer: G. Robledo

FA CUP 1952-53

Fifth round

Blackpool v Southampton	1–1, 2–1
Burnley v Arsenal	0–2
Halifax Town v Tottenham Hotspur	0–3
Chelsea v Birmingham City	0–4
Plymouth Argyle v Gateshead	0–1
Everton v Manchester United	2–1
Rotherham United v Aston Villa	1–3
Luton Town v Bolton Wanderers	0–1

Quarter-finals

Arsenal v Blackpool	1–2
Birmingham City v Tottenham H.	1–1, 2–2, 0–1
Aston Villa v Everton	0–1
Gateshead v Bolton Wanderers	0–1

Semi-finals

Blackpool v Tottenham Hotspur	2–1
Bolton Wanderers v Everton	4–3

Final

Blackpool 4 Bolton Wanderers 3
(Wembley, 2.5.53, 100,000)

Blackpool: Farm, Shimwell, Garrett, Fenton, Johnston, Robinson, Matthews, Taylor, Mortensen, Mudie, Perry
Bolton: Hanson, Ball, Banks, Wheeler, Barrass, Bell, Holden, Moir, Lofthouse, Hassall, Langton
Scorers: Mortensen 3, Perry; Lofthouse, Moir, Bell

FA CUP 1953-54

Fifth round

West Bromwich Albion v Newcastle United	3–2
Hull City v Tottenham Hotspur	1–1, 1–2
Leyton Orient v Doncaster Rovers	3–1
Port Vale v Blackpool	2–0
Sheffield Wednesday v Everton	3–1
Bolton Wanderers v Portsmouth	0–0, 2–1
Norwich City v Leicester City	1–2
Preston North End v Ipswich Town	6–1

Quarter-finals

West Bromwich Albion v Tottenham Hotspur	3–0
Leyton Orient v Port Vale	0–1
Sheffield Wednesday v Bolton W.	1–1, 2–0
Leicester City v Preston North End	1–1, 2–2, 1–3

Semi-finals

West Bromwich Albion v Port Vale	2–1
Sheffield Wednesday v Preston North End	0–2

Final

West Bromwich Albion 3 Preston N. E. 2
(Wembley, 1.5.54, 100,000)

WBA: Sanders, Kennedy, Millard, Dudley, Dugdale, Barlow, Griffin, Ryan, Allen, Nicholls, Lee
Preston: Thompson, Cunningham, Walton, Docherty, Marston, Forbes, Finney, Foster, Wayman, Baxter, Morrison
Scorers: Allen 2 (1 pen), Griffin; Morrison, Wayman

FA CUP 1954-55

Fifth round

Nottingham Forest v Newcastle U.	1–1, 2–2, 1–2
Liverpool v Huddersfield Town	0–2
Notts County v Chelsea	1–0
York City v Tottenham Hotspur	3–1
Swansea Town v Sunderland	2–2, 0–1
Wolverhampton W. v Charlton Athletic	4–1
Birmingham City v Doncaster Rovers	2–1
Luton Town v Manchester City	0–2

Quarter-finals

Huddersfield Town v Newcastle U.	1–1, 0–2
Notts County v York City	0–1
Sunderland v Wolverhampton Wanderers	2–0
Birmingham City v Manchester City	0–1

Semi-finals

Newcastle United v York City	1–1, 2–0
Sunderland v Manchester City	0–1

Finals

Newcastle United 3 Manchester City 1
(Wembley, 7.5.55, 100,000)

Newcastle: Simpson, Cowell, Batty, Scoular, Stokoe, Casey, White, Milburn, Keeble, Hannah, Mitchell
City: Trautmann, Meadows, Little, Barnes, Ewing, Paul, Spurdle, Hayes, Revie, Johnstone, Fagan
Scorers: Milburn, Mitchell, Hannah; Johnstone

FA CUP 1955-56

Fifth round

Manchester City v Liverpool	0–0, 2–1
Charlton Athletic v Arsenal	0–2
Newcastle United v Stoke City	2–1
Sheffield United v Sunderland	0–0, 0–1
Doncaster Rovers v Tottenham Hotspur	0–2
West Ham United v Blackburn Rovers	0–0, 3–2
Everton v Chelsea	1–0
West Bromwich Albion v Birmingham City	0–1

Quarter-finals

Manchester City v Everton	2–1
Newcastle United v Sunderland	0–2
Tottenham Hotspur v West Ham U.	3–3, 2–1
Arsenal v Birmingham City	1–3

Semi-finals

Tottenham Hotspur v Manchester City	0–1
Birmingham City v Sunderland	3–0

Final

Manchester City 3 Birmingham City 1
(Wembley, 5.5.56, 100,000)

City: Trautmann, Leivers, Little, Barnes, Ewing, Paul, Johnstone, Hayes, Revie, Dyson, Clarke
Birmingham: Merrick, Hall, Green, Newman, Smith, Boyd, Astall, Kinsey, Brown, Murphy, Govan
Scorers: Hayes, Dyson, Johnstone; Kinsey

FA CUP 1956-57

Fifth round

Aston Villa v Bristol City	2–1
Huddersfield Town v Burnley	1–2
Preston North End v Arsenal	3–3, 1–2
Blackpool v West Bromwich Albion	0–0, 1–2
Bournemouth v Tottenham Hotspur	3–1
Millwall v Birmingham City	1–4
Barnsley v Nottingham Forest	1–2
Manchester United v Everton	1–0

Quarter-finals

Burnley v Aston Villa	1–1, 0–2
West Bromwich Albion v Arsenal	2–2, 1–0
Birmingham City v Nottingham Forest	0–0, 1–0
Bournemouth v Manchester United	1–2

Semi-finals

Aston Villa v West Bromwich Albion	2–2, 1–0
Manchester United v Birmingham City	2–0

Final

Aston Villa 2 Manchester United 1
(Wembley, 4.5.57, 100,000)

Villa: Sims, Lynn, Aldis, Crowther, Dugdale, Saward, Smith, Sewell, Myerscough, Dixon, McParland
United: Wood, Foulkes, Byrne, Colman, J. Blanchflower, Edwards, Berry, Whelan, T. Taylor, R. Charlton, Pegg
Scorers: McParland 2; Taylor

ENTRIES

Every year: Great Marlow and Maidenhead are the only clubs to have entered the competition every year since its foundation.

Cities represented: Blackburn was represented in the final for 5 consecutive years – 1882 to 1886. The closest any other city has come to this record is Manchester, with two appearances by City and two by United between 1955 and 1958.

Shortest FA Cup career: Donington School, near Spalding in Lincolnshire, who were one of the 15 entrants for the first FA Cup in 1871–72, were drawn against Queen's Park but scratched before the game was played and never entered again.

Refused to compete: Several clubs have refused to compete in the tournament, the first being in 1888–89 when Sunderland would not play local rivals Sunderland Albion. Albion were a breakaway club set up because of disagreements over Sunderland's policy of importing Scottish professionals. The clubs played a friendly instead, which Sunderland won 2–0, and Albion soon faded away. Five clubs newly elected to the League have refused to play in the Cup because they were not excluded until the first round proper (or its equivalent) – Charlton and Halifax in 1921–22, Bournemouth in 1923–24, Torquay in 1927–28 and Shrewsbury in 1950–51.

Failed to enter: Birmingham forgot to send in their entry in 1921–22. QPR failed to enter in 1926–27, and Hull City did not enter because their ground was unfit in 1945–46.

The Wednesday sent their entry in too late in 1886–87. Newport County were not allowed to enter in 1931–32 after an investigation into a lottery they were running. **Met in consecutive seasons:** Brighton and Watford were drawn together in the Cup for four consecutive seasons – 1924–28. Manchester City and Leicester City also met in four consecutive seasons, 1965–69, culminating in the 1969 final. Everton and Sheffield Wednesday have met 11 times in all, including the 1966 final.

GOALSCORING

Consecutive finals: Jimmy Brown, captain of Blackburn Rovers, is the only man to have scored in three consecutive finals – 1884, 1885 and 1886 – though he did not actually score in the first 1886 game against WBA but got the second in the replay at Derby. Three other Blackburn players, James Forrest in 1884 and 1885, and John Southworth and William Townley in 1890 and 1891 scored in consecutive games. James Kenrick and Arthur Kinnaird scored in both the 1877 and 1878 finals, when they played for Wanderers. Kinnaird's 1877 goal, however, was an own-goal for Oxford.

Consecutive Wembley finals: Bobby Johnstone scored for Manchester City in 1955 and 1956 and Bobby Smith scored for Spurs in 1961 and 1962. Spurs Glenn Hoddle recorded three scoring shots in the four games that made up the 1981 and 1982 finals; his free-kick against Manchester City was deflected for a goal by Tommy Hutchison in the first 1981 game, his shot was deflected for a goal against QPR in the first 1982 game and his penalty in the 1982 replay won the trophy for Spurs.

Most goals in Cup finals: 4 – William Townley (Blackburn) and Stan Mortensen (Blackpool).

Most goals, Wembley finals: 4 – Stan Mortensen (1948 and 1953). Both Jackie Milburn of Newcastle (who appeared in 1951, 1952 and 1955) and Nat Lofthouse of Bolton (1953 and 1958) have scored three goals. Frank Stapleton (Arsenal 1979 *against* Manchester United and 1983 for United) is the only man to have scored goals in a Cup final for two different clubs.

EARLIER ROUNDS

Semi-final appearances: West Bromwich have appeared in 19, Everton in 18, Aston Villa in 17 (up to 1 January 1985).

Semi-final successes: Old Etonians reached the semi-final round on 5 occasions and reached 5 finals (though they did not have to win a game on every occasion) but Wanderers have a rather better record with 3 semi-final appearances and 5 Cup wins. In fact Wanderers had to win only 2 games at the semi-final stage to reach their 5 finals (*see tabular section*). In more modern times, Blackpool won all 3 of their semi-finals, (1948, 1951 and 1953) and Newcastle won 11 out of 13.

Semi-final defeats: Everton have lost 12 semi-

GREAT CENTRAL RAILWAY
ENGLISH CUP FINAL CRYSTAL PALACE
APRIL 23rd 1904

BILLY MEREDITH SECURES THE CUP.

HE WANTS YOU TO

SEE THE MATCH AND TRAVEL IN COMFORT BY THE GREAT CENTRAL RAILWAY COMPANY
CHEAP EXCURSIONS.
TICKETS HAND... ...PARTICULARS MAY BE OBTAINED WITHIN

Lou Macari turns away after Greenhoff's 1977 goal had broken Liverpool's treble.

ABOVE: The astonishing poster that the Great Central put up at Manchester London Road before the 1904 Cup final to persuade fans to travel on their excursions to Crystal Palace for the first all-Lancashire final, between Bolton and Manchester City. The poster's suggestion that Billy Meredith would score the winning goal was borne out (top, the only existing picture of the game's only goal) even to the extent of correctly predicting which end it would be scored at! Bolton keeper Dai Davies, who was understandably horrified to have to pass the poster for weeks before the game, found his own place in the record books by coming on as a substitute for Wales in the 1908 international v England and also being the only man to win caps at both soccer and rugby league. By a remarkable coincidence, John Sutcliffe, Bolton's keeper in their only previous Cup final appearance (in 1894) was also the last Englishman to wins caps at both soccer and rugby, in his case rugby union. His last soccer cap was v Wales in 1902. (The poster is produced by kind permission of George Dow Esq, of Audlem, Cheshire, who owns copyright in the original, which was used in his book "Great Central".)

Alan Sunderland is mobbed by Arsenal players after scoring the third goal in as many minutes to win the 1979 Cup final.

Brian Kidd puts Everton into the lead from a penalty in the semi-final at Villa Park on 12 April 1980. But West Ham were to win a replay and Kidd was later to be sent off.

Charles Alcock, creator of the FA Cup and that competition's critical figure.

Chelsea's Ron Harris lifts the FA Cup at Old Trafford in 1970 after the only final ever to last a full 240 minutes.

Jack Devey, scorer in 1895 of the fastest FA Cup final goal, after just 30 seconds.

Stan Mortensen scores his and Blackpool's second goal in the 1953 final. Not only did he score the only Wembley hat-trick, but he also achieved a record 4 goals in FA Cup finals.

FA CUP 1957-58

Fifth round
Bolton Wanderers v Stoke City	3–1
Cardiff City v Blackburn Rovers	0–0, 1–2
Scunthorpe United v Liverpool	0–1
Wolverhampton Wanderers v Darlington	6–1
Sheffield U. v West Bromwich Albion	1–1, 1–4
Bristol City v Bristol Rovers	3–4
West Ham United v Fulham	2–3
Manchester United v Sheffield Wednesday	3–0

Quarter-finals
Bolton Wanderers v Wolverhampton W.	2–1
Blackburn Rovers v Liverpool	2–1
Fulham v Bristol Rovers	3–1
WBA v Manchester U.	2–2, 0–1

Semi-finals
Blackburn Rovers v Bolton Wanderers	1–2
Manchester United v Fulham	2–2, 5–3

Final

Bolton Wanderers 2 Manchester United 0
(Wembley, 3.5.58, 100,000)

Bolton: Hopkinson, Hartle, Banks, Hennin, Higgins, Edwards, Birch, Stevens, Lofthouse, Parry, Holden
United: Gregg, Foulkes, Greaves, Goodwin, Cope, Crowther, Dawson, E. Taylor, R. Charlton, Viollet, Webster
Scorer: Lofthouse 2

FA CUP 1959-60

Fifth round
Luton Town v Wolverhampton Wanderers	1–4
Leicester City v West Bromwich Albion	2–1
Preston North End v Brighton	2–1
Port Vale v Aston Villa	1–2
Sheffield United v Watford	3–2
Manchester United v Sheffield Wednesday	0–1
Bradford City v Burnley	2–2, 0–5
Tottenham Hotspur v Blackburn Rovers	1–3

Quarter-finals
Leicester City v Wolverhampton Wanderers	1–2
Aston Villa v Preston North End	2–0
Sheffield United v Sheffield Wednesday	0–2
Burnley v Blackburn Rovers	3–3, 0–2

Semi-finals
Wolverhampton Wanderers v Aston Villa	1–0
Sheffield Wednesday v Blackburn Rovers	1–2

Final

Wolverhampton W. 3 Blackburn Rovers 0
(Wembley, 7.5.60, 100,000)

Wolves: Finlayson, Showell, Harris, Clamp, Slater, Flowers, Deeley, Stobart, Murray, Broadbent, Horne
Blackburn: Leyland, Bray, Whelan, Clayton, Woods, McGrath, Bimpson, Dobing, Dougan, Douglas, McLeod
Scorers: McGrath (og), Deeley 2

FA CUP 1961-62

Fifth round
WBA v Tottenham Hotspur	2–4
Sheffield United v Norwich City	3–1
Fulham v Port Vale	1–0
Blackburn Rovers v Middlesbrough	2–1
Liverpool v Preston North End	0–0, 0–0, 0–1
Manchester U. v Sheffield Wednesday	0–0, 2–0
Aston Villa v Charlton Athletic	2–1
Burnley v Everton	3–1

Quarter-finals
Tottenham Hotspur v Aston Villa	2–0
Fulham v Blackburn Rovers	2–2, 1–0
Preston N. E. v Manchester United	0–0, 1–2
Sheffield United v Burnley	0–1

Semi-finals
Manchester United v Tottenham Hotspur	1–3
Burnley v Fulham	1–1, 2–1

Final

Tottenham Hotspur 3 Burnley 1
(Wembley, 5.5.62, 100,000)

Tottenham: Brown, Baker, Henry, D. Blanchflower, Norman, Mackay, Medwin, White, Smith, Greaves, Jones
Burnley: Blacklaw, Angus, Elder, Adamson, Cummings, Miller, Connelly, McIlroy, Pointer, Robson, Harris
Scorers: Greaves, Smith, Blanchflower (pen); Robson

FA CUP 1958-59

Fifth round
Birmingham City v Nottingham F.	1–1, 1–1, 0–5
Bolton W. v Preston North End	2–2, 1–1, 1–0
Everton v Aston Villa	1–4
Burnley v Portsmouth	1–0
Arsenal v Sheffield United	2–2, 0–3
Tottenham Hotspur v Norwich City	1–1, 0–1
Blackpool v West Bromwich Albion	3–1
Ipswich Town v Luton Town	2–5

Quarter-finals
Nottingham Forest v Bolton Wanderers	2–1
Aston Villa v Burnley	0–0, 2–0
Sheffield United v Norwich City	1–1, 2–3
Blackpool v Luton Town	1–1, 0–1

Semi-fnals
Nottingham Forest v Aston Villa	1–0
Norwich City v Luton Town	1–1, 0–1

Final

Nottingham Forest 2 Luton Town 1
(Wembley, 2.5.59, 100,000)

Forest: Thomson, Whare, McDonald, Whitefoot, McKinlay, Burkitt, Dwight, Quigley, Wilson, Gray, Imlach
Luton: Baynham, McNally, Hawkes, Groves, Owen, Pacey, Bingham, Brown, Morton, Cummins, Gregory
Scorers: Dwight, Wilson; Pacey

FA CUP 1960-61

Fifth round
Aston Villa v Tottenham Hotspur	0–2
Barnsley v Luton Town	1–0
Newcastle United v Stoke City	3–1
Sheffield United v Blackburn Rovers	2–1
Leyton Orient v Sheffield Wednesday	0–2
Burnley v Swansea Town	4–0
Norwich City v Sunderland	0–1
Birmingham City v Leicester City	1–1, 1–2

Quarter-finals
Sunderland v Tottenham Hotspur	1–1, 0–5
Newcastle United v Sheffield United	1–3
Sheffield Wednesday v Burnley	0–0, 0–2
Leicester City v Barnsley	0–0, 2–1

Semi-finals
Burnley v Tottenham Hotspur	0–3
Leicester City v Sheffield United	0–0, 0–0, 2–0

Final

Tottenham Hotspur 2 Leicester City 0
(Wembley, 6.5.61, 100,000)

Tottenham: Brown, Baker, Henry, D. Blanchflower, Norman, Mackay, Jones, White, Smith, Allen, Dyson
Leicester: Banks, Chalmers, Norman, McLintock, King, Appleton, Riley, Walsh, McIlmoyle, Keyworth, Cheesebrough
Scorers: Smith, Dyson

FA CUP 1962-63

Fifth round
Leicester City v Leyton Orient	1–0
Manchester City v Norwich City	1–2
Arsenal v Liverpool	1–2
West Ham United v Everton	1–0
Nottingham Forest v Leeds United	3–0
Southampton v Sheffield United	1–0
Coventry City v Sunderland	2–1
Manchester United v Chelsea	2–1

Quarter-finals
Norwich City v Leicester City	0–2
Liverpool v West Ham United	1–0
Nottingham Forest v Southampton	1–1, 3–3, 0–5
Coventry City v Manchester United	1–3

Semi-finals
Leicester City v Liverpool	1–0
Southampton v Manchester United	0–1

Final

Manchester United 3 Leicester City 1
(Wembley, 25.5.63, 100,000)

United: Gaskell, Dunne, Cantwell, Crerand, Foulkes, Setters, Giles, Quixall, Herd, Law, R. Charlton
Leicester: Banks, Sjoberg, Norman, McLintock, King, Appleton, Riley, Cross, Keyworth, Gibson, Stringfellow
Scorers: Law, Herd 2; Keyworth

---

finals (out of 18), while Derby have lost 9 out of 13. Statistically both Birmingham and Nottingham Forest have worse records, with 7 defeats out of 9. Oddly Forest have won all other semi-finals they have contested – 3 in the League Cup and 2 in the European Cup (up to 1 January 1984).
Non-League semi-finalists: Since 1888, the following non-League clubs have reached the semi-finals:
1890 The Wednesday (reached final)
1892 Nottingham Forest

1898 Southampton
1900 Southampton (final) and Millwall
1901 Tottenham Hotspur (won Cup)
1902 Southampton (reached final)
1903 Millwall
1910 Swindon Town
1912 Swindon Town
Apart from The Wednesday and Nottingham Forest (both in Football Alliance) all of these clubs were in the Southern League.
Division 3 semi-finalists: Six Division 3 clubs have reached the semi-finals though none

has gone further:
1936–37 Millwall
1953–54 Port Vale
1954–55 York City
1958–59 Norwich City
1975–76 Crystal Palace
1983–84 Plymouth Argyle
Division 4 clubs: Three have reached the quarter-finals, none has gone further:
1963–64 Oxford United
1970–71 Colchester United
1975–76 Bradford City

FA CUP 1963-64

Fifth round

West Ham United v Swindon Town	3–1
Burnley v Huddersfield Town	3–0
Sunderland v Everton	3–1
Barnsley v Manchester United	0–4
Stoke City v Swansea Town	2–2, 0–2
Arsenal v Liverpool	0–1
Oxford United v Blackburn Rovers	3–1
Carlisle United v Preston North End	0–1

Quarter-finals

West Ham United v Burnley	3–2
Manchester United v Sunderland	3–3, 2–2, 5–1
Liverpool v Swansea Town	1–2
Oxford United v Preston North End	1–2

Semi-finals

West Ham United v Manchester United	3–1
Swansea Town v Preston North End	1–2

Final

West Ham United 3 Preston North End 2
(Wembley, 2.5.64, 100,000)

West Ham: Standen, Bond, Burkett, Bovington, Brown, Moore, Brabrook, Boyce, Byrne, Hurst, Sissons
Preston: Kelly, Ross, Smith, Lawton, Singleton, Kendall, Wilson, Ashworth, Dawson, Spavin, Holden
Scorers: Sissons, Hurst, Boyce; Holden, Dawson

FA CUP 1965-66

Fifth round

Everton v Coventry City	3–0
Manchester City v Leicester City	2–2, 1–0
Wolverhampton W. v Manchester United	2–4
Preston North End v Tottenham Hotspur	2–1
Chelsea v Shrewsbury Town	3–2
Hull City v Southport	2–0
Norwich City v Blackburn Rovers	2–2, 2–3
Huddersfield Town v Sheffield Wednesday	1–2

Quarter-finals

Manchester City v Everton	0–0, 0–0, 0–2
Preston N. E. v Manchester United	1–1, 1–3
Chelsea v Hull City	2–2, 3–1
Blackburn Rovers v Sheffield Wednesday	1–2

Semi-finals

Everton v Manchester United	1–0
Sheffield Wednesday v Chelsea	2–0

Final

Everton 3 Sheffield Wednesday 2
(Wembley, 14.5.66, 100,000)

Everton: West, Wright, Wilson, Gabriel, Labone, Harris, Scott, Trebilcock, Young, Harvey, Temple
Wednesday: Springett, Smith, Megson, Eustace, Ellis, Young, Pugh, Fantham, McCalliog, Ford, Quinn
Scorers: Trebilcock 2, Temple; McCalliog, Ford

FA CUP 1967-68

Fifth round

Portsmouth v West Bromwich Albion	1–2
Rotherham United v Leicester City	1–1, 0–2
Leeds United v Bristol City	2–0
West Ham United v Sheffield United	1–2
Arsenal v Birmingham City	1–1, 1–2
Sheffield Wednesday v Chelsea	2–2, 0–2
Tottenham Hotspur v Liverpool	1–1, 1–2
Everton v Tranmere Rovers	2–0

Quarter-finals

WBA v Liverpool	0–0, 1–1, 2–1
Leeds United v Sheffield United	1–0
Birmingham City v Chelsea	1–0
Everton v Leicester City	3–1

Semi-finals

West Bromwich Albion v Birmingham City	2–0
Everton v Leeds United	1–0

Final

West Bromwich Albion 1 Everton 0 [aet]
(Wembley, 18.5.68, 100,000)

WBA: Osborne, Fraser, Williams, Brown, Talbut, Kaye (Clarke), Lovett, Collard, Astle, Hope, Clark
Everton: West, Wright, Wilson, Kendall, Labone, Harvey, Husband, Ball, Royle, Hurst, Morrissey. (Kenyon)
Scorer: Astle

FA CUP 1964-65

Fifth round

Bolton Wanderers v Liverpool	0–1
Middlesbrough v Leicester City	0–3
Chelsea v Tottenham Hotspur	1–0
Peterborough United v Swansea Town	0–0, 2–0
Aston Villa v Wolverhampton W.	1–1, 0–0, 1–3
Manchester United v Burnley	2–1
Crystal Palace v Nottingham Forest	3–1
Leeds United v Shrewsbury Town	2–0

Quarter-finals

Leicester City v Liverpool	0–0, 0–1
Chelsea v Peterborough United	5–1
Wolverhampton W. v Manchester United	3–5
Crystal Palace v Leeds United	0–3

Semi-finals

Liverpool v Chelsea	2–0
Manchester United v Leeds United	0–0, 0–1

Final

Liverpool 2 Leeds United 1 [aet]
(Wembley, 1.5.65, 100,000)

Liverpool: Lawrence, Lawler, Byrne, Strong, Yeats, Stevenson, Callaghan, Hunt, St John, Smith, Thompson
Leeds: Sprake, Reaney, Bell, Bremner, J. Charlton, Hunter, Giles, Storrie, Peacock, Collins, Johanneson
Scorers: Hunt, St John; Bremner

FA CUP 1966-67

Fifth round

Tottenham Hotspur v Bristol City	2–0
Norwich City v Sheffield Wednesday	1–3
Sunderland v Leeds United	1–1, 1–1, 1–2
Manchester City v Ipswich Town	1–1, 3–0
Birmingham City v Arsenal	1–0
Nottingham Forest v Swindon T.	0–0, 1–1, 3–0
Everton v Liverpool	1–0
Chelsea v Sheffield United	2–0

Quarter-finals

Birmingham City v Tottenham Hotspur	0–0, 0–6
Leeds United v Manchester City	1–0
Nottingham Forest v Everton	3–2
Chelsea v Sheffield Wednesday	1–0

Semi-finals

Tottenham Hotspur v Nottingham Forest	2–1
Chelsea v Leeds United	1–0

Final

Tottenham Hotspur 2 Chelsea 1
(Wembley, 20.5.67, 100,000)

Tottenham: Jennings, Kinnear, Knowles, Mullery, England, Mackay, Robertson, Greaves, Gilzean, Venables, Saul. (Jones)
Chelsea: Bonetti, A. Harris, McCreadie, Hollins, Hinton, R. Harris, Cooke, Baldwin, Hateley, Tambling, Boyle. (Kirkup)
Scorers: Robertson, Saul; Tambling

FA CUP 1968-69

Fifth round

Manchester City v Blackburn Rovers	4–1
Tottenham Hotspur v Aston Villa	3–2
Birmingham City v Manchester United	2–2, 2–6
Bristol Rovers v Everton	0–1
West Bromwich Albion v Arsenal	1–0
Chelsea v Stoke City	3–2
Mansfield Town v West Ham United	3–0
Liverpool v Leicester City	0–0, 0–1

Quarter-finals

Manchester City v Tottenham Hotspur	1–0
Manchester United v Everton	0–1
Chelsea v West Bromwich Albion	1–2
Mansfield Town v Leicester City	0–1

Semi-finals

Manchester City v Everton	1–0
West Bromwich Albion v Leicester City	0–1

Final

Manchester City 1 Leicester City 0
(Wembley, 26.4.69, 100,000)

City: Dowd, Book, Pardoe, Doyle, Booth, Oakes, Summerbee, Bell, Lee, Young, Coleman. (Connor)
Leicester: Shilton, Rodrigues, Nish, Roberts, Woollet, Cross, Fern, Gibson, Lochhead, Clarke, Glover. (Manley)
Scorer: Young

No home ties: Arsenal set up a remarkable record by reaching both the 1971 and 1972 Cup finals without being drawn at home once either year. But in 1950 they also set up another record by becoming the first club to win the Cup without having to leave their home town since the amateur days of the 1870s. Arsenal had home ties versus Sheffield Wednesday, Swansea, Burnley and Leeds, beat Chelsea in the semi-final at Tottenham and Liverpool 2-0 in the final at Wembley.
Toughest Cup run: Manchester United, in

1947–48, are the only side apart from Arsenal and Bury in 1899–1900 to win the Cup without a single home draw. In addition, they were also drawn against six Division 1 sides in succession. Their record was: 6-4 v Aston Villa at Villa Park, 3-0 v Liverpool at Goodison, 2-0 v Charlton at Huddersfield, 4-1 v Preston at Maine Road, 3-1 v Derby in the semi-final in Sheffield and 4-2 v Blackpool at Wembley. As Old Trafford was bomb damaged, they had to use other grounds for their 'home' fixtures. As as

result Preston, who beat Manchester City away in the fifth round, played consecutive rounds against different opponents on the same away ground – another record of sorts. United are also the only team to beat six Division 1 sides in a season – those sides were placed, out of interest, 4th, 6th, 7th, 9th, 11th and 13th in the League that year.
Cup ties in 4 countries: Nottingham Forest have been drawn to play Cup matches in all 4 home countries. In 1885, they drew their

FA CUP 1969-70

Fifth round

Chelsea v Crystal Palace	4–1
Queen's Park Rangers v Derby County	1–0
Watford v Gillingham	2–1
Liverpool v Leicester City	0–0, 2–0
Northampton Town v Manchester United	2–8
Carlisle United v Middlesbrough	1–2
Swindon Town v Scunthorpe United	3–1
Mansfield Town v Leeds United	0–2

Quarter-finals

Queen's Park Rangers v Chelsea	2–4
Watford v Liverpool	1–0
Manchester United v Middlesbrough	1–1, 2–1
Swindon Town v Leeds United	0–2

Semi-finals

Chelsea v Watford	5–1
Manchester United v Leeds U.	0–0, 0–0, 0–1

Final

Chelsea 2 Leeds United 2 [aet]
(Wembley, 11.4.70, 100,000)

Chelsea: Bonetti, Webb, McCreadie, Hollins, Dempsey, Harris (Hinton), Baldwin, Houseman, Osgood, Hutchinson, Cooke
Leeds: Sprake, Madeley, Cooper, Bremner, J. Charlton, Hunter, Lorimer, Clarke, Jones, Giles, Gray, (Bates)
Scorers: Houseman, Hutchinson; Charlton, Jones

Replay
Chelsea 2 Leeds United 1 [aet]
(Old Trafford, 29.4.70, 62,000)

Chelsea: Unchanged: Hinton came on for Osgood
Leeds: Harvey for Sprake
Scorers: Osgood, Webb; Jones

FA CUP 1970-71

Fifth round

Manchester City v Arsenal	1–2
Tottenham Hotspur v Nottingham Forest	2–1
Everton v Derby County	1–0
Colchester United v Leeds United	3–2
Hull City v Brentford	2–1
Stoke City v Ipswich Town	0–0, 1–0
Leicester City v Oxford United	1–1, 3–1
Liverpool v Southampton	1–0

Quarter-finals

Leicester City v Arsenal	0–0, 0–1
Everton v Colchester United	5–0
Hull City v Stoke City	2–3
Liverpool v Tottenham Hotspur	0–0, 1–0

Semi-finals

Stoke City v Arsenal	2–2, 0–2
Liverpool v Everton	2–1

Final

Arsenal 2 Liverpool 1 [aet]
(Wembley, 8.5.71, 100,000)

Arsenal: Wilson, Rice, McNab, Storey (Kelly), McLintock, Simpson, Armstrong, Graham, Radford, R. Kennedy, George
Liverpool: Clemence, Lawler, Lindsay, Smith, Lloyd, Hughes, Callaghan, Evans (Peter Thompson), Heighway, Toshack, Hall
Scorers: Kelly, George; Heighway

FA CUP 1971-72

Fifth round

Cardiff City v Leeds United	0–2
Everton v Tottenham Hotspur	0–2
Birmingham City v Portsmouth	3–1
Huddersfield v West Ham	4–2
Manchester United v Middlesbrough	0–0, 3–0
Stoke City v Hull City	4–1
Orient v Chelsea	3–2
Derby County v Arsenal	2–2, 0–0, 0–1

Quarter-finals

Leeds United v Tottenham Hotspur	2–1
Birmingham City v Huddersfield Town	3–1
Manchester United v Stoke City	1–1, 1–2
Orient v Arsenal	0–1

Semi-finals

Leeds United v Birmingham City	3–0
Arsenal v Stoke City	1–1, 2–1

Final

Leeds United 1 Arsenal 0
(Wembley, 6.5.72, 100,000)

Leeds: Harvey, Reaney, Madeley, Bremner, J. Charlton, Hunter, Lorimer, Clarke, Jones, Giles, E. Gray, (Bates)
Arsenal: Barnett, Rice, McNab, Storey, McLintock, Simpson, Armstrong, Ball, George, Radford (R. Kennedy), Graham
Scorer: Clarke

FA CUP 1972-73

Fifth round

Manchester City v Sunderland	2–2, 1–3
Bolton Wanderers v Luton Town	0–1
Carlisle United v Arsenal	1–2
Coventry City v Hull City	3–0
Derby County v Queen's Park Rangers	4–2
Sheffield Wednesday v Chelsea	1–2
Wolverhampton Wanderers v Millwall	1–0
Leeds United v West Bromwich Albion	2–0

Quarter-finals

Sunderland v Luton Town	2–0
Chelsea v Arsenal	2–2, 1–2
Wolverhampton Wanderers v Coventry City	2–0
Derby County v Leeds United	0–1

Semi-finals

Arsenal v Sunderland	1–2
Leeds United v Wolverhampton Wanderers	1–0

Final

Sunderland 1 Leeds United 0
(Wembley, 5.5.73, 100,000)

Sunderland: Montgomery, Malone, Guthrie, Horswill, Watson, Pitt, Kerr, Hughes, Halom, Porterfield, Tueart. (Young)
Leeds: Harvey, Reaney, Cherry, Bremner, Madeley, Hunter, Lorimer, Clarke, Jones, Giles, E. Gray (Yorath)
Scorer: Porterfield

FA CUP 1973-74

Fifth round

Liverpool v Ipswich Town	2–0
Bristol City v Leeds United	1–1, 1–0
Burnley v Aston Villa	1–0
Coventry City v Queen's Park Rangers	0–0, 2–3
Luton Town v Leicester City	0–4
Nottingham Forest v Portsmouth	1–0
Southampton v Wrexham	0–1
West Bromwich Albion v Newcastle United	0–3

Quarter-finals

Bristol City v Liverpool	0–1
Burnley v Wrexham	1–0
Queen's Park Rangers v Leicester City	0–2
Newcastle United v Nottingham Forest	4–3*, 0–0, 1–0

Semi-finals

Burnley v Newcastle United	0–2
Leicester City v Liverpool	0–0, 1–3

Final

Liverpool 3 Newcastle United 0
(Wembley, 4.5.74, 100,000)

Liverpool: Clemence, Smith, Lindsay, Phil Thompson, Cormack, Hughes, Keegan, Hall, Heighway, Toshack, Callaghan (Lawler)
Newcastle: McFaul, Clark, A. Kennedy, McDermott, Howard, Moncur, Smith (Gibb), Cassidy, Macdonald, Tudor, Hibbitt
Scorers: Keegan 2, Heighway

*replay ordered after invasion by crowd; replays at Goodison Park

FA CUP 1974-75

Fifth round

West Ham United v Queen's Park Rangers	2–1
Arsenal v Leicester City	0–0, 1–0
Birmingham City v Walsall	2–1
Ipswich Town v Aston Villa	3–2
Mansfield Town v Carlisle United	0–1
Peterborough United v Middlesbrough	1–1, 2–0
Derby County v Leeds United	0–1
Everton v Fulham	1–2

Quarter-finals

Arsenal v West Ham United	0–2
Birmingham City v Middlesbrough	1–0
Ipswich Town v Leeds United	0–0, 1–1, 0–0, 3–2
Carlisle United v Fulham	0–1

Semi-finals

West Ham United v Ipswich Town	0–0, 2–1
Fulham v Birmingham City	1–1, 1–0

Final

West Ham United 2 Fulham 0
(Wembley, 2.5.75, 100,000)

West Ham: Day, McDowell, T. Taylor, Lock, Lampard, Bonds, Paddon, Brooking, Jennings, A. Taylor, Holland (Gould)
Fulham: Mellor, Cutbush, Lacy, Moore, Fraser, Mullery, Conway, Slough, Mitchell, Busby, Barrett. (Lloyd)
Scorer: A. Taylor 2

semi-final with Queen's Park at Derby and then lost the replay in the grounds of Merchiston Castle School, Edinburgh. In 1888–89 they were drawn to play Linfield in Belfast, travelled to Ireland but found that Linfield had scratched while they were en route and played a friendly, which ended 3-1 to Linfield, instead. They also lost 4-1 at Cardiff in 1921–22. No other team has ever played ties in more than two countries.

Won on toss of coin: The only known instance in the FA Cup was in the first round of 1873–74 when Sheffield drew twice with Shropshire Wanderers and went through on a tossed coin. The system has become common in recent years in England in both European competition and the League Cup.
Disqualified: This was quite common in the early seasons, particularly for professionalism in the 1880s. The worst year was 1885–86 when Clapham Rovers, Old Harrovians and Preston (for professionalism) were disqualified in the third round and Bolton Wanderers were disqualified in the fifth. Protests around

FA CUP — 1975-76

Fifth round

Bolton Wanderers v Newcastle	3–3, 0–0, 1–2
West Bromwich Albion v Southampton	1–1, 0–4
Chelsea v Crystal Palace	2–3
Derby County v Southend United	1–0
Norwich City v Bradford City	1–2
Stoke City v Sunderland	0–0, 1–2
Wolverhampton W. v Charlton Athletic	3–0
Leicester City v Manchester United	1–2

Quarter-finals

Bradford City v Southampton	0–1
Derby County v Newcastle United	4–2
Sunderland v Crystal Palace	0–1
Manchester Utd v Wolverhampton W.	1–1, 3–2

Semi-finals

Southampton v Crystal Palace	2–0
Manchester United v Derby County	2–0

Final

Southampton 1 Manchester United 0
(Wembley, 1.5.76, 100,000)

Southampton: Turner, Rodrigues, Peach, Holmes, Blyth, Steele, Gilchrist, Channon, Osgood, McCalliog, Stokes. (Fisher)
United: Stepney, Forsyth, Houston, Daly, B. Greenhoff, Buchan, Coppell, McIlroy, Pearson, Macari, Hill (McCreery)
Scorer: Stokes

FA CUP — 1976-77

Fifth round

Southampton v Manchester United	2–2, 1–2
Aston Villa v Port Vale	3–0
Cardiff City v Everton	1–2
Derby County v Blackburn Rovers	3–1
Leeds United v Manchester City	1–0
Middlesbrough v Arsenal	4–1
Wolverhampton Wanderers v Chester	1–0
Liverpool v Oldham Athletic	3–1

Quarter-finals

Manchester United v Aston Villa	2–1
Everton v Derby County	2–0
Wolverhampton Wanderers v Leeds United	0–1
Liverpool v Middlesbrough	2–0

Semi-finals

Leeds United v Manchester United	1–2
Everton v Liverpool	2–2, 0–3

Final

Manchester United 2 Liverpool 1
(Wembley, 21.5.77, 100,000)

United: Stepney, Nicholl, Albiston, McIlroy, B. Greenhoff, Buchan, Coppell, J. Greenhoff, Pearson, Macari, Hill (McCreery)
Liverpool: Clemence, Neal, Jones, Smith, R. Kennedy, Hughes, Keegan, Case, Heighway, Johnson (Callaghan), McDermott
Scorers: Pearson, J. Greenhoff; Case

FA CUP — 1977-78

Fifth round

Bristol Rovers v Ipswich Town	2–2, 0–3
Derby County v West Bromwich Albion	2–3
Orient v Chelsea	0–0, 2–1
Middlesbrough v Bolton Wanderers	2–0
Millwall v Notts County	2–1
Queen's P. R. v Nottingham F.	1–1, 1–1, 1–3
Wrexham v Blyth Spartans	1–1, 2–1
Arsenal v Walsall	4–1

Quarter-finals

Middlesbrough v Orient	0–0, 1–2
Wrexham v Arsenal	2–3
West Bromwich Albion v Nottingham Forest	2–0
Millwall v Ipswich Town	1–6

Semi-finals

Ipswich Town v West Bromwich Albion	3–1
Arsenal v Orient	3–0

Final

Ipswich Town 1 Arsenal 0
(Wembley, 6.5.78, 100,000)

Ipswich: Cooper, Burley, Mills, Osborne (Lambert), Hunter, Beattie, Talbot, Wark, Mariner, Geddis, Woods
Arsenal: Jennings, Rice, Nelson, Price, O'Leary, Young, Brady (Rix), Hudson, Macdonald, Stapleton, Sunderland
Scorer: Osborne

FA CUP — 1978-79

Fifth round

Nottingham Forest v Arsenal	0–1
West Bromwich Albion v Southampton	1–1, 1–2
Aldershot v Shrewsbury Town	2–2, 1–3
Crystal Palace v Wolverhampton W.	0–1
Liverpool v Burnley	3–0
Ipswich Town v Bristol Rovers	6–1
Oldham Athletic v Tottenham Hotspur	0–1
Colchester United v Manchester United	0–1

Quarter-finals

Southampton v Arsenal	1–1, 0–2
Wolverhampton W. v Shrewsbury T.	1–1, 3–1
Ipswich Town v Liverpool	0–1
Tottenham H. v Manchester United	1–1, 0–2

Semi-finals

Arsenal v Wolverhampton Wanderers	2–0
Manchester United v Liverpool	2–2, 1–0

Final

Arsenal 3 Manchester United 2
(Wembley, 12.5.79, 100,000)

Arsenal: Jennings, Rice, Nelson, Talbot, O'Leary, Young, Brady, Sunderland, Stapleton, Price (Walford), Rix
United: Bailey, Nicholl, Albiston, McIlroy, McQueen, Buchan, Coppell, J. Greenhoff, Jordan, Macari, Thomas. (B. Greenhoff)
Scorers: Talbot, Stapleton, Sunderland; McQueen, McIlroy

FA CUP — 1979-80

Fifth round

West Ham United v Swansea City	2–0
Blackburn Rovers v Aston Villa	1–1, 0–1
Ipswich Town v Chester	2–1
Everton v Wrexham	5–2
Liverpool v Bury	2–0
Tottenham Hotspur v Birmingham City	3–1
Wolverhampton Wanderers v Watford	0–3
Bolton Wanderers v Arsenal	1–1, 0–3

Quarter-finals

West Ham United v Aston Villa	1–0
Everton v Ipswich Town	2–1
Tottenham Hotspur v Liverpool	0–1
Watford v Arsenal	1–2

Semi-finals

West Ham United v Everton	1–1, 2–1
Arsenal v Liverpool	0–0, 1–1, 1–1, 1–0

Final

West Ham United 1 Arsenal 0
(Wembley, 10.5.80, 100,000)

West Ham: Parkes, Stewart, Lampard, Bonds, Martin, Devonshire, Allen, Pearson, Cross, Brooking, Pike. (Holland)
Arsenal: Jennings, Rice, Devine (Nelson), Talbot, O'Leary, Young, Brady, Sunderland, Stapleton, Price, Rix
Scorer: Brooking

FA CUP — 1980-81

Quarter-finals

Tottenham Hotspur v Exeter City	2–0
Middlesbrough v Wolverhampton Wanderers	1–1, 1–3
Nottingham Forest v Ipswich Town	3–3, 0–1
Everton v Manchester City	2–2, 1–3

Semi-finals

Tottenham Hotspur v Wolverhampton W.	2–2, 3–0
Ipswich Town v Manchester City	0–1

Final

Tottenham Hotspur 1 Manchester City 1 [aet]
(Wembley, 9.5.81, 100,000)

Tottenham: Aleksic, Perryman, Miller, Roberts, Hughton, Hoddle, Ardiles, Villa (Brooke); Crooks, Archibald, Galvin
City: Corrigan, Ranson, Reid, Caton, McDonald, Gow, Mackenzie, Power, Hutchison (Henry), Bennett, Reeves
Scorer: Hutchison (og); Hutchison

Replay
Tottenham Hotspur 3 Manchester City 2
(Wembley, 14.5.81, 92,000)

Tottenham: Unchanged
City: Unchanged; Tueart came on for McDonald
Scorers: Villa 2, Crooks; Mackenzie, Reeves (pen)

---

this time became so common that, in 1891, the FA insisted that all protests be made before a game and not afterwards – clubs had been investigating their opponents and then not revealing what they had found unless they lost the game. The oddest disqualification probably came in 1879–80 when Sheffield were thrown out of the competition for refusing to play extra time against Nottingham Forest. The only comparable event this century was in the fourth qualifying round, 1980–81, when Gateshead were awarded a tie they had lost 1-0 because opponents Marine fielded an ineligible player.

GIANTKILLING

Over Division 1 sides: Since the Third Division was added in 1920, there have been 5 victories by non-League sides over Division 1 clubs:

1923–24 Corinthians 1 Blackburn 0
1947–48 Colchester 1 Huddersfield 0
1948–49 Yeovil Town 2 Sunderland 1
1971–72 Hereford 2 Newcastle 1
1974–75 Burnley 0 Wimbledon 1

Hereford had previously earned a draw at St James' Park, but Wimbledon remain the only non-League club to have won on a First Division ground since the Third Division was created. Mention might be made of Darlington who in 1919–20, as a Northern League club, beat The Wednesday 2-0 at Hillsborough after a 0-0 draw at home. The Third Division North was not introduced until 1921, but their per-

Colchester's Ray Crawford hooks home his second goal to destroy Leeds' FA Cup hopes and provide the shock of 1971 – Colchester 3 Leeds 2.

FA CUP 1981-82

Fifth round

Tottenham Hotspur v Aston Villa	1–0
Chelsea v Liverpool	2–0
Leicester v Watford	2–0
Shrewsbury v Ipswich	2–1
West Bromwich Albion v Norwich	1–0
Coventry v Oxford United	4–0
Crystal Palace v Orient	0–0, 1–0
Queen's Park Rangers v Grimsby	3–1

Quarter-finals

Chelsea v Tottenham Hotspur	2–3
Leicester v Shrewsbury	5–2
West Bromwich Albion v Coventry	2–0
Queen's Park Rangers v Crystal Palace	1–0

Semi-finals

Tottenham Hotspur v Leicester	2–0
West Bromwich Albion v Queen's Park Rangers	0–1

Final

Tottenham Hotspur 1 Queen's Park Rangers 1
(aet)
(Wembley, 22.5.82, 100,000)
Tottenham: Clemence, Hughton, Miller, Price, Hazard (Brooke), Perryman, Roberts, Archibald, Galvin, Hoddle, Crooks
QPR: Hucker, Fenwick, Gillard, Waddock, Hazell, Roeder, Currie, Flanagan, Allen (Micklewhite), Stainrod, Gregory
Scorers: Hoddle; Fenwick

Replay
Tottenham Hotspur 1 Queen's Park Rangers 0
(Wembley, 27.5.82, 90,000)
Tottenham: Unchanged; Brooke again substituted for Hazard
QPR: Neill replaced Roeder, Micklewhite replaced Allen and was substituted by Burke
Scorer: Hoddle (pen)

FA CUP 1982-83

Fifth round

Derby County v Manchester United	0–1
Everton v Tottenham Hotspur	2–0
Aston Villa v Watford	4–1
Middlesbrough v Arsenal	1–1, 1–2
Cambridge United v Sheffield Wednesday	1–2
Crystal Palace v Burnley	0–0, 0–1
Norwich City v Ipswich Town	1–0
Liverpool v Brighton	1–2

Quarter-finals

Manchester United v Everton	1–0
Arsenal v Aston Villa	2–0
Burnley v Sheffield Wednesday	1–1, 0–5
Brighton v Norwich City	1–0

Semi-finals

Manchester United v Arsenal	2–1
Brighton v Sheffield Wednesday	2–1

Final

Manchester United 2 Brighton & Hove Albion 2
(aet)
(Wembley, 21.5.83, 100,000)
United: Bailey, Duxbury, Moran, McQueen, Albiston, Davies, Wilkins, Robson, Muhren, Stapleton, Whiteside. (Grimes)
Brighton: Moseley, Ramsey (Ryan), Stevens, Gatting, Pearce, Smillie, Case, Grealish, Howlett, Robinson, Smith
Scorers: Stapleton, Wilkins; Smith, Stevens

Replay
Manchester United 4 Brighton & Hove Albion 0
(Wembley, 26.5.83, 100,000)
United: Unchanged
Brighton: Foster replaced Ramsey
Scorers: Robson 2, Whiteside, Muhren (pen)

FA CUP 1983-84

Fifth round

Birmingham v West Ham	3–0
Derby v Norwich	2–1
Everton v Shrewsbury	3–0
Notts Co v Middlesbrough	1–0
Oxford Utd v Sheff Wed	0–3
Watford v Brighton	3–1
West Bromwich v Plymouth	0–1
Blackburn v Southampton	0–1

Quarter-finals

Birmingham v Watford	1–3
Notts Co v Everton	1–2
Plymouth v Derby	0–0, 1–0
Sheff Wed v Southampton	0–0, 1–5

Semi-finals

Everton v Southampton	1–0
Watford v Plymouth	1–0

Final

Everton 2 Watford 0
(Wembley, 19.5.84, 100,000)
Everton: Southall, Stevens, Ratcliffe, Mountfield, Bailey, Steven, Reid, Heath, Richardson, Sharp, Gray. (Harper)
Watford: Sherwood, Bardsley, Terry, Sinnott, Price (Atkinson), Taylor, Jackett, Callaghan, Johnston, Reilly, Barnes.
Scorers: Sharp, Gray.

TOP : Southern League Millwall Athletic losing a 1903 semi-final v Derby at Villa Park.
CENTRE : Bingham scores for Luton in a 1959 semi-final replay and Div 3 Norwich are out.
BOTTOM: Yeovil 2 Sunderland 1 in 1949 – one of 5 defeats of Div 1 clubs by non-Leaguers.

formance against Division 1 Wednesday still remains the club's best Cup performance.

Over Division 2 sides: There have been 12 victories by non-League clubs over Division 2 sides since 1920, five of which were accomplished away from home:

1928–29 Wolves 0 Mansfield 1
1938–39 Chelmsford 4 Southampton 1
1947–48 Colchester 3 Bradford PA 2
1948–49 Yeovil Town 3 Bury 1
1954–55 Ipswich 2:1 B. Auckland 2:3
1956–57 Lincoln 2:4 Peterboro 2:5
1956–57 Notts County 1 Rhyl 3
1958–59 Worcester City 2 Liverpool 1
1959–60 Ipswich 2 Peterborough 3
1963–64 Newcastle 1 Bedford Town 2
1977–78 Stoke City 2 Blyth Spartans 3
1979–80 Leicester City 1:0 Harlow Town 1:1

Biggest wins over League clubs:

1934–35 Carlisle 1 Wigan Athletic 6
1936–37 Walthamstow 6 Northampton 1
1955–56 Derby County 1 Boston United 6
1957–58 Hereford United 6 QPR 1
1970–71 Barnet 6 Newport County 1

Walthamstow Avenue were an amateur club at the time, but Boston's victory is surely the most creditable as Derby, a Division 1 club only a couple of years before, were second in Division 3N at the time and were at home. Boston, perhaps significantly, had 6 ex-Derby players in their team.

Most in a season: Five non-League sides have beaten three League clubs in a single season of the FA Cup. Colchester, then a Southern League club, beat Wrexham, Bradford PA and Huddersfield (all at home) in 1947–48. In 1952–53 Walthamstow Avenue, an amateur side who won the Isthmian League that season, beat Gillingham, Watford and Stockport before drawing with Manchester United. New Brighton also beat 3 League clubs in 1956–57, Peterborough did so in 1959–60 and Stafford Rangers beat Stockport County, Halifax and Rotherham as recently as 1974–75. Cup finalists Southampton beat 3 League clubs in 1900 and Tottenham beat 4 in 1901, but as they were Southern League sides the comparisons are not exact.

Total number of victories: While a non-League club, Southampton defeated 17 of their betters in the FA Cup. Since the competition was reorganised to allow 80 clubs to compete in the first round proper in 1925–26, Yeovil Town have recorded no less than 13 victories over League clubs.

NON-LEAGUE APPEARANCES

In the semi-finals: No non-League club has reached the last 4 since Swindon Town in 1909–10 and 1911–12.

In the quarter-finals: Three non-League clubs have reached the last 16 of the FA Cup since 1920 – Colchester United in 1947–48, Yeovil Town in 1948–49 and Blyth in 1977–78. Cardiff and Plymouth both reached the last 16 in 1919–20 and, in fact, between 1888–89 and 1914–15 there were only 7 seasons on which a non-League club did *not* reach the last 8. In 1890–91 three non-League clubs (The Wednesday, Stoke, Nottingham Forest) reached the last 8. When Cardiff and Plymouth reached the last 16 in 1919–20 it was the last season of a separate Southern League before the formation of Division 3. The only occasion since 1945 when a non-League club has appeared in the quarter-final draw was on 18 February 1978 after Blyth Spartans had drawn 1-1 at Wrexham in the fifth round and thus went into the hat. They lost their replay 2-1 at Newcastle before 42,000 after a famous last minute incident when Wrexham scored after retaking a corner because the corner-flag had fallen over.

In last 64: The most non-League sides to reach the last 64 (current third round) since the reorganisation of the competition in 1925–26 was 6 in 1977–78.

In competition proper: Since 1925–26, Yeovil have appeared in the first round on 36 occasions, more than any other side who have never played in the Football League.

Consecutive appearances: While still a non-League club, Hereford United appeared in the first round for 21 consecutive seasons.

Worst year: In both 1929–30 and 1950–51, no non-League side reached the third round.

Third round: Altrincham of the Alliance Premier League set up a remarkable record on 2 January 1982 when they beat York City 4-3 and hence reached the third round of the FA Cup for the fourth consecutive season, a performance unmatched by any other non-League side.

Defeats by non-League sides: Three League

clubs – Rochdale, Stockport and, surprisingly, Notts County – have been beaten by non-League clubs on 11 separate occasions. Of the First and Second Division clubs, only Charlton, Leeds, Portsmouth and West Ham have never been beaten by non-League opposition in the FA Cup since joining the League.

Terry Yorath and Graham Rix contest a 1980 North London derby between Arsenal and Spurs. These clubs are alone in having completed the double of League and Cup this century and it was at Tottenham that Arsenal won the Championship on 3 May 1971.

Football League

The oldest competition of its kind in the World, the Football League was basically instituted by William McGregor of Aston Villa, who was tired of Villa either having fixtures called off because of Cup replays or of having to play too many easy local games. The idea was that a set programme of matches – originally 22 for each of 12 founding members – would allow a guaranteed income for a season. He arranged a preliminary meeting at Anderton's Hotel, Fleet Street, on Thursday 22 March 1888 (just before the Cup final) and the first formal meeting took place at the Royal Hotel, Piccadilly, Manchester on Tuesday 17 April that year.

The original 12 members were: Accrington, Aston Villa, Blackburn Rovers, Bolton Wanderers, Burnley, Derby County, Everton, Notts County, Preston North End, Stoke, West Bromwich Albion and Wolverhampton Wanderers. Of those 12, both Accrington and Stoke were soon disbanded, though another Stoke club was reformed almost immediately. Of the 10 survivors, only Notts County have spent the majority of the first 90-odd years outside the First Division. All but Accrington, Bolton, Notts County and Stoke have won the League Championship.

The League absorbed the old Football Alliance to create a Second Division in 1892 and the Southern League in 1920 to add a third. A year later, 20 senior northern clubs formed Division 3N.

Eric Gates and Paul Mariner resist the attentions of Phil Thompson and Alan Hansen in a First Division clash between Ipswich and Liverpool in 1980-81.

ABOVE: *In Portsmouth's first season in Division 4, Steve Davey (blue) challenges the Aldershot defence in September 1978. Portsmouth, Sheffield United and Huddersfield are the only clubs to have won the League and to have played in all four divisions.*
LEFT: *David Johnson and David O'Leary, representing the two most successful clubs in the history of the Football League.*

FOOTBALL COMBINATION

Year	Winners	Year	Winners
		1949	Chelsea
		1950	Charlton A.
1916	Chelsea*	1951	Arsenal
1917	West Ham U.*	1952	Reading
1918	Chelsea*	1953	Tottenham H.
1919	Brentford*	1954	West Ham U.
1920	Tottenham H.	1955	Chelsea
1921	West Ham U.	1956	Tottenham H.
1922	Tottenham H.	1957	Tottenham H.
1923	Arsenal	1958	Chelsea
1924	West Ham U.	1959	Leicester C.
1925	West Ham U.	1960	Chelsea
1926	Tottenham H.	1961	Chelsea
1927	Arsenal	1962	Tottenham H.
1928	Arsenal	1963	Arsenal
1929	Arsenal	1964	Tottenham H.
1930	Arsenal	1965	Chelsea
1931	Arsenal	1966	Tottenham H.
1932	Brentford	1967	Tottenham H.
1933	Brentford	1968	Tottenham H.
1934	Arsenal	1969	Arsenal
1935	Arsenal	1970	Arsenal
1936	Portsmouth	1971	Tottenham H.
1937	Arsenal	1972	Tottenham H.
1938	Arsenal	1973	Ipswich Town
1939	Arsenal	1974	Bournemouth
1940	*Not contested*	1975	Chelsea
1941	*Not contested*	1976	Ipswich T.
1942	*Not contested*	1977	Chelsea
1943	*Not contested*	1978	West Ham U.
1944	*Not contested*	1979	Tottenham H.
1945	*Not contested*	1980	Tottenham H.
1946	*Not contested*	1981	Southampton
1947	Arsenal	1982	QPR
1948	West Ham U.	1983	QPR

*first team (all others reserve teams)

ABOVE: *The Football Combination was a continuation of the First World War London League and developed for the reserve sides of southern clubs. The most interesting record set up by a Football Combination side was that of Brentford, who won 44 consecutive home games between November 1931 and November 1933.*

FOOTBALL LEAGUE 1888-89

1	Preston	22	18	4	0	74:15	40
2	Aston Villa	22	12	5	5	61:43	29
3	Wolverhampton	22	12	4	6	50:37	28
4	Blackburn	22	10	6	6	66:45	26
5	Bolton	22	10	2	10	63:59	22
6	West Bromwich	22	10	2	10	40:46	22
7	Accrington	22	6	8	8	48:48	20
8	Everton	22	9	2	11	35:46	20
9	Burnley	22	7	3	12	42:62	17
10	Derby	22	7	2	13	41:61	16
11	Notts Co.	22	5	2	15	40:73	12
12	Stoke	22	4	4	14	26:51	12

FOOTBALL LEAGUE 1889-90

1	Preston	22	15	3	4	71:30	33
2	Everton	22	14	3	5	65:40	31
3	Blackburn	22	12	3	7	78:41	27
4	Wolverhampton	22	10	5	7	51:38	25
5	West Bromwich	22	11	3	8	47:50	25
6	Accrington	22	9	6	7	53:56	24
7	Derby	22	9	3	10	43:55	21
8	Aston Villa	22	7	5	10	43:51	19
9	Bolton	22	9	1	12	54:65	19
10	Notts Co.	22	6	5	11	43:51	17
11	Burnley	22	4	5	13	36:65	13
12	Stoke	22	3	4	15	27:69	10

FOOTBALL LEAGUE 1890-91

1	Everton	22	14	1	7	63:29	29
2	Preston	22	12	3	7	44:23	27
3	Notts Co.	22	11	4	7	52:35	26
4	Wolverhampton	22	12	2	8	39:50	26
5	Bolton	22	12	1	9	47:34	25
6	Blackburn	22	11	2	9	52:43	24
7	Sunderland‡	22	10	5	7	51:31	23
8	Burnley	22	9	3	10	52:63	21
9	Aston Villa	22	7	4	11	45:58	18
10	Accrington	22	6	4	12	28:50	16
11	Derby	22	7	1	14	47:81	15
12	West Bromwich	22	5	2	15	34:57	12

FOOTBALL LEAGUE 1891-92

1	Sunderland	26	21	0	5	93:36	42
2	Preston	26	18	1	7	61:31	37
3	Bolton	26	17	2	7	51:37	36
4	Aston Villa	26	15	0	11	89:56	30
5	Everton	26	12	4	10	49:49	28
6	Wolverhampton	26	11	4	11	59:46	26
7	Burnley	26	11	4	11	49:45	26
8	Notts Co.	26	11	4	11	55:51	26
9	Blackburn	26	10	6	10	58:65	26
10	Derby	26	10	4	12	46:52	24
11	Accrington	26	8	4	14	40:78	20
12	West Bromwich	26	6	6	14	51:58	18
13	Stoke	26	5	4	17	38:61	14
14	Darwen†	26	4	3	19	38:112	11

DIVISION 1 1892-93

1	Sunderland	30	22	4	4	100:36	48
2	Preston	30	17	3	10	57:39	37
3	Everton	30	16	4	10	74:51	36
4	Aston Villa	30	16	3	11	73:62	35
5	Bolton	30	13	6	11	56:55	32
6	Burnley	30	13	4	13	51:44	30
7	Stoke	30	12	5	13	58:48	29
8	West Bromwich	30	12	5	13	58:69	29
9	Blackburn	30	8	13	9	47:56	29
10	Nottingham F.	30	10	8	12	48:52	28
11	Wolverhampton	30	12	4	14	47:68	28
12	The Wednesday	30	12	3	15	55:65	27
13	Derby	30	9	9	12	52:64	27
14	Notts Co.†	30	10	4	16	53:61	24
15	Accrington §	30	6	11	13	57:81	23
16	Newton Heath	30	6	6	18	50:85	18

DIVISION 2 1892-93

1	Small Heath	22	17	2	3	90:35	36
2	Sheffield U.*	22	16	3	3	62:19	35
3	Darwen*	22	14	2	6	60:36	30
4	Grimsby	22	11	1	10	42:41	23
5	Ardwick	22	9	3	10	45:40	21
6	Burton Swifts	22	9	2	11	47:47	20
7	Northwich Victoria	22	9	2	11	42:58	20
8	Bootle §	22	8	3	11	49:63	19
9	Lincoln	22	7	3	12	45:51	17
10	Crewe	22	6	3	13	42:69	15
11	Burslem P. Vale	22	6	3	13	30:57	15
12	Walsall T. Swifts	22	5	3	14	37:75	13

DIVISION 1 1893-94

1	Aston Villa	30	19	6	5	84:42	44
2	Sunderland	30	17	4	9	72:44	38
3	Derby	30	16	4	10	73:62	36
4	Blackburn	30	16	2	12	69:53	34
5	Burnley	30	15	4	11	61:51	34
6	Everton	30	15	3	12	90:57	33
7	Nottingham F.	30	14	4	12	57:48	32
8	West Bromwich	30	14	4	12	66:59	32
9	Wolverhampton	30	14	3	13	52:63	31
10	Sheffield U.	30	13	5	12	47:61	31
11	Stoke	30	13	3	14	65:79	29
12	The Wednesday	30	9	8	13	48:57	26
13	Bolton	30	10	4	16	38:52	24
14	Preston	30	10	3	17	44:56	23
15	Darwen†	30	7	5	18	37:83	19
16	Newton Heath†	30	6	2	22	36:72	14

DIVISION 2 1893-94

1	Liverpool*	28	22	6	0	77:18	50
2	Small Heath*	28	21	0	7	103:44	42
3	Notts Co.	28	18	3	7	70:31	39
4	Newcastle	28	15	6	7	66:39	36
5	Grimsby	28	15	2	11	71:58	32
6	Burton Swifts	28	14	3	11	79:61	31
7	Burslem P. Vale	28	13	4	11	66:64	30
8	Lincoln	28	11	6	11	59:58	28
9	Woolwich Arsenal	28	12	4	12	52:55	28
10	Walsall T. Swifts	28	10	3	15	51:61	23
11	Middlesbr' Iron.	28	8	4	16	37:72	20
12	Crewe	28	6	7	15	42:73	19
13	Ardwick	28	8	2	18	47:71	18
14	Rotherham Town	28	6	3	19	44:91	15
15	Northwich Victoria	28	3	3	22	30:98	9

DIVISION 1 1894-95

1	Sunderland	30	21	5	4	80:37	47
2	Everton	30	18	6	6	82:50	42
3	Aston Villa	30	17	5	8	82:43	39
4	Preston	30	15	5	10	62:46	35
5	Blackburn	30	11	10	9	59:49	32
6	Sheffield U.	30	14	4	12	57:55	32
7	Nottingham F.	30	13	5	12	50:56	31
8	The Wednesday	30	12	4	14	50:55	28
9	Burnley	30	11	4	15	44:56	26
10	Bolton	30	9	7	14	61:62	25
11	Wolverhampton	30	9	7	14	43:63	25
12	Small Heath	30	9	7	14	50:74	25
13	West Bromwich	30	10	4	16	51:66	24
14	Stoke	30	9	6	15	50:67	24
15	Derby	30	7	9	14	45:68	23
16	Liverpool†	30	7	8	15	51:70	22

DIVISION 2 1894-95

1	Bury*	30	23	2	5	78:33	48
2	Notts Co.	30	17	5	8	75:45	39
3	Newton Heath	30	15	8	7	78:44	38
4	Leicester Fosse	30	15	8	7	72:53	38
5	Grimsby	30	18	1	11	79:52	37
6	Darwen	30	16	4	10	74:43	36
7	Burton W.	30	14	7	9	67:39	35
8	Woolwich Arsenal	30	14	6	10	75:58	34
9	Manchester C.	30	14	3	13	82:72	31
10	Newcastle	30	12	3	15	72:84	27
11	Burton Swifts	30	11	3	16	52:74	25
12	Rotherham Town	30	11	2	17	55:62	24
13	Lincoln	30	10	0	20	52:92	20
14	Walsall T. Swifts	30	10	0	20	47:92	20
15	Burslem P. Vale	30	7	4	19	39:77	18
16	Crewe	30	3	4	23	26:103	10

DIVISION 1 1895-96

1	Aston Villa	30	20	5	5	78:45	45
2	Derby	30	17	7	6	68:35	41
3	Everton	30	16	7	7	66:43	39
4	Bolton	30	16	5	9	49:37	37
5	Sunderland	30	15	7	8	52:41	37
6	Stoke	30	15	0	15	56:47	30
7	The Wednesday	30	12	5	13	44:53	29
8	Blackburn	30	12	5	13	40:50	29
9	Preston	30	11	6	13	44:48	28
10	Burnley	30	10	7	13	48:44	27
11	Bury	30	12	3	15	50:54	27
12	Sheffield U.	30	10	6	14	40:50	26
13	Nottingham F.	30	11	3	16	42:57	25
14	Wolverhampton	30	10	1	19	61:65	21
15	Small Heath†	30	8	4	18	39:79	20
16	West Bromwich	30	6	7	17	30:59	19

DIVISION 2 1895-96

1	Liverpool*	30	22	2	6	106:32	46
2	Manchester C.	30	21	4	5	63:38	46
3	Grimsby	30	20	2	8	82:38	42
4	Burton W.	30	19	4	7	69:40	42
5	Newcastle	30	16	2	12	73:50	34
6	Newton Heath	30	15	3	12	66:57	33
7	Woolwich Arsenal	30	14	4	12	59:42	32
8	Leicester Fosse	30	14	4	12	57:44	32
9	Darwen	30	12	6	12	72:67	30
10	Notts Co.	30	12	2	16	57:54	26
11	Burton Swifts	30	10	4	16	39:69	24
12	Loughborough	30	9	5	16	40:67	23
13	Lincoln	30	9	4	17	53:75	22
14	Burslem P. Vale	30	7	4	19	43:78	18
15	Rotherham Town	30	7	3	20	34:97	17
16	Crewe	30	5	3	22	30:95	13

DIVISION 1 1896-97

1	Aston Villa	30	21	5	4	73:38	47
2	Sheffield U.	30	13	10	7	42:29	36
3	Derby	30	16	4	10	70:50	36
4	Preston	30	11	12	7	55:40	34
5	Liverpool	30	12	9	9	46:38	33
6	The Wednesday	30	10	11	9	42:37	31
7	Everton	30	14	3	13	62:57	31
8	Bolton	30	12	6	12	40:43	30
9	Bury	30	10	10	10	39:44	30
10	Wolverhampton	30	11	6	13	45:41	28
11	Nottingham F.	30	9	8	13	44:49	26
12	West Bromwich	30	10	6	14	33:56	26
13	Stoke	30	11	3	16	48:59	25
14	Blackburn	30	11	3	16	35:62	25
15	Sunderland	30	7	9	14	34:47	23
16	Burnley†	30	6	7	17	43:61	19

DIVISION 2 1896-97

1	Notts Co.*	30	19	4	7	92:43	42
2	Newton Heath	30	17	5	8	56:34	39
3	Grimsby	30	17	4	9	66:45	38
4	Small Heath	30	16	5	9	69:47	37
5	Newcastle	30	17	1	12	56:52	35
6	Manchester C.	30	12	8	10	58:50	32
7	Gainsborough	30	12	7	11	50:47	31
8	Blackpool	30	13	5	12	59:56	31
9	Leicester Fosse	30	13	4	13	59:56	30
10	Woolwich Arsenal	30	13	4	13	68:70	30
11	Darwen	30	14	0	16	67:61	28
12	Walsall	30	11	4	15	53:69	26
13	Loughborough	30	12	1	17	50:64	25
14	Burton Swifts	30	9	6	15	46:61	24
15	Burton W.	30	9	2	19	31:67	20
16	Lincoln	30	5	2	23	27:85	12

DIVISION 1 1897-98

1	Sheffield U.	30	17	8	5	56:31	42
2	Sunderland	30	16	5	9	43:30	37
3	Wolverhampton	30	14	7	9	57:41	35
4	Everton	30	13	9	8	48:39	35
5	The Wednesday	30	15	3	12	51:42	33
6	Aston Villa	30	14	5	11	61:51	33
7	West Bromwich	30	11	10	9	44:45	32
8	Nottingham F.	30	11	9	10	47:49	31
9	Liverpool	30	11	6	13	48:45	28
10	Derby	30	11	6	13	57:61	28
11	Bolton	30	11	4	15	28:41	26
12	Preston	30	8	8	14	35:43	24
13	Notts Co.	30	8	8	14	36:46	24
14	Bury	30	8	8	14	39:51	24
15	Blackburn	30	7	10	13	39:54	24
16	Stoke	30	8	8	14	35:55	24

DIVISION 2 1897-98

1	Burnley*	30	20	8	2	80:24	48
2	Newcastle*	30	21	3	6	64:32	45
3	Manchester C.	30	15	9	6	66:36	39
4	Newton Heath	30	16	6	8	64:35	38
5	Woolwich Arsenal	30	16	5	9	69:49	37
6	Small Heath	30	16	4	10	58:50	36
7	Leicester Fosse	30	13	7	10	46:35	33
8	Luton	30	13	4	13	68:50	30
9	Gainsborough	30	12	6	12	50:54	30
10	Walsall	30	12	5	13	58:58	29
11	Blackpool	30	10	5	15	49:61	25
12	Grimsby	30	10	4	16	52:62	24
13	Burton Swifts	30	8	5	17	38:69	21
14	Lincoln	30	6	5	19	43:83	17
15	Darwen	30	6	2	22	31:76	14
16	Loughborough	30	6	2	22	24:87	14

*promoted †relegated ‡Sunderland penalised two points for fielding ineligible player (Ned Doig) v WBA, 20.9.90 §resigned

DIVISION 1 1898-99

1	Aston Villa	34	19	7	8	76:40	45
2	Liverpool	34	19	5	10	49:33	43
3	Burnley	34	15	9	10	45:47	39
4	Everton	34	15	8	11	48:41	38
5	Notts Co.	34	12	13	9	47:51	37
6	Blackburn	34	14	8	12	60:52	36
7	Sunderland	34	15	6	13	41:41	36
8	Wolverhampton	34	14	7	13	54:48	35
9	Derby	34	12	11	11	62:57	35
10	Bury	34	14	7	13	48:49	35
11	Nottingham F.	34	11	11	12	42:42	33
12	Stoke	34	13	7	14	47:52	33
13	Newcastle	34	11	8	15	49:48	30
14	West Bromwich	34	12	6	16	42:57	30
15	Preston	34	10	9	15	44:47	29
16	Sheffield U.	34	9	11	14	45:51	29
17	Bolton†	34	9	7	18	37:51	25
18	The Wednesday†	34	8	8	18	32:61	24

DIVISION 2 1898-99

1	Manchester C.*	34	23	6	5	92:35	52
2	Glossop*	34	20	6	8	76:38	46
3	Leicester Fosse	34	18	9	7	64:42	45
4	Newton Heath	34	19	5	10	67:43	43
5	New Brighton Tower	34	18	7	9	71:52	43
6	Walsall	34	15	12	7	79:36	42
7	Woolwich Arsenal	34	18	5	11	72:41	41
8	Small Heath	34	17	7	10	85:50	41
9	Burslem P. Vale	34	17	5	12	56:34	39
10	Grimsby	34	15	5	14	71:60	35
11	Barnsley	34	12	7	15	52:56	31
12	Lincoln	34	12	7	15	51:56	31
13	Burton Swifts	34	10	8	16	51:70	28
14	Gainsborough	34	10	5	19	56:72	25
15	Luton	34	10	3	21	51:95	23
16	Blackpool	34	8	4	22	49:90	20
17	Loughborough	34	6	6	22	38:92	18
18	Darwen	34	2	5	27	22:141	9

DIVISION 1 1899-1900

1	Aston Villa	34	22	6	6	77:35	50
2	Sheffield U.	34	18	12	4	63:33	48
3	Sunderland	34	19	3	12	50:35	41
4	Wolverhampton	34	15	9	10	48:37	39
5	Newcastle	34	13	10	11	53:43	36
6	Derby	34	14	8	12	45:43	36
7	Manchester C.	34	13	8	13	50:44	34
8	Nottingham F.	34	13	8	13	56:55	34
9	Stoke	34	13	8	13	37:45	34
10	Liverpool	34	14	5	15	49:45	33
11	Everton	34	13	7	14	47:49	33
12	Bury	34	13	6	15	40:44	32
13	West Bromwich	34	11	8	15	43:51	30
14	Blackburn	34	13	4	17	49:61	30
15	Notts Co.	34	9	11	14	46:60	29
16	Preston	34	12	4	18	38:48	28
17	Burnley†	34	11	5	18	34:54	27
18	Glossop†	34	4	10	20	31:74	18

DIVISION 2 1899-1900

1	The Wednesday*	34	25	4	5	84:22	54
2	Bolton*	34	22	8	4	79:25	52
3	Small Heath	34	20	6	8	78:38	46
4	Newton Heath	34	20	4	10	63:27	44
5	Leicester Fosse	34	17	9	8	53:36	43
6	Grimsby	34	17	6	11	67:46	40
7	Chesterfield	34	16	6	12	65:60	38
8	Woolwich Arsenal	34	16	4	14	61:43	36
9	Lincoln	34	14	8	12	46:43	36
10	New Brighton Tower	34	13	9	12	66:58	35
11	Burslem P. Vale	34	14	6	14	39:49	34
12	Walsall	34	12	8	14	50:55	32
13	Gainsborough	34	9	7	18	47:75	25
14	Middlesbrough	34	8	8	18	39:69	24
15	Burton Swifts	34	9	6	19	43:84	24
16	Barnsley	34	8	7	19	46:79	23
17	Luton	34	5	8	21	40:75	18
18	Loughborough	34	1	6	27	18:100	8

DIVISION 1 1900-01

1	Liverpool	34	19	7	8	59:35	45
2	Sunderland	34	15	13	6	57:26	43
3	Notts Co.	34	18	4	12	54:46	40
4	Nottingham F.	34	16	7	11	53:36	39
5	Bury	34	16	7	11	53:37	39
6	Newcastle	34	14	10	10	42:37	38
7	Everton	34	16	5	13	55:42	37
8	The Wednesday	34	13	10	11	52:42	36
9	Blackburn	34	12	9	13	39:47	33
10	Bolton	34	13	7	14	39:55	33
11	Manchester C.	34	13	6	15	48:58	32
12	Derby	34	12	7	15	55:42	31
13	Wolverhampton	34	9	13	12	39:55	31
14	Sheffield U.	34	12	7	15	35:52	31
15	Aston Villa	34	10	10	14	45:51	30
16	Stoke	34	11	5	18	46:57	27
17	Preston†	34	9	7	18	49:75	25
18	West Bromwich†	34	7	8	19	35:62	22

DIVISION 2 1900-01

1	Grimsby*	34	20	9	5	60:33	49
2	Small Heath*	34	19	10	5	57:24	48
3	Burnley	34	20	4	10	53:29	44
4	New Brighton Tower	34	17	8	9	57:38	42
5	Glossop	34	15	8	11	51:33	38
6	Middlesbrough	34	15	7	12	50:40	37
7	Woolwich Arsenal	34	15	6	13	39:35	36
8	Lincoln	34	13	7	14	43:39	33
9	Burslem P. Vale	34	11	11	12	45:47	33
10	Newton Heath	34	14	4	16	42:38	32
11	Leicester Fosse	34	11	10	13	39:37	32
12	Blackpool	34	12	7	15	33:58	31
13	Gainsborough	34	10	10	14	45:60	30
14	Chesterfield	34	9	10	15	46:58	28
15	Barnsley	34	11	5	18	47:60	27
16	Walsall	34	7	13	14	40:56	27
17	Stockport	34	11	3	20	38:68	25
18	Burton Swifts	34	8	4	22	34:66	20

DIVISION 1 1901-02

1	Sunderland	34	19	6	9	50:35	44
2	Everton	34	17	7	10	53:35	41
3	Newcastle	34	14	9	11	48:34	37
4	Blackburn	34	15	6	13	52:48	36
5	Nottingham F.	34	13	9	12	43:43	35
6	Derby	34	13	9	12	39:41	35
7	Bury	34	13	8	13	44:38	34
8	Aston Villa	34	13	8	13	42:40	34
9	The Wednesday	34	13	8	13	48:52	34
10	Sheffield U.	34	13	7	14	53:48	33
11	Liverpool	34	10	12	12	42:38	32
12	Bolton	34	12	8	14	51:56	32
13	Notts Co.	34	14	4	16	51:57	32
14	Wolverhampton	34	13	6	15	46:57	32
15	Grimsby	34	13	6	15	44:60	32
16	Stoke	34	11	9	14	45:55	31
17	Small Heath†	34	11	8	15	47:45	30
18	Manchester C.†	34	11	6	17	42:58	28

DIVISION 2 1901-02

1	West Bromwich*	34	25	5	4	82:29	55
2	Middlesbrough*	34	23	5	6	90:24	51
3	Preston	34	18	6	10	71:32	42
4	Woolwich Arsenal	34	18	6	10	50:26	42
5	Lincoln	34	14	13	7	45:35	41
6	Bristol C.	34	17	6	11	52:35	40
7	Doncaster	34	13	8	13	49:58	34
8	Glossop	34	10	12	12	36:40	32
9	Burnley	34	10	10	14	41:45	30
10	Burton U.	34	11	8	15	46:54	30
11	Barnsley	34	12	6	16	51:63	30
12	Burslem P. Vale	34	10	9	15	43:59	29
13	Blackpool	34	11	7	16	40:56	29
14	Leicester Fosse	34	12	5	17	38:56	29
15	Newton Heath	34	11	6	17	38:53	28
16	Chesterfield	34	11	6	17	47:68	28
17	Stockport	34	8	7	19	36:72	23
18	Gainsborough	34	4	11	19	30:80	19

DIVISION 1 1902-03

1	The Wednesday	34	19	4	11	54:36	42
2	Aston Villa	34	19	3	12	61:40	41
3	Sunderland	34	16	9	9	51:36	41
4	Sheffield U.	34	17	5	12	58:44	39
5	Liverpool	34	17	4	13	68:49	38
6	Stoke	34	15	7	12	46:38	37
7	West Bromwich	34	16	4	14	54:53	36
8	Bury	34	16	3	15	54:43	35
9	Derby	34	16	3	15	50:47	35
10	Nottingham F.	34	14	7	13	49:47	35
11	Wolverhampton	34	14	5	15	48:57	33
12	Everton	34	13	6	15	45:47	32
13	Middlesbrough	34	14	4	16	41:50	32
14	Newcastle	34	14	4	16	41:51	32
15	Notts Co.	34	12	7	15	41:49	31
16	Blackburn	34	12	5	17	44:63	29
17	Grimsby†	34	8	9	17	43:62	25
18	Bolton†	34	8	3	23	37:73	19

DIVISION 2 1902-03

1	Manchester C.*	34	25	4	5	95:29	54
2	Small Heath*	34	24	3	7	74:36	51
3	Woolwich Arsenal	34	20	8	6	66:30	48
4	Bristol C.	34	17	8	9	59:38	42
5	Manchester U.	34	15	8	11	53:38	38
6	Chesterfield	34	14	9	11	67:40	37
7	Preston	34	13	10	11	56:40	36
8	Barnsley	34	13	8	13	55:51	34
9	Burslem P. Vale	34	13	8	13	57:62	34
10	Lincoln	34	12	6	16	46:53	30
11	Glossop	34	11	7	16	43:58	29
12	Gainsborough	34	11	7	16	41:59	29
13	Burton U.	34	11	7	16	39:59	29
14	Blackpool	34	9	10	15	44:59	28
15	Leicester Fosse	34	10	8	16	41:65	28
16	Doncaster	34	9	7	18	35:72	25
17	Stockport	34	7	6	21	39:74	20
18	Burnley	34	6	8	20	30:77	20

DIVISION 1 1903-04

1	The Wednesday	34	20	7	7	48:28	47
2	Manchester C.	34	19	6	9	71:45	44
3	Everton	34	19	5	10	59:32	43
4	Newcastle	34	18	6	10	58:45	42
5	Aston Villa	34	17	7	10	70:48	41
6	Sunderland	34	17	5	12	63:49	39
7	Sheffield U.	34	15	8	11	62:57	38
8	Wolverhampton	34	14	8	12	44:66	36
9	Nottingham F.	34	11	9	14	57:57	31
10	Middlesbrough	34	9	12	13	46:47	30
11	Small Heath	34	11	8	15	39:52	30
12	Bury	34	7	15	12	40:53	29
13	Notts Co.	34	12	5	17	37:61	29
14	Derby	34	9	10	15	58:60	28
15	Blackburn	34	11	6	17	48:60	28
16	Stoke	34	10	7	17	54:57	27
17	Liverpool†	34	9	8	17	49:62	26
18	West Bromwich†	34	7	10	17	36:60	24

DIVISION 2 1903-04

1	Preston*	34	20	10	4	62:24	50
2	Woolwich Arsenal*	34	21	7	6	91:22	49
3	Manchester U.	34	20	8	6	65:33	48
4	Bristol C.	34	18	6	10	73:41	42
5	Burnley	34	15	9	10	50:55	39
6	Grimsby	34	14	8	12	50:49	36
7	Bolton	34	12	10	12	59:41	34
8	Barnsley	34	11	10	13	38:57	32
9	Gainsborough	34	14	3	17	53:60	31
10	Bradford C.	34	12	7	15	45:59	31
11	Chesterfield	34	11	8	15	37:45	30
12	Lincoln	34	11	8	15	41:58	30
13	Burslem P. Vale	34	10	9	15	54:52	29
14	Burton U.	34	11	7	16	45:61	29
15	Blackpool	34	11	5	18	40:67	27
16	Stockport	34	8	11	15	40:72	27
17	Glossop	34	10	6	18	57:64	26
18	Leicester Fosse	34	6	10	18	42:82	22

DIVISION 1 — 1904-05

1	Newcastle	34	23	2	9	72:33	48
2	Everton	34	21	5	8	63:36	47
3	Manchester C.	34	20	6	8	66:37	46
4	Aston Villa	34	19	4	11	63:43	42
5	Sunderland	34	16	8	10	60:44	40
6	Sheffield U.	34	19	2	13	64:56	40
7	Small Heath	34	17	5	12	54:38	39
8	Preston	34	13	10	11	42:37	36
9	The Wednesday	34	14	5	15	61:57	33
10	Woolwich Arsenal	34	12	9	13	36:40	33
11	Derby	34	12	8	14	37:48	32
12	Stoke	34	13	4	17	40:58	30
13	Blackburn	34	11	5	18	40:51	27
14	Wolverhampton	34	11	4	19	47:73	26
15	Middlesbrough	34	9	8	17	36:56	26
16	Nottingham F.	34	9	7	18	40:61	25
17	Bury	34	10	4	20	47:67	24
18	Notts Co.	34	5	8	21	36:69	18

DIVISION 2 — 1904-05

1	Liverpool *	34	27	4	3	93:25	58
2	Bolton *	34	27	2	5	87:32	56
3	Manchester U.	34	24	5	5	81:30	53
4	Bristol C.	34	19	4	11	66:45	42
5	Chesterfield Town	34	14	11	9	44:35	39
6	Gainsborough	34	14	8	12	61:58	36
7	Barnsley	34	14	5	15	38:56	33
8	Bradford C.	34	12	8	14	45:49	32
9	Lincoln	34	12	7	15	42:40	31
10	West Bromwich	34	13	4	17	56:48	30
11	Burnley	34	12	6	16	43:52	30
12	Glossop	34	10	10	14	37:46	30
13	Grimsby	34	11	8	15	33:46	30
14	Leicester Fosse	34	11	7	16	40:55	29
15	Blackpool	34	9	10	15	36:48	28
16	Burslem P. Vale	34	10	7	17	47:72	27
17	Burton U.	34	8	4	22	30:84	20
18	Doncaster	34	3	2	29	23:81	8

DIVISION 1 — 1905-06

1	Liverpool	38	23	5	10	79:46	51
2	Preston	38	17	13	8	54:39	47
3	The Wednesday	38	18	8	12	63:52	44
4	Newcastle	38	18	7	13	74:48	43
5	Manchester C.	38	19	5	14	73:54	43
6	Bolton	38	17	7	14	81:67	41
7	Birmingham	38	17	7	14	65:59	41
8	Aston Villa	38	17	6	15	72:56	40
9	Blackburn	38	16	8	14	54:52	40
10	Stoke	38	16	7	15	54:55	39
11	Everton	38	15	7	16	70:66	37
12	Woolwich Arsenal	38	15	7	16	62:64	37
13	Sheffield U.	38	15	6	17	57:62	36
14	Sunderland	38	15	5	18	61:70	35
15	Derby	38	14	7	17	39:58	35
16	Notts Co.	38	11	12	15	55:71	34
17	Bury	38	11	10	17	57:74	32
18	Middlesbrough	38	10	11	17	56:71	31
19	Nottingham F.†	38	13	5	20	58:79	31
20	Wolverhampton†	38	8	7	23	58:99	23

DIVISION 2 — 1905-06

1	Bristol C. *	38	30	6	2	83:28	66
2	Manchester U. *	38	28	6	4	90:28	62
3	Chelsea	38	22	9	7	90:37	53
4	West Bromwich	38	22	8	8	79:36	52
5	Hull	38	19	6	13	67:54	44
6	Leeds C.	38	17	9	12	59:47	43
7	Leicester Fosse	38	15	12	11	53:48	42
8	Grimsby	38	15	10	13	46:46	40
9	Burnley	38	15	8	15	42:53	38
10	Stockport	38	13	9	16	44:56	35
11	Bradford C.	38	13	8	17	46:60	34
12	Barnsley	38	12	9	17	60:62	33
13	Lincoln	38	12	6	20	69:72	30
14	Blackpool	38	10	9	19	37:62	29
15	Gainsborough	38	12	4	22	44:57	28
16	Glossop	38	10	8	20	49:71	28
17	Burslem P. Vale	38	12	4	22	49:82	28
18	Chesterfield Town	38	10	8	20	40:72	28
19	Burton U.	38	10	6	22	34:67	26
20	Clapton Orient	38	7	7	24	35:78	21

DIVISION 1 — 1906-07

1	Newcastle	38	22	7	9	74:46	51
2	Bristol C.	38	20	8	10	66:47	48
3	Everton	38	20	5	13	70:46	45
4	Sheffield U.	38	17	11	10	57:55	45
5	Aston Villa	38	19	6	13	78:52	44
6	Bolton	38	18	8	12	59:47	44
7	Woolwich Arsenal	38	20	4	14	66:59	44
8	Manchester U.	38	17	8	13	53:56	42
9	Birmingham	38	15	8	15	52:52	38
10	Sunderland	38	14	9	15	65:66	37
11	Middlesbrough	38	15	6	17	56:63	36
12	Blackburn	38	14	7	17	56:59	35
13	The Wednesday	38	12	11	15	49:60	35
14	Preston	38	14	7	17	44:57	35
15	Liverpool	38	13	7	18	64:65	33
16	Bury	38	13	6	19	58:68	32
17	Manchester C.	38	10	12	16	53:77	32
18	Notts Co.	38	8	15	15	46:50	31
19	Derby†	38	9	9	20	41:59	27
20	Stoke†	38	8	10	20	41:64	26

DIVISION 2 — 1906-07

1	Nottingham F. *	38	28	4	6	74:36	60
2	Chelsea *	38	26	5	7	80:34	57
3	Leicester Fosse	38	20	8	10	62:39	48
4	West Bromwich	38	21	5	12	83:45	47
5	Bradford C.	38	21	5	12	70:53	47
6	Wolverhampton	38	17	7	14	66:53	41
7	Burnley	38	17	6	15	62:47	40
8	Barnsley	38	15	8	15	73:55	38
9	Hull	38	15	7	16	65:57	37
10	Leeds C.	38	13	10	15	55:63	36
11	Grimsby	38	16	3	19	57:62	35
12	Stockport	38	12	11	15	42:52	35
13	Blackpool	38	11	11	16	33:51	33
14	Gainsborough	38	14	5	19	45:72	33
15	Glossop	38	13	6	19	53:79	32
16	Burslem P. Vale	38	12	7	19	60:83	31
17	Clapton Orient	38	11	8	19	45:67	30
18	Chesterfield Town	38	11	7	20	50:66	29
19	Lincoln	38	12	4	22	46:73	28
20	Burton U.	38	8	7	23	34:68	23

DIVISION 1 — 1907-08

1	Manchester U.	38	23	6	9	81:48	52
2	Aston Villa	38	17	9	12	77:59	43
3	Manchester C.	38	16	11	11	62:54	43
4	Newcastle	38	15	12	11	65:54	42
5	The Wednesday	38	19	4	15	73:64	42
6	Middlesbrough	38	17	7	14	54:45	41
7	Bury	38	14	11	13	58:61	39
8	Liverpool	38	16	6	16	68:61	38
9	Nottingham F.	38	13	11	14	59:62	37
10	Bristol C.	38	12	12	14	58:61	36
11	Everton	38	15	6	17	58:64	36
12	Preston	38	12	12	14	47:53	36
13	Chelsea	38	14	8	16	53:62	36
=14	Blackburn	38	12	12	14	51:63	36
=14	Woolwich Arsenal	38	12	12	14	51:63	36
16	Sunderland	38	16	3	19	78:75	35
17	Sheffield U.	38	12	11	15	52:58	35
18	Notts Co.	38	13	8	17	39:51	34
19	Bolton†	38	14	5	19	52:58	33
20	Birmingham†	38	9	12	17	40:60	30

DIVISION 2 — 1907-08

1	Bradford C. *	38	24	6	8	90:42	54
2	Leicester Fosse *	38	21	10	7	72:47	52
3	Oldham	38	22	6	10	76:42	50
4	Fulham	38	22	5	11	82:49	49
5	West Bromwich	38	19	9	10	61:39	47
6	Derby	38	21	4	13	77:45	46
7	Burnley	38	20	6	12	67:50	46
8	Hull	38	21	4	13	73:62	46
9	Wolverhampton	38	15	7	16	50:45	37
10	Stoke	38	16	5	17	57:52	37
11	Gainsborough	38	14	7	17	47:71	35
12	Leeds C.	38	12	8	18	53:65	32
13	Stockport	38	12	8	18	48:67	32
14	Clapton Orient	38	11	10	17	40:65	32
15	Blackpool	38	11	9	18	51:58	31
16	Barnsley	38	12	6	20	54:68	30
17	Glossop	38	11	8	19	54:74	30
18	Grimsby	38	11	8	19	43:71	30
19	Chesterfield Town	38	6	11	21	46:92	23
20	Lincoln	38	9	3	26	46:83	21

DIVISION 1 — 1908-09

1	Newcastle	38	24	5	9	65:41	53
2	Everton	38	18	10	10	82:57	46
3	Sunderland	38	21	2	15	78:63	44
4	Blackburn	38	14	13	11	61:50	41
5	The Wednesday	38	17	6	15	67:61	40
6	Woolwich Arsenal	38	14	10	14	52:49	38
7	Aston Villa	38	14	10	14	58:56	38
8	Bristol C.	38	13	12	13	45:58	38
9	Middlesbrough	38	14	9	15	59:53	37
10	Preston	38	13	11	14	48:44	37
11	Chelsea	38	14	9	15	56:61	37
12	Sheffield U.	38	14	9	15	51:59	37
13	Manchester U.	38	15	7	16	58:68	37
14	Nottingham F.	38	14	8	16	66:57	36
15	Notts C.	38	14	8	16	51:48	36
16	Liverpool	38	15	6	17	57:65	36
17	Bury	38	14	8	16	63:77	36
18	Bradford C.	38	12	10	16	47:47	.34
19	Manchester C.†	38	15	4	19	67:69	34
20	Leicester Fosse†	38	8	9	21	54:102	25

DIVISION 2 — 1908-09

1	Bolton *	38	24	4	10	59:28	52
2	Tottenham *	38	20	11	7	67:32	51
3	West Bromwich	38	19	13	6	56:27	51
4	Hull	38	19	6	13	63:39	44
5	Derby	38	16	11	11	55:41	43
6	Oldham	38	17	6	15	55:43	40
7	Wolverhampton	38	14	11	13	56:48	39
8	Glossop	38	15	8	15	57:53	38
9	Gainsborough	38	15	8	15	49:70	38
10	Fulham	38	13	11	14	58:48	37
11	Birmingham	38	14	9	15	58:61	37
12	Leeds C.	38	14	7	17	43:53	35
13	Grimsby	38	14	7	17	41:54	35
14	Burnley	38	13	7	18	51:58	33
15	Clapton Orient	38	12	9	17	37:49	33
16	Bradford P.A.	38	13	6	19	51:59	32
17	Barnsley	38	11	10	17	48:57	32
18	Stockport	38	14	3	21	39:71	31
19	Chesterfield Town	38	11	8	19	37:67	30
20	Blackpool	38	9	11	18	46:68	29

DIVISION 1 — 1909-10

1	Aston Villa	38	23	7	8	84:42	53
2	Liverpool	38	21	6	11	78:57	48
3	Blackburn	38	18	9	11	73:55	45
4	Newcastle	38	19	7	12	70:56	45
5	Manchester U.	38	19	7	12	69:61	45
6	Sheffield U.	38	16	10	12	62:41	42
7	Bradford C.	38	17	8	13	64:47	42
8	Sunderland	38	18	5	15	66:51	41
9	Notts Co.	38	15	10	13	67:59	40
10	Everton	38	16	8	14	51:56	40
11	The Wednesday	38	15	9	14	60:63	39
12	Preston	38	15	5	18	52:58	35
13	Bury	38	12	9	17	62:66	33
14	Nottingham F.	38	11	11	16	54:72	33
15	Tottenham	38	11	10	17	53:69	32
16	Bristol C.	38	12	8	18	45:60	32
17	Middlesbrough	38	11	9	18	56:73	31
18	Woolwich Arsenal	38	11	9	18	37:67	31
19	Chelsea†	38	11	7	20	47:70	29
20	Bolton†	38	9	6	23	44:71	24

DIVISION 2 — 1909-10

1	Manchester C. *	38	23	8	7	81:40	54
2	Oldham *	38	23	7	8	79:39	53
3	Hull	38	23	7	8	80:46	53
4	Derby	38	22	9	7	72:47	53
5	Leicester Fosse	38	20	4	14	79:58	44
6	Glossop	38	18	7	13	64:57	43
7	Fulham	38	14	13	11	51:43	41
8	Wolverhampton	38	17	6	15	64:63	40
9	Barnsley	38	16	7	15	62:59	39
10	Bradford P.A.	38	17	4	17	64:59	38
11	West Bromwich	38	16	5	17	58:56	37
12	Blackpool	38	14	8	16	50:52	36
13	Stockport	38	13	8	17	50:47	34
14	Burnley	38	14	6	18	62:61	34
15	Lincoln	38	10	11	17	42:69	31
16	Clapton Orient	38	12	6	20	37:60	30
17	Leeds C.	38	10	7	21	46:80	27
18	Gainsborough	38	10	6	22	33:75	26
19	Grimsby	38	9	6	23	50:77	24
20	Birmingham	38	8	7	23	42:78	23

DIVISION 1 1910-11

1	Manchester U.	38	22	8	8	72:40	52
2	Aston Villa	38	22	7	9	69:41	51
3	Sunderland	38	15	15	8	67:48	45
4	Everton	38	19	7	12	50:36	45
5	Bradford C.	38	20	5	13	51:42	45
6	The Wednesday	38	17	8	13	47:48	42
7	Oldham	38	16	9	13	44:41	41
8	Newcastle	38	15	10	13	61:43	40
9	Sheffield U.	38	15	8	15	49:43	38
10	Woolwich Arsenal	38	13	12	13	41:49	38
11	Notts Co.	38	14	10	14	37:45	38
12	Blackburn	38	13	11	14	62:54	37
13	Liverpool	38	15	7	16	53:53	37
14	Preston	38	12	11	15	40:49	35
15	Tottenham	38	13	6	19	52:63	32
16	Middlesbrough	38	11	10	17	49:63	32
17	Manchester C.	38	9	13	16	43:58	31
18	Bury	38	9	11	18	43:71	29
19	Bristol C.†	38	11	5	22	43:66	27
20	Nottingham F.†	38	9	7	22	55:75	25

DIVISION 2 1910-11

1	West Bromwich*	38	22	9	7	67:41	53
2	Bolton*	38	21	9	8	69:40	51
3	Chelsea	38	20	9	9	71:35	49
4	Clapton Orient	38	19	7	12	44:35	45
5	Hull	38	14	16	8	55:39	44
6	Derby	38	17	8	13	73:52	42
7	Blackpool	38	16	10	12	49:38	42
8	Burnley	38	13	15	10	45:45	41
9	Wolverhampton	38	15	8	15	51:52	38
10	Fulham	38	15	7	16	52:48	37
11	Leeds C.	38	15	7	16	58:56	37
12	Bradford P. A.	38	14	9	15	53:55	37
13	Huddersfield	38	13	8	17	57:58	34
14	Glossop	38	13	8	17	48:62	34
15	Leicester Fosse	38	14	5	19	52:62	33
16	Birmingham	38	12	8	18	42:64	32
17	Stockport	38	11	8	19	47:79	30
18	Gainsborough	38	9	11	18	37:55	29
19	Barnsley	38	7	14	17	52:62	28
20	Lincoln	38	7	10	21	28:72	24

DIVISION 1 1911-12

1	Blackburn	38	20	9	9	60:43	49
2	Everton	38	20	6	12	46:42	46
3	Newcastle	38	18	8	12	64:50	44
4	Bolton	38	20	3	15	54:43	43
5	The Wednesday	38	16	9	13	69:49	41
6	Aston Villa	38	17	7	14	76:63	41
7	Middlesbrough	38	16	8	14	56:45	40
8	Sunderland	38	14	11	13	58:51	39
9	West Bromwich	38	15	9	14	43:47	39
10	Woolwich Arsenal	38	15	8	15	55:59	38
11	Bradford C.	38	15	8	15	46:50	38
12	Tottenham	38	14	9	15	53:53	37
13	Manchester U.	38	13	11	14	45:60	37
14	Sheffield U.	38	13	10	15	63:56	36
15	Manchester C.	38	13	9	16	56:58	35
16	Notts Co.	38	14	7	17	46:63	35
17	Liverpool	38	12	10	16	49:55	34
18	Oldham	38	12	10	16	46:54	34
19	Preston†	38	13	7	18	40:57	33
20	Bury†	38	6	9	23	32:59	21

DIVISION 2 1911-12

1	Derby*	38	23	8	7	74:28	54
2	Chelsea*	38	24	6	8	64:34	54
3	Burnley	38	22	8	8	77:41	52
4	Clapton Orient	38	21	3	14	61:44	45
5	Wolverhampton	38	16	10	12	57:33	42
6	Barnsley	38	15	12	11	45:42	42
7	Hull	38	17	8	13	54:51	42
8	Fulham	38	16	7	15	66:58	39
9	Grimsby	38	15	9	14	48:55	39
10	Leicester Fosse	38	15	7	16	49:66	37
11	Bradford P.A.	38	13	9	16	44:45	35
12	Birmingham	38	14	6	18	55:59	34
13	Bristol C.	38	14	6	18	41:60	34
14	Blackpool	38	13	8	17	32:52	34
15	Nottingham F.	38	13	7	18	46:48	33
16	Stockport	38	11	11	16	47:54	33
17	Huddersfield	38	13	6	19	50:64	32
18	Glossop	38	8	12	18	42:56	28
19	Leeds C.	38	10	8	20	50:78	28
20	Gainsborough	38	5	13	20	30:64	23

DIVISION 1 1912-13

1	Sunderland	38	25	4	9	86:43	54
2	Aston Villa	38	19	12	7	86:52	50
3	The Wednesday	38	21	7	10	75:55	49
4	Manchester U.	38	19	8	11	69:43	46
5	Blackburn	38	16	13	9	79:43	45
6	Manchester C.	38	18	8	12	53:37	44
7	Derby	38	17	8	13	69:66	42
8	Bolton	38	16	10	12	62:63	42
9	Oldham	38	14	14	10	50:55	42
10	West Bromwich	38	13	12	13	57:50	38
11	Everton	38	15	7	16	48:54	37
12	Liverpool	38	16	5	17	61:71	37
13	Bradford C.	38	12	11	15	50:60	35
14	Newcastle	38	13	8	17	47:47	34
15	Sheffield U.	38	14	6	18	56:70	34
16	Middlesbrough	38	11	10	17	55:69	32
17	Tottenham	38	12	6	20	45:72	30
18	Chelsea	38	11	6	21	51:73	28
19	Notts Co.†	38	7	9	22	28:56	23
20	Woolwich Arsenal†	38	3	12	23	26:74	18

DIVISION 2 1912-13

1	Preston*	38	19	15	4	56:33	53
2	Burnley*	38	21	8	9	88:53	50
3	Birmingham	38	18	10	10	59:44	46
4	Barnsley	38	19	7	12	57:47	45
5	Huddersfield	38	17	9	12	66:40	43
6	Leeds C.	38	15	10	13	70:64	40
7	Grimsby	38	15	10	13	51:50	40
8	Lincoln	38	15	10	13	50:52	40
9	Fulham	38	17	5	16	65:55	39
10	Wolverhampton	38	14	10	14	56:54	38
11	Bury	38	15	8	15	53:57	38
12	Hull	38	15	6	17	60:56	36
13	Bradford P.A.	38	14	8	16	60:60	36
14	Clapton Orient	38	10	14	14	34:47	34
15	Leicester Fosse	38	13	7	18	50:65	33
16	Bristol C.	38	9	15	14	46:72	33
17	Nottingham F.	38	12	8	18	58:59	32
18	Glossop	38	12	8	18	49:68	32
19	Stockport	38	8	10	20	56:78	26
20	Blackpool	38	9	8	21	39:69	26

DIVISION 1 1913-14

1	Blackburn	38	20	11	7	78:42	51
2	Aston Villa	38	19	6	13	65:50	44
3	Middlesbrough	38	19	5	14	77:60	43
4	Oldham	38	17	9	12	55:45	43
5	West Bromwich	38	15	13	10	46:42	43
6	Bolton	38	16	10	12	65:52	42
7	Sunderland	38	17	6	15	63:52	40
8	Chelsea	38	16	7	15	46:55	39
9	Bradford C.	38	12	14	12	40:40	38
10	Sheffield U.	38	16	5	17	63:60	37
11	Newcastle	38	13	11	14	39:48	37
12	Burnley	38	12	12	14	61:53	36
13	Manchester C.	38	14	8	16	51:53	36
14	Manchester U.	38	15	6	17	52:62	36
15	Everton	38	12	11	15	46:55	35
16	Liverpool	38	14	7	17	46:62	35
17	Tottenham	38	12	10	16	50:62	34
18	The Wednesday	38	13	8	17	53:70	34
19	Preston†	38	12	6	20	52:69	30
20	Derby†	38	8	11	19	55:71	27

DIVISION 2 1913-14

1	Notts Co.*	38	23	7	8	77:36	53
2	Bradford P.A.*	38	23	3	12	71:47	49
3	The Arsenal	38	20	9	9	54:38	49
4	Leeds C.	38	20	7	11	76:46	47
5	Barnsley	38	19	7	12	51:45	45
6	Clapton Orient	38	16	11	11	47:35	43
7	Hull	38	16	9	13	53:37	41
8	Bristol C.	38	16	9	13	52:50	41
9	Wolverhampton	38	18	5	15	51:52	41
10	Bury	38	15	10	13	39:40	40
11	Fulham	38	16	6	16	46:43	38
12	Stockport	38	13	10	15	55:57	36
13	Huddersfield	38	13	8	17	47:53	34
14	Birmingham	38	12	10	16	48:60	34
15	Grimsby	38	13	8	17	42:58	34
16	Blackpool	38	9	14	15	33:44	32
17	Glossop	38	11	6	21	51:67	28
18	Leicester Fosse	38	11	4	23	45:61	26
19	Lincoln	38	10	6	22	36:66	26
20	Nottingham F.	38	7	9	22	37:76	23

DIVISION 1 1914-15

1	Everton	38	19	8	11	76:47	46
2	Oldham	38	17	11	10	70:56	45
3	Blackburn	38	18	7	13	83:61	43
4	Burnley	38	18	7	13	61:47	43
5	Manchester C.	38	15	13	10	49:39	43
6	Sheffield U.	38	15	13	10	49:41	43
7	The Wednesday	38	15	13	10	61:54	43
8	Sunderland	38	18	5	15	81:72	41
9	Bradford P.A.	38	17	7	14	69:65	41
10	West Bromwich	38	15	10	13	51:43	40
11	Bradford C.	38	13	14	11	55:51	40
12	Middlesbrough	38	13	12	13	62:74	38
13	Liverpool	38	14	9	15	65:75	37
14	Aston Villa	38	13	11	14	62:72	37
15	Newcastle	38	11	10	17	46:48	32
16	Notts Co.	38	9	13	16	41:57	31
17	Bolton	38	11	8	19	68:84	30
18	Manchester U.	38	9	12	17	46:62	30
19	Chelsea‡	38	8	13	17	51:65	29
20	Tottenham†	38	8	12	18	57:90	28

DIVISION 2 1914-15

1	Derby*	38	23	7	8	71:33	53
2	Preston*	38	20	10	8	61:42	50
3	Barnsley	38	22	3	13	51:51	47
4	Wolverhampton	38	19	7	12	77:52	45
5	The Arsenal§	38	19	5	14	69:41	43
6	Birmingham	38	17	9	12	62:39	43
7	Hull	38	19	5	14	65:54	43
8	Huddersfield	38	17	8	13	61:42	42
9	Clapton Orient	38	16	9	13	50:48	41
10	Blackpool	38	17	5	16	58:57	39
11	Bury	38	15	8	15	61:56	38
12	Fulham	38	15	7	16	53:47	37
13	Bristol C.	38	15	7	16	62:56	37
14	Stockport	38	15	7	16	54:60	37
15	Leeds C.	38	14	4	20	65:64	32
16	Lincoln	38	11	9	18	46:65	31
17	Grimsby	38	11	9	18	48:76	31
18	Nottingham F.	38	10	9	19	43:77	29
19	Leicester Fosse	38	10	4	24	47:88	24
20	Glossop	38	6	6	26	31:87	18

DIVISION 1 1919-20

1	West Bromwich	42	28	4	10	104:47	60
2	Burnley	42	21	9	12	65:59	51
3	Chelsea	42	22	5	15	56:51	49
4	Liverpool	42	19	10	13	59:44	48
5	Sunderland	42	22	4	16	72:59	48
6	Bolton	42	19	9	14	72:65	47
7	Manchester C.	42	18	9	15	71:62	45
8	Newcastle	42	17	9	16	44:39	43
9	Aston Villa	42	18	6	18	75:73	42
10	The Arsenal	42	15	12	15	56:58	42
11	Bradford P.A.	42	15	12	15	60:63	42
12	Manchester U.	42	13	14	15	54:50	40
13	Middlesbrough	42	15	10	17	61:65	40
14	Sheffield U.	42	16	8	18	59:69	40
15	Bradford C.	42	14	11	17	54:63	39
16	Everton	42	12	14	16	69:68	38
17	Oldham	42	15	8	19	49:52	38
18	Derby	42	13	12	17	47:57	38
19	Preston	42	14	10	18	57:73	38
20	Blackburn	42	13	11	18	64:77	37
21	Notts Co.†	42	12	12	18	56:74	36
22	The Wednesday†	42	7	9	26	28:64	23

DIVISION 2 1919-20

1	Tottenham*	42	32	6	4	102:32	70
2	Huddersfield*	42	28	8	6	97:38	64
3	Birmingham	42	24	8	10	85:34	56
4	Blackpool	42	21	10	11	65:47	52
5	Bury	42	20	8	14	60:44	48
6	Fulham	42	19	9	14	61:50	47
7	West Ham	42	19	9	14	47:40	47
8	Bristol C.	42	13	17	12	46:43	43
9	South Shields	42	15	12	15	58:48	42
10	Stoke	42	18	6	18	60:54	42
11	Hull	42	18	6	18	78:72	42
12	Barnsley	42	15	10	17	61:55	40
13	Port Vale	42	16	8	18	59:62	40
14	Leicester	42	15	10	17	41:61	40
15	Clapton Orient	42	16	6	20	51:59	38
16	Stockport	42	14	9	19	52:61	37
17	Rotherham Co.	42	13	8	21	51:83	34
18	Nottingham F.	42	11	9	22	43:73	31
19	Wolverhampton	42	10	10	22	55:80	30
20	Coventry	42	9	11	22	35:73	29
21	Lincoln	42	9	9	24	44:101	27
22	Grimsby	42	10	5	27	34:75	25

‡Chelsea were later re-elected to larger Division 1 after the war §Arsenal also joined larger Division 1 when League restarted after the war ¶Port Vale replaced Leeds City, who were expelled on 4.10.19 when their record read 8-4-2-2-17-10-10

DIVISION 1 1920-21

1	Burnley	42	23	13	6	79:36	59
2	Manchester C.	42	24	6	12	70:50	54
3	Bolton	42	19	14	9	77:53	52
4	Liverpool	42	18	15	9	63:35	51
5	Newcastle	42	20	10	12	66:45	50
6	Tottenham	42	19	9	14	70:48	47
7	Everton	42	17	13	12	66:55	47
8	Middlesbrough	42	17	12	13	53:53	46
9	The Arsenal	42	15	14	13	59:63	44
10	Aston Villa	42	18	7	17	63:70	43
11	Blackburn	42	13	15	14	57:59	41
12	Sunderland	42	14	13	15	57:60	41
13	Manchester U.	42	15	10	17	64:68	40
14	West Bromwich	42	13	14	15	54:58	40
15	Bradford C.	42	12	15	15	61:63	39
16	Preston	42	15	9	18	61:65	39
17	Huddersfield	42	15	9	18	42:49	39
18	Chelsea	42	13	13	16	48:58	39
19	Oldham	42	9	15	18	49:86	33
20	Sheffield U.	42	6	18	18	42:68	30
21	Derby†	42	5	16	21	32:58	26
22	Bradford P.A.†	42	8	8	26	43:76	24

DIVISION 2 1920-21

1	Birmingham*	42	24	10	8	79:38	58
2	Cardiff*	42	24	10	8	59:32	58
3	Bristol C.	42	19	13	10	49:29	51
4	Blackpool	42	20	10	12	54:42	50
5	West Ham	42	19	10	13	51:30	48
6	Notts Co.	42	18	11	13	55:40	47
7	Clapton Orient	42	16	13	13	43:42	45
8	South Shields	42	17	10	15	61:46	44
9	Fulham	42	16	10	16	43:47	42
10	The Wednesday	42	15	11	16	48:48	41
11	Bury	42	15	10	17	45:49	40
12	Leicester	42	12	16	14	39:46	40
13	Hull	42	10	20	12	43:53	40
14	Leeds	42	14	10	18	40:45	38
15	Wolverhampton	42	16	6	20	49:66	38
16	Barnsley	42	10	16	16	48:50	36
17	Port Vale	42	11	14	17	43:49	36
18	Nottingham F.	42	12	12	18	48:55	36
19	Rotherham Co.	42	12	12	18	37:53	36
20	Stoke	42	12	11	19	46:56	35
21	Coventry	42	12	11	19	39:70	35
22	Stockport†	42	9	12	21	42:75	30

DIVISION 3 1920-21

1	Crystal Palace*	42	24	11	7	70:34	59
2	Southampton	42	19	16	7	64:28	54
3	QPR	42	22	9	11	61:32	53
4	Swindon	42	21	10	11	73:49	52
5	Swansea	42	18	15	9	56:45	51
6	Watford	42	20	8	14	59:44	48
7	Millwall Athletic	42	18	11	13	42:30	47
8	Merthyr Town	42	15	15	12	60:49	45
9	Luton	42	16	12	14	61:56	44
10	Bristol R.	42	18	7	17	68:57	43
11	Plymouth	42	11	21	10	35:34	43
12	Portsmouth	42	12	15	15	46:48	39
13	Grimsby	42	15	9	18	49:59	39
14	Northampton	42	15	8	19	59:75	38
15	Newport	42	14	9	19	43:64	37
16	Norwich	42	10	16	16	44:53	36
17	Southend	42	14	8	20	44:61	36
18	Brighton	42	14	8	20	42:61	36
19	Exeter	42	10	15	17	39:54	35
20	Reading	42	12	7	23	42:59	31
21	Brentford	42	9	12	21	42:67	30
22	Gillingham	42	8	12	22	34:74	28

DIVISION 1 1921-22

1	Liverpool	42	22	13	7	63:36	57
2	Tottenham	42	21	9	12	65:39	51
3	Burnley	42	22	5	15	72:54	49
4	Cardiff	42	19	10	13	61:53	48
5	Aston Villa	42	22	3	17	74:55	47
6	Bolton	42	20	7	15	68:59	47
7	Newcastle	42	18	10	14	59:45	46
8	Middlesbrough	42	16	14	12	79:69	46
9	Chelsea	42	17	12	13	40:43	46
10	Manchester C.	42	18	9	15	65:70	45
11	Sheffield U.	42	15	10	17	59:54	40
12	Sunderland	42	16	8	18	60:62	40
13	West Bromwich	42	15	10	17	51:63	40
14	Huddersfield	42	15	9	18	53:54	39
15	Blackburn	42	13	12	17	54:57	38
16	Preston	42	13	12	17	42:65	38
17	The Arsenal	42	15	7	20	47:56	37
18	Birmingham	42	15	7	20	48:60	37
19	Oldham	42	13	11	18	38:50	37
20	Everton	42	12	12	18	57:55	36
21	Bradford C.†	42	11	10	21	48:72	32
22	Manchester U.†	42	8	12	22	41:73	28

DIVISION 2 1921-22

1	Nottingham F.*	42	22	12	8	51:30	56
2	Stoke*	42	18	16	8	60:44	52
3	Barnsley	42	22	8	12	67:52	52
4	West Ham	42	20	8	14	52:39	48
5	Hull	42	19	10	13	51:41	48
6	South Shields	42	17	12	13	43:38	46
7	Fulham	42	18	9	15	57:38	45
8	Leeds	42	16	13	13	48:38	45
9	Leicester	42	14	17	11	39:34	45
10	The Wednesday	42	15	14	13	47:50	44
11	Bury	42	15	10	17	54:55	40
12	Derby	42	15	9	18	60:64	39
13	Notts Co.	42	12	15	15	47:51	39
14	Crystal Palace	42	13	13	16	45:51	39
15	Clapton Orient	42	15	9	18	43:50	39
16	Rotherham Co.	42	14	11	17	32:43	39
17	Wolverhampton	42	13	11	18	44:49	37
18	Port Vale	42	14	8	20	43:57	36
19	Blackpool	42	15	5	22	44:57	35
20	Coventry	42	12	10	20	51:60	34
21	Bradford P.A.†	42	12	9	21	46:62	33
22	Bristol C.†	42	12	9	21	37:58	33

DIVISION 3N 1921-22

1	Stockport*	38	24	8	6	60:21	56
2	Darlington	38	22	6	10	81:37	50
3	Grimsby	38	21	8	9	72:47	50
4	Hartlepools	38	17	8	13	52:39	42
5	Accrington	38	19	3	16	73:57	41
6	Crewe	38	18	5	15	60:56	41
7	Stalybridge	38	18	5	15	62:63	41
8	Walsall	38	18	3	17	66:65	39
9	Southport	38	14	10	14	55:44	38
10	Ashington	38	17	4	17	59:66	38
11	Durham	38	17	3	18	68:67	37
12	Wrexham	38	14	9	15	51:56	37
13	Chesterfield	38	16	3	19	48:67	35
14	Lincoln	38	14	6	18	48:59	34
15	Barrow	38	14	5	19	42:54	33
16	Nelson	38	13	7	18	48:66	33
17	Wigan Borough	38	11	9	18	46:72	31
18	Tranmere	38	9	11	18	51:61	29
19	Halifax	38	10	9	19	56:76	29
20	Rochdale	38	11	4	23	52:77	26

DIVISION 3S 1921-22

1	Southampton*	42	23	15	4	68:21	61
2	Plymouth	42	25	11	6	63:24	61
3	Portsmouth	42	18	17	7	62:39	53
4	Luton	42	22	8	12	64:35	52
5	QPR	42	18	13	11	53:44	49
6	Swindon	42	16	13	13	72:60	45
7	Watford	42	13	18	11	54:48	44
8	Aberdare	42	17	10	15	57:51	44
9	Brentford	42	16	11	15	52:43	43
10	Swansea	42	13	15	14	50:47	41
11	Merthyr Town	42	17	6	19	45:56	40
12	Millwall Athletic	42	10	18	14	38:42	38
13	Reading	42	14	10	18	40:47	38
14	Bristol R.	42	14	10	18	52:67	38
15	Norwich	42	12	13	17	50:62	37
16	Charlton	42	13	11	18	43:56	37
17	Northampton	42	13	11	18	47:71	37
18	Gillingham	42	14	8	20	47:60	36
19	Brighton	42	13	9	20	45:51	35
20	Newport	42	11	12	19	44:61	34
21	Exeter	42	11	12	19	38:59	34
22	Southend	42	8	11	23	34:74	27

DIVISION 1 1922-23

1	Liverpool	42	26	8	8	70:31	60
2	Sunderland	42	22	10	10	72:54	54
3	Huddersfield	42	21	11	10	60:32	53
4	Newcastle	42	18	12	12	45:37	48
5	Everton	42	20	7	15	63:59	47
6	Aston Villa	42	18	10	14	64:51	46
7	West Bromwich	42	17	11	14	58:49	45
8	Manchester C.	42	17	11	14	50:49	45
9	Cardiff	42	18	7	17	73:59	43
10	Sheffield U.	42	16	10	16	68:64	42
11	The Arsenal	42	16	10	16	61:62	42
12	Tottenham	42	17	7	18	50:50	41
13	Bolton	42	14	12	16	50:58	40
14	Blackburn	42	14	12	16	47:62	40
15	Burnley	42	16	6	20	58:59	38
16	Preston	42	13	11	18	60:64	37
17	Birmingham	42	13	11	18	41:57	37
18	Middlesbrough	42	13	10	19	57:63	36
19	Chelsea	42	9	18	15	45:53	36
20	Nottingham F.	42	13	8	21	41:70	34
21	Stoke†	42	10	10	22	47:67	30
22	Oldham†	42	10	10	22	35:65	30

DIVISION 2 1922-23

1	Notts Co.*	42	23	7	12	46:34	53
2	West Ham*	42	20	11	11	63:38	51
3	Leicester	42	21	9	12	65:44	51
4	Manchester U.	42	17	14	11	51:36	48
5	Blackpool	42	18	11	13	60:43	47
6	Bury	42	18	11	13	55:46	47
7	Leeds	42	18	11	13	43:36	47
8	The Wednesday	42	17	12	13	54:47	46
9	Barnsley	42	17	11	14	62:51	45
10	Fulham	42	16	12	14	43:32	44
11	Southampton	42	14	14	14	40:40	42
12	Hull	42	14	14	14	43:45	42
13	South Shields	42	15	10	17	35:44	40
14	Derby	42	14	11	17	46:50	39
15	Bradford C.	42	12	13	17	41:45	37
16	Crystal Palace	42	13	11	18	54:62	37
17	Port Vale	42	14	9	19	39:51	37
18	Coventry	42	15	7	20	46:63	37
19	Clapton Orient	42	12	12	18	40:50	36
20	Stockport	42	14	8	20	43:58	36
21	Rotherham Co.†	42	13	9	20	44:63	35
22	Wolverhampton†	42	9	9	24	42:77	27

DIVISION 3N 1922-23

1	Nelson*	38	24	3	11	61:41	51
2	Bradford P.A.	38	19	9	10	67:38	47
3	Walsall	38	19	8	11	51:44	46
4	Chesterfield	38	19	7	12	68:52	45
5	Wigan Borough	38	18	8	12	64:39	44
6	Crewe	38	17	9	12	48:38	43
7	Halifax	38	17	7	14	53:46	41
8	Accrington	38	17	7	14	59:65	41
9	Darlington	38	15	10	13	59:46	40
10	Wrexham	38	14	10	14	38:48	38
11	Stalybridge	38	15	6	17	42:47	36
12	Rochdale	38	13	10	15	42:53	36
13	Lincoln	38	13	10	15	39:55	36
14	Grimsby	38	14	5	19	55:52	33
15	Hartlepools	38	10	12	16	48:54	32
16	Tranmere	38	12	8	18	49:59	32
17	Southport	38	12	7	19	32:46	31
18	Barrow	38	13	4	21	50:60	30
19	Ashington	38	11	8	19	51:77	30
20	Durham	38	9	10	19	43:59	28

DIVISION 3S 1922-23

1	Bristol C.*	42	24	11	7	66:40	59
2	Plymouth	42	23	7	12	61:29	53
3	Swansea	42	22	9	11	78:45	53
4	Brighton	42	20	11	11	52:34	51
5	Luton	42	21	7	14	68:49	49
6	Millwall Athletic	42	14	18	10	45:40	46
7	Portsmouth	42	19	8	15	58:52	46
8	Northampton	42	17	11	14	54:44	45
9	Swindon	42	17	11	14	62:56	45
10	Watford	42	17	10	15	57:54	44
11	QPR	42	16	10	16	54:49	42
12	Charlton	42	14	14	14	55:51	42
13	Bristol R.	42	13	16	13	35:36	42
14	Brentford	42	13	12	17	41:51	38
15	Southend	42	12	13	17	49:54	37
16	Gillingham	42	15	7	20	51:59	37
17	Merthyr Town	42	11	14	17	39:48	36
18	Norwich	42	13	10	19	51:71	36
19	Reading	42	10	14	18	36:55	34
20	Exeter	42	13	7	22	47:84	33
21	Aberdare	42	9	11	22	42:70	29
22	Newport	42	8	11	23	40:70	27

DIVISION 1 1923-24

1	Huddersfield	42	23	11	8	60:33	57
2	Cardiff	42	22	13	7	61:34	57
3	Sunderland	42	22	9	11	71:54	53
4	Bolton	42	18	14	10	68:34	50
5	Sheffield U.	42	19	12	11	69:49	50
6	Aston Villa	42	18	13	11	52:37	49
7	Everton	42	18	13	11	62:53	49
8	Blackburn	42	17	11	14	54:50	45
9	Newcastle	42	17	10	15	60:54	44
10	Notts Co.	42	14	14	14	44:49	42
11	Manchester C.	42	15	12	15	54:71	42
12	Liverpool	42	15	11	16	49:48	41
13	West Ham	42	13	15	14	40:43	41
14	Birmingham	42	13	13	16	41:49	39
15	Tottenham	42	12	14	16	50:56	38
16	West Bromwich	42	12	14	16	51:62	38
17	Burnley	42	12	12	18	55:60	36
18	Preston	42	12	10	20	52:67	34
19	The Arsenal	42	12	9	21	40:63	33
20	Nottingham F.	42	10	12	20	42:64	32
21	Chelsea†	42	9	14	19	31:53	32
22	Middlesbrough†	42	7	8	27	37:60	22

DIVISION 2 1923-24

1	Leeds*	42	21	12	9	61:35	54
2	Bury*	42	21	9	12	63:35	51
3	Derby	42	21	9	12	75:42	51
4	Blackpool	42	18	13	11	72:47	49
5	Southampton	42	17	14	11	52:31	48
6	Stoke	42	14	18	10	44:42	46
7	Oldham	42	14	17	11	45:52	45
8	The Wednesday	42	16	12	14	54:51	44
9	South Shields	42	17	10	15	49:50	44
10	Clapton Orient	42	14	15	13	40:36	43
11	Barnsley	42	16	11	15	57:61	43
12	Leicester	42	17	8	17	64:54	42
13	Stockport	42	13	16	13	44:52	42
14	Manchester U.	42	13	14	15	52:44	40
15	Crystal Palace	42	13	13	16	53:65	39
16	Port Vale	42	13	12	17	50:66	38
17	Hull	42	10	17	15	46:51	37
18	Bradford C.	42	11	15	16	35:48	37
19	Coventry	42	11	13	18	52:68	35
20	Fulham	42	10	14	18	45:56	34
21	Nelson†	42	10	13	19	40:74	33
22	Bristol C.†	42	7	15	20	32:65	29

DIVISION 3N 1923-24

1	Wolverhampton*	42	24	15	3	76:27	63
2	Rochdale	42	25	12	5	60:26	62
3	Chesterfield	42	22	10	10	70:39	54
4	Rotherham Co.	42	23	6	13	70:43	52
5	Bradford P.A.	42	21	10	11	69:43	52
6	Darlington	42	20	8	14	70:53	48
7	Southport	42	16	14	12	44:42	46
8	Ashington	42	18	8	16	59:61	44
9	Doncaster	42	15	12	15	59:53	42
10	Wigan Borough	42	14	14	14	55:53	42
11	Grimsby	42	14	13	15	49:47	41
12	Tranmere	42	13	15	14	51:60	41
13	Accrington	42	16	8	18	48:61	40
14	Halifax	42	15	10	17	42:59	40
15	Durham	42	15	9	18	59:60	39
16	Wrexham	42	10	18	14	37:44	38
17	Walsall	42	14	8	20	44:59	36
18	New Brighton	42	11	13	18	40:53	35
19	Lincoln	42	10	12	20	48:59	32
20	Crewe	42	7	13	22	32:58	27
21	Hartlepools	42	7	11	24	33:70	25
22	Barrow	42	8	9	25	35:80	25

DIVISION 3S 1923-24

1	Portsmouth*	42	24	11	7	87:30	59
2	Plymouth	42	23	9	10	70:34	55
3	Millwall Athletic	42	22	10	10	64:38	54
4	Swansea	42	22	8	12	60:48	52
5	Brighton	42	21	9	12	68:37	51
6	Swindon	42	17	13	12	58:44	47
7	Luton	42	16	14	12	50:44	46
8	Northampton	42	17	11	14	64:47	45
9	Bristol R.	42	15	13	14	52:46	43
10	Newport	42	17	9	16	56:64	43
11	Norwich	42	16	8	18	60:59	40
12	Aberdare	42	12	14	16	45:58	38
13	Merthyr Town	42	11	16	15	45:65	38
14	Charlton	42	11	15	16	38:45	37
15	Gillingham	42	12	13	17	43:58	37
16	Exeter	42	15	7	20	37:52	37
17	Brentford	42	14	8	20	54:71	36
18	Reading	42	13	9	20	51:57	35
19	Southend	42	12	10	20	53:84	34
20	Watford	42	9	15	18	45:54	33
21	Bournemouth	42	11	11	20	40:65	33
22	QPR	42	11	9	22	37:77	31

DIVISION 1 1924-25

1	Huddersfield	42	21	16	5	69:28	58
2	West Bromwich	42	23	10	9	58:34	56
3	Bolton	42	22	11	9	76:34	55
4	Liverpool	42	20	10	12	63:55	50
5	Bury	42	17	15	10	54:51	49
6	Newcastle	42	16	16	10	61:42	48
7	Sunderland	42	19	10	13	64:51	48
8	Birmingham	42	17	12	13	49:53	46
9	Notts Co.	42	16	13	13	42:31	45
10	Manchester C.	42	17	9	16	76:68	43
11	Cardiff	42	16	11	15	56:51	43
12	Tottenham	42	15	12	15	52:43	42
13	West Ham	42	15	12	15	62:60	42
14	Sheffield U.	42	13	13	16	55:63	39
15	Aston Villa	42	13	13	16	58:71	39
16	Blackburn	42	11	13	18	53:66	35
17	Everton	42	12	11	19	40:60	35
18	Leeds	42	11	12	19	46:59	34
19	Burnley	42	11	12	19	46:75	34
20	The Arsenal	42	14	5	23	46:58	33
21	Preston†	42	10	6	26	37:74	26
22	Nottingham F.†	42	6	12	24	29:65	24

DIVISION 2 1924-25

1	Leicester*	42	24	11	7	90:32	59
2	Manchester U.*	42	23	11	8	57:23	57
3	Derby	42	22	11	9	71:36	55
4	Portsmouth	42	15	18	9	58:50	48
5	Chelsea	42	16	15	11	51:37	47
6	Wolverhampton	42	20	6	16	55:51	46
7	Southampton	42	13	18	11	40:36	44
8	Port Vale	42	17	8	17	48:56	42
9	South Shields	42	12	17	13	42:38	41
10	Hull	42	15	11	16	50:49	41
11	Clapton Orient	42	14	12	16	42:42	40
12	Fulham	42	15	10	17	41:56	40
13	Middlesbrough	42	10	19	13	36:44	39
14	The Wednesday	42	15	8	19	50:56	38
15	Barnsley	42	13	12	17	46:59	38
16	Bradford C.	42	13	12	17	37:50	38
17	Blackpool	42	14	9	19	65:61	37
18	Oldham	42	13	11	18	35:51	37
19	Stockport	42	13	11	18	37:57	37
20	Stoke	42	12	11	19	34:46	35
21	Crystal Palace†	42	12	10	20	38:54	34
22	Coventry†	42	11	9	22	45:84	31

DIVISION 3N 1924-25

1	Darlington*	42	24	10	8	78:33	58
2	Nelson	42	23	7	12	79:50	53
3	New Brighton	42	23	7	12	75:50	53
4	Southport	42	22	7	13	59:37	51
5	Bradford P.A.	42	19	12	11	84:42	50
6	Rochdale	42	21	7	14	75:53	49
7	Chesterfield	42	17	11	14	60:44	45
8	Lincoln	42	18	8	16	53:58	44
9	Halifax	42	16	11	15	56:52	43
10	Ashington	42	16	10	16	68:76	42
11	Wigan Borough	42	15	11	16	62:65	41
12	Grimsby	42	15	9	18	60:60	39
13	Durham	42	13	13	16	50:68	39
14	Barrow	42	16	7	19	51:74	39
15	Crewe	42	13	13	16	53:78	39
16	Wrexham	42	15	8	19	53:61	38
17	Accrington	42	15	8	19	60:72	38
18	Doncaster	42	14	10	18	54:65	38
19	Walsall	42	13	11	18	44:53	37
20	Hartlepools	42	12	11	19	45:63	35
21	Tranmere	42	14	4	24	59:78	32
22	Rotherham Co.	42	7	7	28	42:88	21

DIVISION 3S 1924-25

1	Swansea*	42	23	11	8	68:35	57
2	Plymouth	42	23	10	9	77:38	56
3	Bristol C.	42	22	9	11	60:41	53
4	Swindon	42	20	11	11	66:38	51
5	Millwall Athletic	42	18	13	11	58:38	49
6	Newport	42	20	9	13	62:42	49
7	Exeter	42	19	9	14	59:48	47
8	Brighton	42	19	8	15	59:45	46
9	Northampton	42	20	6	16	51:44	46
10	Southend	42	19	5	18	51:61	43
11	Watford	42	17	9	16	38:47	43
12	Norwich	42	14	13	15	53:51	41
13	Gillingham	42	13	14	15	35:44	40
14	Reading	42	14	10	18	37:38	38
15	Charlton	42	13	12	17	46:48	38
16	Luton	42	10	17	15	49:57	37
17	Bristol R.	42	12	13	17	42:49	37
18	Aberdare	42	14	9	19	54:67	37
19	QPR	42	14	8	20	42:63	36
20	Bournemouth	42	13	8	21	40:58	34
21	Brentford	42	9	7	26	38:91	25
22	Merthyr Town	42	8	5	29	35:77	21

DIVISION 1 1925-26

1	Huddersfield	42	23	11	8	92:60	57
2	The Arsenal	42	22	8	12	87:63	52
3	Sunderland	42	21	6	15	96:80	48
4	Bury	42	20	7	15	85:77	47
5	Sheffield U.	42	19	8	15	102:82	46
6	Aston Villa	42	16	12	14	86:76	44
7	Liverpool	42	14	16	12	70:63	44
8	Bolton	42	17	10	15	75:76	44
9	Manchester U.	42	19	6	17	66:73	44
10	Newcastle	42	16	10	16	84:75	42
11	Everton	42	12	18	12	72:70	42
12	Blackburn	42	15	11	16	91:80	41
13	West Bromwich	42	16	8	18	79:78	40
14	Birmingham	42	16	8	18	66:81	40
15	Tottenham	42	15	9	18	66:79	39
16	Cardiff	42	16	7	19	61:76	39
17	Leicester	42	14	10	18	70:80	38
18	West Ham	42	15	7	20	63:76	37
19	Leeds	42	14	8	20	64:76	36
20	Burnley	42	13	10	19	85:108	36
21	Manchester C.†	42	12	11	19	89:100	35
22	Notts Co.†	42	13	7	22	54:74	33

DIVISION 2 1925-26

1	The Wednesday*	42	27	6	9	88:48	60
2	Derby*	42	25	7	10	77:42	57
3	Chelsea	42	19	14	9	76:49	52
4	Wolverhampton	42	21	7	14	84:60	49
5	Swansea	42	19	11	12	77:57	49
6	Blackpool	42	17	11	14	76:69	45
7	Oldham	42	18	8	16	74:62	44
8	Port Vale	42	19	6	17	79:69	44
9	Middlesbrough	42	21	2	19	77:68	44
10	South Shields	42	18	8	16	74:65	44
11	Portsmouth	42	17	10	15	79:74	44
12	Preston	42	18	7	17	71:84	43
13	Hull	42	16	9	17	63:61	41
14	Southampton	42	15	8	19	63:63	38
15	Darlington	42	14	10	18	72:77	38
16	Bradford C.	42	13	10	19	47:66	36
17	Nottingham F.	42	14	8	20	51:73	36
18	Barnsley	42	12	12	18	58:84	36
19	Fulham	42	11	12	19	46:77	34
20	Clapton Orient	42	12	9	21	50:65	33
21	Stoke†	42	12	8	22	54:77	32
22	Stockport†	42	8	9	25	51:97	25

DIVISION 3N 1925-26

1	Grimsby*	42	26	9	7	91:40	61
2	Bradford P.A.	42	26	8	8	101:43	60
3	Rochdale	42	27	5	10	104:58	59
4	Chesterfield	42	25	5	12	100:54	55
5	Halifax	42	17	11	14	53:50	45
6	Hartlepools	42	18	8	16	82:73	44
7	Tranmere	42	19	6	17	73:83	44
8	Nelson	42	16	11	15	89:71	43
9	Ashington	42	16	11	15	70:62	43
10	Doncaster	42	16	11	15	80:72	43
11	Crewe	42	17	9	16	63:61	43
12	New Brighton	42	17	8	17	69:67	42
13	Durham	42	18	6	18	63:70	42
14	Rotherham	42	17	7	18	69:92	41
15	Lincoln	42	17	5	20	66:82	39
16	Coventry	42	16	6	20	73:82	38
17	Wigan Borough	42	13	11	18	68:74	37
18	Accrington	42	17	3	22	81:105	37
19	Wrexham	42	11	10	21	63:92	32
20	Southport	42	11	10	21	62:92	32
21	Walsall	42	10	6	26	58:107	26
22	Barrow	42	7	4	31	50:98	18

DIVISION 3S 1925-26

1	Reading*	42	23	11	8	77:52	57
2	Plymouth	42	24	8	10	107:67	56
3	Millwall	42	21	11	10	73:39	53
4	Bristol C.	42	21	9	12	72:51	51
5	Brighton	42	19	9	14	84:73	47
6	Swindon	42	20	6	16	69:64	46
7	Luton	42	18	7	17	80:75	43
8	Bournemouth	42	17	9	16	75:91	43
9	Aberdare	42	17	8	17	74:66	42
10	Gillingham	42	17	8	17	53:49	42
11	Southend	42	19	4	19	78:73	42
12	Northampton	42	17	7	18	82:80	41
13	Crystal Palace	42	19	3	20	75:79	41
14	Merthyr Town	42	14	11	17	69:75	39
15	Watford	42	15	9	18	73:89	39
16	Norwich	42	15	9	18	58:73	39
17	Newport	42	14	10	18	64:74	38
18	Brentford	42	16	6	20	69:94	38
19	Bristol R.	42	15	6	21	66:69	36
20	Exeter	42	15	5	22	72:70	35
21	Charlton	42	11	13	18	48:68	35
22	QPR	42	6	9	27	37:84	21

DIVISION 1 1926-27

1	Newcastle	42	25	6	11	96:58	56
2	Huddersfield	42	17	17	8	76:60	51
3	Sunderland	42	21	7	14	98:70	49
4	Bolton	42	19	10	13	84:62	48
5	Burnley	42	19	9	14	91:80	47
6	West Ham	42	19	8	15	86:70	46
7	Leicester	42	17	12	13	85:70	46
8	Sheffield U.	42	17	10	15	74:86	44
9	Liverpool	42	18	7	17	69:61	43
10	Aston Villa	42	18	7	17	81:83	43
11	The Arsenal	42	17	9	16	77:86	43
12	Derby	42	17	7	18	86:73	41
13	Tottenham	42	16	9	17	76:78	41
14	Cardiff	42	16	9	17	55:65	41
15	Manchester U.	42	13	14	15	52:64	40
16	The Wednesday	42	15	9	18	75:92	39
17	Birmingham	42	17	4	21	64:73	38
18	Blackburn	42	15	8	19	77:96	38
19	Bury	42	12	12	18	68:77	36
20	Everton	42	12	10	20	64:90	34
21	Leeds†	42	11	8	23	69:88	30
22	West Bromwich†	42	11	8	23	65:86	30

DIVISION 1 1927-28

1	Everton	42	20	13	9	102:66	53
2	Huddersfield	42	22	7	13	91:68	51
3	Leicester	42	18	12	12	96:72	48
4	Derby	42	17	10	15	96:83	44
5	Bury	42	20	4	18	80:80	44
6	Cardiff	42	17	10	15	70:80	44
7	Bolton	42	16	11	15	81:66	43
8	Aston Villa	42	17	9	16	78:73	43
9	Newcastle	42	15	13	14	79:81	43
10	Arsenal	42	13	15	14	82:86	41
11	Birmingham	42	13	15	14	70:75	41
12	Blackburn	42	16	9	17	66:78	41
13	Sheffield U.	42	15	10	17	79:86	40
14	The Wednesday	42	13	13	16	81:78	39
15	Sunderland	42	15	9	18	74:76	39
16	Liverpool	42	13	13	16	84:87	39
17	West Ham	42	14	11	17	81:88	39
18	Manchester U.	42	16	7	19	72:80	39
19	Burnley	42	16	7	19	82:98	39
20	Portsmouth	42	16	7	19	66:90	39
21	Tottenham†	42	15	8	19	74:86	38
22	Middlesbrough†	42	11	15	16	81:88	37

DIVISION 1 1928-29

1	The Wednesday	42	21	10	11	86:62	52
2	Leicester	42	21	9	12	96:67	51
3	Aston Villa	42	23	4	15	98:81	50
4	Sunderland	42	20	7	15	93:75	47
5	Liverpool	42	17	12	13	90:64	46
6	Derby	42	18	10	14	86:71	46
7	Blackburn	42	17	11	14	72:63	45
8	Manchester C.	42	18	9	15	95:86	45
9	Arsenal	42	16	13	13	77:72	45
10	Newcastle	42	19	6	17	70:72	44
11	Sheffield U.	42	15	11	16	86:85	41
12	Manchester U.	42	14	13	15	66:76	41
13	Leeds	42	16	9	17	71:84	41
14	Bolton	42	14	12	16	73:80	40
15	Birmingham	42	15	10	17	68:77	40
16	Huddersfield	42	14	11	17	70:61	39
17	West Ham	42	15	9	18	86:96	39
18	Everton	42	17	4	21	63:75	38
19	Burnley	42	15	8	19	81:103	38
20	Portsmouth	42	15	6	21	56:80	36
21	Bury†	42	12	7	23	62:99	31
22	Cardiff†	42	8	13	21	43:59	29

DIVISION 2 1926-27

1	Middlesbrough*	42	27	8	7	122:60	62
2	Portsmouth*	42	23	8	11	87:49	54
3	Manchester C.	42	22	10	10	108:61	54
4	Chelsea	42	20	12	10	62:52	52
5	Nottingham F.	42	18	14	10	80:55	50
6	Preston	42	20	9	13	74:72	49
7	Hull	42	20	7	15	63:52	47
8	Port Vale	42	16	13	13	88:78	45
9	Blackpool	42	18	8	16	95:80	44
10	Oldham	42	19	6	17	74:84	44
11	Barnsley	42	17	9	16	88:87	43
12	Swansea	42	16	11	15	68:72	43
13	Southampton	42	15	12	15	60:62	42
14	Reading	42	16	8	18	64:72	40
15	Wolverhampton	42	14	7	21	73:75	35
16	Notts Co.	42	15	5	22	70:96	35
17	Grimsby	42	11	12	19	74:91	34
18	Fulham	42	13	8	21	58:92	34
19	South Shields	42	11	11	20	71:96	33
20	Clapton Orient	42	12	7	23	60:96	31
21	Darlington†	42	12	6	24	79:98	30
22	Bradford C.†	42	7	9	26	50:88	23

DIVISION 2 1927-28

1	Manchester C.*	42	25	9	8	100:59	59
2	Leeds*	42	25	7	10	98:49	57
3	Chelsea	42	23	8	11	75:45	54
4	Preston	42	22	9	11	100:66	53
5	Stoke	42	22	8	12	78:59	52
6	Swansea	42	18	12	12	75:63	48
7	Oldham	42	19	8	15	75:51	46
8	West Bromwich	42	17	12	13	90:70	46
9	Port Vale	42	18	8	16	68:57	44
10	Nottingham F.	42	15	10	17	83:84	40
11	Grimsby	42	14	12	16	69:83	40
12	Bristol C.	42	15	9	18	76:79	39
13	Barnsley	42	14	11	17	65:85	39
14	Hull	42	12	15	15	41:54	39
15	Notts Co.	42	13	12	17	68:74	38
16	Wolverhampton	42	13	10	19	63:91	36
17	Southampton	42	14	7	21	68:77	35
18	Reading	42	11	13	18	53:75	35
19	Blackpool	42	13	8	21	83:101	34
20	Clapton Orient	42	11	12	19	55:85	34
21	Fulham†	42	13	7	22	68:89	33
22	South Shields†	42	7	9	26	56:111	23

DIVISION 2 1928-29

1	Middlesbrough*	42	22	11	9	92:57	55
2	Grimsby*	42	24	5	13	82:61	53
3	Bradford P.A.	42	22	4	16	88:70	48
4	Southampton	42	17	14	11	74:60	48
5	Notts Co.	42	19	9	14	78:65	47
6	Stoke	42	17	12	13	74:51	46
7	West Bromwich	42	19	8	15	80:79	46
8	Blackpool	42	19	7	16	92:76	45
9	Chelsea	42	17	10	15	64:65	44
10	Tottenham	42	17	9	16	75:81	43
11	Nottingham F.	42	15	12	15	71:70	42
12	Hull	42	13	14	15	58:63	40
13	Preston	42	15	9	18	78:79	39
14	Millwall	42	16	7	19	71:86	39
15	Reading	42	15	9	18	63:86	39
16	Barnsley	42	16	6	20	69:66	38
17	Wolverhampton	42	15	7	20	77:81	37
18	Oldham	42	16	5	21	54:75	37
19	Swansea	42	13	10	19	62:75	36
20	Bristol C.	42	13	10	19	58:72	36
21	Port Vale†	42	15	4	23	71:86	34
22	Clapton Orient†	42	12	8	22	45:72	32

DIVISION 3N 1926-27

1	Stoke*	42	27	9	6	92:40	63
2	Rochdale	42	26	6	10	105:65	58
3	Bradford P.A.	42	24	7	11	101:59	55
4	Halifax	42	21	11	10	70:53	53
5	Nelson	42	22	7	13	104:75	51
6	Stockport‡	42	22	7	13	93:69	49
7	Chesterfield	42	21	5	16	92:68	47
8	Doncaster	42	18	11	13	81:65	47
9	Tranmere	42	19	8	15	85:67	46
10	New Brighton	42	18	10	14	79:67	46
11	Lincoln	42	15	12	15	90:78	42
12	Southport	42	15	9	18	80:85	39
13	Wrexham	42	14	10	18	65:73	38
14	Walsall	42	14	10	18	68:81	38
15	Crewe	42	14	9	19	71:81	37
16	Ashington	42	12	12	18	60:90	36
17	Hartlepools	42	14	6	22	66:81	34
18	Wigan Borough	42	11	10	21	66:83	32
19	Rotherham	42	10	12	20	70:92	32
20	Durham	42	12	6	24	58:105	30
21	Accrington	42	10	7	25	62:98	27
22	Barrow	42	7	8	27	34:117	22

DIVISION 3N 1927-28

1	Bradford P.A.*	42	27	9	6	101:45	63
2	Lincoln	42	24	7	11	91:64	55
3	Stockport	42	23	8	11	89:51	54
4	Doncaster	42	23	7	12	80:44	53
5	Tranmere	42	22	9	11	105:72	53
6	Bradford C.	42	18	12	12	85:60	48
7	Darlington	42	21	5	16	89:74	47
8	Southport	42	20	5	17	79:70	45
9	Accrington	42	18	8	16	76:67	44
10	New Brighton	42	14	14	14	72:62	42
11	Wrexham	42	18	6	18	64:67	42
12	Halifax	42	13	15	14	73:71	41
13	Rochdale	42	17	7	18	74:77	41
14	Rotherham	42	14	11	17	65:69	39
15	Hartlepools	42	16	6	20	69:81	38
16	Chesterfield	42	13	10	19	71:78	36
17	Crewe	42	12	10	20	77:86	34
18	Ashington	42	11	11	20	77:103	33
19	Barrow	42	10	11	21	54:102	31
20	Wigan Borough	42	10	10	22	56:97	30
21	Durham	42	11	7	24	53:100	29
22	Nelson	42	10	6	26	76:136	26

DIVISION 3N 1928-29

1	Bradford C.*	42	27	9	6	128:43	63
2	Stockport	42	28	6	8	111:58	62
3	Wrexham	42	21	10	11	91:69	52
4	Wigan Borough	42	21	9	12	82:49	51
5	Doncaster	42	20	10	12	76:66	50
6	Lincoln	42	21	6	15	91:67	48
7	Tranmere	42	22	3	17	79:77	47
8	Carlisle	42	19	8	15	86:77	46
9	Crewe	42	18	8	16	80:68	44
10	South Shields	42	18	8	16	83:74	44
11	Chesterfield	42	18	5	19	71:77	41
12	Southport	42	16	8	18	75:85	40
13	Halifax	42	13	13	16	63:62	39
14	New Brighton	42	15	9	18	64:71	39
15	Nelson	42	17	5	20	77:90	39
16	Rotherham	42	15	9	18	60:77	39
17	Rochdale	42	13	10	19	79:96	36
18	Accrington	42	13	8	21	68:82	34
19	Darlington	42	13	7	22	64:88	33
20	Barrow	42	10	8	24	64:93	28
21	Hartlepools	42	10	6	26	59:112	26
22	Ashington	42	8	7	27	45:115	23

DIVISION 3S 1926-27

1	Bristol C.*	42	27	8	7	104:54	62
2	Plymouth	42	25	10	7	95:61	60
3	Millwall	42	23	10	9	89:51	56
4	Brighton	42	21	11	10	79:50	53
5	Swindon	42	21	9	12	100:85	51
6	Crystal Palace	42	18	9	15	84:81	45
7	Bournemouth	42	18	8	16	78:66	44
8	Luton	42	15	14	13	68:66	44
9	Newport	42	19	6	17	57:71	44
10	Bristol R.	42	16	9	17	78:80	41
11	Brentford	42	13	14	15	70:61	40
12	Exeter	42	15	10	17	76:73	40
13	Charlton	42	16	8	18	60:61	40
14	QPR	42	15	9	18	65:71	39
15	Coventry	42	15	7	20	71:86	37
16	Norwich	42	12	11	19	59:71	35
17	Merthyr Town	42	13	9	20	63:80	35
18	Northampton	42	15	5	22	59:87	35
19	Southend	42	14	6	22	64:77	34
20	Gillingham	42	11	10	21	54:72	32
21	Watford	42	12	8	22	57:87	32
22	Aberdare	42	9	7	26	62:101	25

DIVISION 3S 1927-28

1	Millwall*	42	30	5	7	127:50	65
2	Northampton	42	23	9	10	102:64	55
3	Plymouth	42	23	7	12	85:54	53
4	Brighton	42	19	10	13	81:69	48
5	Crystal Palace	42	18	12	12	79:72	48
6	Swindon	42	19	9	14	90:69	47
7	Southend	42	20	6	16	80:64	46
8	Exeter	42	17	12	13	70:60	46
9	Newport	42	18	9	15	81:84	45
10	QPR	42	17	9	16	72:71	43
11	Charlton	42	15	13	14	60:70	43
12	Brentford	42	16	8	18	76:74	40
13	Luton	42	16	7	19	94:87	39
14	Bournemouth	42	13	12	17	72:79	38
15	Watford	42	14	10	18	68:78	38
16	Gillingham	42	13	11	18	62:81	37
17	Norwich	42	10	16	16	66:70	36
18	Walsall	42	12	9	21	75:101	33
19	Bristol R.	42	14	4	24	67:93	32
20	Coventry	42	11	9	22	67:96	31
21	Merthyr Town	42	9	13	20	53:91	31
22	Torquay	42	8	14	20	53:103	30

DIVISION 3S 1928-29

1	Charlton*	42	23	8	11	86:60	54
2	Crystal Palace	42	23	8	11	81:67	54
3	Northampton	42	20	12	10	96:57	52
4	Plymouth	42	20	12	10	83:51	52
5	Fulham	42	21	10	11	101:71	52
6	QPR	42	19	14	9	82:61	52
7	Luton	42	19	11	12	89:73	49
8	Watford	42	19	10	13	79:74	48
9	Bournemouth	42	19	9	14	84:77	47
10	Swindon	42	15	13	14	75:72	43
11	Coventry	42	14	14	14	62:57	42
12	Southend	42	15	11	16	80:75	41
13	Brentford	42	14	10	18	56:60	38
14	Walsall	42	13	12	17	73:79	38
15	Brighton	42	16	6	20	58:76	38
16	Newport	42	13	9	20	69:86	35
17	Norwich	42	14	6	22	69:81	34
18	Torquay	42	14	6	22	66:84	34
19	Bristol R.	42	13	7	22	60:79	33
20	Merthyr Town	42	11	8	23	55:103	30
21	Exeter	42	9	11	22	67:88	29
22	Gillingham	42	10	9	23	43:83	29

‡Stockport were penalised two points for fielding ineligible player (Joe Smith) v Stoke City on 19.3.27

DIVISION 1 1929-30

1	Sheffield W.	42	26	8	8	105:57	60
2	Derby	42	21	8	13	90:82	50
3	Manchester C.	42	19	9	14	91:81	47
4	Aston Villa	42	21	5	16	92:83	47
5	Leeds	42	20	6	16	79:63	46
6	Blackburn	42	19	7	16	99:93	45
7	West Ham	42	19	5	18	86:79	43
8	Leicester	42	17	9	16	86:90	43
9	Sunderland	42	18	7	17	76:80	43
10	Huddersfield	42	17	9	16	63:69	43
11	Birmingham	42	16	9	17	67:62	41
12	Liverpool	42	16	9	17	63:79	41
13	Portsmouth	42	15	10	17	66:62	40
14	Arsenal	42	14	11	17	78:66	39
15	Bolton	42	15	9	18	74:74	39
16	Middlesbrough	42	16	6	20	82:84	38
17	Manchester U.	42	15	8	19	67:88	38
18	Grimsby	42	15	7	20	73:89	37
19	Newcastle	42	15	7	20	71:92	37
20	Sheffield U.	42	15	6	21	91:96	36
21	Burnley†	42	14	8	20	79:97	36
22	Everton†	42	12	11	19	80:92	35

DIVISION 2 1929-30

1	Blackpool*	42	27	4	11	98:67	58
2	Chelsea*	42	22	11	9	74:46	55
3	Oldham	42	21	11	10	90:51	53
4	Bradford P.A.	42	19	12	11	91:70	50
5	Bury	42	22	5	15	78:67	49
6	West Bromwich	42	21	5	16	105:73	47
7	Southampton	42	17	11	14	77:76	45
8	Cardiff	42	18	8	16	61:59	44
9	Wolverhampton	42	16	9	17	77:79	41
10	Nottingham F.	42	13	15	14	55:69	41
11	Stoke	42	16	8	18	74:72	40
12	Tottenham	42	15	9	18	59:61	39
13	Charlton	42	14	11	17	59:63	39
14	Millwall	42	12	15	15	57:73	39
15	Swansea	42	14	9	19	57:61	37
16	Preston	42	13	11	18	65:80	37
17	Barnsley	42	14	8	20	56:71	36
18	Bradford C.	42	12	12	18	60:77	36
19	Reading	42	12	11	19	54:67	35
20	Bristol C.	42	13	9	20	61:83	35
21	Hull†	42	14	7	21	51:78	35
22	Notts Co.†	42	9	15	18	54:70	33

DIVISION 3N 1929-30

1	Port Vale*	42	30	7	5	103:37	67
2	Stockport	42	28	7	7	106:44	63
3	Darlington	42	22	6	14	108:73	50
4	Chesterfield	42	22	6	14	76:56	50
5	Lincoln	42	17	14	11	83:61	48
6	York	42	15	16	11	77:64	46
7	South Shields	42	18	10	14	77:74	46
8	Hartlepools	42	17	11	14	81:74	45
9	Southport	42	15	13	14	81:74	43
10	Rochdale	42	18	7	17	89:91	43
11	Crewe	42	17	8	17	82:71	42
12	Tranmere	42	16	9	17	83:86	41
13	New Brighton	42	16	8	18	69:79	40
14	Doncaster	42	15	9	18	62:69	39
15	Carlisle	42	16	7	19	90:101	39
16	Accrington	42	14	9	19	84:81	37
17	Wrexham	42	13	8	21	67:88	34
18	Wigan Borough	42	13	7	22	60:88	33
19	Nelson	42	13	7	22	51:80	33
20	Rotherham	42	11	8	23	67:113	30
21	Halifax	42	10	8	24	44:79	28
22	Barrow	42	11	5	26	41:98	27

DIVISION 3S 1929-30

1	Plymouth*	42	30	8	4	98:38	68
2	Brentford	42	28	5	9	94:44	61
3	QPR	42	21	9	12	80:68	51
4	Northampton	42	21	8	13	82:58	50
5	Brighton	42	21	8	13	87:63	50
6	Coventry	42	19	9	14	88:73	47
7	Fulham	42	18	11	13	87:83	47
8	Norwich	42	18	10	14	88:77	46
9	Crystal Palace	42	17	12	13	81:74	46
10	Bournemouth	42	15	13	14	72:61	43
11	Southend	42	15	13	14	69:59	43
12	Clapton Orient	42	14	13	15	55:62	41
13	Luton	42	14	12	16	64:78	40
14	Swindon	42	13	12	17	73:83	38
15	Watford	42	15	8	19	60:73	38
16	Exeter	42	12	11	19	67:73	35
17	Walsall	42	13	8	21	71:78	34
18	Newport	42	12	10	20	74:85	34
19	Torquay	42	10	11	21	64:94	31
20	Bristol R.	42	11	8	23	67:93	30
21	Gillingham	42	11	8	23	51:80	30
22	Merthyr Town	42	6	9	27	60:135	21

DIVISION 1 1930-31

1	Arsenal	42	28	10	4	127:59	66
2	Aston Villa	42	25	9	8	128:78	59
3	Sheffield W.	42	22	8	12	102:75	52
4	Portsmouth	42	18	13	11	84:67	49
5	Huddersfield	42	18	12	12	81:65	48
6	Derby	42	18	10	14	94:79	46
7	Middlesbrough	42	19	8	15	98:90	46
8	Manchester C.	42	18	10	14	75:70	46
9	Liverpool	42	15	12	15	86:85	42
10	Blackburn	42	17	8	17	83:84	42
11	Sunderland	42	16	9	17	89:85	41
12	Chelsea	42	15	10	17	64:67	40
13	Grimsby	42	17	5	20	82:87	39
14	Bolton	42	15	9	18	68:81	39
15	Sheffield U.	42	14	10	18	78:84	38
16	Leicester	42	16	6	20	80:95	38
17	Newcastle	42	15	6	21	78:87	36
18	West Ham	42	14	8	20	79:94	36
19	Birmingham	42	13	10	19	55:70	36
20	Blackpool	42	11	10	21	71:125	32
21	Leeds†	42	12	7	23	68:81	31
22	Manchester U.†	42	7	8	27	53:115	22

DIVISION 2 1930-31

1	Everton*	42	28	5	9	121:66	61
2	West Bromwich*	42	22	10	10	83:49	54
3	Tottenham	42	22	7	13	88:55	51
4	Wolverhampton	42	21	5	16	84:67	47
5	Port Vale	42	21	5	16	67:61	47
6	Bradford P.A.	42	18	10	14	97:66	46
7	Preston	42	17	11	14	83:64	45
8	Burnley	42	17	11	14	81:77	45
9	Southampton	42	19	6	17	74:62	44
10	Bradford C.	42	17	10	15	61:63	44
11	Stoke	42	17	10	15	64:71	44
12	Oldham	42	16	10	16	61:72	42
13	Bury	42	19	3	20	75:82	41
14	Millwall	42	16	7	19	71:80	39
15	Charlton	42	15	9	18	59:86	39
16	Bristol C.	42	15	8	19	54:82	38
17	Nottingham F.	42	14	9	19	80:85	37
18	Plymouth	42	14	8	20	76:84	36
19	Barnsley	42	13	9	20	59:79	35
20	Swansea	42	12	10	20	51:74	34
21	Reading†	42	12	6	24	72:96	30
22	Cardiff†	42	8	9	25	47:87	25

DIVISION 3N 1930-31

1	Chesterfield*	42	26	6	10	102:57	58
2	Lincoln	42	25	7	10	102:59	57
3	Wrexham	42	21	12	9	94:62	54
4	Tranmere	42	24	6	12	111:74	54
5	Southport	42	22	9	11	88:56	53
6	Hull	42	20	10	12	99:55	50
7	Stockport	42	20	9	13	77:61	49
8	Carlisle	42	20	5	17	98:81	45
9	Gateshead	42	16	13	13	71:73	45
10	Wigan Borough	42	19	5	18	76:86	43
11	Darlington	42	16	10	16	71:59	42
12	York	42	18	6	18	85:82	42
13	Accrington	42	15	9	18	84:108	39
14	Rotherham	42	13	12	17	81:83	38
15	Doncaster	42	13	11	18	65:65	37
16	Barrow	42	15	7	20	68:89	37
17	Halifax	42	13	9	20	55:89	35
18	Crewe	42	14	6	22	66:93	34
19	New Brighton	42	13	7	22	49:76	33
20	Hartlepools	42	12	6	24	67:86	30
21	Rochdale	42	12	6	24	62:107	30
22	Nelson	42	6	7	29	43:113	19

DIVISION 3S 1930-31

1	Notts Co.*	42	24	11	7	97:46	59
2	Crystal Palace	42	22	7	13	107:71	51
3	Brentford	42	22	6	14	90:64	50
4	Brighton	42	17	15	10	68:53	49
5	Southend	42	22	5	15	76:60	49
6	Northampton	42	18	12	12	77:59	48
7	Luton	42	19	8	15	76:51	46
8	QPR	42	20	3	19	82:75	43
9	Fulham	42	18	7	17	77:75	43
10	Bournemouth	42	15	13	14	72:73	43
11	Torquay	42	17	9	16	80:84	43
12	Swindon	42	18	6	18	89:94	42
13	Exeter	42	17	8	17	84:90	42
14	Coventry	42	16	9	17	75:65	41
15	Bristol R.	42	16	8	18	75:92	40
16	Gillingham	42	14	10	18	61:76	38
17	Walsall	42	14	9	19	78:95	37
18	Watford	42	14	7	21	72:75	35
19	Clapton Orient	42	14	7	21	63:91	35
20	Thames	42	13	8	21	54:93	34
21	Newport	42	11	6	25	69:111	28
22	Norwich	42	10	8	24	47:76	28

DIVISION 1 1931-32

1	Everton	42	26	4	12	116:64	56
2	Arsenal	42	22	10	10	90:48	54
3	Sheffield W.	42	22	6	14	96:82	50
4	Huddersfield	42	19	10	13	80:63	48
5	Aston Villa	42	19	8	15	104:72	46
6	West Bromwich	42	20	6	16	77:55	46
7	Sheffield U.	42	20	6	16	80:75	46
8	Portsmouth	42	19	7	16	62:62	45
9	Birmingham	42	18	8	16	78:67	44
10	Liverpool	42	19	6	17	81:93	44
11	Newcastle	42	18	6	18	80:87	42
12	Chelsea	42	16	8	18	69:73	40
13	Sunderland	42	15	10	17	67:73	40
14	Manchester C.	42	13	12	17	83:73	38
15	Derby	42	14	10	18	71:75	38
16	Blackburn	42	16	6	20	89:95	38
17	Bolton	42	17	4	21	72:80	38
18	Middlesbrough	42	15	8	19	64:89	38
19	Leicester	42	15	7	20	74:94	37
20	Blackpool	42	12	9	21	65:102	33
21	Grimsby†	42	13	6	23	67:98	32
22	West Ham†	42	12	7	23	62:107	31

DIVISION 2 1931-32

1	Wolverhampton*	42	24	8	10	115:49	56
2	Leeds*	42	22	10	10	78:54	54
3	Stoke	42	19	14	9	69:48	52
4	Plymouth	42	20	9	13	100:66	49
5	Bury	42	21	7	14	70:58	49
6	Bradford P.A.	42	21	7	14	72:63	49
7	Bradford C.	42	16	13	13	80:61	45
8	Tottenham	42	16	11	15	87:78	43
9	Millwall	42	17	9	16	61:61	43
10	Charlton	42	17	9	16	61:66	43
11	Nottingham F.	42	16	10	16	77:72	42
12	Manchester U.	42	17	8	17	71:72	42
13	Preston	42	16	10	16	75:77	42
14	Southampton	42	17	7	18	66:77	41
15	Swansea	42	16	7	19	73:75	39
16	Notts Co.	42	13	12	17	75:75	38
17	Chesterfield	42	13	11	18	64:86	37
18	Oldham	42	13	10	19	62:84	36
19	Burnley	42	13	9	20	59:87	35
20	Port Vale	42	13	7	22	58:89	33
21	Barnsley†	42	12	9	21	55:91	33
22	Bristol C.†	42	6	11	25	39:78	23

DIVISION 3N 1931-32

1	Lincoln*	40	26	5	9	106:47	57
2	Gateshead	40	25	7	8	94:48	57
3	Chester	40	21	8	11	78:60	50
4	Tranmere	40	19	11	10	107:58	49
5	Barrow	40	24	1	15	86:59	49
6	Crewe	40	21	6	13	95:66	48
7	Southport	40	18	10	12	58:53	46
8	Hull	40	20	5	15	82:53	45
9	York	40	18	7	15	76:81	43
10	Wrexham	40	18	7	15	64:69	43
11	Darlington	40	17	4	19	66:69	38
12	Stockport	40	13	11	16	55:53	37
13	Hartlepools	40	16	5	19	78:100	37
14	Accrington	40	15	6	19	75:80	36
15	Doncaster	40	16	4	20	59:80	36
16	Walsall	40	16	3	21	57:85	35
17	Halifax	40	13	8	19	61:87	34
18	Carlisle	40	11	11	18	64:79	33
19	Rotherham	40	14	4	22	63:72	32
20	New Brighton	40	8	8	24	38:76	24
21	Rochdale	40	4	3	33	48:135	11

Wigan resigned 26.10.31; results declared void

DIVISION 3S 1931-32

1	Fulham*	42	24	9	9	111:62	57
2	Reading	42	23	9	10	97:67	55
3	Southend	42	21	11	10	77:53	53
4	Crystal Palace	42	20	11	11	74:63	51
5	Brentford	42	19	10	13	68:52	48
6	Luton	42	20	7	15	95:70	47
7	Exeter	42	20	7	15	77:62	47
8	Brighton	42	17	12	13	73:58	46
9	Cardiff	42	19	8	15	87:73	46
10	Norwich	42	17	12	13	76:67	46
11	Watford	42	19	8	15	81:79	46
12	Coventry	42	18	8	16	108:97	44
13	QPR	42	15	12	15	79:73	42
14	Northampton	42	16	7	19	69:69	39
15	Bournemouth	42	13	12	17	70:78	38
16	Clapton Orient	42	12	11	19	77:90	35
17	Swindon	42	14	6	22	70:84	34
18	Bristol R.	42	13	8	21	65:92	34
19	Torquay	42	12	9	21	72:106	33
20	Mansfield	42	11	10	21	75:108	32
21	Gillingham	42	10	8	24	40:82	28
22	Thames	42	7	9	26	53:109	23

DIVISION 1 1932-33

1	Arsenal	42	25	8	9	118:61	58
2	Aston Villa	42	23	8	11	92:67	54
3	Sheffield W.	42	21	9	12	80:68	51
4	West Bromwich	42	20	9	13	83:70	49
5	Newcastle	42	22	5	15	71:63	49
6	Huddersfield	42	18	11	13	66:53	47
7	Derby	42	15	14	13	76:69	44
8	Leeds	42	15	14	13	59:62	44
9	Portsmouth	42	18	7	17	74:76	43
10	Sheffield U.	42	17	9	16	74:80	43
11	Everton	42	16	9	17	81:74	41
12	Sunderland	42	15	10	17	63:80	40
13	Birmingham	42	14	11	17	57:57	39
14	Liverpool	42	14	11	17	79:84	39
15	Blackburn	42	14	10	18	76:102	38
16	Manchester C.	42	16	5	21	68:71	37
17	Middlesbrough	42	14	9	19	63:73	37
18	Chelsea	42	14	7	21	63:73	35
19	Leicester	42	11	13	18	75:89	35
20	Wolverhampton	42	13	9	20	80:96	35
21	Bolton†	42	12	9	21	78:92	33
22	Blackpool†	42	14	5	23	69:85	33

DIVISION 1 1933-34

1	Arsenal	42	25	9	8	75:47	59
2	Huddersfield	42	23	10	9	90:61	56
3	Tottenham	42	21	7	14	79:56	49
4	Derby	42	17	11	14	68:54	45
5	Manchester C.	42	17	11	14	65:72	45
6	Sunderland	42	16	12	14	81:56	44
7	West Bromwich	42	17	10	15	78:70	44
8	Blackburn	42	18	7	17	74:81	43
9	Leeds	42	17	8	17	75:66	42
10	Portsmouth	42	15	12	15	52:55	42
11	Sheffield W.	42	16	9	17	62:67	41
12	Stoke	42	15	11	16	58:71	41
13	Aston Villa	42	14	12	16	78:75	40
14	Everton	42	12	16	14	62:63	40
15	Wolverhampton	42	14	12	16	74:86	40
16	Middlesbrough	42	16	7	19	68:80	39
17	Leicester	42	14	11	17	59:74	39
18	Liverpool	42	14	10	18	79:87	38
19	Chelsea	42	14	8	20	67:69	36
20	Birmingham	42	12	12	18	54:56	36
21	Newcastle†	42	10	14	18	68:77	34
22	Sheffield U.†	42	12	7	23	58:101	31

DIVISION 1 1934-35

1	Arsenal	42	23	12	7	115:46	58
2	Sunderland	42	19	16	7	90:51	54
3	Sheffield W.	42	18	13	11	70:64	49
4	Manchester C.	42	20	8	14	82:67	48
5	Grimsby	42	17	11	14	78:60	45
6	Derby	42	18	9	15	81:66	45
7	Liverpool	42	19	7	16	85:88	45
8	Everton	42	16	12	14	89:88	44
9	West Bromwich	42	17	10	15	83:83	44
10	Stoke	42	18	6	18	71:70	42
11	Preston	42	15	12	15	62:67	42
12	Chelsea	42	16	9	17	73:82	41
13	Aston Villa	42	14	13	15	74:88	41
14	Portsmouth	42	15	10	17	71:72	40
15	Blackburn	42	14	11	17	66:78	39
16	Huddersfield	42	14	10	18	76:71	38
17	Wolverhampton	42	15	8	19	88:94	38
18	Leeds	42	13	12	17	75:92	38
19	Birmingham	42	13	10	19	63:81	36
20	Middlesbrough	42	10	14	18	70:90	34
21	Leicester†	42	12	9	21	61:86	33
22	Tottenham†	42	10	10	22	54:93	30

DIVISION 2 1932-33

1	Stoke*	42	25	6	11	78:39	56
2	Tottenham*	42	20	15	7	96:51	55
3	Fulham	42	20	10	12	78:65	50
4	Bury	42	20	9	13	84:59	49
5	Nottingham F.	42	17	15	10	67:59	49
6	Manchester U.	42	15	13	14	71:68	43
7	Millwall	42	16	11	15	59:57	43
8	Bradford P.A.	42	17	8	17	77:71	42
9	Preston	42	16	10	16	74:70	42
10	Swansea	42	19	4	19	50:54	42
11	Bradford C.	42	14	13	15	65:61	41
12	Southampton	42	18	5	19	66:66	41
13	Grimsby	42	14	13	15	79:84	41
14	Plymouth	42	16	9	17	63:67	41
15	Notts Co.	42	15	10	17	67:78	40
16	Oldham	42	15	8	19	67:80	38
17	Port Vale	42	14	10	18	66:79	38
18	Lincoln	42	12	13	17	72:87	37
19	Burnley	42	11	14	17	67:79	36
20	West Ham	42	13	9	20	75:93	35
21	Chesterfield†	42	12	10	20	61:84	34
22	Charlton†	42	12	7	23	60:91	31

DIVISION 2 1933-34

1	Grimsby*	42	27	5	10	103:59	59
2	Preston*	42	23	6	13	71:52	52
3	Bolton	42	21	9	12	79:55	51
4	Brentford	42	22	7	13	85:60	51
5	Bradford P.A.	42	23	3	16	86:67	49
6	Bradford C.	42	20	6	16	73:67	46
7	West Ham	42	17	11	14	78:70	45
8	Port Vale	42	19	7	16	60:55	45
9	Oldham	42	17	10	15	72:60	44
10	Plymouth	42	15	13	14	69:70	43
11	Blackpool	42	15	13	14	62:64	43
12	Bury	42	17	9	16	70:73	43
13	Burnley	42	18	6	18	60:72	42
14	Southampton	42	15	8	19	54:58	38
15	Hull	42	13	12	17	52:68	38
16	Fulham	42	15	7	20	48:67	37
17	Nottingham F.	42	13	9	20	73:74	35
18	Notts Co.	42	12	11	19	53:62	35
19	Swansea	42	10	15	17	51:60	35
20	Manchester U.	42	14	6	22	59:85	34
21	Millwall†	42	11	11	20	39:68	33
22	Lincoln†	42	9	8	25	44:75	26

DIVISION 2 1934-35

1	Brentford*	42	26	9	7	93:48	61
2	Bolton*	42	26	4	12	96:48	56
3	West Ham	42	26	4	12	80:63	56
4	Blackpool	42	21	11	10	79:57	53
5	Manchester U.	42	23	4	15	76:55	50
6	Newcastle	42	22	4	16	89:68	48
7	Fulham	42	17	12	13	76:56	46
8	Plymouth	42	19	8	15	75:64	46
9	Nottingham F.	42	17	8	17	76:70	42
10	Bury	42	19	4	19	62:73	42
11	Sheffield U.	42	16	9	17	79:70	41
12	Burnley	42	16	9	17	63:73	41
13	Hull	42	16	8	18	63:74	40
14	Norwich	42	14	11	17	71:61	39
15	Bradford P.A.	42	11	16	15	55:63	38
16	Barnsley	42	13	12	17	60:83	38
17	Swansea	42	14	8	20	56:67	36
18	Port Vale	42	11	12	19	55:74	34
19	Southampton	42	11	12	19	46:75	34
20	Bradford C.	42	12	8	22	50:68	32
21	Oldham†	42	10	6	26	56:95	26
22	Notts Co.†	42	9	7	26	46:97	25

DIVISION 3N 1932-33

1	Hull*	42	26	7	9	100:45	59
2	Wrexham	42	24	9	9	106:51	57
3	Stockport	42	21	12	9	99:58	54
4	Chester	42	22	8	12	94:66	52
5	Walsall	42	19	10	13	75:58	48
6	Doncaster	42	17	14	11	77:79	48
7	Gateshead	42	19	9	14	78:67	47
8	Barnsley	42	19	8	15	92:80	46
9	Barrow	42	18	7	17	60:60	43
10	Crewe	42	20	3	19	80:84	43
11	Tranmere	42	17	8	17	70:66	42
12	Southport	42	17	7	18	70:67	41
13	Accrington	42	15	10	17	78:76	40
14	Hartlepools	42	16	7	19	87:116	39
15	Halifax	42	15	8	19	71:90	38
16	Mansfield	42	14	7	21	84:100	35
17	Rotherham	42	14	6	22	60:84	34
18	Rochdale	42	13	7	22	58:80	33
19	Carlisle	42	13	7	22	51:75	33
20	York	42	13	6	23	72:92	32
21	New Brighton	42	11	10	21	63:88	32
22	Darlington	42	10	8	24	66:109	28

DIVISION 3N 1933-34

1	Barnsley*	42	27	8	7	118:61	62
2	Chesterfield	42	27	7	8	86:43	61
3	Stockport	42	24	11	7	115:52	59
4	Walsall	42	23	7	12	97:60	53
5	Doncaster	42	22	9	11	83:61	53
6	Wrexham	42	23	5	14	102:73	51
7	Tranmere	42	20	7	15	84:63	47
8	Barrow	42	19	9	14	116:94	47
9	Halifax	42	20	4	18	80:91	44
10	Chester	42	17	6	19	89:86	40
11	Hartlepools	42	16	7	19	89:93	39
12	York	42	15	8	19	71:74	38
13	Carlisle	42	15	8	19	66:81	38
14	Crewe	42	15	6	21	81:97	36
15	New Brighton	42	14	8	20	62:87	36
16	Darlington	42	13	9	20	70:101	35
17	Mansfield	42	11	12	19	81:88	34
18	Southport	42	8	17	17	63:90	33
19	Gateshead	42	12	9	21	76:110	33
20	Accrington	42	13	7	22	65:101	33
21	Rotherham	42	10	8	24	53:91	28
22	Rochdale	42	9	6	27	53:103	24

DIVISION 3N 1934-35

1	Doncaster*	42	26	5	11	87:44	57
2	Halifax	42	25	5	12	76:67	55
3	Chester	42	20	14	8	91:58	54
4	Lincoln	42	22	7	13	87:58	51
5	Darlington	42	21	9	12	80:59	51
6	Tranmere	42	20	11	11	74:55	51
7	Stockport	42	22	3	17	90:72	47
8	Mansfield	42	19	9	14	75:62	47
9	Rotherham	42	19	7	16	86:73	45
10	Chesterfield	42	17	10	15	71:52	44
11	Wrexham	42	16	11	15	76:69	43
12	Hartlepools	42	17	7	18	80:78	41
13	Crewe	42	14	11	17	66:86	39
14	Walsall	42	13	10	19	81:72	36
15	York	42	15	6	21	76:82	36
16	New Brighton	42	14	8	20	59:76	36
17	Barrow	42	13	9	20	58:87	35
18	Accrington	42	12	10	20	63:89	34
19	Gateshead	42	13	8	21	58:96	34
20	Rochdale	42	11	11	20	53:71	33
21	Southport	42	10	12	20	55:85	32
22	Carlisle	42	8	7	27	51:102	23

DIVISION 3S 1932-33

1	Brentford*	42	26	10	6	90:49	62
2	Exeter	42	24	10	8	88:48	58
3	Norwich	42	22	13	7	88:55	57
4	Reading	42	19	13	10	103:71	51
5	Crystal Palace	42	19	8	15	78:64	46
6	Coventry	42	19	6	17	106:77	44
7	Gillingham	42	18	8	16	72:61	44
8	Northampton	42	18	8	16	76:66	44
9	Bristol R.	42	15	14	13	61:56	44
10	Torquay	42	16	12	14	72:67	44
11	Watford	42	16	12	14	66:63	44
12	Brighton	42	17	8	17	66:65	42
13	Southend	42	15	11	16	65:82	41
14	Luton	42	13	13	16	78:78	39
15	Bristol C.	42	12	13	17	83:90	37
16	QPR	42	13	11	18	72:87	37
17	Aldershot	42	13	10	19	61:72	36
18	Bournemouth	42	12	12	18	60:81	36
19	Cardiff	42	12	7	23	69:99	31
20	Clapton Orient	42	8	13	21	59:93	29
21	Newport	42	11	7	24	61:105	29
22	Swindon	42	9	11	22	60:105	29

DIVISION 3S 1933-34

1	Norwich*	42	25	11	6	88:49	61
2	Coventry	42	21	12	9	100:54	54
3	Reading	42	21	12	9	82:50	54
4	QPR	42	24	6	12	70:51	54
5	Charlton	42	22	8	12	83:56	52
6	Luton	42	21	10	11	83:61	52
7	Bristol R.	42	20	11	11	77:47	51
8	Swindon	42	17	11	14	64:68	45
9	Exeter	42	16	11	15	68:57	43
10	Brighton	42	15	13	14	68:60	43
11	Clapton Orient	42	16	10	16	75:69	42
12	Crystal Palace	42	16	9	17	71:67	41
13	Northampton	42	14	12	16	71:78	40
14	Aldershot	42	13	12	17	52:71	38
15	Watford	42	15	7	20	71:63	37
16	Southend	42	12	10	20	51:74	34
17	Gillingham	42	11	11	20	75:96	33
18	Newport	42	8	17	17	49:70	33
19	Bristol C.	42	10	13	19	58:85	33
20	Torquay	42	13	7	22	53:93	33
21	Bournemouth	42	9	9	24	60:102	27
22	Cardiff	42	9	6	27	57:105	24

DIVISION 3S 1934-35

1	Charlton*	42	27	7	8	103:52	61
2	Reading	42	21	11	10	89:65	53
3	Coventry	42	21	9	12	86:50	51
4	Luton	42	19	12	11	92:60	50
5	Crystal Palace	42	19	10	13	86:64	48
6	Watford	42	19	9	14	76:49	47
7	Northampton	42	19	8	15	65:67	46
8	Bristol R.	42	17	10	15	73:77	44
9	Brighton	42	17	9	16	69:62	43
10	Torquay	42	18	6	18	81:75	42
11	Exeter	42	16	9	17	70:75	41
12	Millwall	42	17	7	18	57:62	41
13	QPR	42	16	9	17	63:72	41
14	Clapton Orient	42	15	10	17	65:65	40
15	Bristol C.	42	15	9	18	52:68	39
16	Swindon	42	13	12	17	67:78	38
17	Bournemouth	42	15	7	20	54:71	37
18	Aldershot	42	13	10	19	50:75	36
19	Cardiff	42	13	9	20	62:82	35
20	Gillingham	42	11	13	18	55:75	35
21	Southend	42	11	9	22	65:78	31
22	Newport	42	10	5	27	54:112	25

DIVISION 1 1935-36

1	Sunderland	42	25	6	11	109:74	56
2	Derby	42	18	12	12	61:52	48
3	Huddersfield	42	18	12	12	59:56	48
4	Stoke	42	20	7	15	57:57	47
5	Brentford	42	17	12	13	81:60	46
6	Arsenal	42	15	15	12	78:48	45
7	Preston	42	18	8	16	67:64	44
8	Chelsea	42	15	13	14	65:72	43
9	Manchester C.	42	17	8	17	68:60	42
10	Portsmouth	42	17	8	17	54:67	42
11	Leeds	42	15	11	16	66:64	41
12	Birmingham	42	15	11	16	61:63	41
13	Bolton	42	14	13	15	67:76	41
14	Middlesbrough	42	15	10	17	84:70	40
15	Wolverhampton	42	15	10	17	77:76	40
16	Everton	42	13	13	16	89:89	39
17	Grimsby	42	17	5	20	65:73	39
18	West Bromwich	42	16	6	20	89:88	38
19	Liverpool	42	13	12	17	60:64	38
20	Sheffield W.	42	13	12	17	63:77	38
21	Aston Villa†	42	13	9	20	81:110	35
22	Blackburn†	42	12	9	21	55:96	33

DIVISION 2 1935-36

1	Manchester U.*	42	22	12	8	85:43	56
2	Charlton*	42	22	11	9	85:58	55
3	Sheffield U.	42	20	12	10	79:50	52
4	West Ham	42	22	8	12	90:68	52
5	Tottenham	42	18	13	11	91:55	49
6	Leicester	42	19	10	13	79:57	48
7	Plymouth	42	20	8	14	71:57	48
8	Newcastle	42	20	6	16	88:79	46
9	Fulham	42	15	14	13	76:52	44
10	Blackpool	42	18	7	17	93:72	43
11	Norwich	42	17	9	16	72:65	43
12	Bradford C.	42	15	13	14	55:65	43
13	Swansea	42	15	9	18	67:76	39
14	Bury	42	13	12	17	66:84	38
15	Burnley	42	12	13	17	50:59	37
16	Bradford P.A.	42	14	9	19	62:84	37
17	Southampton	42	14	9	19	47:65	37
18	Doncaster	42	14	9	19	51:71	37
19	Nottingham F.	42	12	11	19	69:76	35
20	Barnsley	42	12	9	21	54:80	33
21	Port Vale†	42	12	8	22	56:106	32
22	Hull†	42	5	10	27	47:111	20

DIVISION 3N 1935-36

1	Chesterfield*	42	24	12	6	92:39	60
2	Chester	42	22	11	9	100:45	55
3	Tranmere	42	22	11	9	93:58	55
4	Lincoln	42	22	9	11	91:51	53
5	Stockport	42	20	8	14	65:49	48
6	Crewe	42	19	9	14	80:76	47
7	Oldham	42	18	9	15	86:73	45
8	Hartlepools	42	15	12	15	57:61	42
9	Accrington	42	17	8	17	63:72	42
10	Walsall	42	16	9	17	79:59	41
11	Rotherham	42	16	9	17	69:66	41
12	Darlington	42	17	6	19	74:79	40
13	Carlisle	42	14	12	16	56:62	40
14	Gateshead	42	13	14	15	56:76	40
15	Barrow	42	13	12	17	58:65	38
16	York	42	13	12	17	62:95	38
17	Halifax	42	15	7	20	57:61	37
18	Wrexham	42	15	7	20	66:75	37
19	Mansfield	42	14	9	19	80:91	37
20	Rochdale	42	10	13	19	58:88	33
21	Southport	42	11	9	22	48:90	31
22	New Brighton	42	9	6	27	43:102	24

DIVISION 3S 1935-36

1	Coventry*	42	24	9	9	102:45	57
2	Luton	42	22	12	8	81:45	56
3	Reading	42	26	2	14	87:62	54
4	QPR	42	22	9	11	84:53	53
5	Watford	42	20	9	13	80:54	49
6	Crystal Palace	42	22	5	15	96:74	49
7	Brighton	42	18	8	16	70:63	44
8	Bournemouth	42	16	11	15	60:56	43
9	Notts Co.	42	15	12	15	60:57	42
10	Torquay	42	16	9	17	62:62	41
11	Aldershot	42	14	12	16	53:61	40
12	Millwall	42	14	12	16	58:71	40
13	Bristol C.	42	15	10	17	48:59	40
14	Clapton Orient	42	16	6	20	55:61	38
15	Northampton	42	15	8	19	62:90	38
16	Gillingham	42	14	9	19	66:77	37
17	Bristol R.	42	14	9	19	69:95	37
18	Southend	42	13	10	19	61:62	36
19	Swindon	42	14	8	20	64:73	36
20	Cardiff	42	13	10	19	60:73	36
21	Newport	42	11	9	22	60:111	31
22	Exeter	42	8	11	23	59:93	27

DIVISION 1 1936-37

1	Manchester C.	42	22	13	7	107:61	57
2	Charlton	42	21	12	9	58:49	54
3	Arsenal	42	18	16	8	80:49	52
4	Derby	42	21	7	14	96:90	49
5	Wolverhampton	42	21	5	16	84:67	47
6	Brentford	42	18	10	14	82:78	46
7	Middlesbrough	42	19	8	15	74:71	46
8	Sunderland	42	19	6	17	89:87	44
9	Portsmouth	42	17	10	15	62:66	44
10	Stoke	42	15	12	15	72:57	42
11	Birmingham	42	13	15	14	64:60	41
12	Grimsby	42	17	7	18	86:81	41
13	Chelsea	42	14	13	15	52:55	41
14	Preston	42	14	13	15	56:67	41
15	Huddersfield	42	12	15	15	62:64	39
16	West Bromwich	42	16	6	20	77:98	38
17	Everton	42	14	9	19	81:78	37
18	Liverpool	42	12	11	19	62:84	35
19	Leeds	42	15	4	23	60:80	34
20	Bolton	42	10	14	18	43:66	34
21	Manchester U.†	42	10	12	20	55:78	32
22	Sheffield W.†	42	9	12	21	53:69	30

DIVISION 2 1936-37

1	Leicester*	42	24	8	10	89:57	56
2	Blackpool*	42	24	7	11	88:53	55
3	Bury	42	22	8	12	74:55	52
4	Newcastle	42	22	5	15	80:56	49
5	Plymouth	42	18	13	11	71:53	49
6	West Ham	42	19	11	12	73:55	49
7	Sheffield U.	42	18	10	14	66:54	46
8	Coventry	42	17	11	14	66:54	45
9	Aston Villa	42	16	12	14	82:70	44
10	Tottenham	42	17	9	16	88:66	43
11	Fulham	42	15	13	14	71:61	43
12	Blackburn	42	16	10	16	70:62	42
13	Burnley	42	16	10	16	57:61	42
14	Barnsley	42	16	9	17	50:64	41
15	Chesterfield	42	16	8	18	84:89	40
16	Swansea	42	15	7	20	50:65	37
17	Norwich	42	14	8	20	63:71	36
18	Nottingham F.	42	12	10	20	68:90	34
19	Southampton	42	11	12	19	53:77	34
20	Bradford P.A.	42	12	9	21	52:88	33
21	Bradford C.†	42	9	12	21	54:94	30
22	Doncaster†	42	7	10	25	30:84	24

DIVISION 3N 1936-37

1	Stockport*	42	23	14	5	84:39	60
2	Lincoln	42	25	7	10	103:57	57
3	Chester	42	22	9	11	87:57	53
4	Oldham	42	20	11	11	77:59	51
5	Hull	42	17	12	13	68:69	46
6	Hartlepools	42	19	7	16	75:69	45
7	Halifax	42	18	9	15	68:63	45
8	Wrexham	42	16	12	14	71:57	44
9	Mansfield	42	18	8	16	91:76	44
10	Carlisle	42	18	8	16	65:68	44
11	Port Vale	42	17	10	15	58:64	44
12	York	42	16	11	15	79:70	43
13	Accrington	42	16	9	17	76:69	41
14	Southport	42	12	13	17	73:87	37
15	New Brighton	42	13	11	18	55:70	37
16	Barrow	42	13	10	19	70:86	36
17	Rotherham	42	14	7	21	78:91	35
18	Rochdale	42	13	9	20	69:86	35
19	Tranmere	42	12	9	21	71:88	33
20	Crewe	42	10	12	20	55:83	32
21	Gateshead	42	11	10	21	63:98	32
22	Darlington	42	8	14	20	66:96	30

DIVISION 3S 1936-37

1	Luton*	42	27	4	11	103:53	58
2	Notts Co.	42	23	10	9	74:52	56
3	Brighton	42	24	5	13	74:43	53
4	Watford	42	19	11	12	85:60	49
5	Reading	42	19	11	12	76:60	49
6	Bournemouth	42	20	9	13	65:59	49
7	Northampton	42	20	6	16	85:68	46
8	Millwall	42	18	10	14	64:54	46
9	QPR	42	18	9	15	73:52	45
10	Southend	42	17	11	14	78:67	45
11	Gillingham	42	18	8	16	52:66	44
12	Clapton Orient	42	14	15	13	52:52	43
13	Swindon	42	14	11	17	75:73	39
14	Crystal Palace	42	13	12	17	62:61	38
15	Bristol R.	42	16	4	22	71:80	36
16	Bristol C.	42	15	6	21	58:70	36
17	Walsall	42	13	10	19	62:84	36
18	Cardiff	42	14	7	21	54:87	35
19	Newport	42	12	10	20	67:98	34
20	Torquay	42	11	10	21	57:80	32
21	Exeter	42	10	12	20	59:88	32
22	Aldershot	42	7	9	26	50:89	23

DIVISION 1 1937-38

1	Arsenal	42	21	10	11	77:44	52
2	Wolverhampton	42	20	11	11	72:49	51
3	Preston	42	16	17	9	64:44	49
4	Charlton	42	16	14	12	65:51	46
5	Middlesbrough	42	19	8	15	72:65	46
6	Brentford	42	18	9	15	69:59	45
7	Bolton	42	15	15	12	64:60	45
8	Sunderland	42	14	16	12	55:57	44
9	Leeds	42	14	15	13	64:69	43
10	Chelsea	42	14	13	15	65:65	41
11	Liverpool	42	15	11	16	65:71	41
12	Blackpool	42	16	8	18	61:66	40
13	Derby	42	15	10	17	66:87	40
14	Everton	42	16	7	19	79:75	39
15	Huddersfield	42	17	5	20	55:68	39
16	Leicester	42	14	11	17	54:75	39
17	Stoke	42	13	12	17	58:59	38
18	Birmingham	42	10	18	14	58:62	38
19	Portsmouth	42	13	12	17	62:68	38
20	Grimsby	42	13	12	17	51:68	38
21	Manchester C.†	42	14	8	20	80:77	36
22	West Bromwich†	42	14	8	20	74:91	36

DIVISION 2 1937-38

1	Aston Villa*	42	25	7	10	73:35	57
2	Manchester U.*	42	22	9	11	82:50	53
3	Sheffield U.	42	22	9	11	73:56	53
4	Coventry	42	20	12	10	66:45	52
5	Tottenham	42	19	6	17	76:54	44
6	Burnley	42	17	10	15	54:54	44
7	Bradford P.A.	42	17	9	16	69:56	43
8	Fulham	42	16	11	15	61:57	43
9	West Ham	42	14	14	14	53:52	42
10	Bury	42	18	5	19	63:60	41
11	Chesterfield	42	16	9	17	63:63	41
12	Luton	42	15	10	17	89:86	40
13	Plymouth	42	14	12	16	57:65	40
14	Norwich	42	14	11	17	56:75	39
15	Southampton	42	15	9	18	55:77	39
16	Blackburn	42	14	10	18	71:80	38
17	Sheffield W.	42	14	10	18	49:56	38
18	Swansea	42	13	12	17	45:73	38
19	Newcastle	42	14	8	20	51:58	36
20	Nottingham F.	42	14	8	20	47:60	36
21	Barnsley†	42	11	14	17	50:64	36
22	Stockport†	42	11	9	22	43:70	31

DIVISION 3N 1937-38

1	Tranmere*	42	23	10	9	81:41	56
2	Doncaster	42	21	12	9	74:49	54
3	Hull	42	20	13	9	80:43	53
4	Oldham	42	19	13	10	67:46	51
5	Gateshead	42	20	11	11	84:59	51
6	Rotherham	42	20	10	12	68:56	50
7	Lincoln	42	19	8	15	66:50	46
8	Crewe	42	18	9	15	71:53	45
9	Chester	42	16	12	14	77:72	44
10	Wrexham	42	16	11	15	58:63	43
11	York	42	16	10	16	70:68	42
12	Carlisle	42	15	9	18	57:67	39
13	New Brighton	42	15	8	19	60:61	38
14	Bradford C.	42	14	10	18	66:69	38
15	Port Vale	42	12	14	16	65:73	38
16	Southport	42	12	14	16	53:82	38
17	Rochdale	42	13	11	18	67:78	37
18	Halifax	42	12	12	18	44:66	36
19	Darlington	42	11	10	21	54:79	32
20	Hartlepools	42	10	12	20	53:80	32
21	Barrow	42	11	10	21	41:71	32
22	Accrington	42	11	7	24	45:75	29

DIVISION 3S 1937-38

1	Millwall*	42	23	10	9	83:37	56
2	Bristol C.	42	21	13	8	68:40	55
3	QPR	42	22	9	11	80:47	53
4	Watford	42	21	11	10	73:43	53
5	Brighton	42	21	9	12	64:44	51
6	Reading	42	20	11	11	71:63	51
7	Crystal Palace	42	18	12	12	67:47	48
8	Swindon	42	17	10	15	49:49	44
9	Northampton	42	17	9	16	51:57	43
10	Cardiff	42	15	12	15	67:54	42
11	Notts Co.	42	16	9	17	50:50	41
12	Southend	42	15	10	17	70:68	40
13	Bournemouth	42	14	12	16	56:57	40
14	Mansfield	42	15	9	18	62:67	39
15	Bristol R.	42	13	13	16	46:61	39
16	Newport	42	11	16	15	43:52	38
17	Exeter	42	13	12	17	57:70	38
18	Aldershot	42	15	5	22	39:59	35
19	Clapton Orient	42	13	7	22	42:61	33
20	Torquay	42	9	12	21	38:73	30
21	Walsall	42	11	7	24	52:88	29
22	Gillingham	42	10	6	26	36:77	26

DIVISION 1 1938-39

1	Everton	42	27	5	10	88:52	59
2	Wolverhampton	42	22	11	9	88:39	55
3	Charlton	42	22	6	14	75:59	50
4	Middlesbrough	42	20	9	13	93:74	49
5	Arsenal	42	19	9	14	55:41	47
6	Derby	42	19	8	15	66:55	46
7	Stoke	42	17	12	13	71:68	46
8	Bolton	42	15	15	12	67:58	45
9	Preston	42	16	12	14	63:59	44
10	Grimsby	42	16	11	15	61:69	43
11	Liverpool	42	14	14	14	62:63	42
12	Aston Villa	42	15	11	16	71:60	41
13	Leeds	42	16	9	17	59:67	41
14	Manchester U.	42	11	16	15	57:65	38
15	Blackpool	42	12	14	16	56:68	38
16	Sunderland	42	13	12	17	54:67	38
17	Portsmouth	42	12	13	17	47:70	37
18	Brentford	42	14	8	20	53:74	36
19	Huddersfield	42	12	11	19	58:64	35
20	Chelsea	42	12	9	21	64:80	33
21	Birmingham†	42	12	8	22	62:84	32
22	Leicester†	42	9	11	22	48:82	29

DIVISION 1 1946-47

1	Liverpool	42	25	7	10	84:52	57
2	Manchester U.	42	22	12	8	95:54	56
3	Wolverhampton	42	25	6	11	98:56	56
4	Stoke	42	24	7	11	90:53	55
5	Blackpool	42	22	6	14	71:70	50
6	Sheffield U.	42	21	7	14	89:75	49
7	Preston	42	18	11	13	76:74	47
8	Aston Villa	42	18	9	15	67:53	45
9	Sunderland	42	18	8	16	65:66	44
10	Everton	42	17	9	16	62:67	43
11	Middlesbrough	42	17	8	17	73:68	42
12	Portsmouth	42	16	9	17	66:60	41
13	Arsenal	42	16	9	17	72:70	41
14	Derby	42	18	5	19	73:79	41
15	Chelsea	42	16	7	19	69:84	39
16	Grimsby	42	13	12	17	61:82	38
17	Blackburn	42	14	8	20	45:53	36
18	Bolton	42	13	8	21	57:69	34
19	Charlton	42	11	12	19	57:71	34
20	Huddersfield	42	13	7	22	53:79	33
21	Brentford†	42	9	7	26	45:88	25
22	Leeds†	42	6	6	30	45:90	18

DIVISION 1 1947-48

1	Arsenal	42	23	13	6	81:32	59
2	Manchester U.	42	19	14	9	81:48	52
3	Burnley	42	20	12	10	56:43	52
4	Derby	42	19	12	11	77:57	50
5	Wolverhampton	42	19	9	14	83:70	47
6	Aston Villa	42	19	9	14	65:57	47
7	Preston	42	20	7	15	67:68	47
8	Portsmouth	42	19	7	16	68:50	45
9	Blackpool	42	17	10	15	57:41	44
10	Manchester C.	42	15	12	15	52:47	42
11	Liverpool	42	16	10	16	65:61	42
12	Sheffield U.	42	16	10	16	65:70	42
13	Charlton	42	17	6	19	57:66	40
14	Everton	42	17	6	19	52:66	40
15	Stoke	42	14	10	18	41:55	38
16	Middlesbrough	42	14	9	19	71:73	37
17	Bolton	42	16	5	21	46:58	37
18	Chelsea	42	14	9	19	53:71	37
19	Huddersfield	42	12	12	18	51:60	36
20	Sunderland	42	13	10	19	56:67	36
21	Blackburn†	42	11	10	21	54:72	32
22	Grimsby†	42	8	6	28	45:111	22

DIVISION 2 1938-39

1	Blackburn *	42	25	5	12	94:60	55
2	Sheffield U. *	42	20	14	8	69:41	54
3	Sheffield W.	42	21	11	10	88:59	53
4	Coventry	42	21	8	13	62:45	50
5	Manchester C.	42	21	7	14	96:72	49
6	Chesterfield	42	20	9	13	69:52	49
7	Luton	42	22	5	15	82:66	49
8	Tottenham	42	19	9	14	67:62	47
9	Newcastle	42	18	10	14	61:48	46
10	West Bromwich	42	18	9	15	89:72	45
11	West Ham	42	17	10	15	70:52	44
12	Fulham	42	17	10	15	61:55	44
13	Millwall	42	14	14	14	64:53	42
14	Burnley	42	15	9	18	50:56	39
15	Plymouth	42	15	8	19	49:55	38
16	Bury	42	12	13	17	65:74	37
17	Bradford P.A.	42	12	11	19	61:82	35
18	Southampton	42	13	9	20	56:82	35
19	Swansea	42	11	12	19	50:83	34
20	Nottingham F.	42	10	11	21	49:82	31
21	Norwich†	42	13	5	24	50:91	31
22	Tranmere†	42	6	5	31	39:99	17

DIVISION 2 1946-47

1	Manchester C.*	42	26	10	6	78:35	62
2	Burnley *	42	22	14	6	65:29	58
3	Birmingham	42	25	5	12	74:33	55
4	Chesterfield	42	18	14	10	58:44	50
5	Newcastle	42	19	10	13	95:62	48
6	Tottenham	42	17	14	11	65:53	48
7	West Bromwich	42	20	8	14	88:75	48
8	Coventry	42	16	13	13	66:59	45
9	Leicester	42	18	7	17	69:64	43
10	Barnsley	42	17	8	17	84:86	42
11	Nottingham F.	42	15	10	17	69:74	40
12	West Ham	42	16	8	18	70:76	40
13	Luton	42	16	7	19	71:73	39
14	Southampton	42	15	9	18	69:76	39
15	Fulham	42	15	9	18	63:74	39
16	Bradford P.A.	42	14	11	17	65:77	39
17	Bury	42	12	12	18	80:78	36
18	Millwall	42	14	8	20	56:79	36
19	Plymouth	42	14	5	23	79:96	33
20	Sheffield W.	42	12	8	22	67:88	32
21	Swansea†	42	11	7	24	55:83	29
22	Newport†	42	10	3	29	61:133	23

DIVISION 2 1947-48

1	Birmingham *	42	22	15	5	55:24	59
2	Newcastle *	42	24	8	10	72:41	56
3	Southampton	42	21	10	11	71:53	52
4	Sheffield W.	42	20	11	11	66:53	51
5	Cardiff	42	18	11	13	61:58	47
6	West Ham	42	16	14	12	55:53	46
7	West Bromwich	42	18	9	15	63:58	45
8	Tottenham	42	15	14	13	56:43	44
9	Leicester	42	16	11	15	60:57	43
10	Coventry	42	14	13	15	59:52	41
11	Fulham	42	15	10	17	47:46	40
12	Barnsley	42	15	10	17	62:64	40
13	Luton	42	14	12	16	56:59	40
14	Bradford P.A.	42	16	8	18	68:72	40
15	Brentford	42	13	14	15	44:61	40
16	Chesterfield	42	16	7	19	54:55	39
17	Plymouth	42	9	20	13	40:58	38
18	Leeds	42	14	8	20	62:72	36
19	Nottingham F.	42	12	11	19	54:60	35
20	Bury	42	9	16	17	58:68	34
21	Doncaster†	42	9	11	22	40:66	29
22	Millwall†	42	9	11	22	44:74	29

DIVISION 3N 1938-39

1	Barnsley*	42	30	7	5	94:34	67
2	Doncaster	42	21	14	7	87:47	56
3	Bradford C.	42	22	8	12	89:56	52
4	Southport	42	20	10	12	75:54	50
5	Oldham	42	22	5	15	76:59	49
6	Chester	42	20	9	13	88:70	49
7	Hull	42	18	10	14	83:74	46
8	Crewe	42	19	6	17	82:70	44
9	Stockport	42	17	9	16	91:77	43
10	Gateshead	42	14	14	14	74:67	42
11	Rotherham	42	17	8	17	64:64	42
12	Halifax	42	13	16	13	52:54	42
13	Barrow	42	16	9	17	66:65	41
14	Wrexham	42	17	7	18	66:79	41
15	Rochdale	42	15	9	18	92:82	39
16	New Brighton	42	15	9	18	68:73	39
17	Lincoln	42	12	9	21	66:92	33
18	Darlington	42	13	7	22	62:92	33
19	Carlisle	42	13	7	22	64:111	33
20	York	42	12	8	22	66:92	32
21	Hartlepools	42	12	7	23	55:94	31
22	Accrington	42	7	6	29	49:103	20

DIVISION 3N 1946-47

1	Doncaster *	42	33	6	3	123:40	72
2	Rotherham	42	29	6	7	114:53	64
3	Chester	42	25	6	11	95:51	56
4	Stockport	42	24	2	16	78:53	50
5	Bradford C.	42	20	10	12	62:47	50
6	Rochdale	42	19	10	13	80:64	48
7	Wrexham	42	17	12	13	65:51	46
8	Crewe	42	17	9	16	70:74	43
9	Barrow	42	17	7	18	54:62	41
10	Tranmere	42	17	7	18	66:77	41
11	Hull	42	16	8	18	49:53	40
12	Lincoln	42	17	5	20	86:87	39
13	Hartlepools	42	15	9	18	64:73	39
14	Gateshead	42	16	6	20	62:72	38
15	York	42	14	9	19	67:81	37
16	Carlisle	42	14	9	19	70:93	37
17	Darlington	42	15	6	21	68:80	36
18	New Brighton	42	14	8	20	57:77	36
19	Oldham	42	12	8	22	55:80	32
20	Accrington	42	14	4	24	56:92	32
21	Southport	42	7	11	24	53:85	25
22	Halifax	42	8	6	28	43:92	22

DIVISION 3N 1947-48

1	Lincoln *	42	26	8	8	81:40	60
2	Rotherham	42	25	9	8	95:49	59
3	Wrexham	42	21	8	13	74:54	50
4	Gateshead	42	19	11	12	75:57	49
5	Hull	42	18	11	13	59:48	47
6	Accrington	42	20	6	16	62:59	46
7	Barrow	42	16	13	13	49:40	45
8	Mansfield	42	17	11	14	57:51	45
9	Carlisle	42	18	7	17	88:77	43
10	Crewe	42	18	7	17	61:63	43
11	Oldham	42	14	13	15	63:64	41
12	Rochdale	42	15	11	16	48:72	41
13	York	42	13	14	15	65:60	40
14	Bradford C.	42	15	10	17	65:66	40
15	Southport	42	14	11	17	60:63	39
16	Darlington	42	13	13	16	54:70	39
17	Stockport	42	13	12	17	63:67	38
18	Tranmere	42	16	4	22	54:72	36
19	Hartlepools	42	14	8	20	51:73	36
20	Chester	42	13	9	20	64:67	35
21	Halifax	42	7	13	22	43:76	27
22	New Brighton	42	8	9	25	38:81	25

DIVISION 3S 1938-39

1	Newport *	42	22	11	9	58:45	55
2	Crystal Palace	42	20	12	10	71:52	52
3	Brighton	42	19	11	12	68:49	49
4	Watford	42	17	12	13	62:51	46
5	Reading	42	16	14	12	69:59	46
6	QPR	42	15	14	13	68:49	44
7	Ipswich	42	16	12	14	62:52	44
8	Bristol C.	42	16	12	14	61:63	44
9	Swindon	42	18	8	16	72:77	44
10	Aldershot	42	16	12	14	53:66	44
11	Notts Co.	42	17	9	16	59:54	43
12	Southend	42	16	9	17	61:64	41
13	Cardiff	42	15	11	16	61:65	41
14	Exeter	42	13	14	15	65:82	40
15	Bournemouth	42	13	13	16	52:58	39
16	Mansfield	42	12	15	15	44:62	39
17	Northampton	42	15	8	19	51:58	38
18	Port Vale	42	14	9	19	52:58	37
19	Torquay	42	14	9	19	54:70	37
20	Clapton Orient	42	11	13	18	53:55	35
21	Walsall	42	11	11	20	68:69	33
22	Bristol R.	42	10	13	19	55:61	33

DIVISION 3S 1946-47

1	Cardiff *	42	30	6	6	93:30	66
2	QPR	42	23	11	8	74:40	57
3	Bristol C.	42	20	11	11	94:56	51
4	Swindon	42	19	11	12	84:73	49
5	Walsall	42	17	12	13	74:59	46
6	Ipswich	42	16	14	12	61:53	46
7	Bournemouth	42	18	8	16	72:54	44
8	Southend	42	17	10	15	71:60	44
9	Reading	42	16	11	15	83:74	43
10	Port Vale	42	17	9	16	68:63	43
11	Torquay	42	15	12	15	52:61	42
12	Notts Co.	42	15	10	17	63:63	40
13	Northampton	42	15	10	17	72:75	40
14	Bristol R.	42	16	8	18	59:69	40
15	Exeter	42	15	9	18	60:69	39
16	Watford	42	17	5	20	61:76	39
17	Brighton	42	13	12	17	54:72	38
18	Crystal Palace	42	13	11	18	49:62	37
19	Leyton Orient	42	12	8	22	54:75	32
20	Aldershot	42	10	12	20	48:78	32
21	Norwich	42	10	8	24	64:100	28
22	Mansfield	42	9	10	23	48:96	28

DIVISION 3S 1947-48

1	QPR *	42	26	9	7	74:37	61
2	Bournemouth	42	24	9	9	76:35	57
3	Walsall	42	21	9	12	70:40	51
4	Ipswich	42	23	3	16	67:61	49
5	Swansea	42	18	12	12	70:52	48
6	Notts Co.	42	19	8	15	68:59	46
7	Bristol C.	42	18	7	17	77:65	43
8	Port Vale	42	16	11	15	63:54	43
9	Southend	42	15	13	14	51:58	43
10	Reading	42	15	11	16	56:58	41
11	Exeter	42	15	11	16	55:63	41
12	Newport	42	14	13	15	61:73	41
13	Crystal Palace	42	13	13	16	49:49	39
14	Northampton	42	14	11	17	58:72	39
15	Watford	42	14	10	18	57:79	38
16	Swindon	42	10	16	16	41:46	36
17	Leyton Orient	42	13	10	19	51:73	36
18	Torquay	42	11	13	18	63:62	35
19	Aldershot	42	10	15	17	45:67	35
20	Bristol R.	42	13	8	21	71:75	34
21	Norwich	42	13	8	21	61:76	34
22	Brighton	42	11	12	19	43:73	34

DIVISION 1 1948-49

1	Portsmouth	42	25	8	9	84:42	58
2	Manchester U.	42	21	11	10	77:44	53
3	Derby	42	22	9	11	74:55	53
4	Newcastle	42	20	12	10	70:56	52
5	Arsenal	42	18	13	11	74:44	49
6	Wolverhampton	42	17	12	13	79:66	46
7	Manchester C.	42	15	15	12	47:51	45
8	Sunderland	42	13	17	12	49:58	43
9	Charlton	42	15	12	15	63:67	42
10	Aston Villa	42	16	10	16	60:76	42
11	Stoke	42	16	9	17	66:68	41
12	Liverpool	42	13	14	15	53:43	40
13	Chelsea	42	12	14	16	69:68	38
14	Bolton	42	14	10	18	59:68	38
15	Burnley	42	12	14	16	43:50	38
16	Blackpool	42	11	16	15	54:67	38
17	Birmingham	42	11	15	16	36:38	37
18	Everton	42	13	11	18	41:63	37
19	Middlesbrough	42	11	12	19	46:57	34
20	Huddersfield	42	12	10	20	40:69	34
21	Preston †	42	11	11	20	62:75	33
22	Sheffield U. †	42	11	11	20	57:78	33

DIVISION 2 1948-49

1	Fulham *	42	24	9	9	77:37	57
2	West Bromwich *	42	24	8	10	69:39	56
3	Southampton	42	23	9	10	69:36	55
4	Cardiff	42	19	13	10	62:47	51
5	Tottenham	42	17	16	9	72:44	50
6	Chesterfield	42	15	17	10	51:45	47
7	West Ham	42	18	10	14	56:58	46
8	Sheffield W.	42	15	13	14	63:56	43
9	Barnsley	42	14	12	16	62:61	40
10	Luton	42	14	12	16	55:57	40
11	Grimsby	42	15	10	17	72:76	40
12	Bury	42	17	6	19	67:76	40
13	QPR	42	14	11	17	44:62	39
14	Blackburn	42	15	8	19	53:63	38
15	Leeds	42	12	13	17	55:63	37
16	Coventry	42	15	7	20	55:64	37
17	Bradford P.A.	42	13	11	18	65:78	37
18	Brentford	42	11	14	17	42:53	36
19	Leicester	42	10	16	16	62:79	36
20	Plymouth	42	12	12	18	49:64	36
21	Nottingham F. †	42	14	7	21	50:54	35
22	Lincoln †	42	8	12	22	53:91	28

DIVISION 3N 1948-49

1	Hull *	42	27	11	4	93:28	65
2	Rutherham	42	28	6	8	90:46	62
3	Doncaster	42	20	10	12	53:40	50
4	Darlington	42	20	6	16	83:74	46
5	Gateshead	42	16	13	13	69:58	45
6	Oldham	42	18	9	15	75:67	45
7	Rochdale	42	18	9	15	55:53	45
8	Stockport	42	16	11	15	61:56	43
9	Wrexham	42	17	9	16	56:62	43
10	Mansfield	42	14	14	14	52:48	42
11	Tranmere	42	13	15	14	46:57	41
12	Crewe	42	16	9	17	52:74	41
13	Barrow	42	14	12	16	41:48	40
14	York	42	15	9	18	74:74	39
15	Carlisle	42	14	11	17	60:77	39
16	Hartlepools	42	14	10	18	45:58	38
17	New Brighton	42	14	8	20	46:58	36
18	Chester	42	11	13	18	57:56	35
19	Halifax	42	12	11	19	45:62	35
20	Accrington	42	12	10	20	55:64	34
21	Southport	42	11	9	22	45:64	31
22	Bradford C.	42	10	9	23	48:77	29

DIVISION 3S 1948-49

1	Swansea *	42	27	8	7	87:34	62
2	Reading	42	25	5	12	77:50	55
3	Bournemouth	42	22	8	12	69:48	52
4	Swindon	42	18	15	9	64:56	51
5	Bristol R.	42	19	10	13	61:51	48
6	Brighton	42	15	18	9	55:55	48
7	Ipswich	42	18	9	15	78:77	45
8	Millwall	42	17	11	14	63:64	45
9	Torquay	42	17	11	14	65:70	45
10	Norwich	42	16	12	14	67:49	44
11	Notts Co.	42	19	5	18	102:68	43
12	Exeter	42	15	10	17	63:76	40
13	Port Vale	42	14	11	17	51:54	39
14	Walsall	42	15	8	19	56:64	38
15	Newport	42	14	9	19	68:92	37
16	Bristol C.	42	11	14	17	44:62	36
17	Watford	42	10	15	17	41:54	35
18	Southend	42	9	16	17	41:46	34
19	Leyton Orient	42	11	12	19	58:80	34
20	Northampton	42	12	9	21	51:62	33
21	Aldershot	42	11	11	20	48:59	33
22	Crystal Palace	42	8	11	23	38:76	27

DIVISION 1 1949-50

1	Portsmouth	42	22	9	11	74:38	53
2	Wolverhampton	42	20	13	9	76:49	53
3	Sunderland	42	21	10	11	83:62	52
4	Manchester U.	42	18	14	10	69:44	50
5	Newcastle	42	19	12	11	77:55	50
6	Arsenal	42	19	11	12	79:55	49
7	Blackpool	42	17	15	10	46:35	49
8	Liverpool	42	17	14	11	64:54	48
9	Middlesbrough	42	20	7	15	59:48	47
10	Burnley	42	16	13	13	40:40	45
11	Derby	42	17	10	15	69:61	44
12	Aston Villa	42	15	12	15	61:61	42
13	Chelsea	42	12	16	14	58:65	40
14	West Bromwich	42	14	12	16	47:53	40
15	Huddersfield	42	14	9	19	52:73	37
16	Bolton	42	10	14	18	45:59	34
17	Fulham	42	10	14	18	41:54	34
18	Everton	42	10	14	18	42:66	34
19	Stoke	42	11	12	19	45:75	34
20	Charlton	42	13	6	23	53:65	32
21	Manchester C †	42	8	13	21	36:68	29
22	Birmingham †	42	7	14	21	31:67	28

DIVISION 2 1949-50

1	Tottenham *	42	27	7	8	81:35	61
2	Sheffield W. *	42	18	16	8	67:48	52
3	Sheffield U.	42	19	14	9	68:49	52
4	Southampton	42	19	14	9	64:48	52
5	Leeds	42	17	13	12	54:45	47
6	Preston	42	18	9	15	60:49	45
7	Hull	42	17	11	14	64:72	45
8	Swansea	42	17	9	16	53:49	43
9	Brentford	42	15	13	14	44:49	43
10	Cardiff	42	16	10	16	41:44	42
11	Grimsby	42	16	8	18	74:73	40
12	Coventry	42	13	13	16	55:55	39
13	Barnsley	42	13	13	16	64:67	39
14	Chesterfield	42	15	9	18	43:47	39
15	Leicester	42	12	15	15	55:65	39
16	Blackburn	42	14	10	18	55:60	38
17	Luton	42	10	18	14	41:51	38
18	Bury	42	14	9	19	60:65	37
19	West Ham	42	12	12	18	53:61	36
20	QPR	42	11	12	19	40:57	34
21	Plymouth †	42	8	16	18	44:65	32
22	Bradford P.A. †	42	10	11	21	51:77	31

DIVISION 3N 1949-50

1	Doncaster *	42	19	17	6	66:38	55
2	Gateshead	42	23	7	12	87:54	53
3	Rochdale	42	21	9	12	68:41	51
4	Lincoln	42	21	9	12	60:39	51
5	Tranmere	42	19	11	12	51:48	49
6	Rotherham	42	19	10	13	80:59	48
7	Crewe	42	17	14	11	68:55	48
8	Mansfield	42	18	12	12	66:54	48
9	Carlisle	42	16	15	11	68:51	47
10	Stockport	42	19	7	16	55:52	45
11	Oldham	42	16	11	15	58:63	43
12	Chester	42	17	6	19	70:79	40
13	Accrington	42	16	7	19	57:62	39
14	New Brighton	42	14	10	18	45:63	38
15	Barrow	42	14	9	19	47:53	37
16	Southport	42	12	13	17	51:71	37
17	Darlington	42	11	13	18	56:69	35
18	Hartlepools	42	14	5	23	52:79	33
19	Bradford C.	42	12	8	22	61:76	32
20	Wrexham	42	10	12	20	39:54	32
21	Halifax	42	12	8	22	58:85	32
22	York	42	9	13	20	52:70	31

DIVISION 3S 1949-50

1	Notts Co. *	42	25	8	9	95:50	58
2	Northampton	42	20	11	11	72:50	51
3	Southend	42	19	13	10	66:48	51
4	Nottingham F.	42	20	9	13	67:39	49
5	Torquay	42	19	10	13	66:63	48
6	Watford	42	16	13	13	45:35	45
7	Crystal Palace	42	15	14	13	55:54	44
8	Brighton	42	16	12	14	57:69	44
9	Bristol R.	42	19	5	18	51:51	43
10	Reading	42	17	8	17	70:64	42
11	Norwich	42	16	10	16	65:63	42
12	Bournemouth	42	16	10	16	57:56	42
13	Port Vale	42	15	11	16	47:42	41
14	Swindon	42	15	11	16	59:62	41
15	Bristol C.	42	15	10	17	60:61	40
16	Exeter	42	14	11	17	63:75	39
17	Ipswich	42	12	11	19	57:86	35
18	Leyton Orient	42	12	11	19	53:85	35
19	Walsall	42	9	16	17	61:62	34
20	Aldershot	42	13	8	21	48:60	34
21	Newport	42	13	8	21	67:98	34
22	Millwall	42	14	4	24	55:63	32

DIVISION 1 1950-51

1	Tottenham	42	25	10	7	82:44	60
2	Manchester U.	42	24	8	10	74:40	56
3	Blackpool	42	20	10	12	79:53	50
4	Newcastle	42	18	13	11	62:53	49
5	Arsenal	42	19	9	14	73:56	47
6	Middlesbrough	42	18	11	13	76:65	47
7	Portsmouth	42	16	15	11	71:68	47
8	Bolton	42	19	7	16	64:61	45
9	Liverpool	42	16	11	15	53:59	43
10	Burnley	42	14	14	14	48:43	42
11	Derby	42	16	8	18	81:75	40
12	Sunderland	42	12	16	14	63:73	40
13	Stoke	42	13	14	15	50:59	40
14	Wolverhampton	42	15	8	19	74:61	38
15	Aston Villa	42	12	13	17	66:68	37
16	West Bromwich	42	13	11	18	53:61	37
17	Charlton	42	14	9	19	63:80	37
18	Fulham	42	13	11	18	52:68	37
19	Huddersfield	42	15	6	21	64:92	36
20	Chelsea	42	12	8	22	53:65	32
21	Sheffield W. †	42	12	8	22	64:83	32
22	Everton †	42	12	8	22	48:86	32

DIVISION 2 1950-51

1	Preston *	42	26	5	11	91:49	57
2	Manchester C. *	42	19	14	9	89:61	52
3	Cardiff	42	17	16	9	53:45	50
4	Birmingham	42	20	9	13	64:53	49
5	Leeds	42	20	8	14	63:55	48
6	Blackburn	42	19	8	15	65:66	46
7	Coventry	42	19	7	16	75:59	45
8	Sheffield U.	42	16	12	14	72:62	44
9	Brentford	42	18	8	16	75:74	44
10	Hull	42	16	11	15	74:70	43
11	Doncaster	42	15	13	14	64:68	43
12	Southampton	42	15	13	14	66:73	43
13	West Ham	42	16	10	16	68:69	42
14	Leicester	42	15	11	16	68:58	41
15	Barnsley	42	15	10	17	74:68	40
16	QPR	42	15	10	17	71:82	40
17	Notts Co.	42	13	13	16	61:60	39
18	Swansea	42	16	4	22	54:77	36
19	Luton	42	9	14	19	57:70	32
20	Bury	42	12	8	22	60:86	32
21	Chesterfield †	42	9	12	21	44:69	30
22	Grimsby †	42	8	12	22	61:95	28

DIVISION 3N 1950-51

1	Rotherham *	46	31	9	6	103:41	71
2	Mansfield	46	26	12	8	78:48	64
3	Carlisle	46	25	12	9	79:50	62
4	Tranmere	46	24	11	11	83:62	59
5	Lincoln	46	25	8	13	89:58	58
6	Bradford P.A.	46	23	8	15	90:72	54
7	Bradford C.	46	21	10	15	90:63	52
8	Gateshead	46	21	8	17	84:62	50
9	Crewe	46	19	10	17	61:60	48
10	Stockport	46	20	8	18	63:63	48
11	Rochdale	46	17	11	18	69:62	45
12	Scunthorpe	46	13	18	15	58:57	44
13	Chester	46	17	9	20	62:64	43
14	Wrexham	46	15	12	19	55:71	42
15	Oldham	46	16	8	22	73:73	40
16	Hartlepools	46	16	7	23	64:66	39
17	York	46	12	15	19	66:77	39
18	Darlington	46	13	13	20	59:77	39
19	Barrow	46	16	6	24	51:76	38
20	Shrewsbury	46	15	7	24	43:74	37
21	Southport	46	13	10	23	56:72	36
22	Halifax	46	11	12	23	50:69	34
23	Accrington	46	11	10	25	42:101	32
24	New Brighton	46	11	8	27	40:90	30

DIVISION 3S 1950-51

1	Nottingham F. *	46	30	10	6	110:40	70
2	Norwich	46	25	14	7	82:45	64
3	Reading	46	21	15	10	88:53	57
4	Plymouth	46	24	9	13	85:55	57
5	Millwall	46	23	10	13	80:57	56
6	Bristol R.	46	20	15	11	64:42	55
7	Southend	46	21	10	15	92:69	52
8	Ipswich	46	23	6	17	69:58	52
9	Bournemouth	46	22	7	17	65:57	51
10	Bristol C.	46	20	11	15	64:59	51
11	Newport	46	19	9	18	77:70	47
12	Port Vale	46	16	13	17	60:65	45
13	Brighton	46	13	17	16	71:79	43
14	Exeter	46	18	6	22	62:85	42
15	Walsall	46	15	10	21	52:62	40
16	Colchester	46	14	12	20	63:76	40
17	Swindon	46	18	4	24	55:67	40
18	Aldershot	46	15	10	21	56:88	40
19	Leyton Orient	46	15	8	23	53:75	38
20	Torquay	46	14	9	23	64:81	37
21	Northampton	46	10	16	20	55:67	36
22	Gillingham	46	13	9	24	69:101	35
23	Watford	46	9	11	26	54:88	29
24	Crystal Palace	46	8	11	27	33:84	27

DIVISION 1 1951-52

1	Manchester U.	42	23	11	8	95:52	57
2	Tottenham	42	22	9	11	76:51	53
3	Arsenal	42	21	11	10	80:61	53
4	Portsmouth	42	20	8	14	68:58	48
5	Bolton	42	19	10	13	65:61	48
6	Aston Villa	42	19	9	14	79:70	47
7	Preston	42	17	12	13	74:54	46
8	Newcastle	42	18	9	15	98:73	45
9	Blackpool	42	18	9	15	64:64	45
10	Charlton	42	17	10	15	68:63	44
11	Liverpool	42	12	19	11	57:61	43
12	Sunderland	42	15	12	15	70:61	42
13	West Bromwich	42	14	13	15	74:77	41
14	Burnley	42	15	10	17	56:63	40
15	Manchester C.	42	13	13	16	58:61	39
16	Wolverhampton	42	12	14	16	73:73	38
17	Derby	42	15	7	20	63:80	37
18	Middlesbrough	42	15	6	21	64:88	36
19	Chelsea	42	14	8	20	52:72	36
20	Stoke	42	12	7	23	49:88	31
21	Huddersfield †	42	10	8	24	49:82	28
22	Fulham †	42	8	11	23	58:77	27

DIVISION 1 1952-53

1	Arsenal	42	21	12	9	97:64	54
2	Preston	42	21	12	9	85:60	54
3	Wolverhampton	42	19	13	10	86:63	51
4	West Bromwich	42	21	8	13	66:60	50
5	Charlton	42	19	11	12	77:63	49
6	Burnley	42	18	12	12	67:52	48
7	Blackpool	42	19	9	14	71:70	47
8	Manchester U.	42	18	10	14	69:72	46
9	Sunderland	42	15	13	14	68:82	43
10	Tottenham	42	15	11	16	78:69	41
11	Aston Villa	42	14	13	15	63:61	41
12	Cardiff	42	14	12	16	54:46	40
13	Middlesbrough	42	14	11	17	70:77	39
14	Bolton	42	15	9	18	61:69	39
15	Portsmouth	42	14	10	18	74:83	38
16	Newcastle	42	14	9	19	59:70	37
17	Liverpool	42	14	8	20	61:82	36
18	Sheffield W.	42	12	11	19	62:72	35
19	Chelsea	42	12	11	19	56:66	35
20	Manchester C.	42	14	7	21	72:87	35
21	Stoke †	42	12	10	20	53:66	34
22	Derby †	42	11	10	21	59:74	32

DIVISION 1 1953-54

1	Wolverhampton	42	25	7	10	96:56	57
2	West Bromwich	42	22	9	11	86:63	53
3	Huddersfield	42	20	11	11	78:61	51
4	Manchester U.	42	18	12	12	73:58	48
5	Bolton	42	18	12	12	75:60	48
6	Blackpool	42	19	10	13	80:69	48
7	Burnley	42	21	4	17	78:67	46
8	Chelsea	42	16	12	14	74:68	44
9	Charlton	42	19	6	17	75:77	44
10	Cardiff	42	18	8	16	51:71	44
11	Preston	42	19	5	18	87:58	43
12	Arsenal	42	15	13	14	75:73	43
13	Aston Villa	42	16	9	17	70:68	41
14	Portsmouth	42	14	11	17	81:89	39
15	Newcastle	42	14	10	18	72:77	38
16	Tottenham	42	16	5	21	65:76	37
17	Manchester C.	42	14	9	19	62:77	37
18	Sunderland	42	14	8	20	81:89	36
19	Sheffield W.	42	15	6	21	70:91	36
20	Sheffield U.	42	11	11	20	69:90	33
21	Middlesbrough †	42	10	10	22	60:91	30
22	Liverpool †	42	9	10	23	68:97	28

DIVISION 2 1951-52

1	Sheffield W.*	42	21	11	10	100:66	53
2	Cardiff *	42	20	11	11	72:54	51
3	Birmingham	42	21	9	12	67:56	51
4	Nottingham F.	42	18	13	11	77:62	49
5	Leicester	42	19	9	14	78:64	47
6	Leeds	42	18	11	13	59:57	47
7	Everton	42	17	10	15	64:58	44
8	Luton	42	16	12	14	77:78	44
9	Rotherham	42	17	8	17	73:71	42
10	Brentford	42	15	12	15	54:55	42
11	Sheffield U.	42	18	5	19	90:76	41
12	West Ham	42	15	11	16	67:77	41
13	Southampton	42	15	11	16	61:73	41
14	Blackburn	41	17	6	19	54:63	40
15	Notts Co.	42	16	7	19	71:68	39
16	Doncaster	42	13	12	17	55:60	38
17	Bury	42	15	7	20	57:69	37
18	Hull	42	13	11	18	60:70	37
19	Swansea	42	12	12	18	72:76	36
20	Barnsley	42	11	14	17	59:72	36
21	Coventry †	42	14	6	22	59:82	34
22	QPR †	42	11	12	19	52:81	34

DIVISION 2 1952-53

1	Sheffield U.*	42	25	10	7	97:55	60
2	Huddersfield *	42	24	10	8	84:33	58
3	Luton	42	22	8	12	84:49	52
4	Plymouth	42	20	9	13	65:60	49
5	Leicester	42	18	12	12	89:74	48
6	Birmingham	42	19	10	13	71:66	48
7	Nottingham F.	42	18	8	16	77:67	44
8	Fulham	42	17	10	15	81:71	44
9	Blackburn	42	18	8	16	68:65	44
10	Leeds	42	14	15	13	71:63	43
11	Swansea	42	15	12	15	78:81	42
12	Rotherham	42	16	9	17	75:74	41
13	Doncaster	42	12	16	14	58:64	40
14	West Ham	42	13	13	16	58:60	39
15	Lincoln	42	11	17	14	64:71	39
16	Everton	42	12	14	16	71:75	38
17	Brentford	42	13	11	18	59:76	37
18	Hull	42	14	8	20	57:69	36
19	Notts Co.	42	14	8	20	60:88	36
20	Bury	42	13	9	20	53:81	35
21	Southampton †	42	10	13	19	68:85	33
22	Barnsley †	42	5	8	29	47:108	18

DIVISION 2 1953-54

1	Leicester *	42	23	10	9	97:60	56
2	Everton *	42	20	16	6	92:58	56
3	Blackburn	42	23	9	10	86:50	55
4	Nottingham F.	42	20	12	10	86:59	52
5	Rotherham	42	21	7	14	80:67	49
6	Luton	42	18	12	12	64:59	48
7	Birmingham	42	18	11	13	78:58	47
8	Fulham	42	17	10	15	98:85	44
9	Bristol R.	42	14	16	12	64:58	44
10	Leeds	42	15	13	14	89:81	43
11	Stoke	42	12	17	13	71:60	41
12	Doncaster	42	16	9	17	59:63	41
13	West Ham	42	15	9	18	67:69	39
14	Notts Co.	42	13	13	16	54:74	39
15	Hull	42	16	6	20	64:66	38
16	Lincoln	42	14	9	19	65:83	37
17	Bury	42	11	14	17	54:72	36
18	Derby	42	12	11	19	64:82	35
19	Plymouth	42	9	16	17	65:82	34
20	Swansea	42	13	8	21	58:82	34
21	Brentford †	42	10	11	21	40:78	31
22	Oldham †	42	8	9	25	40:89	25

DIVISION 3N 1951-52

1	Lincoln *	46	30	9	7	121:52	69
2	Grimsby	46	29	8	9	96:45	66
3	Stockport	46	23	13	10	74:40	59
4	Oldham	46	24	9	13	90:61	57
5	Gateshead	46	21	11	14	66:49	53
6	Mansfield	46	22	8	16	73:60	52
7	Carlisle	46	19	13	14	62:57	51
8	Bradford P.A.	46	19	12	15	74:64	50
9	Hartlepools	46	21	8	17	71:65	50
10	York	46	18	13	15	73:52	49
11	Tranmere	46	21	6	19	76:71	48
12	Barrow	46	17	12	17	57:61	46
13	Chesterfield	46	17	11	18	65:66	45
14	Scunthorpe	46	14	16	16	65:74	44
15	Bradford C.	46	16	10	20	61:68	42
16	Crewe	46	17	8	21	63:82	42
17	Southport	46	15	11	20	53:71	41
18	Wrexham	46	15	9	22	63:73	39
19	Chester	46	15	9	22	72:85	39
20	Halifax	46	14	7	25	61:97	35
21	Rochdale	46	11	13	22	47:79	35
22	Accrington	46	10	12	24	61:92	32
23	Darlington	46	11	9	26	64:103	31
24	Workington	46	11	7	28	50:91	29

DIVISION 3N 1952-53

1	Oldham *	46	22	15	9	77:45	59
2	Port Vale	46	20	18	8	67:35	58
3	Wrexham	46	24	8	14	86:66	56
4	York	46	20	13	13	60:45	53
5	Grimsby	46	21	10	15	75:59	52
6	Southport	46	20	11	15	63:60	51
7	Bradford P.A.	46	19	12	15	75:61	50
8	Gateshead	46	17	15	14	76:60	49
9	Carlisle	46	18	13	15	82:68	49
10	Crewe	46	20	8	18	70:68	48
11	Stockport	46	17	13	16	82:69	47
=12	Chesterfield	46	18	11	17	65:63	47
=12	Tranmere	46	21	5	20	65:63	47
14	Halifax	46	16	15	15	68:68	47
15	Scunthorpe	46	16	14	16	62:56	46
16	Bradford C.	46	14	18	14	75:80	46
17	Hartlepools	46	16	14	16	57:61	46
18	Mansfield	46	16	14	16	55:62	46
19	Barrow	46	16	12	18	66:71	44
20	Chester	46	11	15	20	64:85	37
21	Darlington	46	14	6	26	58:96	34
22	Rochdale	46	14	5	27	62:83	33
23	Workington	46	11	10	25	55:91	32
24	Accrington	46	8	11	27	39:89	27

DIVISION 3N 1953-54

1	Port Vale *	46	26	17	3	74:21	69
2	Barnsley	46	24	10	12	77:57	58
3	Scunthorpe	46	21	15	10	77:56	57
4	Gateshead	46	21	13	12	74:55	55
5	Bradford C.	46	22	9	15	60:55	53
6	Chesterfield	46	19	14	13	76:64	52
7	Mansfield	46	20	11	15	88:67	51
8	Wrexham	46	21	9	16	81:68	51
9	Bradford P.A.	46	18	14	14	77:68	50
10	Stockport	46	18	11	17	77:67	47
11	Southport	46	17	12	17	63:60	46
12	Barrow	46	16	12	18	72:71	44
13	Carlisle	46	14	15	17	83:71	43
14	Tranmere	46	18	7	21	59:70	43
15	Accrington	46	16	10	20	66:74	42
16	Crewe	46	14	13	19	49:67	41
17	Grimsby	46	16	9	21	51:77	41
18	Hartlepools	46	13	14	19	59:65	40
19	Rochdale	46	15	10	21	59:77	40
20	Workington	46	13	14	19	59:80	40
21	Darlington	46	12	14	20	50:71	38
22	York	46	12	13	21	64:86	37
23	Halifax	46	12	10	24	44:73	34
24	Chester	46	11	10	25	48:67	32

DIVISION 3S 1951-52

1	Plymouth *	46	29	8	9	107:53	66
2	Reading	46	29	3	14	112:60	61
3	Norwich	46	26	9	11	89:50	61
4	Millwall	46	23	12	11	74:53	58
5	Brighton	46	24	10	12	87:63	58
6	Newport	46	21	12	13	77:76	54
7	Bristol R.	46	20	12	14	89:53	52
8	Northampton	46	22	5	19	93:74	49
9	Southend	46	19	10	17	75:66	48
10	Colchester	46	17	12	17	56:77	46
11	Torquay	46	17	10	19	86:98	44
12	Aldershot	46	18	8	20	78:89	44
13	Port Vale	46	14	15	17	50:66	43
14	Bournemouth	46	16	10	20	69:75	42
15	Bristol C.	46	15	12	19	58:69	42
16	Swindon	46	14	14	18	51:68	42
17	Ipswich	46	16	9	21	53:74	41
18	Leyton Orient	46	16	9	21	55:68	41
19	Crystal Palace	46	15	9	22	61:80	39
20	Shrewsbury	46	13	10	23	62:86	36
21	Watford	46	13	10	23	57:81	36
22	Gillingham	46	11	13	22	71:81	35
23	Exeter	46	13	9	24	65:86	35
24	Walsall	46	13	5	28	55:94	31

DIVISION 3S 1952-53

1	Bristol R.*	46	26	12	8	92:46	64
2	Millwall	46	24	14	8	82:44	62
3	Northampton	46	26	10	10	109:70	62
4	Norwich	46	25	10	11	99:55	60
5	Bristol C.	46	22	15	9	95:61	59
6	Coventry	46	19	12	15	77:62	50
7	Brighton	46	19	12	15	81:75	50
8	Southend	46	18	13	15	69:74	49
9	Bournemouth	46	19	9	18	74:69	47
10	Watford	46	15	17	14	62:63	47
11	Reading	46	19	8	19	69:64	46
12	Torquay	46	18	9	19	87:88	45
13	Crystal Palace	46	15	13	18	66:82	43
14	Leyton Orient	46	16	10	20	68:73	42
15	Newport	46	16	10	20	70:82	42
16	Ipswich	46	13	15	18	60:69	41
17	Exeter	46	13	14	19	61:71	40
18	Swindon	46	14	12	20	64:79	40
19	Aldershot	46	12	15	19	61:77	39
20	QPR	46	12	15	19	61:82	39
21	Gillingham	46	12	15	19	55:74	39
22	Colchester	46	12	14	20	59:76	38
23	Shrewsbury	46	12	12	22	68:91	36
24	Walsall	46	7	10	29	56:118	24

DIVISION 3S 1953-54

1	Ipswich *	46	27	10	9	82:51	64
2	Brighton	46	26	9	11	86:61	61
3	Bristol C.	46	25	6	15	88:68	56
4	Watford	46	21	10	15	85:69	52
5	Northampton	46	20	11	15	82:55	51
6	Southampton	46	22	7	17	76:63	51
7	Norwich	46	20	11	15	73:66	51
8	Reading	46	20	9	17	86:73	49
9	Exeter	46	20	8	18	68:58	48
10	Gillingham	46	19	10	17	61:66	48
11	Leyton Orient	46	18	11	17	79:73	47
12	Millwall	46	19	9	18	74:77	47
13	Torquay	46	17	12	17	81:88	46
14	Coventry	46	18	9	19	61:56	45
15	Newport	46	19	6	21	61:81	44
16	Southend	46	18	7	21	69:71	43
17	Aldershot	46	17	9	20	74:86	43
18	QPR	46	16	10	20	60:68	42
=19	Bournemouth	46	16	8	22	67:70	40
=19	Swindon	46	15	10	21	67:70	40
21	Shrewsbury	46	14	12	20	65:76	40
22	Crystal Palace	46	14	12	20	60:86	40
23	Colchester	46	10	10	26	50:78	30
24	Walsall	46	9	8	29	40:87	26

DIVISION 1 1954-55

1	Chelsea	42	20	12	10	81:57	52
2	Wolverhampton	42	19	10	13	89:70	48
3	Portsmouth	42	18	12	12	74:62	48
4	Sunderland	42	15	18	9	64:54	48
5	Manchester U.	42	20	7	15	84:74	47
6	Aston Villa	42	20	7	15	72:73	47
7	Manchester C.	42	18	10	14	76:69	46
8	Newcastle	42	17	9	16	89:77	43
9	Arsenal	42	17	9	16	69:63	43
10	Burnley	42	17	9	16	51:48	43
11	Everton	42	16	10	16	62:68	42
12	Huddersfield	42	14	13	15	63:68	41
13	Sheffield U.	42	17	7	18	70:86	41
14	Preston	42	16	8	18	83:64	40
15	Charlton	42	15	10	17	76:75	40
16	Tottenham	42	16	8	18	72:73	40
17	West Bromwich	42	16	8	18	76:96	40
18	Bolton	42	13	13	16	62:69	39
19	Blackpool	42	14	10	18	60:64	38
20	Cardiff	42	13	11	18	62:76	37
21	Leicester †	42	12	11	19	74:86	35
22	Sheffield W. †	42	8	10	24	63:100	26

DIVISION 2 1954-55

1	Birmingham *	42	22	10	10	92:47	54
2	Luton *	42	23	8	11	88:53	54
3	Rotherham	42	25	4	13	94:64	54
4	Leeds	42	23	7	12	70:53	53
5	Stoke	42	21	10	11	69:46	52
6	Blackburn	42	22	6	14	114:79	50
7	Notts Co.	42	21	6	15	74:71	48
8	West Ham	42	18	10	14	74:70	46
9	Bristol R.	42	19	7	16	75:70	45
10	Swansea	42	17	9	16	86:83	43
11	Liverpool	42	16	10	16	92:96	42
12	Middlesbrough	42	18	6	18	73:82	42
13	Bury	42	15	11	16	77:72	41
14	Fulham	42	14	11	17	76:79	39
15	Nottingham F.	42	16	7	19	58:62	39
16	Lincoln	42	13	10	19	68:79	36
17	Port Vale	42	12	11	19	48:71	35
18	Doncaster	42	14	7	21	58:95	35
19	Hull	42	12	10	20	44:69	34
20	Plymouth	42	12	7	23	57:82	31
21	Ipswich †	42	11	6	25	57:92	28
22	Derby †	42	7	9	26	53:82	23

DIVISION 3N 1954-55

1	Barnsley *	46	30	5	11	86:46	65
2	Accrington	46	25	11	10	96:67	61
3	Scunthorpe	46	23	12	11	81:53	58
4	York	46	24	10	12	92:63	58
5	Hartlepools	46	25	5	16	64:49	55
6	Chesterfield	46	24	6	16	81:70	54
7	Gateshead	46	20	12	14	65:69	52
8	Workington	46	18	14	14	68:55	50
9	Stockport	46	18	12	16	84:70	48
10	Oldham	46	19	10	17	74:68	48
11	Southport	46	16	16	14	47:44	48
12	Rochdale	46	17	14	15	69:66	48
13	Mansfield	46	18	9	19	65:71	45
14	Halifax	46	15	13	18	63:67	43
15	Darlington	46	14	14	18	62:73	42
16	Bradford P.A.	46	15	11	20	56:70	41
17	Barrow	46	17	6	23	70:89	40
18	Wrexham	46	13	12	21	65:77	38
19	Tranmere	46	13	11	22	55:70	37
20	Carlisle	46	15	6	25	78:89	36
21	Bradford C.	46	13	10	23	47:55	36
22	Crewe	46	10	14	22	68:91	34
23	Grimsby	46	13	8	25	47:78	34
24	Chester	46	12	9	25	44:77	33

DIVISION 3S 1954-55

1	Bristol C.*	46	30	10	6	101:47	70
2	Leyton Orient	46	26	9	11	89:47	61
3	Southampton	46	24	11	11	75:51	59
4	Gillingham	46	20	15	11	77:66	55
5	Millwall	46	20	11	15	72:68	51
6	Brighton	46	20	10	16	76:63	50
7	Watford	46	18	14	14	71:62	50
8	Torquay	46	18	12	16	82:82	48
9	Coventry	46	18	11	17	67:59	47
10	Southend	46	17	12	17	83:80	46
=11	Brentford	46	16	14	16	82:82	46
=11	Norwich	46	18	10	18	60:60	46
13	Northampton	46	19	8	19	73:81	46
14	Aldershot	46	16	13	17	75:71	45
15	QPR	46	15	14	17	69:75	44
16	Shrewsbury	46	16	10	20	70:78	42
17	Bournemouth	46	12	18	16	57:65	42
18	Reading	46	13	15	18	65:73	41
19	Newport	46	11	16	19	60:73	38
20	Crystal Palace	46	11	16	19	52:80	38
21	Swindon	46	11	15	20	46:64	37
22	Exeter	46	11	15	20	47:73	37
23	Walsall	46	10	14	22	75:86	34
24	Colchester	46	9	13	24	53:91	31

DIVISION 1 1955-56

1	Manchester U.	42	25	10	7	83:51	60
2	Blackpool	42	20	9	13	86:62	49
3	Wolverhampton	42	20	9	13	89:65	49
4	Manchester C.	42	18	10	14	82:69	46
5	Arsenal	42	18	10	14	60:61	46
6	Birmingham	42	18	9	15	75:57	45
7	Burnley	42	18	8	16	64:54	44
8	Bolton	42	18	7	17	71:58	43
9	Sunderland	42	17	9	16	80:95	43
10	Luton	42	17	8	17	66:64	42
11	Newcastle	42	17	7	18	85:70	41
12	Portsmouth	42	16	9	17	78:85	41
13	West Bromwich	42	18	5	19	58:70	41
14	Charlton	42	17	6	19	75:81	40
15	Everton	42	15	10	17	55:69	40
16	Chelsea	42	14	11	17	64:77	39
17	Cardiff	42	15	9	18	55:69	39
18	Tottenham	42	15	7	20	61:71	37
19	Preston	42	14	8	20	73:72	36
20	Aston Villa	42	11	13	18	52:69	35
21	Huddersfield †	42	14	7	21	54:83	35
22	Sheffield U. †	42	12	9	21	63:77	33

DIVISION 2 1955-56

1	Sheffield W.*	42	21	13	8	101:62	55
2	Leeds *	42	23	6	13	80:60	52
3	Liverpool	42	21	6	15	85:63	48
4	Blackburn	42	21	6	15	84:65	48
5	Leicester	42	21	6	15	94:78	48
6	Bristol R.	42	21	6	15	84:70	48
7	Nottingham F.	42	19	9	14	68:63	47
8	Lincoln	42	18	10	14	79:65	46
9	Fulham	42	20	6	16	89:79	46
10	Swansea	42	20	6	16	83:81	46
11	Bristol C.	42	19	7	16	80:64	45
12	Port Vale	42	16	13	13	60:58	45
13	Stoke	42	20	4	18	71:62	44
14	Middlesbrough	42	16	8	18	76:78	40
15	Bury	42	16	8	18	86:90	40
16	West Ham	42	14	11	17	74:69	39
17	Doncaster	42	12	11	19	69:96	35
18	Barnsley	42	11	12	19	47:84	34
19	Rotherham	42	12	9	21	56:75	33
20	Notts Co.	42	11	9	22	55:82	31
21	Plymouth †	42	10	8	24	54:87	28
22	Hull †	42	10	6	26	53:97	26

DIVISION 3N 1955-56

1	Grimsby *	46	31	6	9	76:29	68
2	Derby	46	28	7	11	110:55	63
3	Accrington	46	25	9	12	92:57	59
4	Hartlepools	46	26	5	15	81:60	57
5	Southport	46	23	11	12	66:53	57
6	Chesterfield	46	25	4	17	94:66	54
7	Stockport	46	21	9	16	90:61	51
8	Bradford C.	46	18	13	15	78:64	49
9	Scunthorpe	46	20	8	18	75:63	48
10	Workington	46	19	9	18	75:63	47
11	York	46	19	9	18	85:72	47
12	Rochdale	46	17	13	16	66:84	47
13	Gateshead	46	17	11	18	77:84	45
14	Wrexham	46	16	10	20	66:73	42
15	Darlington	46	16	9	21	60:73	41
16	Tranmere	46	16	9	21	59:84	41
17	Chester	46	13	14	19	52:82	40
18	Mansfield	46	14	11	21	84:81	39
19	Halifax	46	14	11	21	66:76	39
20	Oldham	46	10	18	18	76:86	38
21	Carlisle	46	15	8	23	71:95	38
22	Barrow	46	12	9	25	61:83	33
23	Bradford P.A.	46	13	7	26	61:122	33
24	Crewe	46	9	10	27	50:105	28

DIVISION 3S 1955-56

1	Leyton Orient *	46	29	8	9	106:49	66
2	Brighton	46	29	7	10	112:50	65
3	Ipswich	46	25	14	7	106:60	64
4	Southend	46	21	11	14	88:80	53
5	Torquay	46	20	12	14	86:63	52
6	Brentford	46	19	14	13	69:66	52
7	Norwich	46	19	13	14	86:82	51
8	Coventry	46	20	9	17	73:60	49
9	Bournemouth	46	19	10	17	63:51	48
10	Gillingham	46	19	10	17	69:71	48
11	Northampton	46	20	7	19	67:71	47
12	Colchester	46	18	11	17	76:81	47
13	Shrewsbury	46	17	12	17	69:66	46
14	Southampton	46	18	8	20	91:81	44
15	Aldershot	46	12	16	18	70:90	40
16	Exeter	46	15	10	21	58:77	40
17	Reading	46	15	9	22	70:79	39
18	QPR	46	14	11	21	64:86	39
19	Newport	46	15	9	22	58:79	39
20	Walsall	46	15	8	23	68:84	38
21	Watford	46	13	11	22	52:85	37
22	Millwall	46	15	6	25	83:100	36
23	Crystal Palace	46	12	10	24	54:83	34
24	Swindon	46	8	14	24	34:78	30

DIVISION 1 1956-57

1	Manchester U.	42	28	8	6	103:54	64
2	Tottenham	42	22	12	8	104:56	56
3	Preston	42	23	10	9	84:56	56
4	Blackpool	42	22	9	11	93:65	53
5	Arsenal	42	21	8	13	85:69	50
6	Wolverhampton	42	20	8	14	94:70	48
7	Burnley	42	18	10	14	56:50	46
8	Leeds	42	15	14	13	72:63	44
9	Bolton	42	16	12	14	65:65	44
10	Aston Villa	42	14	15	13	65:55	43
11	West Bromwich	42	14	14	14	59:61	42
=12	Birmingham	42	15	9	18	69:69	39
=12	Chelsea	42	13	13	16	73:73	39
14	Sheffield W.	42	16	6	20	82:88	38
15	Everton	42	14	10	18	61:79	38
16	Luton	42	14	9	19	58:76	37
17	Newcastle	42	14	8	20	67:87	36
18	Manchester C.	42	13	9	20	78:88	35
19	Portsmouth	42	10	13	19	62:92	33
20	Sunderland	42	12	8	22	67:88	32
21	Cardiff †	42	10	9	23	53:88	29
22	Charlton †	42	9	4	29	62:120	22

DIVISION 2 1956-57

1	Leicester *	42	25	11	6	109:67	61
2	Nottingham F *	42	22	10	10	94:55	54
3	Liverpool	42	21	11	10	82:54	53
4	Blackburn	42	21	10	11	83:75	52
5	Stoke	42	20	8	14	83:58	48
6	Middlesbrough	42	19	10	13	84:60	48
7	Sheffield U.	42	19	8	15	87:76	46
8	West Ham	42	19	8	15	59:63	46
9	Bristol R.	42	18	9	15	81:67	45
10	Swansea	42	19	7	16	90:90	45
11	Fulham	42	19	4	19	84:76	42
12	Huddersfield	42	18	6	18	68:74	42
13	Bristol C.	42	16	9	17	74:79	41
14	Doncaster	42	15	10	17	77:77	40
15	Leyton Orient	42	15	10	17	66:84	40
16	Grimsby	42	17	5	20	61:62	39
17	Rotherham	42	13	11	18	74:75	37
18	Lincoln	42	14	6	22	54:80	34
19	Barnsley	42	12	10	20	59:89	34
20	Notts Co.	42	9	12	21	58:86	30
21	Bury †	42	8	9	25	60:96	25
22	Port Vale †	42	8	6	28	57:101	22

DIVISION 3N 1956-57

1	Derby *	46	26	11	9	111:53	63
2	Hartlepools	46	25	9	12	90:63	59
3	Accrington	46	25	8	13	95:64	58
4	Workington	46	24	10	12	93:63	58
5	Stockport	46	23	8	15	91:75	54
6	Chesterfield	46	22	9	15	96:79	53
7	York	46	21	10	15	75:61	52
8	Hull	46	21	10	15	84:69	52
9	Bradford C.	46	22	8	16	78:68	52
10	Barrow	46	21	9	16	76:62	51
11	Halifax	46	21	7	18	65:70	49
12	Wrexham	46	19	10	17	97:74	48
13	Rochdale	46	18	12	16	65:65	48
14	Scunthorpe	46	15	15	16	71:69	45
15	Carlisle	46	16	13	17	76:85	45
16	Mansfield	46	17	10	19	91:90	44
17	Gateshead	46	17	10	19	72:90	44
18	Darlington	46	17	8	21	82:95	42
19	Oldham	46	12	15	19	66:74	39
20	Bradford P.A.	46	16	3	27	66:93	35
21	Chester	46	10	13	23	55:84	33
22	Southport	46	10	12	24	52:94	32
23	Tranmere	46	7	13	26	51:91	27
24	Crewe	46	6	9	31	43:110	21

DIVISION 3S 1956-57

1	Ipswich *	46	25	9	12	101:54	59
2	Torquay	46	24	11	11	89:64	59
3	Colchester	46	22	14	10	84:56	58
4	Southampton	46	22	10	14	76:52	54
5	Bournemouth	46	19	14	13	88:62	52
6	Brighton	46	19	14	13	86:65	52
7	Southend	46	18	12	16	73:65	48
8	Brentford	46	16	16	14	78:76	48
9	Shrewsbury	46	15	18	13	72:79	48
10	QPR	46	18	11	17	61:60	47
11	Watford	46	18	10	18	72:75	46
12	Newport	46	16	13	17	65:62	45
13	Reading	46	18	9	19	80:81	45
14	Northampton	46	18	9	19	66:73	45
15	Walsall	46	16	12	18	80:74	44
16	Coventry	46	16	12	18	74:84	44
17	Millwall	46	16	12	18	64:84	44
18	Plymouth	46	16	11	19	68:73	43
19	Aldershot	46	15	12	19	79:92	42
20	Crystal Palace	46	11	18	17	62:75	40
21	Exeter	46	12	13	21	61:79	37
22	Gillingham	46	12	13	21	54:85	37
23	Swindon	46	15	6	25	66:96	36
24	Norwich	46	8	15	23	61:94	31

DIVISION 1 1957-58

1	Wolverhampton	42	28	8	6	103:47	64
2	Preston	42	26	7	9	100:51	59
3	Tottenham	42	21	9	12	93:77	51
4	West Bromwich	42	18	14	10	92:70	50
5	Manchester C.	42	22	5	15	104:100	49
6	Burnley	42	21	5	16	80:74	47
7	Blackpool	42	19	6	17	80:67	44
8	Luton	42	19	6	17	69:63	44
9	Manchester U.	42	16	11	15	85:75	43
10	Nottingham F.	42	16	10	16	69:63	42
11	Chelsea	42	15	12	15	83:79	42
12	Arsenal	42	16	7	19	73:85	39
13	Birmingham	42	14	11	17	76:89	39
14	Aston Villa	42	16	7	19	73:86	39
15	Bolton	42	14	10	18	65:87	38
16	Everton	42	13	11	18	65:75	37
17	Leeds	42	14	9	19	51:63	37
18	Leicester	42	14	5	23	91:112	33
19	Newcastle	42	12	8	22	73:81	32
20	Portsmouth	42	12	8	22	73:88	32
21	Sunderland†	42	10	12	20	54:97	32
22	Sheffield W.†	42	12	7	23	69:92	31

DIVISION 2 1957-58

1	West Ham*	42	23	11	8	101:54	57
2	Blackburn*	42	22	12	8	93:57	56
3	Charlton	42	24	7	11	107:69	55
4	Liverpool	42	22	10	10	79:54	54
5	Fulham	42	20	12	10	97:59	52
6	Sheffield U.	42	21	10	11	75:50	52
7	Middlesbrough	42	19	7	16	83:74	45
8	Ipswich	42	16	12	14	68:69	44
9	Huddersfield	42	14	16	12	63:66	44
10	Bristol R.	42	17	8	17	85:80	42
11	Stoke	42	18	6	18	75:73	42
12	Leyton Orient	42	18	5	19	77:79	41
13	Grimsby	42	17	6	19	86:83	40
14	Barnsley	42	14	12	16	70:74	40
15	Cardiff	42	14	9	19	63:77	37
16	Derby	42	14	8	20	60:81	36
17	Bristol C.	42	13	9	20	63:88	35
18	Rotherham	42	14	5	23	65:101	33
19	Swansea	42	11	9	22	72:99	31
20	Lincoln	42	11	9	22	55:82	31
21	Notts Co.†	42	12	6	24	44:80	30
22	Doncaster†	42	8	11	23	56:88	27

DIVISION 3N ‡ 1957-58

1	Scunthorpe*	46	29	8	9	88:50	66
2	Accrington	46	25	9	12	83:61	59
3	Bradford C.	46	21	15	10	73:49	57
4	Bury	46	23	10	13	94:62	56
5	Hull	46	19	15	12	78:67	53
6	Mansfield	46	22	8	16	100:92	52
7	Halifax	46	20	11	15	83:69	51
8	Chesterfield	46	18	15	13	71:69	51
9	Stockport	46	18	11	17	74:67	47
10	Rochdale	46	19	8	19	79:67	46
11	Tranmere	46	18	10	18	82:76	46
12	Wrexham	46	17	12	17	61:63	46
13	York†	46	17	12	17	68:76	46
14	Gateshead†	46	15	15	16	68:76	45
15	Oldham†	46	14	17	15	72:84	45
16	Carlisle†	46	19	6	21	80:78	44
17	Hartlepools†	46	16	12	18	73:76	44
18	Barrow†	46	13	15	18	66:74	41
19	Workington†	46	14	13	19	72:81	41
20	Darlington†	46	17	7	22	78:89	41
21	Chester†	46	13	13	20	73:81	39
22	Bradford P.A.†	46	13	11	22	68:95	37
23	Southport†	46	11	6	29	52:88	28
24	Crewe†	46	8	7	31	47:93	23

DIVISION 3S ‡ 1957-58

1	Brighton*	46	24	12	10	88:64	60
2	Brentford	46	24	10	12	82:56	58
3	Plymouth	46	25	8	13	67:48	58
4	Swindon	46	21	15	10	79:50	57
5	Reading	46	21	13	12	79:51	55
6	Southampton	46	22	10	14	112:72	54
7	Southend	46	21	12	13	90:58	54
8	Norwich	46	19	15	12	75:70	53
9	Bournemouth	46	21	9	16	81:74	51
10	QPR	46	18	14	14	64:65	50
11	Newport	46	17	14	15	73:67	48
12	Colchester	46	17	13	16	77:79	47
13	Northampton†	46	19	6	21	87:79	44
14	Crystal Palace†	46	15	13	18	70:72	43
15	Port Vale†	46	16	10	20	67:58	42
16	Watford†	46	13	16	17	59:77	42
17	Shrewsbury†	46	15	10	21	49:71	40
18	Aldershot†	46	12	16	18	59:89	40
19	Coventry†	46	13	13	20	61:81	39
20	Walsall†	46	14	9	23	61:75	37
21	Torquay†	46	11	13	22	49:74	35
22	Gillingham†	46	13	9	24	52:81	35
23	Millwall†	46	11	9	26	63:91	31
24	Exeter†	46	11	9	26	57:99	31

DIVISION 1 1958-59

1	Wolverhampton	42	28	5	9	110:49	61
2	Manchester U.	42	24	7	11	103:66	55
3	Arsenal	42	21	8	13	88:68	50
4	Bolton	42	20	10	12	79:66	50
5	West Bromwich	42	18	13	11	88:68	49
6	West Ham	42	21	6	15	85:70	48
7	Burnley	42	19	10	13	81:70	48
8	Blackpool	42	18	11	13	66:49	47
9	Birmingham	42	20	6	16	84:68	46
10	Blackburn	42	17	10	15	76:70	44
11	Newcastle	42	17	7	18	80:80	41
12	Preston	42	17	7	18	70:77	41
13	Nottingham F.	42	17	6	19	71:74	40
14	Chelsea	42	18	4	20	77:98	40
15	Leeds	42	15	9	18	57:74	39
16	Everton	42	17	4	21	71:87	38
17	Luton	42	12	13	17	68:71	37
18	Tottenham	42	13	10	19	85:95	36
19	Leicester	42	11	10	21	67:98	32
20	Manchester C.	42	11	9	22	64:95	31
21	Aston Villa†	42	11	8	23	58:87	30
22	Portsmouth†	42	6	9	27	64:112	21

DIVISION 2 1958-59

1	Sheffield W.*	42	28	6	8	106:48	62
2	Fulham*	42	27	6	9	96:61	60
3	Sheffield U.	42	23	7	12	82:48	53
4	Liverpool	42	24	5	13	87:62	53
5	Stoke	42	21	7	14	72:58	49
6	Bristol R.	42	18	12	12	80:64	48
7	Derby	42	20	8	14	74:71	48
8	Charlton	42	18	7	17	92:90	43
9	Cardiff	42	18	7	17	65:65	43
10	Bristol C.	42	17	7	18	74:70	41
11	Swansea	42	16	9	17	79:81	41
12	Brighton	42	15	11	16	74:90	41
13	Middlesbrough	42	15	10	17	87:71	40
14	Huddersfield	42	16	8	18	62:55	40
15	Sunderland	42	16	8	18	64:75	40
16	Ipswich	42	17	6	19	62:77	40
17	Leyton Orient	42	14	8	20	71:78	36
18	Scunthorpe	42	12	9	21	55:84	33
19	Lincoln	42	11	7	24	63:93	29
20	Rotherham	42	10	9	23	42:82	29
21	Grimsby†	42	9	10	23	62:90	28
22	Barnsley†	42	10	7	25	55:91	27

DIVISION 3 1958-59

1	Plymouth*	46	23	16	7	89:59	62
2	Hull*	46	26	9	11	90:55	61
3	Brentford	46	21	15	10	76:49	57
4	Norwich	46	22	13	11	89:62	57
5	Colchester	46	21	10	15	71:67	52
6	Reading	46	21	8	17	78:63	50
7	Tranmere	46	21	8	17	82:67	50
8	Southend	46	21	8	17	85:80	50
9	Halifax	46	21	8	17	80:77	50
10	Bury	46	17	14	15	69:58	48
11	Bradford C.	46	18	11	17	84:76	47
12	Bournemouth	46	17	12	17	69:69	46
13	QPR	46	19	8	19	74:77	46
14	Southampton	46	17	11	18	88:80	45
15	Swindon	46	16	13	17	59:57	45
16	Chesterfield	46	17	10	19	67:64	44
17	Newport	46	17	9	20	69:68	43
18	Wrexham	46	14	14	18	63:77	42
19	Accrington	46	15	12	19	71:87	42
20	Mansfield	46	14	13	19	73:98	41
21	Stockport†	46	13	10	23	65:78	36
22	Doncaster†	46	14	5	27	50:90	33
23	Notts Co.†	46	8	13	25	55:96	29
24	Rochdale†	46	8	12	26	37:79	28

DIVISION 4 1958-59

1	Port Vale*	46	26	12	81	10:58	64
2	Coventry*	46	24	12	10	84:47	60
3	York*	46	21	18	7	73:52	60
4	Shrewsbury*	46	24	10	12	101:63	58
5	Exeter	46	23	11	12	87:61	57
6	Walsall	46	21	10	15	95:64	52
7	Crystal Palace	46	20	12	14	90:71	52
8	Northampton	46	21	9	16	85:78	51
9	Millwall	46	20	10	16	76:69	50
10	Carlisle	46	19	12	15	62:65	50
11	Gillingham	46	20	9	17	82:77	49
12	Torquay	46	16	12	18	78:77	44
13	Chester	46	16	12	18	72:84	44
14	Bradford P.A.	46	18	7	21	75:77	43
15	Watford	46	16	10	20	81:79	42
16	Darlington	46	13	16	17	66:68	42
17	Workington	46	12	17	17	63:78	41
18	Crewe	46	15	10	21	70:82	40
19	Hartlepools	46	15	10	21	74:88	40
20	Gateshead	46	16	8	22	56:85	40
21	Oldham	46	16	4	26	59:84	36
22	Aldershot	46	14	7	25	63:97	35
23	Barrow	46	9	10	27	51:104	28
24	Southport	46	7	12	27	41:86	26

DIVISION 1 1959-60

1	Burnley	42	24	7	11	85:61	55
2	Wolverhampton	42	24	6	12	106:67	54
3	Tottenham	42	21	11	10	86:50	53
4	West Bromwich	42	19	11	12	83:57	49
5	Sheffield W.	42	19	11	12	80:59	49
6	Bolton	42	20	8	14	59:51	48
7	Manchester U.	42	19	7	16	102:80	45
8	Newcastle	42	18	8	16	82:78	44
9	Preston	42	16	12	14	79:76	44
10	Fulham	42	17	10	15	73:80	44
11	Blackpool	42	15	10	17	59:71	40
12	Leicester	42	13	13	16	66:75	39
13	Arsenal	42	15	9	18	68:80	39
14	West Ham	42	16	6	20	75:91	38
15	Everton	42	13	11	18	73:78	37
16	Manchester C.	42	17	3	22	78:84	37
17	Blackburn	42	16	5	21	60:70	37
18	Chelsea	42	14	9	19	76:91	37
19	Birmingham	42	13	10	19	63:80	36
20	Nottingham F.	42	13	9	20	50:74	35
21	Leeds†	42	12	10	20	65:92	34
22	Luton†	42	9	12	21	50:73	30

DIVISION 2 1959-60

1	Aston Villa*	42	25	9	8	89:43	59
2	Cardiff*	42	23	12	7	90:62	58
3	Liverpool	42	20	10	12	90:66	50
4	Sheffield U.	42	19	12	11	68:51	50
5	Middlesbrough	42	19	10	13	90:64	48
6	Huddersfield	42	19	9	14	73:52	47
7	Charlton	42	17	13	12	90:87	47
8	Rotherham	42	17	13	12	61:60	47
9	Bristol R.	42	18	11	13	72:78	47
10	Leyton Orient	42	15	14	13	76:61	44
11	Ipswich	42	19	6	17	78:68	44
12	Swansea	42	15	10	17	82:84	40
13	Lincoln	42	16	7	19	75:78	39
14	Brighton	42	13	12	17	67:76	38
15	Scunthorpe	42	13	10	19	57:71	36
16	Sunderland	42	12	12	18	52:65	36
17	Stoke	42	14	7	21	66:83	35
18	Derby	42	14	7	21	61:77	35
19	Plymouth	42	13	9	20	61:89	35
20	Portsmouth	42	10	12	20	59:77	32
21	Hull†	42	10	10	22	48:76	30
22	Bristol C.†	42	11	5	26	60:97	27

DIVISION 3 1959-60

1	Southampton*	46	26	9	11	106:75	61
2	Norwich*	46	24	11	11	82:54	59
3	Shrewsbury	46	18	16	12	97:75	52
4	Grimsby	46	18	16	12	87:70	52
5	Coventry	46	21	10	15	78:63	52
6	Brentford	46	21	9	16	78:61	51
7	Bury	46	21	9	16	64:51	51
8	QPR	46	18	13	15	73:54	49
9	Colchester	46	18	11	17	83:74	47
10	Bournemouth	46	17	13	16	72:72	47
11	Reading	46	18	10	18	84:77	46
12	Southend	46	19	8	19	76:74	46
=13	Newport	46	20	6	20	80:79	46
=13	Port Vale	46	19	8	19	80:79	46
15	Halifax	46	18	10	18	70:72	46
16	Swindon	46	19	8	19	69:78	46
17	Barnsley	46	15	14	17	65:66	44
18	Chesterfield	46	18	7	21	71:84	43
19	Bradford C.	46	15	12	19	66:74	42
20	Tranmere	46	14	13	19	72:75	41
21	York†	46	13	12	21	57:73	38
22	Mansfield†	46	15	6	25	81:112	36
23	Wrexham†	46	14	8	24	68:101	36
24	Accrington†	46	11	5	30	57:123	27

DIVISION 4 1959-60

1	Walsall*	46	28	9	9	102:60	65
2	Notts Co.*	46	26	8	12	107:69	60
3	Torquay*	46	26	8	12	84:58	60
4	Watford*	46	24	9	13	92:67	57
5	Millwall	46	18	17	11	84:61	53
6	Northampton	46	22	9	15	85:63	53
7	Gillingham	46	21	10	15	74:69	52
8	Crystal Palace	46	19	12	15	84:64	50
9	Exeter	46	19	11	16	80:70	49
10	Stockport	46	19	11	16	58:54	49
11	Bradford P.A.	46	17	15	14	70:68	49
12	Rochdale	46	18	10	18	65:60	46
13	Aldershot	46	18	9	19	77:74	45
14	Crewe	46	18	9	19	79:88	45
15	Darlington	46	17	9	20	63:73	43
16	Workington	46	14	14	18	68:60	42
17	Doncaster	46	16	10	20	69:76	42
18	Barrow	46	15	11	20	77:87	41
19	Carlisle	46	15	11	20	51:66	41
20	Chester	46	14	12	20	59:77	40
21	Southport	46	10	14	22	48:92	34
22	Gateshead	46	12	9	25	58:86	33
23	Oldham	46	8	12	26	41:83	28
24	Hartlepools	46	10	7	29	59:109	27

‡the lower 12 clubs of Division 3N & 3S formed the new Division 4; clubs 2-12, plus the relegated clubs from Division 2, formed the revived Division 3

DIVISION 1 1960-61

1	Tottenham	42	31	4	7	115:55	66
2	Sheffield W.	42	23	12	7	78:47	58
3	Wolverhampton	42	25	7	10	103:75	57
4	Burnley	42	22	7	13	102:77	51
5	Everton	42	22	6	14	87:69	50
6	Leicester	42	18	9	15	87:70	45
7	Manchester U.	42	18	9	15	88:76	45
8	Blackburn	42	15	13	14	77:76	43
9	Aston Villa	42	17	9	16	78:77	43
10	West Bromwich	42	18	5	19	67:71	41
11	Arsenal	42	15	11	16	77:85	41
12	Chelsea	42	15	7	20	98:100	37
13	Manchester C.	42	13	11	18	79:90	37
14	Nottingham F.	42	14	9	19	62:78	37
15	Cardiff	42	13	11	18	60:85	37
16	West Ham	42	13	10	19	77:88	36
17	Fulham	42	14	8	20	72:95	36
18	Bolton	42	12	11	19	58:73	35
19	Birmingham	42	14	6	22	62:84	34
20	Blackpool	42	12	9	21	68:73	33
21	Newcastle†	42	11	10	21	86:109	32
22	Preston†	42	10	10	22	43:71	30

DIVISION 2 1960-61

1	Ipswich*	42	26	7	9	100:55	59
2	Sheffield U.*	42	26	6	10	81:51	58
3	Liverpool	42	21	10	11	87:58	52
4	Norwich	42	20	9	13	70:53	49
5	Middlesbrough	42	18	12	12	83:74	48
6	Sunderland	42	17	13	12	75:60	47
7	Swansea	42	18	11	13	77:73	47
8	Southampton	42	18	8	16	84:81	44
9	Scunthorpe	42	14	15	13	69:64	43
10	Charlton	42	16	11	15	97:91	43
11	Plymouth	42	17	8	17	81:82	42
12	Derby	42	15	10	17	80:80	40
13	Luton	42	15	9	18	71:79	39
14	Leeds	42	14	10	18	75:83	38
15	Rotherham	42	12	13	17	65:64	37
16	Brighton	42	14	9	19	61:75	37
17	Bristol R.	42	15	7	20	73:92	37
18	Stoke	42	12	12	18	51:59	36
19	Leyton Orient	42	14	8	20	55:78	36
20	Huddersfield	42	13	9	20	62:71	35
21	Portsmouth†	42	11	11	20	64:91	33
22	Lincoln†	42	8	8	26	48:95	24

DIVISION 3 1960-61

1	Bury*	46	30	8	8	108:45	68
2	Walsall*	46	28	6	12	98:60	62
3	QPR	46	25	10	11	93:60	60
4	Watford	46	20	12	14	85:72	52
5	Notts Co.	46	21	9	16	82:77	51
6	Grimsby	46	20	10	16	77:69	50
7	Port Vale	46	17	15	14	96:79	49
8	Barnsley	46	21	7	18	83:80	49
9	Halifax	46	16	17	13	71:78	49
10	Shrewsbury	46	15	16	15	83:75	46
11	Hull	46	17	12	17	73:73	46
12	Torquay	46	14	17	15	75:83	45
13	Newport	46	17	11	18	81:90	45
14	Bristol C.	46	17	10	19	70:68	44
15	Coventry	46	16	12	18	80:83	44
16	Swindon	46	14	15	17	62:55	43
17	Brentford	46	13	17	16	56:70	43
18	Reading	46	14	12	20	72:83	40
19	Bournemouth	46	15	10	21	58:76	40
20	Southend	46	14	11	21	60:76	39
21	Tranmere†	46	15	8	23	79:115	38
22	Bradford C.†	46	11	14	21	65:87	36
23	Colchester†	46	11	11	24	68:101	33
24	Chesterfield†	46	10	12	24	67:87	32

DIVISION 4 1960-61

1	Peterborough*	46	28	10	8	134:65	66
2	Crystal Palace*	46	29	6	11	110:69	64
3	Northampton*	46	25	10	11	90:62	60
4	Bradford P.A.*	46	26	8	12	84:74	60
5	York	46	21	9	16	80:60	51
6	Millwall	46	21	8	17	97:86	50
7	Darlington	46	18	13	15	78:70	49
8	Workington	46	21	7	18	74:76	49
9	Crewe	46	20	9	17	61:67	49
10	Aldershot	46	18	9	19	79:69	45
11	Doncaster	46	19	7	20	76:78	45
12	Oldham	46	19	7	20	79:88	45
13	Stockport	46	18	9	19	57:66	45
14	Southport	46	19	6	21	69:67	44
15	Gillingham	46	15	13	18	64:66	43
16	Wrexham	46	17	8	21	62:56	42
17	Rochdale	46	17	8	21	60:66	42
18	Accrington	46	16	8	22	74:88	40
19	Carlisle	46	13	13	20	61:79	39
20	Mansfield	46	16	6	24	71:78	38
21	Exeter	46	14	10	22	66:94	38
22	Barrow	46	13	11	22	52:79	37
23	Hartlepools	46	12	8	26	71:103	32
24	Chester	46	11	9	26	61:104	31

DIVISION 1 1961-62

1	Ipswich	42	24	8	10	93:67	56
2	Burnley	42	21	11	10	101:67	53
3	Tottenham	42	21	10	11	88:69	52
4	Everton	42	20	11	11	88:54	51
5	Sheffield U.	42	19	9	14	61:69	47
6	Sheffield W.	42	20	6	16	72:58	46
7	Aston Villa	42	18	8	16	65:56	44
8	West Ham	42	17	10	15	76:82	44
9	West Bromwich	42	15	13	14	83:67	43
10	Arsenal	42	16	11	15	71:72	43
11	Bolton	42	16	10	16	62:66	42
12	Manchester C.	42	17	7	18	78:81	41
13	Blackpool	42	15	11	16	70:75	41
14	Leicester	42	17	6	19	72:71	40
15	Manchester U.	42	15	9	18	72:75	39
16	Blackburn	42	14	11	17	50:58	39
17	Birmingham	42	14	10	18	65:81	38
18	Wolverhampton	42	13	10	19	73:86	36
19	Nottingham F.	42	13	10	19	63:79	36
20	Fulham	42	13	7	22	66:74	33
21	Cardiff†	42	9	14	19	50:81	32
22	Chelsea†	42	9	10	23	63:94	28

DIVISION 2 1961-62

1	Liverpool*	42	27	8	7	99:43	62
2	Leyton Orient*	42	22	10	10	69:40	54
3	Sunderland	42	22	9	11	85:50	53
4	Scunthorpe	42	21	7	14	86:71	49
5	Plymouth	42	19	8	15	75:75	46
6	Southampton	42	18	9	15	77:62	45
7	Huddersfield	42	16	12	14	67:59	44
8	Stoke	42	17	8	17	55:57	42
9	Rotherham	42	16	9	17	70:76	41
10	Preston	42	15	10	17	55:57	40
11	Newcastle	42	15	9	18	64:58	39
12	Middlesbrough	42	16	7	19	76:72	39
13	Luton	42	17	5	20	69:71	39
14	Walsall	42	14	11	17	70:75	39
15	Charlton	42	15	9	18	69:75	39
16	Derby	42	14	11	17	68:75	39
17	Norwich	42	14	11	17	61:70	39
18	Bury	42	17	5	20	52:76	39
19	Leeds	42	12	12	18	50:61	36
20	Swansea	42	12	12	18	61:83	36
21	Bristol R.†	42	13	7	22	53:81	33
22	Brighton†	42	10	11	21	42:86	31

DIVISION 3 1961-62

1	Portsmouth*	46	27	11	8	87:47	65
2	Grimsby*	46	28	6	12	80:56	62
3	Bournemouth	46	21	17	8	69:45	59
4	QPR	46	24	11	11	111:73	59
5	Peterborough	46	26	6	14	107:82	58
6	Bristol C.	46	23	8	15	94:72	54
7	Reading	46	22	9	15	77:66	53
8	Northampton	46	20	11	15	85:57	51
9	Swindon	46	17	15	14	78:71	49
10	Hull	46	20	8	18	67:54	48
11	Bradford P.A.	46	20	7	19	80:78	47
12	Port Vale	46	17	11	18	65:58	45
13	Notts County	46	17	9	20	67:74	43
14	Coventry	46	16	11	19	64:71	43
15	Crystal Palace	46	14	14	18	83:80	42
16	Southend	46	13	16	17	57:69	42
17	Watford	46	14	13	19	63:74	41
18	Halifax	46	15	10	21	62:84	40
19	Shrewsbury	46	13	12	21	73:84	38
20	Barnsley	46	13	12	21	71:95	38
21	Torquay†	46	15	6	25	76:100	36
22	Lincoln†	46	9	17	20	57:87	35
23	Brentford	46	13	8	25	53:93	34
24	Newport†	46	7	8	31	46:102	22

DIVISION 4 1961-62

1	Millwall*	44	23	10	11	87:62	56
2	Colchester*	44	23	9	12	104:71	55
3	Wrexham*	44	22	9	13	96:56	53
4	Carlisle*	44	22	8	14	64:63	52
5	Bradford C.	44	21	9	14	94:86	51
6	York	44	20	10	14	84:53	50
7	Aldershot	44	22	5	17	81:60	49
8	Workington	44	19	11	14	69:70	49
9	Barrow	44	17	14	13	74:58	48
10	Crewe	44	20	6	18	79:70	46
11	Oldham	44	17	12	15	77:70	46
12	Rochdale	44	19	7	18	71:71	45
13	Darlington	44	18	9	17	61:73	45
14	Mansfield	44	19	6	19	77:66	44
15	Tranmere	44	20	4	20	70:81	44
16	Stockport	44	17	9	18	70:69	43
17	Southport	44	17	9	18	61:71	43
18	Exeter	44	13	11	20	62:77	37
19	Chesterfield	44	14	9	21	70:87	37
20	Gillingham	44	13	11	20	73:94	37
21	Doncaster	44	11	7	26	60:85	29
22	Hartlepools	44	8	11	25	52:101	27
23	Chester	44	7	12	25	54:96	26
24	Accrington‡						

‡Accrington Stanley resigned from the League after playing 33 matches; results declared void

DIVISION 1 1962-63

1	Everton	42	25	11	6	84:42	61
2	Tottenham	42	23	9	10	111:62	55
3	Burnley	42	22	10	10	78:57	54
4	Leicester	42	20	12	10	79:53	52
5	Wolverhampton	42	20	10	12	93:65	50
6	Sheffield W.	42	19	10	13	77:63	48
7	Arsenal	42	18	10	14	86:77	46
8	Liverpool	42	17	10	15	71:59	44
9	Nottingham F.	42	17	10	15	67:69	44
10	Sheffield U.	42	16	12	14	58:60	44
11	Blackburn	42	15	12	15	79:71	42
12	West Ham	42	14	12	16	73:69	40
13	Blackpool	42	13	14	15	58:64	40
14	West Bromwich	42	16	7	19	71:79	39
15	Aston Villa	42	15	8	19	62:68	38
16	Fulham	42	14	10	18	50:71	38
17	Ipswich	42	12	11	19	59:78	35
18	Bolton	42	15	5	22	55:75	35
19	Manchester U.	42	12	10	20	67:81	34
20	Birmingham	42	10	13	19	63:90	33
21	Manchester C.†	42	10	11	21	58:102	31
22	Leyton Orient†	42	6	9	27	37:81	21

DIVISION 2 1962-63

1	Stoke*	42	20	13	9	73:50	53
2	Chelsea*	42	24	4	14	81:42	52
3	Sunderland	42	20	12	10	84:55	52
4	Middlesbrough	42	20	9	13	86:85	49
5	Leeds	42	19	10	13	79:53	48
6	Huddersfield	42	17	14	11	63:50	48
7	Newcastle	42	18	11	13	79:59	47
8	Bury	42	18	11	13	51:47	47
9	Scunthorpe	42	16	12	14	57:59	44
10	Cardiff	42	18	7	17	83:73	43
11	Southampton	42	17	8	17	72:67	42
12	Plymouth	42	15	12	15	76:73	42
13	Norwich	42	17	8	17	80:79	42
14	Rotherham	42	17	6	19	67:74	40
15	Swansea	42	15	9	18	51:72	39
16	Portsmouth	42	13	11	18	63:79	37
17	Preston	42	13	11	18	59:74	37
18	Derby	42	12	12	18	61:72	36
19	Grimsby	42	11	13	18	55:66	35
20	Charlton	42	13	5	24	62:94	31
21	Walsall†	42	11	9	22	53:89	31
22	Luton†	42	11	7	24	61:84	29

DIVISION 3 1962-63

1	Northampton*	46	26	10	10	109:60	62
2	Swindon*	46	22	14	10	87:56	58
3	Port Vale	46	23	8	15	72:58	54
4	Coventry	46	18	17	11	83:69	53
5	Bournemouth	46	18	16	12	63:46	52
6	Peterborough	46	20	11	15	93:75	51
7	Notts Co.	46	19	13	14	73:74	51
8	Southend	46	19	12	15	75:77	50
9	Wrexham	46	20	9	17	84:83	49
10	Hull	46	19	10	17	74:69	48
11	Crystal Palace	46	17	13	16	68:58	47
12	Colchester	46	18	11	17	73:93	47
13	QPR	46	17	11	18	85:76	45
14	Bristol C.	46	16	13	17	100:92	45
15	Shrewsbury	46	16	12	18	83:81	44
16	Millwall	46	15	13	18	82:87	43
17	Watford	46	17	8	21	82:85	42
18	Barnsley	46	15	11	20	63:74	41
19	Bristol R.	46	15	11	20	70:88	41
20	Reading	46	16	8	22	74:78	40
21	Bradford P.A.†	46	14	12	20	79:97	40
22	Brighton†	46	12	12	22	58:84	36
23	Carlisle†	46	13	9	24	61:89	35
24	Halifax†	46	9	12	25	64:106	30

DIVISION 4 1962-63

1	Brentford*	46	27	8	11	98:64	62
2	Oldham*	46	24	11	11	95:60	59
3	Crewe*	46	24	11	11	86:58	59
4	Mansfield*	46	24	9	13	108:69	57
5	Gillingham	46	22	13	11	71:49	57
6	Torquay	46	20	16	10	75:56	56
7	Rochdale	46	20	11	15	67:59	51
8	Tranmere	46	20	10	16	81:67	50
9	Barrow	46	19	12	15	82:80	50
10	Workington	46	17	13	16	76:68	47
11	Aldershot	46	15	17	14	73:69	47
12	Darlington	46	19	6	21	72:87	44
13	Southport	46	15	14	17	72:106	44
14	York	46	16	11	19	67:62	43
15	Chesterfield	46	13	16	17	70:64	42
16	Doncaster	46	14	14	18	64:77	42
17	Exeter	46	16	10	20	57:77	42
18	Oxford	46	13	15	18	70:71	41
19	Stockport	46	15	11	20	56:70	41
20	Newport	46	14	11	21	76:90	39
21	Chester	46	15	9	22	51:66	39
22	Lincoln	46	13	9	24	68:89	35
23	Bradford C.	46	11	10	25	64:93	32
24	Hartlepools	46	7	11	28	56:104	25

DIVISION 1 1963-64

1	Liverpool	42	26	5	11	92:45	57
2	Manchester U.	42	23	7	12	90:62	53
3	Everton	42	21	10	11	84:64	52
4	Tottenham	42	22	7	13	97:81	51
5	Chelsea	42	20	10	12	72:56	50
6	Sheffield W.	42	19	11	12	84:67	49
7	Blackburn	42	18	10	14	89:65	46
8	Arsenal	42	17	11	14	90:82	45
9	Burnley	42	17	10	15	71:64	44
10	West Bromwich	42	16	11	15	70:61	43
11	Leicester	42	16	11	15	61:58	43
12	Sheffield U.	42	16	11	15	61:64	43
13	Nottingham F.	42	16	9	17	64:68	41
14	West Ham	42	14	12	16	69:74	40
15	Fulham	42	13	13	16	58:65	39
16	Wolverhampton	42	12	15	15	70:80	39
17	Stoke	42	14	10	18	77:78	38
18	Blackpool	42	13	9	20	52:73	35
19	Aston Villa	42	11	12	19	62:71	34
20	Birmingham	42	11	7	24	54:92	29
21	Bolton†	42	10	8	24	48:80	28
22	Ipswich†	42	9	7	26	56:121	25

DIVISION 2 1963-64

1	Leeds *	42	24	15	3	71:34	63
2	Sunderland *	42	25	11	6	81:37	61
3	Preston	42	23	10	9	79:54	56
4	Charlton	42	19	10	13	76:70	48
5	Southampton	42	19	9	14	100:73	47
6	Manchester C.	42	18	10	14	84:66	46
7	Rotherham	42	19	7	16	90:78	45
8	Newcastle	42	20	5	17	74:69	45
9	Portsmouth	42	16	11	15	79:70	43
10	Middlesbrough	42	15	11	16	67:52	41
11	Northampton	42	16	9	17	58:60	41
12	Huddersfield	42	15	10	17	57:64	40
13	Derby	42	14	11	17	56'67	39
14	Swindon	42	14	10	18	57:69	38
15	Cardiff	42	14	10	18	56:81	38
16	Leyton Orient	42	13	10	19	54:72	36
17	Norwich	42	11	13	18	64:80	35
18	Bury	42	13	9	20	57:73	35
19	Swansea	42	12	9	21	63:74	33
20	Plymouth	42	8	16	18	45:67	32
21	Grimsby†	42	9	14	19	47:75	32
22	Scunthorpe†	42	10	10	22	52:82	30

DIVISION 3 1963-64

1	Coventry *	46	22	16	8	98:61	60
2	Crystal Palace *	46	23	14	9	73:51	60
3	Watford	46	23	12	11	79:59	58
4	Bournemouth	46	24	8	14	79:58	56
5	Bristol C.	46	20	15	11	84:64	55
6	Reading	46	21	10	15	79:62	52
7	Mansfield	46	20	11	15	76:62	51
8	Hull	46	16	17	13	73:68	49
9	Oldham	46	20	8	18	73:70	48
10	Peterborough	46	18	11	17	75:70	47
11	Shrewsbury	46	18	11	17	73:80	47
12	Bristol R.	46	19	8	19	91:79	46
13	Port Vale	46	16	14	16	53:49	46
14	Southend	46	15	15	16	77:78	45
15	QPR	46	18	9	19	76:78	45
16	Brentford	46	15	14	17	87:80	44
17	Colchester	46	12	19	15	70:68	43
18	Luton	46	16	10	20	64:80	42
19	Walsall	46	13	14	19	59:76	40
20	Barnsley	46	12	15	19	68:94	39
21	Millwall†	46	14	10	22	53:67	38
22	Crewe†	46	11	12	23	50:77	34
23	Wrexham†	46	13	6	27	75:107	32
24	Notts Co.†	46	9	9	28	45:92	27

DIVISION 4 1963-64

1	Gillingham *	46	23	14	9	59:30	60
2	Carlisle *	46	25	10	11	113:58	60
3	Workington *	46	24	11	11	76:52	59
4	Exeter *	46	20	18	8	62:37	58
5	Bradford C.	46	25	6	15	76:62	56
6	Torquay	46	20	11	15	80:54	51
7	Tranmere	46	20	11	15	85:73	51
8	Brighton	46	19	12	15	71:52	50
9	Aldershot	46	19	10	17	83:78	48
10	Halifax	46	17	14	15	77:77	48
11	Lincoln	46	19	9	18	67:75	47
12	Chester	46	19	8	19	65:60	46
13	Bradford P.A.	46	18	9	19	75:81	45
14	Doncaster	46	15	12	19	70:75	42
15	Newport	46	17	8	21	64:73	42
16	Chesterfield	46	15	12	19	57:71	42
17	Stockport	46	15	12	19	50:68	42
18	Oxford	46	14	13	19	59:63	41
19	Darlington	46	14	12	20	66:93	40
20	Rochdale	46	12	15	19	56:59	39
21	Southport	46	15	9	22	63:88	39
22	York	46	14	7	25	52:66	35
23	Hartlepools	46	12	9	25	54:93	33
24	Barrow	46	6	18	22	51:93	30

DIVISION 1 1964-65

1	Manchester U.	42	26	9	7	89:39	61
2	Leeds	42	26	9	7	83:52	61
3	Chelsea	42	24	8	10	89:54	56
4	Everton	42	17	15	10	69:60	49
5	Nottingham F.	42	17	13	12	71:67	47
6	Tottenham	42	19	7	16	87:71	45
7	Liverpool	42	17	10	15	67:73	44
8	Sheffield W.	42	16	11	15	57:55	43
9	West Ham	42	19	4	19	82:71	42
10	Blackburn	42	16	10	16	83:79	42
11	Stoke	42	16	10	16	67:66	42
12	Burnley	42	16	10	16	70:70	42
13	Arsenal	42	17	7	18	69:75	41
14	West Bromwich	42	13	13	16	70:65	39
15	Sunderland	42	14	9	19	64:74	37
16	Aston Villa	42	16	5	21	57:82	37
17	Blackpool	42	12	11	19	67:78	35
18	Leicester	42	11	13	18	69:85	35
19	Sheffield U.	42	12	11	19	50:64	35
20	Fulham	42	11	12	19	60:78	34
21	Wolverhampton†	42	13	4	25	59:89	30
22	Birmingham†	42	8	11	23	64:96	27

DIVISION 2 1964-65

1	Newcastle *	42	24	9	9	81:45	57
2	Northampton *	42	20	16	6	66:50	56
3	Bolton	42	20	10	12	80:58	50
4	Southampton	42	17	14	11	83:63	48
5	Ipswich	42	15	17	10	74:67	47
6	Norwich	42	20	7	15	61:57	47
7	Crystal Palace	42	16	13	13	55:51	45
8	Huddersfield	42	17	10	15	53:51	44
9	Derby	42	16	11	15	84:79	43
10	Coventry	42	17	9	16	72:70	43
11	Manchester C.	42	16	9	17	63:62	41
12	Preston	42	14	13	15	76:81	41
13	Cardiff	42	13	14	15	64:57	40
14	Rotherham	42	14	12	16	70:69	40
15	Plymouth	42	16	8	18	63:79	40
16	Bury	42	14	10	18	60:66	38
17	Middlesbrough	42	13	9	20	70:76	35
18	Charlton	42	13	9	20	64:75	35
19	Leyton Orient	42	12	11	19	50:72	35
20	Portsmouth	42	12	10	20	56:77	34
21	Swindon†	42	14	5	23	63:81	33
22	Swansea†	42	11	10	21	62:84	32

DIVISION 3 1964-65

1	Carlisle *	46	25	10	11	76:53	60
2	Bristol C. *	46	24	11	11	92:55	59
3	Mansfield	46	24	11	11	95:61	59
4	Hull	46	23	12	11	91:57	58
5	Brentford	46	24	9	13	83:55	57
6	Bristol R.	46	20	15	11	82:58	55
7	Gillingham	46	23	9	14	70:50	55
8	Peterborough	46	22	7	17	85:74	51
9	Watford	46	17	16	13	71:64	50
10	Grimsby	46	16	17	13	68:67	49
11	Bournemouth	46	18	11	17	72:63	47
12	Southend	46	19	8	19	78:71	46
13	Reading	46	16	14	16	70:70	46
14	QPR	46	17	12	17	72:80	46
15	Workington	46	17	12	17	58:69	46
16	Shrewsbury	46	15	12	19	76:84	42
17	Exeter	46	12	17	17	51:52	41
18	Scunthorpe	46	14	12	20	65:72	40
19	Walsall	46	15	7	24	55:80	37
20	Oldham	46	13	10	23	61:83	36
21	Luton†	46	11	11	24	51:94	33
22	Port Vale†	46	9	14	23	41:76	32
23	Colchester†	46	10	10	26	50:89	30
24	Barnsley†	46	9	11	26	54:90	29

DIVISION 4 1964-65

1	Brighton*	46	26	11	9	102:57	63
2	Millwall*	46	23	16	7	78:45	62
3	York*	46	28	6	12	91:56	62
4	Oxford*	46	23	15	8	87:44	61
5	Tranmere	46	27	6	13	99:56	60
6	Rochdale	46	22	14	10	74:53	58
7	Bradford P.A.	46	20	17	9	86:62	57
8	Chester	46	25	6	15	119:81	56
9	Doncaster	46	20	11	15	84:72	51
10	Crewe	46	18	13	15	90:81	49
11	Torquay	46	21	7	18	70:70	49
12	Chesterfield	46	20	8	18	58:70	48
13	Notts Co.	46	15	14	17	61:73	44
14	Wrexham	46	17	9	20	84:92	43
15	Hartlepools	46	15	13	18	61:85	43
16	Newport	46	17	8	21	85:81	42
17	Darlington	46	18	6	22	84:87	42
18	Aldershot	46	15	7	24	64:84	37
19	Bradford C.	46	12	8	26	70:88	32
20	Southport	46	8	16	22	58:89	32
21	Barrow	46	12	6	28	59:105	30
22	Lincoln	46	11	6	29	58:99	28
23	Halifax	46	11	6	29	54:103	28
24	Stockport	46	10	7	29	44:87	27

DIVISION 1 1965-66

1	Liverpool	42	26	9	7	79:34	61
2	Leeds	42	23	9	10	79:38	55
3	Burnley	42	24	7	11	79:47	55
4	Manchester U.	42	18	15	9	84:59	51
5	Chelsea	42	22	7	13	65:53	51
6	West Bromwich	42	19	12	11	91:69	50
7	Leicester	42	21	7	14	80:65	49
8	Tottenham	42	16	12	14	75:66	44
9	Sheffield U.	42	16	11	15	56:59	43
10	Stoke	42	15	12	15	65:64	42
11	Everton	42	15	11	16	56:62	41
12	West Ham	42	15	9	18	70:83	39
13	Blackpool	42	14	9	19	55:65	37
14	Arsenal	42	12	13	17	62:75	37
15	Newcastle	42	14	9	19	50:63	37
16	Aston Villa	42	15	6	21	69:80	36
17	Sheffield W.	42	14	8	20	56:66	36
18	Nottingham F.	42	14	8	20	56:72	36
19	Sunderland	42	14	8	20	51:72	36
20	Fulham	42	14	7	21	67:85	35
21	Northampton†	42	10	13	19	55:92	33
22	Blackburn†	42	8	4	30	57:88	20

DIVISION 2 1965-66

1	Manchester C.*	42	22	15	5	76:44	59
2	Southampton*	42	22	10	10	85:56	54
3	Coventry	42	20	13	9	73:53	53
4	Huddersfield	42	19	13	10	62:36	51
5	Bristol C.	42	17	17	8	63:48	51
6	Wolverhampton	42	20	10	12	87:61	50
7	Rotherham	42	16	14	12	75:74	46
8	Derby	42	16	11	15	71:68	43
9	Bolton	42	16	9	17	62:59	41
10	Birmingham	42	16	9	17	70:75	41
11	Crystal Palace	42	14	13	15	47:52	41
12	Portsmouth	42	16	8	18	74:78	40
13	Norwich	42	12	15	15	52:52	39
14	Carlisle	42	17	5	20	60:63	39
15	Ipswich	42	15	9	18	58:66	39
16	Charlton	42	12	14	16	61:70	38
17	Preston	42	11	15	16	62:70	37
18	Plymouth	42	12	13	17	54:63	37
19	Bury	42	14	7	21	62:76	35
20	Cardiff	42	12	10	20	71:91	34
21	Middlesbrough†	42	10	13	19	58:86	33
22	Leyton Orient†	42	5	13	24	38:80	23

DIVISION 3 1965-66

1	Hull *	46	31	7	8	109:62	69
2	Millwall *	46	27	11	8	76:43	65
3	QPR	46	24	9	13	95:65	57
4	Scunthorpe	46	21	11	14	80:67	53
5	Workington	46	19	14	13	67:57	52
6	Gillingham	46	22	8	16	62:54	52
7	Swindon	46	19	13	14	74:48	51
8	Reading	46	19	13	14	70:63	51
9	Walsall	46	20	10	16	77:64	50
10	Shrewsbury	46	19	11	16	73:64	49
11	Grimsby	46	17	13	16	68:62	47
12	Watford	46	17	13	16	55:51	47
13	Peterborough	46	17	12	17	80:66	46
14	Oxford	46	19	8	19	70:74	46
15	Brighton	46	16	11	19	67:65	43
16	Bristol R.	46	14	14	18	64:64	42
17	Swansea	46	15	11	20	81:96	41
18	Bournemouth	46	13	12	21	38:56	38
19	Mansfield	46	15	8	23	59:89	38
20	Oldham	46	12	13	21	55:81	37
21	Southend†	46	16	4	26	54:83	36
22	Exeter†	46	12	11	23	53:79	35
23	Brentford†	46	10	12	24	48:69	32
24	York†	46	9	9	28	53:106	27

DIVISION 4 1965-66

1	Doncaster*	46	24	11	11	85:54	59
2	Darlington*	46	25	9	12	72:53	59
3	Torquay*	46	24	10	12	72:49	58
4	Colchester*	46	23	10	13	70:47	56
5	Tranmere	46	24	8	14	93:66	56
6	Luton	46	24	8	14	90:70	56
7	Chester	46	20	12	14	79:70	52
8	Notts Co.	46	19	12	15	61:53	50
9	Newport	46	18	12	16	75:75	48
10	Southport	46	18	12	16	68:69	48
11	Bradford P.A.	46	21	5	20	102:92	47
12	Barrow	46	16	15	15	72:76	47
13	Stockport	46	18	6	22	71:70	42
14	Crewe	46	16	9	21	61:63	41
15	Halifax	46	15	11	20	67:75	41
16	Barnsley	46	15	10	21	74:78	40
17	Aldershot	46	15	10	21	75:84	40
18	Hartlepools	46	16	8	22	63:75	40
19	Port Vale	46	15	9	22	48:59	39
20	Chesterfield	46	13	13	20	62:78	39
21	Rochdale	46	16	5	25	71:87	37
22	Lincoln	46	13	11	22	57:82	37
23	Bradford C.	46	12	13	21	63:94	37
24	Wrexham	46	13	9	24	72:104	35

DIVISION 1 1966-67

1	Manchester U.	42	24	12	6	84:45	60
2	Nottingham F.	42	23	10	9	64:41	56
3	Tottenham	42	24	8	10	71:48	56
4	Leeds	42	22	11	9	62:42	55
5	Liverpool	42	19	13	10	64:47	51
6	Everton	42	19	10	13	65:46	48
7	Arsenal	42	16	14	12	58:47	46
8	Leicester	42	18	8	16	78:71	44
9	Chelsea	42	15	14	13	67:62	44
10	Sheffield U.	42	16	10	16	52:59	42
11	Sheffield W.	42	14	13	15	56:47	41
12	Stoke	42	17	7	18	63:58	41
13	West Bromwich	42	16	7	19	77:73	39
14	Burnley	42	15	9	18	66:76	39
15	Manchester C.	42	12	15	15	43:52	39
16	West Ham	42	14	8	20	80:84	36
17	Sunderland	42	14	8	20	58:72	36
18	Fulham	42	11	12	19	71:83	34
19	Southampton	42	14	6	22	74:92	34
20	Newcastle	42	12	9	21	39:81	33
21	Aston Villa†	42	11	7	24	54:85	29
22	Blackpool†	42	6	9	27	41:76	21

DIVISION 2 1966-67

1	Coventry*	42	23	13	6	74:43	59
2	Wolverhampton*	42	25	8	9	88:48	58
3	Carlisle	42	23	6	13	71:54	52
4	Blackburn	42	19	13	10	56:46	51
5	Ipswich	42	17	16	9	70:54	50
6	Huddersfield	42	20	9	13	58:46	49
7	Crystal Palace	42	19	10	13	61:55	48
8	Millwall	42	18	9	15	49:58	45
9	Bolton	42	14	14	14	64:58	42
10	Birmingham	42	16	8	18	70:66	40
11	Norwich	42	13	14	15	49:55	40
12	Hull	42	16	7	19	77:72	39
13	Preston	42	16	7	19	65:67	39
14	Portsmouth	42	13	13	16	59:70	39
15	Bristol C.	42	12	14	16	56:62	38
16	Plymouth	42	14	9	19	59:58	37
17	Derby	42	12	12	18	68:72	36
18	Rotherham	42	13	10	19	61:70	36
19	Charlton	42	13	9	20	49:53	35
20	Cardiff	42	12	9	21	61:87	33
21	Northampton†	42	12	6	24	47:84	30
22	Bury†	42	11	6	25	49:83	28

DIVISION 3 1966-67

1	QPR*	46	26	15	5	103:38	67
2	Middlesbrough*	46	23	9	14	87:64	55
3	Watford	46	20	14	12	61:46	54
4	Reading	46	22	9	15	76:57	53
5	Bristol R.	46	20	13	13	76:67	53
6	Shrewsbury	46	20	12	14	77:62	52
7	Torquay	46	21	9	16	73:54	51
8	Swindon	46	20	10	16	81:59	50
9	Mansfield	46	20	9	17	84:79	49
10	Oldham	46	19	10	17	80:63	48
11	Gillingham	46	15	16	15	58:62	46
12	Walsall	46	18	10	18	65:72	46
13	Colchester	46	17	10	19	76:73	44
14	Leyton Orient	46	13	18	15	58:68	44
15	Peterborough	46	14	15	17	66:71	43
16	Oxford	46	15	13	18	61:66	43
17	Grimsby	46	17	9	20	61:68	43
18	Scunthorpe	46	17	8	21	58:73	42
19	Brighton	46	13	15	18	61:71	41
20	Bournemouth	46	12	17	17	39:57	41
21	Swansea†	46	12	15	19	85:89	39
22	Darlington†	46	13	11	22	47:81	37
23	Doncaster†	46	12	8	26	58:117	32
24	Workington†	46	12	7	27	55:89	31

DIVISION 4 1966-67

1	Stockport*	46	26	12	8	69:42	64
2	Southport*	46	23	13	10	69:42	59
3	Barrow*	46	24	11	11	76:54	59
4	Tranmere*	46	22	14	10	66:43	58
5	Crewe	46	21	12	13	70:55	54
6	Southend	46	22	9	15	70:49	53
7	Wrexham	46	16	20	10	76:62	52
8	Hartlepools	46	22	7	17	66:64	51
9	Brentford	46	18	13	15	58:56	49
10	Aldershot	46	18	12	16	72:57	48
11	Bradford C.	46	19	10	17	74:62	48
12	Halifax	46	15	14	17	59:68	44
13	Port Vale	46	14	15	17	55:58	43
14	Exeter	46	14	15	17	50:60	43
15	Chesterfield	46	17	8	21	60:63	42
16	Barnsley	46	13	15	18	60:64	41
17	Luton	46	16	9	21	59:73	41
18	Newport	46	12	16	18	56:63	40
19	Chester	46	15	10	21	54:78	40
20	Notts Co.	46	13	11	22	53:72	37
21	Rochdale	46	13	11	22	53:75	37
22	York	46	12	11	23	65:79	35
23	Bradford P.A.	46	11	13	22	52:79	35
24	Lincoln	46	9	13	24	58:82	31

DIVISION 1 1967-68

1	Manchester C.	42	26	6	10	86:43	58
2	Manchester U.	42	24	8	10	89:55	56
3	Liverpool	42	22	11	9	71:40	55
4	Leeds	42	22	9	11	71:41	53
5	Everton	42	23	6	13	67:40	52
6	Chelsea	42	18	12	12	62:68	48
7	Tottenham	42	19	9	14	70:59	47
8	West Bromwich	42	17	12	13	75:62	46
9	Arsenal	42	17	10	15	60:56	44
10	Newcastle	42	13	15	14	54:67	41
11	Nottingham F.	42	14	11	17	52:64	39
12	West Ham	42	14	10	18	73:69	38
13	Leicester	42	13	12	17	64:69	38
14	Burnley	42	14	10	18	64:71	38
15	Sunderland	42	13	11	18	51:61	37
16	Southampton	42	13	11	18	66:83	37
17	Wolverhampton	42	14	8	20	66:75	36
18	Stoke	42	14	7	21	50:73	35
19	Sheffield W.	42	11	12	19	51:63	34
20	Coventry	42	9	15	18	51:71	33
21	Sheffield U.†	42	11	10	21	49:70	32
22	Fulham†	42	10	7	25	56:98	27

DIVISION 2 1967-68

1	Ipswich*	42	22	15	5	79:44	59
2	QPR*	42	25	8	9	67:36	58
3	Blackpool	42	24	10	8	71:43	58
4	Birmingham	42	19	14	9	83:51	52
5	Portsmouth	42	18	13	11	68:55	49
6	Middlesbrough	42	17	12	13	60:54	46
7	Millwall	42	14	17	11	62:50	45
8	Blackburn	42	16	11	15	56:49	43
9	Norwich	42	16	11	15	60:65	43
10	Carlisle	42	14	13	15	58:52	41
11	Crystal Palace	42	14	11	17	56:56	39
12	Bolton	42	13	13	16	60:63	39
13	Cardiff	42	13	12	17	60:66	38
14	Huddersfield	42	13	12	17	46:61	38
15	Charlton	42	12	13	17	63:68	37
16	Aston Villa	42	15	7	20	54:64	37
17	Hull	42	12	13	17	58:73	37
18	Derby	42	13	10	19	71:78	36
19	Bristol C.	42	13	10	19	48:62	36
20	Preston	42	12	11	19	43:65	35
21	Rotherham†	42	10	11	21	42:76	31
22	Plymouth†	42	9	9	24	38:72	27

DIVISION 3 1967-68

1	Oxford*	46	22	13	11	69:47	57
2	Bury*	46	24	8	14	91:65	56
3	Shrewsbury	46	20	15	11	61:49	55
4	Torquay	46	21	11	14	60:56	53
5	Reading	46	21	9	16	70:60	51
6	Watford	46	21	8	17	74:50	50
7	Walsall	46	19	12	15	74:61	50
8	Barrow	46	21	8	17	65:54	50
9	Swindon	46	16	17	13	74:51	49
10	Brighton	46	16	16	14	57:55	48
11	Gillingham	46	18	12	16	59:63	48
12	Bournemouth	46	16	15	15	56:51	47
13	Stockport	46	19	9	18	70:75	47
14	Southport	46	17	12	17	65:65	46
15	Bristol R.	46	17	9	20	72:78	43
16	Oldham	46	18	7	21	60:65	43
17	Northampton	46	14	13	19	58:72	41
18	Orient	46	12	17	17	46:62	41
19	Tranmere	46	14	12	20	62:74	40
20	Mansfield	46	12	13	21	51:67	37
21	Grimsby†	46	14	9	23	52:69	37
22	Colchester†	46	9	15	22	50:87	33
23	Scunthorpe†	46	10	12	24	56:87	32
24	Peterborough†‡	46	20	10	16	79:67	31

DIVISION 4 1967-68

1	Luton*	46	27	12	7	87:44	66
2	Barnsley*	46	24	13	9	68:46	61
3	Hartlepools*	46	25	10	11	60:46	60
4	Crewe*	46	20	18	8	74:49	58
5	Bradford C.	46	23	11	12	72:51	57
6	Southend	46	20	14	12	77:58	54
7	Chesterfield	46	21	11	14	71:50	53
8	Wrexham	46	20	13	13	72:53	53
9	Aldershot	46	18	17	11	70:55	53
10	Doncaster	46	18	15	13	66:56	51
11	Halifax	46	15	16	15	52:49	46
12	Newport	46	16	13	17	58:63	45
13	Lincoln	46	17	9	20	71:68	43
14	Brentford	46	18	7	21	61:64	43
15	Swansea	46	16	10	20	63:77	42
16	Darlington	46	12	17	17	47:53	41
17	Notts Co.	46	15	11	20	53:79	41
18	Port Vale§	46	12	15	19	61:72	39
19	Rochdale	46	12	14	20	51:72	38
20	Exeter	46	11	16	19	45:65	38
21	York	46	11	14	21	65:68	36
22	Chester	46	9	14	23	57:78	32
23	Workington	46	10	11	25	54:87	31
24	Bradford P.A.	46	4	15	27	30:82	23

DIVISION 1 1968-69

1	Leeds	42	27	13	2	66:26	67
2	Liverpool	42	25	11	6	63:24	61
3	Everton	42	21	15	6	77:36	57
4	Arsenal	42	22	12	8	56:27	56
5	Chelsea	42	20	10	12	73:53	50
6	Tottenham	42	14	17	11	61:51	45
7	Southampton	42	16	13	13	57:48	45
8	West Ham	42	13	18	11	66:50	44
9	Newcastle	42	15	14	13	61:55	44
10	West Bromwich	42	16	11	15	64:67	43
11	Manchester U.	42	15	12	15	57:53	42
12	Ipswich	42	15	11	16	59:60	41
13	Manchester C.	42	15	10	17	64:55	40
14	Burnley	42	15	9	18	55:82	39
15	Sheffield W.	42	10	16	16	41:54	36
16	Wolverhampton	42	10	15	17	41:58	35
17	Sunderland	42	11	12	19	43:67	34
18	Nottingham F.	42	10	13	19	45:57	33
19	Stoke	42	9	15	18	40:63	33
20	Coventry	42	10	11	21	46:64	31
21	Leicester†	42	9	12	21	39:68	30
22	QPR†	42	4	10	28	39:95	18

DIVISION 2 1968-69

1	Derby*	42	26	11	5	65:32	63
2	Crystal Palace*	42	22	12	8	70:47	56
3	Charlton	42	18	14	10	61:52	50
4	Middlesbrough	42	19	11	12	58:49	49
5	Cardiff	42	20	7	15	67:54	47
6	Huddersfield	42	17	12	13	53:46	46
7	Birmingham	42	18	8	16	73:59	44
8	Blackpool	42	14	15	13	51:41	43
9	Sheffield U.	42	16	11	15	61:50	43
10	Millwall	42	17	9	16	57:49	43
11	Hull	42	13	16	13	59:52	42
12	Carlisle	42	16	10	16	46:49	42
13	Norwich	42	15	10	17	53:56	40
14	Preston	42	12	15	15	38:44	39
15	Portsmouth	42	12	14	16	58:58	38
16	Bristol C.	42	11	16	15	46:53	38
17	Bolton	42	12	14	16	55:67	38
18	Aston Villa	42	12	14	16	37:48	38
19	Blackburn	42	13	11	18	52:63	37
20	Oxford	42	12	9	21	34:55	33
21	Bury†	42	11	8	23	51:80	30
22	Fulham†	42	7	11	24	40:81	25

DIVISION 3 1968-69

1	Watford*	46	27	10	9	74:34	64
2	Swindon*	46	27	10	9	71:35	64
3	Luton	46	25	11	10	74:38	61
4	Bournemouth	46	21	9	16	60:45	51
5	Plymouth	46	17	15	14	53:49	49
6	Torquay	46	18	12	16	54:46	48
7	Tranmere	46	19	10	17	70:68	48
8	Southport	46	17	13	16	71:64	47
9	Stockport	46	16	14	16	67:68	46
10	Barnsley	46	16	14	16	58;63	46
11	Rotherham	46	16	13	17	56:50	45
12	Brighton	46	16	13	17	72:65	45
13	Walsall	46	14	16	16	50:49	44
14	Reading	46	15	13	18	67:66	43
15	Mansfield	46	16	11	19	58:62	43
16	Bristol R.	46	16	11	19	63:71	43
17	Shrewsbury	46	16	11	19	51:67	43
18	Orient	46	14	14	18	51:58	42
19	Barrow	46	17	8	21	56:75	42
20	Gillingham	46	13	15	18	54:63	41
21	Northampton†	46	14	12	20	54:61	40
22	Hartlepool†	46	10	19	17	40:70	39
23	Crewe†	46	13	9	24	52:76	35
24	Oldham†	46	13	9	24	50:83	35

DIVISION 4 1968-69

1	Doncaster*	46	21	17	8	65:38	59
2	Halifax*	46	20	17	9	53:37	57
3	Rochdale*	46	18	20	8	68:35	56
4	Bradford C.*	46	18	20	8	65:46	56
5	Darlington	46	17	18	11	62:45	52
6	Colchester	46	20	12	14	57:53	52
7	Southend	46	19	13	14	78:61	51
8	Lincoln	46	17	17	12	54:52	51
9	Wrexham	46	18	14	14	61:52	50
10	Swansea	46	19	11	16	58:54	49
11	Brentford	46	18	12	16	64:65	48
12	Workington	46	15	17	14	40:43	47
13	Port Vale	46	16	14	16	46:46	46
14	Chester	46	16	13	17	76:66	45
15	Aldershot	46	19	7	20	66:66	45
16	Scunthorpe	46	18	8	20	61:60	44
17	Exeter	46	16	11	19	66:65	43
18	Peterborough	46	13	16	17	60:57	42
19	Notts Co.	46	12	18	16	48:57	42
20	Chesterfield	46	13	15	18	43:50	41
21	York	46	14	11	21	53:75	39
22	Newport	46	11	14	21	49:74	36
23	Grimsby	46	9	15	22	47:69	33
24	Bradford P.A.	46	5	10	31	32:106	20

‡Peterborough were 'fined' 19 points and relegated for offering illegal bonuses §Port Vale forced to seek re-election for offering illegal bonuses

DIVISION 1 1969-70

1	Everton	42	29	8	5	72:34	66
2	Leeds	42	21	15	6	84:49	57
3	Chelsea	42	21	13	8	70:50	55
4	Derby	42	22	9	11	64:37	53
5	Liverpool	42	20	11	11	65:42	51
6	Coventry	42	19	11	12	58:48	49
7	Newcastle	42	17	13	12	57:35	47
8	Manchester U.	42	14	17	11	66:61	45
9	Stoke	42	15	15	12	56:52	45
10	Manchester C.	42	16	11	15	55:48	43
11	Tottenham	42	17	9	16	54:55	43
12	Arsenal	42	12	18	12	51:49	42
13	Wolverhampton	42	12	16	14	55:57	40
14	Burnley	42	12	15	15	56:61	39
15	Nottingham F.	42	10	18	14	50:71	38
16	West Bromwich	42	14	9	19	58:66	37
17	West Ham	42	12	12	18	51:60	36
18	Ipswich	42	10	11	21	40:63	31
19	Southampton	42	6	17	19	46:67	29
20	Crystal Palace	42	6	15	21	34:68	27
21	Sunderland†	42	6	14	22	30:68	26
22	Sheffield W.†	42	8	9	25	40:71	25

DIVISION 2 1969-70

1	Huddersfield*	42	24	12	6	68:37	60
2	Blackpool*	42	20	13	9	56:45	53
3	Leicester	42	19	13	10	64:50	51
4	Middlesbrough	42	20	10	12	55:45	50
5	Swindon	42	17	16	9	57:47	50
6	Sheffield U.	42	22	5	15	73:38	49
7	Cardiff	42	18	13	11	61:41	49
8	Blackburn	42	20	7	15	54:50	47
9	QPR	42	17	11	14	66:57	45
10	Millwall	42	15	14	13	56:56	44
11	Norwich	42	16	11	15	49:46	43
12	Carlisle	42	14	13	15	58:56	41
13	Hull	42	15	11	16	72:70	41
14	Bristol C.	42	13	13	16	54:50	39
15	Oxford	42	12	15	15	35:42	39
16	Bolton	42	12	12	18	54:61	36
17	Portsmouth	42	13	9	20	66:80	35
18	Birmingham	42	11	11	20	51:78	33
19	Watford	42	9	13	20	44:57	31
20	Charlton	42	7	17	18	35:76	31
21	Aston Villa†	42	8	13	21	36:62	29
22	Preston†	42	8	12	22	43:63	28

DIVISION 3 1969-70

1	Orient*	46	25	12	9	67:36	62
2	Luton*	46	23	14	9	77:43	60
3	Bristol R.	46	20	16	10	80:59	56
4	Fulham	46	20	15	11	81:55	55
5	Brighton	46	23	9	14	57:43	55
6	Mansfield	46	21	11	14	70:49	53
7	Barnsley	46	19	15	12	68:59	53
8	Reading	46	21	11	14	87:77	53
9	Rochdale	46	18	10	18	69:60	46
10	Bradford C.	46	17	12	17	57:50	46
11	Doncaster	46	17	12	17	52:54	46
12	Walsall	46	17	12	17	54:67	46
13	Torquay	46	14	17	15	62:59	45
14	Rotherham	46	15	14	17	62:54	44
15	Shrewsbury	46	13	18	15	62:63	44
16	Tranmere	46	14	16	16	56:72	44
17	Plymouth	46	16	11	19	56:64	43
18	Halifax	46	14	15	17	47:63	43
19	Bury	46	15	11	20	75:80	41
20	Gillingham	46	13	13	20	52:64	39
21	Bournemouth†	46	12	15	19	48:71	39
22	Southport†	46	14	10	22	48:66	38
23	Barrow†	46	8	14	24	46:81	30
24	Stockport†	46	6	11	29	27:71	23

DIVISION 4 1969-70

1	Chesterfield*	46	27	10	9	77:32	64
2	Wrexham*	46	26	9	11	84:49	61
3	Swansea*	46	21	18	7	66:45	60
4	Port Vale*	46	20	19	7	61:33	59
5	Brentford	46	20	16	10	58:39	56
6	Aldershot	46	20	13	13	78:65	53
7	Notts Co.	46	22	8	16	73:62	52
8	Lincoln	46	17	16	13	66:52	50
9	Peterborough	46	17	14	15	77:69	48
10	Colchester	46	17	14	15	64:63	48
11	Chester	46	21	6	19	58:66	48
12	Scunthorpe	46	18	10	18	67:65	46
13	York	46	16	14	16	55:62	46
14	Northampton	46	16	12	18	64:55	44
15	Crewe	46	16	12	18	51:51	44
16	Grimsby	46	14	15	17	54:58	43
17	Southend	46	15	10	21	59:85	40
18	Exeter	46	14	11	21	57:59	39
19	Oldham	46	13	13	20	60:65	39
20	Workington	46	12	14	20	46:64	38
21	Newport	46	13	11	22	53:74	37
22	Darlington	46	13	10	23	53:73	36
23	Hartlepool	46	10	10	26	42:82	30
24	Bradford P.A.	46	6	11	29	41:96	23

DIVISION 1 1970-71

1	Arsenal	42	29	7	6	71:29	65
2	Leeds	42	27	10	5	72:30	64
3	Tottenham	42	19	14	9	54:33	52
4	Wolverhampton	42	22	8	12	64:54	52
5	Liverpool	42	17	17	8	42:24	51
6	Chelsea	42	18	15	9	52:42	51
7	Southampton	42	17	12	13	56:44	46
8	Manchester U.	42	16	11	15	65:66	43
9	Derby	42	16	10	16	56:54	42
10	Coventry	42	16	10	16	37:38	42
11	Manchester C.	42	12	17	13	47:42	41
12	Newcastle	42	14	13	15	44:46	41
13	Stoke	42	12	13	17	44:48	37
14	Everton	42	12	13	17	54:60	37
15	Huddersfield	42	11	14	17	40:49	36
16	Nottingham F.	42	14	8	20	42:61	36
17	West Bromwich	42	10	15	17	58:75	35
18	Crystal Palace	42	12	11	19	39:57	35
19	Ipswich	42	12	10	20	42:48	34
20	West Ham	42	10	14	18	47:60	34
21	Burnley†	42	7	13	22	29:63	27
22	Blackpool†	42	4	15	23	34:66	23

DIVISION 2 1970-71

1	Leicester*	42	23	13	6	57:30	59
2	Sheffield U.*	42	21	14	7	73:39	56
3	Cardiff	42	20	13	9	64:41	53
4	Carlisle	42	20	13	9	65:43	53
5	Hull	42	19	13	10	54:41	51
6	Luton	42	18	13	11	62:43	49
7	Middlesbrough	42	17	14	11	60:43	48
8	Millwall	42	19	9	14	59:42	47
9	Birmingham	42	17	12	13	58:48	46
10	Norwich	42	15	14	13	54:52	44
11	QPR	42	16	11	15	58:53	43
12	Swindon	42	15	12	15	61:51	42
13	Sunderland	42	15	12	15	52:54	42
14	Oxford	42	14	14	14	41:48	42
15	Sheffield W.	42	12	12	18	51:69	36
16	Portsmouth	42	10	14	18	46:61	34
17	Orient	42	9	16	17	29:51	34
18	Watford	42	10	13	19	38:60	33
19	Bristol C.	42	10	11	21	46:64	31
20	Charlton	42	8	14	20	41:65	30
21	Blackburn†	42	6	15	21	37:69	27
22	Bolton†	42	7	10	25	35:74	24

DIVISION 3 1970-71

1	Preston*	46	22	17	7	63:39	61
2	Fulham*	46	24	12	10	68:41	60
3	Halifax	46	22	12	12	74:55	56
4	Aston Villa	46	19	15	12	54:46	53
5	Chesterfield	46	17	17	12	66:38	51
6	Bristol R.	46	19	13	14	69:50	51
7	Mansfield	46	18	15	13	64:62	51
8	Rotherham	46	17	16	13	64:60	50
9	Wrexham	46	18	13	15	72:65	49
10	Torquay	46	19	11	16	54:57	49
11	Swansea	46	15	16	15	59:56	46
12	Barnsley	46	17	11	18	49:52	45
13	Shrewsbury	46	16	13	17	58:62	45
14	Brighton	46	14	16	16	50:47	44
15	Plymouth	46	12	19	15	63:63	43
16	Rochdale	46	14	15	17	61:68	43
17	Port Vale	46	15	12	19	52:59	42
18	Tranmere	46	10	22	14	45:55	42
19	Bradford C.	46	13	14	19	49:62	40
20	Walsall	46	14	11	21	51:57	39
21	Reading†	46	14	11	21	48:85	39
22	Bury†	46	12	13	21	52:60	37
23	Doncaster†	46	13	9	24	45:66	35
24	Gillingham†	46	10	13	23	42:67	33

DIVISION 4 1970-71

1	Notts Co.*	46	30	9	7	89:36	69
2	Bournemouth*	46	24	12	10	81:46	60
3	Oldham*	46	24	11	11	88:63	59
4	York*	46	23	10	13	78:54	56
5	Chester	46	24	7	15	69:55	55
6	Colchester	46	21	12	13	70:54	54
7	Northampton	46	19	13	14	63:59	51
8	Southport	46	21	6	19	63:57	48
9	Exeter	46	17	14	15	67:68	48
10	Workington	46	18	12	16	48:49	48
11	Stockport	46	16	14	16	49:65	46
12	Darlington	46	17	11	18	58:57	45
13	Aldershot	46	14	17	15	66:71	45
14	Brentford	46	18	8	20	66:62	44
15	Crewe	46	18	8	20	75:76	44
16	Peterborough	46	18	7	21	70:71	43
17	Scunthorpe	46	15	13	18	56:61	43
18	Southend	46	14	15	17	53:66	43
19	Grimsby	46	18	7	21	57:71	43
20	Cambridge	46	15	13	18	51:66	43
21	Lincoln	46	13	13	20	70:71	39
22	Newport	46	10	8	28	55:85	28
23	Hartlepool	46	8	12	26	34:74	28
24	Barrow	46	7	8	31	51:90	22

DIVISION 1 1971-72

1	Derby	42	24	10	8	69:33	58
2	Leeds	42	24	9	9	73:31	57
3	Liverpool	42	24	9	9	64:30	57
4	Manchester C.	42	23	11	8	77:45	57
5	Arsenal	42	22	8	12	58:40	52
6	Tottenham	42	19	13	10	63:42	51
7	Chelsea	42	18	12	12	58:49	48
8	Manchester U.	42	19	10	13	69:61	48
9	Wolverhampton	42	18	11	13	65:57	47
10	Sheffield U.	42	17	12	13	61:60	46
11	Newcastle	42	15	11	16	49:52	41
12	Leicester	42	13	13	16	41:46	39
13	Ipswich	42	11	16	15	39:53	38
14	West Ham	42	12	12	18	47:51	36
15	Everton	42	9	18	15	37:48	36
16	West Bromwich	42	12	11	19	42:54	35
17	Stoke	42	10	15	17	39:56	35
18	Coventry	42	9	15	18	44:67	33
19	Southampton	42	12	7	23	52:80	31
20	Crystal Palace	42	8	13	21	39:65	29
21	Nottingham F.†	42	8	9	25	47:81	25
22	Huddersfield†	42	6	13	23	27:59	25

DIVISION 2 1971-72

1	Norwich*	42	21	15	6	60:36	57
2	Birmingham*	42	19	18	5	60:31	56
3	Millwall	42	19	17	6	64:46	55
4	QPR	42	20	14	8	57:28	54
5	Sunderland	42	17	16	9	67:57	50
6	Blackpool	42	20	7	15	70:50	47
7	Burnley	42	20	6	16	70:55	46
8	Bristol C.	42	18	10	14	61:49	46
9	Middlesbrough	42	19	8	15	50:48	46
10	Carlisle	42	17	9	16	61:57	43
11	Swindon	42	15	12	15	47:47	42
12	Hull	42	14	10	18	49:53	38
13	Luton	42	10	18	14	43:48	38
14	Sheffield W.	42	13	12	17	51:58	38
15	Oxford	42	12	14	16	43:55	38
16	Portsmouth	42	12	13	17	59:68	37
17	Orient	42	14	9	19	50:61	37
18	Preston	42	12	12	18	52:58	36
19	Cardiff	42	10	14	18	56:69	34
20	Fulham	42	12	10	20	45:68	34
21	Charlton†	42	12	9	21	55:77	33
22	Watford†	42	5	9	28	24:75	19

DIVISION 3 1971-72

1	Aston Villa*	46	32	6	8	85:32	70
2	Brighton*	46	27	11	8	82:47	65
3	Bournemouth	46	23	16	7	73:37	62
4	Notts Co.	46	25	12	9	74:44	62
5	Rotherham	46	20	15	11	69:52	55
6	Bristol R.	46	21	12	13	75:56	54
7	Bolton	46	17	16	13	51:41	50
8	Plymouth	46	20	10	16	74:64	50
9	Walsall	46	15	18	13	62:57	48
10	Blackburn	46	19	9	18	54:57	47
11	Oldham	46	17	11	18	59:63	45
12	Shrewsbury	46	17	10	19	73:65	44
13	Chesterfield	46	18	8	20	57:57	44
14	Swansea	46	17	10	19	46:59	44
15	Port Vale	46	13	15	18	43:59	41
16	Wrexham	46	16	8	22	59:63	40
17	Halifax	46	13	12	21	48:61	38
18	Rochdale	46	12	13	21	57:83	37
19	York	46	12	12	22	57:66	36
20	Tranmere	46	10	16	20	50:71	36
21	Mansfield†	46	8	20	18	41:63	36
22	Barnsley†	46	9	18	19	32:64	36
23	Torquay†	46	10	12	24	41:69	32
24	Bradford C.†	46	11	10	25	45:77	32

DIVISION 4 1971-72

1	Grimsby*	46	28	7	11	88:56	63
2	Southend*	46	24	12	10	81:55	60
3	Brentford*	46	24	11	11	76:44	59
4	Scunthorpe*	46	22	13	11	56:37	57
5	Lincoln	46	21	14	11	77:59	56
6	Workington	46	16	19	11	50:34	51
7	Southport	46	18	14	14	66:46	50
8	Peterborough	46	17	16	13	82:64	50
9	Bury	46	19	12	15	73:59	50
10	Cambridge	46	17	14	15	62:60	48
11	Colchester	46	19	10	17	70:69	48
12	Doncaster	46	16	14	16	56:63	46
13	Gillingham	46	16	13	17	61:67	45
14	Newport	46	18	8	20	60:72	44
15	Exeter	46	16	11	19	61:68	43
16	Reading	46	17	8	21	56:76	42
17	Aldershot	46	9	22	15	48:54	40
18	Hartlepool	46	17	6	23	58:69	40
19	Darlington	46	14	11	21	64:82	39
20	Chester	46	10	18	18	47:56	38
21	Northampton	46	12	13	21	66:79	37
22	Barrow	46	13	11	22	40:71	37
23	Stockport	46	9	14	23	55:87	32
24	Crewe	46	10	9	27	43:69	29

DIVISION 1 1972-73

1	Liverpool	42	25	10	7	72:42	60
2	Arsenal	42	23	11	8	57:43	57
3	Leeds	42	21	11	10	71:45	53
4	Ipswich	42	17	14	11	55:45	48
5	Wolverhampton	42	18	11	13	66:54	47
6	West Ham	42	17	12	13	67:53	46
7	Derby	42	19	8	15	56:54	46
8	Tottenham	42	16	13	13	58:48	45
9	Newcastle	42	16	13	13	60:51	45
10	Birmingham	42	15	12	15	53:54	42
11	Manchester C.	42	15	11	16	57:60	41
12	Chelsea	42	13	14	15	49:51	40
13	Southampton	42	11	18	13	47:52	40
14	Sheffield U.	42	15	10	17	51:59	40
15	Stoke	42	14	10	18	61:56	38
16	Leicester	42	10	17	15	40:46	37
17	Everton	42	13	11	18	41:49	37
18	Manchester U.	42	12	13	17	44:60	37
19	Coventry	42	13	9	20	40:55	35
20	Norwich	42	11	10	21	36:63	32
21	Crystal Palace†	42	9	12	21	41:58	30
22	West Bromwich†	42	9	10	23	38:62	28

DIVISION 2 1972-73

1	Burnley*	42	24	14	4	72:35	62
2	QPR*	42	24	13	5	81:37	61
3	Aston Villa	42	18	14	10	51:47	50
4	Middlesbrough	42	17	13	12	46:43	47
5	Bristol C.	42	17	12	13	63:51	46
6	Sunderland	42	17	12	13	59:49	46
7	Blackpool	42	18	10	14	56:51	46
8	Oxford	42	19	7	16	52:43	45
9	Fulham	42	16	12	14	58:49	44
10	Sheffield W.	42	17	10	15	59:55	44
11	Millwall	42	16	10	16	55:47	42
12	Luton	42	15	11	16	44:53	41
13	Hull	42	14	12	16	64:59	40
14	Nottingham F.	42	14	12	16	47:52	40
15	Orient	42	12	12	18	49:53	36
16	Swindon	42	10	16	16	46:60	36
17	Portsmouth	42	12	11	19	42:59	35
18	Carlisle	42	11	12	19	50:52	34
19	Preston	42	11	12	19	37:64	34
20	Cardiff	42	11	11	20	43:58	33
21	Huddersfield†	42	8	17	17	36:56	33
22	Brighton†	42	8	13	21	46:83	29

DIVISION 3 1972-73

1	Bolton*	46	25	11	10	73:39	61
2	Notts Co.*	46	23	11	12	67:47	57
3	Blackburn	46	20	15	11	57:47	55
4	Oldham	46	19	16	11	72:54	54
5	Bristol R.	46	20	13	13	77:56	53
6	Port Vale	46	21	11	14	56:69	53
7	Bournemouth	46	17	16	13	66:44	50
8	Plymouth	46	20	10	16	74:66	50
9	Grimsby	46	20	8	18	67:61	48
10	Tranmere	46	15	16	15	56:52	46
11	Charlton	46	17	11	18	69:67	45
12	Wrexham	46	14	17	15	55:54	45
13	Rochdale	46	14	17	15	48:54	45
14	Southend	46	17	10	19	61:54	44
15	Shrewsbury	46	15	14	17	46:54	44
16	Chesterfield	46	17	9	20	57:61	43
17	Walsall	46	18	7	21	56:66	43
18	York	46	13	15	18	42:46	41
19	Watford	46	12	17	17	43:48	41
20	Halifax	46	13	15	18	43:53	41
21	Rotherham†	46	17	7	22	51:65	41
22	Brentford†	46	15	7	24	51:69	37
23	Swansea†	46	14	9	23	51:73	37
24	Scunthorpe†	46	10	10	26	33:72	30

DIVISION 4 1972-73

1	Southport*	46	26	10	10	71:48	62
2	Hereford*	46	23	12	11	56:38	58
3	Cambridge*	46	20	17	9	67:57	57
4	Aldershot*	46	22	12	12	60:38	56
5	Newport	46	22	12	12	64:44	56
6	Mansfield	46	20	14	12	78:51	54
7	Reading	46	17	18	11	51:38	52
8	Exeter	46	18	14	14	57:51	50
9	Gillingham	46	19	11	16	63:58	49
10	Lincoln	46	16	16	14	64:57	48
11	Stockport	46	18	12	16	53:53	48
12	Bury	46	14	18	14	58:51	46
13	Workington	46	17	12	17	59:61	46
14	Barnsley	46	14	16	16	58:60	44
15	Chester	46	14	15	17	61:52	43
16	Bradford C.	46	16	11	19	61:65	43
17	Doncaster	46	15	12	19	49:58	42
18	Torquay	46	12	17	17	44:47	41
19	Peterborough	46	14	13	19	71:76	41
20	Hartlepool	46	12	17	17	34:49	41
21	Crewe	46	9	18	19	38:61	36
22	Colchester	46	10	11	25	48:76	31
23	Northampton	46	10	11	25	40:73	31
24	Darlington	46	7	15	24	42:85	29

DIVISION 1 1973-74

1	Leeds	42	24	14	4	66:31	62
2	Liverpool	42	22	13	7	52:31	57
3	Derby	42	17	14	11	52:42	48
4	Ipswich	42	18	11	13	67:58	47
5	Stoke	42	15	16	11	54:42	46
6	Burnley	42	16	14	12	56:53	46
7	Everton	42	16	12	14	50:48	44
8	QPR	42	13	17	12	56:52	43
9	Leicester	42	13	16	13	51:41	42
10	Arsenal	42	14	14	14	49:51	42
11	Tottenham	42	14	14	14	45:50	42
12	Wolverhampton	42	13	15	14	49:49	41
13	Sheffield U.	42	14	12	16	44:49	40
14	Manchester C.	42	14	12	16	39:46	40
15	Newcastle	42	13	12	17	49:48	38
16	Coventry	42	14	10	18	43:54	38
17	Chelsea	42	12	13	17	56:60	37
18	West Ham	42	11	15	16	55:60	37
19	Birmingham	42	12	13	17	52:64	37
20	Southampton†	42	11	14	17	47:68	36
21	Manchester U.†	42	10	12	20	38:48	32
22	Norwich†	42	7	15	20	37:62	29

DIVISION 2 1973-74

1	Middlesbrough*	42	27	11	4	77:30	65
2	Luton*	42	19	12	11	64:51	50
3	Carlisle*	42	20	9	13	61:48	49
4	Orient	42	15	18	9	55:42	48
5	Blackpool	42	17	13	12	57:40	47
6	Sunderland	42	19	9	14	58:44	47
7	Nottingham F.	42	15	15	12	57:43	45
8	West Bromwich	42	14	16	12	48:45	44
9	Hull	42	13	17	12	46:47	43
10	Notts Co.	42	15	13	14	55:60	43
11	Bolton	42	15	12	15	44:40	42
12	Millwall	42	14	14	14	51:51	42
13	Fulham	42	16	10	16	39:43	42
14	Aston Villa	42	13	15	14	48:45	41
15	Portsmouth	42	14	12	16	45:62	40
16	Bristol C.	42	14	10	18	47:54	38
17	Cardiff	42	10	16	16	49:62	36
18	Oxford	42	10	16	16	35:46	36
19	Sheffield W.	42	12	11	19	51:63	35
20	Crystal Palace†	42	11	12	19	43:56	34
21	Preston†‡	42	9	14	19	40:62	31
22	Swindon†	42	7	11	24	36:72	25

DIVISION 3 1973-74

1	Oldham*	46	25	12	9	83:47	62
2	Bristol R.*	46	22	17	7	65:33	61
3	York*	46	21	19	6	67:38	61
4	Wrexham	46	22	12	12	63:43	56
5	Chesterfield	46	21	14	11	55:42	56
6	Grimsby	46	18	15	13	67:50	51
7	Watford	46	19	12	15	64:56	50
8	Aldershot	46	19	11	16	65:52	49
9	Halifax	46	14	21	11	48:51	49
10	Huddersfield	46	17	13	16	56:55	47
11	Bournemouth	46	16	15	15	54:58	47
12	Southend	46	16	14	16	62:62	46
13	Blackburn	46	18	10	18	62:64	46
14	Charlton	46	19	8	19	66:73	46
15	Walsall	46	16	13	17	57:48	45
16	Tranmere	46	15	15	16	50:44	45
17	Plymouth	46	17	10	19	59:54	44
18	Hereford	46	14	15	17	53:57	43
19	Brighton	46	16	11	19	52:58	43
20	Port Vale	46	14	14	18	52:58	42
21	Cambridge†	46	13	9	24	48:81	35
22	Shrewsbury†	46	10	11	25	41:62	31
23	Southport†	46	6	16	24	35:82	28
24	Rochdale†	46	2	17	27	38:94	21

DIVISION 4 1973-74

1	Peterborough*	46	27	11	8	75:38	65
2	Gillingham*	46	25	12	9	90:49	62
3	Colchester*	46	24	12	10	73:36	60
4	Bury*	46	24	11	11	81:49	59
5	Northampton	46	20	13	13	63:48	53
6	Reading	46	16	19	11	58:37	51
7	Chester	46	17	15	14	54:55	49
8	Bradford C.	46	17	14	15	58:52	48
9	Newport‡	46	16	14	16	56:65	45
10	Exeter§	45	18	8	19	58:55	44
11	Hartlepool	46	16	12	18	48:47	44
12	Lincoln	46	16	12	18	63:67	44
13	Barnsley	46	17	10	19	58:64	44
14	Swansea	46	16	11	19	45:46	43
15	Rotherham	46	15	13	18	56:58	43
16	Torquay	46	13	17	16	52:57	43
17	Mansfield	46	13	17	16	62:69	43
18	Scunthorpe§	45	14	12	19	47:64	42
19	Brentford	46	12	16	18	48:50	40
20	Darlington	46	13	13	20	40:62	39
21	Crewe	46	14	10	22	43:71	38
22	Doncaster	46	12	11	23	47:80	35
23	Workington	46	11	13	22	43:74	35
24	Stockport	46	7	20	19	44:69	34

DIVISION 1 1974-75

1	Derby	42	21	11	10	67:49	53
2	Liverpool	42	20	11	11	60:39	51
3	Ipswich	42	23	5	14	66:44	51
4	Everton	42	16	18	8	56:42	50
5	Stoke	42	17	15	10	64:48	49
6	Sheffield U.	42	18	13	11	58:51	49
7	Middlesbrough	42	18	12	12	54:40	48
8	Manchester C.	42	18	10	14	54:54	46
9	Leeds	42	16	13	13	57:49	45
10	Burnley	42	17	11	14	68:67	45
11	QPR	42	16	10	16	54:54	42
12	Wolverhampton	42	14	11	17	57:54	39
13	West Ham	42	13	13	16	58:59	39
14	Coventry	42	12	15	15	51:62	39
15	Newcastle	42	15	9	18	59:72	39
16	Arsenal	42	13	11	18	47:49	37
17	Birmingham	42	14	9	19	53:61	37
18	Leicester	42	12	12	18	46:60	36
19	Tottenham	42	13	8	21	52:63	34
20	Luton†	42	11	11	20	47:65	33
21	Chelsea†	42	9	15	18	42:72	33
22	Carlisle†	42	12	5	25	43:59	29

DIVISION 2 1974-75

1	Manchester U.*	42	26	9	7	66:30	61
2	Aston Villa*	42	25	8	9	69:32	58
3	Norwich*	42	20	13	9	58:37	53
4	Sunderland	42	19	13	10	65:35	51
5	Bristol C.	42	21	8	13	47:33	50
6	West Bromwich	42	18	9	15	54:42	45
7	Blackpool	42	14	17	11	38:33	45
8	Hull	42	15	14	13	40:53	44
9	Fulham	42	13	16	13	44:39	42
10	Bolton	42	15	12	15	45:41	42
11	Oxford	42	15	12	15	41:51	42
12	Orient	42	11	20	11	28:39	42
13	Southampton	42	15	11	16	53:54	41
14	Notts Co.	42	12	16	14	49:59	40
15	York	42	14	10	18	51:55	38
16	Nottingham F.	42	12	14	16	43:55	38
17	Portsmouth	42	12	13	17	44:54	37
18	Oldham	42	10	15	17	40:48	35
19	Bristol R.	42	12	11	19	42:64	35
20	Millwall†	42	10	12	20	44:56	32
21	Cardiff†	42	9	14	19	36:62	32
22	Sheffield W.†	42	5	11	26	29:64	21

DIVISION 3 1974-75

1	Blackburn*	46	22	16	8	68:45	60
2	Plymouth*	46	24	11	11	79:58	59
3	Charlton*	46	22	11	13	76:61	55
4	Swindon	46	21	11	14	64:58	53
5	Crystal Palace	46	18	15	13	66:57	51
6	Port Vale	46	18	15	13	61:54	51
7	Peterborough	46	19	12	15	47:53	50
8	Walsall	46	18	13	15	67:52	49
9	Preston	46	19	11	16	63:56	49
10	Gillingham	46	17	14	15	65:60	48
11	Colchester	46	17	13	16	70:63	47
12	Hereford	46	16	14	16	64:66	46
13	Wrexham	46	15	15	16	65:55	45
14	Bury	46	16	12	18	53:50	44
15	Chesterfield	46	16	12	18	62:66	44
16	Grimsby	46	15	13	18	55:64	43
17	Halifax	46	13	17	16	49:65	43
18	Southend	46	13	16	17	46:51	42
19	Brighton	46	16	10	20	56:64	42
20	Aldershot‡	46	14	11	21	53:63	38
21	Bournemouth†	46	13	12	21	44:58	38
22	Tranmere†	46	14	9	23	55:57	37
23	Watford†	46	10	17	19	52:75	37
24	Hudderfield†	46	11	10	25	47:76	32

DIVISION 4 1974-75

1	Mansfield*	46	28	12	6	90:40	68
2	Shrewsbury*	46	26	10	10	80:43	62
3	Rotherham*	46	22	15	9	71:41	59
4	Chester*	46	23	11	12	64:38	57
5	Lincoln	46	21	15	10	79:48	57
6	Cambridge	46	20	14	12	62:44	54
7	Reading	46	21	10	15	63:47	52
8	Brentford	46	18	13	15	53:45	49
9	Exeter	46	19	11	16	60:63	49
10	Bradford C.	46	17	13	16	56:51	47
11	Southport	46	15	17	14	56:56	47
12	Newport	46	19	9	18	68:75	47
13	Hartlepool	46	16	11	19	52:62	43
14	Torquay	46	14	14	18	46:61	42
15	Barnsley	46	15	11	20	62:65	41
16	Northampton	46	15	11	20	67:73	41
17	Doncaster	46	14	12	20	65:79	40
18	Crewe	46	11	18	17	34:47	40
19	Rochdale	46	13	13	20	59:75	39
20	Stockport	46	12	14	20	43:70	38
21	Darlington	46	13	10	23	54:67	36
22	Swansea	46	15	6	25	46:73	36
23	Workington	46	10	11	25	36:66	31
24	Scunthorpe	46	7	15	24	41:78	29

‡Preston (1973–74), Newport (1973–74) & Aldershot (1974–75) had one point deducted for fielding an ineligible player §Scunthorpe awarded both points after Exeter failed to turn up, 2.4.74

DIVISION 1 1975-76

1	Liverpool	42	23	14	5	66:31	60
2	QPR	42	24	11	7	67:33	59
3	Manchester U.	42	23	10	10	68:42	56
4	Derby	42	21	11	10	75:58	53
5	Leeds	42	21	9	12	65:46	51
6	Ipswich	42	16	14	12	54:48	46
7	Leicester	42	13	19	10	48:51	45
8	Manchester C.	42	16	12	15	64:46	43
9	Tottenham	42	14	15	13	63:63	43
10	Norwich	42	16	10	16	58:58	42
11	Everton	42	15	12	15	60:66	42
12	Stoke	42	15	11	16	48:50	41
13	Middlesbrough	42	15	10	17	46:45	40
14	Coventry	42	13	14	15	47:57	40
15	Newcastle	42	15	9	18	71:62	39
16	Aston Villa	42	11	17	14	51:59	39
17	Arsenal	42	13	10	19	47:53	36
18	West Ham	42	13	10	19	48:71	36
19	Birmingham	42	13	7	22	57:75	33
20	Wolverhampton†	42	10	10	22	51:68	30
21	Burnley†	42	9	10	23	43:66	28
22	Sheffield U.†	42	6	10	26	33:82	22

DIVISION 2 1975-76

1	Sunderland*	42	24	8	10	67:36	56
2	Bristol C.*	42	19	15	8	59:35	53
3	West Bromwich*	42	20	13	9	50:33	53
4	Bolton	42	20	12	10	64:38	52
5	Notts Co.	42	19	11	12	60:41	49
6	Southampton	42	21	7	14	66:50	49
7	Luton	42	19	10	13	61:51	48
8	Nottingham F.	42	17	12	13	55:40	46
9	Charlton	42	15	12	15	61:72	42
10	Blackpool	42	14	14	14	40:49	42
11	Chelsea	42	12	16	14	53:54	40
12	Fulham	42	13	14	15	45:47	40
13	Orient	42	13	14	15	37:39	40
14	Hull	42	14	11	17	45:49	39
15	Blackburn	42	12	14	16	45:50	38
16	Plymouth	42	13	12	17	48:54	38
17	Oldham	42	13	12	17	57:68	38
18	Bristol R.	42	11	16	15	38:50	38
19	Carlisle	42	12	13	17	45:59	37
20	Oxford†	42	11	11	20	39:59	33
21	York†	42	10	8	24	39:71	28
22	Portsmouth†	42	9	7	26	32:61	25

DIVISION 3 1975-76

1	Hereford*	46	26	11	9	86:55	63
2	Cardiff*	46	22	13	11	69:48	57
3	Millwall*	46	20	16	10	54:43	56
4	Brighton	46	22	9	15	78:53	53
5	Crystal Palace	46	18	17	11	61:46	53
6	Wrexham	46	20	12	14	66:55	52
7	Walsall	46	18	14	14	74:61	50
8	Preston	46	19	10	17	62:57	48
9	Shrewsbury	46	19	10	17	61:59	48
10	Peterborough	46	15	18	13	63:63	48
11	Mansfield.	46	16	15	15	58:52	47
12	Port Vale	46	15	16	15	55:54	46
13	Bury	46	14	16	16	51:46	44
14	Chesterfield	46	17	9	20	69:69	43
15	Gillingham	46	12	19	15	58:68	43
16	Rotherham	46	15	12	19	54:65	42
17	Chester	46	15	12	19	43:62	42
18	Grimsby	46	15	10	21	62:74	40
19	Swindon	46	16	8	22	62:75	40
20	Sheffield W.	46	12	16	18	48:59	40
21	Aldershot†	46	13	13	20	59:75	39
22	Colchester†	46	12	14	20	41:65	38
23	Southend†	46	12	13	21	65:75	37
24	Halifax†	46	11	13	22	41:61	35

DIVISION 4 1975-76

1	Lincoln*	46	32	10	4	111:39	74
2	Northampton*	46	29	10	7	87:40	68
3	Reading*	46	24	12	10	70:51	60
4	Tranmere*	46	24	10	12	89:55	58
5	Huddersfield	46	21	14	11	56:41	56
6	Bournemouth	46	20	12	14	57:48	52
7	Exeter	46	18	14	14	56:47	50
8	Watford	46	22	6	18	62:62	50
9	Torquay	46	18	14	14	55:63	50
10	Doncaster	46	19	11	16	75:69	49
11	Swansea	46	16	15	15	66:57	47
12	Barnsley	46	14	16	16	52:48	44
13	Cambridge	46	14	15	17	58:62	43
14	Hartlepool	46	16	10	20	62:78	42
15	Rochdale	46	12	18	16	40:54	42
16	Crewe	46	13	15	18	58:57	41
17	Bradford C.	46	12	17	17	63:65	41
18	Brentford	46	14	13	19	56:60	41
19	Scunthorpe	46	14	10	22	50:59	38
20	Darlington	46	14	10	22	48:57	38
21	Stockport	46	13	12	21	43:76	38
22	Newport	46	13	9	24	57:90	35
23	Southport	46	8	10	28	41:77	26
24	Workington	46	7	7	32	30:87	27

DIVISION 1 1976-77

1	Liverpool	42	23	11	8	62:33	57
2	Manchester C.	42	21	14	7	60:34	56
3	Ipswich	42	22	8	12	66:39	56
4	Aston Villa	42	22	7	13	76:50	51
5	Newcastle	42	18	13	11	64:49	49
6	Manchester U.	42	18	11	13	71:62	47
7	West Bromwich	42	16	13	13	62:56	45
8	Arsenal	42	16	11	15	64:59	43
9	Everton	42	14	14	14	62:64	42
10	Leeds	42	15	12	15	48:51	42
11	Leicester	42	12	18	12	47:60	42
12	Middlesbrough	42	14	13	15	40:45	41
13	Birmingham	42	13	12	17	63:61	38
14	QPR	42	13	12	17	47:52	38
15	Derby	42	9	19	14	50:55	37
16	Norwich	42	14	9	19	47:64	37
17	West Ham	42	11	14	17	46:65	36
18	Bristol C.	42	11	13	18	38:48	35
19	Coventry	42	10	15	17	48:59	35
20	Sunderland†	42	11	12	19	46:54	34
21	Stoke†	42	10	14	18	28:51	34
22	Tottenham†	42	12	9	21	48:72	33

DIVISION 2 1976-77

1	Wolverhampton*	42	22	13	7	84:45	57
2	Chelsea*	42	21	13	8	73:53	55
3	Nottingham F.*	42	21	10	11	77:43	52
4	Bolton	42	20	11	11	74:54	51
5	Blackpool	42	17	17	8	58:42	51
6	Luton	42	23	6	15	67:48	48
7	Charlton	42	16	16	10	71:58	48
8	Notts Co.	42	19	10	13	65:60	48
9	Southampton	42	17	10	15	72:67	44
10	Millwall	42	17	13	14	57:53	43
11	Sheffield U.	42	14	12	16	54:63	40
12	Blackburn	42	15	9	18	42:54	39
13	Oldham	42	14	10	18	52:64	38
14	Hull	42	10	17	15	45:53	37
15	Bristol R.	42	12	13	17	53:68	37
16	Burnley	42	11	14	17	46:64	36
17	Fulham	42	11	13	18	44:61	35
18	Cardiff	42	12	10	20	56:67	34
19	Orient	42	9	16	17	37:55	34
20	Carlisle†	42	11	12	19	49:75	34
21	Plymouth†	42	8	16	18	46:65	32
22	Hereford†	42	8	15	19	57:78	31

DIVISION 3 1976-77

1	Mansfield*	46	28	8	10	78:33	64
2	Brighton*	46	25	11	10	83:39	61
3	Crystal Palace*	46	23	13	10	68:40	59
4	Rotherham	46	22	15	9	69:44	59
5	Wrexham	46	24	10	12	80:54	58
6	Preston	46	21	12	13	64:43	54
7	Bury	46	23	8	15	64:59	54
8	Sheffield W.	46	22	9	15	65:55	53
9	Lincoln	46	19	14	13	77:70	52
10	Shrewsbury	46	18	11	17	65:59	47
11	Swindon	46	15	15	16	68:75	45
12	Gillingham	46	14	12	18	55:64	44
13	Chester	46	18	8	20	48:58	44
14	Tranmere	46	13	17	16	51:53	43
15	Walsall	46	13	15	18	57:65	41
16	Peterborough	46	13	15	18	55:65	41
17	Oxford	46	12	15	19	55:65	39
18	Chesterfield	46	14	10	22	56:64	38
19	Port Vale	46	11	16	19	47:71	38
20	Portsmouth	46	11	14	21	43:70	35
21	Reading†	46	13	9	24	49:73	35
22	Northampton†	46	13	8	25	60:75	34
23	Grimsby†	46	12	9	25	45:69	33
24	York†	46	10	12	24	50:89	32

DIVISION 4 1976-77

1	Cambridge*	46	26	13	7	87:40	65
2	Exeter*	46	25	12	9	70:46	62
3	Colchester*	46	25	9	12	77:43	59
4	Bradford C.*	46	23	13	10	71:51	59
5	Swansea	46	25	8	13	82:68	58
6	Barnsley	46	23	9	14	62:39	55
7	Watford	46	18	15	13	67:55	51
8	Doncaster	46	21	9	16	61:65	51
9	Huddersfield	46	19	12	15	60:49	50
10	Southend	46	15	19	12	52:45	49
11	Darlington	46	18	13	15	59:64	49
12	Crewe	46	19	11	16	47:60	49
13	Bournemouth	46	15	18	13	55:44	48
14	Stockport	46	13	19	14	53:57	45
15	Brentford	46	18	7	21	77:76	43
16	Torquay	46	17	9	20	59:67	43
17	Aldershot	46	16	11	19	45:59	43
18	Rochdale	46	13	12	21	50:59	38
19	Newport	46	14	10	22	42:58	38
20	Scunthorpe	46	13	11	22	49:73	37
21	Halifax	46	11	14	21	47:58	36
22	Hartlepool	46	10	12	24	47:73	32
23	Southport	46	3	19	24	53:77	25
24	Workington	46	4	11	31	41:102	19

DIVISION 1 1977-78

1	Nottingham F.	42	25	14	3	69:24	64
2	Liverpool	42	24	9	9	65:34	57
3	Everton	42	22	11	9	76:45	55
4	Manchester C.	42	20	12	10	74:51	52
5	Arsenal	42	21	10	11	60:37	52
6	West Bromwich	42	18	14	10	62:53	50
7	Coventry	42	18	12	12	75:62	48
8	Aston Villa	42	18	10	14	57:42	46
9	Leeds	42	18	10	14	63:53	46
10	Manchester U.	42	16	10	16	67:63	42
11	Birmingham	42	16	9	17	55:60	41
12	Derby	42	14	13	15	54:59	41
13	Norwich	42	11	18	13	52:66	40
14	Middlesbrough	42	12	15	15	42:54	39
15	Wolverhampton	42	12	12	18	51:64	36
16	Chelsea	42	11	14	17	46:69	36
17	Bristol C.	42	11	13	18	49:53	35
18	Ipswich	42	11	13	18	47:61	35
19	QPR	42	9	15	18	47:64	33
20	West Ham†	42	12	8	22	52:69	32
21	Newcastle†	42	6	10	26	42:78	22
22	Leicester†	42	5	12	25	26:70	22

DIVISION 2 1977-78

1	Bolton*	42	24	10	8	63:33	58
2	Southampton*	42	22	13	7	70:39	57
3	Tottenham*	42	20	16	6	83:49	56
4	Brighton	42	22	12	8	63:38	56
5	Blackburn	42	16	13	13	56:60	45
6	Sunderland	42	14	16	12	67:59	44
7	Stoke	42	16	10	16	53:49	42
8	Oldham	42	13	16	13	54:58	42
9	Crystal Palace	42	13	15	14	50:47	41
10	Fulham	42	14	13	15	49:49	41
11	Burnley	42	15	10	17	56:64	40
12	Sheffield U.	42	16	8	18	62:73	40
13	Luton	42	14	10	18	54:52	38
14	Orient	42	10	18	14	43:49	38
15	Notts Co.	42	11	16	15	54:62	38
16	Millwall	42	12	14	16	49:57	38
17	Charlton	42	13	12	17	55:68	38
18	Bristol R.	42	13	12	17	61:77	38
19	Cardiff	42	13	12	17	51:71	38
20	Blackpool†	42	12	13	17	59:60	37
21	Mansfield†	42	10	11	21	49:69	31
22	Hull†	42	8	12	22	34:52	28

DIVISION 3 1977-78

1	Wrexham*	46	23	15	8	78:45	61
2	Cambridge*	46	23	12	11	72:51	58
3	Preston*	46	20	16	10	63:38	56
4	Peterborough	46	20	16	10	47:33	56
5	Chester	46	16	22	8	59:56	54
6	Walsall	46	18	17	11	61:50	53
7	Gillingham	46	15	20	11	67:60	50
8	Colchester	46	15	18	13	55:44	48
9	Chesterfield	46	17	14	15	58:49	48
10	Swindon	46	16	16	14	67:60	48
11	Shrewsbury	46	16	15	15	63:57	47
12	Tranmere	46	16	15	15	57:52	47
13	Carlisle	46	14	19	13	59:59	47
14	Sheffield W.	46	15	16	15	50:52	46
15	Bury	46	13	19	14	62:56	45
16	Lincoln	46	15	15	16	53:61	45
17	Exeter	46	15	14	17	49:59	44
18	Oxford	46	13	14	19	64:67	40
19	Plymouth	46	11	17	18	61:68	39
20	Rotherham	46	13	13	20	51:68	39
21	Port Vale†	46	8	20	18	46:67	36
22	Bradford C.†	46	12	10	24	56:86	34
23	Hereford†	46	9	14	23	34:60	32
24	Portsmouth†	46	7	17	22	31:75	31

DIVISION 4 1977-78

1	Watford*	46	30	11	5	85:38	71
2	Southend*	46	25	10	11	66:39	60
3	Swansea*	46	23	10	13	87:47	56
4	Brentford*	46	21	14	11	86:54	56
5	Aldershot	46	19	16	11	67:47	54
6	Grimsby	46	21	11	14	57:51	53
7	Barnsley	46	18	14	14	61:49	50
8	Reading	46	18	14	14	55:52	50
9	Torquay	46	16	15	15	57:56	47
10	Northampton	46	17	13	16	63:68	47
11	Huddersfield	46	15	15	16	63:55	45
12	Doncaster	46	14	17	15	52:65	45
13	Wimbledon	46	14	16	16	66:67	44
14	Scunthorpe	46	14	16	16	50:55	44
15	Crewe	46	15	14	17	50:69	44
16	Newport	46	16	11	19	65:73	43
17	Bournemouth	46	14	15	17	41:51	43
18	Stockport	46	16	10	20	56:56	42
19	Darlington	46	14	13	19	52:59	41
20	Halifax	46	10	21	15	52:62	41
21	Hartlepool	46	15	7	24	51:84	37
22	York	46	12	12	22	50:69	36
23	Southport	46	6	19	21	52:76	31
24	Rochdale	46	8	8	30	43:85	24

DIVISION 1 1978-79

1	Liverpool	42	30	8	4	85:16	68
2	Nottingham F.	42	21	18	3	61:26	60
3	West Bromwich	42	24	11	7	72:35	59
4	Everton	42	17	17	8	52:40	51
5	Leeds	42	18	14	10	70:52	50
6	Ipswich	42	20	9	13	63:49	49
7	Arsenal	42	17	14	11	61:48	48
8	Aston Villa	42	15	16	11	59:49	46
9	Manchester U.	42	15	15	12	60:63	45
10	Coventry	42	14	16	12	58:68	44
11	Tottenham	42	13	15	14	48:61	41
12	Middlesbrough	42	15	10	17	57:50	40
13	Bristol C.	42	15	10	17	47:51	40
14	Southampton	42	12	16	14	47:53	40
15	Manchester C.	42	13	13	16	58:56	39
16	Norwich	42	7	23	12	51:57	37
17	Bolton	42	12	11	19	54:75	35
18	Wolverhampton	42	13	8	21	44:68	34
19	Derby	42	10	11	21	44:71	31
20	QPR†	42	6	13	23	45:73	25
21	Birmingham†	42	6	10	26	37:64	22
22	Chelsea†	42	5	10	27	44:92	20

DIVISION 2 1978-79

1	Crystal Palace*	42	19	19	4	51:24	57
2	Brighton*	42	23	10	9	72:39	56
3	Stoke*	42	20	16	6	58:31	56
4	Sunderland	42	22	11	9	70:44	55
5	West Ham	42	18	14	10	70:39	50
6	Notts Co.	42	14	16	12	48:60	44
7	Preston	42	12	18	12	59:57	42
8	Newcastle	42	17	8	17	51:55	42
9	Cardiff	42	16	10	16	56:70	42
10	Fulham	42	13	15	14	50:47	41
11	Orient	42	15	10	17	51:51	40
12	Cambridge	42	12	16	14	44:52	40
13	Burnley	42	14	12	16	51:62	40
14	Oldham	42	13	13	16	52:61	39
15	Wrexham	42	12	14	16	45:42	38
16	Bristol R.	42	14	10	18	48:60	38
17	Leicester	42	10	17	15	43:52	37
18	Luton	42	13	10	19	60:57	36
19	Charlton	42	11	13	18	60:69	35
20	Sheffield U.†	42	11	12	19	52:69	34
21	Millwall†	42	11	10	21	42:61	32
22	Blackburn†	42	10	10	22	41:72	30

DIVISION 3 1978-79

1	Shrewsbury*	46	21	19	6	61:41	61
2	Watford*	46	24	12	10	83:52	60
3	Swansea*	46	24	12	10	83:61	60
4	Gillingham	46	21	17	8	65:42	59
5	Swindon	46	25	7	14	74:52	57
6	Carlisle	46	15	22	9	53:42	52
7	Colchester	46	17	17	12	60:55	51
8	Hull	46	19	11	16	66:61	49
9	Exeter	46	17	15	14	61:56	49
10	Brentford	46	19	9	18	53:49	47
11	Oxford	46	14	18	14	44:50	46
12	Blackpool	46	18	9	19	61:59	45
13	Southend	46	15	15	16	51:49	45
14	Sheffield W.	46	13	19	14	53:53	45
15	Plymouth	46	15	14	17	67:68	44
16	Chester	46	14	16	16	57:61	44
17	Rotherham	46	17	10	19	49:55	44
18	Mansfield	46	12	19	15	51:52	43
19	Bury	46	11	20	15	59:65	42
20	Chesterfield	46	13	14	19	51:65	40
21	Peterborough†	46	11	14	21	44:63	36
22	Walsall†	46	10	12	24	56:71	32
23	Tranmere†	46	6	16	24	45:78	28
24	Lincoln†	46	7	11	28	41:88	25

DIVISION 4 1978-79

1	Reading*	46	26	13	7	76:35	65
2	Grimsby*	46	26	9	11	82:49	61
3	Wimbledon*	46	25	11	10	78:46	61
4	Barnsley*	46	24	13	9	73:42	61
5	Aldershot	46	20	17	9	63:47	57
6	Wigan	46	21	13	12	63:48	55
7	Portsmouth	46	20	12	14	62:48	52
8	Newport	46	21	10	15	66:55	52
9	Huddersfield	46	18	11	17	57:53	47
10	York	46	18	11	17	51:55	47
11	Torquay	46	19	8	19	58:65	46
12	Scunthorpe	46	17	11	18	54:60	45
13	Hartlepool	46	13	18	15	57:66	44
14	Hereford	46	15	13	18	53:53	43
15	Bradford C.	46	17	9	20	62:68	43
16	Port Vale	46	14	14	18	57:70	42
17	Stockport	46	14	12	20	58:60	40
18	Bournemouth	46	14	11	21	47:48	39
19	Northampton	46	15	9	22	64:76	39
20	Rochdale	46	15	9	22	47:64	39
21	Darlington	46	11	15	20	49:66	37
22	Doncaster	46	13	11	22	50:73	37
23	Halifax	46	9	8	29	39:72	26
24	Crewe	46	6	14	26	43:90	26

DIVISION 1 1979-80

1	Liverpool	42	25	10	7	81:30	60
2	Manchester U.	42	24	10	8	65:35	58
3	Ipswich	42	22	9	11	68:39	53
4	Arsenal	42	18	16	8	52:36	52
5	Nottingham F.	42	20	8	14	63:43	48
6	Wolverhampton	42	19	9	14	58:47	47
7	Aston Villa	42	16	14	12	51:50	46
8	Southampton	42	18	9	15	65:53	45
9	Middlesbrough	42	16	12	14	50:44	44
10	West Bromwich	42	11	19	12	54:50	41
11	Leeds	42	13	14	15	46:50	40
12	Norwich	42	13	14	15	58:66	40
13	Crystal Palace	42	12	16	14	41:50	40
14	Tottenham	42	15	10	17	52:62	40
15	Coventry	42	16	7	19	56:66	39
16	Brighton	42	11	15	16	47:57	37
17	Manchester C.	42	12	13	17	43:66	37
18	Stoke	42	13	10	19	44:58	36
19	Everton	42	9	17	16	43:51	35
20	Bristol C.†	42	9	13	20	37:66	31
21	Derby†	42	11	8	23	47:67	30
22	Bolton†	42	5	15	22	38:73	25

DIVISION 2 1979-80

1	Leicester*	42	21	13	8	58:38	55
2	Sunderland*	42	21	12	9	69:42	54
3	Birmingham*	42	21	11	10	58:38	53
4	Chelsea	42	23	7	12	66:52	53
5	QPR	42	18	13	11	75:53	49
6	Luton	42	16	17	9	66:45	49
7	West Ham	42	20	7	15	54:43	47
8	Cambridge	42	14	16	12	61:53	44
9	Newcastle	42	15	14	13	53:49	44
10	Preston	42	12	19	11	56:52	43
11	Oldham	42	16	11	15	49:53	43
12	Swansea	42	17	9	16	48:53	43
13	Shrewsbury	42	18	5	19	60:53	41
14	Orient	42	12	17	13	48:54	41
15	Cardiff	42	16	8	18	41:48	40
16	Wrexham	42	16	6	20	40:49	38
17	Notts Co.	42	11	15	16	51:52	37
18	Watford	42	12	13	17	39:46	37
19	Bristol R.	42	11	13	18	50:64	35
20	Fulham†	42	11	7	24	42:74	29
21	Burnley†	42	6	15	21	39:73	27
22	Charlton†	42	6	10	26	39:78	22

DIVISION 3 1979-80

1	Grimsby*	46	26	10	10	73:42	62
2	Blackburn*	46	25	9	12	58:36	59
3	Sheffield W.*	46	21	16	9	81:47	58
4	Chesterfield	46	23	11	12	71:46	57
5	Colchester	46	20	12	14	64:56	52
6	Carlisle	46	18	12	16	66:56	48
7	Reading	46	16	16	14	66:65	48
8	Exeter	46	19	10	17	60:68	48
9	Chester	46	17	13	16	49:57	47
10	Swindon	46	19	8	19	71:63	46
11	Barnsley	46	16	14	16	53:56	46
12	Sheffield U.	46	18	10	18	60:66	46
13	Rotherham	46	18	10	18	58:66	46
14	Millwall	46	16	13	17	65:59	45
15	Plymouth	46	16	12	18	59:55	44
16	Gillingham	46	14	14	18	49:51	42
17	Oxford	46	14	13	19	57:62	41
18	Blackpool	46	15	11	20	62:74	41
19	Brentford	46	15	11	20	59:73	41
20	Hull	46	12	16	18	51:69	40
21	Bury†	46	16	7	23	45:59	39
22	Southend†	46	14	10	22	47:58	38
23	Mansfield†	46	10	16	20	47:58	36
24	Wimbledon†	46	10	14	22	52:81	34

DIVISION 4 1979-80

1	Huddersfield*	46	27	12	7	101:48	66
2	Walsall*	46	23	18	5	75:47	64
3	Newport*	46	27	7	12	83:50	61
4	Portsmouth*	46	24	12	10	91:49	60
5	Bradford C.	46	24	12	10	77:50	60
6	Wigan	46	21	13	12	76:61	55
7	Lincoln	46	18	17	11	64:42	53
8	Peterborough	46	21	10	15	58:47	52
9	Torquay	46	15	17	14	70:69	47
10	Aldershot	46	16	13	17	62:53	45
11	Bournemouth	46	13	18	15	52:51	44
12	Doncaster	46	15	14	17	62:63	44
13	Northampton	46	16	12	18	51:66	44
14	Scunthorpe	46	14	15	17	58:75	43
15	Tranmere	46	14	13	19	50:56	41
16	Stockport	46	14	12	20	48:72	40
17	York	46	14	11	21	65:82	39
18	Halifax	46	13	13	20	46:72	39
19	Hartlepool	46	14	10	22	59:64	38
20	Port Vale	46	12	12	22	56:70	36
21	Hereford	46	11	14	21	38:52	36
22	Darlington	46	9	17	20	50:74	35
23	Crewe	46	11	13	22	35:68	35
24	Rochdale	46	7	13	26	33:79	27

DIVISION 1 1980-81

1	Aston Villa	42	26	8	8	72:40	60
2	Ipswich	42	23	10	9	77:43	56
3	Arsenal	42	19	15	8	61:45	53
4	West Bromwich	42	20	12	10	60:42	52
5	Liverpool	42	17	17	8	62:46	51
6	Southampton	42	20	10	12	76:56	50
7	Nottingham F.	42	19	12	11	62:45	50
8	Manchester U.	42	15	18	9	51:36	48
9	Leeds	42	17	10	15	39:47	44
10	Tottenham	42	14	15	13	70:68	43
11	Stoke	42	12	18	12	51:60	42
12	Manchester C.	42	14	11	17	56:59	39
13	Birmingham	42	13	12	17	50:61	38
14	Middlesbrough	42	16	5	21	53:61	37
15	Everton	42	13	10	19	55:58	36
16	Coventry	42	13	10	19	48:68	36
17	Sunderland	42	14	7	21	58:53	35
18	Wolverhampton	42	13	9	20	47:55	35
19	Brighton	42	14	7	21	54:67	35
20	Norwich†	42	13	7	22	49:73	33
21	Leicester †	42	13	6	23	40:67	32
22	Crystal Palace †	42	6	7	29	47:83	19

DIVISION 2 1980-81

1	West Ham*	42	28	10	4	79:29	66
2	Notts Co.*	42	18	17	7	49:38	53
3	Swansea*	42	18	14	10	64:44	50
4	Blackburn	42	16	18	8	42:29	50
5	Luton	42	18	12	12	61:46	48
6	Derby	42	15	15	12	57:52	45
7	Grimsby	42	15	15	12	44:42	45
8	QPR	42	15	13	14	56:46	43
9	Watford	42	16	11	15	50:45	43
10	Sheffield W.	42	17	8	17	53:51	42
11	Newcastle	42	14	14	14	30:45	42
12	Chelsea	42	14	12	16	46:41	40
13	Cambridge	42	17	6	17	53:65	40
14	Shrewsbury	42	11	17	14	46:47	39
15	Oldham	42	12	15	15	39:48	39
16	Wrexham	42	12	14	16	43:45	38
17	Orient	42	13	12	17	52:56	38
18	Bolton	42	14	10	18	61:66	38
19	Cardiff	42	12	12	18	44:60	36
20	Preston†	42	11	14	17	41:62	36
21	Bristol C.†	42	7	16	19	29:51	30
22	Bristol R.†	42	5	13	24	34:65	23

DIVISION 3 1980-81

1	Rotherham*	46	24	13	9	62:32	61
2	Barnsley*	46	21	17	8	72:45	59
3	Charlton*	46	25	9	12	63:44	59
4	Huddersfield	46	21	14	11	71:40	56
5	Chesterfield	46	23	10	13	72:48	56
6	Portsmouth	46	22	9	15	55:47	53
7	Plymouth	46	19	14	13	56:44	52
8	Burnley	46	18	14	14	60:48	50
9	Brentford	46	14	19	13	52:49	47
10	Reading	46	18	10	18	62:62	46
11	Exeter	46	16	13	17	62:66	45
12	Newport	46	15	13	18	64:61	43
13	Fulham	46	15	13	18	57:64	43
14	Oxford	46	13	17	16	39:47	43
15	Gillingham	46	12	18	16	48:58	42
16	Millwall	46	14	14	18	43:60	42
17	Swindon	46	13	15	18	51:56	41
18	Chester	46	15	11	20	41:48	41
19	Carlisle	46	14	13	19	57:70	41
20	Walsall	46	13	15	18	59:74	41
21	Sheffield U.†	46	14	13	19	65:62	40
22	Colchester†	46	14	11	21	45:65	39
23	Blackpool†	46	9	14	23	45:75	32
24	Hull†	46	8	16	22	40:71	32

DIVISION 4 1980-81

1	Southend*	46	30	7	9	79:31	67
2	Lincoln*	46	25	15	6	66:25	65
3	Doncaster*	46	22	12	12	59:49	56
4	Wimbledon*	46	23	9	14	64:46	55
5	Peterborough	46	17	18	11	68:54	52
6	Aldershot	46	18	14	14	43:41	50
7	Mansfield	46	20	9	17	58:44	49
8	Darlington	46	19	11	16	65:59	49
9	Hartlepool	46	20	9	17	64:61	49
10	Northampton	46	18	13	15	65:67	49
11	Wigan	46	18	11	17	51:55	47
12	Bury	46	17	11	18	70:62	45
13	Bournemouth	46	16	13	17	47:48	45
14	Bradford C.	46	14	16	16	53:60	44
15	Rochdale	46	14	15	17	60:70	43
16	Scunthorpe	46	11	20	15	60:69	42
17	Torquay	46	18	5	23	55:63	41
18	Crewe	46	13	14	19	48:61	40
19	Port Vale	46	12	15	19	57:68	39
20	Stockport	46	16	7	23	44:57	39
21	Tranmere	46	13	10	23	59:73	36
22	Hereford	46	11	13	22	38:62	35
23	Halifax	46	11	12	23	44:71	34
24	York	46	12	9	25	47:66	33

DIVISION 1 1981-82

1	Liverpool	42	26	9	7	80:32	87
2	Ipswich	42	26	5	11	75:53	83
3	Man United	42	22	12	8	59:29	78
4	Tottenham	42	20	11	11	67:48	71
5	Arsenal	42	20	11	11	48:37	71
6	Swansea	42	21	6	15	58:51	69
7	Southampton	42	19	9	14	72:67	66
8	Everton	42	17	13	12	56:50	64
9	West Ham	42	14	16	12	66:57	58
10	Man City	42	15	13	14	49:50	58
11	Aston Villa	42	15	12	15	55:53	57
12	Nottm Forest	42	15	12	15	42:48	57
13	Brighton	42	13	13	16	43:52	52
14	Coventry	42	13	11	18	56:62	50
15	Notts County	42	13	8	21	45:69	47
16	Birmingham	42	10	14	18	53:61	44
17	WBA	42	11	11	20	46:57	44
18	Stoke	42	12	8	22	44:63	44
19	Sunderland	42	11	11	20	38:58	44
20	Leeds†	42	10	12	20	39:61	42
21	Wolves†	42	10	10	22	32:63	40
22	Middlesbrough†	42	8	15	19	34:52	39

DIVISION 2 1981-82

1	Luton*	42	25	13	4	86:46	88
2	Watford*	42	23	11	8	76:42	80
3	Norwich*	42	22	5	15	64:50	71
4	Sheff Wed	42	20	10	12	55:51	70
5	QPR	42	21	6	15	65:43	69
6	Barnsley	42	19	10	13	59:41	67
7	Rotherham	42	20	7	15	66:54	67
8	Leicester	42	18	12	12	56:48	66
9	Newcastle	42	18	8	16	52:50	62
10	Blackburn	42	16	11	15	47:43	59
11	Oldham	42	15	14	13	50:51	59
12	Chelsea	42	15	12	15	60:60	57
13	Charlton	42	13	12	17	50:65	51
14	Cambridge	42	13	9	20	48:53	48
15	Crystal Palace	42	13	9	20	34:45	48
16	Derby	42	12	12	18	53:68	48
17	Grimsby	42	11	13	18	53:65	46
18	Shrewsbury	42	11	3	18	37:57	46
19	Bolton	42	13	7	22	39:61	46
20	Cardiff†	42	12	8	22	45:61	44
21	Wrexham†	42	11	11	20	40:56	44
22	Orient†	42	10	9	23	39:61	39

DIVISION 3 1981-82

1	Burnley*	46	21	17	8	66:49	80
2	Carlisle*	46	23	11	12	65:50	80
3	Fulham*	46	21	15	10	77:51	78
4	Lincoln	46	21	14	11	66:40	77
5	Oxford	46	19	14	13	63:49	71
6	Gillingham	46	20	11	15	64:56	71
7	Southend	46	18	15	13	63:51	69
8	Brentford	46	19	11	16	56:47	68
9	Millwall	46	18	13	15	62:62	67
10	Plymouth	46	18	11	17	64:56	65
11	Chesterfield	46	18	10	18	67:58	64
12	Reading	46	17	11	18	67:75	62
13	Portsmouth	46	14	19	13	56:51	61
14	Preston	46	16	13	17	50:56	61
15	Bristol Rovers‡	46	18	9	19	58:65	61
16	Newport	46	14	16	16	54:54	58
17	Huddersfield	46	15	12	19	64:59	57
18	Exeter	46	16	9	21	71:84	57
19	Doncaster	46	13	17	16	55:68	56
20	Walsall	46	13	14	19	51:55	53
21	Wimbledon†	46	14	11	21	61:75	53
22	Swindon†	46	13	13	20	55:71	52
23	Bristol City†	46	11	13	22	40:65	46
24	Chester†	46	7	11	28	36:78	32

DIVISION 4 1981-82

1	Sheff United*	46	27	15	4	94:41	96
2	Bradford City*	46	26	13	7	88:45	91
3	Wigan*	46	26	13	7	80:46	91
4	Bournemouth*	46	23	19	4	62:30	88
5	Peterborough	46	24	10	12	71:57	82
6	Colchester	46	20	12	14	82:57	72
7	Port Vale	46	18	16	12	56:49	70
8	Hull	46	19	12	15	70:61	69
9	Bury	46	17	17	12	80:59	68
10	Hereford	46	16	19	11	64:58	67
11	Tranmere	46	14	18	14	51:56	60
12	Blackpool	46	15	13	18	66:60	58
13	Darlington	46	15	13	18	61:62	58
14	Hartlepool	46	13	16	17	73:84	55
15	Torquay	46	14	13	19	47:59	55
16	Aldershot	46	13	15	18	57:68	54
17	York	46	14	8	24	69:91	50
18	Stockport	46	12	13	21	48:67	49
19	Halifax	46	9	22	15	51:72	49
20	Mansfield‡	46	13	10	23	63:81	47
21	Rochdale	46	10	16	20	50:62	46
22	Northampton	46	11	9	26	57:84	42
23	Scunthorpe	46	9	15	22	43:79	42
24	Crewe	46	6	9	31	29:84	27

DIVISION 1 1982-83

1	Liverpool	42	24	10	8	87:37	82
2	Watford	42	22	5	15	74:57	71
3	Man United	42	19	13	8	56:38	70
4	Tottenham	42	20	9	13	65:50	69
5	Nottm Forest	42	20	9	13	62:50	69
6	Aston Villa	42	21	5	16	62:50	68
7	Everton	42	18	10	14	66:48	64
8	West Ham	42	20	4	18	68:62	64
9	Ipswich	42	15	13	14	64:50	58
10	Arsenal	42	16	10	16	58:56	58
11	WBA	42	15	12	15	51:49	57
12	Southampton	42	15	12	15	54:58	57
13	Stoke	42	16	9	17	53:64	57
14	Norwich	42	14	12	16	52:58	54
15	Sunderland	42	12	14	16	48:61	50
16	Notts County	42	15	7	21	55:71	52
17	Birmingham	42	12	15	16	40:55	50
18	Luton	42	12	13	17	65:84	49
19	Coventry	42	13	9	20	48:59	48
20	Man City†	42	13	8	21	47:70	47
21	Swansea†	42	10	11	21	51:69	41
22	Brighton†	42	9	13	20	38:67	40

DIVISION 2 1982-83

1	QPR*	42	26	7	9	77:36	85
2	Wolves*	42	20	15	7	68:44	75
3	Leicester*	42	20	10	12	72:44	70
4	Fulham	42	20	9	13	64:47	69†
5	Newcastle	42	18	13	11	75:53	67
6	Sheff Wed	42	16	15	11	60:47	63
7	Oldham	42	14	19	9	64:47	61
8	Leeds	42	13	21	8	51:46	60
9	Shrewsbury	42	15	14	13	48:48	59
10	Barnsley	42	14	15	13	57:55	57
11	Blackburn	42	15	12	15	58:58	57
12	Cambridge	42	13	12	17	42:60	51
13	Derby	42	10	19	13	49:58	49†
14	Carlisle	42	12	12	18	68:70	48
15	Crystal Palace	42	12	12	18	43:52	48
16	Middlesbrough	42	11	15	16	46:67	48
17	Charlton	42	13	9	20	63:86	48
18	Chelsea	42	11	14	17	51:61	47
19	Grimsby	42	12	11	19	45:70	47
20	Rotherham†	42	10	15	17	45:68	45
21	Burnley†	42	12	8	22	56:66	44
22	Bolton†	42	11	11	20	42:61	44

DIVISION 3 1982-83

1	Portsmouth*	46	27	10	9	74:41	91
2	Cardiff*	46	25	11	10	76:50	86
3	Huddersfield*	46	23	13	10	84:49	82
4	Newport	46	23	9	14	76:54	78
5	Oxford	46	22	12	12	71:53	78
6	Lincoln	46	23	7	16	77:51	76
7	Bristol Rovers	46	22	9	15	84:57	75
8	Plymouth	46	19	8	19	61:66	65
9	Brentford	46	18	10	18	88:77	64
10	Walsall	46	17	13	16	64:63	64
11	Sheff United	46	19	7	20	62:64	64
12	Bradford City	46	16	13	17	68:69	61
13	Gillingham	46	16	13	17	58:59	61
14	Bournemouth	46	16	13	17	59:68	61
15	Southend	46	15	14	17	66:65	59
16	Preston	46	15	13	18	60:69	58
17	Millwall	46	14	13	19	64:78	55
18	Wigan	46	15	9	22	60:72	54
19	Exeter	46	14	12	20	81:104	54
20	Orient	46	15	9	22	64:88	54
21	Reading†	46	12	17	17	63:80	53
22	Wrexham†	46	12	15	19	57:76	51
23	Doncaster†	46	9	11	26	57:97	38
24	Chesterfield†	46	8	13	25	44:68	37

DIVISION 4 1982-83

1	Wimbledon*	46	29	11	6	96:45	98
2	Hull*	46	25	15	6	75:34	90
3	Port Vale*	46	26	10	10	67:34	88
4	Scunthorpe*	46	23	14	9	71:42	83
5	Bury	46	24	12	11	76:44	81
6	Colchester	46	24	9	13	75:55	81
7	York	46	22	13	11	88:58	79
8	Swindon	46	19	11	16	61:54	68
9	Peterborough	46	17	13	16	58:52	64
10	Mansfield	46	16	13	17	61:70	61
11	Halifax	46	16	12	18	59:66	60
12	Torquay	46	17	7	22	56:65	58
13	Chester	46	15	11	20	55:60	56
14	Bristol City	46	13	17	16	59:70	56
15	Northampton	46	14	12	20	67:75	54
16	Stockport	46	14	12	20	60:79	54
17	Darlington	46	13	13	20	61:71	52
18	Aldershot	46	12	15	19	61:82	51
19	Tranmere	46	13	11	22	49:71	50
20	Rochdale	46	11	16	19	55:73	49
21	Blackpool	46	13	12	21	55:74	49
22	Hartlepool	46	13	9	24	46:76	48
23	Crewe	46	11	8	27	53:71	41
24	Hereford	46	11	8	27	43:79	41

DIVISION 1 1983-84

1	Liverpool	42	22	14	6	73:32	80
2	Southampton	42	22	11	9	66:38	77
3	Nottingham F.	42	22	8	12	76:45	74
4	Manchester U.	42	20	14	8	71:41	74
5	QPR	42	22	7	13	67:37	73
6	Arsenal	42	19	9	15	74:60	63
7	Everton	42	16	14	12	44:42	62
8	Tottenham	42	17	10	15	64:65	61
9	West Ham	42	17	9	16	60:55	60
10	Aston Villa	42	17	9	16	59:61	60
11	Watford	42	16	9	17	68:77	57
12	Ipswich	42	15	8	19	55:57	53
13	Sunderland	42	13	13	16	42:53	52
14	Norwich	42	12	15	15	48:49	51
15	Leicester	42	13	12	17	65:68	51
16	Luton	42	14	9	19	53:66	51
17	West Bromwich	42	14	9	19	48:62	51
18	Stoke	42	13	11	18	44:63	50
19	Coventry	42	13	11	18	57:77	50
20	Birmingham†	42	12	12	18	39:50	48
21	Notts Co†	42	10	11	21	50:72	41
22	Wolves†	42	6	11	25	27:80	29

DIVISION 2 1983-84

1	Chelsea*	42	25	13	4	90:40	89
2	Sheffield W*	42	26	10	6	72:34	89
3	Newcastle*	42	24	8	10	85:53	80
4	Manchester C.	42	20	10	12	66:48	70
5	Grimsby	42	19	13	10	60:47	70
6	Blackburn	42	17	16	9	57:46	67
7	Carlisle	42	16	16	10	48:41	64
8	Shrewsbury	42	17	10	15	49:53	61
9	Brighton	42	17	9	16	69:60	60
10	Leeds	42	16	12	14	55:56	60
11	Fulham	42	15	12	15	60:53	57
12	Huddersfield	42	14	15	13	56:49	57
13	Charlton	42	16	9	17	53:64	57
14	Barnsley	42	15	7	20	57:53	52
15	Cardiff	42	15	6	21	53:66	51
16	Portsmouth	42	14	7	21	73:64	49
17	Middlesbrough	42	12	13	17	41:47	49
18	Crystal Palace	42	12	11	19	42:52	47
19	Oldham	42	13	8	21	47:73	47
20	Derby†	42	11	9	22	36:72	42
21	Swansea†	42	7	8	27	36:85	29
22	Cambridge†	42	4	12	26	28:77	24

DIVISION 3 1983-84

1	Oxford*	46	28	11	7	91:50	95
2	Wimbledon*	46	26	9	11	97:76	87
3	Sheffield U.	46	24	11	11	86:53	83
4	Hull	46	23	14	9	71:38	83
5	Bristol R.	46	22	13	11	68:54	79
6	Walsall	46	22	9	15	68:61	75
7	Bradford C.	46	20	11	15	73:65	71
8	Gillingham	46	20	10	16	74:69	70
9	Millwall	46	18	13	15	71:65	67
10	Bolton	46	18	10	18	56:60	64
11	Orient	46	18	9	19	71:81	63
12	Burnley	46	16	14	16	76:61	62
13	Newport	46	16	14	16	58:75	62
14	Lincoln	46	17	10	19	59:62	61
15	Wigan	46	16	13	17	46:56	61
16	Preston	46	15	11	20	66:66	56
17	Bournemouth	46	16	7	23	63:73	55
18	Rotherham	46	15	9	22	57:64	54
19	Plymouth	46	13	12	21	56:62	51
20	Brentford	46	11	16	19	69:79	49
21	Scunthorpe†	46	9	19	18	54:73	46
22	Southend†	46	10	14	22	55:76	44
23	Port Vale†	46	11	10	25	51:83	43
24	Exeter†	46	6	15	25	50:84	33

DIVISION 4 1983-84

1	York*	46	31	8	7	96:39	101
2	Doncaster*	46	24	13	9	82:54	85
3	Reading*	46	22	16	8	84:56	82
4	Bristol C.*	46	24	10	12	70:44	82
5	Aldershot	46	22	9	15	76:69	75
6	Blackpool	46	21	9	16	70:52	72
7	Peterborough	46	18	14	14	72:48	68
8	Colchester	46	17	16	13	69:53	67
9	Torquay	46	18	13	15	59:64	67
10	Tranmere	46	17	15	14	53:53	66
11	Hereford	46	16	15	15	54:53	63
12	Stockport	46	17	11	18	60:64	62
13	Chesterfield	46	15	15	16	59:61	60
14	Darlington	46	17	8	21	49:50	59
15	Bury	46	15	14	17	61:64	59
16	Crewe	46	16	11	19	56:67	59
17	Swindon	46	15	13	18	58:56	58
18	Northampton	46	13	14	19	53:78	53
19	Mansfield	46	13	13	20	66:70	52
20	Wrexham	46	11	15	20	59:74	48
21	Halifax	46	12	12	22	55:89	48
22	Rochdale	46	11	13	22	52:80	46
23	Hartlepool	46	10	10	26	47:85	40
24	Chester	46	7	13	26	45:82	34

‡Two points deduced by League. †Game between Derby and Fulham abandoned after 88 minutes but result allowed to stand at 1-0.

CHAMPIONS

Most Championships: Liverpool have won the League on 14 occasions. Arsenal have the next best record with 8 (up to 1 January 1984).

Division 2 Championships: Leicester City and Manchester City have both won the Second Division title 6 times.

Division 3 Championships: Barnsley, Bristol City, Doncaster, Grimsby, Portsmouth and Lincoln have all won Division 3, 3S or 3N Championships on 3 occasions. No side has won the reconstituted Division 3 more than once.

Division 4 Championships: Doncaster, Peterborough and Walsall have all won Division 4 twice.

Never led the League: Burnley did not lead Division 1 in 1959–60 until after their very last game, on Monday 2 May against Manchester City at Maine Road. They won 2-1 to go past Wolves to the top for the first time – and to win the Championship by a point. Wolves had a much better goal average, won the Cup that year, and had beaten Burnley 6-1 on Wednesday 30 March 1960. Needless to say, the nature of Burnley's success is unparalleled.

Worst start: Burnley also had the worst ever start of a Championship winning side when they lost their first 3 games of the 1920–21 season – 4-1 at home to Bradford City (their only home defeat of the season) on Saturday 28 August, 1-0 at Huddersfield on Monday 30 August and 2-0 at Bradford City on Saturday 4 September. Their fourth game, a 3-0 win over Huddersfield on Monday 6 September, was the start of a run of 30 games without defeat, broken by Manchester City 3-0 at Hyde Road on Saturday 26 March 1921. After their 30-game run, Burnley won only 2 games. Hence their season's record was 3 defeats, then 30 games without defeat, finishing with only 2 wins out of 9 games – but they still won the Championship by 5 points from Manchester City.

Sunderland did not win until their 8th game in 1912–13, but still set a record for a 38-game season with 54 points. After 7 games they had only 2 points and had lost 4-2 at home to Blackburn, 2-0 at home to Derby, 4-0 away to Blackburn and 3-0 away to Oldham. Yet they came within an ace of the double in winning the League and losing the Cup final by a single goal to Aston Villa.

Championship play-offs: On only two occasions have two clubs effectively played off for the Championship – and both involved Liverpool:

1898–99 season: On the morning of Saturday 22 April 1899 Liverpool had 41 points with 2 matches to play and Aston Villa had 39 points with 3 matches left. Liverpool beat Blackburn 2-0 and Villa beat Notts County 6-1 that day. On 24 April Villa beat WBA 7-1. On Saturday 29 April Villa and Liverpool met at Villa Park in the final game of the season, both having 43 points. Villa won 5-0 and took the League, having had an aggregate of 18-2 in their final 3 games in the space of a week (all 3 were played at Villa Park).

1946–47 season: On Saturday 31 May Liverpool beat Wolves 2-1 at Molineux in their last game of the season and took over from them at the top of Division 1 with 57 points to Wolves' 56. Manchester United, despite

---

Frank Stapleton equalises for Manchester United against Brighton and Hove Albion in the 1983 FA Cup final. The game finished 2-2 and was therefore the third consecutive final to go to a replay. This had not happened since 1912. Stapleton's goal also made him the only man to score for two different clubs in an FA Cup final (excluding Kinnaird, Turner and Hutchison, who all scored own goals). He had scored for Arsenal against Manchester United in 1979 (inset).

defeating Sheffield United 6-2 in their last game, could also only finish with 56 points. Liverpool then had to wait until Saturday 14 June to see whether Stoke would overhaul them, as Stoke had 2 points less but a better goal difference and one game to play. That game was at Bramall Lane, where Stoke lost 2-1 to Sheffield United and hence finished fourth. That day, 14 June, is the latest date on which the Championship of any division has been decided.

CLUB MISCELLANY

Joined League without kicking a ball: Two sides have been accepted for membership of the Football League without ever having played a game. In 1903 Manningham Rugby Club changed to playing soccer, applied to the League as Bradford City, and were accepted for membership. This had more than a little to do with the establishment of the rival Northern Rugby League Championship in 1902, which had Bradford as something of a stronghold. Chelsea were also accepted into Division 2 on Monday 29 May 1905 after chairman Gus Mears had founded his stadium (Stamford Bridge, previously home of the London Athletic Club), found some players and then looked for a League in which to play. Bradford City

finished 10th in their first season, Chelsea 3rd.

Played against all other clubs: Brentford were the first club to play against all other 91 sides in the League – achieving this in their first ever Division 4 season, 1962–63. Grimsby have met more clubs in the League than any other – 112 in all, which in fact includes every side they could have technically met excepting just Thames and Aberdare Athletic. There are now 15 other clubs who have met at least 100 different opponents in the Football League; one of those 15 is Bradford Park Avenue, who no longer exist.

Original members: Everton were the last of the original 12 League clubs to lose their First Division status, in 1930. Aston Villa and Blackburn Rovers had never actually played in Division 2 at that time but both had been relegated and then re-elected back to Division 1 on its extension before the following season. Villa and Blackburn were finally relegated in the same season, 1935–36.

Player revolt: In March 1902 the Stockport County team, unpaid for some time in Division 2, revolted against the club's management, picked their own side and shared out the gate money to compensate for the

lack of wages.

Parent club: In 1931 Clapton Orient (Division 3S) had a receiver appointed and Arsenal effectively took them over, paying the players' wages and having an agreement that any Orient player could be transferred to Highbury as and when Arsenal wished. The League objected and told manager Herbert Chapman to abandon the plan after a season. The result was that Arsenal withdrew their money and Orient manager Jimmy Seed was left without a single player on his books at the start of the following season. For their part Arsenal went off and took on Margate of the Southern League as their nursery club instead.

Failing to turn up: The only instance of a

Arsenal's Colin Hill and Graham Rix are unable to hold Liverpool's leading scorer Ian Rush at Highbury on 10 September 1983. Liverpool and England midfield man Sammy Lee looks on. At this date Liverpool had just won their 14th Championship. Arsenal had the highest number of wins otherwise, with six less. Liverpool, however, had achieved neither of the feats which still made Arsenal the more celebrated club – the hat-trick of Championship wins between 1932 and 1935 and the Double in 1970–71.

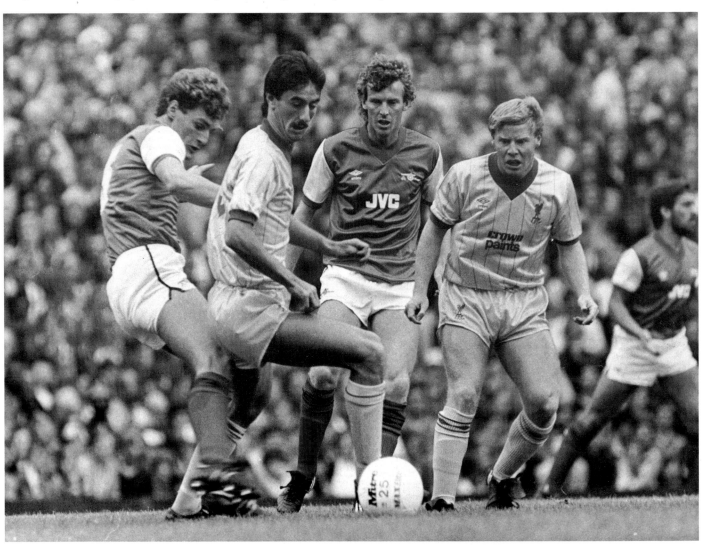

club refusing to turn up for a Football League fixture was on Tuesday 2 April 1974 when Exeter City, who had several players down with 'flu, did not turn up at Scunthorpe. The League had refused to postpone the Division 4 fixture and fined Exeter £5,000, as well as awarding Scunthorpe both points.

Directors: When Workington increased their board to 13 members in October 1966 it was reported that they then had more directors than professionals on their books.

Fog determines Championship: Everton and Newcastle were neck and neck for the League Championship at the end of the 1904–05 season. On 26 November, Everton had been beating Woolwich Arsenal 3-1 after 78 minutes at Woolwich, when dense fog rolled in and the game had to be abandoned. It was replayed on Saturday 22 April 1905 and Everton lost 2-1. Even though Newcastle lost 3-1 at home to Sunderland on the same day, they took the title. Had the fog not intervened, Everton would certainly have won the Championship by a single point.

Most Championship teams: Phil Thompson of Liverpool played in a total of seven Championship winning teams – 1973, 1976, 1977, 1979, 1980, 1982 and 1983.

Oldest director: George Cox was 95 when he left the Spurs board in the 1950s.

Oldest player: The oldest player to complete a whole season of 42 League games was Bob McGrory of Stoke City in 1934–35. He was then aged 43.

Not promoted: The only club currently in the Football League not to have attained its present position by promotion or relegation is Arsenal. In 1919, having finished just 5th in the pre-war Second Division, Arsenal were awarded one of two new places in the First Division (effectively at Spurs expense). They have never been relegated since and have therefore never had to gain promotion.

Goal average: The highest goal average achieved by a Championship winning side was 3.57 goals per game by Sunderland in 1892. The lowest was by the 1904 champions The Wednesday, with only 1.41 goals per game.

Points system: It was not until the League was 10 weeks old that it was finally decided that clubs who drew be awarded one point. Previously the intention had been that points should only be given for wins. The League were heavily influenced by Accrington having drawn 5-5 away at Blackburn on 15 September and 4-4 at home to Wolves on 6 October.

Memorable debuts: The biggest debut win by a League side was Swindon's 9-1 defeat of Luton in Division 3S on 28 August 1920. Swindon had reached the FA Cup semi-finals in 1910 and 1912 and four of their nine goals were scored by England international Harold Fleming.

Disastrous debuts: Crewe Alexandra lost their first ever League game 7-1 away to Burton Swifts on 3 September 1892. Disastrous would be a better description for Norwich City's first professional game against Plymouth in the Southern League at the start of the 1905–06 season. On their way to Plymouth, Norwich's train crashed and, though no player was badly injured, several other passengers lost their lives. During the match Norwich lost two players through injury, ended the match with 9 men and lost 2-0.

Debut attendances: Peterborough's first away game in the Football League, against Crystal Palace on 7 September 1960, was watched by 36,487 people, then a Division 4 record and a record for a club's first appearance at an away ground. Peterborough won 2-0 and the crowd were remarkably prescient, as Peterborough won the League by two points from Palace.

Spurs Alan Brazil has a header saved on the line at Watford on 19 March 1983; but Mark Falco scored from the rebound to give Spurs a 1-0 win. It was a rare home defeat for Watford, who surprised the Division by finishing second in their debut season. Only Ipswich, who won the Championship at their first attempt in 1962, had ever done better.

Footballer of the Year

LEFT: *Cyrille Regis in West Bromwich Albion's second strip. Born in French Guyana, Regis was elected Young Player of the Year in 1978-79.*

ABOVE: *Kenny Burns in Munich completing the most remarkable rehabilitation in modern football. During his time with Birmingham, he was the archetype bad boy of football, but under Brian Clough at Nottingham Forest he became a magnificent sweeper and Footballer of the Year in 1978.*

BELOW: *Burns' team-mate Peter Shilton, PFA winner in 1978 when Forest uniquely swept all of the available individual awards, with Tony Woodcock elected Young Player and Brian Clough Manager of the Year.*

FOOTBALLER OF THE YEAR AWARDS

FWA FOOTBALLER OF THE YEAR

1947–48	Stanley Matthews *(Blackpool)*
1948–49	Johnny Carey *(Manchester United)*
1949–50	Joe Mercer *(Arsenal)*
1950–51	Harry Johnston *(Blackpool)*
1951–52	Billy Wright *(Wolverhampton W.)*
1952–53	Nat Lofthouse *(Bolton Wanderers)*
1953–54	Tom Finney *(Preston North End)*
1954–55	Don Revie *(Manchester City)*
1955–56	Bert Trautmann *(Manchester City)*
1956–57	Tom Finney *(Preston North End)*
1957–58	Danny Blanchflower *(Tottenham H.)*
1958–59	Syd Owen *(Luton Town)*
1959–60	Bill Slater *(Wolverhampton W.)*
1960–61	Danny Blanchflower *(Tottenham H.)*
1961–62	Jimmy Adamson *(Burnley)*
1962–63	Stanley Matthews *(Stoke City)*
1963–64	Bobby Moore *(West Ham United)*
1964–65	Bobby Collins *(Leeds United)*
1965–66	Bobby Charlton *(Manchester United)*
1966–67	Jackie Charlton *(Leeds United)*
1967–68	George Best *(Manchester United)*
1968–69	Tony Book *(Manchester City)*
	Dave Mackay *(Derby County)*
1969–70	Billy Bremner *(Leeds United)*
1970–71	Frank McLintock *(Arsenal)*
1971–72	Gordon Banks *(Stoke City)*
1972–73	Pat Jennings *(Tottenham Hotspur)*
1973–74	Ian Callaghan *(Liverpool)*
1974–75	Alan Mullery *(Fulham)*
1975–76	Kevin Keegan *(Liverpool)*
1976–77	Emlyn Hughes *(Liverpool)*
1977–78	Kenny Burns *(Nottingham Forest)*
1978–79	Kenny Dalglish *(Liverpool)*
1979–80	Terry McDermott *(Liverpool)*
1980–81	Frans Thijssen *(Ipswich)*
1981–82	Steve Perryman *(Tottenham Hotspur)*
1982–83	Kenny Dalglish *(Liverpool)*

PFA PLAYER OF THE YEAR

1973–74	Norman Hunter *(Leeds United)*
1974–75	Colin Todd *(Derby County)*
1975–76	Pat Jennings *(Tottenham Hotspur)*
1976–77	Andy Gray *(Aston Villa)*
1977–78	Peter Shilton *(Nottingham Forest)*
1978–79	Liam Brady *(Arsenal)*
1979–80	Terry McDermott *(Liverpool)*
1980–81	John Wark *(Ipswich)*
1981–82	Kevin Keegan *(Southampton)*
1982–83	Kenny Dalglish *(Liverpool)*

PFA YOUNG PLAYER OF THE YEAR

1973–74	Kevin Beattie *(Ipswich)*
1974–75	Mervyn Day *(West Ham United)*
1975–76	Peter Barnes *(Manchester City)*
1976–77	Andy Gray *(Aston Villa)*
1977–78	Tony Woodcock *(Nottingham Forest)*
1978–79	Cyrille Regis *(West Bromwich Albion)*
1979–80	Glenn Hoddle *(Tottenham Hotspur)*
1980–81	Gary Shaw *(Aston Villa)*
1981–82	Steve Moran *(Southampton)*
1982–83	Ian Rush *(Liverpool)*

SCOTTISH FWA FOOTBALLER OF THE YEAR

1964–65	Billy McNeill *(Celtic)*
1965–66	John Greig *(Rangers)*
1966–67	Ronnie Simpson *(Celtic)*
1967–68	Gordon Wallace *(Raith Rovers)*
1968–69	Bobby Murdoch *(Celtic)*
1969–70	Pat Stanton *(Hibernian)*
1970–71	Martin Buchan *(Aberdeen)*
1971–72	Davie Smith *(Rangers)*
1972–73	George Connelly *(Celtic)*
1973–74	Scottish World Cup Squad
1974–75	Sandy Jardine *(Rangers)*
1975–76	John Greig *(Rangers)*
1976–77	Danny McGrain *(Celtic)*
1977–78	Derek Johnstone *(Rangers)*
1978–79	Andy Ritchie *(Morton)*
1979–80	Gordon Strachan *(Aberdeen)*
1980–81	Alan Rough *(Partick Thistle)*
1981–82	Paul Sturrock *(Dundee United)*
1982–83	Charlie Nicholas *(Celtic)*

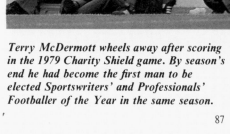

Terry McDermott wheels away after scoring in the 1979 Charity Shield game. By season's end he had become the first man to be elected Sportswriters' and Professionals' Footballer of the Year in the same season.

Goal average & difference

HISTORY AND PLAY-OFFS

First introduced: The problem of separating teams with the same number of points did not occur in the Football League until 1894–95, when Lincoln City and Walsall tied for 13th place in Division 2 with 20 points. One of the two should have had to apply for re-election, but the League could not separate them and made them both apply. From the following season goal average applied to all positions. Goal difference was introduced in 1976–77.

Scotland: Up to 1921–22, the Scottish League decided Championship issues (there was no automatic relegation and promotion before that season) with play-offs. There were four such play-offs:

Scottish League, 1890–91: Dumbarton and Rangers finished the first League season with 29 points and played off at Cathkin Park (Second Hampden Park) on Thursday 21 May 1891. They drew 2-2 and were declared joint champions – one of only two occasions on which this has happened in Scottish or Football League history. On the basis of either goal average or goal difference Dumbarton would have won easily.

Division 1, 1904–05: Celtic and Rangers ended with 41 points. Rangers had much the better goal average, but Celtic won a play-off 2-1 at Hampden Park on Saturday 6 May 1905.

Division 2, 1909–10: Leith Athletic and Raith Rovers, who finished with 33 points each, decided not to play-off and were declared joint champions. Leith had a much better goal average but Raith were elected to Division 1 and Leith stayed down.

Division 2, 1914–15: The only three-way tie in Scottish history: Cowdenbeath, Leith and St Bernard's all ended with 37 points and had a three-way play-off. Cowdenbeath beat Leith 1-0 and St Bernard's 3-1, while Leith beat St Bernard's 2-1. Cowdenbeath were hence declared champions, but this was the last Division 2 for seven seasons because of war. At the end of it, Cowdenbeath were not given a Division 1 place, despite being Division 2 champions in both 1914 and 1915. In 1921–22 they came second, but, uniquely, only champions Alloa were promoted that year. Cowdenbeath were to suffer the same fate in 1939, being champions the season before war intervened again (strangely with Alloa second) but again failed to be awarded a Division 1 place in 1946–47. At this stage they obviously decided there was little point trying, and finished the next season bottom of Division 2. The Scottish League changed from using goal average to goal difference in 1970–71.

CHAMPIONSHIPS DECIDED

Football League: Since 1894–95, 17 divi-

DIVISION 1						1923-24	
1 Huddersfield	42	23	11	8	60:33	57
2 Cardiff	42	22	13	7	61:34	57
3 Sunderland	42	22	9	11	71:54	53
4 Bolton	42	18	14	10	68:34	50
5 Sheffield U.	42	19	12	11	69:49	50
	42	18	13	11	52:37	49
	42	14	11	11	62:53	49

DIVISION 1						1964-65	
1 Manchester U.	42	26	9	7	89:39	61
2 Leeds	42	26	9	7	83:52	61
3 Chelsea	42	24	8	10	89:54	56
4 Everton	42	17	15	10	69:60	49
5 Nottingham F.	42	17	13	12		

SCOTTISH DIVISION 2						1914-15	
1 Cowdenbeath‡	26	16	5	5	49:17	37
2 Leith‡	26	15	7	4	54:31	37
3 St Bernard's‡	26	18	1	7	66:34	37
4 E. Stirlingshire	26	13	5	8	53:46	31
5 Clydebank	26	13	4	9	68:37	30
6 Dunfermline	26	13	2	11	49:39	28
7 Johnstone	26	11	5	10	41:52	27
8 St Johnstone	26	10	6	10	56:53	26
9 Albion	26	9	7	10	47:42	25

TOP AND LEFT ABOVE: The two most important goals in Kilmarnock's history; Dave Sneddon's header from Tom McLean's cross (left) puts Kilmarnock 1-0 up at Hearts' Tynecastle on 24 April 1965, the last day of the Scottish Division 1 season. Had the game ended this way, then Hearts would have won the Championship on goal average. Two minutes later Brian McIlroy's shot (top) put Kilmarnock 2-0 up and leap-frogged them into the Championship spot. Had Hearts scored later, they would have gone top again. This is by far the tightest end to any Championship – largely because the contestants played each other on the last day.
LEFT: Bobby and Jack Charlton face each other during the 1964-65 season, the last time Division 1 was won on goal average. Bobby's Manchester United pipped Jack's Leeds United (above).
ABOVE: The top of the table from the tightest ever Championship race, 1923-24. If it happened today, Cardiff would be champions. Also shown is the only three-way tie in Scottish League history.

sional championships, including four in Division 1, have been decided on goal average. None to 1980 has had to be decided by goal difference. In addition, numerous promotion, relegation and re-election issues have been settled by both methods.

The first championship to be decided by goal average was Division 2 in 1895–96, when Liverpool had a record of 106-32 and Manchester City's was 63-38. The four League Championships decided by goal average were: 1923–24 Huddersfield (60-33) over Cardiff (61-34); 1949–50 Portsmouth (74-38) over Wolves (76-49); 1952–53 Arsenal (97-64) over Preston (85-60); 1964–65 Manchester United (89-39) over Leeds (83-52).

Only one of these Championships would have gone the other way under the goal difference system; Cardiff and Huddersfield had the same goal difference (27 each in 1924) but Cardiff would have won the Championship by virtue of having scored one more goal (see Closest Finishes, below.)

Five Division 2 titles have been decided on goal average (the closest being between Leicester and Everton in 1953–54), four in Divisions 3 and 4, and there were four in Divisions 3S and 3N before 1958. These were in some ways the most critical as only one club went up – Ipswich over Torquay in 1957 was one instance.

Scottish League: Two Scottish League Championships have been decided by goal average: 1952–53 Rangers (80-39) over Hibs (93-51); 1964–65 Kilmarnock (62-33) over Hearts (90-49).

Both would have been won by the runner – up if goal difference had been in operation.

Three-way ties: This has happened at the top of a division only twice. Cowdenbeath, Leith and St Bernard's (see History, above) and in Division 2 in 1954–55 when Birmingham, Luton and Rotherham all finished with 54 points. Birmingham finished their programme on Wednesday 4 May with a 5-1 win at Doncaster, while Rotherham's 6-1 defeat of Liverpool on Monday 2 May was just not enough to get them into Division 1, a status they have never achieved in their history.

Greatest: The biggest positive goal difference of any British side was by Hearts in 1957–58 in Scottish Division 1 with 103 (132-29). In England Bradford City had a difference of 85 (128-43) in Division 3N in 1928–29.

CLOSEST FINISHES

Championship: There are two possible contenders for the title of closest finish, but Kilmarnock and Hearts in the Scottish League in 1964–65 is probably the most appropriate, as the clubs played each other at Tynecastle (Edinburgh) on the very last day of the season, Saturday 24 April. Before the game Hearts had a lead of 2 points and a slightly better goal average – but Kilmarnock won the game 2-0 and took the Championship by 0.04 of a goal. The differences were so slight that had Kilmarnock won 2-1 or 1-0, then Hearts would have become Champions.

Football League: The Huddersfield – Cardiff conclusion of 1923–24 is easily the closest as the clubs had virtually identical records (see above). On the last day of the season, Saturday 3 May 1924, Cardiff started a point ahead with a better goal average. Huddersfield won 3-0 against Nottingham Forest at Leeds Road, but Cardiff could only draw 0-0 at Birmingham – after missing a penalty. When they were awarded the penalty, for a defender's hand ball on the line, none of the senior players was prepared to take it and it fell to young Len Davies to take the first penalty of his career, and Birmingham's Dan Tremelling saved it. Had Davies scored, or had Huddersfield beaten Forest only 2-0 or 3-1, or had goal difference been in use, then Cardiff would have won the only Championship in their history. It was also enormously significant for Huddersfield as it was their first Championship and the first of their hat-trick of League titles. In mathematical terms Gillingham's (59-30) Division 4 title over Carlisle (113-58) in 1964 was even closer, but obviously of much less significance as both clubs were promoted anyway.

Tightest finish: The tightest mathematical promotion race was in Division 2 in 1926–27 when Portsmouth and Manchester City both finished on Saturday 7 May 1927 with 54 points, contesting the second promotion place. Manchester City beat Bradford City 8-0 at Maine Road that day, but Portsmouth had kicked off 15 minutes later at Fratton Park against Preston and were leading 4-1 when the news of City's win came through. If the score had remained at 4-1, City would have been promoted, but Portsmouth scored once more in the last few minutes and went up. The actual goal averages were 1.7755 and 1.77049.

Manchester City were remarkably unlucky in interwar promotion and relegation situations. They had scored 108 goals in 1926–27, and the previous year had been relegated having scored more goals (89) than any other relegated club in history. In 1937–38 they also managed to become the first club ever to be relegated with a positive goal difference (80-77) in Division 1. On 30 April 1938, one week before the end of that season, they were 16th, but 6 clubs had 36 points and the two sides who were bottom on 30 April (Grimsby and Huddersfield) both escaped relegation. City's 80 goals that year were also the most scored by any First Division club. Everton, who scored the second highest with 79, only came 14th and West Bromwich, who scored the fourth highest total with 74, finished bottom.

Best goal differences, relegated: Manchester City (above) were the first club to be relegated with a positive goal difference. Sheffield United were relegated from Division 3 with a 65:62 record in 1980–81. The best unrewarded difference was probably Dundee's 91-44 in Scottish Division 1 in 1977–78, which was the best goal average in the division and the best difference in the League but they were not promoted.

See also: PROMOTION, RELEGATION

ABOVE: *England World Cup star Roger Hunt tussles with Manchester United keeper Alex Stepney at Old Trafford in 1969. Hunt led the League scorers in 1961-62 with 41 goals and also led the First Division in 1965-66 with 30 goals. He is Liverpool's all-time leading scorer with 245 goals as well as holding the single season record with those 41. Roger Hunt was also instrumental in establishing another very personal record on 11 April 1972, when the crowd for his testimonial match at Anfield (56,000) was then the biggest ever recorded at a friendly in England. Liverpool played a 1966 England eleven.*
BELOW: *Tony Brown, whose 28 goals for WBA made him Division 1 leading scorer in 1971.*

Goalscorers

SINGLE GAME

Overall record: 13 – by John Petrie for Arbroath against Bon Accord on Saturday 12 September 1885. On the same day one Alisdair D'Arcy scored 10 goals in Dundee Harp's 35-0 win over Aberdeen Rovers.

Any League game: 10 – Joe Payne of Luton Town against Bristol Rovers in Division 3S on Monday 13 April 1936. It was Payne's first game at centre-forward and Luton won 12-0.

Ten goals: Apart from Payne and D'Arcy above, the only other instance of 10 goals being scored in a first-class game was by Gerry Baker for St Mirren against Glasgow University in the first round of the Scottish Cup on Saturday 30 January 1960. St Mirren won 15-0.

Nine goals: There have been five instances in a first-class game, two in England:

● Thursday 26 December 1935 – Robert 'Bunny' Bell for Tranmere against Oldham in Division 3N. Tranmere won 13-4 – and Bell also missed a penalty;

● Saturday 20 November 1971 – Ted Mac-Dougall for Bournemouth against Margate in the first round of the FA Cup. Bournemouth won 11-0.

The three instances in Scotland are:

● Saturday 17 January 1931 – Johnny Simpson for Partick Thistle against Royal Albert in the first round of the Scottish Cup. Partick won 16-0;

● Saturday 20 January 1934 – Jim Fleming for Rangers against Blairgowrie, also in the first round of the Scottish Cup. Rangers won 14-2;

● Saturday 11 February 1961 – Joe Baker (Gerry's brother, *see Ten goals*) for Hibs against Peebles Rovers in the second round of the Scottish Cup. Hibernian won 15-1.

Eight goals: No players other than Payne, Bell and MacDougall (*above*) have scored eight goals or more in a recognised English first-class fixture, but six Scottish players have managed this feat:

● Saturday 1 October 1927 – Owen McNally for Arthurlie against Armadale in Division 2;

● Saturday 14 January 1928 – Jimmy McGrory for Celtic against Dunfermline in Division 1;

● Thursday 2 January 1930 – Jim Dyet (on his debut) for King's Park against Forfar in Division 2;

● Saturday 18 April 1936 – John Calder for Morton against Raith in Division 2;

● Saturday 13 February 1937 – William Walsh for Hearts against King's Park in the second round of the Scottish Cup.

● Saturday 20 August 1937 – Norman Haywood for Raith v Brechin in Division 2.

Division 1: 7 – Jimmy Ross Jnr for Preston against Stoke on Saturday 6 October 1888 and by Ted Drake for Arsenal against Aston Villa on Saturday 14 December 1935. The latter game was played at Villa Park, making Drake's feat of seven goals from just eight shots all the more remarkable.

Division 2: 7 – Tommy Briggs for Blackburn against Bristol Rovers on Saturday 5 February 1955 (Blackburn won 8-3), and Neville Coleman for Stoke against Lincoln on Saturday 23 February 1957 (Stoke won 8-0). Both were home games.

Division 3: 10 – Joe Payne (*above*).

Division 4: 6 – Herbert Lister for Oldham against Southport on Wednesday 26 December 1962. Oldham won 11-0.

Scottish Division 1/Premier: 8 – Jimmy McGrory (*above*).

Scottish non-Division 1/Premier: 8 – Calder, Dyet, Haywood and McNally (*above*).

FA Cup: 9 – Ted MacDougall (*above*).

Scottish Cup: 13 – John Petrie (*above*).

Football League Cup: 5 – Derek Reeves of Southampton against Leeds in the fourth round, Monday 5 December 1960 and Alan

---

RIGHT: *A picture of the great Steve Bloomer taken at Crystal Palace on 1 April 1905 before the England v Scotland match. Twice the League's leading scorer, Bloomer's 352 League goals for Derby and Middlesbrough remained a record until broken by Dixie Dean in the 1930s. Bloomer once scored 6 goals for Derby v The Wednesday, on 21 January 1899.*

LEADING FOOTBALL & SCOTTISH LEAGUE SCORERS

Season	Football League	Div.	Gls.
1888–89	John Goodall (Preston)		21
1889–90	James Ross (Preston)		24
1890–91	Jack Southworth (Blackburn)		26
1891–92	Johnny Campbell (Sunderland)		32
1892–93	Johnny Campbell (Sunderland)	(1)	31
1893–94	Jack Southworth (Everton)	(1)	27
1894–95	Johnny Campbell (Sunderland)	(1)	22
	David Skea (Leicester Fosse)	(2)	22
1895–96	Geo Allan (Liverpool)	(2)	26
1896–97	Steve Bloomer (Derby)	(1)	22
	John Murphy (Notts Co)	(2)	22
	Tommy Boucher (Notts Co)	(2)	22
1897–98	Harry Boyd (Newton Heath)	(2)	23
1898–99	Walter Abbott (Small Heath)	(2)	33
1899–00	William Garraty (Aston Villa)	(1)	27
1900–01	Steve Bloomer (Derby)	(1)	24
1901–02	Charles Simmons (WBA)	(2)	23
1902–03	Alec Reybould (Liverpool)	(1)	31
1903–04	Tom Shanks (Woolwich Arsenal)	(2)	25
1904–05	Samuel Marsh (Bolton)	(2)	26
1905–06	Albert Shepherd (Bolton)	(1)	26
	William Jones (Birmingham)	(1)	26
	William Maxwell (Bristol City)	(2)	26
1906–07	Alf Young (Everton)	(1)	30
1907–08	Enoch West (Nottingham Forest)	(1)	27
1908–09	Bert Freeman (Everton)	(1)	38
1909–10	John Smith (Hull)	(2)	32
1910–11	Robert Whittingham (Chelsea)	(2)	30
1911–12	Bert Freeman (Burnley)	(2)	32
1912–13	Bert Freeman (Burnley)	(2)	31
1913–14	George Elliott (Middlesbrough)	(1)	32
1914–15	Bob Parker (Everton)	(1)	35

Season	Football League	Div.	Gls.	Scottish League	Div.	Gls.
1919–20	Fred Morris (WBA)	(1)	37	Hugh Ferguson (Motherwell)	(1)	33
1920–21	Joe Smith (Bolton Wanderers)	(1)	38	Hugh Ferguson (Motherwell)	(1)	43
1921–22	James Carmichael (Grimsby)	(3N)	37	Wee Crilley (Alloa Athletic)	(2)	49
1922–23	Harry Bedford (Blackpool)	(2)	32	John White (Hearts)	(1)	30
1923–24	Harry Bedford (Blackpool)	(2)	34	Dave Halliday (Dundee)	(1)	38
1924–25	Doug Brown (Darlington)	(3N)	39	Willie Devlin (Cowdenbeath)	(1)	33
1925–26	Jimmy Cookson (Chesterfield)	(3N)	44	Bobby Skinner (Dunfermline)	(2)	53
1926–27	George Camsell (Middlesbro)	(2)	59	Jimmy McGrory (Celtic)	(1)	49
1927–28	Dixie Dean (Everton)	(1)	60	Jimmy Smith (Ayr)	(2)	66
1928–29	Dave Halliday (Sunderland)	(2)	43	Evelyn Morrison (Falkirk)	(1)	43
	Jimmy McConnell (Carlisle)	(3N)	43			
	Andy Rennie (Luton Town)	(3S)	43			
1929–30	Jimmy Hampson (Blackpool)	(2)	45	Davie Kilgour (Forfar Athletic)	(2)	45
1930–31	Pongo Waring (Aston Villa)	(1)	49	Barney Battles (Hearts)	(1)	44
1931–32	Clarrie Bourton (Coventry C.)	(3S)	49	Willie McFadyen (Motherwell)	(1)	52
1932–33	Clarrie Bourton (Coventry C.)	(3S)	40	Willie McFadyen (Motherwell)	(1)	45
1933–34	Alf Lythgoe (Stockport Co.)	(3N)	46	Jimmy Smith (Rangers)	(1)	41
1934–35	Ted Drake (Arsenal)	(1)	42	Gordon Hay (Third Lanark)	(2)	44
1935–36	Albert Dawes (Crystal Palace)	(3S)	38	Jimmy McGrory (Celtic)	(1)	50
1936–37	Ted Harston (Mansfield T.)	(3N)	55	Terry McGibbon (Ayr United)	(2)	39
	Joe Payne (Luton Town)	(3S)	55			
1937–38	Tommy Lawton (Everton)	(1)	28	Andy Black (Hearts)	(1)	40
	John Roberts (Port Vale)	(3N)	28			
1938–39	Tommy Lawton (Everton)	(1)	35	Malcolm Morrison (E. Stirling)	(2)	36
1946–47	Clarrie Jordan (Doncaster R.)	(3N)	42	Bobby Flavell (Airdrie)	(2)	38
1947–48	Ronnie Rooke (Arsenal)	(1)	33	Henry Morris (East Fife)	(2)	41
1948–49	Charlie Wayman (South'ton)	(2)	32	Willie Penman (Raith Rovers)	(2)	35
1949–50	Tommy Briggs (Grimsby T.)	(2)	35	Willie Bauld (Hearts)	(1)	30
1950–51	Jack Shaw (Rotherham U.)	(3N)	37	Peter McKay (Dundee United)	(2)	34
1951–52	Derek Dooley (Sheffield W.)	(2)	46	Billy McPhail (Clyde)	(2)	36
1952–53	Arthur Rowley (Leicester C.)	(2)	39	Charlie Fleming (East Fife)	(1)	30
				Lawrie Reilly (Hibernian)	(1)	30
1953–54	John Charles (Leeds United)	(2)	42	Ian Rodger (St Johnstone)	(2)	30
1954–55	Tommy Briggs (Blackburn R.)	(2)	33	Hugh Baird (Airdrie)	(2)	34
1955–56	Sam Collins (Torquay United)	(3S)	40	John Coyle (Dundee United)	(2)	41
1956–57	Arthur Rowley (Leicester C.)	(2)	44	Pat Keogh (Clyde)	(2)	35
1957–58	Brian Clough (Middlesbrough)	(2)	40	Peter Price (Ayr United)	(2)	45
1958–59	Brian Clough (Middlesbrough)	(2)	42	Dave Easson (Arbroath)	(2)	45
1959–60	Cliff Holton (Watford)	(4)	42	Joe Baker (Hibernian)	(1)	42
1960–61	Terry Bly (Peterborough U.)	(4)	52	Alex Harley (Third Lanark)	(1)	42
1961–62	Roger Hunt (Liverpool)	(2)	41	Peter Smith (Alloa Athletic)	(2)	29
1962–63	Jimmy Greaves (Tottenham H.)	(1)	37	Allan McGraw (Morton)	(2)	30
1963–64	Hugh McIlmoyle (Carlisle U.)	(4)	39	Allan McGraw (Morton)	(2)	41
1964–65	Alick Jeffrey (Doncaster R.)	(4)	36	Willie Forsyth (Hamilton A.)	(2)	33
1965–66	Kevin Hector (Bradford P.A.)	(4)	44	Tommy Murray (Airdrie)	(2)	33
1966–67	Ron Davies (Southampton)	(1)	37	Joe Mason (Morton)	(2)	35
1967–68	Ron Davies (Southampton)	(1)	28	Bobby Lennox (Celtic)	(1)	32
	George Best (Manchester U.)	(1)	28	Dennis Bruce (Arbroath)	(2)	32
1968–69	Jimmy Greaves (Tottenham H.)	(1)	27	Dixie Deans (Motherwell)	(2)	29
1969–70	Albert Kinsey (Wrexham)	(4)	27	John Dickson (Cowdenbeath)	(2)	28
1970–71	Ted MacDougall (Bournemouth)	(4)	42	Kenny Wilson (Dumbarton)	(2)	28
1971–72	Ted MacDougall (Bournemouth)	(3)	35	Kenny Wilson (Dumbarton)	(2)	38
	Alf Wood (Shrewsbury Town)	(4)	35			
1972–73	Pop Robson (West Ham)	(1)	28	Brian Third (Montrose)	(2)	28
	Fred Binney (Exeter City)	(4)	28			
1973–74	Brian Yeo (Gillingham)	(4)	31	Ian Fleming (Kilmarnock)	(2)	32
1974–75	Dixie McNeil (Hereford U.)	(3)	31	Ian Reid (Queen of the South)	(2)	27
1975–76	Dixie McNeil (Hereford U.)	(3)	35	Kenny Dalglish (Celtic)		24
1976–77	Peter Ward (Brighton)	(3)	32	Billy Pirie (Dundee)	(1)	36
1977–78	Alan Curtis (Swansea)	(4)	32	Billy Pirie (Dundee)	(1)	35
	Steve Phillips (Brentford)	(4)	32			
1978–79	Ross Jenkins (Watford)	(3)	29	Blair Miller (Clydebank)	(1)	28
1979–80	Clive Allen (QPR)	(2)	28	Doug Somner (St Mirren)	(P)	25
				Ian Campbell (Brechin City)	(2)	25
1980–81	Tony Kellow (Exeter)	(3)	25	Frank McGarvey (Celtic)	(P)	23
1981–82	Keith Edwards (Sheffield United)	(4)	36	Daniel Masterton (Clyde)	(1)	23
1982–83	Luther Blissett (Watford)	(1)	27	Charlie Nicholas (Celtic)	(P)	29

LEADING POSTWAR FOOTBALL LEAGUE SCORERS

SEASON	DIVISION 1		DIVISION 2		DIVISION 3N/ DIVISION 3*		DIVISION 3S/ DIVISION 4*	
1946–47	Dennis Westcott (Wolves)	37	Charlie Wayman (Newcastle)	30	Clarrie Jordan (Doncaster)	42	Don Clark (Bristol C.)	36
1947–48	Ronnie Rooke (Arsenal)	33	Eddie Quigley (Sheffield W.)	23	Jim Hutchinson (Lincoln)	32	Len Townsend (Bristol C.)	29
1948–49	Willie Moir (Bolton)	25	Charlie Wayman (South'ton)	32	Wally Ardron (Rotherham)	29	Don McGibbon (B'mouth)	30
1949–50	Dick Davis (Sunderland)	25	Tommy Briggs (Grimsby)	35	Peter Doherty (Doncaster)	26	Tommy Lawton (Notts Co.)	31
					Reg Phillips (Crewe)	26		
1950–51	Stan Mortensen (Blackpool)	30	Cecil McCormack (Barnsley)	33	Jack Shaw (Rotherham)	37	Wally Ardron (Nottm F.)	36
1951–52	George Robledo (Newcastle)	33	Derek Dooley (Sheffield W.)	46	Andy Graver (Lincoln)	37	Ronnie Blackman (Reading)	39
1952–53	Charlie Wayman (Preston)	24	Arthur Rowley (Leicester)	39	Jack Whitehouse (Carlisle)	29	Geoff Bradford (Bristol R.)	33
1953–54	Jimmy Glazzard (Huddersf'd)	29	John Charles (Leeds)	42	Jack Connor (Stockport)	31	Jack English (Northampton)	30
	Johnny Nicholls (WBA)	29						
1954–55	Ronnie Allen (WBA)	27	Tommy Briggs (Blackburn)	33	Don Travis (Oldham)	32	Ernie Morgan (Gillingham)	31
1955–56	Nat Lofthouse (Bolton)	33	Bob Gardiner (Leicester)	34	Bob Crosbie (Grimsby)	36	Sam Collins (Torquay)	40
1956–57	John Charles (Leeds)	38	Arthur Rowley (Leicester)	44	Ray Straw (Derby)	37	Ted Phillips (Ipswich)	41
1957–58	Bobby Smith (Tottenham)	36	Brian Clough (Middlesbro)	40	Alf Ackerman (Carlisle)	35	Sam McCrory (Southend)	31
							Derek Reeves (Southampton)	31
1958–59	Jimmy Greaves (Chelsea)	32	Brian Clough (Middlesbro)	42	Eddie Towers (Brentford)	32	Arthur Rowley (Shrewsbury)	38
1959–60	Dennis Viollet (Man. U.)	32	Brian Clough (Middlesbro)	39	Derek Reeves (Southampton)	39	Cliff Holton (Watford)	42
1960–61	Jimmy Greaves (Chelsea)	41	Ray Crawford (Ipswich)	39	Tony Richards (Walsall)	36	Terry Bly (Peterborough)	52
1961–62	Ray Crawford (Ipswich)	33	Roger Hunt (Liverpool)	41	Cliff Holton (Northampton)	†37	Bobby Hunt (Colchester)	39
1962–63	Jimmy Greaves (Tottenham)	37	Bobby Tambling (Chelsea)	35	George Hudson (Coventry)	30	Ken Wagstaff (Mansfield)	34
1963–64	Jimmy Greaves (Tottenham)	35	Ron Saunders (Portsmouth)	33	Alf Biggs (Bristol R.)	30	Hugh McIlmoyle (Carlisle)	39
1964–65	Jimmy Greaves (Tottenham)	29	George O'Brien (South'ton)	32	Ken Wagstaff (Hull)	‡35	Alick Jeffrey (Doncaster)	36
	Andy McEvoy (Blackburn)	29						
1965–66	Roger Hunt (Liverpool)	30	Martin Chivers (South'ton)	30	Les Allen (QPR)	30	Kevin Hector (Bradford P.A.)	44
1966–67	Ron Davies (Southampton)	37	Derek Dougan (Wolves)	§25	Rodney Marsh (QPR)	30	Ernie Phythian (Hartlepools)	23
1967–68	Ron Davies (Southampton)	28	John Hickton (Middlesbro)	24	Bobby Owen (Bury)	25	Roy Chapman (Port Vale)	25
	George Best (Manchester U.)	28			Don Rogers (Swindon)	25	Len Massie (Halifax)	25
1968–69	Jimmy Greaves (Tottenham)	27	John Toshack (Cardiff)	22	Alex Dawson (Brighton)	24	Gary Talbot (Chester)	22
1969–70	Jeff Astle (WBA)	25	John Hickton (Middlesbro)	24	George Jones (Burry)	26	Albert Kinsey (Wrexham)	27
1970–71	Tony Brown (WBA)	28	John Hickton (Middlesbro)	25	Gerry Ingram (Preston)	22	Ted MacDougall (B'mouth)	42
					Dudley Roberts (Mansfield)	22		
1971–72	Francis Lee (Manchester C.)	33	Bob Latchford (Birmingham)	23	Ted MacDougall (B'mouth)	35	Alf Wood (Shrewsbury)	35
1972–73	Pop Robson (West Ham)	28	Don Givens (QPR)	23	Bruce Bannister (Bristol R.)	25	Fred Binney (Exeter)	28
1973–74	Mike Channon (South'ton)	21	Duncan McKenzie (Nottm F.)	26	Billy Jennings (Watford)	26	Brian Yeo (Gillingham)	31
1974–75	Malcolm Macdonald (N'castle)	21	Brian Little (Aston Villa)	20	Dixie McNeil (Hereford)	31	Ray Clarke (Mansfield)	28
1975–76	Ted MacDougall (Norwich)	23	Derek Hales (Charlton)	28	Dixie McNeil (Hereford)	35	Ronnie Moore (Tranmere)	34
1976–77	Andy Gray (Aston Villa)	25	Mickey Walsh (Blackpool)	26	Peter Ward (Brighton)	32	Brian Joicey (Barnsley)	25
	Malcolm Macdonald (Arsenal)	25						
1977–78	Bob Latchford (Everton)	30	Bob Hatton (Blackpool)	22	Alex Bruce (Preston)	27	Alan Curtis (Swansea)	32
							Steve Phillips (Brentford)	32
1978–79	Frank Worthington (Bolton)	24	Pop Robson (West Ham)	24	Ross Jenkins (Watford)	29	John Dungworth (Aldershot)	26
1979–80	Phil Boyer (Southampton)	23	Clive Allen (QPR)	28	Terry Curran (Sheffield W.)	22	Colin Garwood (Aldershot)	¶27
1980–81	Steve Archibald (Tottenham)	20	David Cross (West Ham)	22	Tony Kellow (Exeter)	25	Alan Cork (Wimbledon)	23
	Peter Withe (Aston Villa)	20						
1981–82	Kevin Keegan (Southampton)	26	Ronnie Moore (Rotherham)	22	Gordon Davies (Fulham)	24	Keith Edwards (Sheffield U)[1]	36
1982–83	Luther Blissett (Watford)	27	Gary Lineker (Leicester)	26	Kerry Dixon (Reading)	26	Steve Cammack (Scunthorpe)	25

*first season of Divisions 3 & 4 was 1958–59 †inc. 1 with Watford (Division 3) ‡inc. 12 with Mansfield (Division 3)
§inc. 16 with Leicester (Division 1); in strict terms the 'Division 2' leading scorer for 1966–67 was Bobby Gould (Coventry)
with 24 goals ¶inc. 17. with Portsmouth (Division 4) [1]inc. 1 with Hull City (Division 4)

Wilks for QPR v Oxford on 10 October 1967 in the third round. Wilks scored just 3 goals in 15 other appearances that season.

Scottish League Cup: 5 – Jim Fraser for Ayr United against Dumbarton on Wednesday 13 August 1952 and Jim Forrest for Rangers against Stirling Albion on Wednesday 17 August 1966. Forrest also holds the record for a Scottish League Cup final with 4 goals against Morton at Hampden Park on Saturday 26 October 1963. Rangers won 5-0.

FA Cup final: 3 – by William Townley of Blackburn Rovers in 1890, Jimmy Logan of Notts County in 1894 and Stan Mortensen of Blackpool in 1953. Mortensen remains one of only two players (Geoff Hurst in the 1966 World Cup final being the other) to have scored a hat-trick in a major final at Wembley.

LEFT: Vivian Woodward, who twice scored six goals for England in amateur internationals.

Six goals in two games: Only four players have scored double hat-tricks in two first-class games – Vivian Woodward, Jim Fleming, Ted MacDougall and Albert Juliussen. Juliussen's is by far the most remarkable feat for he achieved this in **consecutive** games. The first was for Dundee v Alloa on 8 March 1947, when he scored 6 goals, and Dundee's next game was at home to Dunfermline on 22 March 1947, when Juliussen scored 7! Dundee won both games 10-0, a record for two consecutive League games while Juliussen's is also a scoring record for consecutive matches.

Wingers: 7 – Neville Coleman scored 7 for Stoke from the wing against Lincoln on 23 February 1957 (Stoke won 8-0).

Full backs: 4 – Sam Wynne scored with a penalty and a free-kick for his own side, Oldham, on Saturday 6 October 1923 and also scored two own goals for Manchester United. Oldham won the Division 2 game 3-2. The only hat-trick known to have been scored by a full-back *without* a penalty

among the three was by John Brown for Hamilton v Berwick on 9 August 1980. Hamilton won 9-1. Only one full-back has ever scored from open play in an FA Cup final (Terry Fenwick for QPR in 1982) but Alan Kennedy of Liverpool scored Liverpool's only goal in both the 1981 League Cup final at Wembley and the 1981 European Cup final against Real Madrid.

Centre-backs and midfield: Hat-tricks from this area are not unknown in the past two decades, but Graham Roberts of Spurs managed all 3 from open play against Southampton on 20 March 1982. Normally a centre-back, he was playing in midfield; Spurs won the game 3-2 and removed Southampton from the top of the First Division. Brian Stanton, playing in Huddersfield's midfield, scored 4 goals in a 6-3 defeat of Bradford City on 1 January 1983. Three of his goals came within the space of 6 minutes, a fast-scoring record for any player but a forward.

Losing side: 7 – Billy Minter of St Albans City scored all 7 of his side's goals against Dulwich Hamlet in an FA Cup fourth preliminary round replay on Wednesday 22 November 1922, when Dulwich Hamlet won 8-7. Denis Law had scored all 6 Manchester City goals against Luton Town in a fourth round FA Cup tie at Kenilworth Road on Saturday 28 January 1961 when the game was abandoned at 6-2. He also scored in the replay but City lost 3-1.

SINGLE GAME INTERNATIONALS

Record in a single game: 6 – Joe Bambrick of Linfield for Northern Ireland against Wales at Celtic Park, Belfast, on Saturday 1 February 1930. This is the most any player from the United Kingdom has scored in a recognised first-class international. Vivian Woodward scored 8 goals for England against France in an amateur international

LEADING SCOTTISH LEAGUE SCORERS

SEASON	SCOTTISH DIVISION 1/ PREMIER*		SCOTTISH DIVISION 2/ DIVISION 1*	
1946–47	Bobby Mitchell (T. Lanark)	22	Bobby Flavell (Airdrie)	38
1947–48	Archie Aikman (Falkirk)	20	Henry Morris (East Fife)	41
1948–49	Alec Scott (Dundee)	30	Willie Penman (Raith)	35
1949–50	Willie Bauld (Hearts)	30	Neil Mochan (Morton)	24
1950–51	Lawrie Reilly (Hibs)	22	Peter McKay (Dundee U.)	34
1951–52	Lawrie Reilly (Hibs)	27	Billy McPhail (Clyde)	36
1952–53	Lawrie Reilly (Hibs)	30	Jim Cunningham (Alloa)	25
	Charlie Fleming (East Fife)	30		
1953–54	Jimmy Wardhaugh (Hearts)	27	Ian Rodger (St. Johnstone)	30
1954–55	Willie Bauld (Hearts)	21	Hugh Baird (Airdrie)	34
1955–56	Jimmy Wardhaugh (Hearts)	28	John Coyle (Dundee United)	41
1956–57	Hugh Baird (Airdrie)	33	Pat Keogh (Clyde)	35
1957–58	Jimmy Wardhaugh (Hearts)	28	Peter Price (Ayr United)	45
	Jimmy Murray (Hearts)	28		
1958–59	Joe Baker (Hibs)	25	Dave Easson (Arbroath)	45
1959–60	Joe Baker (Hibs)	42	Jack Liddell (St Johnstone)	28
1960–61	Alex Harley (Third Lanark)	42	Jackie Coburn (Forfar)	29
			Doug Moran (Falkirk)	29
1961–62	Alan Gilzean (Dundee)	24	Peter Smith (Alloa)	29
1962–63	Jimmy Millar (Rangers)	27	Allan McGraw (Morton)	30
1963–64	Alan Gilzean (Dundee)	32	Allan McGraw (Morton)	41
1964–65	Jim Forrest (Rangers)	30	Willie Forsyth (Hamilton)	33
1965–66	Joe McBride (Celtic)	31	Tommy Murray (Airdrie)	33
	Alex Ferguson (Dunf'line)	31		
1966–67	Steve Chalmers (Celtic)	21	Joe Mason (Morton)	35
1967–68	Bobby Lennox (Celtic)	32	Dennis Bruce (Arbroath)	32
1968–69	Kenny Cameron (Dundee U.)	26	Dixie Deans (Motherwell)	29
1969–70	Colin Stein (Rangers)	24	John Dickson (Cowdenbeath)	28
1970–71	Harry Hood (Celtic)	22	Kenny Wilson (Dumbarton)	28
1971–72	Joe Harper (Aberdeen)	33	Kenny Wilson (Dumbarton)	38
1972–73	Alex Gordon (Hibs)	27	Brian Third (Montrose)	28
1973–74	Ian Fleming (Kilmarnock)	32	Ian Reid (Q. of the South)	22
1974–75	Willie Pettigrew (Motherwell)	20	Ian Reid (Q. of the South)	27
	Andy Gray (Dundee United)	20		
1975–76	Kenny Dalglish (Celtic)	24	David Whiteford (Falkirk)	17
1976–77	Willie Pettigrew (Motherwell)	21	Billy Pirie (Dundee)	36
1977–78	Derek Johnstone (Rangers)	25	Billy Pirie (Dundee)	35
1978–79	Andy Ritchie (Morton)	22	Blair Miller (Clydebank)	28
1979–80	Doug Somner (St Mirren)	25	Jim Brogan (St Johnstone)	22
1980–81	Frank McGarvey (Celtic)	23	Ally McCoist (St Johnstone)	22
1981–82	George McCluskey (Celtic)	21	Daniel Masterton (Clyde)	23
1982–83	Charlie Nicholas (Celtic)	29	Ian Campbell (Brechin)	24

*Division 1 and Division 2 were split into Premier (10 clubs), First Division (14 clubs) and Second Division (14 clubs) in 1975.

in Paris on 1 November 1906 and R. E. Foster scored 6 goals for an English representative side against Germany in September 1901, but neither of these games is regarded as a full international.

Inter-League game: 6 – Nat Lofthouse (Bolton Wanderers) for the Football League against the League of Ireland at Wolverhampton on Wednesday 24 September 1952.

England: 5 – five players have been credited with scoring 5 goals in a full England international, but there has to be some doubt about the 3 examples from the last century as goalscorers were not automatically recorded at the time. They are:

O. Howard Vaughton (Aston Villa) against Ireland at Belfast on 18 February 1882. England won 13-0;

Steve Bloomer (Derby County) against Wales at Cardiff on 16 March 1896. England won 9-1;

Gilbert Oswald Smith (Corinthians) against Ireland at Sunderland on 18 February 1899. England won 13-2;

Willie Hall (Spurs) against Northern Ireland at Old Trafford on 16 November 1938 (including 3 timed in no more than 210 seconds). England won 7-0;

Malcolm Macdonald (Newcastle United) against Cyprus at Wembley on 16 April 1975. England won 5-0;

Scotland: 5 – two players have been credited with scoring 5 goals in a full international, but in both cases some sources give only 4 goals. They are:

Charles Heggie (Rangers) against Ireland at Ballynafeigh Park, Belfast, on 20 March 1886. Scotland won 7-2 in what was to be Heggie's only international appearance;

Hughie Gallacher (Newcastle United) against Northern Ireland at Windsor Park, Belfast, on 23 February 1929. Scotland won 7-3.

Wales: 4 – on four recorded occasions:

James Price (Wrexham) against Ireland at Wrexham on 25 February 1882. Wales won 7-1;

Jack Doughty (Druids) against Ireland on 3 March 1888 at Wrexham. Wales won 11-0, and Jack's brother Roger also scored 3 goals;

Mel Charles (Cardiff City) against Northern Ireland at Ninian Park on 11 April 1962. Wales won 4-0;

Ian Edwards (Chester) against Malta at Wrexham on 25 October 1978. Wales won 7-0;

Eire: 4 – on two occasions:

OPPOSITE TOP: Notts County full-back Ray O'Brien, 10-goal record holder in 1979-80.
LEFT: Southampton's Ron Davies rises above John Sjoberg and the Leicester defence during a spell which saw him as the leading scorer in both 1966-67 and 1967-68.
ABOVE: The unfortunate St Albans centre-forward Billy Minter, who scored 7 goals in an FA Cup preliminary game on 22 Nov 1922, only to see Dulwich Hamlet win 8-7.
TOP: Jimmy McGrory's (left) shot is mishandled by Clyde keeper Brown during a Scottish Cup semi-final at Hampden on 3 April 1937. Celtic won 2-0. McGrory scored a Scottish record 410 goals in 408 League matches for Celtic and their nursery club, Clydebank.

Paddy Moore (Shamrock Rovers) against Belgium in Dublin on 25 February 1934. The game was a 4-4 draw;
Don Givens (QPR) against Turkey in Dublin on 29 October 1975. Eire won the European Championship qualifying game 4-0.

IN A SEASON

Overall record aggregate: 96 – Frederick Roberts of Glentoran scored 96 goals in recognised Irish first-class fixtures in 1930–31, mainly in the Irish League and Belfast City Cup. Joe Bambrick of Linfield scored 94 in 1929–30, including his 6 against Wales, and 4 in the Irish Cup final, but Irish fixtures cannot be compared in status with English or Scottish competitions.

British and Scottish aggregate: 84 – Jim Smith of Ayr United in 1927–28, including a record 66 in Scottish Division 2. Two goals were scored in the Scottish Cup and the other 16 in local competitions.

English aggregate: 82 – William 'Dixie' Dean in 1927–28, including a record 60 in Division 1 for Everton and 11 in international and inter-league games. With 2 league games to go, Dean was on 53, 7 away from breaking the league record. He then scored 4 at Burnley on 28 April 1928 and a hat-trick v Arsenal at Goodison in the last game, on 5 May. His 60th goal came with 5 minutes of the season left.

League aggregate: 66 – Jim Smith for Ayr United in Scottish Division 2 in 1927–28. This is the highest total in a single season by any English or Scottish League footballer.

Football League: 60 – Dixie Dean for Everton in 1927–28 in Division 1 (39 games).

Division 2: 59 – George Camsell for Middlesbrough in 1926–27 (37 games) including 29 in the space of 12 matches.

Division 3: 55 – Joe Payne for Luton Town in Division 3S in 1936–37 (39 games) and Ted Harston for Mansfield in Division 3N, also in 1936–37 (41 games). Since reorganisation in 1958, the record for Division 3 is 39 by Derek Reeves for Southampton in 1959–60 (46 games).

Division 4: 52 – Terry Bly for Peterborough United in 1960–61 (46 games). Bly is the only player to score more than 50 goals in a single season since the Second World War.

Wingers: 39 – Ken Dawson scored 39 at outside-left for Falkirk in Scottish Division 2 in 1935–36. In England, Billy Meredith is credited with 34 goals as the outside-right for Manchester City in Division 2 in 1898–99, but the records are not entirely reliable. Since records became reasonably accurate, the English record is 33 from Cliff Bastin for Arsenal in 1932–33 (Division 1) and Colin Taylor of Walsall in 1960–61 (Division 3).

Half-backs: 15 – as the role of the half-back has become so indistinct in recent years, aggregate goals have become almost meaningless, but Jack Lewis, a recognised half-back for Reading, scored 15 goals in Division 3S in 1951–52.

Full-backs: 10 – again, positional roles have become less distinct in recent years,

95

RECORD LEAGUE SCORERS (IN A SEASON) OF CURRENT LEAGUE CLUBS

FOOTBALL LEAGUE

Aldershot	26, John Dungworth, Division 4, 1978–79
Arsenal	42, Ted Drake, Division 1, 1934–35*
Aston Villa	49, Pongo Waring, Division 1, 1930–31
Barnsley	33, Cecil McCormack, Division 2, 1950–51
Birmingham City	33, Walter Abbott, Division 2, 1898–99
Blackburn Rovers	43, Ted Harper, Division 1, 1925–26
Blackpool	45, Jimmy Hampson, Division 2, 1929–30†
Bolton Wanderers	38, Joe Smith, Division 1, 1920–21
Bournemouth	42, Ted MacDougall, Division 4, 1970–71†
Bradford City	34, David 'Bronco' Layne, Division 4, 1961–62
Brentford	37, Jack Holliday, Davision 3S, 1932–33*
Brighton	32, Peter Ward, Division 3, 1976–77†
Bristol City	36, Don Clark, Division 3S, 1946–47
Bristol Rovers	33, Geoff Bradford, Division 3S, 1952–53†
Burnley	35, George Beel, Division 1, 1927–28
Bury	35, Craig Madden, Division 4, 1981–82
Cambridge United	21, Alan Biley, Division 3, 1977–78†
Cardiff City	31, Stan Richards, Division 3S, 1946–47*
Carlisle United	43, Jimmy McConnell, Division 3N, 1928–29
Charlton Athletic	32, Ralph Allen, Division 3S, 1934–35*
Chelsea	41, Jimmy Greaves, Division 1, 1960–61
Chester	36, Dick Yates, Division 3N, 1946–47
Chesterfield	44, Jimmy Cookson, Division 3N, 1925–26
Colchester United	39, Bobby Hunt, Division 4, 1961–62†
Coventry City	49, Clarrie Bourton, Division 3S, 1931–32
Crewe Alexandra	34, Terry Harkin, Division 4, 1964–65
Crystal Palace	46, Peter Simpson, Division 3S, 1930–31*
Darlington	39, Doug Brown, Division 3N, 1924–25
Derby County	37, Jack Bowers, Division 1, 1930–31
	& Ray Straw, Division 3N, 1956–57*
Doncaster Rovers	42, Clarrie Jordan, Division 3, 1946–47*
Everton	60, Dixie Dean, Division 1, 1927–28*
Exeter City	34, Fred Whitlow, Division 3S, 1932–33
Fulham	41, Frank Newton, Division 3S, 1931–32*
Gillingham	31, Ernie Morgan, Division 3S, 1954–55
	& Brian Yeo, Division 4, 1973–74
Grimsby Town	42, Pat Glover, Division 2, 1933–34*
Halifax Town	34, Albert Valentine, Division 3N, 1934–35
Hartlepool United	28, Billy Robinson, Division 3N, 1927–28
Hereford United	35, Dixie McNeil, Division 3, 1975–76*
Huddersfield Town	35, Sam Taylor, Division 2, 1919–20†
	& George Brown, Division 1, 1925–26*
Hull City	41, Bill McNaughton, Division 3N, 1932–33*
Ipswich Town	41, Ted Phillips, Division 3S, 1956–57*
Leeds United	42, John Charles, Division 2, 1953–54
Leicester City	44, Arthur Rowley, Division 2, 1956–57*
Lincoln City	42, Alan Hall, Division 3N, 1931–32*
Liverpool	41, Roger Hunt, Division 2, 1961–62*
Luton Town	55, Joe Payne, Division 3S, 1936–37

FOOTBALL LEAGUE

Manchester City	38, Tom Johnson, Division 1, 1928–29
Manchester United	32, Dennis Viollet, Division 1, 1959–60
Mansfield Town	55, Ted Harston, Division 3N, 1936–37
Middlesbrough	59, George Camsell, Division 2, 1926–27*
Millwall	37, Dick Parker, Division 3S, 1926–27
Newcastle United	36, Hughie Gallacher, Division 1, 1926–27*
Newport County	34, Tudor Martin, Division 3S, 1929–30
Northampton Town	36, Cliff Holton, Division 3, 1961–62
Norwich City	31, Ralph Hunt, Division 3S, 1955–56
Nottingham Forest	36, Wally Ardron, Division 3S, 1950–51*
Notts County	39, Tom Keetley, Division 3S, 1930–31*
Oldham Athletic	33, Tom Davis, Division 3N, 1936–37
Orient	35, Tom Johnston, Division 2, 1957–58
Oxford United	23, Colin Booth, Division 4, 1964–65†
Peterborough United	52, Terry Bly, Division 4, 1960–61†
Plymouth Argyle	32, Jack Cock, Division 3S, 1925–26
Portsmouth	40, Billy Haines, Division 2, 1926–27†
Port Vale	38, Wilf Kirkham, Division 2, 1926–27
Preston North End	37, Ted Harper, Division 2, 1932–33
Queen's Park Rangers	37, George Goddard, Division 3S, 1929–30
Reading	39, Ronnie Blackman, Division 3S, 1951–52
Rochdale	44, Bert Whitehurst, Division 3N, 1926–27
Rotherham United	38, Wally Ardron, Division 3N, 1946–47
Scunthorpe United	31, Barry Thomas, Division 2, 1961–62
Sheffield United	41, Jimmy Dunne, Division 1, 1930–31*
Sheffield Wednesday	46, Derek Dooley, Division 2, 1951–52
Shrewsbury Town	38, Arthur Rowley, Division 4, 1958–59†
Southampton	39, Derek Reeves, Division 3, 1959–60*
Southend United	31, Jim Shankly, Division 3S, 1928–29
	& Sammy McCrory, Division 3S, 1957–58
Stockport County	46, Alf Lythgoe, Division 3N, 1933–34
Stoke City	33, Freddie Steele, Division 1, 1936–37
Sunderland	43, Dave Halliday, Division 1, 1928–29
Swansea City	35, Cyril Pearce, Division 2, 1931–32
Swindon Town	47, Harry Morris, Division 3S, 1926–27
Torquay United	40, Sam Collins, Division 3S, 1955–56
Tottenham Hotspur	37, Jimmy Greaves, Division 1, 1962–63
Tranmere Rovers	35, Robert 'Bunny' Bell, Division 3N, 1933–34
Walsall	40, Gilbert Alsop, Division 3N, 1933–34 & 1934–35
Watford	42, Cliff Holton, Division 4, 1959–60†
West Bromwich Albion	39, William 'Ginger' Richardson, Division 1, 1935–36
West Ham United	41, Vic Watson, Division 1, 1929–30
Wigan Athletic	19, Les Bradd, Division 4, 1981–82
Wimbledon	23, Alan Cork, Division 4, 1980–81
Wolverhampton W.	37, Dennis Westcott, Division 1, 1946–47
Wrexham	44, Tom Bamford, Division 3N, 1933–34
York City	31, Bill Fenton, Division 3N, 1951–52
	& Alf Bottom, Division 3N, 1955–56

*champions that season †promoted that season

but 4 recognised full-backs have scored 10 goals in a season. Chris Lawler of Liverpool did so in Division 1 in 1969–70, and without a single one coming from a penalty or a free-kick. Jimmy Evans of Southend scored all 10 of his goals from penalties in Division 3S in 1921–22, Stan Lynn of Birmingham scored 8 of his 10 from penalties in Division 1 in 1964–65, and Ray O'Brien of Notts County scored 6 out of 10 from penalties in Division 2 in 1979–80.

FA Cup: 15 – Alexander Brown became the first player to score in every round in 1900–01 and his aggregate of 15 goals has never been beaten. Brown scored both Tottenham's goals in the 2-2 draw with Sheffield United in the final at Crystal Palace and the last goal in the 3-1 win in the replay at Bolton. The players who have scored in every round of a series are:

Alex Brown (Tottenham), 1900–01;
Ellis Rimmer (Sheffield W.), 1934–35;
Frank O'Donnell (Preston), 1936–37;
Stan Mortensen (Blackpool), 1947–48;
Jackie Milburn (Newcastle), 1950–51;

Nat Lofthouse (Bolton), 1952–53;
Charlie Wayman (Preston), 1953–54;
Jeff Astle (WBA), 1967–68;
Peter Osgood (Chelsea), 1969–70, though he did not score in the Wembley final.

League Cup: 11 – four players have scored 11 goals in the League Cup in a single season. They are:

Gerry Hitchens (Aston Villa), 1960–61;
Tony Brown (WBA), 1965–66;
Geoff Hurst (West Ham United) 1965–66;
Rodney Marsh (QPR), 1966–67.

Whole squad scoring: Every single Morton player who appeared for them in the Scottish Division 1 in 1912–13 scored, the goalkeeper from a penalty. All Northampton's regular Division 4 side, including the keeper, scored in 1975–76; in fact all but 4 of their 19 man squad scored during the season.

Leading scorers: Bob Hatton, who scored 22 of Blackpool's 59 goals in Division 2 in 1977–78, is one of only two leading scorers from any division of the Football League whose team has been relegated in the same season. Blackpool went down by a point

with 37 that year, while 7 clubs had 38 points. The other example is Mike Channon, who lead the First Division with 21 goals in 1973–74 when Southampton were relegated. In 1933–34 Oliver Brown was Brighton's leading scorer with 12 goals, yet he played in only 8 games.

Leading scorer for two clubs: Colin Garwood was leading scorer for both Portsmouth (17) and Aldershot (10) in Division 4 in 1979–80. A more remarkable record is that of Andy Wilson in 1923–24. Playing only in the First Division, he scored 8 goals for Middlesbrough and 5 for Chelsea and was leading scorer for both sides. They were both relegated to Division 2 at the end of the season!

CAREER AGGREGATE

Overall League record: Only two players have scored more than 400 goals in Football League and/or Scottish League matches. Arthur Rowley scored 434 goals in 619 games between 1946 and 1965 for West Bromwich Albion, Fulham, Leicester and

SCOTTISH LEAGUE

Aberdeen	38, Benny Yorston, Division 1, 1929–30
Airdrieonians	45, Harry Yarnall, Division 1, 1916–17
Albion Rovers	41, Jim Renwick, Division 2, 1932–33
Alloa Athletic	49, Wee Crilley, Division 2, 1921–22*
Arbroath	45, Dave Easson, Division 2, 1958–59†
Ayr United	66, Jimmy Smith, Division 2, 1927–28*
Berwick Rangers	38, Ken Bowron, Division 2, 1963–64
Brechin City	26, Bill McIntosh, Division 2, 1959–60
Celtic	50, Jimmy McGrory, Division 1, 1935–36*
Clyde	36, Billy McPhail, Division 2, 1951–52.
Clydebank	28, Blair Miller, Division 1, 1978–79
Cowdenbeath	40, Willie Devlin, Division 1, 1925–26
Dumbarton	38, Kenny Wilson, Division 2, 1971–72*
Dundee	38, Dave Halliday, Division 1, 1923–24
Dundee United	41, John Coyle, Division 2, 1955–56
Dunfermline Athletic	53, Robert Skinner, Division 2, 1925–26*
East Fife	42, Jimmy Wood, Division 2, 1926–27
East Stirlingshire	36, Malcolm Morrison, Division 2, 1938–39
Falkirk	43, Evelyn Morrison, Division 1, 1928–29
Forfar Athletic	45, Davie Kilgour, Division 2, 1929–30
Hamilton Adademicals	34, David Wilson, Division 1, 1936–37
Heart of Midlothian	44, Barney Battles Junior, Division 1, 1930–31
Hibernian	42, Joe Baker, Division 1, 1959–60
Kilmarnock	35, Peerie Cunningham, Division 1, 1927–28
Meadowbank Thistle	17, John Jobson, Division 2, 1979–80
Montrose	28, Brian Third, Division 2, 1972–73
Morton	41, Allan McGraw, Division 2, 1963–64*
Motherwell	52, Bill McFadyen, Division 1, 1931–32*
Partick Thistle	41, Alec Hair, Division 1, 1926–27
Queen of the South	33, Jimmy Gray, Division 2, 1927–28
Queen's Park	30, Willie Martin, Division 1, 1937–38
Raith Rovers	38, Norman Haywood, Division 2, 1937–38*
Rangers	44, Sam English, Division 1, 1931–32
St Johnstone	36, Jimmy Benson, Division 2, 1931–32†
St Mirren	45, Dunky Walker, Division 1, 1921–22
Stenhousemuir	29, Evelyn Morrison, Division 2, 1928–29 & Ralph Murray, Division 2, 1936–37
Stirling Albion	26, Mick Lawson, Division 2, 1975–76
Stranraer	27, Derek Fry, Division 2, 1977–78

ABOVE: A sequence showing Jimmy Greaves playing for Chelsea at Tottenham on 26 August 1957 and beating Ryden, Brittan and Norman. The picture was captioned: "Jimmy Greaves is predicted to become one of the greatest names in British football." Between 1958-59 and 1968-69 he led the First Division scorers six times.
LEFT: G. O. Smith, who scored 5 goals for England against Ireland on 18 February 1899. Five players share this record for England but there are doubts about the 19th-century examples.

RECORD LEAGUE SCORERS (AGGREGATE) OF CURRENT LEAGUE CLUBS

FOOTBALL LEAGUE

Aldershot	171, Jack Howarth, 1965–1971 & 1972–1977
Arsenal	150, Cliff Bastin, 1930–1947
Aston Villa	213, Harry Hampton, 1904–1920 & Billy Walker, 1919–1934
Barnsley	123, Ernie Hine, 1921–1926 & 1934–38
Birmingham City	250, Joe Bradford, 1921–1935
Blackburn Rovers	140, Tom Briggs, 1952–1958
Blackpool	247, Jimmy Hampson, 1927–1938
Bolton Wanderers	255, Nat Lofthouse, 1946–1961
Bournemouth	202, Ron Eyre, 1924–1933
Bradford City	88, Frank O'Rourke, 1906–1913
Brentford	153, Jim Towers, 1954–1961
Brighton	113, Tommy Cook, 1922–1929
Bristol City	315, John Atyeo, 1951–1966
Bristol Rovers	245, Geoff Bradford, 1949–1964
Burnley	178, George Beel, 1923–1932
Bury	124, Norman Bullock, 1920–1935
Cambridge United	75, Alan Biley, 1975–1980
Cardiff City	127, Len Davies, 1922–1929
Carlisle United	126, Jimmy McConnell, 1928–1932
Charlton Athletic	153, Stuart Leary, 1953–1962
Chelsea	164, Bobby Tambling, 1958–1970
Chester	83, Gary Talbot, 1963–1967 & 1968–1970
Chesterfield	112, Herbert Munday, 1899–1909
Colchester United	131, Martyn King, 1959–1965
Coventry City	171, Clarrie Bourton, 1931–1937
Crewe Alexandra	126, Bert Swindells, 1928–1937
Crystal Palace	154, Peter Simpson, 1930–1936
Darlington	74, Doug Brown, 1923–1926
Derby County	291, Steve Bloomer, 1892–1906 & 1910–1914
Doncaster Rovers	179, Tom Keetley, 1923–1929
Everton	349, Dixie Dean, 1925–1937
Exeter City	105, Alan Banks, 1963–1966 & 1967–1973
Fulham	159, Johnny Haynes, 1952–1970
Gillingham	135, Brian Yeo, 1963–1975
Grimsby Town	182, Pat Glover, 1930–1939
Halifax Town	129, Ernie Dixon, 1922–1930
Hartlepool United	98, Ken Johnson, 1949–1964
Hereford United	85, Dixie McNeil, 1974–1977
Huddersfield Town	142, George Brown, 1921–1929
Hull City	195, Chris Chilton, 1960–1971
Ipswich Town	203, Ray Crawford, 1958–1963 & 1966–1969
Leeds United	154, John Charles, 1949–1957 & 1961–1962
Leicester City	262, Arthur Chandler, 1923–1935
Lincoln City	144, Andy Graver, 1950–1961
Liverpool	245, Roger Hunt, 1959–1969
Luton Town	243, Gordon Turner, 1949–1964
Manchester City	158, Tom Johnson, 1919–1930
Manchester United	198, Bobby Charlton, 1956–1973
Mansfield Town	104, Harry Johnson, 1931–1936
Middlesbrough	326, George Camsell, 1925–1939
Millwall	79, Derek Possee, 1967–1973
Newcastle United	178, Jackie Milburn, 1946–1957
Newport County	99, Reg Parker, 1948–1954
Northampton Town	135, Jack English, 1947–1960
Norwich City	122, Johnny Gavin, 1945–1958

FOOTBALL LEAGUE

Nottingham Forest	199, Grenville Morris, 1898–1913
Notts County	125, Les Bradd, 1967–1978
Oldham Athletic	110, Eric Gemmell, 1947–1954
Orient	121, Tom Johnston, 1956–1961
Oxford United	73, Graham Atkinson, 1962–1973
Peterborough United	120, Jim Hall, 1967–1975
Plymouth Argyle	180, Sam Black, 1924–1938
Portsmouth	194, Peter Harris, 1946–1960
Port Vale	154, Wilf Kirkham, 1923–1929 & 1931–1933
Preston North End	187, Tom Finney, 1946–1960
Queen's Park Rangers	172, George Goddard, 1926–1934
Reading	156, Ronnie Blackman, 1947–1954
Rochdale	119, Reg Jenkins, 1964–75
Rotherham United	130, Gladstone Guest, 1946–1956
Scunthorpe United	92, Barry Thomas, 1959–1962 & 1964–1966
Sheffield United	205, Harry Johnson, 1919–1930
Sheffield Wednesday	200, Andy Wilson, 1900–1920
Shrewsbury Town	152, Arthur Rowley, 1958–1965
Southampton	160, Terry Paine, 1956–1974
Southend United	122, Roy Hollis, 1953–1960
Stockport County	132, Jack Connor, 1951–1956
Stoke City	142, Freddie Steele, 1934–1939
Sunderland	209, Charlie Buchan, 1911–1925
Swansea City	166, Ivor Allchurch, 1949–1958 & 1965–1968
Swindon Town	216, Harry Morris, 1926–1933
Torquay United	204, Sammy Collins, 1948–1958
Tottenham Hotspur	220, Jimmy Greaves, 1961–1970
Tranmere Rovers	104, Robert 'Bunny' Bell, 1931–1936
Walsall	184, Tony Richards, 1954–1963 & Colin Taylor, 1958–1973
Watford	144, Tom Barnett, 1928–1939
West Bromwich Albion	218, Tony Brown, 1963–1.8.1980
West Ham United	306, Vic Watson, 1920–1935
Wigan Athletic	61, Peter Houghton, 1978–83
Wimbledon	86, John Leslie, 1978–83
Wolverhampton W.	164, Bill Hartill, 1928–1935
Wrexham	175, Tom Bamford, 1928–1934
York City	125, Norman Wilkinson, 1954–1966

SCOTTISH LEAGUE

The information is recorded for the following clubs only:

Aberdeen	160, Harry Yorston, 1950–1957
Arbroath	120, Jimmy Jack, 1966–1971
Berwick Rangers	98, Ken Bowron, 1963–1966 & 1968–1969
Celtic	397, Jimmy McGrory, 1922–1923 & 1924–1938
Dundee	111, Alan Gilzean, 1960–1964
Dundee United	202, Peter McKay, 1947–1954
Dunfermline Athletic	154, Charlie Dickson, 1955–1964
Hamilton Academicals	246, Andy Wilson, 1928–1939
Heart of Midlothian	206, Jimmy Wardhaugh, 1946–1959
Hibernian	185, Lawrie Reilly, 1946–1958
Kilmarnock	102, Jimmy Maxwell, 1931–1934
Motherwell	283, Hugh Ferguson, 1916–1925
Rangers	233, Bob McPhail, 1927–1939

Shrewsbury; Jimmy McGrory scored 410 goals in 408 games between 1922 and 1938 for Celtic and Clydebank.

Overall League average: McGrory is the only player to have averaged more than a goal a game in League football, his 410 in 408 games giving a figure of 1.005 per game. His nearest major competitor is Brian Clough with 251 in 274 League games, for an average of 0.916.

International aggregates: Bobby Charlton has scored 49 goals in recognised internationals (106 appearances), more than any other UK player. The Scottish record is 30 (56 appearances) by Denis Law. The Welsh record is 23 (38) by Trevor Ford, and the Northern Ireland best is 13 (25) by Billy Gillespie.

International average: George Camsell has the best figure over a reasonable number of games with 18 goals in only 9 full appearances, though Charles Heggie (*above*) scored 5 goals on his only appearance for Scotland in 1886.

MISCELLANEOUS SCORING RECORDS

Longest range goals are those scored by keepers such as Marc de Clerc (*see* KEEPERS). The longest range headed goal in a League game is reputed to be one of 35 yards by Peter Aldis of Aston Villa against Sunderland on Monday 1 September 1952 in Division 1. It was Aldis's first goal in League football, and Villa won 3-0. Goals from clearances by goalkeepers are uncommon but not unknown. In the Football League the last example was by Steve Sherwood for Watford at Coventry, Division 1, on 14 January 1984. Pat Jennings had done the same thing for Tottenham Hotspur at Old Trafford in the Charity Shield game versus Manchester United on Saturday 12 August 1967. Charlie Williams of Manchester City also scored from his own area at Sunderland on Saturday 14 April 1900.

Throw-ins: The only goal known to have been scored direct from a throw-in was by Frank Bokas of Barnsley in fourth round FA Cup tie against Manchester United on Saturday 22 January 1938. United keeper Tom Breen just touched the ball as it sailed over his head – otherwise the referee would have given a goal-kick.

Most headers in a final: When Wimbledon beat Sutton United 4-2 in the Amateur Cup final of 1963 at Wembley, Eddie Reynolds headed all 4 Wimbledon goals.

Fastest 100 goals: Jimmy Cookson of Chesterfield and West Bromwich reached his century of League goals after only 87 games on Saturday 17 December 1927.

ABOVE: *Keeper Wilson and centre-back Herbie Roberts combine to deny Dixie Dean (right) in an Arsenal v Everton game on 29 August 1936. Dean's total of 349 goals for Everton is the highest recorded by any player for a single Football League club.*
LEFT: *Jimmy McGrory, scorer of 397 goals for Celtic between 1922 and 1938 and later manager of the club. No other player has scored more goals for any single British club.*
BELOW: *Bobby Charlton, all-time leading scorer for Manchester United with 198 goals.*

Goalscoring

MOST IN SEASON

Overall League record: 142 – Raith Rovers in 34 games in Scottish Division 2, 1937–38.

Football League record: 134 – Peterborough United in 46 games in Division 4, 1960–61 (their first season in the League).

Division 1: 128 – Aston Villa in 42 games in 1930–31. Villa scored 4 or more goals on 20 occasions, including losing one game 6-4 at home to Derby and drawing 5-5 away to West Ham. On only 6 occasions at home did they score *less* than 4 goals – and yet they ended the season 7 points behind Arsenal.

Division 2: 122 – Middlesbrough in 42 games in 1926–27, despite scoring only once in their first 4 games.

Division 3: 128 – Bradford City in 42 games in Division 3N, 1928–29. As late as 1961–62, QPR scored 111 goals in 46 Division 3 games, but finished only 4th.

Scottish Division 1/Premier: 132 – Hearts in 34 games, 1957–58.

Goals per game: The best record in the Football League is that of Small Heath, who scored 103 in 28 games in Division 2, 1893–94. That average of 3.67 goals per game was surprisingly not good enough to win them the Championship, which went to Liverpool.

At home: Millwall scored 87 goals in Division 3S in 1927–28.

Away from home: Arsenal scored 60 goals in Division 1 in season 1930–31.

Complete League season: The record for the Football League is the 6985 goals recorded in season 1960–61. The record for a single division is 1855 in Division 3 in 1962–63.

FA Cup: Aston Villa scored 47 goals in the FA Cup in 1886–87. Derby scored 37 goals in winning the FA Cup in 1945–46. Arbroath scored 55 times in the 1885–86 Scottish Cup (before losing to Hibs at Easter Road in the fourth round) and Preston scored 50 goals in 1887–88, but neither won the trophy. Nonetheless, the record is probably Queen's Park's 60 goals in 1881–82.

Most without reward: When Manchester City scored 89 goals and were relegated from Division 1 in 1925–26 (the most ever scored by a relegated club), they also scored 31 in just five rounds of the FA Cup, only to lose the final 1-0 to Bolton. St Bernard's scored 100 goals in 3 consecutive seasons (1934–37) in Scottish Division 2, but still failed to gain promotion. In 1934–35 they scored 103 goals and finished third, three points away from the promotion place. In 1935–36 they scored 106 goals but could only finish fifth (five teams scored over 100 goals in the division, despite playing only 34 games) and in 1936–37 they scored 102, finished third again and were still three points short of promotion. They thus scored over three goals a game for three years.

CONSECUTIVE MATCHES

Best consecutive English record: 17-0 –

RECORD TOTALS OF CURRENT LEAGUE CLUBS

FOOTBALL LEAGUE

Aldershot	83, Division 4, 1963–64
Arsenal	127, Division 1, 1930–31
Aston Villa	128, Division 1, 1930–31
Barnsley	118, Division 3N, 1933–34
Birmingham City	103, Division 2, 1893–94*
Blackburn Rovers	114, Division 2, 1954–55
Blackpool	98, Division 2, 1929–30
Bolton Wanderers	96, Division 2, 1934–35
Bournemouth	88, Division 3S, 1956–57
Bradford City	128, Division 3N, 1928–29
Brentford	98, Division 4, 1962–63
Brighton	112, Division 3S, 1955–56
Bristol City	104, Division 3S, 1926–27
Bristol Rovers	92, Division 3S, 1952–53
Burnley	102, Division 1, 1960–61
Bury	108, Division 3, 1960–61
Cambridge United	87, Division 4, 1976–77
Cardiff City	93, Division 3S, 1946–47
Carlisle United	113, Division 4, 1963–64
Charlton Athletic	107, Division 2, 1957–58
Chelsea	98, Division 1, 1960–61
Chester	119, Division 4, 1964–65
Chesterfield	102, Division 3N, 1930–31
Colchester United	104, Division 4, 1961–62
Coventry City	108, Division 3S, 1931–32
Crewe Alexandra	95, Division 3N, 1931–32
Crystal Palace	110, Division 4, 1960–61
Darlington	108, Division 3N, 1929–30
Derby County	111, Division 3N, 1956–57
Doncaster Rovers	123, Division 3N, 1946–47
Everton	121, Division 2, 1930–31
Exeter City	88, Division 3S, 1932–33
Fulham	111, Division 3S, 1931–32
Gillingham	90, Division 4, 1973–74
Grimsby Town	103, Division 2, 1933–34
Halifax Town	83, Division 3N, 1957–58
Hartlepool United	90, Division 3N, 1956–57
Hereford United	86, Division 3, 1975–76
Huddersfield Town	101, Division 4, 1979–80
Hull City	109, Division 3, 1965–66
Ipswich Town	106, Division 3S, 1955–56
Leeds United	98, Division 2, 1927–28
Leicester City	109, Division 2, 1956–57
Lincoln City	121, Division 3N, 1951–52
Liverpool	106, Division 2, 1895–96†
Luton Town	103, Division 3S, 1936–37
Manchester City	108, Division 2, 1926–27
Manchester United	103, Division 1, 1956–57

FOOTBALL LEAGUE

	& Division 1, 1958–59
Mansfield Town	108, Division 4, 1962–63
Middlesbrough	122, Division 2, 1926–27
Millwall	127, Division 3S, 1927–28
Newcastle United	98, Division 1, 1951–52
Newport County	85, Division 4, 1964–65
Northampton Town	109, Division 3S, 1952–53
	& Division 3, 1962–63
Norwich City	99, Division 3S, 1952–53
Nottingham Forest	110, Division 3S, 1950–51
Notts County	107, Division 3S, 1959–60
Oldham Athletic	95, Division 4, 1962–63
Orient	106, Division 3S, 1955–56
Oxford United	87, Division 4, 1964–65
Peterborough United	134, Division 4, 1960–61
Plymouth Argyle	107, Division 3S, 1925–26
	& Division 3S, 1951–52
Portsmouth	91, Division 4, 1979–80
Port Vale	110, Division 4, 1958–59
Preston North End	100, Division 2, 1927–28
	& Division 1, 1957–58
Queen's Park Rangers	111, Division 3, 1961–62
Reading	112, Division 3S, 1951–52
Rochdale	105, Division 3N, 1926–27
Rotherham United	114, Division 3N, 1946–47
Scunthorpe United	88, Division 3N, 1957–58
Sheffield United	102, Division 1, 1925–26
Sheffield Wednesday	106, Division 2, 1958–59
Shrewsbury Town	101, Division 4, 1958–59
Southampton	112, Division 3S, 1957–58
Southend United	92, Division 3S, 1950–51
Stockport County	115, Division 3N, 1933–34
Stoke City	92, Division 3N, 1926–27
Sunderland	109, Division 1, 1935–36
Swansea City	90, Division 2, 1956–57
Swindon Town	100, Division 3S, 1926–27
Torquay United	89, Division 3S, 1956–57
Tottenham Hotspur	115, Division 1, 1960–61
Tranmere Rovers	111, Division 3N, 1930–31
Walsall	102, Division 4, 1959–60
Watford	92, Division 4, 1959–60
West Bromwich Albion	105, Division 2, 1929–30
West Ham United	101, Division 2, 1957–58
Wigan Athletic	80, Division 4, 1981–82
Wimbledon	96, Division 4, 1982–83
Wolverhampton W.	115, Division 2, 1931–32
Wrexham	106, Division 3N, 1932–33
York City	92, Division 3N, 1954–55

SCOTTISH LEAGUE

Aberdeen	96,	Division 1,	1935–36
Airdrieonians	107,	Division 2,	1965–66
Albion Rovers	101,	Division 2,	1929–30
Alloa Athletic	92,	Division 2,	1961–62
Arbroath	87,	Division 2,	1967–68
Ayr United	122,	Division 2,	1936–37
Berwick Rangers	83,	Division 2,	1961–62
Brechin City	80,	Division 2,	1957–58
Celtic	116,	Division 1,	1915–16
Clyde	122,	Division 2,	1956–57
Clydebank	78,	Division 1,	1978–79
Cowdenbeath	120,	Division 2,	1938–39
Dumbarton	101,	Division 2,	1956–57
Dundee	113,	Division 2,	1946–47
Dundee United	99,	Division 2,	1928–29
Dunfermline Athletic	120,	Division 2,	1957–58
East Fife	114,	Division 2,	1929–30
East Stirlingshire	111,	Division 2,	1931–32
Falkirk	132,	Division 2,	1935–36
Forfar Athletic	90,	Division 2,	1931–32
Hamilton Acad.	92,	Division 1,	1932–33
Heart of Midlothian	132,	Division 1,	1957–58
Hibernian	106,	Division 1,	1959–60
Kilmarnock	92,	Division 1,	1962–63
Meadowbank Thistle	64,	Division 2,	1982–83
Montrose	78,	Division 2,	1970–71
Morton	135,	Division 2,	1963–64
Motherwell	119,	Division 1,	1931–32
Partick Thistle	91,	Division 1,	1928–29
Queen of the South	94,	Division 2,	1959–60
Queen's Park	100,	Division 2,	1928–29
Raith Rovers	142,	Division 2,	1937–38
Rangers	118,	Division 1,	1931–32
	&	Division 1,	1933–34
St Johnstone	102,	Division 2,	1931–32
St Mirren	114,	Division 2,	1935–36
Stenhousemuir	99,	Division 2,	1959–60
Stirling Albion	105,	Division 2,	1957–58
Stranraer	83,	Division 2,	1960–61

*in only 28 games †in only 30 games

Charlton's Bert Turner (centre) scores Derby's first goal (an own goal) in the 1946 Cup final; Derby won 4–1 and ended the game having scored a 20th-century record 37 goals that season.

The two closest grounds in Britain are Dundee's Dens Park (bottom) and Dundee United's Tannadice Park, a mere goal-kick apart on Tannadice Road. On 6 December 1980 the two clubs met at Dens Park in the Scottish League Cup final, only the second time this century that a side has played a major final on its own ground (Celtic played the 1902 Scottish Cup final versus Hibernian at Parkhead). Celtic lost 1–0, Dundee lost 3–0.

Small Heath beat Luton 9–0 in Division 2 on Saturday 12 November 1898, did not play the following Saturday and then beat Darwen 8–0 on Saturday 26 November. Both games were at home. Reading nearly equalled this record in Division 3S, beating Crystal Palace 10–2 on Wednesday 4 September 1946 and Southend 7–2 on Saturday 7 September. Both of these games were at home and Reading finished only ninth in the division that season. On the more conventional basis of consecutive home and away matches alternating, the record is held by Arsenal. They beat Leicester 8–2 at Highbury on Saturday 29 October 1932 and then beat Wolves 7–1 at Molineux the following Saturday. The Scottish, and British, record is held by Dundee who won consecutive Scottish Division B games 10–0 – at Alloa on 8 March 1947 and at home to Dunfermline on 22 March 1947. This is the only occasion on which a British club has reached double figures in consecutive matches.

Worst consecutive record: 20–2 – Newport County, contesting their only season in Division 2, were beaten 2–7 at home on Saturday 28 September 1946 by West Brom and the following Saturday travelled to Newcastle to suffer the biggest defeat in League history – 0–13.

Consecutive home games: 20–2 – Chester, competing in Division 3N, defeated York 12–0 on Saturday 1 February 1936 and New Brighton 8–2 on Saturday 15 February.

Consecutive away games: 12–1 – Sunderland, champions of the Football League, won 6–0 at Accrington on 3 September 1892 and 6–1 at Aston Villa on 17 September 1892.

Biggest reversals: In Division 2 in 1895–96, Darwen beat Rotherham Town 10–2 on 13 January 1896 and then lost their next game, away at Grimsby on 25 January, 5–0. This is the biggest reversal of fortune in consecutive games known in the Football League. A much more interesting and unlikely reversal, however, was that by Manchester City in the First Division on 1925–26. On Saturday 24 October 1925 City defeated Burnley 8–3 at home; two days later, on Monday 26 October, they lost by the very same score, 8–3, away at Sheffield United.

FEWEST IN SEASON

Overall League record: 16 – Dundee scored only 16 goals in 18 Scottish Division 1 games in 1901–02. The following season they conceded only 12 goals and hence established records for the worst attacking and best defensive performance in consecutive seasons. These records still stand for England and Scotland. Mathematically, the worst ever record is 18 by Stirling Albion in 39 games in the Scottish Division 1 in 1980–81.

Football League record: 18 – Loughborough Town in 34 games in Division 2 in 1899–1900. In a full 42-game season, the worst record is held by Watford with 24 in Division 2 in 1971–72.

Division 1: 26 – Leicester (in 42 games) in 1977–78, Stoke (in 22 games) in 1888–89 and Woolwich Arsenal (in 38 games) in 1912–13.

Division 2: Loughborough Town and Watford (*above*).

Division 3: 27 – Stockport County (in 46

games) in 1969–70.

Division 4: 29 – Crewe Alexandra in 46 games in 1981–82.

Scottish Division 1/Premier: 16 – Dundee (*above*). In a season of 34 games or more, Ayr United have the worst record with only 20 goals in 1966–67 (34 games).

Scottish non-Division 1/Premier: 18 – Stirling Albion in 1980–81 (39 games).

Away from home: 4 – Lincoln City in Division 2 in 1900–01, Gainsborough Trinity in Division 2 in 1901–02 and Exeter City in Division 3S in 1923–24.

At home: 11 – Woolwich Arsenal in Division 1 in 1912–13, their last season at Plumstead before moving to Highbury.

Grounds

GENERAL

Largest ground: The largest ground in Britain is Wembley, with a capacity of 100,000. The largest in Scotland is the Third Hampden Park, with a capacity now reduced to 88,000.

Largest club ground: The largest club ground in Britain – apart from Queen's Park's (Hampden) which is more in the nature of a national stadium – is Charlton's The Valley, which is the only English stadium never to have been filled. It has held 75,000 (in 1938) and has an official capacity today of 66,000.

Longest occupancy: Chesterfield have used the Recreation Ground, Saltergate, since their formation in 1866. Dumbarton have used Boghead Park since 1872.

Smallest ground: Cambridge United have the smallest Football League ground at Abbey Road with an official capacity of only 12,000.

All seated: Aberdeen's Pittodrie (a Gaelic word meaning, literally, hill of dung) was the first all-seater stadium in the country. It has a capacity of 24,000 and was opened as an all-seater with a friendly against Tottenham Hotspur on Saturday 5 August 1978. Clydebank followed this pattern at New Kilbowie Park, which holds 9,900 all seated and Coventry became the first club in England to do so in 1982 when they turned Highfield Road into an all-seated, 20,500 capacity stadium. Rangers have abandoned plans to do the same at Ibrox Park. Meadowbank Thistle claim that their Meadowbank Stadium is all-seated because all spectators have to sit during matches. The stadium does, however, have standing room which is never used on match days.

Gates closed: The first recorded occasion was for the 1880–81 Scottish Cup final replay between Queen's Park and Dumbarton at Kinning Park, when the crowd was about 15,000. The first occasion in England was for the 1888 FA Cup final at Kennington Oval between West Bromwich and Preston, when the crowd was about 18,000.

Closest grounds: Dundee and Dundee United have grounds just 200 yards apart either side of Tannadice Street. The closest in England are the grounds of Notts County and Nottingham Forest, 400 yards apart and separated by the River Trent.

Goal nets: Raith Rovers were ordered to replay their 1894–95 Scottish Cup first round tie against 5th Kings Rifle Volunteers because they had failed to provide goal nets. They lost the second game 3-4 having won the first 6-3.

Not in club's home town: Before local government reorganisation, there were three clubs whose grounds were not in their home town. Manchester United's Old Trafford was (and still is) in Stretford, Grimsby Town's Blundell Park is in Cleethorpes and Nottingham Forest's City Ground is in West Bridgford. While Forest's misnamed City Ground is actually in the county of Nottinghamshire, Notts County's Meadow Lane is in the city of Nottingham.

Smallest town with a League club: Currently the smallest in Britain is Brechin, with a population of 6,000.

Smallest town in England/Wales: Until Workington's failure to gain re-election in 1977, their home town was easily the smallest to have a League club, with a population of 25,000. The smallest now is Hereford with 47,000, though Aldershot, without its heavily populated hinterland, claims a population of only 33,000. In the 1920s Ashington, Durham, Stalybridge, Gainsborough, Northwich and Nelson all supported Division 3N clubs on populations smaller than either Workington or Hereford. Glossop, in Derbyshire, is the smallest town ever to have hosted a Division 1 club.

Largest town without a League club: Salford (150,000) is the largest separate town (i.e. excluding London boroughs) never to have had a League club, although Manchester United play right on its border.

Largest town without Division 1 club: The largest towns in Britain never to have had a Division 1 club are Hull (280,000) and Plymouth (250,000).

Largest towns without a trophy: The largest major urban centres never to have had a club win any of the major trophies are Bristol and the Cleveland/Teesside/Middlesbrough conurbation. Both have a population just under 500,000 and Middlesbrough have never even reached an FA Cup semi-final. Bournemouth, Coventry, Hull, Plymouth and Swansea are other major centres never to have welcomed a major trophy won by their clubs.

GROUND ADVANTAGE

Small Heath: The first known instance of a club selling its ground advantage in a Cup tie (no longer allowed by the FA) was in the 1879 Birmingham Cup, when Wednesbury Old Athletic (then the strongest team in the Midlands) offered Small Heath Alliance £5 to switch a game to Wednesbury. Small Heath accepted the money and then proceeded to win the game. In the second round of the 1891–92 FA Cup Small Heath also accepted £200 from The Wednesday to play a game in Sheffield – but this time they lost 2-0. Small Heath became Birming-

ham in 1905.

Blackpool sold their home rights in the second round in 1905–06 to Sheffield United for £250. They then proceeded to win 2-1 at Bramall Lane. In the same decade Blackpool sold similar ground rights to both Arsenal and Spurs.

Notts County sold their rights in the first round of the FA Cup to Bradford City in 1909–10 for £1,000. Bradford won 4-2.

Northampton Town: Non-League Northampton, managed by Herbert Chapman, drew 1-1 in a second round tie away to Cup holders Newcastle United in 1910–11. They accepted £900 to replay in Newcastle, where they lost 1-0. Newcastle went on to the final. Nottingham Forest did exactly the same with Newcastle in 1920–21.

Southport forfeited ground advantage when they drew Newcastle United in the second round of the 1975–76 League Cup. They lost 6-0 but drew a crowd of 23,000 and their share of the receipts was higher than they could have hoped for at home. No money changed hands on this occasion, which was not unlike the decisions of many non-League clubs to play games on their opponents' grounds in the FA Cup (or on neutral League grounds) to get a bigger gate.

In 1976–77 Northwich Victoria were forced to transfer their home fourth round FA Cup tie against Oldham to Maine Road when it was discovered that they had sold more tickets than their official capacity allowed.

UNUSUAL CIRCUMSTANCES

Shared use: There are several instances of grounds being used for more than one sport. The most notable was probably at Valley Parade where Bradford City and the the rugby league club Bradford Northern played in the 1920s and 1930s. City had originally been formed as a bridgehead against rugby penetration in the city. In a similar arrangement, Workington and rugby league's Workington Town shared Borough Park in 1951–52 while in recent years the arrangement has become very common at Fulham, Cardiff, Carlisle and elsewhere. Chesterfield and Northampton still share county cricket grounds, while Sheffield United shared Bramall Lane for nearly a century with Yorkshire CCC. Both Notts County and Nottingham Forest have shared Trent Bridge with Notts CCC, and County were named after their association with the county cricket team. The only instance of a rugby union club sharing a ground is thought to be at Ashton Gate, which has been used by Bristol RFC.

Played elsewhere: There are numerous instances of League clubs having to play away from their home ground for various reasons – in fact it has affected no fewer than 26 current English and Scottish League clubs. The most common reasons are damaged grounds (such as when Forest moved to Notts County after their main stand burned down or when Stoke moved to Port Vale after their stand roof had blown off) or a ban after violent crowd behaviour.

Elsewhere most often: Celtic have played

ABOVE: Bristol Rovers' Eastville Stadium which, despite appearances, has the smallest pitch in the country – 7700 sq yds. A fire in the main stand at the beginning of the 1980-81 season caused the club to play several games at Bristol City's Ashton Gate.

LEFT: Celtic's Bobby Lennox (13) passes Aberdeen's Steve Archibald in a game at Pittodrie on 7 October 1978. Aberdeen had opened the first all-seated stadium in the country just 2 months previously. The picture illustrates two other interesting points – that the Scottish League allows two substitutes (hence Lennox wearing 13) and the fact that Celtic are the only club not to number players' shirts. They number only shorts, except in European games when UEFA insist that they conform.

official home games at Alloa (a Scottish Cup match v Partick Thistle on 19 March 1904), Shawfield, Easter Road, Firhill, Cappielow and, of course, numerous big matches at Hampden.

No home to go to: The most clear-cut example of this was in 1908–09 when Partick Thistle's Meadowside Park ground was judged unfit and closed down and Partick had no home ground for a full season until Firhill was ready. Between 1908 and 1910 Notts County, who were building Meadow Lane, had no home ground other than the cricket pitch at Trent Bridge and would use the City Ground if there was a cricket match in progress. Chelsea have been asked

to move away from Stamford Bridge in 1987 by the freeholders so that the site may be redeveloped.

Two grounds: Queen's Park are the only club in the country to actually have two home grounds – Hampden Park and New Lesser Hampden (capacity 6000). In addition their old ground, Cathkin Park, lies empty close by.

Most grounds used: 13 – Queen's Park Rangers. Rangers have had 11 official home grounds and also played matches at White City in 1931–32 and 1932–33 and for the whole of the 1962–62 season. In 1930 they had to play Coventry at Highbury when Loftus Road was under suspension. That

makes 13 grounds on which QPR have played home fixtures and in the 1960s they also tried to negotiate a move to Brentford's Griffin Park.

PITCHES

Biggest: Maine Road (Manchester City), 9410 sq. yds. [119 × 79].

Biggest in Scotland: Hampden Park (Queen's Park), 8625 sq. yds. [115 × 75].

Smallest: Eastville (Bristol Rovers), 7700 sq. yds. [110 × 70].

Longest: County Ground, Northampton (Northampton Town), 120 yards.

Widest: Edgar Street (Hereford United), 80 yards.

FLOODLIGHTING

First floodlit game: This was probably on Monday 14 October 1878 at Bramall Lane, when two teams chosen by the Sheffield Association drew a crowd of around 20,000 to a demonstration game. This was four times bigger than the crowd at the Cup final that year.

First ban: In 1930 the FA prohibited the use of floodlights for games played under its jurisdiction.

First competitive game: A Football Combination game between the Southampton and Tottenham Hotspur reserve teams on Monday 1 October 1951 at The Dell. The first game in Scotland was a friendly between Stenhousemuir and Hibernian at Ochilview Park in November 1951.

First game between two League clubs: An FA Cup first round second replay between Carlisle and Darlington at St James' Park, Newcastle on Monday 28 November 1955. The first first-class fixtures played under floodlights in Scotland were in the Scottish Cup on Wednesday 8 February 1956 between Hibernian and Raith and East Fife and Stenhousemuir.

First League game: Portsmouth against Newcastle United at Fratton Park on Wednesday 22 February 1956 in Division 1. Newcastle won 2-0. It was 1958 before the Football League lifted its controls over floodlit games.

CHOICE OF GROUND

FA Cup: Initially, all FA Cup games were supposed to be played at Kennington Oval. This was changed from the second season to all games after the second round being played at The Oval, with the captains tossing for choice of ground. The only exception to The Oval rule was the 1873 final, played at Lillie Bridge.

Geographical grouping: This was first introduced for the early rounds in 1879–80 to avoid too much travelling and has been the rule ever since.

Semi-final outside The Oval: The first was Blackburn Rovers against The Wednesday, played at Huddersfield in 1882. The game ended 0-0 and was replayed at the ground of the Manchester Athletic Club, Fallowfield, where Blackburn won 5-1.

Scottish Cup: Scottish Cup semi-finals were not played on neutral grounds until 1912. In 1902 the Scottish FA allowed Celtic to play the final as well as the semi-final on their own Celtic Park pitch.

First final decided outside London: Saturday 10 April 1886, at The Racecourse, Derby, where Blackburn Rovers beat WBA 2-0 in a replay.

Tossed for choice of ground: After Manchester City and Preston North End drew 1-1 at Manchester and 0-0 at Preston in the FA Cup first round 1901–02, they decided to toss for choice of ground for the replay. Preston won the toss, but City won the third game 4-2. On 21 January 1907 Spurs played an FA Cup second replay against Hull City at White Hart Lane after two draws and won the game 1-0. This has become common practice in the League Cup in recent years, but has never been generally accepted for the FA Cup. Clubs can, however, elect to play a third game on one of their home grounds – as happened in the fifth round in 1977–78 when Nottingham Forest played both their first and second replays against Queen's Park Rangers at the City Ground.

Hat-tricks

HOME INTERNATIONAL (BRITISH) CHAMPIONSHIP

Year	Winners						
		1909	England	1938	England	1960	England
		1910	Scotland	1939	England		Scotland
1884	Scotland	1911	England		Scotland		Wales
1885	Scotland	1912	England		Wales	1961	England
1886	England		Scotland	1940	Not contested	1962	Scotland
	Scotland	1913	Scotland	1941	Not contested	1963	Scotland
1887	Scotland	1914	Ireland	1942	Not contested	1964	England
1888	England	1915	Not contested	1943	Not contested		N. Ireland
1889	Scotland	1916	Not contested	1944	Not contested		Scotland
1890	England	1917	Not contested	1945	Not contested	1965	England
	Scotland	1918	Not contested	1946	Not contested	1966	England
1891	England	1919	Not contested	1947	England	1967	Scotland
1892	England	1920	Wales	1948	England	1968	England
1893	England	1921	Scotland	1949	Scotland	1969	England
1894	Scotland	1922	Scotland	1950	England	1970	England
1895	England	1923	Scotland	1951	Scotland		Scotland
1896	Scotland	1924	Wales	1952	England		Wales
1897	Scotland	1925	Scotland		Wales	1971	England
1898	England	1926	Scotland	1953	England	1972	England
1899	England	1927	England		Scotland		Scotland
1900	Scotland		Scotland	1954	England	1973	England
1901	England	1928	Wales	1955	England	1974	England
1902	Scotland	1929	Scotland	1956	England		Scotland
1903	England	1930	England		N. Ireland	1975	England
	Ireland	1931	England		Scotland	1976	Scotland
	Scotland		Scotland		Wales	1977	Scotland
1904	England	1932	England	1957	England	1978	England
1905	England	1933	Wales	1958	England	1979	England
1906	England	1934	Wales		N. Ireland	1980	N. Ireland
	Scotland	1935	England	1959	England	1981	Incomplete
1907	Wales		Scotland		N. Ireland	1982	England
1908	England	1936	Scotland			1983	England
	Scotland	1937	Wales			1984	

TOP LEFT: In the 90th minute of normal time, Stanley Mortensen's free-kick makes it 3-3 in the 1953 Cup final and completes the only hat-trick scored in a Wembley FA Cup or League Cup final.
CENTRE LEFT: The Nottingham Forest side, photographed at Trent Bridge, which defeated Leicester 12-0 on 21 April 1909 for the Div 1 record score. The three players on the far right (Hooper, Spouncer and West) each scored a hat-trick. Enoch West later received the longest ever suspension.
LEFT: Dixie Dean, scorer of 37 hat-tricks.

Career: Dixie Dean scored 37 hat-tricks in his career.

Season: George Camsell scored 9 hat-tricks (out of 59 goals) for Middlesbrough in Division 2 in the 1926–27 season.

Consecutive days: Cliff Holton of Watford is the only man known to have scored hat-tricks on consecutive days in first-class fixtures. On Friday 15 April 1960 Watford beat Chester 4-2 and on Saturday 16 April they beat Gateshead 5-0 in Division 4.

Three consecutive hat-tricks: There have been four known instances of a player scoring hat-tricks in three consecutive games:

● The most remarkable, but least well documented, example is that of Alex Haddow of King's Park who scored a hat-trick in five consecutive Division 2 matches in 1932. They were against Armadale on 23 January (4 goals), Stenhousemuir on 6 February (5 goals), Edinburgh City on 13 February (away, 3 goals), Montrose on 20 February (3 goals) and Brechin on 27 February (away, 3 goals). King's Park did not have a game on 30 January. During this five game spell they scored 34 goals and conceded only 6, winning all the matches.

● Jack White of Hearts scored hat-tricks against Dundee United on 1 February 1926, against Alloa away in the Scottish Cup on 8 February and against Hamilton on 13 February 1926.

● Barney Battles, also of Hearts, repeated White's feat in November 1930. On 15 November Hearts beat Motherwell 5-1, on 22 November they won 3-1 at Dundee and on 29 November beat St Mirren 3-1.

● Jackie Balmer of Liverpool is the only man to have managed the feat in England in the following matches: Saturday 9 November 1946 v Portsmouth (home) – Liverpool won 3-0; Saturday 16 November 1946 v Derby (away) – Liverpool won 4-1; Saturday 23 November 1946 v Arsenal (home) – Liverpool won 4-2. All were Division 1 games and Liverpool won the Championship that season.

Fraternal hat-tricks: Nick Ross of Preston scored 3 goals against Burnley on 28 September 1889. His brother Jimmy scored 3 the following week, on 5 October, against West Brom and Nick then came back to score another 3 against Bolton on 12 October. Each of the brothers scored 3 hat-tricks that season, in only 22 League games. The Capes brothers, Arthur and Adrian, both scored a hat-trick for Burton Wanderers when they defeated Newcastle 9-0 in the Second Division on 15 April 1895. Adrian, in fact, scored 4 of the 9.

Consecutive away games: Tom Keetley of Notts County scored hat-tricks in three consecutive away Division 2 games – against Plymouth on 10 October 1931 (won 4-3), against Manchester United on 24 October 1931 (drew 3-3), and against Chesterfield on 7 November 1931 (won 4-1).

Three times three: There are two certain occasions on which three players from the same side scored a hat-trick in the same League game. Enoch West, Arthur Spouncer and Bill Hooper did so for Nottingham Forest against Leicester Fosse in Division 1 on Wednesday 21 April 1909, when Forest won 12-0; Ron Barnes, Roy Ambler and Wyn Davies also did so for Wrexham against Hartlepools United in Division 4 on Saturday 3 March 1962, when Wrexham won 10-1.

Without another player intervening: The Reverend R.W.S. Vidal (the original 'Prince of Dribblers') is recorded (by Charles Alcock, secretary of the FA) as having scored three goals for Oxford University in 1873 without any other player touching the ball. Under certain rules at the time, the team that scored a goal also kicked off and the ball did not have to be touched to another player at a kick-off.

FA Cup finals: Three hat-tricks have been recorded – by William Townley for Blackburn Rovers in 1890, by Jimmy Logan for Notts County in 1894 and by Stan Mortensen

RIGHT: *Noel Brotherston (green) breaks away from the Welsh defence to score the only goal of the Wales v N. Ireland game at Cardiff on 23 May 1980. In their centenary year, that goal gave the Irish the Championship outright for only the second time in their history – the first was in 1914.*

BELOW: *John Mahoney and Graeme Souness clash in May 1978 at Hampden in the annual Home International (now renamed British Championship) fixture. Scotland were Wales' first ever opponents back on 23 March 1876, though the Scots only billed the Welsh as North Wales FA rather than a side representing the whole principality and the game is of doubtful status. Wales lost 4-0 in 1876 and drew 1-1 in 1978.*

for Blackpool in 1953. Logan was to die tragically only 2 years after his hat-trick feat, in May 1896. He had, by then, been transferred to Loughborough Town.

Scottish Cup finals: Only two hat-tricks have been scored in Scottish Cup finals – by Jimmy Quinn for Celtic against Rangers in 1904 (Celtic won 3-2) and by Dixie Deans for Celtic v Hibs in 1972 (Celtic won 6-1). There have been several hat-tricks in the Scottish League Cup final, the most remarkable being by Joe Harper for Hibernian against Celtic in the 1974–75 game. Hibs lost 6–3 and Harper's is the only hat-trick to be scored by a member of the losing side in a major final. Dixie Deans scored a hat-trick for Celtic in the same match.

See also: CONSECUTIVE SEQUENCES

Home Championship

VICTORIES

Outright winners: England have won the

pionship games for Wales between 1895 and 1920.

Consecutive: Danny Blanchflower appeared in 33 consecutive games for Northern Ireland from Wednesday 19 March 1952 against Wales at Swansea to Wednesday 7 November 1962 against Scotland at Hampden.

Non-British player: The only non-British player (i.e. neither he nor one of his parents were born in the British Isles) known to have appeared in the Championship was Willie Andrews, born in Kansas City, Missouri, who played 3 times for Ireland (once in 1908 and twice in 1913). His clubs at the time were Glentoran and Grimsby.

Played elsewhere: Two Championship games have been played outside either of the two countries involved. On 8 February 1890 Wales beat Ireland 5-2 at Shrewsbury and on 19 May 1973 Northern Ireland beat Wales 1-0 at Goodison Park, Liverpool. In addition, Wales played their final 1978 World Cup qualifying game against Scotland at Anfield, Liverpool on Wednesday 12 October 1977 as Ninian Park had a severe capacity restriction at the time.

Home Games

Most wins in a season: There are numerous instances of clubs going undefeated throughout a whole season at home, but only 7 have won every League game:
Brentford, Division 3S, 1929–30 (21 games);
The Wednesday, Division 2, 1899–1900 (18);
Small Heath, Division 2, 1902–03 (18);
Liverpool, Division 2, 1893–94 (15);
Bury, Division 2, 1894–95 (15);
Sunderland, Division 1, 1891–92 (13);
Rangers, Scottish Division 1, 1898–99 (9).

Fewest wins in a season: O – Raith Rovers are the only team to have failed to win a single home league game in a season. They achieved this feat in Division 1 in 1962–63 when they lost 15 and drew 2 of their 17 home games. Raith did manage to win 2 games away from home and also won a home Scottish Cup game against Peebles Rovers.

Fewest wins, England: Five teams have won just one home Football League match:
- Loughborough, Division 2, 1899–1900
- Notts County, Division 1, 1904–05
- Woolwich Arsenal, Division 1, 1912–13
- Blackpool, Division 1, 1966–67
- Rochdale, Division 4, 1973–74
Rochdale's is the worst record as it encompassed 23 matches. Blackpool's one home win in 1966–67 was 6-0 against Newcastle on Saturday 22 October 1966.

Most wins in a season: 21 – by Brentford in Division 3S in 1929–30 (100% record) and by Lincoln in Division 4 in 1975–76.

Home defeats: The most suffered by a Football League club in a season is 15, by Barrow in Division 3N in 1925–26 and by Blackpool in Division 1 in 1966–67.

FA Cup: Wanderers were allowed to choose their own venue for the 1873 final. They did not have a home (hence their name) but chose Lillie Bridge (near the current Stamford Bridge). Chelsea would have played the 1920 final at home had they not lost their semi-final 3-1 to Aston Villa.

GOALS FOR AND AGAINST

Least conceded at home: 4 – by Lincoln City in Division 2 in 1901–02. Oddly Lincoln had just established the record for least goals scored *away* from home with 4 in 1900–01. Liverpool conceded 4 in 21 games in 1978–79.

Least scored at home: 11 – by Woolwich Arsenal in 1912–13.

See also: AWAY FROM HOME, CONSECUTIVE SEQUENCES

Denis Smith of Stoke City, probably the holder of the record for the most broken bones in first-class football. When he retired in 1981 he had suffered 12 major and 6 minor fractures in his 12-year career.

Championship (now known as the British Championship) outright on 34 occasions, Scotland 24, Wales 7 and Northern Ireland 2 (once as Ireland) (not including 1984). Since 1979 goal difference has been used so joint champions are now less likely.

Four-way split: 1955–56 was the only occasion on which all four countries obtained 3 points each and the trophy was shared (meaninglessly) four ways.

Goalless draws: Scotland and England drew 0-0 in the very first international (1872) and did not do so again in peacetime for 98 years, until 1970.

Incomplete: The 1980–81 Championship was left incomplete after both England and Wales refused to travel to Belfast at the time of the IRA hunger strikes. In 1983 England announced that they would no longer play Wales and Northern Ireland as they could not spare the dates from their crowded calendar. Scotland quickly followed suit and, as a result, the 1983–84 British Championship was due to be the last – exactly 100 years after the first.

APPEARANCES
Most: Billy Meredith played in 48 Cham-

ABOVE: *Football League keeper Gil Merrick saves from Scotland's Graham Leggat in an Inter-League game at Stamford Bridge on 28 April 1954. The Football League won 4-0.*
BELOW: *John Thomson, Celtic and Scotland goalkeeper, was fatally injured at Ibrox diving at the feet of Rangers Irish forward Sam English on 5 September 1931.*

Injuries

DEATHS

William Walker of Leith Athletic died after being accidentally kicked in the stomach during a Division 2 game v Vale of Leven on Saturday 12 January 1907.

John Main, Hibernian full-back, was injured during a game v Partick on 25 December 1909 and died four days later in hospital.

Joshua Williamson died after a Division 1 game v Rangers on Saturday 12 November 1921. He was playing in goal for Dumbarton.

Sam Wynne was the first player to die during a first-class fixture, when on Saturday 30 April 1927 he collapsed while taking a free-kick after 40 minutes of a Bury against Sheffield United Division 1 game. He died in the dressing-room and a post-mortem showed he had been suffering from pneumonia. The game was abandoned and replayed the following Thursday, with all receipts going to Wynne's widow. Wynne had found a place in the record books with his four goals in a game from full-back for Oldham (see GOALSCORERS).

John Thomson, Celtic and Scotland goalkeeper, fractured his skull in a collision with Rangers' Irish forward Sam English on Saturday 5 September 1931.

Samuel Raleigh, Gillingham full-back, was carried off with concussion during a home game against Brighton on Saturday 1 December 1934 and died soon afterwards.

Tommy Allden, Highgate United defender, died after the pitch was struck by lightning during an FA Amateur Cup quarter-final game against Enfield on Saturday 25 February 1967. Four other players were seriously hurt. Two players were also killed during the Army Cup final replay at Aldershot in April 1948 when the pitch was struck by lightning. The King and Queen were watching the game at the time.

FRACTURES

Most: Denis Smith of Stoke City is thought to hold the record for the total number of fractures to various major bones – with 12 up to 1980 plus 6 minor fractures to fingers and toes.

Both full-backs: On Saturday 1 January 1966, Chester lost both full-backs, Ray and Bryn Jones (not related), with broken legs in a Division 4 fixture against Aldershot – and still won the game 3-2.

Inter-League Games

First game: The first Inter-League game which is still recognised as official was played on Monday 11 April 1892 at Pike's Lane, Bolton (then the ground of Bolton Wanderers) between the Football League and the Scottish League. The result was 2-2 before a crowd of 9,500. There had been a game between the Football League and the Football Alliance on Monday 20 April 1891 at Olive Grove, Sheffield, but as the Football Alliance became Division 2 of the League a year later this is no longer regarded as official.

Biggest win: Football League 12 Irish League 0 at Home Park, Plymouth, on Wednesday 21 September 1966.

Biggest crowd: 96,000 saw the game between the Scottish League and Football League at Hampden Park on Saturday 1 March 1913, when the home team won 4-1.

Foreign appearances: Four Scots – H. Gardiner, D. Gow, W. Groves and T. McInnes – played for the Football League in the first ever game at Bolton in 1892. Another Scot, A. Maitland, played for the Football League against the Irish League in 1922. Welshman Ron Burgess of Spurs played for the Football League in the 1950s after which the League changed previous policy and put out teams with numerous non-English players. On 12 October 1960, versus the Irish League at Blackpool, only 4 of the side were English and German-born Bert Trautmann was in goal. The team against the Italian League in Milan on 1 November 1960 included 6 non-Englishmen, one being Denis Law who scored in a 2-4 defeat. Englishman Bob Ferrier (of Motherwell) played 7 times for the Scottish League between 1923 and 1931, another Englishman Willie Lyon (of Celtic) played for the Scottish League twice in 1938–39 and Welshman Ben Ellis also played for the Scottish League against the Irish League on Wednesday 30 August 1939. The most interesting example was Denis Law's appearance for the Italian League against the Scottish League at Hampden Park on Wednesday 1 November 1961. John Charles and Gerry Hitchens were also in the Italian team, Hitchens scoring in a 1-1 draw.

Football League record: The Football League abandoned Inter-League fixtures in 1976. Their last game was at Hampden on Wednesday 17 March 1976, when the Football League won 1-0 in front of a mere 9,000 spectators. Since 1892, the Football League had won 40 of these annual fixtures, the Scottish League had won 16 and 7 were drawn. In all their fixtures over the whole 84 years, the Football League had won 120, drawn 22 and lost 26 out of a total of 168 games.

Scottish League record: The Scottish League did not give up Inter-League games in the

Dave Mackay and Billy Bremner confer during a Spurs v Leeds game on 20 August 1966. Mackay was one of the first non-English players to turn out for the Football League this century, playing against the Scottish League on 23 March 1960. Mackay also holds a unique set of winners medals comprising Scottish League and Cup when he was with Hearts and Football League and FA Cup while at Tottenham.

1970s but now tends not to put out its strongest teams for the remaining fixtures – for example, the Scots lost 2-1 in Dublin on Monday 17 March 1980 and then fielded 11 entirely different players the following night against the Irish League in Belfast. Overall, the Scottish League had completed 166 fixtures by 1 January 1984, winning 94 and drawing 21.

Irish League record: The Belfast-based League's best result was undoubtedly the 5-2 defeat of the Football League at Windsor Park on Wednesday 25 April 1956. This was one of only three defeats that the Irish League ever inflicted on the Football League, though they have done slightly better against the Scots with five victories. Up to 1 January 1984, the Irish had won just 23 and drawn 15 of their 169 fixtures.

League of Ireland record: The Dublin-based League of Ireland has recorded only 3 wins against major League opposition in its history – on Friday 17 March 1939 against the Scottish League (in their first ever fixture), on the very same date in 1980 against the same opposition, and in 1964 against the Football League. All the games were played in Dublin and all ended 2-1. The League of Ireland are now the most

prolific competitors of Inter-League games, with the side acting as a sort of reserve national squad and providing international football without all the attendant problems of recalling players from England, Scotland and, recently, Italy. The League team now arranges matches against full international sides – against New Zealand in 1979 and against Argentina in Buenos Aires in 1980, for instance – and there is some doubt as to the exact status of these games. Certainly the New Zealanders and the Argentinians regarded themselves as playing the national side. Up to the end of 1983, the League of Ireland had played 95 'official' games, winning 22 and drawing 14.

Southern League: The Southern League has perhaps the most interesting history of fixtures. Between 1910 and 1981, that League has played just 33 official fixtures, but against as many as 10 different opponents – the Football League, Scottish League, Irish League, Welsh League, Cheshire League, South-Western League, Italian Semi-Professional League (Serie B), Isthmian League, Western League and Northern Premier League. Of these fixtures, the Southern League won 16 and drew 7. On Monday 14 November 1910 the Southern recorded its

most famous win – 3-2 over the Football League at White Hart Lane. The Southern also beat the Scottish League twice – a week later (21 November 1910) and also on Monday 14 October 1912. On both occasions the score was 1-0 and the games were played at Millwall. The Southern League's most remarkable result, however, was on Saturday 16 October 1937 when they beat the Cheshire League 7-5. This aggregate matches the Football League's 12-0 defeat of the Irish.

Undefeated record: The Football League was undefeated in 24 consecutive fixtures between Saturday 21 March 1914, when they lost 3-2 to the Scottish League at Burnley, and Saturday 2 November 1929, when the Scottish League also won 2-1 in Glasgow.

Goalscoring: Nat Lofthouse scored 6 goals for the Football League against League of Ireland at Wolverhampton on Wednesday 24 September 1952. The Scottish record is 5, shared between Barney Battles Jr (Hearts) against the Irish League at Firhill on Wednesday 31 October 1928, Hughie Gallacher (Airdrie) against the Irish League at Windsor Park on Wednesday 11 November 1925 and Bobby Flavell (Airdrie) v Irish League at Windsor Park on Wednesday 30 April 1947.

Internationals

MATCHES

First international: The Football Association organised a game between Englishmen and Scotsmen at Kennington Oval on Saturday 5 March 1870, which ended as a 1-1 draw. This cannot be seriously regarded as a full international as the English FA selected both sides and several of the Scottish team were chosen because of Scottish family connections or because of their Scottish names. The first 'official' international was on Saturday 30 November 1872 at the West of Scotland Cricket Club, Partick, Glasgow (Hamilton Crescent) in front of a healthy crowd of 4,000 spectators. This was billed as Scotland against England but was, in reality, just a continuation of the Queen's Park against Wanderers rivalry established in the previous year's FA Cup. No Scottish FA existed at the time and the Queen's Park captain chose the Scottish team. Though this match, which ended 0-0, is generally taken to be the first international, such an interpretation is a little generous. Indeed, it can be argued that the first ever international between genuinely independent states did not take place until 1 May 1904, when France played Belgium.

First game outside the UK: England's game against Austria in Vienna on Saturday 6 June 1908 (England won 6-1) was the first recognised international by a British side against foreign opposition. Two games against a German side in September 1901, and various games against Empire countries, are not regarded as official. Scotland did not play foreign opposition until 26 May 1929, Wales until 25 May 1933 and Northern Ireland until 8 February 1921 (against France in Paris).

First foreign defeat: England's 4-3 defeat in Madrid on Wednesday 15 May 1929 was the first by a British side against foreign opposition. Spain's scorers were Lazcano (2), Rubio and Goiburu and Carter (2) and Hill scored for England. The English amateur side (which was still of considerable strength and importance at the time) was first beaten by Denmark in Copenhagen, on Thursday 5 May 1910, by 2-1. The game in Madrid was England's 25th match against foreign sides.

Scotland's first defeat: Scotland's first defeat by foreign opposition was 5-0 by Austria in Vienna on Monday 16 May 1931 – their sixth game abroad.

First home defeat: The first occasion on which a British side lost at home to a full foreign international side was Wednesday 21 September 1949 when Eire beat England 2-0 at Goodison Park. All but 2 of the Irish team (Tommy Goodwin the keeper and outside-left Tom O'Conner both played for Shamrock Rovers) played for Football League sides.

Undefeated runs: The longest by a home country was 22 by Scotland between 7 April 1879 and 17 March 1888, when England won 5-0 at the Second Hampden Park.

Unchanged team: England played a completely unchanged team for the quarter-final, semi-final, and final of the 1966 World Cup, plus the subsequent 3 games – a run of 6 in all.

Cancellation: The first time England ever cancelled a full international for avoidable reasons was the game against Northern Ireland due to be played on 16 May 1981. England excused themselves by saying their fixture list was just too crowded with international and club commitments.

CLUB HONOURS

Most from one club: Rangers had produced 125 players who had won international caps while on their books by the beginning of the 1983–84 season, all but 9 for Scotland. Next in line came Everton with 110, Celtic with 109 and Manchester United with 105.

Most English internationals: Corinthians produced an astonishing 85 England internationals in their late nineteenth-century heyday. Of current senior clubs, Aston Villa had produced 49 and Everton 44 by the beginning of 1983–84.

Most Welsh internationals: Wrexham had provided Wales with 58 internationals by the 1 January 1984. Non-League Druids produced as many as 31 players for Wales in the last century.

Most Irish internationals: Cliftonville of Belfast have provided Ireland/Northern Ireland with 60 players, while Shamrock Rovers have produced 57 for Eire.

Caps first awarded: England first awarded official caps in 1886. They were named after the coloured caps worn in the 1870s and early 1880s which were, for a time, the only means of distinguishing the teams. As heading became more common, the caps were naturally dropped and players began to wear distinctive shirts instead.

Most at one time: Manchester United had 18 full internationals on their books in the 1977–78 season (6 Scotland, 5 England, 5 Northern Ireland and 2 Eire). In one game in December 1976 United fielded 8 full internationals in their reserve side for a Central League game. United also hold the record for providing most players to an association other than their own for a single game: on Wednesday 14 February 1973 Scotland had 5 United players – Alex Forsyth, Martin Buchan, Lou Macari, George Graham and Willie Morgan – playing against England in the Scottish FA Centenary match at Hampden Park. Scotland lost 5-0.

Cardiff had 17 internationals on their books in 1925–26 (9 Wales, 4 Scotland and 4 Ireland). On Saturday 16 February 1924, when Wales played Scotland at Ninian Park, both captains were Cardiff players, the only time that both captains have come from the same club in a home international match. Fred Keenor captained Wales while Jock Blair captained Scotland – and they were, of course, playing on their home ground. Wales won 2-0.

Most in a single game: There have been 3 occasions on which a single club has selected the whole of a national side. Queen's Park chose the Scottish side in the first international, against England on 30 November 1872, though two of the players chosen (the brothers James and Robert Smith) were no longer with the Glasgow club but were playing for South Norwood in London: In fact, the Scottish side was picked solely by the Queen's Park captain, Robert Gardner.

Corinthians were asked by the FA to select the England side against Wales on Monday 12 March 1894 (England won 5-1 at Wrexham) and on Monday 18 March 1895 (drew 1-1 at Queen's Club, Kensington). As Corinthians regularly drew their sides from other amateur clubs and from the universities, they cannot be regarded as a club in the usual meaning of the word.

Nine from one club: Corinthians supplied 9 of the players for England against Scotland in 1886. The other two came from Blackburn Rovers, but the same reservations as the previous entry apply (continues p. 120)

Butterflies for Kevin Keegan during England's 3-1 defeat of Scotland at Wembley in 1979. Keegan is the only British player to have twice been elected European Footballer of the Year.

ENGLAND'S FULL INTERNATIONAL RECORD

Date	Venue	Country	Result
30.11.72	Hamilton Cr.	Scotland	D 0-0
8.3.73	The Oval	Scotland	W 4-2
7.3.74	Hamilton Cr.	Scotland	L 1-2
6.3.75	The Oval	Scotland	D 2-2
4.3.76	Hamilton Cr.	Scotland	L 0-3
3.3.77	The Oval	Scotland	L 1-3
2.3.78	1st Hampden	Scotland	L 2-7
18.1.79	The Oval	Wales	W 2-1
5.4.79	The Oval	Scotland	W 5-4
13.3.80	1st Hampden	Scotland	L 4-5
15.3.80	Wrexham	Wales	W 3-2
26.2.81	Alex Mdws B'burn	Wales	L 0-1
12.3.81	The Oval	Scotland	L 1-6
18.2.82	Belfast	Ireland	W 13-0
11.3.82	1st Hampden	Scotland	L 1-5
13.3.82	Wrexham	Wales	L 3-5
3.2.83	The Oval	Wales	W 5-0
24.2.83	Aigburth	Ireland	W 7-0
10.3.83	Bramall Lane	Scotland	L 2-3
23.2.84	Belfast	Ireland	W 8-1
15.3.84	1st Cathkin	Scotland	L 0-1
17.3.84	Wrexham	Wales	W 4-0
28.2.85	Whalley Range	Ireland	W 4-0
14.3.85	Leamtn Rd B'burn	Wales	D 1-1
21.3.85	The Oval	Scotland	D 1-1
13.3.86	Belfast	Ireland	W 6-1
27.3.86	2nd Hampden	Scotland	D 1-1
29.3.86	Wrexham	Wales	W 3-1
5.2.87	Bramall Lane	Ireland	W 7-0
26.2.87	The Oval	Wales	W 4-0
19.3.87	Leamtn Rd B'burn	Scotland	L 2-3
4.2.88	Crewe	Wales	W 5-1
17.3.88	2nd Hampden	Scotland	W 5-0
7.4.88	Belfast	Ireland	W 5-1
23.2.89	Stoke	Wales	W 4-1
2.3.89	Anfield	Ireland	W 6-1
13.4.89	The Oval	Scotland	L 2-3
15.3.90	Belfast	Ireland	W 9-1
15.3.90	Wrexham	Wales	W 3-1
5.4.90	2nd Hampden	Scotland	D 1-1
7.3.91	Wolver'ton	Ireland	W 6-1
7.3.91	Sunderland	Wales	W 4-1
4.4.91	Ewood Park	Scotland	W 2-1
5.3.92	Belfast	Ireland	W 2-0
5.3.92	Wrexham	Wales	W 2-0
2.4.92	Ibrox	Scotland	W 4-0
25.2.93	Perry Barr	Ireland	W 6-1
13.3.93	Stoke	Wales	W 6-0
1.4.93	Richmond	Scotland	W 5-2
3.3.94	Belfast	Ireland	D 2-2
12.3.94	Wrexham	Wales	W 5-1
7.4.94	Parkhead	Scotland	D 2-2
9.3.95	Derby R'course	Ireland	W 9-0
18.3.95	Kensington	Wales	D 1-1
6.4.95	Goodison	Scotland	W 3-0
7.3.96	Belfast	Ireland	W 2-0
16.3.96	Cardiff	Wales	W 9-1
4.4.96	Parkhead	Scotland	L 1-2
20.2.97	Trent Bridge	Ireland	W 6-0
29.3.97	Bramall Lane	Wales	W 4-0
3.4.97	Crystal Pal.	Scotland	L 1-2
5.3.98	Belfast	Ireland	W 3-2
28.3.98	Wrexham	Wales	W 3-0
2.4.98	Parkhead	Scotland	W 3-1
18.2.99	Roker	Ireland	W 13-2
20.3.99	Ashton Gate	Wales	W 4-0
8.4.99	Villa Park	Scotland	W 2-1
17.3.00	Dublin	Ireland	W 2-0
26.3.00	Cardiff	Wales	D 1-1
7.4.00	Parkhead	Scotland	L 1-4
9.3.01	Southampton	Ireland	W 3-0
18.3.01	Newcastle	Wales	W 6-0
30.3.01	Crystal Pal.	Scotland	D 2-2
3.3.02	Wrexham	Wales	D 0-0
22.3.02	Belfast	Ireland	W 1-0
3.5.02	Villa Park	Scotland	D 2-2
14.2.03	Wolver'ton	Ireland	W 4-0
2.3.03	Portsmouth	Wales	W 2-1
4.4.03	Bramall Lane	Scotland	L 1-2
29.2.04	Wrexham	Wales	D 2-2
12.3.04	Belfast	Ireland	W 3-1
9.4.04	Parkhead	Scotland	W 1-0
25.2.05	Middlesbr'	Ireland	D 1-1
27.3.05	Anfield	Wales	W 3-1
1.4.05	Crystal Pal.	Scotland	W 1-0
17.2.06	Belfast	Ireland	W 5-0
19.3.06	Cardiff	Wales	W 1-0
7.4.06	Hampden	Scotland	L 1-2
16.2.07	Goodison	Ireland	W 1-0
18.3.07	Fulham	Wales	D 1-1
6.4.07	Newcastle	Scotland	D 1-1
15.2.08	Belfast	Ireland	W 3-1
16.3.08	Wrexham	Wales	W 7-1
4.4.08	Hampden	Scotland	D 1-1
6.6.08	Vienna	Austria	W 6-1
8.6.08	Vienna	Austria	W 11-1
10.6.08	Budapest	Hungary	W 7-0
13.6.08	Prague	Bohemia	W 4-0
13.2.09	Valley Parade	Ireland	W 4-0
15.3.09	Trent Bridge	Wales	W 2-0
3.4.09	Crystal Pal.	Scotland	W 2-0
29.5.09	Budapest	Hungary	W 4-2
31.5.09	Budapest	Hungary	W 8-2
1.6.09	Vienna	Austria	W 8-1
12.2.10	Belfast	Ireland	D 1-1
14.3.10	Cardiff	Wales	W 1-0
2.4.10	Hampden	Scotland	L 0-2
11.2.11	Baseball Gd	Ireland	W 2-1
13.3.11	Millwall	Wales	W 3-0
1.4.11	Goodison	Scotland	D 1-1
10.2.12	Dublin	Ireland	W 6-1
11.3.12	Wrexham	Wales	W 2-0
23.3.12	Hampden	Scotland	D 1-1
15.2.13	Belfast	Ireland	L 1-2
17.3.13	Ashton Gate	Wales	W 4-3
5.4.13	Stamford Br.	England	W 1-0
14.2.14	Middlesbr'	Ireland	W 4-3
16.3.14	Cardiff	Wales	W 2-0
4.4.14	Hampden	Scotland	L 1-3
25.10.19	Belfast	Ireland	D 1-1
15.3.20	Highbury	Wales	L 1-2
10.4.20	Bramall Lane	Scotland	W 5-4
23.10.20	Roker	Ireland	W 2-0
14.3.21	Cardiff	Wales	D 0-0
9.4.21	Hampden	Scotland	L 0-3
21.5.21	Brussels	Belgium	W 2-0
22.10.21	Belfast	N. Ireland	D 1-1
13.3.22	Anfield	Wales	W 1-0
8.4.22	Villa Park	Scotland	L 0-1
21.10.22	W. Bromwich	N. Ireland	W 2-0
5.3.23	Cardiff	Wales	D 2-2
19.3.23	Highbury	Belgium	W 6-1
14.4.23	Hampden	Scotland	D 2-2
10.5.23	Paris	France	W 4-1
21.5.23	Stockholm	Sweden	W 4-2
24.5.23	Stockholm	Sweden	W 3-1
20.10.23	Belfast	N. Ireland	L 1-2
1.11.23	Antwerp	Belgium	D 2-2
3.3.24	Ewood Park	Wales	L 1-2
12.4.24	Wembley	Scotland	D 1-1
17.5.24	Paris	France	W 3-1
22.10.24	Goodison	N. Ireland	W 3-1
8.12.24	W. Bromwich	Belgium	W 4-0
28.2.25	Swansea	Wales	W 2-1
4.4.25	Hampden	Scotland	L 0-2
21.5.25	Paris	France	W 3-0
24.10.25	Belfast	N. Ireland	D 0-0
1.3.26	Selhurst Park	Wales	L 1-3
17.4.26	Old Trafford	Scotland	L 0-1
24.5.26	Antwerp	Belgium	W 5-3
20.10.26	Anfield	N. Ireland	D 3-3
12.2.27	Wrexham	Wales	D 3-3
2.4.27	Hampden	Scotland	W 2-1
11.5.27	Brussels	Belgium	W 9-1
21.5.27	Luxembourg	Luxembourg	W 5-2
26.5.27	Paris	France	W 6-0
22.10.27	Belfast	N. Ireland	L 0-2
28.11.27	Burnley	Wales	L 1-2
31.3.28	Wembley	Scotland	L 1-5
17.5.28	Paris	France	W 5-1
19.5.28	Antwerp	Belgium	W 3-1
22.10.28	Goodison	N. Ireland	W 2-1
17.11.28	Swansea	Wales	W 3-2
13.4.29	Hampden	Scotland	L 0-1
9.5.29	Paris	France	W 4-1
11.5.29	Brussels	Belgium	W 5-1
15.5.29	Madrid	Spain	L 3-4
19.10.29	Belfast	N. Ireland	W 3-0
20.11.29	Stamford Br.	Wales	W 6-0
5.4.30	Wembley	Scotland	W 5-2
10.5.30	Berlin	Germany	D 3-3
14.5.30	Vienna	Austria	D 0-0
20.10.30	Bramall Lane	N. Ireland	W 5-1
22.11.30	Wrexham	Wales	W 4-0
28.3.31	Hampden	Scotland	L 0-2
14.5.31	Paris	France	L 2-5
16.5.31	Brussels	Belgium	W 4-1
17.10.31	Belfast	N. Ireland	W 6-2
18.11.31	Anfield	Wales	W 3-1
9.12.31	Highbury	Spain	W 7-1
9.4.32	Wembley	Scotland	W 3-0
17.10.32	Blackpool	N. Ireland	W 1-0
16.11.32	Wrexham	Wales	D 0-0
7.12.32	Stamford Br.	Austria	W 4-3
1.4.33	Hampden	Scotland	L 1-2
13.5.33	Rome	Italy	D 1-1
20.5.33	Bern	Switzerland	W 4-0
14.10.33	Belfast	N. Ireland	W 3-0
15.11.33	Newcastle	Wales	L 1-2
6.12.33	Tottenham	France	W 4-1
14.4.34	Wembley	Scotland	W 3-0
10.5.34	Budapest	Hungary	L 1-2
16.5.34	Prague	Czechoslovakia	L 1-2
29.9.34	Cardiff	Wales	W 4-0
14.11.34	Highbury	Italy	W 3-2
6.2.35	Goodison	N. Ireland	W 2-1
6.4.35	Hampden	Scotland	L 0-2
18.5.35	Amsterdam	Holland	W 1-0
19.10.35	Belfast	N. Ireland	W 3-1
4.12.35	Tottenham	Germany	W 3-0
5.2.36	Wolver'ton	Wales	L 1-2
4.4.36	Wembley	Scotland	D 1-1
6.5.36	Vienna	Austria	L 1-2
9.5.36	Brussels	Belgium	L 2-3
17.10.36	Cardiff	Wales	L 1-2
18.11.36	Stoke	N. Ireland	W 3-1
2.12.36	Highbury	Hungary	W 6-2
17.4.37	Hampden	Scotland	L 1-3
14.5.37	Oslo	Norway	W 6-0
17.5.37	Stockholm	Sweden	W 4-0
20.5.37	Helsinki	Finland	W 8-0
23.10.37	Belfast	N. Ireland	W 5-1
17.11.37	Middlesbr'	Wales	W 2-1
1.12.37	Tottenham	Czechoslovakia	W 5-4
9.4.38	Wembley	Scotland	L 0-1
14.5.38	Berlin	Germany	W 6-3
21.5.38	Zurich	Switzerland	L 1-2
26.5.38	Paris	France	W 4-2
22.10.38	Cardiff	Wales	L 2-4
26.10.38	Highbury	FIFA	W 3-0
9.11.38	Newcastle	Norway	W 4-0
16.11.38	Maine Road	N. Ireland	W 7-0
15.4.39	Hampden	Scotland	W 2-1
13.5.39	Milan	Italy	D 2-2
18.5.39	Belgrade	Yugoslavia	L 1-2
24.5.39	Bucharest	Rumania	W 2-0
28.9.46	Belfast	N. Ireland	W 7-2
30.9.46	Dublin	Eire	W 1-0
13.11.46	Maine Road	Wales	W 3-0
27.11.46	Huddersfield	Holland	W 8-2
12.4.47	Wembley	Scotland	D 1-1
3.5.47	Highbury	France	W 3-0
18.5.47	Zurich	Switzerland	L 0-1
25.5.47	Lisbon	Portugal	W 10-0
21.9.47	Brussels	Belgium	W 5-2
18.10.47	Cardiff	Wales	W 3-0
5.11.47	Goodison	N. Ireland	D 2-2
19.11.47	Highbury	Sweden	W 4-2
10.4.48	Hampden	Scotland	W 2-0
16.5.48	Turin	Italy	W 4-0
26.9.48	Copenhagen	Denmark	D 0-0
9.10.48	Belfast	N. Ireland	W 6-2
10.11.48	Villa Park	Wales	W 1-0
2.12.48	Highbury	Switzerland	W 6-0
9.4.49	Wembley	Scotland	L 1-3
13.5.49	Stockholm	Sweden	L 1-3
18.5.49	Oslo	Norway	W 4-1
22.5.49	Paris	France	W 3-1
21.9.49	Goodison	Eire	L 0-2
15.10.49	Cardiff	*(W)Wales	W 4-1

Date	Venue	Country	Result
16.11.49	Maine Road	*(W)N. Ireland	W 9-2
30.11.49	Tottenham	Italy	W 2-0
15.4.50	Hampden	*(W)Scotland	W 1-0
14.5.50	Lisbon	Portugal	W 5-3
18.5.50	Brussels	Belgium	W 4-1
25.6.50	Rio	(W)Chile	W 2-0
29.6.50	B. Horizonte	(W)United States	L 0-1
2.7.50	Rio	(W)Spain	L 0-1
7.10.50	Belfast	N. Ireland	W 4-1
15.11.50	Sunderland	Wales	W 4-2
22.11.50	Highbury	Yugoslavia	D 2-2
14.4.51	Wembley	Scotland	L 2-3
9.5.51	Wembley	Argentina	W 2-1
19.5.51	Goodison	Portugal	W 5-2
3.10.51	Highbury	France	D 2-2
20.10.51	Cardiff	Wales	D 1-1
14.11.51	Villa Park	N. Ireland	W 2-0
28.11.51	Wembley	Austria	D 2-2
5.4.52	Hampden	Scotland	W 2-1
18.5.52	Florence	Italy	D 1-1
25.5.52	Vienna	Austria	W 3-2
28.5.52	Zurich	Switzerland	W 3-0
4.10.52	Belfast	N. Ireland	D 2-2
12.11.52	Wembley	Wales	W 5-2
26.11.52	Wembley	Belgium	W 5-0
18.4.53	Wembley	Scotland	D 2-2
17.5.53	Buenos Aires†	Argentina	D 0-0
24.5.53	Santiago	Chile	W 2-1
31.5.53	Montevideo	Uruguay	L 1-2
8.6.53	New York	United States	W 6-3
10.10.53	Cardiff	*(W)Wales	W 4-1
21.10.53	Wembley	FIFA	D 4-4
11.11.53	Anfield	*(W)N. Ireland	W 3-1
25.11.53	Wembley	Hungary	L 3-6
3.4.54	Hampden	*(W)Scotland	W 4-2
16.5.54	Belgrade	Yugoslavia	L 0-1
23.5.54	Budapest	Hungary	L 1-7
17.6.54	Basel	(W)Belgium	D 4-4
20.6.54	Bern	(W)Switzerland	W 2-0
26.6.54	Basel	(W)Uruguay	L 2-4
2.10.54	Belfast	N. Ireland	W 2-0
10.11.54	Wembley	Wales	W 3-2
1.12.54	Wembley	West Germany	W 3-1
2.4.55	Wembley	Scotland	W 7-2
15.5.55	Paris	France	L 0-1
18.5.55	Madrid	Spain	D 1-1
22.5.55	Oporto	Portugal	L 1-3
2.10.55	Copenhagen	Denmark	W 5-1
22.10.55	Cardiff	Wales	L 1-2
2.11.55	Wembley	N. Ireland	W 3-0
30.11.55	Wembley	Spain	W 4-1
14.4.56	Hampden	Scotland	D 1-1
9.5.56	Wembley	Brazil	W 4-2
16.5.56	Stockholm	Sweden	D 0-0
20.5.56	Helsinki	Finland	W 5-1
26.5.56	West Berlin	West Germany	W 3-1
6.10.56	Belfast	N. Ireland	D 1-1
14.11.56	Wembley	Wales	W 3-1
28.11.56	Wembley	Yugoslavia	W 3-0
5.12.56	Wolver'ton	(W)Denmark	W 5-2
6.4.57	Wembley	Scotland	W 2-1
8.5.57	Wembley	(W)Eire	W 5-1
15.5.57	Copenhagen	(W)Denmark	W 4-1
19.5.57	Dublin	(W)Eire	D 1-1
19.10.57	Cardiff	Wales	W 4-0
6.11.57	Wembley	N. Ireland	L 2-3
27.11.57	Wembley	France	W 4-0
19.4.58	Hampden	Scotland	W 4-0
7.5.58	Wembley	Portugal	W 2-1
11.5.58	Belgrade	Yugoslavia	L 0-5
18.5.58	Moscow	USSR	D 1-1
8.6.58	Gothenburg	(W)USSR	D 2-2
11.6.58	Gothenburg	(W)Brazil	D 0-0
15.6.58	Boras	(W)Austria	D 2-2
17.6.58	Gothenburg	(W)USSR	L 0-1
4.10.58	Belfast	N. Ireland	D 3-3
22.10.58	Wembley	USSR	W 5-0
26.11.58	Villa Park	Wales	D 2-2
11.4.59	Wembley	Scotland	W 1-0
6.5.59	Wembley	Italy	D 2-2
13.5.59	Rio	Brazil	L 0-2
17.5.59	Lima	Peru	L 1-4
24.5.59	Mexico City	Mexico	L 1-2
28.5.59	Los Angeles	United States	W 8-1
17.10.59	Cardiff	Wales	D 1-1
28.10.59	Wembley	Sweden	L 2-3
18.11.59	Wembley	N. Ireland	W 2-1
9.4.60	Hampden	Scotland	D 1-1
11.5.60	Wembley	Yugoslavia	D 3-3
15.5.60	Madrid	Spain	L 0-3
22.5.60	Budapest	Hungary	L 0-2
8.10.60	Belfast	N. Ireland	W 5-2
19.10.60	Luxembourg	(W)Luxembourg	W 9-0
26.10.60	Wembley	Spain	W 4-2
23.11.60	Wembley	Wales	W 5-1
15.4.61	Wembley	Scotland	W 9-3
10.5.61	Wembley	Mexico	W 8-0
21.5.61	Lisbon	(W)Portugal	D 1-1
24.5.61	Rome	Italy	W 3-2
27.5.61	Vienna	Austria	L 1-3
28.9.61	Highbury	(W)Luxembourg	W 4-1
14.10.61	Cardiff	Wales	D 1-1
25.10.61	Wembley	(W)Portugal	W 2-0
22.11.61	Wembley	N. Ireland	D 1-1
4.4.62	Wembley	Austria	W 3-1
14.4.62	Hampden	Scotland	L 0-2
9.5.62	Wembley	Switzerland	W 3-1
20.5.62	Lima	Peru	W 4-0
31.5.62	Rancagua	(W)Hungary	L 1-2
2.6.62	Rancagua	(W)Argentina	W 3-1
7.6.62	Rancagua	(W)Bulgaria	D 0-0
10.6.62	Vina del Mar	(W)Brazil	L 1-3
3.10.62	Hillsborough	(E)France	D 1-1
20.10.62	Belfast	N. Ireland	W 3-1
21.11.62	Wembley	Wales	W 4-0
27.2.63	Paris	(E)France	L 2-5
6.4.63	Wembley	Scotland	L 1-2
8.5.63	Wembley	Brazil	D 1-1
29.5.63	Bratislava	Czechoslovakia	W 4-2
2.6.63	Leipzig	East Germany	W 2-1
5.6.63	Basel	Switzerland	W 8-1
12.10.63	Cardiff	Wales	W 4-0
23.10.63	Wembley	FIFA	W 2-1
20.11.63	Wembley	N. Ireland	W 8-3
11.4.64	Hampden	Scotland	L 0-1
6.5.64	Wembley	Uruguay	W 2-1
17.5.64	Lisbon	Portugal	W 4-3
24.5.64	Dublin	Eire	W 3-1
27.5.64	New York	United States	W 10-0
30.5.64	Rio	Brazil	L 1-5
4.6.64	Sao Paulo	Portugal	D 1-1
6.6.64	Rio	Argentina	L 0-1
3.10.64	Belfast	N. Ireland	W 4-3
21.10.64	Wembley	Belgium	D 2-2
18.11.64	Wembley	Wales	W 2-1
9.12.64	Amsterdam	Holland	D 1-1
10.4.65	Wembley	Scotland	D 2-2
5.5.65	Wembley	Hungary	W 1-0
9.5.65	Belgrade	Yugoslavia	D 1-1
12.5.65	Nurnberg	West Germany	W 1-0
16.5.65	Gothenburg	Sweden	W 2-1
2.10.65	Cardiff	Wales	D 0-0
20.10.65	Wembley	Austria	L 2-3
10.11.65	Wembley	N. Ireland	W 2-1
8.12.65	Madrid	Spain	W 2-0
5.1.66	Goodison	Poland	D 1-1
23.2.66	Wembley	West Germany	W 1-0
2.4.66	Hampden	Scotland	W 4-3
4.5.66	Wembley	Yugoslavia	W 2-0
26.6.66	Helsinki	Finland	W 3-0
29.6.66	Oslo	Norway	W 6-1
3.7.66	Copenhagen	Denmark	W 2-0
5.7.66	Chorzow	Poland	W 1-0
11.7.66	Wembley	(W)Uruguay	D 0-0
16.7.66	Wembley	(W)Mexico	W 2-0
20.7.66	Wembley	(W)France	W 2-0
23.7.66	Wembley	(W)Argentina	W 1-0
26.7.66	Wembley	(W)Portugal	W 2-1
30.7.66	Wembley	(W)West Germany	W 4-2
22.10.66	Belfast	*(E)N. Ireland	W 2-0
2.11.66	Wembley	Czechoslovakia	D 0-0
16.11.66	Wembley	*(E)Wales	W 5-1
15.4.67	Wembley	*(E)Scotland	L 2-3
24.5.67	Wembley	Spain	W 2-0
27.5.67	Vienna	Austria	W 1-0
21.10.67	Cardiff	*(E)Wales	W 3-0
22.11.67	Wembley	*(E)N. Ireland	W 2-0
6.12.67	Wembley	USSR	D 2-2
24.2.68	Hampden	*(E)Scotland	D 1-1
3.4.68	Wembley	(E)Spain	W 1-0
8.5.68	Madrid	(E)Spain	W 2-1
22.5.68	Wembley	Sweden	W 3-1
1.6.68	Hanover	West Germany	L 0-1
5.6.68	Florence	(E)Yugoslavia	L 0-1
8.6.68	Rome	(E)USSR	W 2-0
6.11.68	Bucharest	Rumania	D 0-0
11.12.68	Wembley	Bulgaria	D 1-1
15.1.69	Wembley	Rumania	D 1-1
12.3.69	Wembley	France	W 5-0
3.5.69	Belfast	N. Ireland	W 3-1
7.5.69	Wembley	Wales	W 2-1
10.5.69	Wembley	Scotland	W 4-1
1.6.69	Mexico City	Mexico	D 0-0
8.6.69	Montevideo	Uruguay	W 2-1
12.6.69	Rio	Brazil	L 1-2
5.11.69	Amsterdam	Holland	W 1-0
10.12.69	Wembley	Portugal	W 1-0
14.1.70	Wembley	Holland	D 0-0
25.2.70	Brussels	Belgium	W 3-1
18.4.70	Cardiff	Wales	D 1-1
21.4.70	Wembley	N. Ireland	W 3-1
25.4.70	Hampden	Scotland	D 0-0
20.5.70	Bogota	Colombia	W 4-0
24.5.70	Quito	Ecuador	W 2-0
2.6.70	Guadalajara	(W)Rumania	W 1-0
7.6.70	Guadalajara	(W)Brazil	L 0-1
11.6.70	Guadalajara	(W)Czechoslovakia	W 1-0
14.6.70	Leon	(W)West Germany	L 2-3
25.11.70	Wembley	East Germany	W 3-1
3.2.71	Valletta	(E)Malta	W 1-0
21.4.71	Wembley	(E)Greece	W 3-0
12.5.71	Wembley	(E)Malta	W 5-0
15.5.71	Belfast	N. Ireland	W 1-0
19.5.71	Wembley	Wales	D 0-0
22.5.71	Wembley	Scotland	W 3-1
13.10.71	Basel	(E)Switzerland	W 3-2
10.11.71	Wembley	(E)Switzerland	D 1-1
1.12.71	Athens	(E)Greece	W 2-0
29.4.72	Wembley	(E)West Germany	L 1-3
13.5.72	West Berlin	(E)West Germany	D 0-0
20.5.72	Cardiff	Wales	W 3-0
23.5.72	Wembley	N. Ireland	L 0-1
27.5.72	Hampden	Scotland	W 1-0
11.10.72	Wembley	Yugoslavia	D 1-1
15.11.72	Cardiff	(W)Wales	W 1-0
24.1.73	Wembley	(W)Wales	D 1-1
14.2.73	Hampden	Scotland	W 5-0
12.5.73	Goodison‡	N. Ireland	W 2-1
15.5.73	Wembley	Wales	W 3-0
19.5.73	Wembley	Scotland	W 1-0
27.5.73	Prague	Czechoslovakia	D 1-1
6.6.73	Katowice	(W)Poland	L 0-2
10.6.73	Moscow	USSR	W 2-1
14.6.73	Turin	Italy	L 0-2
26.9.73	Wembley	Austria	W 7-0
17.10.73	Wembley	(W)Poland	D 1-1
14.11.73	Wembley	Italy	L 0-1
3.4.74	Lisbon	Portugal	D 0-0
11.5.74	Cardiff	Wales	W 2-0
15.5.74	Wembley	N. Ireland	W 1-0
18.5.74	Hampden	Scotland	L 0-2
22.5.74	Wembley	Argentina	D 2-2
29.5.74	Leipzig	East Germany	D 1-1
1.6.74	Sofia	Bulgaria	W 1-0
5.6.74	Belgrade	Yugoslavia	D 2-2
30.10.74	Wembley	(E)Czechoslovakia	W 3-0
20.11.74	Wembley	(E)Portugal	D 0-0
12.3.75	Wembley	West Germany	W 2-0
16.4.75	Wembley	(E)Cyprus	W 5-0
11.5.75	Limassol	(E)Cyprus	W 1-0
17.5.75	Belfast	N. Ireland	D 0-0
21.5.75	Wembley	Wales	D 2-2
24.5.75	Wembley	Scotland	W 5-1
3.9.75	Basel	Switzerland	W 2-1
30.10.75	Bratislava	(E)Czechoslovakia	L 1-2
19.11.75	Lisbon	(E)Portugal	D 1-1
24.3.76	Wrexham	Wales	W 2-1
8.5.76	Cardiff	Wales	W 1-0
11.5.76	Wembley	N. Ireland	W 4-0
15.5.76	Hampden	Scotland	L 1-2
23.5.76	Los Angeles	Brazil	L 0-1
28.5.76	New York	Italy	W 3-2
13.6.76	Helsinki	(W)Finland	W 4-1
8.9.76	Wembley	Eire	D 1-1
13.10.76	Wembley	(W)Finland	W 2-1
17.11.76	Rome	(W)Italy	L 0-2
9.2.77	Wembley	Holland	L 0-2
30.3.77	Wembley	(W)Luxembourg	W 5-0
28.5.77	Belfast	N. Ireland	W 2-1
31.5.77	Wembley	Wales	L 0-1
4.6.77	Wembley	Scotland	L 1-2
8.6.77	Rio	Brazil	D 0-0
12.6.77	Buenos Aires	Argentina	D 1-1
15.6.77	Montevideo	Uruguay	D 0-0

Date	Venue	Country	Result
7.9.77	Wembley	Switzerland	D 0-0
12.10.77	Luxembourg	(W)Luxembourg	W 2-0
16.11.77	Wembley	(W)Italy	W 2-0
22.2.78	W. Berlin	West Germany	L 1-2
19.4.78	Wembley	Brazil	D 1-1
13.5.78	Cardiff	Wales	W 3-1
16.5.78	Wembley	N. Ireland	W 1-0
20.5.78	Hampden	Scotland	W 1-0
24.5.78	Wembley	Hungary	W 4-1
20.9.78	Copenhagen	(E)Denmark	W 4-3
25.10.78	Dublin	(E)Eire	D 1-1
29.11.78	Wembley	Czechoslovakia	W 1-0
7.2.79	Wembley	(E)N. Ireland	W 4-0
19.5.79	Belfast	N. Ireland	W 2-0
23.5.79	Wembley	Wales	D 0-0
26.5.79	Wembley	Scotland	W 3-1
6.6.79	Sofia	(E)Bulgaria	W 3-0
10.6.79	Stockholm	Sweden	D 0-0
13.6.79	Vienna	Austria	L 3-4
12.9.79	Wembley	(E)Denmark	W 1-0
17.10.79	Belfast	(E)N. Ireland	W 4-0
21.11.79	Wembley	(E)Bulgaria	W 2-0
6.2.80	Wembley	(E)Eire	W 2-0
26.3.80	Barcelona	Spain	W 2-0
13.5.80	Wembley	Argentina	W 3-1
17.5.80	Wrexham	Wales	L 1-4
20.5.80	Wembley	N. Ireland	D 1-1
24.5.80	Hampden	Scotland	W 1-0
12.6.80	Turin	(E)Belgium	D 1-1
15.6.80	Turin	(E)Italy	L 0-1
18.6.80	Naples	(E)Spain	W 2-1
10.9.80	Wembley	(W)Norway	W 4-0
15.10.80	Bucharest	(W)Rumania	L 1-2
19.11.80	Wembley	(W)Switzerland	W 2-1
25.3.81	Wembley	Spain	L 1-2
29.4.81	Wembley	(W)Rumania	D 0-0
12.5.81	Wembley	Brazil	L 0-1
16.5.81	Belfast	N. Ireland	Cancelled
19.5.81	Wembley	Wales	D 0-0
23.5.81	Wembley	Scotland	L 0-1
30.5.81	Basel	(W)Switzerland	L 1-2
6.6.81	Budapest	(W)Hungary	W 3-1
9.9.81	Oslo	(W)Norway	L 1-2
18.11.81	Wembley	(W)Hungary	W 1-0
23.2.82	Wembley	N Ireland	W 4-0
27.4.82	Cardiff	Wales	W 1-0
25.5.82	Wembley	Holland	W 2-0
29.5.82	Glasgow	Scotland	W 1-0
2.6.82	Reykjavik	Iceland	D 1-1
3.6.82	Helsinki	Finland	W 4-1
16.6.82	Bilbao	(W)France	W 3-1
20.6.82	Bilbao	(W)Czechoslovakia	W 2-0
25.6.82	Bilbao	(W)Kuwait	W 1-0
29.6.82	Madrid	(W)West Germany	D 0-0
5.7.82	Madrid	(W)Spain	D 0-0
22.9.82	Copenhagen	(E)Denmark	D 2-2

Date	Venue	Country	Result
13.10.82	Wembley	West Germany	L 1-2
17.11.82	Salonika	(E)Greece	W 3-0
15.12.82	Wembley	(E)Luxembourg	W 9-0
23.2.83	Wembley	Wales	W 2-1
30.3.83	Wembley	(E)Greece	D 0-0
27.4.83	Wembley	(E)Hungary	W 2-0
28.5.83	Belfast	N. Ireland	D 0-0
1.6.83	Wembley	Scotland	W 2-0
11.6.83	Sydney	Australia	D 0-0
15.6.83	Brisbane	Australia	L 0-1
19.6.83	Melbourne	Australia	D 1-1
21.9.83	Wembley	Denmark	L 0-1

(W) World Cup (E) European Nations Cup/European Championship *Home International Championship used as qualifying tournament †abandoned after 20 minutes because of downpour ‡switched from Belfast due to political troubles

N IRELAND'S FULL INTERNATIONAL RECORD

Date	Venue	Country	Result
18.2.82	Belfast	England	L 0-13
25.2.82	Wrexham	Wales	L 1-7
24.2.83	Aigburth	England	L 0-7
17.3.83	Wrexham	Wales	D 1-1
26.1.84	Belfast	Scotland	L 0-5
9.2.84	Wrexham	Wales	L 0-6
23.2.84	Belfast	England	L 1-8
28.2.85	Whalley Range	England	L 0-4
14.3.85	1st Hampden	Scotland	L 2-8
11.4.85	Belfast	Wales	L 2-8
27.2.86	Wrexham	Wales	L 0-5
13.3.86	Belfast	England	L 1-6
20.3.86	Belfast	Scotland	L 2-7
5.2.87	Bramall Lane	England	L 0-7
19.2.87	2nd Hampden	Scotland	L 1-4
12.3.87	Belfast	Wales	W 4-1
3.3.88	Wrexham	Wales	L 0-11
24.3.88	Belfast	Scotland	L 2-10
7.4.88	Belfast	England	L 1-5
2.3.89	Anfield	England	L 1-6
9.3.89	Ibrox	Scotland	L 0-7
27.4.89	Belfast	Wales	L 1-3
8.2.90	Shrewsbury	Wales	L 2-5
15.3.90	Belfast	England	L 1-9
29.3.90	Belfast	Scotland	L 1-4
7.2.91	Belfast	Wales	W 7-2
7.3.91	Wolver'ton	England	L 1-6
28.3.91	Parkhead	Scotland	L 1-2
27.2.92	Bangor (Wa.)	Wales	D 1-1
5.3.92	Belfast	England	L 0-2
19.3.92	Belfast	Scotland	L 2-3
25.2.93	Villa Park	England	L 1-6
25.3.93	Parkhead	Scotland	L 1-6
8.4.93	Belfast	Wales	W 4-3
24.2.94	Swansea	Wales	L 1-4
3.3.94	Belfast	England	D 2-2
31.3.94	Belfast	Scotland	L 1-2
9.3.95	Derby	England	L 0-9
16.3.95	Belfast	Wales	D 2-2
30.3.95	Parkhead	Scotland	L 1-3
29.2.96	Wrexham	Wales	L 1-6
7.3.96	Belfast	England	L 0-2
28.3.96	Belfast	Scotland	D 3-3
20.2.97	Trent Bridge	England	L 0-6
6.3.97	Belfast	Wales	W 4-3
27.3.97	Ibrox	Scotland	L 1-5
19.2.98	Llandudno	Wales	W 1-0
5.3.98	Belfast	England	L 2-3
26.3.98	Belfast	Scotland	L 0-3
18.2.99	Sunderland	England	L 2-13
4.3.99	Belfast	Wales	W 1-0
25.3.99	Parkhead	Scotland	L 1-9
24.2.00	Llandudno	Wales	L 0-2
3.3.00	Belfast	Scotland	L 0-3
17.3.00	Dublin	England	L 0-2
23.2.01	Parkhead	Scotland	L 0-11
9.3.01	Southampton	England	L 0-3
23.3.01	Belfast	Wales	L 0-1
22.2.02	Cardiff	Wales	W 3-0
1.3.02	Belfast	Scotland	L 1-5
22.3.02	Belfast	England	L 0-1
14.2.03	Wolver'ton	England	L 0-4
21.3.03	Parkhead	Scotland	W 2-0
28.3.03	Belfast	Wales	W 2-0
12.3.04	Belfast	England	L 1-3
21.3.04	Bangor (Wa.)	Wales	W 1-0
26.3.04	Dublin	Scotland	D 1-1
25.2.05	Middlesbr'	England	D 1-1
18.3.05	Parkhead	Scotland	L 0-4
8.4.05	Belfast	Wales	D 2-2
17.2.06	Belfast	England	L 0-5
17.3.06	Dublin	Scotland	L 0-1
2.4.06	Wrexham	Wales	D 4-4
16.2.07	Goodison	England	L 0-1
23.2.07	Belfast	Wales	L 2-3
16.3.07	Parkhead	Scotland	L 0-3

ABOVE: *Holland's Kuijlen scores the first of his two goals against Scotland at Hampden Park on 11 May 1966. The Scots lost 3-0 and this was the last time they played a full international without a player from an English club (an 'Anglo') in the starting line-up.*

Date	Venue	Country	Result		Date	Venue	Country	Result		Date	Venue	Country	Result
15.2.08	Belfast	England	L 1-3		10.3.48	Wrexham	Wales	L 0-2		16.11.66	Hampden	*(E)Scotland	L 1-2
14.3.08	Dublin	Scotland	L 0-5		9.10.48	Belfast	England	L 2-6		12.4.67	Belfast	*(E)Wales	D 0-0
11.4.08	Aberdare	Wales	W 1-0		17.11.48	Hampden	Scotland	L 2-3		21.10.67	Belfast	*(E)Scotland	W 1-0
13.2.09	Bradford (V.P.)	England	L 0-4		9.3.49	Belfast	Wales	L 0-2		22.11.67	Wembley	*(E)England	L 0-2
15.3.09	Ibrox	Scotland	L 0-5		1.10.49	Belfast	*(W)Scotland	L 2-8		28.2.68	Wrexham	*(E)Wales	L 0-2
20.3.09	Belfast	Wales	L 2-3		16.11.49	Maine Road	*(W)England	L 2-9		10.9.68	Jaffa	Israel	W 3-2
12.2.10	Belfast	England	D 1-1		8.3.50	Wrexham	*(W)Wales	D 0-0		23.10.68	Belfast	(W)Turkey	W 4-1
19.3.10	Belfast	Scotland	W 1-0		7.10.50	Belfast	England	L 1-4		11.12.68	Istanbul	(W)Turkey	W 3-0
11.4.10	Wrexham	Wales	L 1-4		1.11.50	Hampden	Scotland	L 1-6		3.5.69	Belfast	England	L 1-3
28.1.11	Belfast	Wales	L 1-2		7.3.51	Belfast	Wales	L 1-2		6.5.69	Hampden	Scotland	D 1-1
11.2.11	Derby	England	L 1-2		12.5.51	Belfast	France	D 2-2		10.5.69	Belfast	Wales	D 0-0
18.3.11	Parkhead	Scotland	L 0-2		6.10.51	Belfast	Scotland	L 0-3		10.9.69	Belfast	(W)USSR	D 0-0
10.2.12	Dublin	England	L 1-6		14.11.51	Villa Park	England	L 0-2		22.10.69	Moscow	(W)USSR	L 0-2
16.3.12	Belfast	Scotland	L 1-4		19.3.52	Swansea	Wales	L 0-3		18.4.70	Belfast	Scotland	L 0-1
13.4.12	Cardiff	Wales	W 3-2		4.10.52	Belfast	England	D 2-2		21.4.70	Wembley	England	L 1-3
18.1.13	Belfast	Wales	L 0-1		5.11.52	Hampden	Scotland	D 1-1		25.4.70	Swansea	Wales	L 0-1
15.2.13	Belfast	England	W 2-1		11.11.52	Paris	France	L 1-3		11.11.70	Seville	(E)Spain	L 0-3
15.3.13	Dublin	Scotland	L 1-2		15.4.53	Belfast	Wales	L 2-3		3.2.71	Nicosia	(E)Cyprus	W 3-0
19.1.14	Wrexham	Wales	W 2-1		3.10.53	Belfast	*(W)Scotland	L 1-3		21.4.71	Belfast	(E)Cyprus	W 5-0
14.2.14	Middlesbr'	England	W 3-0		11.11.53	Goodison	*(W)England	L 1-3		15.5.71	Belfast	England	L 0-1
14.3.14	Belfast	Scotland	D 1-1		31.3.54	Wrexham	*(W)Wales	W 2-1		18.5.71	Hampden	Scotland	W 1-0
25.10.19	Belfast	England	D 1-1		2.10.54	Belfast	England	L 0-2		22.5.71	Belfast	Wales	W 1-0
14.2.20	Belfast	Wales	D 2-2		3.11.54	Hampden	Scotland	D 2-2		22.9.71	Moscow	(E)USSR	L 0-1
13.3.20	Parkhead	Scotland	L 0-3		20.4.55	Belfast	Wales	L 2-3		13.10.71	Belfast	(E)USSR	D 1-1
23.10.20	Sunderland	England	L 0-2		8.10.55	Belfast	Scotland	W 2-1		16.2.72	Hull†	(E)Spain	D 1-1
8.2.21	Paris	France	W 2-1		2.11.55	Wembley	England	L 0-3		20.5.72	Hampden†	Scotland	L 0-2
26.2.21	Belfast	Scotland	L 0-2		11.4.56	Cardiff	Wales	D 1-1		23.5.72	Wembley	England	W 1-0
9.4.21	Swansea	Wales	L 1-2		6.10.56	Belfast	England	D 1-1		27.5.72	Wrexham	Wales	D 0-0
22.10.21	Belfast	England	D 1-1		7.11.56	Hampden	Scotland	L 0-1		18.10.72	Sofia	(W)Bulgaria	L 0-3
4.3.22	Parkhead	Scotland	L 1-2		16.1.57	Lisbon	(W)Portugal	D 1-1		14.2.73	Nicosia	(W)Cyprus	L 0-1
1.4.22	Belfast	Wales	D 1-1		10.4.57	Belfast	Wales	D 0-0		28.3.73	Coventry†	(W)Portugal	D 1-1
21.10.22	W. Bromwich	England	L 0-2		25.4.57	Rome	(W)Italy	L 0-1		8.5.73	Fulham†	(W)Cyprus	W 3-0
3.3.23	Belfast	Scotland	L 0-1		1.5.57	Belfast	(W)Portugal	W 3-0		12.5.73	Goodison†	England	L 1-2
14.4.23	Wrexham	Wales	W 3-0		5.10.57	Belfast	Scotland	D 1-1		16.5.73	Hampden	Scotland	W 2-1
20.10.23	Belfast	England	W 2-1		6.11.57	Wembley	England	W 3-2		19.5.73	Goodison†	Wales	W 1-0
1.3.24	Parkhead	Scotland	L 0-2		4.12.57	Belfast	Italy	D 2-2		26.9.73	Hillsborough†	(W)Bulgaria	D 0-0
15.3.24	Belfast	Wales	L 0-1		15.1.58	Belfast	(W)Italy	W 2-1		14.11.73	Lisbon	(W)Portugal	D 1-1
22.10.24	Goodison	England	L 1-3		16.4.58	Cardiff	Wales	D 1-1		11.5.74	Hampden†	Scotland	W 1-0
28.2.25	Belfast	Scotland	L 0-3		8.6.58	Halmstad	(W)Czechoslovakia	W 1-0		15.5.74	Wembley	England	L 0-1
18.4.25	Wrexham	Wales	D 0-0		11.6.58	Halmstad	(W)Argentina	L 1-3		18.5.74	Wrexham	Wales	L 0-1
24.10.25	Belfast	England	D 0-0		15.6.58	Malmo	(W)West Germany	D 2-2		4.9.74	Oslo	(E)Norway	L 1-2
13.2.26	Belfast	Wales	W 3-0		17.6.58	Malmo	(W)Czechoslovakia	W 2-1		30.10.74	Stockholm	(E)Sweden	W 2-0
27.2.26	Ibrox	Scotland	L 0-4		19.6.58	Norrkoping	(W)France	L 0-4		16.4.75	Belfast	(E)Yugoslavia	W 1-0
20.10.26	Anfield	England	D 3-3		4.10.58	Belfast	England	D 3-3		17.5.75	Belfast	England	D 0-0
26.2.27	Belfast	Scotland	L 0-2		15.10.58	Madrid	Spain	L 2-6		20.5.75	Hampden	Scotland	L 0-3
9.4.27	Cardiff	Wales	D 2-2		5.11.58	Hampden	Scotland	D 2-2		23.5.75	Belfast	Wales	W 1-0
22.10.27	Belfast	England	W 2-0		22.4.59	Belfast	Wales	W 4-1		3.9.75	Belfast	(E)Sweden	L 1-2
4.2.28	Belfast	Wales	L 1-2		3.10.59	Belfast	Scotland	L 0-4		29.10.75	Belfast	(E)Norway	W 3-0
21.2.28	Paris	France	L 0-4		18.11.59	Wembley	England	L 1-2		19.11.75	Belgrade	(E)Yugoslavia	L 0-1
25.2.28	Firhill Park	Scotland	W 1-0		6.4.60	Wrexham	Wales	L 2-3		3.3.76	Tel Aviv	Israel	D 1-1
22.10.28	Goodison	England	L 1-2		8.10.60	Belfast	England	L 2-5		8.5.76	Hampden†	Scotland	L 0-3
2.2.29	Wrexham	Wales	D 2-2		26.10.60	Belfast	(W)West Germany	L 3-4		11.5.76	Wembley	England	L 0-4
23.2.29	Belfast	Scotland	L 3-7		9.11.60	Hampden	Scotland	L 2-5		14.5.76	Swansea	Wales	L 0-1
19.10.29	Belfast	England	L 0-3		12.4.61	Belfast	Wales	L 1-5		13.10.76	Rotterdam	(W)Holland	D 2-2
1.2.30	Belfast	Wales	W 7-0		25.4.61	Bologna	Italy	L 2-3		10.11.76	Liege	(W)Belgium	L 0-2
22.2.30	Parkhead	Scotland	L 1-3		3.5.61	Athens	(W)Greece	L 1-2		27.4.77	Cologne	West Germany	L 0-5
20.10.30	Bramall Lane	England	L 1-5		10.5.61	West Berlin	(W)West Germany	L 1-2		28.5.77	Belfast	England	L 1-2
21.2.31	Belfast	Scotland	D 0-0		7.10.61	Belfast	Scotland	L 1-6		1.6.77	Hampden	Scotland	L 0-3
22.4.31	Wrexham	Wales	L 2-3		17.10.61	Belfast	(W)Greece	W 2-0		3.6.77	Belfast	Wales	D 1-1
19.9.31	Ibrox	Scotland	L 1-3		22.11.61	Wembley	England	D 1-1		11.6.77	Reykjavik	(W)Iceland	L 0-1
17.10.31	Belfast	England	L 2-6		11.4.62	Cardiff	Wales	L 0-4		21.9.77	Belfast	(W)Iceland	W 2-0
5.12.31	Belfast	Wales	W 4-0		9.5.62	Rotterdam	Holland	L 0-4		12.10.77	Belfast	(W)Holland	L 0-1
12.9.32	Belfast	Scotland	L 0-4		10.10.62	Katowice	(E)Poland	W 2-0		16.11.77	Belfast	(W)Belgium	W 3-0
17.10.32	Blackpool	England	L 0-1		20.10.62	Belfast	England	L 1-3		13.5.78	Hampden†	Scotland	D 1-1
7.12.32	Wrexham	Wales	L 1-4		7.11.62	Belfast	Scotland	L 1-5		16.5.78	Wembley	England	L 0-1
16.9.33	Parkhead	Scotland	W 2-1		28.11.62	Belfast	(E)Poland	W 2-0		19.5.78	Wrexham	Wales	L 0-1
14.10.33	Belfast	England	L 0-3		3.4.63	Belfast	Wales	L 1-4		20.9.78	Dublin	(E)Eire	D 0-0
4.11.33	Belfast	Wales	D 1-1		30.5.63	Bilbao	(E)Spain	D 1-1		25.10.78	Belfast	(E)Denmark	W 2-1
20.10.34	Belfast	Scotland	W 2-1		12.10.63	Belfast	Scotland	W 2-1		29.11.78	Sofia	(E)Bulgaria	W 2-0
6.2.35	Goodison	England	L 1-2		30.10.63	Belfast	(E)Spain	L 0-1		7.2.79	Wembley	(E)England	L 0-4
27.3.35	Wrexham	Wales	L 1-3		20.11.63	Wembley	England	L 3-8		2.5.79	Belfast	(E)Bulgaria	W 2-0
19.10.35	Belfast	England	L 1-3		15.4.64	Swansea	Wales	W 3-2		19.5.79	Belfast	England	L 0-2
13.11.35	Tynecastle	Scotland	L 1-2		29.4.64	Belfast	Uruguay	W 3-0		22.5.79	Hampden	Scotland	L 0-1
11.3.36	Belfast	Wales	W 3-2		3.10.64	Belfast	England	L 3-4		25.5.79	Belfast	Wales	D 1-1
31.10.36	Belfast	Scotland	L 1-3		14.10.64	Belfast	(W)Switzerland	W 1-0		6.6.79	Copenhagen	(E)Denmark	L 0-4
18.11.36	Stoke	England	L 1-3		14.11.64	Lausanne	(W)Switzerland	L 1-2		17.10.79	Belfast	(E)England	L 1-5
17.3.37	Wrexham	Wales	L 1-4		25.11.64	Hampden	Scotland	L 2-3		21.11.79	Belfast	(E)Eire	W 1-0
23.10.37	Belfast	England	L 1-5		17.3.65	Belfast	(W)Holland	W 2-1		26.3.80	Tel Aviv	(W)Israel	D 0-0
10.11.37	Aberdeen	Scotland	D 1-1		31.3.65	Belfast	Wales	L 0-5		17.5.80	Belfast	Scotland	W 1-0
16.3.38	Belfast	Wales	W 1-0		7.4.65	Rotterdam	(W)Holland	D 0-0		20.5.80	Wembley	England	D 1-1
8.10.38	Belfast	Scotland	L 0-2		7.5.65	Belfast	(W)Albania	W 4-1		23.5.80	Belfast	Wales	W 1-0
16.11.38	Maine Road	England	L 0-7		2.10.65	Belfast	Scotland	W 3-2		11.6.80	Sydney	Australia	W 2-1
15.3.39	Wrexham	Wales	L 1-3		10.11.65	Wembley	England	L 1-2		15.6.80	Melbourne	Australia	D 1-1
28.9.46	Belfast	England	L 2-7		24.11.65	Tirana	(W)Albania	D 1-1		18.6.80	Adelaide	Australia	W 2-1
27.11.46	Hampden	Scotland	D 0-0		30.3.66	Cardiff	Wales	W 4-1		15.10.80	Belfast	(W)Sweden	W 3-0
16.4.47	Belfast	Wales	W 2-1		7.5.66	Belfast	West Germany	L 0-2		19.11.80	Lisbon	(W)Portugal	L 0-1
4.10.47	Belfast	Scotland	W 2-0		22.6.66	Belfast	Mexico	W 4-1		25.3.81	Hampden	(W)Scotland	D 1-1
5.11.47	Goodison	England	D 2-2		22.10.66	Belfast	*(E)England	L 0-2		29.4.81	Belfast	(W)Portugal	W 1-0

114

Date	Venue	Country	Result
19.5.81	Hampden	Scotland	L 0-2
3.6.81	Stockholm	(W)Sweden	L 0-1
14.10.81	Belfast	(W)Scotland	D 0-0
18.11.81	Belfast	(W)Israel	W 1-0
23.2.82	Wembley	England	L 0-4
24.3.82	Paris	France	L 0-4
28.4.82	Belfast	Scotland	D 1-1
27.5.82	Wrexham	Wales	L 0-3
17.6.82	Zaragoza	(W)Yugoslavia	D 0-0
21.6.82	Zaragoza	(W)Honduras	D 1-1
25.6.82	Valencia	(W)Spain	W 1-0
1.7.82	Madrid	(W)Austria	D 2-2
4.7.82	Madrid	(W)France	L 1-4
13.10.82	Vienna	(E)Austria	L 0-2
17.11.82	Belfast	(E)W. Germany	W 1-0
15.12.82	Tirana	(E)Albania	D 0-0
30.3.83	Belfast	(E)Turkey	W 2-1
27.4.83	Belfast	(E)Albania	W 1-0
24.5.83	Hampden	Scotland	D 0-0
28.5.83	Belfast	England	D 0-0
31.5.83	Belfast	Wales	L 0-1
21.9.83	Belfast	(E)Austria	W 3-1

(W) World Cup (E) European Nations Cup/European Championship *Home International Championship used as qualifying tournament †switched from Belfast because of political troubles

EIRE'S FULL INTERNATIONAL RECORD

Date	Venue	Country	Result
28.5.24	Paris	Bulgaria	W 1-0
2.6.24	Paris	Holland	L 1-2
3.6.24	Paris	Estonia	W 3-1
16.6.24	Dublin	United States	W 3-1
21.3.26	Turin	Italy	L 0-3
23.4.27	Dublin	Italy	L 1-2
12.2.28	Liege	Belgium	W 4-2
20.4.29	Dublin	Belgium	W 4-0
11.5.30	Brussels	Belgium	W 3-1
26.4.31	Barcelona	Spain	D 1-1
13.12.31	Dublin	Spain	L 0-5
8.5.32	Amsterdam	Holland	W 2-0
25.2.34	Dublin	(W)Belgium	D 4-4
8.4.34	Amsterdam	(W)Holland	L 2-5
15.12.34	Dublin	Hungary	L 2-4
5.5.35	Basel	Switzerland	L 0-1
8.5.35	Dortmund	Germany	L 1-3
8.12.35	Dublin	Holland	L 3-5
17.3.36	Dublin	Switzerland	W 1-0
3.5.36	Budapest	Hungary	D 3-3
9.5.36	Luxembourg	Luxembourg	W 5-1
17.10.36	Dublin	Germany	W 5-2
6.12.36	Dublin	Hungary	L 2-3
17.5.37	Bern	Switzerland	W 1-0
23.5.37	Paris	France	W 2-0
10.10.37	Oslo	(W)Norway	L 2-3
7.11.37	Dublin	(W)Norway	D 3-3
18.5.38	Prague	Czechoslovakia	D 2-2
22.5.38	Warsaw	Poland	L 0-6
18.9.38	Dublin	Switzerland	W 4-0
13.11.38	Dublin	Poland	W 3-2
19.3.39	Cork	Hungary	D 2-2
18.5.39	Budapest	Hungary	D 2-2
23.5.39	Bremen	Germany	D 1-1
16.6.46	Lisbon	Portugal	L 1-3
23.6.46	Madrid	Spain	W 1-0
30.9.46	Dublin	England	L 0-1
2.3.47	Dublin	Spain	W 3-2
4.5.47	Dublin	Portugal	L 0-2
23.5.48	Lisbon	Portugal	L 0-2
30.5.48	Barcelona	Spain	L 1-2
5.12.48	Dublin	Switzerland	L 0-1
25.4.49	Dublin	Belgium	L 0-2
22.5.49	Dublin	Portugal	W 1-0
2.6.49	Stockholm	(W)Sweden	L 1-3
12.6.49	Dublin	Spain	L 1-4
8.9.49	Dublin	(W)Finland	W 3-0
21.9.49	Goodison	England	W 2-0
9.10.49	Helsinki	(W)Finland	D 1-1
13.11.49	Dublin	(W)Sweden	L 1-3

Date	Venue	Country	Result
10.5.50	Brussels	Belgium	L 1-5
26.11.50	Dublin	Norway	D 2-2
13.5.51	Dublin	Argentina	L 0-1
30.5.51	Oslo	Norway	W 3-1
17.10.51	Dublin	West Germany	W 3-2
4.5.52	Cologne	West Germany	L 0-3
7.5.52	Vienna	Austria	L 0-6
1.6.52	Madrid	Spain	L 0-6
16.11.52	Dublin	France	D 1-1
25.3.53	Dublin	Austria	W 4-0
4.10.53	Dublin	(W)France	L 3-5
28.10.53	Dublin	(W)Luxembourg	W 4-0
25.11.53	Paris	(W)France	L 0-1
7.3.54	Luxembourg	(W)Luxembourg	W 1-0
8.11.54	Dublin	Norway	W 2-1
1.5.55	Dublin	Holland	W 1-0
25.5.55	Oslo	Norway	W 3-1
28.5.55	Hamburg	West Germany	L 1-2
19.9.55	Dublin	Yugoslavia	L 1-4
27.11.55	Dublin	Spain	D 2-2
10.5.56	Rotterdam	Holland	W 4-1
3.10.56	Dublin	(W)Denmark	W 2-1
25.11.56	Dublin	West Germany	W 3-0
8.5.57	Wembley	(W)England	L 1-5
19.5.57	Dublin	(W)England	D 1-1
2.10.57	Copenhagen	(W)Denmark	W 2-0
11.5.58	Katowice	Poland	D 2-2
14.5.58	Vienna	Austria	L 1-3
5.10.58	Dublin	Poland	D 2-2
5.4.59	Dublin	(E)Czechoslovakia	W 2-0
10.5.59	Bratislava	(E)Czechoslovakia	L 0-4
1.11.59	Dublin	Sweden	W 3-2
30.3.60	Dublin	Chile	W 2-0
11.5.60	Dusseldorf	West Germany	W 1-0
18.5.60	Malmo	Sweden	L 1-4
28.9.60	Dublin	Wales	L 2-3
6.11.60	Dublin	Norway	W 3-2
3.5.61	Hampden	(W)Scotland	L 1-4
7.5.61	Dublin	(W)Scotland	L 0-3
8.10.61	Dublin	(W)Czechoslovakia	L 1-3
29.10.61	Prague	(W)Czechoslovakia	L 1-7
8.4.62	Dublin	Austria	L 2-3
12.8.62	Dublin	(E)Iceland	W 4-2
2.9.62	Reykjavik	(E)Iceland	D 1-1
9.6.63	Dublin	Scotland	W 1-0
25.9.63	Vienna	(E)Austria	D 0-0
13.10.63	Dublin	(E)Austria	W 3-2
11.3.64	Seville	(E)Spain	L 1-5
8.4.64	Dublin	(E)Spain	L 0-2
10.5.64	Cracow	Poland	L 1-3
13.5.64	Oslo	Norway	W 4-1
24.5.64	Dublin	England	L 1-3
25.10.64	Dublin	Poland	W 3-2
24.3.65	Dublin	Belgium	L 0-2
5.5.65	Dublin	(W)Spain	W 1-0
27.10.65	Seville	(W)Spain	L 1-4
10.11.65	Paris	(W)Spain	L 0-1
4.5.66	Dublin	West Germany	L 0-4
22.5.66	Vienna	Austria	L 0-1
25.5.66	Liege	Belgium	W 3-2
23.10.66	Dublin	(E)Spain	D 0-0
16.11.66	Dublin	(E)Turkey	W 2-1
7.12.66	Valencia	(E)Spain	L 0-2
22.2.67	Ankara	(E)Turkey	L 1-2
21.5.67	Dublin	(E)Czechoslovakia	L 0-2
22.11.67	Prague	(E)Czechoslovakia	W 2-1
15.5.68	Dublin	Poland	D 2-2
30.10.68	Katowice	Poland	L 0-1
10.11.68	Dublin	Austrlia	D 2-2
4.12.68	Dublin	*(W)Denmark	D 1-1
4.5.69	Dublin	(W)Czechoslovakia	L 1-2
27.5.69	Copenhagen	(W)Denmark	W 2-0
8.6.69	Dublin	(W)Hungary	L 1-2
21.9.69	Dublin	Scotland	D 1-1
7.10.69	Prague	(W)Czechoslovakia	L 0-3
15.10.69	Dublin	(W)Denmark	D 1-1
5.11.69	Budapest	(W)Hungary	L 0-4
6.5.70	Dublin	Poland	L 1-2
9.5.70	West Berlin	West Germany	L 1-2
23.9.70	Dublin	Poland	L 0-2
14.10.70	Dublin	(E)Sweden	D 1-1
28.10.70	Malmo	(E)Sweden	L 0-1
8.12.70	Rome	(E)Italy	L 0-3
10.5.71	Dublin	(E)Italy	L 1-2
30.5.71	Dublin	(E)Austria	L 1-4
10.10.71	Linz	(E)Austria	L 0-6
18.6.72	Recife	Iran	W 2-1
19.6.72	Natal, Brazil	Ecuador	W 3-2

Date	Venue	Country	Result
21.6.72	Recife	Chile	L 1-2
25.6.72	Recife	Portugal	L 1-2
18.10.72	Dublin	(W)USSR	L 1-2
15.11.72	Dublin	(W)France-	W 2-1
13.5.73	Moscow	(W)USSR	L 0-1
16.5.73	Wroclaw	Poland	L 0-2
19.5.73	Paris	(W)France	D 1-1
6.6.73	Oslo	Norway	D 1-1
21.10.73	Dublin	Poland	W 1-0
5.5.74	Rio	Brazil	L 1-2
8.5.74	Montevideo	Uruguay	L 0-2
12.5.74	Santiago	Chile	W 2-1
30.10.74	Dublin	(E)USSR	W 3-0
20.11.74	Izmir	(E)Turkey	D 1-1
10.5.75	Dublin	(E)Switzerland	W 2-1
18.5.75	Kiev	(E)USSR	L 1-2
21.5.75	Bern	(E)Switzerland	L 0-1
29.10.75	Dublin	(E)Turkey	W 4-0
24.3.76	Dublin	Norway	W 3-0
26.5.76	Poznan	Poland	W 2-0
8.9.76	Wembley	England	D 1-1
13.10.76	Ankara	Turkey	D 3-3
17.11.76	Paris	(W)France	L 0-2
9.2.77	Dublin	Spain	L 0-1
30.3.77	Dublin	(W)France	W 1-0
24.4.77	Dublin	Poland	D 0-0
1.6.77	Sofia	(W)Bulgaria	L 1-2
12.10.77	Dublin	(W)Bulgaria	D 0-0
5.4.78	Dublin	Turkey	W 4-2
12.4.78	Lodz	Poland	L 0-3
21.5.78	Oslo	Norway	D 0-0
24.5.78	Copenhagen	(E)Denmark	D 3-3
20.9.78	Dublin	(E)N. Ireland	D 0-0
25.9.78	Dublin	(E)England	D 1-1
2.5.79	Dublin	(E)Denmark	W 2-0
19.5.79	Sofia	(E)Bulgaria	L 0-1
22.5.79	Dublin	West Germany	L 1-3
29.5.79	Dublin	Argentina	D 0-0
11.9.79	Swansea	Wales	L 1-2
26.9.79	Prague	Czechoslovakia	L 1-4
17.10.79	Dublin	(E)Bulgaria	W 3-0
29.10.79	Dublin	United States	W 3-2
21.11.79	Belfast	(E)N. Ireland	L 0-1
6.2.80	Wembley	(E)England	L 0-2
26.3.80	Nicosia	(W)Cyprus	W 3-2
30.4.80	Dublin	Switzerland	W 2-0
16.5.80	Dublin	Argentina	L 0-1
10.9.80	Dublin	(W)Holland	W 2-1
15.10.80	Dublin	(W)Belgium	D 1-1
28.10.80	Paris	(W)France	L 0-2
19.11.80	Dublin	(W)Cyprus	W 6-0
24.2.81	Dublin	Wales	L 1-3
25.3.81	Brussels	(W)Belgium	L 0-1
9.9.81	Amsterdam	(W)Holland	D 2-2
14.10.81	Dublin	(W)France	W 3-2
28.4.82	Algiers	Algeria	L 0-2
22.5.82	Santiago	Chile	L 0-1
27.5.82	Uberlandia	Brazil	L 0-7
30.5.82	Port of Spain	Trinidad	L 1-2
22.9.82	Rotterdam	(E)Holland	W 1-0
13.10.82	Dublin	(E)Iceland	W 2-0
17.11.82	Dublin	(E)Spain	D 3-3
30.3.83	Valletta	(E)Malta	W 1-0
27.4.83	Zaragoza	(E)Spain	L 0-2
21.9.83	Rejkavik	(E)Iceland	W 2-0

(W) World Cup (E) European Nations Cup/European Championship *abandoned after 51 minutes; result void

SCOTLAND'S FULL INTERNATIONAL RECORD

Date	Venue	Country	Result
30.11.72	Hamilton Cr.	England	D 0-0
8.3.73	The Oval	England	L 2-4
7.3.74	Hamilton Cr.	England	W 2-1
6.3.75	The Oval	England	D 2-2
4.3.76	Hamilton Cr.	England	W 3-0
25.3.76	Hamilton Cr.	Wales	W 4-0
3.3.77	The Oval	England	W 3-1
5.3.77	Wrexham	Wales	W 2-0
2.3.78	1st Hampden	England	W 7-2
23.3.78	1st Hampden	Wales	W 9-0
5.4.79	The Oval	England	L 4-5
7.4.79	Wrexham	Wales	W 3-0
13.3.80	1st Hampden	England	W 5-4
3.4.80	1st Hampden	Wales	W 5-1
12.3.81	The Oval	England	W 6-1
14.3.81	Wrexham	Wales	W 5-1
11.3.82	1st Hampden	England	W 5-1
25.3.82	1st Hampden	Wales	W 5-0
10.3.83	Bramall Lane	England	W 3-2
12.3.83	Wrexham	Wales	W 3-0
26.1.84	Belfast	Ireland	W 5-0
15.3.84	1st Cathkin	England	W 1-0
29.3.84	1st Cathkin	Wales	W 4-1
14.3.85	2nd Hampden	Ireland	W 8-2
21.3.85	The Oval	England	D 1-1
23.3.85	Wrexham	Wales	W 8-1
20.3.86	Belfast	Ireland	W 7-2
27.3.86	2nd Hampden	England	D 1-1
10.4.86	2nd Hampden	Wales	W 4-1
19.2.87	2nd Hampden	Ireland	W 4-1
19.3.87	Blackburn	England	W 3-2
21.3.87	Wrexham	Wales	W 2-0
10.3.88	Easter Road	Wales	W 5-1
17.3.88	2nd Hampden	England	L 0-5
24.3.88	Cliftonville	Ireland	W 10-2
9.3.89	Ibrox	Ireland	W 7-0
13.4.89	The Oval	England	W 3-2
15.4.89	Wrexham	Wales	D 0-0
22.3.90	Paisley	Wales	W 5-0
29.3.90	Belfast	Ireland	W 4-1
5.4.90	2nd Hampden	England	D 1-1
21.3.91	Wrexham	Wales	W 4-3
28.3.91	Parkhead	Ireland	W 2-1
4.4.91	Blackburn	England	L 1-2
19.3.92	Cliftonville	Ireland	W 3-2
26.3.92	Tynecastle	Wales	W 6-1
2.4.92	Ibrox	England	L 0-4
18.3.93	Wrexham	Wales	W 8-0
25.3.93	Parkhead	Ireland	W 6-1
1.4.93	Richmond	England	L 2-5
24.3.94	Kilmarnock	Wales	W 5-2
31.3.94	Cliftonville	Ireland	W 2-1
7.4.94	Parkhead	England	D 2-2
23.3.95	Wrexham	Wales	D 2-2
30.3.95	Parkhead	Ireland	W 3-1
6.4.95	Goodison	England	L 0-3
21.3.96	Carolina, D'dee	Wales	W 4-0
28.3.96	Cliftonville	Ireland	D 3-3
4.4.96	Parkhead	England	W 2-1
20.3.97	Wrexham	Wales	D 2-2
27.3.97	Ibrox	Ireland	W 5-1
3.4.97	Crystal Pal.	England	W 2-1
19.3.98	Motherwell	Wales	W 5-2
26.3.98	Cliftonville	Ireland	W 3-0
2.4.98	Parkhead	England	L 1-3
18.3.99	Wrexham	Wales	W 6-0
25.3.99	Parkhead	Ireland	W 9-1
8.4.99	Villa Park	England	L 1-2
3.2.00	Aberdeen	Wales	W 5-2
3.3.00	Cliftonville	Ireland	W 3-0
7.4.00	Parkhead	England	W 4-1
23.2.01	Parkhead	Ireland	W 11-0
2.3.01	Wrexham	Wales	D 1-1
30.3.01	Crystal Pal.	England	D 2-2
1.3.02	Belfast	Ireland	W 5-1
15.3.02	Greenock	Wales	W 5-1
3.5.02	Villa Park	England	D 2-2
9.3.03	Cardiff	Wales	W 1-0
21.3.03	Parkhead	Ireland	L 0-2
4.4.03	Bramall Lane	England	W 2-1
12.3.04	Dens Park	Wales	D 1-1
26.3.04	Dublin	Ireland	D 1-1
9.4.04	Parkhead	England	L 0-1
6.3.05	Wrexham	Wales	L 1-3
18.3.05	Parkhead	Ireland	W 4-0
1.4.05	Crystal Pal.	England	L 0-1
3.3.06	Tynecastle	Wales	L 0-2
17.3.06	Dublin	Ireland	W 1-0
7.4.06	Hampden	England	W 2-1
4.3.07	Wrexham	Wales	L 0-1
16.3.07	Parkhead	Ireland	W 3-0
6.4.07	Newcastle	England	D 1-1
7.3.08	Dens Park	Wales	W 2-1
14.3.08	Dublin	Ireland	W 5-0
4.4.08	Hampden	England	D 1-1
1.3.09	Wrexham	Wales	L 2-3
15.3.09	Ibrox	Ireland	W 5-0
3.4.09	Crystal Pal.	England	L 0-2
5.3.10	Kilmarnock	Wales	W 1-0
19.3.10	Belfast	Ireland	L 0-1
2.4.10	Hampden	England	W 2-0
6.3.11	Cardiff	Wales	D 2-2
18.3.11	Parkhead	Ireland	W 2-0
1.4.11	Goodison	England	D 1-1
2.3.12	Tynecastle	Wales	W 1-0
16.3.12	Belfast	Ireland	W 4-1
23.3.12	Hampden	England	D 1-1
3.3.13	Wrexham	Wales	D 0-0
15.3.13	Dublin	Ireland	W 2-1
5.4.13	Stamford B.	England	L 0-1
28.2.14	Parkhead	Wales	D 0-0
14.3.14	Belfast	Ireland	D 1-1
4.4.14	Hampden	England	W 3-1
26.2.20	Cardiff	Wales	D 1-1
13.3.20	Parkhead	Ireland	W 3-0
10.4.20	Bramall Lane	England	L 4-5
12.2.21	Aberdeen	Wales	W 2-1
26.2.21	Belfast	N. Ireland	W 2-0
9.4.21	Hampden	England	W 3-0
4.2.22	Wrexham	Wales	L 1-2
4.3.22	Parkhead	N. Ireland	W 2-1
8.4.22	Villa Park	England	W 1-0
3.3.23	Belfast	N. Ireland	W 1-0
17.3.23	Paisley	Wales	W 2-0
14.4.23	Hampden	England	D 2-2
16.2.24	Cardiff	Wales	L 0-2
1.3.24	Parkhead	N. Ireland	W 2-0
12.4.24	Wembley	England	D 1-1
14.2.25	Tynecastle	Wales	W 3-1
28.2.25	Belfast	N. Ireland	W 3-0
4.4.25	Hampden	England	W 2-0
31.10.25	Cardiff	Wales	W 3-0
27.2.26	Ibrox	N. Ireland	W 4-0
17.4.26	Old Trafford	England	W 1-0
30.10.26	Ibrox	Wales	W 3-0
26.2.27	Belfast	N. Ireland	W 2-0
2.4.27	Hampden	England	L 1-2
29.10.27	Wrexham	Wales	D 2-2
25.2.28	Partick	N. Ireland	L 0-1
31.3.28	Wembley	England	W 5-1
27.10.28	Ibrox	Wales	W 4-2
23.2.29	Belfast	N. Ireland	W 7-3
13.4.29	Hampden	England	W 1-0
26.5.29	Bergen	Norway	W 7-3
1.6.29	Berlin	Germany	D 1-1
4.6.29	Amsterdam	Holland	W 2-0
26.10.29	Cardiff	Wales	W 4-2
22.2.30	Parkhead	N. Ireland	W 3-1
5.4.30	Wembley	England	L 2-5
18.5.30	Paris	France	W 2-0
25.10.30	Ibrox	Wales	D 1-1
21.2.31	Belfast	N. Ireland	D 0-0
28.3.31	Hampden	England	W 2-0
16.5.31	Vienna	Austria	L 0-5
20.5.31	Rome	Italy	L 0-3
24.5.31	Geneva	Switzerland	W 3-2
19.9.31	Ibrox	N. Ireland	W 3-1
31.10.31	Wrexham	Wales	W 3-2
9.4.32	Wembley	England	L 0-3
8.5.32	Paris	France	W 3-1
17.9.32	Belfast	N. Ireland	W 4-0
26.10.32	Tynecastle	Wales	L 2-5
1.4.33	Hampden	England	W 2-1
16.9.33	Parkhead	N. Ireland	L 1-2
4.10.33	Cardiff	Wales	L 2-3
29.11.33	Hampden	Austria	D 2-2
14.4.34	Wembley	England	L 0-3
20.10.34	Belfast	N. Ireland	L 1-2
21.11.34	Pittodrie	Wales	W 3-2
6.4.35	Hampden	England	W 2-0
5.10.35	Cardiff	Wales	D 1-1
13.11.35	Tynecastle	N. Ireland	W 2-1
4.4.36	Wembley	England	D 1-1
14.10.36	Ibrox	Germany	W 2-0
31.10.36	Belfast	N. Ireland	W 3-1
2.12.36	Dens Park	Wales	L 1-2
17.4.37	Hampden	England	W 3-1
9.5.37	Vienna	Austria	D 1-1
15.5.37	Prague	Czechoslovakia	W 3-1
30.10.37	Cardiff	Wales	L 1-2
10.11.37	Pittodrie	N. Ireland	D 1-1
8.12.37	Hampden	Czechoslovakia	W 5-0
9.4.38	Wembley	England	W 1-0
21.5.38	Amsterdam	Holland	W 3-1
8.10.38	Belfast	N. Ireland	W 2-0
9.11.38	Tynecastle	Wales	W 3-2
7.12.38	Ibrox	Hungary	W 3-1
15.4.39	Hampden	England	L 1-2
19.10.46	Wrexham	Wales	L 1-3
27.11.46	Hampden	N. Ireland	D 0-0
12.4.47	Wembley	England	D 1-1
18.5.47	Brussels	Belgium	L 1-2
24.5.47	Luxembourg	Luxembourg	W 6-0
4.10.47	Belfast	N. Ireland	L 0-2
12.11.47	Hampden	Wales	L 1-2
10.4.48	Hampden	England	L 0-2
28.4.48	Hampden	Belgium	W 2-0
17.5.48	Bern	Switzerland	L 1-2
23.5.48	Paris	France	L 0-3
23.10.48	Cardiff	Wales	W 3-1
17.11.48	Hampden	N. Ireland	W 3-2
9.4.49	Wembley	England	W 3-1
27.4.49	Hampden	France	W 2-0
1.10.49	Belfast	*(W)N. Ireland	W 8-2
9.11.49	Hampden	*(W)Wales	W 2-0
15.4.50	Hampden	*(W)England	L 0-1
26.4.50	Hampden	Switzerland	W 3-1
21.5.50	Lisbon	Portugal	D 2-2
27.5.50	Paris	France	W 1-0
21.10.50	Cardiff	Wales	W 3-1
1.11.50	Hampden	N. Ireland	W 6-1
13.12.50	Hampden	Austria	L 0-1
14.4.51	Wembley	England	W 3-2
12.5.51	Hampden	Denmark	W 3-1
16.5.51	Hampden	France	W 1-0
20.5.51	Brussels	Belgium	W 5-0
27.5.51	Vienna	Austria	L 0-4
6.10.51	Belfast	N. Ireland	W 3-0
14.11.51	Hampden	Wales	L 0-1
5.4.52	Hampden	England	L 1-2
30.4.52	Hampden	USA	W 6-0
25.5.52	Copenhagen	Denmark	W 2-1
30.5.52	Stockholm	Sweden	L 1-3
18.10.52	Cardiff	Wales	W 2-1
5.11.52	Hampden	N. Ireland	D 1-1
18.4.53	Wembley	England	D 2-2
6.5.53	Hampden	Sweden	L 1-2
3.10.53	Belfast	*(W)N. Ireland	W 3-1
4.11.53	Hampden	*(W)Wales	D 3-3
3.4.54	Hampden	*(W)England	L 2-4
5.5.54	Hampden	Norway	W 1-0
19.5.54	Oslo	Norway	D 1-1
25.5.54	Helsinki	Finland	W 2-1
16.6.54	Zurich	(W)Austria	L 0-1
19.6.54	Basel	(W)Uruguay	L 0-7
16.10.54	Cardiff	Wales	W 1-0
3.11.54	Hampden	N. Ireland	D 2-2
8.12.54	Hampden	Hungary	L 2-4
2.4.55	Wembley	England	L 2-7
4.5.55	Hampden	Portugal	W 3-0
15.5.55	Belgrade	Yugoslavia	D 2-2
19.5.55	Vienna	Austria	W 4-1
29.5.55	Budapest	Hungary	L 1-3
8.10.55	Belfast	N. Ireland	L 1-2
9.11.55	Hampden	Wales	W 2-0
14.4.56	Hampden	England	D 1-1
2.5.56	Hampden	Austria	D 1-1
20.10.56	Cardiff	Wales	D 2-2
7.11.56	Hampden	N. Ireland	W 1-0
21.11.56	Hampden	Yugoslavia	W 2-0
6.4.57	Wembley	England	L 1-2
8.5.57	Hampden	(W)Spain	W 4-2

Date	Venue	Country	Result
19.5.57	Basel	(W)Switzerland	W 2-1
22.5.57	Stuttgart	West Germany	W 3-1
26.5.57	Madrid	(W)Spain	L 1-4
5.10.57	Belfast	N. Ireland	D 1-1
6.11.57	Hampden	(W)Switzerland	W 3-2
13.11.57	Hampden	Wales	D 1-1
19.4.58	Hampden	England	L 0-4
7.5.58	Hampden	Hungary	D 1-1
1.6.58	Warsaw	Poland	W 2-1
8.6.58	Vasteras	(W)Yugoslavia	D 1-1
11.6.58	Norrkoping	(W)Paraguay	L 2-3
15.6.58	Orebro	(W)France	L 1-2
18.10.58	Cardiff	Wales	W 3-0
5.11.58	Hampden	N. Ireland	D 2-2
11.4.59	Wembley	England	L 0-1
6.5.59	Hampden	West Germany	W 3-2
27.5.59	Amsterdam	Holland	W 2-1
3.6.59	Lisbon	Portugal	L 0-1
3.10.59	Belfast	N. Ireland	W 4-0
4.11.59	Hampden	Wales	D 1-1
9.4.60	Hampden	England	D 1-1
4.5.60	Hampden	Poland	L 2-3
29.5.60	Vienna	Austria	L 1-4
5.6.60	Budapest	Hungary	D 3-3
8.6.60	Ankara	Turkey	L 2-4
22.10.60	Cardiff	Wales	L 0-2
9.11.60	Hampden	N. Ireland	W 5-2
15.4.61	Wembley	England	L 3-9
3.5.61	Hampden	(W)Eire	W 4-1
7.5.61	Dublin	(W)Eire	W 3-0
14.5.61	Bratislava	(W)Czechoslovakia	L 0-4
26.9.61	Hampden	(W)Czechoslovakia	W 3-2
7.10.61	Belfast	N. Ireland	W 6-1
8.11.61	Hampden	Wales	W 2-0
29.11.61	Brussels	(W)Czechoslovakia	L 2-4
14.4.62	Hampden	England	W 2-0
2.5.62	Hampden	Uruguay	L 2-3
20.10.62	Cardiff	Wales	W 3-2
7.11.62	Hampden	N. Ireland	W 5-1
6.4.63	Wembley	England	W 2-1
8.5.63	Hampden§	Austria	W 4-1
4.6.63	Bergen	Norway	L 3-4
9.6.63	Dublin	Eire	L 0-1
13.6.63	Madrid	Spain	W 6-2
12.10.63	Belfast	N. Ireland	L 1-2
7.11.63	Hampden	Norway	W 6-1
20.11.63	Hampden	Wales	W 2-1
11.4.64	Hampden	England	W 1-0
12.5.64	Hanover	West Germany	D 2-2
3.10.64	Cardiff	Wales	L 2-3
21.10.64	Hampden	(W)Finland	W 3-1
25.11.64	Hampden	N. Ireland	W 3-2
10.4.65	Wembley	England	D 2-2
8.5.65	Hampden	Spain	D 0-0
23.5.65	Chorzow	(W)Poland	D 1-1
27.5.65	Helsinki	(W)Finland	W 2-1
2.10.65	Belfast	N. Ireland	L 2-3
13.10.65	Hampden	(W)Poland	L 1-2
9.11.65	Hampden	(W)Italy	W 1-0
24.11.65	Hampden	Wales	W 4-1
7.12.65	Naples	(W)Italy	L 0-3
2.4.66	Hampden	England	L 3-4
11.5.66	Hampden	Holland	L 0-3
18.6.66	Hampden	Portugal	L 0-1
25.6.66	Hampden	Brazil	D 1-1
22.10.66	Cardiff	*(E)Wales	D 1-1
16.11.66	Hampden	*(E)N. Ireland	W 2-1
15.4.67	Wembley	*(E)England	W 3-2
10.5.67	Hampden	USSR	L 0-2
21.10.67	Belfast	*(E)N. Ireland	L 0-1
22.11.67	Hampden	*(E)Wales	W 3-2
24.2.68	Hampden	*(E)England	D 1-1
30.5.68	Amsterdam	Holland	D 0-0
16.10.68	Copenhagen	Denmark	W 1-0
6.11.68	Hampden	(W)Austria	W 2-1
11.12.68	Nicosia	(W)Cyprus	W 5-0
16.4.69	Hampden	(W)West Germany	D 1-1
3.5.69	Wrexham	Wales	W 5-3
6.5.69	Hampden	N. Ireland	D 1-1
10.5.69	Wembley	England	L 1-4
17.5.69	Hampden	(W)Cyprus	W 8-0
21.9.69	Dublin	Eire	D 1-1
22.10.69	Hamburg	(W)West Germany	L 2-3
5.11.69	Vienna	(W)Austria	L 0-2
18.4.70	Belfast	N. Ireland	W 1-0
22.4.70	Hampden	Wales	D 0-0
25.4.70	Hampden	England	D 0-0
11.11.70	Hampden	(E)Denmark	W 1-0
3.2.71	Liege	(E)Belgium	L 0-3
21.4.71	Lisbon	(E)Portugal	L 0-2
15.5.71	Cardiff	Wales	D 0-0
18.5.71	Hampden	N. Ireland	L 0-1
22.5.71	Wembley	England	L 1-3
9.6.71	Copenhagen	(E)Denmark	L 0-1
14.6.71	Moscow	USSR	L 0-1
13.10.71	Hampden	(E)Portugal	W 2-1
10.11.71	Aberdeen	(E)Belgium	W 1-0
1.12.71	Amsterdam	Holland	L 1-2
26.4.72	Hampden	Peru	W 2-0
20.5.72	Hampden†	N. Ireland	W 2-0
24.5.72	Hampden	Wales	W 1-0
27.5.72	Hampden	England	L 0-1
28.6.72	B. Horizonte	Yugoslavia	D 2-2
2.7.72	Porto Alegre	Czechoslovakia	D 0-0
5.7.72	Rio	Brazil	L 0-1
18.10.72	Copenhagen	(W)Denmark	W 4-1
15.11.72	Hampden	(W)Denmark	W 4-0
14.2.73	Hampden	England	L 0-5
12.5.73	Wrexham	Wales	W 2-0
16.5.73	Hampden	N. Ireland	L 1-2
19.5.73	Wembley	England	L 0-1
22.6.73	Bern	Switzerland	L 0-1
30.6.73	Hampden	Brazil	L 0-1
26.9.73	Hampden	(W)Czechoslovakia	W 2-1
17.10.73	Bratislava	(W)Czechoslovakia	L 0-1
14.11.73	Hampden	West Germany	D 1-1
27.3.74	Frankfurt	West Germany	L 1-2
11.5.74	Hampden†	N. Ireland	L 0-1
14.5.74	Hampden	Wales	W 2-0
18.5.74	Hampden	England	W 2-0
1.6.74	Bruges	Belgium	L 1-2
6.6.74	Oslo	Norway	W 2-1
14.6.74	Dortmund	(W)Zaire	W 2-0
18.6.74	Frankfurt	(W)Brazil	D 0-0
22.6.74	Frankfurt	(W)Yugoslavia	D 1-1
30.10.74	Hampden	East Germany	W 3-0
20.11.74	Hampden	(E)Spain	L 1-2
5.2.75	Valencia	(E)Spain	D 1-1
16.4.75	Gothenburg	Sweden	D 1-1
13.5.75	Hampden	Portugal	W 1-0
17.5.75	Cardiff	Wales	D 2-2
20.5.75	Hampden	N. Ireland	W 3-0
24.5.75	Wembley	England	L 1-5
1.6.75	Bucharest	(E)Rumania	D 1-1
3.9.75	Copenhagen	(E)Denmark	W 1-0
29.10.75	Hampden	(E)Denmark	W 3-1
17.12.75	Hampden	(E)Rumania	D 1-1
7.4.76	Hampden	Switzerland	W 1-0
6.5.76	Hampden	Wales	W 3-1
8.5.76	Hampden†	N. Ireland	W 3-0
15.5.76	Hampden	England	W 2-1
8.9.76	Hampden	Finland	W 6-0
13.10.76	Prague	(W)Czechoslovakia	L 0-2
17.11.76	Hampden	(W)Wales	W 1-0
27.4.77	Hampden	Sweden	W 3-1
28.5.77	Wrexham	Wales	D 0-0
1.6.77	Hampden	N. Ireland	W 3-0
4.6.77	Wembley	England	W 2-1
15.6.77	Santiago	Chile	W 4-2
18.6.77	Buenos Aires	Argentina	D 1-1
23.6.77	Rio	Brazil	L 0-2
7.9.77	East Berlin	East Germany	L 0-1
21.9.77	Hampden	(W)Czechoslovakia	W 3-1
12.10.77	Anfield‡	(W)Wales	W 2-0
22.2.78	Hampden	Bulgaria	W 2-1
13.5.78	Hampden†	N. Ireland	D 1-1
17.5.78	Hampden	Wales	D 1-1
20.5.78	Hampden	England	L 0-1
3.6.78	Cordoba	(W)Peru	L 1-3
7.6.78	Cordoba	(W)Iran	D 1-1
11.6.78	Mendoza	(W)Holland	W 3-2
20.9.78	Vienna	(E)Austria	L 2-3
25.10.78	Hampden	(E)Norway	W 3-2
29.11.78	Lisbon	(E)Portugal	L 0-1
19.5.79	Cardiff	Wales	L 0-3
22.5.79	Hampden	N. Ireland	W 1-0
26.5.79	Wembley	England	L 1-3
2.6.79	Hampden	Argentina	L 1-3
7.6.79	Oslo	(E)Norway	W 4-0
12.9.79	Hampden	Peru	D 1-1
17.10.79	Hampden	(E)Austria	D 1-1
21.11.79	Brussels	(E)Belgium	L 0-2
19.12.79	Hampden	(E)Belgium	L 1-3
26.3.80	Hampden	(E)Portugal	W 4-1
17.5.80	Belfast	N. Ireland	L 0-1
21.5.80	Cardiff	Wales	D 1-1
24.5.80	Hampden	England	L 0-2
28.5.80	Poznan	Poland	L 0-1
31.5.80	Budapest	Hungary	L 1-3
10.9.80	Stockholm	(W)Sweden	W 1-0
15.10.80	Hampden	(W)Portugal	D 0-0
25.2.81	Tel Aviv	(W)Israel	W 1-0
25.3.81	Hampden	(W)N. Ireland	D 1-1
29.4.81	Hampden	(W)Israel	W 3-1
16.5.81	Cardiff	Wales	L 0-2
19.5.81	Hampden	N. Ireland	W 2-0
23.5.81	Wembley	England	W 1-0
10.9.81	Hampden	(W)Sweden	W 2-0
14.10.81	Belfast	(W)N. Ireland	D 0-0
18.11.81	Lisbon	(W)Portugal	L 1-2
24.2.82	Valencia	Spain	L 0-3
23.3.82	Hampden	Holland	W 2-1
28.4.82	Belfast	N Ireland	D 1-1
24.5.82	Hampden	Wales	W 1-0
29.5.82	Hampden	England	L 0-1
15.6.82	Malaga	(W)New Zealand	W 5-2
18.6.82	Seville	(W)Brazil	L 1-4
22.6.82	Malaga	(W)Soviet Union	D 2-2
13.10.82	Hampden	(E)E. Germany	W 2-0
17.11.82	Bern	(E)Switzerland	L 0-2
15.12.82	Brussels	(E)Belgium	L 2-3
30.3.83	Hampden	(E)Switzerland	D 2-2
24.5.83	Hampden	N. Ireland	D 0-0
28.5.83	Cardiff	Wales	W 2-0
1.6.83	Wembley	England	L 0-2
12.6.83	Vancouver	Canada	W 2-0
16.6.83	Edmonton	Canada	W 3-0
19.6.83	Toronto	Canada	W 2-0
21.9.83	Hampden	Uruguay	W 2-0

(W) World Cup (E) European Nations Cup/European Championship *Home International Championship used as qualifying tournament †switched from Belfast because of political troubles ‡played at Anfield because of severe capacity restriction at Ninian Park §abandoned by referee after 79 minutes

WALES' FULL INTERNATIONAL RECORD

Date	Venue	Country	Result
25.3.76	Hamilton Cr.	Scotland	L 0-4
5.3.77	Wrexham	Scotland	L 0-2
23.3.78	1st Hampden	Scotland	L 0-9
18.1.79	The Oval	England	L 1-2
7.4.79	Wrexham	Scotland	L 0-3
15.3.80	Wrexham	England	L 2-3
3.4.80	1st Hampden	Scotland	L 1-5
26.2.81	Blackburn	England	W 1-0
14.3.81	Wrexham	Scotland	L 1-5
25.2.82	Wrexham	Ireland	W 7-1
13.3.82	Wrexham	England	W 5-3
25.3.82	1st Hampden	Scotland	L 0-5
3.2.83	The Oval	England	L 0-5
12.3.83	Wrexham	Scotland	L 0-3
17.3.83	Belfast	Ireland	D 1-1
9.2.84	Wrexham	Ireland	W 6-0
17.3.84	Wrexham	England	L 0-4
29.3.84	1st Cathkin	Scotland	L 1-4
14.3.85	Blackburn	England	D 1-1
23.3.85	Wrexham	Scotland	L 1-8
11.4.85	Belfast	Ireland	W 8-2
27.2.86	Wrexham	Ireland	W 5-0
29.3.86	Wrexham	England	L 1-3
10.4.86	2nd Hampden	Scotland	L 1-4
26.2.87	The Oval	England	L 0-4
12.3.87	Belfast	Ireland	L 1-4
21.3.87	Wrexham	Scotland	L 0-2
4.2.88	Crewe	England	L 1-5
3.3.88	Wrexham	Ireland	W 11-0
10.3.88	Easter Road	Scotland	L 1-5
23.2.89	Stoke	England	L 1-4
15.4.89	Wrexham	Scotland	D 0-0
27.4.89	Belfast	Ireland	W 3-1
8.2.90	Shrewsbury	Ireland	W 5-2
15.3.90	Wrexham	England	L 1-3
22.3.90	Paisley	Scotland	L 0-5
7.2.91	Belfast	Ireland	L 2-7
7.3.91	Sunderland	England	L 1-4
21.3.91	Wrexham	Scotland	L 3-4
27.2.92	Bangor (Wa.)	Ireland	D 1-1
5.3.92	Wrexham	England	L 0-2
26.3.92	Tynecastle	Scotland	L 1-6
13.3.93	Stoke	England	L 0-6
18.3.93	Wrexham	Scotland	L 0-8
8.4.93	Belfast	Ireland	L 3-4
24.2.94	Swansea	Ireland	W 4-1
12.3.94	Wrexham	England	L 1-5
24.3.94	Kilmarnock	Scotland	L 2-5
16.3.95	Belfast	Ireland	D 2-2
18.3.95	Kensington	England	D 1-1
23.3.95	Wrexham	Scotland	D 2-2
29.2.96	Wrexham	Ireland	W 6-1
16.3.96	Cardiff	England	L 1-9
21.3.96	Carolina, D'dee	Scotland	L 0-4
6.3.97	Belfast	Ireland	L 3-4
20.3.97	Wrexham	Scotland	D 2-2
29.3.97	Bramall Lane	England	L 0-4
19.2.98	Llandudno	Ireland	L 0-1
19.3.98	Motherwell	Scotland	L 2-5
28.3.98	Wrexham	England	L 0-3
4.3.99	Belfast	Ireland	L 0-1
18.3.99	Wrexham	Scotland	L 0-6
20.3.99	Bristol	England	L 0-4
3.2.1900	Aberdeen	Scotland	L 2-5
24.2.00	Llandudno	Ireland	W 2-0
26.3.00	Cardiff	England	D 1-1
2.3.01	Wrexham	Scotland	D 1-1
18.3.01	Newcastle	England	L 0-6
23.3.01	Llandudno	Ireland	W 1-0
3.3.02	Wrexham	England	D 0-0
15.3.02	Greenock	Scotland	L 1-5
22.3.02	Cardiff	Ireland	L 0-3
2.3.03	Portsmouth	England	L 1-2
9.3.03	Cardiff	Scotland	L 0-1
28.3.03	Belfast	Ireland	L 0-2
29.2.04	Wrexham	England	D 2-2
12.3.04	Dens Park	Scotland	D 1-1
21.3.04	Bangor (Wa.)	Ireland	L 0-1
6.3.05	Wrexham	Scotland	W 3-1
27.3.05	Goodison	England	L 1-3
8.4.05	Belfast	Ireland	D 2-2
3.3.06	Tynecastle	Scotland	W 2-0
19.3.06	Cardiff	England	L 0-1
2.4.06	Wrexham	Ireland	D 4-4
23.2.07	Belfast	Ireland	W 3-2
4.3.07	Wrexham	Scotland	W 1-0
18.3.07	Fulham	England	D 1-1
7.3.08	Dens Park	Scotland	L 1-2
16.3.08	Wrexham	England	L 1-7
11.4.08	Aberdare	Ireland	L 0-1
1.3.09	Wrexham	Scotland	W 3-2
15.3.09	Trent Bridge	England	L 0-2
20.3.09	Belfast	Ireland	W 3-2
5.3.10	Kilmarnock	Scotland	L 0-1
14.3.10	Cardiff	England	L 0-1
11.4.10	Wrexham	Ireland	W 4-1
28.1.11	Belfast	Ireland	W 2-1
6.3.11	Cardiff	Scotland	D 2-2
13.3.11	Millwall	England	L 0-3
2.3.12	Tynecastle	Scotland	L 0-1
11.3.12	Wrexham	England	L 0-2
13.4.12	Cardiff	Ireland	L 2-3
18.1.13	Belfast	Ireland	W 1-0
3.3.13	Wrexham	Scotland	D 0-0
17.3.13	Bristol	England	L 3-4
19.1.14	Wrexham	Ireland	L 1-2
28.2.14	Parkhead	Scotland	D 0-0
16.3.14	Cardiff	England	L 0-2
14.2.20	Belfast	Ireland	D 2-2
26.2.20	Cardiff	Scotland	D 1-1
15.3.20	Highbury	England	W 2-1
12.2.21	Aberdeen	Scotland	L 1-2
14.3.21	Cardiff	England	D 0-0
9.4.21	Swansea	Ireland	W 2-1
4.2.22	Wrexham	Scotland	W 2-1
13.3.22	Goodison	England	L 0-1
1.4.22	Belfast	N. Ireland	D 1-1
5.3.23	Cardiff	England	D 2-2
17.3.23	Paisley	Scotland	L 0-2
14.4.23	Wrexham	N. Ireland	L 0-3
16.2.24	Cardiff	Scotland	W 2-0
3.3.24	Blackburn	England	W 2-1
15.3.24	Belfast	N. Ireland	W 1-0
14.2.25	Tynecastle	Scotland	L 1-3
28.2.25	Swansea	England	L 1-2
18.4.25	Wrexham	N. Ireland	D 0-0
31.10.25	Cardiff	Scotland	L 0-3
13.2.26	Belfast	N. Ireland	L 0-3
1.3.26	Selhurst Park	England	W 3-1
30.10.26	Ibrox	Scotland	L 0-3
12.2.27	Wrexham	England	D 3-3
9.4.27	Cardiff	N. Ireland	D 2-2
29.10.27	Wrexham	Scotland	D 2-2
28.11.27	Burnley	England	W 2-1
4.2.28	Belfast	N. Ireland	W 2-1
27.10.28	Ibrox	Scotland	L 2-4
17.11.28	Swansea	England	L 2-3
2.2.29	Wrexham	N. Ireland	D 2-2
26.10.29	Cardiff	Scotland	L 2-4
20.11.29	Stamford Br.	England	L 0-6
1.2.30	Belfast	N. Ireland	L 0-7
25.10.30	Ibrox	Scotland	D 1-1
22.11.30	Wrexham	England	L 0-4
22.4.31	Wrexham	N. Ireland	W 3-2
31.10.31	Wrexham	Scotland	L 2-3
18.11.31	Liverpool	England	L 1-3
5.12.31	Belfast	N. Ireland	L 0-4
26.10.32	Tynecastle	Scotland	W 5-2
16.11.32	Wrexham	England	D 0-0
7.12.32	Wrexham	N. Ireland	W 4-1
25.5.33	Paris	France	D 1-1
4.10.33	Cardiff	Scotland	W 3-2
4.11.33	Belfast	N. Ireland	D 1-1
15.11.33	Newcastle	England	W 2-1
29.9.34	Cardiff	England	L 0-4
21.11.34	Aberdeen	Scotland	L 2-3
27.3.35	Wrexham	N. Ireland	W 3-1
5.10.35	Cardiff	Scotland	D 1-1
5.2.36	Wolver'ton	England	W 2-1
11.3.36	Belfast	N. Ireland	L 2-3
17.10.36	Cardiff	England	W 2-1
2.12.36	Dens Park	Scotland	W 2-1
17.3.37	Wrexham	N. Ireland	W 4-1
30.10.37	Cardiff	Scotland	W 2-1
17.11.37	Middlesbr'	England	L 1-2
16.3.38	Belfast	N. Ireland	L 0-1
22.10.38	Cardiff	England	W 4-2
9.11.38	Tynecastle	Scotland	L 2-3
15.3.39	Wrexham	N. Ireland	W 3-1
20.5.39	Paris	France	L 1-2
19.10.46	Wrexham	Scotland	W 3-1
13.11.46	Maine Road	England	L 0-3
16.4.47	Belfast	N. Ireland	L 1-2
18.10.47	Cardiff	England	L 0-3
12.11.47	Hampden	Scotland	W 2-1
10.3.48	Wrexham	N. Ireland	W 2-0
23.10.48	Cardiff	Scotland	L 1-3
10.11.48	Villa Park	England	L 0-1
9.3.49	Belfast	N. Ireland	W 2-0
15.5.49	Lisbon	Portugal	L 2-3
22.5.49	Liege	Belgium	L 1-3
26.5.49	Bern	Switzerland	L 0-4
15.10.49	Cardiff	*(W)England	L 1-4
9.11.49	Hampden	*(W)Scotland	L 0-2
23.11.49	Cardiff	Belgium	W 5-1
8.3.50	Wrexham	*(W)N. Ireland	D 0-0
21.10.50	Cardiff	Scotland	L 1-3
15.11.50	Sunderland	England	L 2-4
7.3.51	Belfast	N. Ireland	W 2-1
12.5.51	Cardiff	Portugal	W 2-1
16.5.51	Wrexham	Switzerland	W 3-2
20.10.51	Cardiff	England	D 1-1
14.11.51	Hampden	Scotland	W 1-0
5.12.51	Cardiff	Rest of UK	W 3-2
19.3.52	Swansea	N. Ireland	W 3-0
18.10.52	Cardiff	Scotland	L 1-2
12.11.52	Wembley	England	L 2-5

England captain A. Bower shakes hands with Welsh captain Fred Keenor at Swansea on 28 Feb 1925, when Wales won 2-1. A full-back with Corinthians, Bower was the last amateur ever to captain the full England side. Keenor was also Welsh captain v Scotland on 16 Feb 1924 when Cardiff team-mate Jock Blair captained the Scots – a unique distinction for club team-mates.

Date	Venue	Country	Result
15.4.53	Belfast	N. Ireland	W 3-2
14.5.53	Paris	France	L 1-6
21.5.53	Belgrade	Yugoslavia	L 2-5
10.10.53	Cardiff	*(W)England	L 1-4
4.11.53	Hampden	*(W)Scotland	D 3-3
31.3.54	Wrexham	*(W)N. Ireland	L 1-2
9.5.54	Vienna	Austria	L 0-2
22.9.54	Cardiff	Yugoslavia	L 1-3
16.10.54	Cardiff	Scotland	L 0-1
10.11.54	Wembley	England	L 2-3
20.4.55	Belfast	N. Ireland	W 3-2
22.10.55	Cardiff	England	W 2-1
9.11.55	Hampden	Scotland	L 0-2
23.11.55	Wrexham	Austria	L 1-2
11.4.56	Cardiff	N. Ireland	D 1-1
20.10.56	Cardiff	Scotland	D 2-2
14.11.56	Wembley	England	L 1-3
10.4.57	Belfast	N. Ireland	D 0-0
1.5.57	Cardiff	(W)Czechoslovakia	W 1-0
19.5.57	Leipzig	(W)East Germany	L 1-2
26.5.57	Prague	(W)Czechoslovakia	L 0-2
25.9.57	Cardiff	(W)East Germany	W 4-1
19.10.57	Cardiff	England	L 0-4
13.11.57	Hampden	Scotland	D 1-1
15.1.58	Tel Aviv	(W)Israel	W 2-0
5.2.58	Cardiff	(W)Israel	W 2-0
16.4.58	Cardiff	N. Ireland	D 1-1
8.6.58	Sandviken	(W)Hungary	D 1-1
11.6.58	Stockholm	(W)Mexico	D 1-1
15.6.58	Stockholm	(W)Sweden	D 0-0
17.6.58	Stockholm	(W)Hungary	W 2-1
19.6.58	Gothenburg	(W)Brazil	L 0-1
18.10.58	Cardiff	Scotland	L 0-3
26.11.58	Villa Park	England	D 2-2
22.4.59	Belfast	N. Ireland	L 1-4
17.10.59	Cardiff	England	D 1-1
4.11.59	Hampden	Scotland	D 1-1
6.4.60	Wrexham	N. Ireland	W 3-2
28.9.60	Dublin	Eire	W 3-2
22.10.60	Cardiff	Scotland	W 2-0
23.11.60	Wembley	England	L 1-5
12.4.61	Belfast	N. Ireland	W 5-1
19.4.61	Cardiff	(W)Spain	L 1-2
18.5.61	Madrid	(W)Spain	D 1-1
28.5.61	Budapest	Hungary	L 2-3
14.10.61	Cardiff	England	D 1-1
8.11.61	Hampden	Scotland	L 0-2
11.4.62	Cardiff	N. Ireland	W 4-0
12.5.62	Rio	Brazil	L 1-3
16.5.62	Sao Paulo	Brazil	L 1-3
22.5.62	Mexico City	Mexico	L 1-2
20.10.62	Cardiff	Scotland	L 2-3
7.11.62	Budapest	(E)Hungary	L 1-3
21.11.62	Wembley	England	L 0-4
20.3.63	Cardiff	(E)Hungary	D 1-1
3.4.63	Belfast	N. Ireland	W 4-1
12.10.63	Cardiff	England	L 0-4
20.11.63	Hampden	Scotland	L 1-2
15.4.64	Swansea	N. Ireland	W 3-2
3.10.64	Cardiff	Scotland	W 3-2
21.10.64	Copenhagen	(W)Denmark	L 0-1
18.11.64	Wembley	England	L 1-2
9.12.64	Athens	(W)Greece	L 0-2
17.3.65	Cardiff	(W)Greece	W 4-1
31.3.65	Belfast	N. Ireland	W 5-0
1.5.65	Florence	Italy	L 1-4
30.5.65	Moscow	(W)USSR	L 1-2
2.10.65	Cardiff	England	D 0-0
27.10.65	Cardiff	(W)USSR	W 2-1
24.11.65	Hampden	Scotland	L 1-4
1.12.65	Wrexham	(W)Denmark	W 4-2
30.3.66	Cardiff	N. Ireland	L 1-4
14.5.66	Rio	Brazil	L 1-3
18.5.66	B. Horizonte	Brazil	L 0-1
22.5.66	Santiago	Chile	L 0-2
22.10.66	Cardiff	*(E)Scotland	D 1-1
16.11.66	Wembley	*(E)England	L 1-5
12.4.67	Belfast	*(E)N. Ireland	D 0-0
21.10.67	Cardiff	*(E)England	L 0-3
22.11.67	Hampden	*(E)Scotland	L 2-3
28.2.68	Wrexham	*(E)N. Ireland	W 2-0
8.5.68	Cardiff	West Germany	D 1-1
23.10.68	Cardiff	(W)Italy	L 0-1
26.3.69	Frankfurt	West Germany	D 1-1
16.4.69	Dresden	(W)East Germany	L 1-2
3.5.69	Wrexham	Scotland	L 3-5
7.5.69	Wembley	England	L 1-2
10.5.69	Belfast	N. Ireland	D 0-0
28.7.69	Cardiff	Rest of UK	L 0-1
22.10.69	Cardiff	(W)East Germany	L 1-3
4.11.69	Rome	(W)Italy	L 1-4
18.4.70	Cardiff	England	D 1-1
22.4.70	Hampden	Scotland	D 0-0
25.4.70	Swansea	N. Ireland	W 1-0
11.11.70	Cardiff	(E)Rumania	D 0-0
21.4.71	Swansea	(E)Czechoslovakia	L 1-3
15.5.71	Cardiff	Scotland	D 0-0
18.5.71	Wembley	England	D 0-0
22.5.71	Belfast	N. Ireland	L 0-1
26.5.71	Helsinki	(E)Finland	W 1-0
13.10.71	Swansea	(E)Finland	W 3-0
27.10.71	Prague	(E)Czechoslovakia	L 0-1
24.11.71	Bucharest	(E)Rumania	L 0-2
20.5.72	Cardiff	England	L 0-3
24.5.72	Hampden	Scotland	L 0-1
28.5.72	Wrexham	N. Ireland	D 0-0
15.11.72	Cardiff	(W)England	L 0-1
24.1.73	Wembley	(W)England	D 1-1
28.3.73	Cardiff	(W)Poland	W 2-0
12.5.73	Wrexham	Scotland	L 0-2
15.5.73	Wembley	England	L 0-3
19.5.73	Goodison†	N. Ireland	L 0-1
26.9.73	Katowice	(W)Poland	L 0-3
11.5.74	Cardiff	England	L 0-2
14.5.74	Hampden	Scotland	L 0-2
18.5.74	Wrexham	N. Ireland	W 1-0
4.9.74	Vienna	(E)Austria	L 1-2
30.10.74	Cardiff	(E)Hungary	W 2-0
20.11.74	Swansea	(E)Luxembourg	W 5-0
16.4.75	Budapest	(E)Hungary	W 2-1
1.5.75	Luxembourg	(E)Luxembourg	W 3-1
17.5.75	Cardiff	Scotland	D 2-2
21.5.75	Wembley	England	D 2-2
23.5.75	Belfast	N. Ireland	L 0-1
19.11.75	Wrexham	(E)Austria	W 1-0
24.3.76	Wrexham	England	L 1-2
24.4.76	Zagreb	(E)Yugoslavia	L 0-2
6.5.76	Hampden	Scotland	L 1-3
8.5.76	Cardiff	England	L 0-1
14.5.76	Swansea	N. Ireland	W 1-0
22.5.76	Cardiff	(E)Yugoslavia	D 1-1
6.10.76	Cardiff	West Germany	L 0-2
17.11.76	Hampden	(W)Scotland	L 0-1
30.3.77	Wrexham	(W)Czechoslovakia	W 3-0
28.5.77	Wrexham	Scotland	D 0-0
31.5.77	Wembley	England	W 1-0
3.6.77	Belfast	N. Ireland	D 1-1
6.9.77	Wrexham	Kuwait	D 0-0
20.9.77	Kuwait	Kuwait	D 0-0
12.10.77	Anfield‡	(W)Scotland	L 0-2
16.11.77	Prague	(W)Czechoslovakia	L 0-1
14.12.77	Dortmund	West Germany	D 1-1
18.4.78	Tehran	Iran	W 1-0
13.5.78	Cardiff	England	L 1-3
17.5.78	Hampden	Scotland	D 1-1
19.5.78	Wrexham	N. Ireland	W 1-0
25.10.78	Wrexham	(E)Malta	W 7-0
29.11.78	Wrexham	(E)Turkey	W 1-0
2.5.79	Wrexham	(E)West Germany	L 0-2
19.5.79	Cardiff	Scotland	W 3-0
23.5.79	Wembley	England	D 0-0
25.5.79	Belfast	N. Ireland	D 1-1
2.6.79	Valletta	(E)Malta	W 2-0
11.9.79	Swansea	Eire	W 2-1
17.10.79	Cologne	(E)West Germany	L 1-5
21.11.79	Izmir	(E)Turkey	L 0-1
16.5.80	Wrexham	England	W 4-1
21.5.80	Hampden	Scotland	L 0-1
23.5.80	Cardiff	N. Ireland	L 0-1
2.6.80	Reykjavik	(W)Iceland	W 4-0
15.10.80	Cardiff	(W)Turkey	W 4-0
19.11.80	Cardiff	(W)Czechoslovakia	W 1-0
24.2.81	Dublin	Eire	W 3-1
25.3.81	Istanbul	(W)Turkey	W 1-0
16.5.81	Cardiff	Scotland	W 2-0
20.5.81	Wembley	England	D 0-0
22.5.81	Belfast	N. Ireland	Cancelled
30.5.81	Cardiff	(W)USSR	D 0-0
9.9.81	Prague	(W)Czechoslovakia	L 0-2
14.10.81	Swansea	(W)Iceland	D 2-2
28.11.81	Tbilisi	(W)USSR	L 0-3
24.3.82	Valencia	Spain	D 1-1
27.4.82	Cardiff	England	L 0-1
24.5.82	Hampden	Scotland	L 0-1
27.5.82	Wrexham	N. Ireland	W 3-0
2.6.82	Toulouse	France	W 1-0
22.9.82	Swansea	(E)Norway	W 1-0
15.12.82	Titograd	(E)Yugoslavia	D 4-4
23.2.83	Wembley	England	L 1-2
27.4.83	Wrexham	(E)Bulgaria	W 1-0
28.5.83	Cardiff	Scotland	L 0-2
31.5.83	Belfast	N. Ireland	W 1-0
12.6.83	Cardiff	Brazil	D 1-1
21.9.83	Oslo	(E)Norway	D 0-0

(W) World Cup (E) European Nations Cup/European Championship *Home International Championship used as qualifying tournament †matches switched from Belfast because of political troubles ‡played at Anfield because of severe capacity restriction at Cardiff

FIRST-CLASS 'UNOFFICIAL' INTERNATIONALS

Date	Venue	Home		Away	
5.3.1870	The Oval	England	1	Scotland	1
19.11.1870	The Oval	England	1	Scotland	0
28.2.1871	The Oval	England	1	Scotland	1
18.11.1871	The Oval	England	2	Scotland	1
24.2.1871	The Oval	England	1	Scotland	0
19.12.1891	The Oval	England	6	Canada	1
15.3.1899	Crystal Palace	England	1	Scotland	2*
5.4.02	Ibrox	Scotland	1	England	1†
19.4.02	Belfast	Ireland	0	Scotland	2
29.5.29	Oslo	Scotland	4	Norway	0
21.8.35	Hampden Park	Scotland	4	England	2
24.8.46	Maine Road	England	2	Scotland	2††
10.5.47	Hampden	Great Britain	6	Rest of Europe	1
30.4.54	Highbury	England	2	Young England	1
6.5.55	Highbury	England	5	Young England	0
13.8.55	Belfast	Great Britain	1	Rest of Europe	4
3.5.56	Highbury	England	1	Young England	2
2.5.58	Stamford Bridge	England	4	Young England	1
1.5.59	Highbury	England	3	Young England	3
6.5.60	Highbury	England	2	Young England	1
5.5.61	Stamford Bridge	England	1	Young England	1
4.5.62	Highbury	England	3	Young England	2
24.5.63	Highbury	England	3	Young England	2
1.5.64	Stamford Bridge	England	3	Young England	0
30.4.65	Highbury	England	2	Young England	2
13.5.66	Stamford Bridge	England	1	Young England	1
19.5.67	Highbury	England	0	Young England	5
17.5.68	Highbury	England	1	Young England	4
25.4.69	Stamford Bridge	England	0	Young England	0
30.5.76	Philadelphia	Team America	1	England	3

* Benefit game for players' union † Ibrox disaster, declared unofficial †† Bolton disaster fund match

'B' AND COMMONWEALTH INTERNATIONALS

Date	Venue	Home		Away	
29.6.10	Durban	South Africa	0	England	3
23.7.10	Johannesburg	South Africa	2	England	6
30.7.10	Cape Town	South Africa	3	England	6
26.6.20	Durban	South Africa	1	England	3
17.7.20	Johannesburg	South Africa	1	England	3
19.7.20	Cape Town	South Africa	1	England	9
27.6.25	Brisbane	Australia	1	England	5
4.7.25	Sydney	Australia	1	England	2
11.7.25	Maitland, Victoria	Australia	0	England	5
25.7.25	Melbourne	Australia	0	England	2
15.6.29	Durban	South Africa	2	England	3
13.7.29	Johannesburg	South Africa	1	England	2
17.7.29	Cape Town	South Africa	1	England	3
17.6.39	Johannesburg	South Africa	0	England	3
24.6.39	Durban	South Africa	2	England	8
1.7.39	Cape Town	South Africa	1	England	2
15.5.49	Helsinki	Finland	0	England	4
18.5.49	Amsterdam	Holland	0	England	4
18.1.50	Hillsborough	England	5	Switzerland	4
22.2.50	Newcastle	England	1	Holland	0
17.3.50	Amsterdam	Holland	3	England	0
11.5.50	Milan	Italy	5	England	0
21.5.50	Luxembourg	Luxembourg	1	England	2
26.5.51	Sydney	Australia	1	England	4
30.6.51	Sydney	Australia	0	England	17
7.7.51	Brisbane	Australia	1	England	4
14.7.51	Sydney	Australia	1	England	6
21.7.51	Newcastle, NSW	Australia	0	England	5
26.3.52	Amsterdam	Holland	0	England	1
22.5.52	Le Havre	France	7	England	1
29.5.52	Toulouse	France	0	Scotland	0
11.3.53	Easter Road	Scotland	2	England	2
3.3.54	Sunderland	England	1	Scotland	1
23.4.54	Gelsenkirchen	West Germany	0	England	4
16.5.54	Lubljana	Yugoslavia	2	England	1
22.5.54	Basel	Switzerland	2	England	0
23.3.55	Hillsborough	England	1	West Germany	1
19.10.55	Old Trafford	England	5	Yugoslavia	1
29.2.56	Dens Park, Dundee	Scotland	2	England	2
21.3.56	Southampton	England	4	Scotland	1
6.2.57	Villa Park	England	4	Scotland	1
24.10.57	Belfast	N. Ireland	6	Rumania	0
11.11.59	Belfast	N. Ireland	1	France	1
16.3.60	Annecy	France	5	N. Ireland	0
10.6.61	Auckland	New Zealand	1	England	6
28.5.67	Sydney	Australia	0	Scotland	1
30.5.67	Adelaide	Australia	1	Scotland	2
3.6.67	Melbourne	Australia	0	Scotland	2
11.6.69	Newmarket	England	5	New Zealand	0
20.5.70	Quito	Ecuador	1	England	4
4.6.70	Guadalajara	Mexico	0	England	0
13.6.71	Sydney	Australia	0	England	1
20.6.71	Melbourne	Australia	0	England	1
10.7.71	Auckland	New Zealand	0	Wales	1
21.2.78	Augsburg	West Germany	2	England	1
26.4.78	Verona	Italy	1	Scotland	1
30.5.78	Kuala Lumpur	Malaysia	1	England	1
7.6.78	Christchurch	New Zealand	0	England	4
11.6.78	Wellington	New Zealand	1	England	3
14.6.78	Auckland	New Zealand	0	England	4
18.6.78	Singapore	Singapore	0	England	8
28.11.78	Prague	Czechoslovakia	0	England	1
12.6.79	Klagenfurt	Austria	0	England	1
29.5.80	Sydney	Australia	1	England	2
14.10.80	Old Trafford	England	1	USA	0
17.11.80	St Andrew's	England	1	Australia	0

CLUB HONOURS

Seven from one club: The most players from one club to appear in a single international in normal circumstances (i.e. ignoring the four previous examples) is 7. The best example of this was the selection of Cliff Bastin, Ray Bowden, Wilf Copping, Ted Drake, Eddie Hapgood, George Male and Frank Moss to play Italy at Highbury on Wednesday 14 November 1934. All 7 were from the home club, Arsenal, and England defeated the world champions 3–2. Liverpool supplied 7 players for England v Switzerland at Wembley on 7 September 1977. Queen's Park also supplied 7 players for the Scotland teams against England in 1873, 1874 and 1877, while the Irish team beaten 6–1 by Scotland in Glasgow on Saturday 25 March 1893 included 7 Linfield players.

All-Anglos: The only occasion on which the Scottish team was entirely composed of 'Anglos' (Scots players with English clubs) was on Wednesday 25 October 1978 against Norway at Hampden Park. The last time a Scottish team was composed entirely of Scottish League players was on Wednesday 11 May 1966, when Holland won 3–0 at Hampden Park.

INDIVIDUAL CAREERS

Most internationals: 108 – Bobby Moore (West Ham United) for England, 1962–1974.

Most Scottish caps: 90 – Kenny Dalglish had won 90 Scottish caps by the beginning of the 1983–84 season.

Most Welsh caps: 68 – Ivor Allchurch of Swansea Town and Newcastle United won 68 caps between 1951 and 1966.

Most Irish caps: 100 – Pat Jennings won his 100th cap for Northern Ireland in the 3–1 defeat of Austria in Belfast on 21 September 1983.

Most Eire internationals: 60 – Johnny Giles (Manchester United, Leeds United, WBA & Shamrock Rovers), 1960–1979.

Shortest international career: 50 seconds – Tommy Bogan (Hibernian) was carried off after 50 seconds of the wartime international against England at Hampden Park on Saturday 14 April 1945. He never played for Scotland again.

Shortest full international career: 8 minutes – Jim Barrett (West Ham) made his debut for England against Northern Ireland in Belfast on 19 October 1929. He was carried off after 8 minutes and never played for England again. Bogan's appearance (*above*) was not in an official international.

Consecutive appearances: 70 – Billy Wright (Wolves) for England between 3 October 1951 and 28 May 1959.

Consecutive Scottish appearances: 43 – Kenny Dalglish from 8 May 1976 up to 25 February 1981 when he scored the only goal of the game against Israel in Tel Aviv.

Different levels: Terry Venables is the only player to have appeared for a home country at five different levels – schoolboy, youth, amateur, under-23 and full. With the amateur status now abolished, this record can no longer be equalled, though it would be possible to appear at under-21, 'B' and full levels as well as schoolboy and youth.

Fastest selection: In recent times, Billy Steel was picked for Scotland after playing only 7 League matches for Morton in 1946. After playing in just 2 more League games, he was also selected to play for Great Britain against The Rest of Europe in a forward line with Matthews, Mannion, Lawton and Liddell. He had, of course, emerged during the war years, so his limited League experience is somewhat deceptive.

Steve Heighway of Liverpool played for the Republic of Ireland against Poland on Wednesday 23 September 1970 (Poland won 2-0) before making his first-team debut for his club. That came a few days later on 3 October 1970 at home to Chelsea, when he came on as a substitute for Bobby Graham. Taffy Day, a Spurs reserve, was chosen to play for Wales versus Northern Ireland in Belfast on 4 November 1933 before he had ever played another first-class match.

First professional to appear in an international game was James Forrest of Blackburn Rovers on Saturday 21 March 1885. He had previously appeared in 3 other internationals but this was the first occasion on which he had been declared to be a professional. The Scots objected to his selection (professionalism was not legalised north of the border until 1893) and the England manager apparently gave Forrest a slightly different jersey to wear to distinguish him from the amateurs.

RUGBY INTERNATIONALS

First: H.W. Renny-Tailyour (Royal Engineers) was the first man to play for his country at both major winter sports. He played for Scotland against England at rugby in 1872 and in the same fixture at soccer in 1873. He also scored for Royal Engineers in their 1875 FA Cup final win and is the only Scot ever to be capped at both codes.

England: Three English players have been capped in both sports – R.H. Birkett (Clapham Rovers), John W. Sutcliffe (Heckmondwike & Bolton Wanderers) and C.P. Wilson (Hendon & Cambridge University). All were amateurs and the last was John Sutcliffe, whose final international was on 3 March 1902 against Wales. He was the most distinguished of the three, appearing in goal for Bolton in the 1894 Cup final.

Most recent: The most recent example was that of the brothers Kevin and Michael O'Flanagan who are, in fact, the only instances this century. Kevin played 7 soccer internationals for Northern Ireland, 3 for Eire and rugby for Ireland against Australia in 1948. Michael played soccer for Eire against England at Dublin on Monday 30 September 1946 (Kevin also played that day) and rugby for Ireland against Scotland in 1948. As a family record this is, of course, unparalleled. Kevin also played 20 League games for Arsenal and Brentford.

Rugby League: Goalkeeper Dai Davies (Bolton Wanderers), who appeared twice for Wales in 1904, is the only soccer international also to be capped as a **Rugby League** international. In 1908 he also entered the record books when Wales were allowed to use him as a substitute after their goal-keeper Leigh Roose was injured in the international against England (*see* KEEPERS).

DUAL NATIONALITY

Several players have appeared for more than one of the countries in the British Isles, most commonly for both Northern Ireland and Eire. This was quite normal after the Second World War, the most celebrated example being Johnny Carey, who made 28 appearances for Eire and 7 for Ireland (as they then called themselves) between 1937 and 1953. On Saturday 28 September 1946 he played for Northern Ireland against England in Belfast (losing 7-2) and two days later played for Eire against England in Dublin (losing 1-0). In May 1947 he played for the Rest of Europe against Great Britain but could presumably have been selected for either side. Four other players, who appeared in the Belfast team against England also appeared for the Republic in internationals that season – A'hearne, Gorman, McAlinden and Vernon.

Excluding the dual-Irish selections, there have been four examples of United Kingdom players appearing for more than one country:

James Horley-Edwards (Shropshire Wanderers) played for England against Scotland in 1874 and, when Treasurer of the Welsh FA, played for Wales against Scotland two years later, in 1876.

John Reynolds (Distillery, WBA & Aston Villa) played 5 times for Ireland when a player with Distillery in 1890 and 1891. When he moved to West Bromwich it was discovered that he had been born in England and he played 8 times for his native country, the last in 1897.

R.E. Evans (Aston Villa & Sheffield United) played for Wales against England in 1906, 1907, 1908 and 1910 and for England against Wales in 1911 and 1912. In all he played 10 times for Wales and 4 for England and he and Reynolds are the only players to appear on both sides of an annual British fixture.

Joe Kennaway played for Canada against USA in 1928, for USA against Canada in 1930 and then made 2 appearances for Scotland – in 1933 against Austria and in 1934 against Wales. He was thus capped for 3 different countries, though his USA and Canada appearances were not taken too seriously by the Scots in 1933.

Non-native internationals: In 1971 FIFA altered the rule which had theoretically restricted players (without too much success in many cases) to appearing for the country of their birth or, in certain circumstances, the country of their father's birth, to one which allowed appearances for the country of the mother's birth. As a result, non-native internationals (such as Bob Wilson and Bruce Rioch) became much more common in the 1970s and are no longer remarkable when appearing for Scotland, Ireland or Wales. Mick Robinson of Brighton played for Eire in Paris on 28 October 1980 by virtue of one of his great grandmothers being Irish. By the 1980s it was not even uncommon for England players to have been born elsewhere. Indeed, in the side which played against Denmark on 21 September 1983 there were no less than three players who had not been born in England – Terry Butcher was born in Singapore and Luther Blissett and John Barnes were both born in Jamaica.

Never visited home: When John Hewie, the Charlton full-back, played for Scotland against England on 14 April 1956 at Hampden Park it was the first time he had ever been to Scotland in his life. Though his parents were Scots, he had been born in South Africa and lived only there and in England. Richard Gough, the Dundee United right-back who was first capped for Scotland against Switzerland on 17 November 1982, was born in Sweden and grew up with his parents in South Africa.

Scottish defectors: Only two Scotland-born men are known to have appeared for other countries – Stewart Macrae played 6 times for England in seasons 1882–83 and 1883–84 and Bob Milne of Linfield played 27 times for Ireland between 1894 and 1906. Milne originally came to Linfield's notice while playing for the Gordon Highlanders' side which won the Irish Cup in 1890. Four players who appeared in the early unofficial England v Scotland internationals in 1870–71 – W. Lindsay (Winchester), F.B. Maddison (Oxford University), A. Morton (Crystal Palace) and A.K. Smith (Oxford University) – playing for Scotland, later appeared for England in full internationals *against* Scotland.

NON-SENIOR PLAYERS

Since 1920: Since the addition of the Third Division, the non-League player with most appearances for one of the home countries is Lieutenant K.E. Hegan, a winger who played for the Army and Corinthians. He played for England 4 times in 1923 and 1924 and scored 4 goals.

Division 4 players: The first Division 4 player to be capped was Vic Rouse (Crystal Palace), who kept goal for Wales against Northern Ireland on Wednesday 22 April 1959. Several other Division 4 players have since been capped for Eire, Northern Ireland and Wales.

Division 3 players: Four Division 3 players have appeared for England since the Second World War:

Tommy Lawton was the first and most celebrated, having been transferred for a then record £20,000 from Chelsea to Notts County of Division 3S in 1947 while still England's first-choice centre-forward. He played 4 more internationals while with County – v Sweden at Highbury on 19 November 1947, Scotland at Hampden on 10 April 1948, Italy in Turin on 16 May 1948 and Denmark in Copenhagen on 26 September 1948.

Reg Matthews played 5 games in goal while with Coventry City of Division 3S between

14 April 1956 and 6 October 1956.

Johnny Byrne played against Northern Ireland at Wembley on 22 November 1961 while still with Crystal Palace of Division 3.

Peter Taylor played 4 games for England while still with Crystal Palace of Division 3 between 24 March 1976, when he came on as a substitute against Wales at Wrexham, and against Scotland at Hampden Park on 15 May 1976.

Before Second War: International appearances by Third Division players before the War were much more common, though every single one was a player from a Third Division South club. No player from the Third Division North ever represented England. Players that did appear were: J. Fort, R. Hill and F. Fox (Millwall), E. Simms and Joe Payne (Luton), W. Rawlings and F. Titmuss (Southampton), H. Miller and G. Armitage (Charlton), Tommy Cook (Brighton) and L. Oliver (Fulham).

Same team: W. Rawlings and F. Titmuss (both from Southampton) appeared for England against Wales at Goodison on Monday 13 March 1922, the only occasion since the Great War that England have fielded two players from outside the top two divisions in the same team.

Non-English club: The first player to appear for any England side while not playing for an English club was Cyril Rutter of Cardiff City, who played for England 'B' against Holland in Amsterdam on Wednesday 26 March 1952.

Joe Baker was the first man to appear for the full England side while playing outside the country. His first appearance was against Yugoslavia on Wednesday 11 May 1960 at Wembley and he made 5 appearances while still with Hibernian. He remains the only player to have appeared for England while with a Scottish League club. Joe's brother Gerry, though born in Scotland, later made international appearances for the United States.

'B' INTERNATIONALS

A limited number of games in recent years have been designated 'B' internationals, mostly by England, reflecting the growth of the squad system and the need to give all players in the squad competitive fixtures. England occasionally arrange 'B' tours with the England second team usually playing first-class national squads of minor soccer nations, such as New Zealand or Malaysia. The England 'B' squad is often effectively as good as the 'A' squad (as the results of the England against Young England games used to suggest) but many countries, most recently Australia, resent a side with a second-rate nomenclature.

In the 1920s, and as late as 1951, the Football Association sent full international squads to play 'Commonwealth Tour' games in the southern hemisphere. The FA remained confused as to how these games should be recorded and insisted that they were not official internationals – but that any player appearing in a game on the tour should receive one international cap – and

only one, no matter how many matches he appeared in. These games have therefore been included separately. The lists above do not, however, include Under-23, Under-21, FA or Scottish FA representative teams for non-official games or tournaments, sides selected by Leagues rather than Associations, or teams selected to play against sides which were not themselves chosen by the FA of a FIFA country as their national first-choice side. The waters became even muddier in 1982 and 1983 when the home countries began to designate certain games which would previously have been 'B' internationals at best as first-class games. This particularly applied to one game against Iceland in Rejkavik and the two close season tours in 1983 – England's to Australia and Scotland's to Canada. Whatever the doubts about the status of these games, however, it is up to the various FAs to decide when a full cap should be awarded.

See also: GOALSCORERS, SENDINGS OFF

RIGHT: Viv Anderson, who became the first coloured player to appear for the full England side when he played right-back against Czechoslovakia at Wembley on 29 November 1978.
BELOW: Taffy Day (left) and Eugene O'Callaghan leave White Hart Lane to join the Welsh team in Belfast before the Home International there on 4 November 1933. The reason the cameras had turned out for such a mundane event was that Day had never played a first-team match for Spurs or any other senior club. This was the first occasion that a player made his senior debut in an international, though it was equalled in 1970 by Steve Heighway for Eire.

Irish Football

IRISH CUP

Oldest club: The oldest Irish club is Cliftonville, founded on Saturday 11 October 1879. Their first game was against a team of rugby players.

LEFT: Drawn together in the same European Championship group, the two Irelands met for the first time at Lansdowne Road, Dublin, on 20 September 1978.

Most wins: Linfield have won the Irish Cup 33 times (to 1 January 1984).

Most final appearances: Linfield have appeared in 50 finals, though they were also awarded the Cup without contesting it in 1912.

First attempt: Ballymena United won the Cup at their first attempt in 1929 (the final was on 30 May), which was also their first year as a senior club.

Withheld: In 1912 Linfield won one semi-final but the clubs contesting the other semi-final refused to compete further due to a dispute between the Irish FA and the County Antrim FA. Linfield were awarded the Cup while the other major clubs organised a County Antrim Irish Cup, which was won by Belfast Celtic, who beat Glentoran 2-0.

Walked off: Linfield were awarded the Cup in 1899 when, with 15 minutes remaining of the final on 18 March, their opponents Glentoran walked off the field in protest at a refereeing decision. A Linfield player had apparently punched the ball out but the referee had not seen the incident and did not give a penalty. Linfield were leading 1-0 at the time.

In 1919–20 the semi-final between Belfast Celtic and Glentoran was disrupted when shots were fired in the crowd. Celtic were held responsible and disqualified, but they then claimed that Glentoran had fielded an ineligible player, and they also were disqualified. This left Shelbourne, winners of the other semi-final, to take the trophy by default. In 1886 the Cup was withheld after a violent final, in which Distillery beat Limavady 1-0 and later sued the Irish FA to try and get the winners' medals.

Last Southern winner: Shelbourne of Dublin were awarded the trophy in 1919–20 (*above*). This was the last occasion on which the senior Southern clubs entered.

Non-senior clubs: Willowfield were not a senior club (and never have been) when they won the Cup in 1928, beating Larne 1-0. Termed an Intermediate club, Willowfield had beaten Belfast Celtic 2-1 in a semi-final replay. Dundela, another Intermediate club, also won the Cup in 1955, convincingly beating Glenavon (of Lurgan) 3-0. Carrick Rangers were a junior club when they won the Irish Cup in 1976.

Goalscoring: Joe Bambrick performed the most notable scoring feat in finals of the Irish Cup on 29 May 1930 (just 4 months after he had set up the British record of 6 goals in an international) when he scored all 4 of Linfield's goals in a 4-3 defeat of Ballymena United in the final, played at the Belfast Oval.

IRISH LEAGUE

Most wins: Linfield have won the Irish League 35 times (to 1 January 1984)

Grand slam: Linfield created an Irish record (both sides of the border) when they carried off all available trophies in 1921–22 – the Irish League, the Irish Cup, the Irish League

IRISH FA CUP FINALS

Yr	Winners		Runners-up		Yr	Winners		Runners-up		Yr	Winners		Runners-up	
1881	Moyola Park	1	Cliftonville	0	1915	Linfield	1	Belfast Celtic	0	1950	Linfield	2	Distillery	1
1882	Queen's Island	2	Cliftonville	1	1916	Linfield	1	Glentoran	0	1951	Glentoran	3	Ballymena Utd	1
1883	Cliftonville	5	Ulster	0	1917	Glentoran	2	Belfast Celtic	0	1952	Ards	1	Glentoran	0
1884	Distillery	5	Wellington Park	0	1918	Belfast Celtic	0:0:2	Linfield	0:0:0	1953	Linfield	5	Coleraine	0
1885	Distillery	2	Limavady	0	1919	Linfield	1:0:2	Glentoran	1:0:1	1954	Derry City	2:0:1	Glentoran	2:0:0
1886	Cup withheld*				1920	Shelbourne‡				1955	Dundela	3	Glenavon	0
1887	Ulster	3	Cliftonville	0	1921	Glentoran	2	Glenavon	0	1956	Distillery	2:1:1	Glentoran	2:1:0
1888	Cliftonville	2	Distillery	1	1922	Linfield	2	Glenavon	0	1957	Glenavon	2	Derry City	0
1889	Distillery	5	YMCA	4	1923	Linfield	2	Glentoran	0	1958	Ballymena Utd	2	Linfield	0
1890	Gordon High.	2:3	Cliftonville	2:1	1924	Queen's Island	1	Willowfield	0	1959	Glenavon	1:2	Ballymena Utd	1:0
1891	Linfield	4	Ulster	2	1925	Distillery	2	Glentoran	1	1960	Linfield	5	Ards	1
1892	Linfield	7	The Black Watch	0	1926	Belfast Celtic	3	Linfield	2	1961	Glenavon	5	Linfield	1
1893	Linfield	5	Cliftonville	1	1927	Ards	3	Cliftonville	2	1962	Linfield	4	Portadown	0
1894	Distillery	2:3	Linfield	2:2	1928	Willowfield	1	Larne	0	1963	Linfield	2	Distillery	1
1895	Linfield	10	Bohemians	1	1929	Ballymena Utd	2	Belfast Celtic	1	1964	Derry City	2	Glentoran	0
1896	Distillery	3	Glentoran	1	1930	Linfield	4	Ballymena Utd	3	1965	Coleraine	2	Glenavon	1
1897	Cliftonville	3	Sherwood For.	1	1931	Linfield	3	Ballymena Utd	0	1966	Glentoran	2	Linfield	0
1898	Linfield	2	St Columb's Hall Celtic	0	1932	Glentoran	2	Linfield	1	1967	Crusaders	3	Glentoran	1
1899	Linfield†				1933	Glentoran	1:1:3	Distillery	1:1:1	1968	Crusaders	2	Linfield	0
1900	Cliftonville	2	Bohemians	1	1934	Linfield	5	Cliftonville	0	1969	Ards	0:4	Distillery	0:2
1901	Cliftonville	1	Freebooters	0	1935	Glentoran	0:0:1	Larne	0:0:0	1970	Linfield	2	Ballymena Utd	1
1902	Linfield	5	Distillery	1	1936	Linfield	0:2	Derry City	0:1	1971	Distillery	3	Derry City	0
1903	Distillery	3	Bohemians	1	1937	Belfast Celtic	3	Linfield	0	1972	Coleraine	2	Portadown	1
1904	Linfield	5	Derry Celtic	0	1938	Belfast Celtic	0:2	Bangor	0:0	1973	Glentoran	3	Linfield	2
1905	Distillery	3	Shelbourne	0	1939	Linfield	2	Ballymena Utd	0	1974	Ards	2	Ballymena Utd	1
1906	Shelbourne	2	Belfast Celtic	0	1940	Ballymena Utd	2	Glenavon	0	1975	Coleraine	1:0:1	Linfield	1:0:0
1907	Cliftonville	0:1	Shelbourne	0:0	1941	Belfast Celtic	1	Linfield	0	1976	Carrick Rangers	2	Linfield	1
1908	Bohemians	1:3	Shelbourne	1:1	1942	Linfield	3	Glentoran	1	1977	Coleraine	4	Linfield	1
1909	Cliftonville	0:2	Bohemians	0:1	1943	Belfast Celtic	1	Glentoran	0	1978	Linfield	3	Ballymena Utd	1
1910	Distillery	1	Cliftonville	0	1944	Belfast Celtic	3	Linfield	1	1979	Cliftonville	3	Portadown	2
1911	Shelbourne	0:2	Bohemians	0:1	1945	Linfield	4	Glentoran	2	1980	Linfield	2	Crusaders	0
1912	Linfield‡				1946	Linfield	3	Distillery	0	1981	Ballymena Utd	1	Glenavon	0
1913	Linfield	2	Glentoran	0	1947	Belfast Celtic	1	Glentoran	0	1982	Linfield	2	Coleraine	1
1914	Glentoran	3	Linfield	1	1948	Linfield	3	Coleraine	0	1983	Glentoran	1:2	Linfield	1:1
					1949	Derry City	3	Glentoran	1					

*Cup withheld after Distillery had won the final against Limavady †Linfield awarded trophy after Glentoran walked off the pitch with the score at 1-0 ‡final not played

IRISH LEAGUE CHAMPIONS

Year	Club	Year	Club
1891	Linfield	1937	Belfast Celtic
1892	Linfield	1938	Belfast Celtic
1893	Linfield	1939	Belfast Celtic
1894	Glentoran	1940	*Not contested*
1895	Linfield	1941	*Not contested*
1896	Distillery	1942	*Not contested*
1897	Glentoran	1943	*Not contested*
1898	Linfield	1944	*Not contested*
1899	Distillery	1945	*Not contested*
1900	Belfast Celtic	1946	*Not contested*
1901	Distillery	1947	Belfast Celtic
1902	Linfield	1948	Belfast Celtic
1903	Distillery	1949	Linfield
1904	Linfield	1950	Linfield
1905	Glentoran	1951	Glentoran
1906	Cliftonville &	1952	Glenavon
	Distillery	1953	Glentoran
1907	Linfield	1954	Linfield
1908	Linfield	1955	Linfield
1909	Linfield	1956	Linfield
1910	Cliftonville	1957	Glenavon
1911	Linfield	1958	Ards
1912	Glentoran	1959	Linfield
1913	Glentoran	1960	Glenavon
1914	Linfield	1961	Linfield
1915	Belfast Celtic	1962	Linfield
1916	*Not contested*	1963	Distillery
1917	*Not contested*	1964	Glentoran
1918	*Not contested*	1965	Derry City
1919	*Not contested*	1966	Linfield
1920	Belfast Celtic	1967	Glentoran
1921	Glentoran	1968	Glentoran
1922	Linfield	1969	Linfield
1923	Linfield	1970	Glentoran
1924	Queen's Island	1971	Linfield
1925	Glentoran	1972	Glentoran
1926	Belfast Celtic	1973	Crusaders
1927	Belfast Celtic	1974	Coleraine
1928	Belfast Celtic	1975	Linfield
1929	Belfast Celtic	1976	Crusaders
1930	Linfield	1977	Glentoran
1931	Glentoran	1978	Linfield
1932	Linfield	1979	Linfield
1933	Belfast Celtic	1980	Linfield
1934	Linfield	1981	Glentoran
1935	Linfield	1982	Linfield
1936	Belfast Celtic	1983	Linfield

LEAGUE OF IRELAND CHAMPIONS

Year	Club	Year	Club
1922	St James' Gate	1953	Shelbourne
1923	Shamrock Rovers	1954	Shamrock Rovers
1924	Bohemians	1955	St Patrick's A.
1925	Shamrock Rovers	1956	St Patrick's A.
1926	Shelbourne	1957	Shamrock Rovers
1927	Shamrock Rovers	1958	Drumcondra
1928	Bohemians	1959	Shamrock Rovers
1929	Shelbourne	1960	Limerick
1930	Bohemians	1961	Drumcondra
1931	Shelbourne	1962	Shelbourne
1932	Shamrock Rovers	1963	Dundalk
1933	Dundalk	1964	Shamrock Rovers
1934	Bohemians	1965	Drumcondra
1935	Dolphin	1966	Waterford
1936	Bohemians	1967	Dundalk
1937	Sligo Rovers	1968	Waterford
1938	Shamrock Rovers	1969	Waterford
1939	Shamrock Rovers	1970	Waterford
1940	St James' Gate	1971	Cork Hibernians
1941	Cork United	1972	Waterford
1942	Cork United	1973	Waterford
1943	Cork United	1974	Cork Celtic
1944	Shelbourne	1975	Bohemians
1945	Cork United	1976	Dundalk
1946	Cork United	1977	Sligo Rovers
1947	Shelbourne	1978	Bohemians
1948	Drumcondra	1979	Dundalk
1949	Drumcondra	1980	Limerick
1950	Cork Athletic	1981	Athlone
1951	Cork Athletic	1982	Dundalk
1952	St Patrick's A	1983	Athlone

FA OF IRELAND CUP WINNERS

Year	Club	Year	Club
1922	St James' Gate	1953	Cork Athletic
1923	Alton United	1954	Drumcondra
1924	Athlone Town	1955	Shamrock Rovers
1925	Shamrock Rovers	1956	Shamrock Rovers
1926	Fordson	1957	Drumcondra
1927	Drumcondra	1958	Dundalk
1928	Bohemians	1959	St Patrick's A.
1929	Shamrock Rovers	1960	Shelbourne
1930	Shamrock Rovers	1961	St Patrick's A.
1931	Shamrock Rovers	1962	Shamrock Rovers
1932	Shamrock Rovers	1963	Shelbourne
1933	Shamrock Rovers	1964	Shamrock Rovers
1934	Cork	1965	Shamrock Rovers
1935	Bohemians	1966	Shamrock Rovers
1936	Shamrock Rovers	1967	Shamrock Rovers
1937	Waterford	1968	Shamrock Rovers
1938	St James' Gate	1969	Shamrock Rovers
1939	Shelbourne	1970	Bohemians
1940	Shamrock Rovers	1971	Limerick
1941	Cork United	1972	Cork Hibernian
1942	Dundalk	1973	Cork Hibernian
1943	Drumcondra	1974	Finn Harps
1944	Shamrock Rovers	1975	Home Farm
1945	Shamrock Rovers	1976	Bohemians
1946	Drumcondra	1977	Dundalk
1947	Cork United	1978	Shamrock Rovers
1948	Shamrock Rovers	1979	Dundalk
1949	Dundalk	1980	Waterford
1950	Transport	1981	Dundalk
1951	Cork Athletic	1982	Limerick
1952	Dundalk	1983	Sligo Rovers

Cup, the Belfast City Cup, the Irish Gold Cup, the Belfast Charity Cup and the County Antrim Shield. Celtic did the same in Scotland in 1907–08 and 1966–67.

FA OF IRELAND CUP

Most wins: Shamrock Rovers have won the Cup 21 times (to 1 January 1984).
Last Northern winners: Alton United in 1923 were the last (and only) club from Northern Ireland to win the FA of Ireland Cup after separation. They were not allowed to carry the trophy back over the border by the Northern authorities.

LEAGUE OF IRELAND

History: The FA of Ireland League was formed on Wednesday 17 August 1921 when the Leinster Association broke away from the Irish FA in Belfast and founded their own League competition in Dublin. Eight Dublin clubs – Bohemians, Dublin United, Frankfort, Olympia, St James's Gate, Shelbourne, YMCA and W & R. Jacobs – formed the first League. Athlone Town, the first provincial club, joined in 1922–23, as did Eire's senior club, Shamrock Rovers. In 1924–25 Fordson (of Cork) joined to make it a truly national league.
Permanent membership: Bohemians (of Dub-

RIGHT: The programme from the Republic of Ireland v Argentina game on 29 May 1979. Ireland drew with the world champions 0-0 but the game was one of the first about which the status of Irish teams was questioned. In actual fact, the team this day eventually included O'Leary, Giles, Grealish, Brady and Stapleton and was therefore a convincing side, but tours of South America with teams composed mainly of League of Ireland players were of complex status at around this time.

lin) are the only club to have competed every year since 1921.
Most wins: Shamrock Rovers have been champions 10 times (to 1 January 1984).
See also: GOALSCORERS, INTERNATIONALS

Journeys

TOURS

First ever: Royal Engineers toured the North Midlands in December 1873, defeating Sheffield 4-0, Derbyshire 2-1 and Nottingham Forest 2-1.

First overseas tour: An Oxford University team tied in an educational visit with a football tour of Germany in 1875.

First outside Europe: Corinthians toured South America in 1897.

First Scottish club: Queen's Park played two matches in Copenhagen against Danish Boldspiel Union in 1898.

First representative: The first official FA team that toured abroad was in 1899, visiting Berlin, Prague and Karlsruhe. The side was not a first-class one, but included such notables as Billy Bassett and Charles Wreford-Brown, the man credited with inventing the name soccer.

First Scottish national tour: May/June 1929 to Norway, Holland and Germany. Their first game was on Sunday 26 May 1929 in Bergen, when they beat Norway 7-3.

Most disastrous tour: Raith Rovers were shipwrecked in the Canary Isles during a tour in the 1920s. All were saved unharmed.

LONGEST

Between League games: On 10 April 1936 (Good Friday) Swansea played Plymouth at Home Park, winning 2-1. The next day they lost 2-0 at St James' Park, Newcastle, having travelled 400 miles. The League apparently paid for first-class sleepers.

Keepers

SCORING GOALS

Career: Ted Scattergood scored 8 goals (all penalties) during his career with Derby and Bradford Park Avenue between 1907 and 1925.

Season: Arnold Birch of Chesterfield scored 5 penalties in Division 3N in 1923–24.

From goal-kicks: Until 1936, defenders were allowed to tap goal-kicks into the keeper's hands, and this led to a goal on Saturday 14 April 1900 when Charlie Williams of Manchester City scored from a goal-kick at Sunderland. Sunderland won 3–1.

Leading scorer: Alex Stepney was Manchester United's joint leading scorer halfway through the 1973-74 season with 2 penalties.

Both keepers scoring: Until 1912 goalkeepers were allowed to handle the ball anywhere in their own half. In 1910 this allowed both Jimmy Brownlie of Third Lanark and Clem Hampton of Motherwell to score in the same game – the only known instance of both keepers scoring in a single match. It was this game which, in part, led to the law being changed in 1912.

Scoring from punts: This was once almost unknown, but with the introduction of lighter balls in recent seasons it occurs much more regularly. Recorded examples are:
- Pat Jennings for Spurs against Manchester United at Old Trafford in the 1967 Charity Shield.
- Peter Shilton for Leicester v Southampton at The Dell on 14 October 1967.
- Ray Cashley for Bristol City versus Hull at Ashton Gate on 18 September 1973.
- Marc de Clerc, Aberdeen's Belgian goalkeeper, away against Berwick in a League Cup second round game on Saturday 30 August 1980.

- Brian Lloyd for Stockport at Bradford City on 10 March 1982. Lloyd's goal put Stockport 1-0 up but Bradford scored five times in the last 17 minutes.
- Jim McDonaugh for Bolton v Burnley on 15 January 1983.
- Steve Sherwood for Watford at Coventry on 14 January 1984. Watford won 2-1.

MOST KEEPERS IN A GAME

Internationals: Welsh keeper Leigh Richmond Roose was injured playing against England at Wrexham on Monday 16 March 1908 and was replaced by full-back Morris. At half-time England agreed to Dai Davies substituting for Morris (*see* SUBSTITUTES) making 3 keepers in all.

None needed: The Arbroath goalkeeper in the 36-0 defeat of Bon Accord in 1885 is reputed not to have touched the ball once. In more recent times, England goalkeeper Gordon Banks did not collect the ball once direct from a Maltese player, nor did it cross the England goal-line, during the 90 minutes of England's 5-0 European Championship defeat of Malta at Wembley on Wednesday 12 May 1971.

In a League game: Several instances of clubs using as many as three keepers in a single game have come to light in recent years:
- Newton Heath played 3 men in goal (Stewart, Fitzsimmons and Clements) on Saturday 7 January 1893 after their usual keeper had missed the train to Stoke. Stoke recorded their biggest win of the season, 7-1.
- West Ham fielded 3 keepers (Ernie Gregory, Tom Moroney, George Dick) versus Lincoln at Sincil Bank on 18 December 1948. Lincoln won 4-3 and Jack Dodds scored against all three keepers.
- Berwick Rangers used 3 keepers against Hamilton in a Division 2 game on Wednesday 24 August 1955. Alex Paterson was injured, replacement defender Runciman was carried off injured 6 minutes later and

another defender, Mitchell, took the jersey. Despite having only 9 fit men, Berwick drew 3-3.
- Huddersfield played three different keepers, (Andy Rankin, Steve Kindon and Mark Lillis) in goal v Shrewsbury in the FA Cup third round on 3 January 1981. Each of the 3 conceded a goal.
- Amazingly, Shrewsbury faced three goalkeepers in the FA Cup again the following season on 6 March 1982 when they played at Leicester in the quarter-finals. Leicester won 5-2 despite having both Wallington and Young injured and Lynex becoming the third keeper.
- Fox, Bracewell and Parkin all kept goal for Stoke v Luton on 25 September 1982. Fox was sent off and Bracewell scored for Stoke after handing over the jersey to Parkin. The game ended 4-4.
- Cardiff City played Andy Dibble, Phil Dwyer (who scored after leaving goal) and Linden Jones in goal v Bradford City on Wednesday 16 February 1983. Bradford won 4-2.

Without conceding a goal: There is some dispute about this record, but it appears that the longest spell a keeper has gone without conceding a goal in first-class football is the 1103 minutes claimed by Steve Death for Reading between 24 March 1979 and a goal scored by one of his defenders for Rochdale in the first game of the next, 1979–80, season. All the games were League matches.

Alan Gilzean turns away in delight, Alex Stepney can't believe it; the best known of all the goals by first-class keepers, and the only one preserved on film was by Pat Jennings for Spurs v Manchester United at Old Trafford in the 1967 Charity Shield. Jennings was the first man to play 1000 first-class matches in England and the first Irishman to win 100 caps.

Longest Matches

SINGLE GAMES

Longest ever: 205 minutes between Stockport and Doncaster in the second leg of a Division 3N War Cup tie (a wartime competition organised by the League and FA) on Saturday 30 March 1946. The aggregate score was 4-4 when bad light forced them to give up.

Longest concluded game: 202 minutes between Cardiff and Bristol City on Saturday 14 April 1945 in a Football League North War Cup tie (another wartime competition) at Ninian Park. After 3 hrs 22 mins Welsh international Billy Rees headed home the decisive goal to give Cardiff a 3-2 win. The game actually kicked off at 3.00 pm and finished at 6.40 pm.

League game: 135 minutes between Sunderland and Derby at Roker Park on Saturday 1 September 1894. The referee did not arrive on time and the game started with one of the linesmen in charge. At half-time, with Sunderland leading 3-0, the referee arrived and insisted on starting the game all over again. Sunderland then scored another 8 and thus ended with an aggregate of 11-0 (though the official score was given as 8-0).

League Cup: 160 minutes (with stoppages) between Southampton and Leeds at The Dell on Monday 5 December 1960. Power failure had cut the floodlights for 62 minutes and Southampton won 5-4 in the last mi-nute. The actual period of play was only 98 minutes.

Scottish game: 142 minutes between Hibernian and Motherwell in the semi-final of the Scottish Cup on Saturday 29 March 1947. The score was 1-1 both at 90 minutes and 120 minutes. They carried on playing until a goal was scored, which Hibs managed after another 22 minutes.

CUP COMPETITIONS

Longest lasting round: The third round of the 1962–63 FA Cup lasted 65 days, from 5 January to 11 March. There were 261 postponements and half the 32 ties were called off 10 times or more.

Longest lasting tie: Stoke and Bury played 5 times before Stoke won the third round of the FA Cup in January 1955 by an aggregate score of 10-9. The tie lasted 9 hrs 22 minutes and ended at Old Trafford. Stoke were knocked out 3-1 by Swansea in the next round. This is a record only for games after qualifying or preliminary rounds.

Finals: No FA Cup final has ever been replayed twice. The 1970 final, when Chelsea beat Leeds, was the only one which lasted 240 minutes and employed extra-time in both games. Four Scottish Cup finals – 1877, 1903, 1910 and 1979 – have gone to two replays.

Semi-finals: Only two semi-finals have gone to four games – and Liverpool lost both of them. In 1899, Sheffield United won after a sequence of 2-2, 4-4, 0-1 (abandoned) and 1-0. In the second game United scored twice in the last 8 minutes (both by Fred Priest) to draw level. United were also fortunate in the third game on Monday 27 March 1899, at Fallowfield, Manchester, after a crowd of 30,000 kept spilling on to the pitch. The game began at 3.30 pm and was eventually abandoned just before 6.00 pm, with only 45 minutes having been completed and Liverpool winning 1-0, United won the fourth game with four reserves in place of injured players, including goalkeeper 'Fatty' Foulke, and went on to beat Derby 4-1 in the final. Receipts from the four games, £3,156, were a world record at the time.

The 1979–80 semi-final series of 4 games between Arsenal and Liverpool actually ran longer – 0-0, 1-1, 1-1 and 1-0, ending after 420 minutes. It was after this series that the FA decided extra-time should be played in the first semi-final if scores were level after 90 minutes. Arsenal, incidentally, lost 1-0 to Second Division West Ham in the final.

See also: FA CUP, REPLAYS

Managers

LONGEST/SHORTEST SERVING

Longest career: William Struth was manager of Glasgow Rangers from August 1920 to April 1953. In this period Rangers won the Championship 15 times, the Scottish Cup 10 times and the Scottish League Cup twice.

Longest English career: Matt Busby was either manager or general manager at Old Trafford from October 1945 to June 1971 – nearly 26 years. His period as sole manager was just over 23 years until Wilf McGuinness came in under him. Other managers

Phil Thompson and Phil Neal (red shirts) exchange despairing glances as Brian Talbot (centre) scores Arsenal's winning goal in the fourth game of the 1979-80 semi-final marathon at Highfield Road. Lasting 420 minutes, this was the longest FA Cup semi-final in history.

have been with a single club for 23 years: Joe Smith was with Blackpool from 1935 to May 1958 and Jimmy Seed was with Charlton from May 1933 to September 1956. Both won the FA Cup for their clubs but could never finish higher than second in the League.

Longest with one club: Willie Maley was with Celtic as player, secretary and manager from December 1887 to February 1939 – over 51 years. He actually played in Celtic's first ever game – a 5-2 win over Rangers. The Celtic captain for that first game, James Kelly, continued his association with the club by becoming Chairman.

Shortest career: Bill Lampton was officially manager of Scunthorpe for just 3 days – from 21 April 1959 to 24 April 1959. In Scotland, the shortest tenure was by Steve Murray, who was appointed manager of Forfar on 18 August 1980 and resigned 5 days later.

Youngest: Carlisle United appointed Ivor Broadis as player-manager in August 1946, when he was aged 23. He had never played first-class professional football, though he had appeared as a wartime amateur for Millwall and Spurs. He created another record when he became the only manager to transfer himself – to Sunderland for £18,000 in September 1949.

Oldest: Joe Fagan was 62 when appointed manager by Liverpool at the start of the 1983–84 season. It was a successful debut Liverpool won the European Cup, Milk Cup and League Championship that season.

Managed most clubs: Bob Stokoe has been appointed manager of a major side on 12 different occasions, though he has been appointed twice at Bury, Rochdale, Blackpool and Carlisle so the record covers only 8 different clubs. Tommy Docherty managed 10 clubs sides, the Scottish national team and was appointed manager of Norwegian club Lillestrom but never arrived to take up the appointment.

Most managers at one club: Doncaster Rovers had 13 managers in 13 years – 1956–69. Walsall have had 20 managers since the Second World War. Crystal Palace had 5 managers in 13 months between October 1980 and November 1981.

MOST SUCCESSFUL

Overall: Only two men can arguably compete for this title – Herbert Chapman and Jock Stein. Chapman, probably the more deserving of the title, managed the only two sides ever to win a hat-trick of League Championships – Huddersfield in 1923–26 and Arsenal in 1932–35. Actually he was with neither for their final success, having left Huddersfield for Highbury in 1925 and dying after a severe cold in 1934. Both clubs also won the FA Cup while he was in charge – Huddersfield in 1922, Arsenal in 1930 (when they beat Huddersfield). Stein won a record 9 consecutive Scottish League titles with Celtic and, in 1966–67, the club won every trophy they contested, including becoming the first British club to win the European Cup.

BELL'S MANAGER OF THE YEAR

Year	Manager
1965–66	Jock Stein (*Celtic*)
1966–67	Jock Stein (*Celtic*)
1967–68	Matt Busby (*Manchester United*)
1968–69	Don Revie (*Leeds United*)
1969–70	Don Revie (*Leeds United*)
1970–71	Bertie Mee (*Arsenal*)
1971–72	Don Revie (*Leeds United*)
1972–73	Bill Shankly (*Liverpool*)
1973–74	Jack Charlton (*Middlesbrough*)
1974–75	Ron Saunders (*Aston Villa*)
1975–76	Bob Paisley (*Liverpool*)
1976–77	Bob Paisley (*Liverpool*)
1977–78	Brian Clough (*Nottingham Forest*)
1978–79	Bob Paisley (*Liverpool*)
1979–80	Bob Paisley (*Liverpool*)
1980–81	Ron Saunders (*Aston Villa*)
1981–82	Bob Paisley (*Liverpool*)
1982–83	Bob Paisley (*Liverpool*)

ABOVE: Taylor and Clough look on as John Robertson's shot hits the post in the 1979 European Cup final. Clough and Herbert Chapman are the only men to manage two separate clubs to the League title.
LEFT: Jock Stein, of Celtic and Scotland.

Two Championship sides: Only Herbert Chapman (*above*) and Brian Clough (Derby in 1972 and Nottingham Forest in 1978) have managed more than one club to a League title.

Two Cup winning sides: Only one man, Billy Walker, has managed two FA Cup winning clubs – Sheffield Wednesday in 1935 and Nottingham Forest in 1959. He also won a Cup winners medal in 1920 with Villa.

127

Medals

MOST WINNERS MEDALS

FA Cup: 5 – Charles H.R. Wollaston (Wanderers) 1872, '73, '76, '77, '78, Lord A.F. Kinnaird (Wanderers) 1873, '77, '78, (Old Etonians) 1879, '82, James H. Forrest (Blackburn Rovers) 1884, '85, '86, '90, '91.

Scottish Cup: 8 – Charles Campbell (Queen's Park) 1874, '75, '76, '80, '81, '82, '84, '86.

Scottish League Cup: 6 – Billy McNeill (Celtic) 1966, '67, '68, '69, '70 and '75.

Football League: 7 – both Phil Thompson and Phil Neal have won 7 Championship winners medals with Liverpool in the period from 1973 to 1984.

Grand slam: Bobby Charlton has come closest to winning all available major awards open to a British player – World Cup 1966, European Cup 1968, League Championship 1957, 1965, 1967, FA Cup 1963, European Footballer of the Year 1966, Footballer of the Year 1966. He did not win a League Cup winners medal, nor appear in a final.

England and Scotland: Dave Mackay is the only man to have been a member of a winning side in the four major domestic competitions – FA Cup with Spurs in 1961,

FAR RIGHT: Alan Sunderland and Pat Rice (right) display their medals at the end of the 1979 FA Cup final. Rice is one of 3 men to receive 5 medals at Wembley.

RIGHT AND BELOW : Alfie Conn established a remarkable record by winning Scottish Cup medals for Rangers against Celtic and vice versa. He scored the second goal for Rangers in 1973 (below) and kept close hold on his Celtic medal in 1977 (right).

1962, 1967, Football League Championship with Spurs in 1961, Scottish Cup with Hearts in 1956 and Scottish League Championship with Hearts in 1958. He also won Scottish League Cup winners medals with Hearts in 1955 and 1959, was joint Footballer of the Year in 1969 and was manager of Derby when that club won the League Championship in 1975. Many Scotsmen have won Scottish and FA Cup winners medals, but only one Englishman has won both – John Welford with Aston Villa in 1895 and with Celtic in 1899.

Aggregate: Billy McNeill won 23 winners medals with Celtic between 1960 and 1975 – 9 Scottish League, 7 Scottish Cup. 6 League Cup and 1 European Cup. He also holds the record aggregate for medals, with 5 Scottish Cup runners-up medals, 3 Scottish League Cup runners-up medals and one European Cup runners-up medal, taking his overall tally to 32 medals. In just Scottish League and Cup, Bob McPhail also won 16 winners medals – 9 Championships with Rangers, 6 Scottish Cups with Rangers and 1 Scottish Cup with Airdrie.

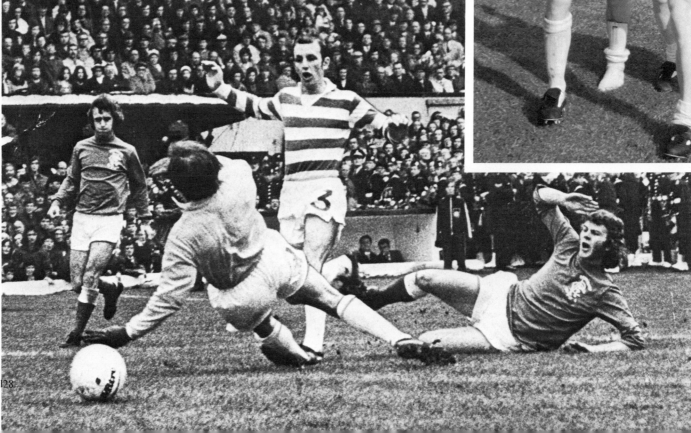

WINNERS AND LOSERS

Aggregate: 32 – Billy McNeill (*above*).

FA Cup: 9 – Lord A.F. Kinnaird played in a record 9 finals with Wanderers and Old Etonians, 5 as a winner.

Scottish Cup: Billy McNeill appeared in 12 Scottish Cup finals.

Four domestic Cups: Jimmy Delaney is the only man to have gained medals in the four major cup competitions in the British Isles. In 1937 he won a Scottish Cup winners medal with Celtic, in 1948 an FA Cup winners medal with Manchester United, in 1954 an Irish Cup winners medal with Derry City and in 1956 a runners-up medal in the FA of Ireland Cup with Cork Athletic.

Appearances at Wembley: Three men made 5 FA Cup final appearances at Wembley:
- Joe Hulme (Arsenal) 1927, '30, '32, '36, (Huddersfield) 1938;
- Johnny Giles (Manchester United) 1963, (Leeds) 1965, '70, '72, '73 (+ League Cup '68);
- Pat Rice (Arsenal) 1971, '72, '78, '79, '80.

Several players have appeared six times in Wembley finals if FA Cup and League Cup are added together, including Pat Jennings, Frank McLintock, Johnny Giles and Ray Clemence.

HAT-TRICKS OF MEDALS

Four consecutive appearances: Five players appeared in four consecutive FA Cup final matches for Wanderers – 1876 plus a replay, 1877 and 1878. They were A.H. Stratford, W. Lindsay, Charles Wollaston, Hubert Heron (whose brother Frank played only in 1876) and J. Kenrick, and they all won 3 winners medals. Seven Blackburn players also appeared in 4 consecutive games in 1884, 1885, 1886 plus a replay. They were goalkeeper Herbert Arthur, Fergus Suter, H. McIntyre, Jimmy Forrest, Jimmy Brown, J. Douglas and J. Sowerbutts. Jimmy Brown scored all 3 years, each of the seven won 3 FA Cup winners medals, and Blackburn used only 17 players in their 4 games.

20th century: 12 players have won three FA Cup winners medals this century:
- Clem Stephenson (Aston Villa and Huddersfield) 1913, '20, '22;
- William Butler, Bob Haworth, Harry Nuttall, Dick Pym and Jimmy Seddon (all of Bolton) 1923, '26, '29;
- David Jack (Bolton Wanderers and Arsenal) 1923, '26, '30;
- Bobby Cowell, Jackie Milburn, Bobby Mitchell (all of Newcastle) 1951, '52, '55;
- Dave Mackay (Tottenham) 1961, '62, '67.
- Cliff Jones (Tottenham) won medals in 1961, 1962 and 1967 but did not play in the 1967 game when he became the first substitute to win an FA Cup winners' medal.

ODDITIES

Amateur Cup/FA Cup: Two players have won both Amateur Cup and FA Cup winners' medals, by coincidence in the same two years. Tom Morren won an Amateur

Cup medal with Middlesbrough in 1895 and an FA Cup medal with Sheffield United in 1899 (plus a runners-up medal in 1901), and Bob Chatt won an FA Cup medal with Aston Villa in 1895 and an Amateur Cup medal with Stockton in 1899.

Four consecutive Wembley finals: Charlton goalkeeper Sam Bartram played in four successive Cup finals at Wembley, two in the Football League Wartime South Cup (which was the premier Cup competition in those war years) and two in the FA Cup

Two games, two medals: Bill Williamson played just two Scottish Cup games for Rangers in 1947–48 and 1948–49, and won 2 Cup winners medals. The games were the replayed 1948 final (1-0 against Morton when he scored the goal) and the 1949 final (4-1 against Clyde, when he again scored).

Amateur and professional: Carlisle-born Seamus O'Connell set up perhaps the most unlikely combination of medals in 1955 when he won both a League Championship medal with Chelsea (an inside-left, he scored 7 goals in 10 appearances) and an Amateur Cup winners medal with Bishop Auckland. Frank Clark gained his League Cup winners medal with Forest in 1978 nearly 16 years after playing for Crook Town in their replay win over Hounslow in the 1962 FA Amateur Cup final. Given a free transfer by Newcastle United in 1975 (the year after his Wembley final for them), Clark went on to get another League Cup winners medal and a European Cup winners medal in 1979.

Glasgow double: Alfie Conn won a Cup winners medal for Rangers against Celtic in 1973 and another Cup winners medal for Celtic against Rangers in 1977.

Different teams: In 1979 Brian Talbot became the only man in the 20th century to gain winners medals with different teams in consecutive FA Cup finals. Lord Kinnaird had done the same with Wanderers in 1878 and Old Etonians in 1879. Talbot and 10 other Arsenal players were the first in the 20th century to win FA Cup medals in three consecutive years, 1978–80. With Nottingham Forest appearing in 3 consecutive League Cup finals from 1978 to 1980 and Liverpool doing the same from 1981 to 1983, the previously almost unknown winning of a hat-trick of medals has become something of a commonplace. In addition, given the relative rarity of players appearing for two different sides in FA Cup finals, this achievement in League Cup finals is surprisingly common. By 1984 as many as 16 players had done so and Ron Saunders had even managed three clubs (Norwich, Manchester City and Aston Villa) to separate League Cup finals.

European Cup: Several Liverpool and Forest players have, of course, won more than one European Cup winners' medal, but Jimmy Rimmer also won two, 14 years apart and played for only 8 minutes in his two finals. In 1968 he was Alex Stepney's deputy and sat on the bench throughout Manchester United's success, while in 1982 he played only the first 8 minutes of Aston

Year	Winner	Year	Winner
1890	Lincoln City	1937	Barnsley Res.
1891	Gainsborough T.	1938	Shrewsbury T.
1892	Rotherham Town	1939	Scunthorpe U.
1893	Rotherham Town	1940	*Not contested*
1894	Burton W.	1941	*Not contested*
1895	Loughborough T.	1942	*Not contested*
1896	Kettering	1943	*Not contested*
1897	Doncaster R.	1944	*Not contested*
1898	Mexborough T.	1945	*Not contested*
1899	Doncaster R.	1946	*Not contested*
1900	Kettering	1947	Grimsby T. Res.
1901	Sheffield U. Res.	1948	Shrewsbury T.
1902	Barnsley Res.	1949	Gainsborough T.
1903	Wednesday Res.	1950	Nottingham F. R.
1904	Sheffield U. Res.	1951	Nottingham F. R.
1905	Sheffield U. Res.	1952	Nottingham F. R.
1906	Wednesday Res.	1953	Nottingham F. R.
1907	Sheffield U. Res.	1954	Nottingham F. R.
1908	Wednesday Res.	1955	Notts Co. Res.
1909	Lincoln City	1956	Peterborough U.
1910	Chesterfield	1957	Peterborough U.
1911	Grimsby Town	1958	Peterborough U.
1912	Rotherham Co.	1959	Peterborough U.
1913	Rotherham Co.	1960	Peterborough U.
1914	Rotherham Co.	1961	*Not contested*
1915	*Not contested*	1962	Matlock Town
1916	*Not contested*	1963	Loughborough U.
1917	*Not contested*	1964	Grantham
1918	*Not contested*	1965	Lockheed Leam.
1919	*Not contested*	1966	Worksop Town
1920	Chesterfield Mun.	1967	Gainsborough T.
1921	Lincoln City	1968	Ilkeston Town
1922	Worksop Town	1969	Matlock Town
1923	Wednesday Res.	1970	Alfreton Town
1924	Mansfield Town	1971	Grantham
1925	Mansfield Town	1972	Grantham
1926	Mexborough T.	1973	Worksop Town
1927	Scunthorpe U.	1974	Alfreton Town
1928	Gainsborough T.	1975	Boston
1929	Mansfield Town	1976	Eastwood Town
1930	Scarborough	1977	Alfreton Town
1931	Grimsby T. Res.	1978	Brigg Town
1932	Bradford Res.	1979	Boston
1933	Grimsby T. Res.	1980	Belper Town
1934	Grimsby T. Res.	1981	Boston
1935	Barnsley Res.	1982	Shepshed
1936	Barnsley Res.	1983	Shepshed

ABOVE: The Midland Counties League, which had a long and proud history of accommodating Football League aspirants such as Peterborough and Scunthorpe, was officially renamed in 1982. In a complete revision of the non-League structure, the major secondary leagues were formed into a pyramid with the Alliance at the top, the Northern Premier, Southern and Isthmian below the Alliance and a group of other leagues below those. The Northern Premier now has two 'feeders', the North West Counties and the Northern Counties East League. The Midland was merged with the Yorkshire League to create the latter and the first winner of the new league was the last winner of the old Midland, Shepshed Charterhouse.

Villa's final against Bayern Munich and was then replaced by Nigel Spink.

England and Scotland: Gordon Smith created a unique record in the 1982–83 season when he appeared in major finals in both England and Scotland in the same season. On 4 December 1982 he was in the Rangers side which lost the Scottish League Cup final to Celtic, and by May 1983 he was in the Brighton side which lost the FA Cup final.

Milk Cup

Name: Originally named the Football League Cup, this competition changed its name in the 1981–82 season, becoming the Milk Cup after its sponsor.

Two Cups: Because the name of the competition was changed in mid-season, Liverpool became the only club ever to be presented with two cups. After defeating Spurs 3-1 in the 1982 final, they were presented with the old Football League Cup and the new Milk Cup.

Winners: Aston Villa have won the Cup on three occasions (1961, 1975 and 1977) and also appeared in two other finals (1963 and 1971). Liverpool won the trophy in three consecutive years (1981, 1982 and 1983) and thus became the first team since Blackburn in 1884–1886 to win a domestic cup competition three years on the trot. Liverpool were also defeated in the 1978 final. Four other sides have also won the trophy on two occasions – Manchester City in 1970 and 1976, Spurs in 1971 and 1973, Wolves in 1974 and 1980 and Nottingham Forest in 1978 and 1979.

Consecutive appearances; Apart from Liverpool (above), Nottingham Forest also appeared in three consecutive finals (1978–1980), winning the first two and losing the third by the only goal of the game to Wolves. Forest thus became the first team this century to appear in three consecutive Cup finals though, oddly, Arsenal did the same in the FA Cup final in the same years and Forest achieved the honour only by virtue of the fact that the League Cup final is traditionally played before the FA Cup final.

(continued on p. 134)

FOOTBALL LG CUP 1960-61

Fourth round

Aston Villa v Plymouth Argyle	3-3, 0-0, 5-3
Blackburn Rovers v Wrexham	1-1, 1-3
Southampton v Leeds United	5-4
Burnley v Nottingham Forest	2-1
Shrewsbury Town v Norwich City	1-0
Tranmere Rovers v Everton	0-4
Portsmouth v Chelsea	1-0
Bolton Wanderers v Rotherham United	0-2

Quarter-finals

Aston Villa v Wrexham	3-0
Southampton v Burnley	2-4
Shrewsbury Town v Everton	2-1
Rotherham United v Portsmouth	3-0

Semi-finals

Burnley v Aston Villa (1-1, 2-2, 1-2*)	4-5
Rotherham U. v Shrewsbury T. (3-2, 1-1)	4-3

Final

Rotherham United 2 Aston Villa 0
(Rotherham, 22.8.61, 12,226)

Rotherham: Ironside, Perry, Morgan, Lambert, Madden, Waterhouse, Webster, Weston, Houghton, Kirkman, Bambridge
Villa: Sims, Lynn, Lee, Crowe, Dugdale, Deakin, McEwan, Thomson, Brown, Wylie, McParland
Scorers: Webster, Kirkman

Aston Villa 3 Rotherham United 0 [aet]
(Villa Park, 5.9.61, 27,000)

Villa: Sidebottom, Neal, Lee, Crowe, Dugdale, Deakin, McEwan, O'Neill, McParland, Thomson, Burrows
Rotherham: Unchanged
Scorers: O'Neill, Burrows, McParland

[Aston Villa won 3-2 on aggregate]

*play-off at Old Trafford

Garry Birtles slips the ball under Terry Gennoe for his and Forest's second goal in the 1979 League Cup final. The first club to retain the trophy, Forest beat Southampton 3-2. Back again playing Wolves in 1980, Forest became the first club to appear in 3 successive Wembley finals.

FOOTBALL LG CUP 1961-62

Fourth round

Blackburn Rovers v Ipswich Town	4-1
Rotherham United v Leeds United	1-1, 2-1
York City v Bournemouth	1-0

[Blackpool, Norwich City, Rochdale, Sheffield United & Sunderland received byes]

Quarter-finals

Sunderland v Norwich City	1-4
Blackpool v Sheffield United	0-0, 2-0
Rotherham United v Blackburn Rovers	0-1
Rochdale v York City	2-1

Semi-finals

Norwich City v Blackpool (4-1, 0-2)	4-3
Rochdale v Blackburn Rovers (3-1, 1-2)	4-3

Final

Rochdale 0 Norwich City 3
(Rochdale, 26.4.62, 11,123)

Rochdale: Burgin, Milburn, Winton, Bodell, Aspden, Thompson, Wragg, Hepton, Bimpson, Cairns, Whitaker
Norwich: Kennon, McCrohan, Ashman, Burton, Butler, Mullett, Mannion, Lythgoe, Scott, Hill, Punton
Scorers: Lythgoe 2, Punton

Norwich City 1 Rochdale 0
(Norwich, 1.5.62, 19,708)

Norwich: Unchanged
Rochdale: Whyke for Wragg, Richardson for Hepton
Scorer: Hill

[Norwich City won 4-0 on aggregate]

FOOTBALL LG CUP 1962-63

Fourth round

Birmingham City v Notts County	3-2
Manchester City v Luton Town	1-0
Leyton Orient v Charlton Athletic	3-2
Bury v Bristol Rovers	3-1
Portsmouth v Sunderland	0-0, 1-2
Blackburn Rovers v Rotherham United	4-1
Norwich City v Fulham	1-0
Aston Villa v Preston North End	6-2

Quarter-finals

Birmingham City v Manchester City	6-0
Leyton Orient v Bury	0-2
Sunderland v Blackburn Rovers	3-2
Aston Villa v Norwich City	4-1

Semi-finals

Birmingham City v Bury (3-2, 1-1)	4-3
Sunderland v Aston Villa (1-3, 0-0)	1-3

Final

Birmingham City 3 Aston Villa 1
(St Andrews, 23.5.63, 31,850)

Birmingham: Schofield, Lynn, Green, Hennessey, Smith, Beard, Hellawell, Bloomfield, Harris, Leek, Auld
Villa: Sims, Fraser, Aitken, Crowe, Sleeuwenhoek, Lee, Baker, Graham, Thomson, Wylie, Burrows
Scorers: Leek 2, Bloomfield; Thomson

Aston Villa 0 Birmingham City 0
(Villa Park, 27.5.63, 37,920)
Villa: Unchanged
Birmingham: Unchanged

[Birmingham City won 3-1 on aggregate]

FOOTBALL LG CUP 1963-64

Fourth round

Leicester City v Gillingham	4-1
Halifax Town v Norwich City	1-7
Workington v Colchester United	2-1
Swindon Town v West Ham United	3-3, 1-4
Manchester City v Leeds United	3-1
Notts County v Portsmouth	3-2
Rotherham United v Millwall	5-2
Stoke City v Bournemouth	2-1

Quarter-finals

Norwich City v Leicester City	1-1, 1-2
West Ham United v Workington	6-0
Notts County v Manchester City	0-1
Stoke City v Rotherham United	3-2

Semi-finals

Leicester City v West Ham United (4-3, 2-0)	6-3
Stoke City v Manchester City (2-1, 0-1)	2-1

Final

Stoke City 1 Leicester City 1
(Stoke, 15.4.64, 22,309)

Stoke: Leslie, Asprey, Allen, Palmer, Kinnell, Skeels, Dobing, Viollet, Ritchie, McIlroy, Bebbington
Leicester: Banks, Sjoberg, Appleton, Heath, King, Cross, Riley, Dougan, Keyworth, Gibson, Stringfellow
Scorers: Bebbington; Gibson

Leicester City 3 Stoke City 2
(Leicester, 22.4.64, 25,372)

Leicester: Unchanged
Stoke: Unchanged
Scorers: Stringfellow, Gibson, Riley; Viollet, Kinnell

[Leicester City won 4-3 on aggregate]

FOOTBALL LG CUP 1964-65

Fourth round

Chelsea v Swansea Town	3-2
Workington v Norwich City	3-0
Charlton Athletic v Bradford City	0-1
Aston Villa v Reading	3-1
Stoke City v Plymouth Argyle	1-1, 1-3
Northampton Town v Chesterfield	4-1
Coventry City v Sunderland	4-2
Leicester City v Crystal Palace	0-0, 2-1

Quarter-finals

Workington v Chelsea	2-2, 0-2
Aston Villa v Bradford City	7-1
Plymouth Argyle v Northampton Town	1-0
Coventry City v Leicester City	1-8

Semi-finals

Aston Villa v Chelsea (2-3, 1-1)	3-4
Leicester City v Plymouth Argyle (3-2, 1-0)	4-2

Final

Chelsea 3 Leicester City 2
(Stamford Bridge, 15.3.65, 20,690)

Chelsea: Bonetti, Hinton, R. Harris, Hollins, Young, Boyle, Murray, Graham, McCreadie, Venables, Tambling
Leicester: Banks, Sjoberg, Norman, Chalmers, King, Appleton, Hodgson, Cross, Goodfellow, Gibson, Sweenie
Scorers: Tambling, Venables (pen); McCreadie; Appleton, Goodfellow

Leicester City 0 Chelsea 0
(Leicester, 5.4.65, 26,958)

Leicester: Unchanged
Chelsea: Bonetti, Hinton, McCreadie, Harris, Mortimore, Upton, Murray, Boyle, Bridges, Venables, Tambling

[Chelsea won 3-2 on aggregate]

FOOTBALL LG CUP 1965-66

Fourth round

Coventry City v West Bromwich Albion	1-1, 1-6
Fulham v Aston Villa	1-1, 0-2
Millwall v Peterborough United	1-4
Stoke City v Burnley	0-0, 1-2
Cardiff City v Reading	5-1
Ipswich Town v Darlington	2-0
Grimsby Town v Preston North End	4-0
Rotherham United v West Ham United	1-2

Quarter-finals

West Bromwich Albion v Aston Villa	3-1
Peterborough United v Burnley	4-0
Cardiff City v Ipswich Town	2-1
Grimsby Town v West Ham United	2-2, 0-1

Semi-finals

WBA v Peterborough United (2-1, 4-2)	6-3
West Ham United v Cardiff City (5-2, 5-1)	10-3

Final

West Ham United 2 West Bromwich A. 1
(Upton Park, 9.3.66, 28,341)

West Ham: Standen, Burnett, Burkett, Peters, Brown, Moore, Brabrook, Boyce, Byrne, Hurst, Dear
WBA: Potter, Cram, Fairfax, Fraser, Campbell, Williams, T. Brown, Astle, Kaye, Lovett, Clark
Scorers: Moore, Byrne; Astle

West Bromwich A. 4 West Ham United 1
(The Hawthorns, 23.3.66, 31,925)

WBA: Hope for Lovett
West Ham: Bovington for Burkett, Sissons for Dear
Scorers: Kaye, Brown, Clark, Williams; Peters

[West Bromwich Albion won 5-3 on aggregate]

[For 1967 the Football League adopted a one-match final. The two-legged semi-final was retained, and from 1975-76 the first round was also played on aggregate over two games]

FOOTBALL LG CUP 1966-67

Fourth round

Queen's Park Rangers v Leicester City	4-2
Carlisle United v Blackburn Rovers	4-0
Sheffield United v Walsall	2-1
Grimsby Town v Birmingham City	2-4
West Ham United v Leeds United	7-0
Blackpool v Fulham	4-2
Brighton v Northampton Town	1-1, 0-8
Swindon Town v West Bromwich Albion	0-2

Quarter-finals

Queen's Park Rangers v Carlisle United	2-1
Sheffield United v Birmingham City	2-3
Blackpool v West Ham United	1-3
Northampton T. v West Bromwich Albion	1-3

Semi-finals

Birmingham City v QPR (1-4, 1-3)	2-7
WBA v West Ham United (4-0, 2-2)	6-2

Final

Queen's Park Rangers 3 West Bromwich 2
(Wembley, 4.3.67, 97,952)

QPR: P. Springett, Hazell, Langley, Sibley, Hunt, Keen, Lazarus, Sanderson, Allen, Marsh, R. Morgan. (I. Morgan)
WBA: Sheppard, Cram, Williams, Collard, Clarke, Fraser, T. Brown, Astle, Kaye, Hope, Clark. (Foggo)
Scorers: R. Morgan, Marsh, Lazarus; Clark 2

FOOTBALL LG CUP 1967-68

Fourth round

Sunderland v Leeds United	0-2
Sheffield Wednesday v Stoke City	0-0, 1-2
Darlington v Millwall	2-0
Derby County v Lincoln City	1-1, 3-0
Huddersfield Town v West Ham United	2-0
Fulham v Manchester City	3-2
Queen's Park Rangers v Burnley	1-2
Arsenal v Blackburn Rovers	2-1

Quarter-finals

Leeds United v Stoke City	2-0
Derby County v Darlington	5-4
Fulham v Huddersfield Town	1-1, 1-2
Burnley v Arsenal	3-3, 1-2

Semi-finals

Derby County v Leeds United (0-1, 2-3)	2-4
Arsenal v Huddersfield Town (3-2, 3-1)	6-3

Final

Leeds United 1 Arsenal 0
(Wembley, 2.3.68, 97,887)

Leeds: Sprake, Reaney, Cooper, Bremner, Charlton, Hunter, J. Greenhoff, Lorimer, Madeley, Giles, E. Gray. (Belfitt)
Arsenal: Furnell, Storey, McNab, McLintock, Ure (Neill) Simpson, Radford, Jenkins, Graham, Sammels, Armstrong.
Scorer: Cooper

FOOTBALL LG CUP 1968-69

Fourth round

Coventry City v Swindon Town	2-2, 0-3
Everton v Derby County	0-0, 0-1
Crystal Palace v Leeds United	2-1
Burnley v Leicester City	4-0
Norwich City v Southampton	0-4
Tottenham Hotspur v Peterborough United	1-0
Blackpool v Wolverhampton Wanderers	2-1
Arsenal v Liverpool	2-1

Quarter-finals

Derby County v Swindon Town	0-0, 0-1
Burnley v Crystal Palace	2-0
Tottenham Hotspur v Southampton	1-0
Arsenal v Blackpool	5-1

Semi-finals

Burnley v Swindon Town (1-2, 2-1, 2-3*)	5-6
Arsenal v Tottenham Hotspur (1-0, 1-1)	2-1

Final

Swindon Town 3 Arsenal 1
(Wembley, 15.3.69, 98,189)

Swindon: Downsborough, Thomas, Trollope, Butler, Burrows, Harland, Heath, Smart, Smith, (Penman) Noble, Rogers.
Arsenal: Wilson, Storey, McNab, McLintock, Ure, Simpson, Radford, Sammels, Court, Gould, Armstrong. (Graham)
Scorers: Smart, Rogers 2; Gould

*play-off at The Hawthorns

FOOTBALL LG CUP 1969-70

Fourth round

Manchester City v Everton	2-0
Queen's Park Rangers v Wolverhampton W.	3-1
Crystal Palace v Derby County	1-1, 0-3
Burnley v Manchester United	0-0, 0-1
Carlisle United v Chelsea	1-0
Nottingham Forest v Oxford United	0-1
Leicester City v Sheffield United	2-0
West Bromwich Albion v Bradford City	4-0

Quarter-finals

Manchester City v Queen's Park Rangers	3-0
Manchester United v Derby County	0-0, 0-1
Oxford United v Carlisle United	0-0, 0-1
Leicester City v West Bromwich Albion	0-0, 1-2

Semi-finals

Manchester C. v Manchester U. (2-1, 2-2)	4-3
Carlisle United v WBA (1-0, 1-4)	2-4

Final

Manchester City 2 West Bromwich A. 1
(Wembley, 7.3.70, 97,963)

City: Corrigan, Book, Mann, Doyle, Booth, Oakes, Heslop, Bell, Summerbee (Bowyer), Lee, Pardoe.
WBA: Osborne, Fraser, Wilson, T. Brown, Talbut, Kaye, Cantello, Suggett, Astle, Hartford (Krzywicki), Hope.
Scorers: Doyle, Pardoe; Astle

FOOTBALL LG CUP 1971-72

Fourth round

Manchester United v Stoke City	1-1, 0-0, 1-2
Queen's Park Rangers v Bristol Rovers	1-1, 0-1
Arsenal v Sheffield United	0-0, 0-2
West Ham United v Liverpool	2-1
Tottenham H. v Preston North End	1-1, 2-1
Blackpool v Aston Villa	4-1
Grimsby Town v Norwich City	1-1, 1-3
Chelsea v Bolton Wanderers	1-1, 6-0

Quarter-finals

Bristol Rovers v Stoke City	2-4
West Ham United v Sheffield United	5-0
Tottenham Hotspur v Blackpool	2-0
Norwich City v Chelsea	0-1

Semi-finals

Stoke C. v West Ham (1-2, 1-0, 0-0*, 3-2†)	5-4
Chelsea v Tottenham Hotspur (3-2, 2-2)	5-4

Final

Stoke City 2 Chelsea 1
(Wembley, 4.3.72, 100,000)

Stoke: Banks, Marsh, Pejic, Bernard, Smith, Bloor, Conroy, J. Greenhoff (Mahoney), Ritchie, Dobing, Eastham
Chelsea: Bonetti, Mulligan (Baldwin), R. Harris, Hollins, Dempsey, Webb, Cooke, Garland, Osgood, Hudson, Houseman
Scorers: Conroy, Eastham; Osgood

*play-off at Hillsborough   †second play-off at Old Trafford

FOOTBALL LG CUP 1973-74

Fourth round

Wolverhampton Wanderers v Exeter City	5-1
Hull City v Liverpool	0-0, 1-3
Millwall v Luton Town	3-1
Southampton v Norwich City	0-2
Queen's Park Rangers v Plymouth Argyle	0-3
Ipswich Town v Birmingham City	1-3
Coventry City v Stoke City	2-1
York City v Manchester City	0-0, 1-4

Quarter-finals

Wolverhampton Wanderers v Liverpool	1-0
Millwall v Norwich City	1-1, 1-2
Birmingham City v Plymouth Argyle	1-2
Coventry City v Manchester City	2-2, 2-4

Semi-finals

Norwich C. v Wolverhampton W. (1-1, 0-1)	1-2
Plymouth A. v Manchester City (1-1, 0-2)	1-3

Final

Wolverhampton W. 2 Manchester City 1
(Wembley, 2.3.74, 100,000)

Wolves: Pierce, Palmer, Parkin, Bailey, Munro, McAlle, Sunderland, Hibbitt, Richards, Dougan, Wagstaffe (Powell)
City: MacRae, Pardoe, Donachie, Doyle, Booth, Towers, Summerbee, Bell, Lee, Law, Marsh
Scorers: Hibbitt, Richards; Bell

FOOTBALL LG CUP 1970-71

Fourth round

Tottenham Hotspur v West Bromwich Albion	5-0
Coventry City v Derby County	1-0
Fulham v Swindon Town	1-0
Leicester City v Bristol City	2-2, 1-2
Manchester United v Chelsea	2-1
Crystal Palace v Arsenal	0-0, 2-0
Bristol Rovers v Birmingham City	3-0
Aston Villa v Carlisle United	1-0

Quarter-finals

Tottenham Hotspur v Coventry City	4-1
Manchester United v Crystal Palace	4-2
Fulham v Bristol City	0-0, 0-1
Bristol Rovers v Aston Villa	1-1, 0-1

Semi-finals

Bristol City v Tottenham Hotspur (1-1, 0-2)	1-3
Manchester United v Aston Villa (1-1, 1-2)	2-3

Final

Tottenham Hotspur 2 Aston Villa 0
(Wembley, 27.2.71, 100,000)

Tottenham: Jennings, Kinnear, Knowles, Mullery, Collins, Beal, Gilzean, Perryman, Chivers, Peters, Neighbour. (Pearce)
Villa: Dunn, Bradley, Aitken, Godfrey, Turnbull, Tiler, McMahon, Rioch, Lochhead, Hamilton, Anderson. (Gibson)
Scorer: Chivers 2

FOOTBALL LG CUP 1972-73

Fourth round

Tottenham Hotspur v Millwall	2-0
Liverpool v Leeds United	2-2, 1-0
Blackpool v Birmingham City	2-0
Wolverhampton Wanderers v Bristol Rovers	4-0
Bury v Chelsea	0-1
Notts County v Stoke City	3-1
Sheffield United v Arsenal	1-2
Stockport County v Norwich City	1-5

Quarter-finals

Liverpool v Tottenham Hotspur	1-1, 1-3
Wolverhampton Wanderers v Blackpool	1-1, 1-0
Chelsea v Notts County	3-1
Arsenal v Norwich City	0-3

Semi-finals

Wolverhampton W. v Tottenham (1-2, 2-2)	3-4
Chelsea v Norwich City (0-2, 0-1)	0-3

Final

Tottenham Hotspur 1 Norwich City 0
(Wembley, 3.3.73, 100,000)

Tottenham: Jennings, Kinnear, Knowles, Pratt (Coates), England, Beal, Gilzean, Perryman, Chivers, Peters, Pearce
Norwich: Keelan, Payne, Butler, Stringer, Forbes, Briggs, Livermore, Blair (Howard), Cross, Paddon, Anderson
Scorer: Coates

FOOTBALL LG CUP 1974-75

Fourth round

Hartlepool v Aston Villa	1-1, 1-6
Colchester United v Southampton	0-0, 1-0
Newcastle United v Fulham	3-0
Chester v Leeds United	3-0
Manchester United v Burnley	3-2
Liverpool v Middlesbrough	0-1
Ipswich Town v Stoke City	2-1
Sheffield United v Norwich City	2-2, 1-2

Quarter-finals

Colchester United v Aston Villa	1-2
Newcastle United v Chester	0-0, 0-1
Middlesbrough v Manchester United	0-0, 0-3
Norwich City v Ipswich Town	1-1, 2-1

Semi-finals

Chester v Aston Villa (2-2, 2-3)	4-5
Manchester U. v Norwich City (2-2, 0-1)	2-3

Final

Aston Villa 1 Norwich City 0
(Wembley, 1.3.75, 100,000)

Villa: Cumbes, Robson, Aitken, Ross, Nicholl, McDonald, Graydon, Little, Leonard, Hamilton, Carrodus
Norwich: Keelan, Machin, Sullivan, Morris, Forbes, Stringer, Miller, MacDougall, Boyer, Suggett, Powell
Scorer: Graydon

FOOTBALL LG CUP   1975-76

Fourth round

Manchester City v Manchester United	4-0
Mansfield Town v Wolverhampton W.	1-0
Burnley v Leicester City	2-0
Middlesbrough v Peterborough United	3-0
Tottenham Hotspur v West Ham United	0-0, 2-0
Doncaster Rovers v Hull City	2-1
Everton v Notts County	2-2, 0-2
Queen's Park Rangers v Newcastle United	1-3

Quarter-finals

Manchester City v Mansfield Town	4-2
Burnley v Middlesbrough	0-2
Tottenham Hotspur v Doncaster Rovers	7-2
Newcastle United v Notts County	1-0

Semi-finals

Middlesbrough v Manchester City (1-0, 0-4)		1-4
Tottenham H. v Newcastle United (1-0, 1-3)		2-3

Final

Manchester City 2 Newcastle United 1
(Wembley, 28.2.76, 100,000)

City: Corrigan, G. Keegan, Donachie, Doyle, Watson, Oakes, Barnes, Booth, Royle, Hartford, Tueart
Newcastle: Mahoney, Nattrass, Kennedy, Barrowclough, Keeley, Howard, Burns, Cassidy, Macdonald, Gowling, Craig
Scorers: Barnes, Tueart; Gowling

FOOTBALL LG CUP   1976-77

Fourth round

Aston Villa v Wrexham	5-1
Millwall v Sheffield Wednesday	3-0
Arsenal v Chelsea	2-1
West Ham United v Queen's Park Rangers	0-2
Swansea City v Bolton Wanderers	1-1, 1-5
Brighton v Derby County	1-1, 1-2
Manchester United v Newcastle United	7-2
Everton v Coventry City	3-0

Quarter-finals

Aston Villa v Millwall	2-0
Queen's Park Rangers v Arsenal	2-1
Derby County v Bolton Wanderers	1-2
Manchester United v Everton	0-3

Semi-finals

QPR v Aston Villa (0-0, 2-2, 0-3*)		2-5
Everton v Bolton Wanderers (1-1, 1-0)		2-1

Final

Aston Villa 0 Everton 0
(Wembley, 12.3.77, 100,000)

Villa: Burridge, Gidman, Robson, Phillips, Nicholl, Mortimer, Deehan, Little, Gray, Cropley, Carrodus
Everton: Lawson, Jones, Darracott, Lyons, McNaught, King, Hamilton, Dobson, Latchford, McKenzie, Goodlass

Replay
Aston Villa 1 Everton 1 [aet]
(Hillsborough, 16.3.77, 55,000)

Villa: Cowans for Cropley
Everton: Bernard for Jones, Kenyon for Dobson; Pearson came on for Hamilton
Scorers: Kenyon (og); Latchford

Second replay
Aston Villa 3 Everton 2 [aet]
(Old Trafford, 13.4.77, 54,749)

Villa: Burridge, Gidman (Smith), Robson, Phillips, Nicholl, Mortimer, Graydon, Little, Deehan, Cropley, Cowans
Everton: Lawson, Robinson, Darracott, Lyons, McNaught, King, Hamilton, Dobson, Latchford, Pearson (Seargeant), Goodlass
Scorers: Little 2, Nicholl; Latchford, Lyons
*play-off at Highbury

FOOTBALL LG CUP   1977-78

Fourth round

Nottingham Forest v Aston Villa	4-2
Bury v West Bromwich Albion	1-0
Sheffield Wednesday v Everton	1-3
Bolton Wanderers v Leeds United	1-3
Arsenal v Hull City	5-1
Ipswich Town v Manchester City	1-2
Wrexham v Swindon Town	2-0
Liverpool v Coventry City	2-2, 2-0

Quarter-finals

Bury v Nottingham Forest	0-3
Leeds United v Everton	4-1
Manchester City v Arsenal	0-0, 0-1
Wrexham v Liverpool	1-3

Semi-finals

Leeds United v Nottingham F. (1-3, 2-4)		3-7
Liverpool v Arsenal (2-1, 0-0)		2-1

Final

Nottingham Forest 0 Liverpool 0 [aet]
(Wembley, 18.3.78, 100,000)

Forest: Woods, Anderson, Clark, McGovern (O'Hare), Lloyd, Burns, O'Neill, Bowyer, Withe, Woodcock, Robertson
Liverpool: Clemence, Neal, Hughes, Smith, Thompson, R. Kennedy (Fairclough), Dalglish, Case, Heighway, McDermott, Callaghan

Replay
Nottingham Forest 1 Liverpool 0
(Old Trafford, 22.3.78, 54,375)

Forest: O'Hare for McGovern
Liverpool: Unchanged; Fairclough came on for Case
Scorer: Robertson (pen)

FOOTBALL LG CUP   1978-79

Fourth round

Everton v Nottingham Forest	2-3
Brighton v Peterborough United	1-0
Charlton Athletic v Stoke City	2-3
Exeter City v Watford	0-2
Queen's Park Rangers v Leeds United	0-2
Aston Villa v Luton Town	0-2
Norwich City v Manchester City	1-3
Reading v Southampton	0-0, 0-2

Quarter-finals

Nottingham Forest v Brighton	3-1
Stoke City v Watford	0-0, 1-3
Leeds United v Luton Town	4-1
Southampton v Manchester City	2-1

Semi-finals

Nottingham Forest v Watford (3-1, 0-0)		3-1
Leeds United v Southampton (2-2, 0-1)		2-3

Final

Nottingham Forest 3 Southampton 2
(Wembley, 17.3.79, 100,000)

Forest: Shilton, Barrett, Clark, McGovern, Lloyd, Needham, O'Neill, Gemmill, Birtles, Woodcock, Robertson
Southampton: Gennoe, Golac, Peach, Williams, Nicholl, Waldron, Ball, Boyer, Hayes (Sealy), Holmes, Curran
Scorers: Birtles 2, Woodcock; Peach, Holmes

FOOTBALL LG CUP   1979-80

Fourth round

Queen's Park Rangers v Wolves	1-1, 0-1
Grimsby Town v Everton	2-1
Brighton v Arsenal	0-0, 0-4
Wimbledon v Swindon Town	1-2
Liverpool v Exeter City	2-0
West Bromwich Albion v Norwich C.	0-0, 0-3
Sunderland v West Ham United	1-1, 1-2
Bristol City v Nottingham Forest	1-1, 0-3

Quarter-finals

Grimsby T. v Wolverhampton W.	0-0, 1-1, 0-2
Arsenal v Swindon Town	1-1, 3-4
Norwich City v Liverpool	1-3
West Ham United v Nottingham F.	0-0, 0-3

Semi-finals

Swindon T. v Wolverhampton W. (2-1, 1-3)		3-4
Nottingham Forest v Liverpool (1-0, 1-1)		2-1

Final

Wolverhampton W. 1 Nottingham F. 0
(Wembley, 15.3.80, 100,000)

Wolves: Bradshaw, Palmer, Parkin, Daniel, Berry, Hughes, Carr, Hibbitt, A. Gray, Richards, Eves
Forest: Shilton, Anderson, F. Gray, McGovern, Needham, Burns, O'Neill, Bowyer, Birtles, Francis, Robertson
Scorer: Gray

FOOTBALL LG CUP   1980-81

Fourth round

Liverpool v Portsmouth	4-1
Birmingham City v Ipswich Town	2-1
West Bromwich A. v Preston N.E.	0-0, 1-1, 2-1
Manchester City v Notts County	5-1
Coventry City v Cambridge United	1-1, 1-0
Watford v Nottingham Forest	4-1
Tottenham Hotspur v Arsenal	1-0
West Ham United v Barnsley	2-1

Quarter-finals

Liverpool v Birmingham City	3-1
Manchester City v West Bromwich Albion	2-1
Watford v Coventry City	2-2, 0-5
West Ham United v Tottenham Hotspur	1-0

Semi-finals

Manchester City v Liverpool (0-1, 1-1)		1-2
Coventry City v West Ham United (3-2, 0-2)		3-4

Final

Liverpool 1 West Ham United 1 [aet]
(Wembley, 14.3.81, 100,000)

Liverpool: Clemence, Neal, Irwin, Hansen, A. Kennedy, Lee, McDermott, Souness, R. Kennedy, Dalglish, Heighway (Case)
West Ham: Parkes, Stewart, Bonds, Martin, Lampard, Pike, Devonshire, Brooking, Neighbour, Cross, Goddard (Pearson)
Scorers: A. Kennedy; Stewart (pen)

Replay
Liverpool 2 West Ham United 1
(Villa Park, 1.4.81, 36,693)

Liverpool: Clemence, Neal, Thompson, Hansen, A. Kennedy, Lee, McDermott, Case, R. Kennedy, Dalglish, Rush
West Ham: Unchanged; Pearson came on for Pike
Scorers: Dalglish, R. Kennedy; Goddard

Non-Division 1 winners: Non-Division 1 clubs have won the trophy on four occasions – Norwich City (Division 2) in 1962, Queen's Park Rangers (Division 3) in 1967, Swindon Town (Division 3) in 1969 and Aston Villa (Division 2) in 1975.

Biggest victory: The largest aggregate victory in a single round is Liverpool 11 Exeter City 0 in the second round of the 1981–82 competition. The two leg results were 6-0 and 5-0. Other record scores are covered under VICTORIES.

See also: CONSECUTIVE SEQUENCES, TIME SPANS, VICTORIES.

LEFT: Ian Rush throws his hands in the air as Ronnie Whelan (number 5) scores Liverpool's second goal in the 1982 Milk Cup final. Spurs, who had lead for most of the game, thus reached the end of their record-breaking sequence of 25 cup ties (in all competitions) without defeat. Liverpool were also the beneficiaries of the game's particular oddity – that two Cups were presented at the end of it. The first was the old Football League Cup, the second the new Milk Cup. The competition had been renamed half-way through. Liverpool were also on their way to a unique four consecutive victories in any domestic competition, 1981, 1982, 1983 and 1984.
OPPOSITE BOTTOM: The only known picture of the only penalty miss in an FA Cup final. The culprit was Charlie Wallace of Aston Villa in the 1913 final against Sunderland at the Crystal Palace. Nonetheless, Villa won the game 1-0. The match was of particular note because it is, oddly, the only Cup final ever contested between the clubs who finished first and second in the League.

MILK CUP — 1981-82

Fourth round

Arsenal v Liverpool	0-0, 0-3
Watford v QPR	4-1
Wigan Athletic v Aston Villa	1-2
Barnsley v Manchester City	1-0
Nottingham Forest v Tranmere Rovers	2-0
Tottenham Hotspur v Fulham	1-0
Crystal Palace v WBA	1-3
Everton v Ipswich	2-3

Quarter-finals

Liverpool v Barnsley	0-0, 3-1
Ipswich v Watford	2-1
Tottenham Hotspur v Nottingham Forest	1-0
Aston Villa v WBA	0-1

Semi-finals (two legs)

Ipswich Town v Liverpool	0-2, 2-2
WBA v Tottenham Hotspur	0-0, 0-1

Final

Liverpool 3 Tottenham Hotspur 1 (aet)
(Wembley, 13.3.82, 100,000)

Liverpool: Grobbelaar, Neal, Kennedy A, Thompson, Whelan, Lawrenson, Dalglish, Lee, Rush, McDermott (Johnson D), Souness
Spurs: Clemence, Hughton, Miller, Price, Hazard (Villa), Perryman, Ardiles, Archibald, Galvin, Hoddle, Crooks
Scorers: Whelan 2, Rush; Archibald

MILK CUP — 1982-83

Fourth round

Arsenal v Huddersfield	1-0
Burnley v Birmingham	3-2
Liverpool v Norwich	2-0
Sheffield Wednesday v Barnsley	1-0
Manchester United v Southampton	2-0
Nottingham Forest v Brentford	2-0
Tottenham Hotspur v Luton	1-0
Notts County v West Ham	3-3, 0-3

Quarter-finals

Arsenal v Sheffield Wednesday	1-0
Liverpool v West Ham	2-1
Manchester United v Nottingham Forest	4-0
Tottenham Hotspur v Burnley	1-4

Semi-finals (two legs)

Liverpool v Burnley	3-0, 0-1
Arsenal v Manchester United	2-4, 1-2

Final

Liverpool 2 Manchester United 1 (aet)
(Wembley, 26.3.83, 100,000)

Liverpool: Grobbelaar, Neal, Kennedy A, Lawrenson, Whelan, Hansen, Dalglish, Lee, Rush, Johnston C (Fairclough), Souness
Manchester United: Bailey, Duxbury, Albiston, Moses, Moran (Macari), McQueen, Wilkins, Muhren, Stapleton, Whiteside, Coppell
Scorers: Kennedy, Whelan; Whiteside

MILK CUP — 1983-84

Fourth round

Arsenal v Walsall	1-2
Rotherham United v Wimbledon	1-0
Ipswich Town v Norwich City	0-1
Oxford v Manchester United	1-1, 1-1, 2-1
Stoke City v Sheffield Wednesday	0-1
West Bromwich v Aston Villa	1-2
West Ham United v Everton	2-2, 0-2
Birmingham City v Liverpool	1-1, 0-3

Quarter-finals

Norwich City v Aston Villa	0-2
Sheffield Wednesday v Liverpool	2-2, 0-3
Oxford United v Everton	1-1, 1-4
Rotherham United v Walsall	2-4

Semi-finals (two legs)

Liverpool v Walsall	2-2, 2-0
Everton v Aston Villa	2-0, 0-1

Final

Liverpool 0 Everton 0 (aet)
(Wembley, 25.3.84, 100,000)
Liverpool: Grobbelaar, Neal, Kennedy, Lawrension, Hansen, Dalglish, Lee, Whelan, Souness, Rush, Johnston C. (Robinson)
Everton: Southall, Stevens, Bailey, Ratcliffe, Mountfield, Reid, Irvine, Heath, Sharp, Richardson, Sheedy (Harper)
Replay
Liverpool 1 Everton 0
(Maine Road, 28.3.84, 52,089)
Everton: Harper for Sheedy; sub King. Liverpool unchanged. **Scorer:** Souness

1908 London

1:      Great Britain 12   Sweden   1
S-F: Great Britain 4   Holland 0
Final: Great Britain 2   Denmark 0
Scorers: Chapman (*South Nottingham*),
Woodward (*Tottenham H.*)

1912 Stockholm

1:      Bye
2:      Great Britain 7   Hungary 0
S-F: Great Britain 4   Finland 0
Final: Great Britain 4   Denmark 2
Scorers: Hoare (*Glossop North End*) 2, Berry
(*Oxford City*), Walden (*Halifax Town*)

1920 Antwerp

1: Great Britain 1   Norway 3

1924 [Paris] & 1928 [Amsterdam]

Did not enter because of dispute over broken
time payments to amateurs, which were allowed
by FIFA but not by the home associations.

1932 [Los Angeles]

No soccer competition was held in the games
that year.

1936 Berlin

1: Great Britain 2   China   0
2: Great Britain 4   Poland 5

1948 London

1:      Great Britain 4   Holland   3
2:      Great Britain 1   France   0
S-F: Great Britain 1   Yugoslavia 3
(Third place match: Great Britain 3 Denmark 5)

1952 Helsinki

Pr: Great Britain 3   Luxembourg 5

1956 Melbourne

1: Great Britain 9   Thailand 0
2: Great Britain 1   Bulgaria 6

1960 Rome

Group game: Great Britain 3   Brazil 4
Group game: Great Britain 2   Italy 2
Group game: Great Britain 3   China 2

1964 (Preliminary round only)

Great Britain 6   Iceland 0 (away)
Great Britain 4   Iceland 0 (home)
Great Britain 2   Greece 1 (home)
Great Britain 1   Greece 4 (away)
(Great Britain eliminated by Greece on goal
difference before final rounds)

1968 (Preliminary round only)

Great Britain 0   Spain 0 (home)
Great Britain 0   Spain 1 (away)

1972 (Preliminary round only)

Great Britain 0   Bulgaria 5 (away)
Great Britain 1   Bulgaria 0 (home)

Oldest Players

Any game: Neil McBain, the New Brighton manager, was forced to play in goal for his side at Hartlepool in Division 3N on Saturday 15 March 1947, at the age of 52. New Brighton lost 3-0.

International: Billy Meredith was 45 years 8 months old when he played his last international for Wales against England at Highbury on Monday 15 March 1920. Wales won 2-1.

Division 1: Stanley Matthews was 5 days past his 50th birthday when he made his last appearance for Stoke against Fulham on Saturday 6 February 1965. Stoke won 3-1. Matthews is the only outfield player ever to appear in a first-class game after his 50th birthday.

FA Cup: Billy Meredith was aged 49 years 8 months when he appeared for Manchester City against Newcastle United in a semi-final on Saturday 29 March 1924. City lost 2-0. Almost exactly 20 years earlier he had captained the Manchester City side and scored the only goal of the 1904 Cup final against Bolton.

Cup final: Walter Hampson, who played for Newcastle against Aston Villa in the 1924 final, is thought to have been the oldest player to appear. He was 41 years 257 days old at the time. It is probable that some players in the 1870s were over 40 when they competed in an FA Cup final.

Complete season: Bob McGrory was 43 years old when he played in all Stoke City's Division 1 games in 1934-35.

Victorious Club: Arsenal's Championship winning team of 1947-48 had the oldest average age of any trophy winning side.

Olympics

The very first side to ever win an Olympic soccer match was named Great Britain. That was an exhibition game at the 1900 Paris Olympics and Upton Park, representing Great Britain, defeated a French side 4-0. After soccer became an official Olympic sport in 1908, the four home associations always entered a single amateur team, though it was usually inaccurately known as Great Britain rather than the United Kingdom. This team won the 1908 and 1912 gold medals but has not competed since the 1972 preliminary competition, shortly after which the English, Welsh and Northern Irish FAs ceased to recognise any separate amateur status. The Scottish Amateur Football Association still exists and could, one supposes, try to enter an Olympic team. As England were the only one of the home countries affiliated to FIFA in 1908, that year's winning team (as well as the one from 1912) was entirely composed of English players. Great Britain retained one Olympic record until the 1984 Los Angeles Games – that of appearing more times in the competition than any other country (11). In 1984, however, the USA surpassed this mark with their 12th appearance.

Own Goals

First known: The first own goal of any significance was in the 1877 FA Cup final between Wanderers and Oxford University. A shot by Waddington was caught by Lord Kinnaird in the Wanderers goal. He stepped back over the line and Oxford were awarded a goal. Kenrick scored to level after 90 minutes and Lindsay got the winner for Wanderers in extra time. This is reminiscent of a similar incident in the 1901 final when Spurs keeper Clawley and Sheffield forward Bennett clashed. The ball went out, Clawley appealed for a goal-kick,

Bennett for a corner and the referee gave a goal – apparently because he thought Clawley had set foot behind his line before colliding with Bennett. A film of the incident apparently showed the referee to have been mistaken.

Other FA Cup final own goals were scored by Bert Turner (Derby) in 1946, Doug McGrath (Blackburn) in 1960, Alan Kelly (Preston) in 1964, and Tommy Hutchison (Manchester City) in 1981.

First in League: Scored by George Cox, of Aston Villa, for Wolves on Saturday 8 September 1888, the very first day of League football. The game finished 1-1.

Quickest: The fastest own goal recorded in first-class football was after 8 seconds, by Pat Kruse of Torquay for Cambridge United on Monday 3 January 1977. Cambridge's other score that day was also an own goal. The quickest Scottish own goal was scored in 12 seconds by J. McDonald of Raith for Kilmarnock in the Scottish League Cup on 2 September 1961. The fastest recorded instance of scoring for both sides was by Desmond Tennant, a Brighton full-back, who scored for both sides in a Division 3S game against Exeter City at St James's Park on 16 February 1957. He did this within the space of 45 seconds and Brighton won 3-1.

Most in one game: 3 – there are three recorded instances. The first was Clyde v Raith in the Scottish Cup on 11 February 1950 when all 3 Raith goals were scored by Clyde players, Campbell, Mennie and Milligan. Sheffield Wednesday players Curtis, Gannon and Kenny all scored for West Bromwich in the Division 1 game at Hillsborough on Friday 26 December 1952. Wednesday lost 5-4. When Carlisle defeated Rochdale 7-2 on Saturday 25 December 1954, three of their goals in the Division 3N game were scored by Rochdale players – Boyle, Murphy and Underwood.

Without touching the ball: 30 seconds – Alan Mullery of Fulham scored for Sheffield Wednesday approximately 30 seconds after the kick-off on Saturday 21 January 1961 without any Sheffield player touching the ball. This is thought to be unique in League history. It was, however, a portent of things to come. Fulham, playing at Craven Cottage, lost 6-1.

Two for each side: Oldham's Sam Wynne scored twice for Manchester United in the Division 2 game on Saturday 6 October 1923, plus a penalty and a free-kick for his own side, who won 3-2. Chris Nicholl matched this feat on Saturday 20 March 1976 with 2 goals for his own side, Aston Villa, and 2 goals for Leicester.

FA Cup final: Bert Turner became the first player to score for both sides in an FA Cup final when he did so within a minute of the Charlton v Derby game in 1946. Tommy Hutchison of Manchester City repeated this feat in the first 1981 FA Cup final when he put Manchester City ahead against Tottenham Hotspur and then deflected Glenn Hoddle's free-kick for an own-goal to level the scores at 1-1. City lost the replay.

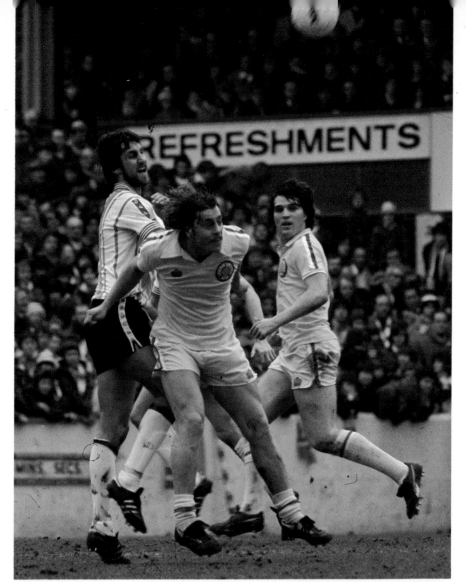

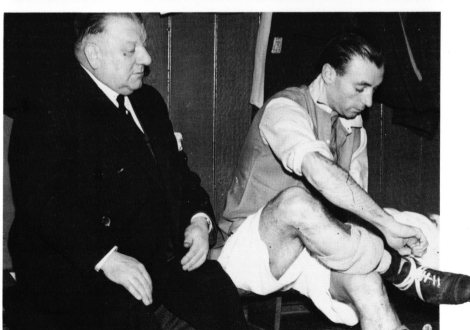

TOP: Southampton's Chris Nicholl rises above Leeds' John Hawley at The Dell. While playing for Aston Villa in Div 1 at Leicester in 1976 Nicholl scored twice for each side. The most remarkable thing about this feat was that, unlike Sam Wynne earlier, none of Nicholl's goals came from set pieces but all from open play.
BOTTOM: Stanley Matthews (right), the oldest man to play in Div 1 and the only outfield player to appear in a League match aged 50, sits with Arsenal manager George Allison.

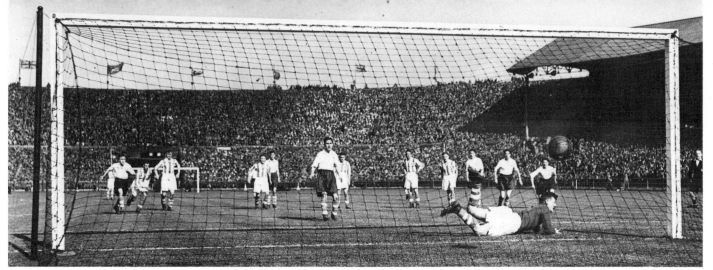

George Mutch scores from the penalty spot and off the bar in the 120th minute of the 1938 Cup final, the latest time at which a final has been decided. For Preston it was ironic revenge over Huddersfield – the Yorkshiremen had beaten them with a penalty in 1922.

Penalties

HISTORY

First ever scored: The first penalty ever awarded was apparently at Airdrie during a minor league game on 6 March 1891. This was three days after the penalty law was adopted but was awarded in error as the rule did not officially come into effect until the beginning of the next season. The first genuine penalty-kick ever converted, therefore, was by Alex McCall for Renton against Leith Athletic at Bank Park, Leith, on Saturday 22 August 1891. The first scored in England was by a Wolves player, John Heath, against Accrington, in a Football League game on Monday 14 September 1891. Wolves won 5-0.

Primary cause: Several officials had suggested penalty kicks in the 1880s but the idea had been rejected as implying that some players were ungentlemanly. The incident which finally swung the balance was in an FA Cup quarter-final between Notts County and Stoke at Trent Bridge in 1891. Stoke had already beaten Preston and Aston Villa and had high hopes of winning their first trophy. In the last minute of the game, with County leading 1-0, their back Hendry punched a Stoke shot off the line when his keeper Toone was beaten. Stoke were given a free-kick on the goal-line but Toone smothered it easily. County won 1-0 and went on to reach the final.

Further rule changes: By unfortunate chance, Stoke were to suffer further with the penalty law the following season when, on Saturday 21 November 1891, they lost 2-1 at Villa Park. With just a few seconds left, Stoke were awarded a penalty, but a Villa player kicked the ball out of the ground and, by the time the ball had been retrieved and the confusion died down, the referee had blown for full-time and Stoke never got to take the penalty. The law was changed to allow time to be added on at the end of that season.

Tie-breakers: Penalties were first used as a tie-breaker in a competition between first-class clubs on Wednesday 5 August 1970 to decide a Watney Cup semi-final between Hull City and Manchester United. United eventually won 4-3.

First-class competitions: Penalties have never been used to decide the result of any first-class domestic game in the later stages of a major competition (though they have been used to decide major European games, such as the 1976 European Championship final between Czechoslovakia and West Germany and the 1980 Cup Winners Cup final between Valencia and Arsenal). Penalties would, however, have been used to conclude the FA Cup semi-final between Arsenal and Liverpool had they been level after a fifth game scheduled for Monday 5 May 1980. Arsenal won the fourth game 1-0 and rendered the eventuality unnecessary. Arsenal lost 1-0 to West Ham in the final. It was also decided that the 1982 FA Cup final replay between Spurs and QPR would be decided on penalties if the sides were level after 120 minutes. As it happened the game was decided on penalties anyway – Glenn Hoddle scoring the only goal of the match from the spot.

Football League/Scottish League Cups: Penalties have been used to decide ties in the early rounds of these competitions, after 3 indecisive games, since 1977. From the 1979–80 season onwards, penalties could also be used to decide early round Football League Cup games which end in an aggregate tie (the early rounds are played on a home and away basis). The first tie to be decided in this way was Barnsley v Lincoln in the first round of the 1979–80 competition. Both won their home legs 2-1 but Barnsley won 4-3 on penalties.

First touch of ball: Tony Coton saved a penalty for Birmingham with his very first touch of the ball in first-class football after just 80 seconds of a Division 1 game v Sunderland at St Andrew's on 27 December 1980. John Hawley took the kick and Birmingham won 3-2.

PENALTIES AWARDED

Most: There are five known instances of games in which 4 penalties were awarded:

- On 9 January 1904 in a Scottish Division 1 game at Love Street, Paisley, St Mirren were awarded three penalties and Rangers one. All 4 were converted and this is the only instance of four penalties being scored in a single first-class game.
- On 13 February 1909, Burnley were awarded 4 penalties against Grimsby Town in Division 2 but scored from only one of them. This is the only instance of one team being awarded four penalties in a single match and is also the record for penalties missed by a team in a single game.
- On 25 February 1928 in Scottish Division 1 Queen's Park were awarded 2 penalties and scored from them both while Kilmarnock were also awarded 2 but missed one. Queen's Park won 5-1.
- On 2 September 1931 in Scottish Division 1 at Dens Park, Dundee, the home side were awarded a penalty, converted by Gilmour, while Ayr were awarded 3 penalties, of which two were converted by Robertson and one was missed. The game ended 2-2.
- On 17 April 1976 at Northampton in Division 4, the home side were awarded 3 penalties against Hartlepool in the first 20 minutes. The first was converted by keeper Alan Starling (thus establishing a record by enabling all first-team members to score at least once in a single season), the second was converted by Don Martin and the third was saved by the keeper from Martin but the Northampton player, following up, scored from the rebound. Hartlepool were later awarded the game's fourth penalty, scored by Kevin Johnson.

PENALTIES SCORED

Most in single game: The only game in which 4 penalties have been scored was the St Mirren v Rangers game at Paisley in 1904 (*above*). David J. Lindsay (a right-winger) scored three for St Mirren, R. Hamilton scored the fourth for Rangers, and St Mirren won 5-4.

Most by single player: There are 17 recorded instances of a player scoring a hat-trick of 3 penalties in a single first-class game:

- Saturday 9 January 1904, David Lindsay

for St Mirren v Rangers (*above*);

• Saturday 12 November 1921, Billy Walker for Aston Villa v Bradford City in Division 1. Villa won 7-1;

• Saturday 27 August 1938, Benjamin Ellis for Motherwell v Kilmarnock in Scottish Division 1. Kilmarnock lost 4-2;

• Saturday 7 June 1947, George Milburn for Chesterfield v Sheffield Wednesday in Division 2, Chesterfield won 4-2;

• Saturday 4 February 1950, Eddie Turnbull for Hibs v Celtic, Scottish Division 1;

• Wednesday 8 March 1950, Charlie Mitten for Manchester United v Aston Villa in Division 1. United won 7-0;

• Friday 23 March 1951, Joe Willetts for Hartlepools United v Darlington in Division 3N. Hartlepools won 6-1;

• Saturday 26 September 1953, Bobby Collins for Celtic v Aberdeen in Scottish Division 1. Celtic won 3-0;

• Saturday 7 December 1957, Ken Barnes for Manchester City v Everton in Division 1. City won 6-2;

• Saturday 8 August 1959, Billy Price for Falkirk v Hamilton in the Scottish League Cup;

• Saturday 20 August 1963, Gordon Wallace for Montrose v Hamilton in Scottish Division 2;

• Saturday 1 September 1973, Donald Ford for Hearts v Morton in Scottish Division 1. Hearts won 3-2, despite having been losing 2-0 at one stage;

• Saturday 16 February 1974, Bobby McKean for St Mirren v Brechin City in Scottish Division 2;

• Saturday 24 April 1976, Trevor Anderson for Swindon v Walsall in Division 3. Swindon won 5-1;

• Saturday 18 September 1976, Gerry Colgan for Queen's Park v East Stirlingshire at Hampden in Scottish Division 2. Queen's won 3-1;

• Saturday 29 April 1978, Alan Slough for Peterborough v Chester in Division 3. The game was played at Chester and, despite Slough's efforts, Peterborough lost 4-3;

• Wednesday 17 September 1980, John Wark for Ipswich v Aris Salonika in the UEFA Cup first round tie at Portman Road. Wark also scored a fourth goal in Ipswich's 5-1 win.

Consecutive games: Everton full-back Billy Cook converted penalties in 3 consecutive Division 1 games within the space of 4 days in 1938:

Saturday 24 December 1938 v Blackpool at Goodison. Everton won 4-0;

Monday 26 December 1938 v Derby County at Goodison. Everton drew 2-2;

Tuesday 27 December 1938 v Derby County at the Baseball Ground. Everton lost 2-1; Everton won the League Championship that season.

Most in a season: Francis Lee scored 13 penalties for Manchester City in a Division 1 total of 33 goals in 1971–72. He had equalled the previous record of 11 as early as 12 February 1972 but scored only 2 after that date.

·**Carried back on the field:** On Friday 26

December 1924, Nottingham Forest, bottom of Division 1, were playing Bolton at home. Harry Martin, Forest's usual penalty taker, had been carried off injured. Losing 1-0, Forest were awarded a penalty but no player would take it. Captain Bob Wallace went back to the dressing-room, Martin was carried back on to the field and took the kick from a standing position. He scored, beating England goalkeeper Dick Pym, and Forest drew 1-1. They were still relegated at the end of the season.

SAVED AND MISSED

Single game: The most penalties actually saved by a goalkeeper in one game is 3, by Grimsby keeper Walter Scott at Burnley on Saturday 13 February 1909. Burnley scored with a fourth penalty. Burnley's total of 3 misses is also the most any side has failed to convert in a single game. On Saturday 27 January 1912 Manchester City also missed all 3 penalties they were awarded against Newcastle at Hyde Road in a Division 1 game. Not all of the shots were saved by the Newcastle keeper, however, and the game ended 1-1. The misses were by Thornley and Fletcher (2)

Taken most often: On 27 October 1945 in the Scottish Southern League during a game between Partick Thistle and Kilmarnock, the latter were ordered to take the same penalty 7 times. On the last occasion it was saved by the keeper and Partick won 5-3.

None awarded: Liverpool are thought to have established a modern record by not having a penalty awarded in their favour between 11 October 1980 and 3 October 1981 when they were awarded 2 in the same game against Swansea. This drought lasted 53 first-class games in all.

Missed same penalty: Three Notts County players – Kevin Randall, Don Masson and Brian Stubbs – all missed with the same penalty against Portsmouth in Division 2 on Saturday 22 September 1973. The first two kicks had to be retaken because of encroachment by Portsmouth defenders. County won the game, at Fratton Park, 2-1.

Consecutive saves: Roy Brown saved 6 consecutive penalty kicks for Notts County in the 1972-73 season.

Most saves in season: Paul Cooper of Ipswich Town saved 8 out of the 10 penalties taken against him in Division 1 matches in the 1979–80 season.

Relegated: On Saturday 1 May 1926 Manchester City went to Newcastle for their last game of the season needing a point to stay in Division 1. They missed a penalty, lost 3-2 and were relegated. Burnley won 4-1 the same day and stayed up, but had City converted the penalty and drawn 3-3 Burnley would have gone down instead. This was in keeping with City's season – their 89 goals that year was the highest ever recorded by a relegated club and they had lost the Cup final 1-0 to Bolton the previous week. An even more dramatic last game of the season occured at Bramall Lane, Sheffield, at the end of the 1980–81 Division 3 season. Walsall and Sheffield United

were playing each other for the last relegation place and United were eventually relegated to Division 4 for the first time in their history while Walsall finished 20th. At 4.39 pm United were awarded a penalty which Don Givens missed; had he scored United would have finished 17th and Walsall gone down. Manager Martin Peters said afterwards: 'Don was not supposed to take the penalty; the nominated player wouldn't.'

Championship: The most costly penalty miss ever was by Len Davies of Cardiff City against Birmingham on Saturday 3 May 1924. Cardiff could only draw 0-0 as a result and the Championship went to Huddersfield on goal average.

Misses in season: 10 different Sheffield Wednesday players missed penalties in first-class games during the 1977–78 season. Wednesday also established a record by missing 7 consecutive penalties in 1983, a sequence broken by Mel Sterland against Barnsley on 5 November 1983.

CUP FINALS

FA Cup final: To 1983, only 10 penalties have been awarded in an FA Cup final. Goals were scored by Albert Shepherd for Newcastle v Barnsley in the 1910 replay, Billy Smith for Huddersfield v Preston in 1922, George Mutch for Preston v Huddersfield in 1938 (in the last minute of extra-time), Eddie Shimwell for Blackpool v Manchester United in 1948, Ronnie Allen for WBA v Preston in 1954, Danny Blanchflower for Spurs v Burnley in 1962, Kevin Reeves for Manchester City v Spurs in the 1981 replay, Glenn Hoddle for Spurs v QPR in the 1982 replay and Arnold Muhren for Manchester United against Brighton in the 1983 replay. Only one penalty has ever been missed in a final – by Charlie Wallace of Aston Villa v Sunderland in 1913, the first penalty to be awarded in the first game of a final.

Scottish Cup final: Penalties have been scored by Willie Orr for Celtic v Hearts in 1907, Davie Meiklejohn for Rangers v Celtic in 1928, George Young (2) for Rangers v Clyde in 1949, John Prentice for Falkirk v Kilmarnock in 1957, Ian Lister for Dunfermline v Hearts in 1968, Joe Harper for Aberdeen v Celtic in 1970, Harry Hood for Celtic v Rangers in 1971, George Connelly for Celtic v Rangers in 1973, Pat McCluskey for Celtic v Airdrie in 1975, Andy Lynch for Celtic v Rangers in 1977 and Ally MacLeod for Hibs v Rangers in 1979. As many as five penalties have been mised in Scottish Cup finals, all by Rangers' players. In 1929 Kilmarnock keeper Clemie saved a penalty by Tully Craig and Rangers lost 2-0, in 1935 Hamilton keeper Jim Morgan saved from Rangers' Bob McPhail, Eric Caldow missed a penalty v Kilmarnock in 1960, Alex Miller missed one v Hibernian in the second replay in 1979, and to complete a sorry tale Ian Redford missed one v Dundee United in the 90th minute in 1981 when the score was 0-0.

See also: CONSECUTIVE SEQUENCES, GOAL AVERAGE

Players

PHYSICAL

Biggest player to appear in first-class football was almost certainly Billy 'Fatty' Foulke of Sheffield United, Chelsea and Bradford City, a goalkeeper who weighed 25 stones at the end of his career. He won a League Championship medal in 1898, FA Cup winners medals in 1899 and 1902 and an England cap against Wales in 1897.

Tallest player was probably Albert Iremonger of Notts County and Lincoln City, who was 6'6" tall and played 600 League games between 1 April 1905 (v Wednesday at Trent Bridge) and 1927. His last game for Notts County was their last in Division 1 for over half a century, on Saturday 1 May 1926 when County beat three times champions Huddersfield 4-2.

All positions: Only one player – James Gordon of Rangers in the decades from 1910 to 1930 – is known to have been picked by his club to play in all 11 positions on the field, including goalkeeper.

Smallest player was probably Fred Le May who played for Thames, Watford and Orient between 1930 and 1932 and was just 5 feet tall. Fanny Walden of Northampton and Spurs may have been 1 inch taller.

SHIRTS

First numbered: The first occasion on which senior players are known to have worn numbers was on Saturday 25 August 1928 when Arsenal did so at Hillsborough and Chelsea did the same against Swansea at Stamford Bridge.

First official numbering was in the 1933 Cup final on 29 April when Everton wore 1-11 and Manchester City 12-22. Everton also wore numbers the following week at Wolverhampton (where they lost 4-2) and were presumably wearing the same shirts. Both English and Scottish players were officially numbered for the first time at the start of the abortive 1939–40 season.

No numbering: Celtic have always refused to number their players' shirts, though they do carry numbers on their shorts. UEFA insist that they number shirts for Europe. The first time that they ever wore numbers, on their shorts only, was for a friendly against Sparta Rotterdam on 14 May 1960.

Points

PERCENTAGE RECORDS

Since the introduction of 3 points for a win in England in 1981, it has become very difficult to compare points totals. Even on a percentage achieved basis there are difficulties – a win and a draw under a two-point system is 75%, under the three-point system it is only 67%. The following records are therefore based on percentages achieved assuming a two-point system only.

Best percentage record: 100% by Rangers in Scottish Division 1 in 1898–99 (18 games). The only other occasions when a figure of 90% has been achieved (to nearest whole number) are:
- 93% – Celtic, Division 1, 1967–68 (34 games)
- 92% – Celtic, Division 1, 1897–98 (18 games)
- 91% – Hearts, Division 1, 1957–58 (34 games)
- 91% – Morton, Division 2, 1966–67 (38 games)
- 91% – Preston, Division 1, 1888–89 (22 games)

Best percentage, England: Preston (above) with 40 points out of 44 in 1888–89. In seasons with at least 40 matches, the record is 86% by Doncaster Rovers in Division 3N in 1946–47 (72 out of a possible 84).

Worst percentage record: Abercorn in Scottish Division 1 in 1896–97 recorded only 3 points out of 36, a percentage of 8.3%. This is the only occasion a team has recorded less than 10%. Stirling Albion achieved exactly 10% in Division 1 in 1954–55 (6 points out of 60).

Worst percentage, England: 11.8% by Loughborough Town in Division 2 in 1899–1900 and by Doncaster Rovers in Division 2 in 1904–05. Both recorded 8 points out of a possible 68. In seasons of at least 40 matches, Rochdale have the worst record with 13.8% (11 points out of 80) in Division 3N in 1931–32.

Lowest Championship percentage: Everton won the 1914–15 League Championship with a record of only 60.5% (46/76).

Lowest promotion percentage: Carlisle were promoted from Division 2 in 1973–74 with a record of just 58.3% (49 points from 42 games), the lowest ever for a promoted club. Since the introduction of 3 and 4 club promotion in England it is obviously easier for a club to be promoted with a low percentage record. The lowest percentage for a club promoted from a conventional two clubs up/two clubs down league is 59.0% (46 out of 78) by Queen of the South from Scottish Division 2 in 1980–81.

MOST AND LEAST

Most points: At 1 January 1985, the record is held by York City with 101 in Division 4 in the 1983–84 season. But the most points ever recorded under a conventional 2 points for a win system was 76 by Rangers in Scottish Division 1 in 1920–21 (42 games). In England the record was held by Lincoln City with 74 in Division 4 in 1975–76 (46 games).

Least points: 3 by Abercorn in Scottish Division 1 in 1896–97. They won one and drew one of their 18 games. The English record is 8 by Loughborough Town and Doncaster (*above*).

None at all: There are two recorded instances in senior leagues. Milford lost all 14 of their Irish League games in 1890–91 while similarly named Ilford lost all 18 of their Southern League games in 1895–96.

Most points in history: Up to the beginning of season 1983–84, Everton had gained 3355 First Division points from 3116 games since 1888. Liverpool were second with 3129 First Division points from 2732 games since they first joined Division 1 in 1894.

Points per goal: Though it may be superseded in a three-point system, Orient did establish an amazing record in Division 2 in 1974–75. They scored only 28 goals but finished in 12th position with 42 points – a record of 1.5 points per goal scored.

DEDUCTED AND AWARDED

Football League: There have only been eight instances of the League deducting points:

Sunderland had 2 points deducted for fielding goalkeeper Ned Doig against WBA on 20 September 1890 before he had completed the necessary 14-day qualifying period following his transfer from Arbroath.

Stockport had 2 points deducted for playing ex-Bolton star Joe Smith in Division 3N on 19 March 1927 while he was unregistered.

Peterborough had 19 points deducted from their total of 50 in Division 3 in 1967–68 to ensure that they were relegated after a commission had discovered financial irregularities in their books.

Preston North End had one point deducted in 1973–74 for fielding an ineligible player.

Newport County had one point deducted in 1973–74 for fielding an unregistered player.

Aldershot had one point deducted in 1974–75 for fielding an unregistered player. Had they had two points deducted, they would have been relegated to Division 4.

Bristol Rovers had two points deducted by the League in 1981–82 for fielding a player, Steve Bailey, against Newport before his registration forms had arrived at Football League headquarters.

Mansfield Town had two points deducted by the League in 1981–82 for fielding an unregistered player. Had the League deducted three points Mansfield would have had to seek re-election.

Points awarded: On two occasions in Scotland, 2 points have been awarded without games being played. Dundee Wanderers received 2 points when Renton failed to play their home game in 1894–95 and Brechin received both points when Dykehead failed to play a Scottish Division 3 game in 1924–25. The first instance of this occuring in England was on Tuesday 2 April 1974 when Exeter failed to turn up at Scunthorpe for a Division 4 fixture and Scunthorpe were awarded both points.

Negative points: Points deductions were quite common in Scotland in the early years of the game (the last was against Alloa in 1947–48) but there was only one occasion on which a side registered negative points. In 1893–94 Port Glasgow Athletic had only 6 points in the Second Division when the 3 they had won by beating Northern and drawing against Clyde were deducted for fielding an unregistered player. They were also fined 4 points and hence had a tally of (−1) until they drew their next game.

Promotion

League Championship: Four clubs have won Division 2 and Division 1 in successive seasons: Liverpool, 1904–05 & 1905–06; Everton, 1930–31 & 1931–32; Tottenham, 1949–50 & 1950–51 and Ipswich, 1960–61 & 1961–62. Both Liverpool and Everton were relegated from Division 1 the season before winning Division 2. Nottingham Forest are the only other club to have been promoted from Division 2 the season before winning the Championship. In 1976–77 they were promoted in third place.

Consecutive seasons: Only two clubs have been promoted from Division 3 to Division 1 in successive seasons. Charlton were Division 3S champions in 1934–35, runners-up in Division 2 in 1935–36 and were then runners-up in Division 1 (3 points behind Manchester City) in 1936–37, to just miss an astonishing record. QPR were Champions of Division 3 in 1966–67 and runners-up in Division 2 in 1967–68. Since the reorganisation of the divisions in 1958, and the introduction of 3 and 4 up and down in 1973, it has obviously become much easier for clubs to rise or fall in consecutive seasons. Since 1958, 7 clubs have risen from Division 4 to Division 2 in consecutive years: Walsall 1959–61, Carlisle 1963–65, Millwall 1964–66, Cambridge 1976–78, Watford 1977–79, Swansea 1977–79 and Grimsby 1978–80. Only one Scottish club has ever been promoted twice in consecutive seasons. Clydebank were champions of Division 2 in 1975–76 and second in Division 1 in 1976–77.

Division 4 to Division 1: Northampton Town are the only club to have gone from one end of the League to the other – and then back. They moved from Division 4 to Division 1 in the space of just four years (1961 to 1965) spending two seasons in Division 3 and two in Division 2. They were relegated straight back with just one season in Division 2 and two in Division 3, and were back playing Division 4 football in 1969. Between their 4-2 defeat at Mansfield on Saturday 29 April 1961 and their 2-0 defeat at Crewe on Saturday 9 August 1969 (both in Division 4) they had travelled the whole length of the Football League in just over 8 years.

Fewest goals: Notts County became Champions of Division 2 in 1922–23, having scored only 46 goals in 42 matches. They scored only 17 goals away from home but ended with 53 points. Their last game of the season was at Upton Park on Saturday 5 May 1923, when they needed to win to go up (West Ham were already promoted). County won 1-0. Surprisingly, County had conceded 6 goals at home to Manchester United and 4 at home to Crystal Palace this season. In 1975–76 both Kilmarnock and Clydebank were promoted with just 44 goals scored but both only played 26 games that season. In 1980–81 Blackburn missed promotion only on goal difference despite having scored just 42 Second Division goals.

Last club promoted: All clubs in the Football League have been promoted at least once. Chester were the last of the clubs who entered the League prior to the Second World War to be promoted when they reached Division 3 (though only on goal average) in 1975. They would not have been promoted if goal difference had been applied. The only club not to have been promoted to its current position is Arsenal. They were elected to Division 1 in 1919, despite having finished only 5th in the 1914–15 Second Division, and have not been relegated since.

Closest miss: There have been many tight finishes to promotion races, but the most interesting is probably Derby's in 1923–24. They went to Leicester for their last Second Division game of the season on 3 May 1924 needing to win 5-0 to go up. In fact they won 4-0 and Bury were promoted by 0.014 of a goal.

See also: RELEGATION, TEST MATCHES; GOAL AVERAGE

The Everton team (minus Dixie Dean) which won the Second Division in 1930–31. They went on to win the Championship a year later. Only one club, Liverpool in 1905 and 1906, had done this before and only Ipswich and Tottenham Hotspur have done it since.

Quickest Goals

SINGLE GOALS

Fastest ever: The quickest ever goal is thought to have been scored by Malcolm Macdonald for Newcastle United v St Johnstone in a friendly at Muirton Park, Perth, before the start of the 1975–76 season. The ball was touched to him at the kick-off and he hit it straight over the keeper's head. It is difficult to see how a quicker goal could be scored.

Fastest recorded: C. Cowperthwaite of Barrow was recorded as scoring in 3½ seconds against Kettering in an Alliance Premier League match on 8 December 1979. Jim Fryatt of Bradford PA was recorded, by referee R.J. Simon, as scoring after 4 seconds against Tranmere in Division 4 on 25 April 1964, but as three other players touched the ball this seems unlikely. Ian Scarlett of Walsall was recorded as scoring after 4 seconds of a Division 3S game against Bournemouth on 7 November 1953. George James of WBA was timed as scoring after 5 seconds against Nottingham Forest on 13 December 1924 at The Hawthorns. None of the above four feats are generally accepted as being undisputably proven and the usual record is given as 6 seconds.

Undisputed fastest: Three players have recorded a goal within 6 seconds of the kick-off: Alf Mundy for Aldershot at Hartlepool in Division 4 on Saturday 25 October 1958, Barry Jones for Notts County against Torquay in Division 3 on Saturday 31 March 1962, Ken Smith for Crystal Palace at Derby in Division 2 on Saturday 12 December 1964.

Fastest, Scotland: Willie Sharp scored for Partick against Queen of the South after 7 seconds of a Scottish Division 1 game at Firhill on Saturday 20 December 1947.

FA Cup: Vic Lambden of Bristol Rovers scored after 8 seconds against Aldershot in the third round on Saturday 6 January 1951.

Scottish Cup: John Hewitt scored for Aberdeen at Motherwell after 9.6 seconds on 30 January 1982. It was the only goal of the game.

FA Cup semi-final: Alan Sunderland scored after 13 seconds of the Arsenal v Liverpool second replay at Villa Park on Monday 28 April 1980.

FA Cup final: Aston Villa scored the only goal of the 1895 final v West Bromwich after just 30 seconds. Charlie Athersmith centred to Bob Chatt, whose shot was blocked by defender Reader but the ball rebounded inadvertently off Jack Devey's knee into the net. The goal is sometimes credited to Chatt. Two other Cup final goals have been scored in under a minute: John Roscamp of Blackburn scored by bundling Huddersfield keeper Mercer into the net after 40 seconds of the 1928 final on 21 April, and Jackie Milburn scored with a rare header after 45 seconds of the 1955 final for Newcastle v Manchester City on 7 May.

SINGLE GAMES (PLAYERS)

6 goals – Frank Keetley, one of 9 brothers who played professional football, scored 6 goals in 21 minutes for Lincoln City against Halifax in Division 3N on Saturday 16 January 1932. Lincoln won the game 9-1.

4 goals – Johnny McIntyre of Blackburn Rovers scored 4 goals in 5 minutes during the 5-1 win over Everton at Ewood Park in Division 1 on Saturday 16 September 1922. Three of the goals came in 3 minutes and, amazingly, they were 4 of only 47 goals Blackburn scored that season. William 'Ginger' Richardson also scored 4 goals in 5 minutes for West Bromwich at West Ham in Division 1 on Saturday 7 November 1931. West Brom also won 5-1.

3 goals – Ian St John scored 3 goals for Motherwell in a League Cup tie away at Hibernian on Saturday 15 August 1959 in 150 seconds. Jim Scarth of Gillingham is also reputed to have scored 3 goals in 150 seconds against Leyton Orient in Division 3S on Saturday 1 November 1952. Gillingham won 3-2. Ian Scanlon scored 3 goals in 165 seconds against Sheffield Wednesday in Division 2 on Saturday 16 November 1974. The oddity here was that one of the three was a penalty. County drew 3-3. Apart from McIntyre, Richardson, St John, Scarth and Scanlon above, 8 other players are credited with having scored a first class hat-trick in 3 minutes:

Bill Lane for Watford v Clapton Orient, Division 3S, Wednesday 20 December 1933;

Jimmy McGrory for Celtic v Motherwell, Scottish Division 1, Saturday 14 March 1936;

Jack Lindsay for Southport v Scunthorpe, Division 3N, Saturday 9 February 1952;

John Hartburn for Leyton Orient v Shrewsbury, Division 3S, Saturday 22 January 1955;

Graham Leggat for Fulham v Ipswich, Division 1, Thursday 26 December 1963 (Fulham won 10-1);

Gerry Talbot for Chester v Crewe, FA Cup first round, Saturday 14 November 1964;

Colin Stein for Rangers v Arbroath, Scottish Division 1, Saturday 2 November 1968;

Billy Best for Southend v Brentwood, FA Cup second round, Saturday 7 December 1968.

There may have been instances before the First World War, but timekeeping was not precise enough to detail such feats with any certainty.

SINGLE GAMES (TEAMS)

10 goals – Arbroath are reputed to have scored 10 goals between the 46th and 60th minutes of their record 36-0 defeat of Bon Accord on 12 September 1885.

8 goals: Sunderland scored 8 goals in the last 28 minutes of their Division 1 game away at Newcastle on Saturday 5 December 1908. Newcastle were League leaders at the time, but Sunderland won 9-1. The last 5 goals came in 8 minutes, easily the fastest burst of scoring in an indisputably senior fixture.

In one half: Apart from Cup victories against minor opposition such as Arbroath's above, the highest number of goals scored in one half is 11. Stockport were leading 2-0 at half-time against Halifax in Division 3N on 6 January 1934 but ended the game 13-0 victors.

5 goals: Alloa scored 5 goals in 10 minutes against Armadale in Scottish Division 2 on 26 March 1927. Alloa won 6-2.

4 goals: Four goals in less than 10 minutes is not particularly uncommon, though it is most interesting at the end of a Cup tie. Cambuslang, for instance, scored 4 times between the 82nd and 90th minutes of a Scottish Cup tie against Queen's Park on 11 December 1886 but still lost 5-4. Darwen scored 4 goals in the last 15 minutes of their FA Cup quarter-final with Old Etonians on 15 February 1879 to draw 5-5. In recent years the most celebrated four goal comeback was by Chelsea, who scored 4 goals in the last 15 minutes of a Division 1 game against Bolton at Stamford Bridge on 14 October 1978 to win 4-3.

In the first minute: There are two recorded instances of a side scoring twice in the first minute of a Football League match. On 10 April 1954, Spurs were two goals ahead after just 54 seconds of a First Division game against Huddersfield at Leeds Road. Spurs won 5-2. On 22 September 1956 Ipswich were two up after 50 seconds at Portman Road in a Division 3S game against Brentford. Ipswich won 4-0.

Arsenal's Alan Sunderland, who scored the fastest ever goal in any Cup semi-final when he put Arsenal ahead of Liverpool after 13 seconds of an FA Cup second replay at Villa Park on Monday 28 April 1980.

TOP: A rare picture of Aberdare Athletic (stripes) in happier days: on 12 January 1924 they lost 5-0 in the Cup at West Ham. Three years later they failed to gain re-election.
ABOVE: Blackburn's John Roscamp charges Huddersfield keeper Mercer and the ball over the line after 40 seconds of the 1928 Cup final for the quickest goal ever at Wembley.

Re-election & Resignation

RE-ELECTION

Applications: Up to the 1983–84 season, Lincoln City and Hartlepools had both applied for re-election on 13 occasions. Before being expelled from the League, both Barrow (1972) and Southport (1978) had made 11 applications.

Consecutive: Hartlepool applied for re-election successfully in five successive seasons – 1959–64. Bradford Park Avenue finished bottom of Division 4 in three consecutive seasons, 1967–70, at the end of which they were not re-elected. In 1966–67 they had finished 23rd.

Come-backs: The following 12 clubs have returned to the League after previously being evicted: Blackpool, Chesterfield, Crewe, Doncaster, Gillingham, Grimsby, Lincoln, Luton, Newport, Port Vale, Stockport and Walsall. This has happened only once since the Second World War – with Gillingham's election in 1950.

Lincolnshire handicap: Between 1908 and 1922 the three Lincolnshire clubs – Lincoln, Grimsby and Gainsborough – conducted an almost comical game of musical chairs, darting in and out of the League. In 1908 Lincoln City, with Stoke, failed to gain re-election. In 1909, Lincoln were elected back to Division 2 in place of neighbouring Chesterfield (actually in Derbyshire). In 1910, Grimsby failed to gain re-election and were replaced by Huddersfield. In 1911, Lincoln were replaced by their county neighbours, Grimsby. In 1912, Gainsborough Trinity failed to gain re-election and Lincoln came back in their place. All was quiet until the first season after the war, 1919–20, when both Grimsby and Lincoln failed to gain re-election. Lincoln (21st) had to leave the League but Grimsby (22nd) were invited to join the new Division 3. Lincoln became founder members of Division 3N in 1921–22.

Close finishes: On four occasions there have been ties between League and non-League clubs in re-election votes – and on each occasion the non-League club won the second ballot. In 1927 Torquay and Aberdare received 21 votes each, Torquay (then in the Southern League) winning the second vote 26-19. In 1931 Chester overcame Nelson on a second ballot. In 1972 Hereford took Barrow's place and in 1978 Wigan took Southport's after identical votes – 26-26 on the first and 29-20 on the second. In 1950 Wigan and Workington drew for one of the new Division 3N places and went to a second ballot, only for Scunthorpe to come through, beat them both, and join the League!

RESIGNATIONS AND EXPULSIONS

The following clubs have either resigned from the Football League or failed to win re-election at the end of a season in which they finished in the bottom 2, 3 or 4 (pre-1921 the number varied) or bottom 4 (after the formation of Division 3N in 1921–22).

Aberdare Athletic: Not re-elected 1927. Torquay replaced them.

Accrington: Failed to gain re-election in 1893 after being founder members of the League in 1888. They were actually relegated from Div 1 and then found themselves unable to finance a place in Div 2.

Accrington Stanley: Not the same club as Accrington, Stanley joined the League in 1921 and resigned on Tuesday 6 March 1962. Their fixtures for the season were expunged.

Ashington: Not re-elected 1929. York replaced them.

Barrow: Not re-elected 1972. Hereford United took their place.

Bootle: Resigned in 1893 (after only one season in the League) despite finishing 8th out of 12.

Bradford Park Avenue: Not re-elected 1970. Cambridge United took their place.

Burton United: Not re-elected 1907. For a time they were also known as Burton Swifts.

Burton Wanderers: Not re-elected 1897.

Darwen: Not re-elected 1899.

Durham City: Not re-elected 1928. Carlisle replaced them.

Gainsborough Trinity: Not re-elected 1912.

Gateshead: Not re-elected 1960 and replaced by Peterborough. South Shields Adelaide was the name of the original club which joined the League in 1919, later changing to plain South Shields. In 1930 this club moved in toto to Gateshead.

Glossop North End: Finished bottom of Division 2 in 1914–15 and then resigned. Stoke took over their place but didn't play until 1919–20.

Leeds City: Expelled from the League on Saturday 4 October 1919 for making illegal payments during wartime football, and Port Vale took over their fixtures. Ironically Port Vale are the only other club to have been expelled from the League, also for illegal payments, in 1968, though they were readmitted immediately. Leeds United were formed soon after Leeds City's demise but cannot be considered the same club.

Loughborough Town: Not re-elected 1900.

Merthyr Town: Not re-elected 1930. Replaced by Thames.

Middlesbrough Ironopolis: Resigned after one season in 1894.

Nelson: Not re-elected 1931. Replaced by Chester.

New Brighton/New Brighton Tower: The Tower club resigned in 1901. A reformed New Brighton were League members from 1923 to 1951, when Workington were elected in their place.

Northwich Victoria: Resigned in 1894 after just two seasons.

Rotherham County/Town/United: Rotherham Town were members of the League from 1893 to 1896, when they resigned. Rotherham County were elected to Division 2 in 1919, and in 1925 County and Town combined to form Rotherham United.

Southport: Not re-elected 1978. Wigan Athletic took their place.

Stalybridge Celtic: Resigned in 1923 when Division 3N was extended from 20 to 22 clubs.

Stoke: Failed to gain re-election in 1890, were elected back in 1891 but resigned on Wednesday 17 June 1908 and the club was disbanded. A new Stoke club was formed soon afterwards and became Stoke City in 1925, but this is not strictly the same club.

Thames: Did not apply for re-election after the 1931–32 season. Replaced by Newport.

Wigan Borough: Resigned from League on Monday 26 October 1931. Their fixtures for the season were expunged. Wigan Athletic, though formed the following year, are not the same club.

Workington: Not re-elected 1977. Wimbledon took their place.

Another 12 clubs who were not re-elected at some point have since returned to the League (see RE-ELECTION).

Most impressive departure: Leeds City played their last ever game at Molineux on Saturday 4 October 1919. The team apparently travelled over-night by bus because of a railway strike but still won the game 4–2. Manager Herbert Chapman, plus all the directors, were suspended for refusing to open their books to a committee investigating financial payments during the First World War and Port Vale took over their fixtures. Leeds had been declared League Champions (despite having been a Division 2 club before the war) in 1918 after play-offs among the various wartime League Champions.

SCOTLAND

Seven Scottish clubs have either been expelled or resigned from one or other of the Scottish Leagues:

Renton were expelled from the Scottish League after just four games of the initial season 1890–91 for playing Edinburgh Saints, a club made up of St Bernard's players who had been suspended for professionalism. Renton, under investigation for professionalism themselves, were found to have spent an enormous amount on chickens. Their secretary, trying to explain this, suggested that the team trained on 'chicken bree' (broth) and Renton were known ever afterwards as 'chicken bree'. When Renton resigned in 1897–98, after 4 matches, Hamilton took their place.

Dumbarton Harp resigned from Division 3 after 16 games in 1924–25.

Galston dropped out of Scottish Division 3 in 1926 after getting into financial difficulties and the whole League was suspended after several other clubs indicated that they were also in trouble. The League thus only existed for 3 years – Arthurlie were winners in 1924, Nithsdale Wanderers in 1925 and Helensburgh were heading the table when it was suspended in 1926 – though it was briefly revived as Division C after the War.

Bathgate and **Arthurlie** both resigned from Division 2 in 1928–29. Arthurlie's record was allowed to stand as they resigned after playing 32 of their 36 games.

Bo'ness and **Armadale** were expelled from Division 2 in November 1932 when they were unable to meet their £50 guarantees.

Third Lanark, one of the founding members of the Scottish FA and winners of both the Scottish Cup and the Scottish League, dropped out of the League at the end of 1966–67 and ceased to exist.

Failed to gain re-election: 26 other teams have played in the Scottish League at some time or another and have either not been re-elected or chose not to apply for re-election: Abercorn, Broxburn, Cambuslang, Clackmannan, Clydebank (not the current club), Cowlairs, Dundee Wanderers, Edinburgh City, Leith Athletic, Linthouse, Lochgelly, Johnstone (not St Johnstone), King's Park, Northern, Port Glasgow, St Bernard's, Thistle and Vale of Leven. This first list excludes those clubs from the short-lived Third Division – namely Peebles Rovers, Dykehead, Solway Star, Helensburgh, Beith, Nithsdale Wanderers, Royal Albert and Mid-Annandale.

Relegation

Never relegated: Aberdeen, Celtic and Rangers have never been relegated, though Aberdeen did finish bottom of the Scottish League in 1917 and dropped out for two years. This was, however, at their own volition and there was no Second Division at the time. Aberdeen also played in Scottish Division 2 in 1904–05 before entering the senior division. Celtic were just one game away from relegation when they played at Dundee on 17 April 1948. They won the game 3–2 and finished 12th but, as it happened, would not have gone down even if they had lost. On 1 January 1984 only one Football League club, Wigan Athletic, had never been relegated. Arsenal have not been relegated since 1913, nor promoted either as they were given a First Division place in 1919.

Longest before relegation: Apart from Rangers and Celtic, Sunderland had the longest run without relegation, remaining in the First Division from 1890 to 1958 when they went down on goal average, two other clubs also having 32 points. Arsenal have already technically surpassed this record, it being over 70 years since they were last relegated, but will equal Sunderland's tenure in 1987, which is coincidentally Arsenal's centenary season.

Consecutive seasons: Bristol City established a remarkable record by falling from Division 1 to Division 4 in three consecutive seasons. On 1 September 1979 they were 6th in Division 1; on Saturday 4 December 1982 they were 92nd in the League, a decline of 86 places in the space of 3 years 95 days. There is no performance strictly comparable with this in League history, though York City were relegated from Division 2 in 1976, from Division 3 in 1977 and had to apply for re-election in 1978. Other clubs which have been relegated in consecutive seasons are as follows:

Division 1-Division 3N: Bradford P.A., 1920–22.

Division 1-Division 3: Northampton, 1965–67; Fulham, 1967–69; Huddersfield. 1971–73; Crystal Palace, 1972–74.

Division 2-Division 4: Port Vale, 1956–58 (on reorganization); Doncaster, 1957–59; Notts County, 1957–59; Lincoln, 1960–62; Brighton, 1961–63; York, 1975–77; Hereford, 1976–78. Apart from Bristol City no club has ever been relegated in three consecutive seasons, but York came closest with relegation from Division 2 in 1976, from Division 3 in 1977 and an application for re-election in 1978.

Championship to relegation: Manchester City are the only team to be relegated the season after winning the Championship, in 1937–38. In that season they scored more goals than any other Division 1 club and had a positive goal difference (80–77). As a counter-point, Cardiff City were relegated in 1928–29 having *conceded* fewer goals than any other side in the Division (59). They scored 43.

Most goals: Manchester City's 89 goals in 1925–26 is the most ever scored by a relegated club, though Newcastle scored 86 in Division 1 in 1960–61. In Division 2 Darlington scored 79 in 1926–27 and in Division 3 Wrexham scored 75 in 1963–64.

Escapes: The most dramatic was by Lincoln City at the foot of Division 2 in 1957–58, when they won their last 6 games in April 1958 – 3–1 on 8 April at Barnsley, 3–1 on 12 April at Doncaster, 2–0 at home to Rotherham on 19 April, 4–0 at home to Bristol City on 23 April, 1–0 at Huddersfield on 26 April and 3–1 at home to Cardiff on 30 April to escape by a point.

Replays

MOST

At senior level: Only one tie in the major Cup competitions has gone to 6 games. That was in the fourth qualifying round of the FA Cup between Alvechurch and Oxford City in 1971–72. Alvechurch eventually won 1–0.

Competitions proper: Five games have been required on 5 occasions in the later rounds of the major Cup competitions:

1908–09: Broxburn and Beith met 5 times in the first round of the Scottish Cup, the last 3 occasions on Wednesday 3rd, Thursday 4th and Friday 5th of February 1909. Beith won and on the 6th lost 3-0 to St Mirren in the second round. Broxburn's four games on consecutive days is unparalleled in first-class football.

1954–55: Stoke and Bury played for a total of 9 hrs 22 minutes in the third round of the FA Cup before Stoke won 3-2 at Old Trafford. Stoke won 10-9 on aggregate. They went out 3-1 to Swansea in the fourth round. In the fourth round Doncaster played Aston Villa 5 times before the former won 3-1 at The Hawthorns.

1955–56: Chelsea and Burnley played for 9 hours in the fourth round before Chelsea won 2-0. Chelsea lost to Everton in the fifth round.

1960–61: Hull City and Darlington played for 9 hours in the second round before Hull won. They lost 1-0 to Bolton in the third round.

Finals: No FA Cup final has gone to a second replay, but the 1976–77 League Cup final between Aston Villa and Everton did so before Villa won 3-2. Four Scottish Cup finals, in 1877, 1903, 1910 and 1979, went to two replays.

Ordered: Only one FA Cup tie has been ordered to be replayed twice. That was an 1889–90 quarter-final between The Wednesday and Notts County. The Sheffield club won the first game 5-0 but County's protests about the pitch were upheld and the game was replayed, County winning 3-2. Wednesday then protested about an ineligible player and a third game was played, which they won 2-1. Wednesday went on to the final, which they lost to Blackburn by the then record score of 6-1. Wednesday are one of only two clubs to have reached a final after losing a game. In 1946, when the series was played on a two-legged basis, Charlton lost 2-1 at Fulham in the third round but won 3-1 at home. Both of these clubs lost the final. Protests over ineligible players lead to numerous replays in both the FA Cup and Scottish Cup in the 1880s. Clubs would investigate the opposition, but only protest if they lost the tie. As a result, in 1891 the FA insisted that protests would only be valid if lodged *before* a game and replayed matches therefore became a rarity after this date.

GAMES REPLAYED FOR SPECIAL REASONS

Arbroath 2 Rangers 1, 1884: Rangers complained that they had been 'beaten on a back green' as the pitch was only 49 yds 1 ft wide on the centre-line. Rangers won the legalities, Arbroath had to widen the pitch, and Rangers won the replay.

Pollockshields Athletic v St Andrew's, 1886: St Andrew's protested that the Pollockshields' pitch had the goal-line several feet behind the goal-posts and the Scottish FA, not surprisingly, ordered a replay.

Celtic 0 Clyde 1, 1889: Celtic protested that the referee should not have allowed the game to proceed because of bad light and a waterlogged pitch. The Scottish FA agreed

David Webb's 'Golden Shoulder' carries the ball into the net from Ian Hutchinson's throw for Chelsea in 1970 to win the first Cup final replay in 60 years. The final against Leeds was the only one ever to last 240 minutes and involved the first drawn Wembley game.

and Celtic won the replay 9-2. It was a great year for Celtic protests – they reached the final and protested about the state of the pitch after Third Lanark's 3-1 win. The final had to be replayed, with Celtic again losing, 2-1. Abercorn had also protested at a 5-4 defeat by Third Lanark in an earlier round and the game was replayed. After two 2-2 draws, Third Lanark finally won 3-1 at the end of a fourth game.

Celtic 2 Royal Albert 2, 1890: The first Scottish Cup tie between the two clubs on 29 November 1890 was ordered replayed because of the state of the pitch. The replay, played on 6 December 1890, which Celtic won 4-0, was ordered to be replayed because of a crowd invasion, and Celtic finally won the match 2-0 at Ibrox on 13 December.

Darwen 3 Kidderminster 1, 1891: Kidderminster protested at the state of the pitch in an FA Cup first round match on Saturday

17 January 1891, and the FA ordered the game replayed. Darwen obviously decided to punish their less celebrated opponents and won the replay 13-0. On the same day, Blackburn Rovers won 2-1 at Middlesbrough Ironopolis, but the FA also ordered that game replayed. Blackburn won again, 3-0, and went on to win the Cup. Strangely, both they and their final opponents The Wednesday (*above*) were ordered to replay a tie in the same season – the only time that anything like this had happened.

Rotherham Town 0 Grimsby 1, Saturday 22 December 1894: Grimsby arrived an hour late for this Division 2 game and it eventually had to be abandoned because of bad light. The League Management Committee ordered it replayed, allowed Rotherham Town to keep the whole of the two gates, and thus presented the Yorkshiremen with an extra bonus when they won the second game 3-2 on Monday 7 January 1895.

Barnsley 1 Liverpool 2, 1895: The score in this first round FA Cup tie was 1-1 at full time but the referee ordered an extra 15 minutes each way, and Liverpool scored once more to win 2-1. The Barnsley committee objected that the extra 30 minutes should not have been played and the FA ordered a replay – which Liverpool won 4-0.

FA Cup semi-final, 1899: The replayed semi-final between Sheffield United and Liverpool at the Manchester Athletic Club, Fallowfield, was abandoned at half-time, with Liverpool leading 1-0, after the crowd continually encroached on the pitch. This was due more to the pressure of over 30,000 people then any intent to disrupt the game, which was scheduled to kick-off at 3.30 pm but was actually abandoned, with only 45 minutes played, $2\frac{1}{4}$ hours later. Of course, numerous other FA Cup and League matches have been abandoned because of weather conditions and have had to be replayed.

Newcastle v Sunderland, 1901: During the Division 1 game at St James's Park on 20 April 1901, fighting broke out in the crowd and spilled onto the pitch. The goal-posts were torn down and subsequent riots caused the game to be abandoned. It was replayed on 24 April, the result being a 2-0 win for Sunderland. This is the first recorded example of an English game being abandoned as a result of deliberate unruly behaviour by the crowd, as opposed to the crowd simply being too large.

Tottenham v Aston Villa in the second round of the FA Cup of 1904 was abandoned when Spurs fans invaded the pitch after Villa had gone into a 1-0 lead. Spurs were fined £350 and the FA ordered that the replay should be held at Villa Park. Unfortunately for Villa, Tottenham won the replay 1-0. Similar incidents have happened several times in the 1970s, notably at Leeds and Newcastle. On 1 February 1913 the second round tie between Manchester City and Sunderland was abandoned because of overcrowding and the FA ordered the game to be replayed at Sunderland, where City lost 2-0.

Croydon Common v Grimsby, 1911: Grimsby were ordered to replay their FA Cup first round tie with Croydon Common on 14 January 1911. The Lincolnshire team had restudded their boots at half-time and, as a result, the interval lasted more than 20 minutes. Grimsby won the first game 3-0 and the replay 8-1.

Ayr v Falkirk, 1935: This is the only instance of a normal League fixture having two complete playings. On 9 March 1935 Falkirk visited Ayr for a vital Scottish First Division relegation battle and won 3-2. It emerged later that the Falkirk manager had approached an Ayr player to throw the match. The SFA suspended the manager and ordered the game replayed, which it was on Wednesday 10 April with Ayr winning 3-1. Falkirk were relegarted at the end of the season and Ayr stayed up.

Newcastle 4 Nottingham Forest 3, 9 March 1974: In the only incident of its kind this century, the Newcastle crowd invaded the pitch of a quarter-final tie when Newcastle defender Pat Howard was sent off and Forest went 3-1 up from a penalty. The game was held up for 20 minutes, and, when it restarted, Newcastle came back to win 4-3. The FA ordered the game replayed because of the crowd invasion and two more matches were played out at neutral Goodison Park. After a 0-0 draw Newcastle won 1-0 and went on to the final, where Liverpool beat them 3-0. The game was also peculiar in that Forest were ordered (despite their protests) to play three games in the same round away from home. There is no precedent for this in the FA Cup except, of course, at the semi-final stage.

ABANDONED

Over the years large numbers of games have been abandoned because of weather conditions and ordered replayed. There are one or two exceptional instances, however:

Umpires failed to agree: The semi-final between Dumbarton and Renton in the Scottish Cup on Saturday 6 March 1875 was abandoned 10 minutes from time when the umpires (one from each side) and referee could not reach agreement on whether Renton had scored a goal. The game was replayed the following week, Renton winning 1-0 and going though to the final.

Fog determines Championship: Everton and Newcastle were neck and neck for the League Championship at the end of the 1904-05 season. On 26 November, Everton had been beating Woolwich Arsenal 3-1 after 78 minutes at Woolwich, when dense fog rolled in and the game had to be abandoned. It was replayed on Saturday 22 April 1905 and Everton lost 2-1. Even though Newcastle lost 3-1 at home to Sunderland on the same day, they took the title. Had the fog not intervened, Everton would certainly have won the Championship by a single point.

Internationals: Only one England international has ever been abandoned – that against Argentina in Buenos Aires on Sunday 17 May 1953, when torrential rain water-logged the pitch after 23 minutes. The score at the time was 0-0. Scotland have also had one game abandoned – on Wednesday 8 May 1963 at Hampden after 79 minutes when the referee felt unable to control the persistent fouling of their Austrian opponents. Scotland were leading 4-1.

Anglo-Italian Trophy: The first final of this competition, played in Naples in 1970, was abandoned after 79 minutes through crowd disturbances, with Swindon Town leading Napoli 3-0.

Unfinished Cup matches: On 7 November 1953, in the fourth qualifying round of the FA Cup, the Runcorn team walked off the field in the 31st minute when the referee awarded a goal to opponents Witton. The ball had passed through a hole in the side of the net and Runcorn refused to return to the pitch. Witton were awarded the match 2-0. On 28 August 1950 the Scottish League Cup tie between Hibernian and Dundee was abandoned after 45 minutes because of a waterlogged pitch. The game was never completed because Hibernian had already won the section into which the match fell.

Scottish Cup finals: A whole string were replayed or disrupted in the 19th century. In 1878-79 Rangers drew 1-1 with Vale of Leven but refused to replay because of a disputed goal; in 1881 Queen's Park and Dumbarton had to replay because of the state of the pitch; in 1884 the final was not played at all and in 1889, 1892 and 1893 the finals were ordered replayed because of snow, frost or crowd trouble.

POSTPONED

Most often: The Scottish Cup second round tie between Inverness Thistle and Falkirk was postponed 29 times before finally being played on Thursday 22 February 1979 (the original date had been Saturday 6 January 1979). Falkirk won 4-0.

Most often, England: The Coventry City v Lincoln City third round FA Cup tie was postponed 15 times in 1962-63.

Most games called off: 57 first-class fixtures were called off and only 7 played (all in the Football League) on Saturday 9 February 1963.

Fewest games played: All but 1 of the 56 scheduled Regional League games were called off on Saturday 3 February 1940. The one that was played made up for this a little, ending Plymouth 10 Bristol City 3.

Fewest Football League games played: Only 4 Football League matches were played on 12 January 1963 and Saturday 2 February 1963.

See also: UNFINISHED MATCHES

The programme for the Scottish Cup second round tie between Inverness Thistle and Falkirk – postponed for a record 29 times in 1979. Falkirk won 4-0.

Scottish Cup

FINALS

Most wins: 26 – up to and including 1983, Celtic had won the Cup 26 times.

Most appearances: 41 – up to and including 1983, Celtic had made the most final appearances, having played in almost half of the 98 games thus far.

Division 2 winners: Only one non-Division 1/Premier Division club has ever won the Scottish Cup – East Fife in 1938, when they beat Kilmarnock 4-2 after a 1-1 draw. They had to sign two players just to send out a full team in the final as they were so depleted by injuries. Danny McKerrall, a Falkirk reserve, was signed as outside-left, while Hearts reserve left-back John Harvey was actually played at left-half. Neither had played in the competition before that season and hence won Scottish Cup winners medals in their first games with their new club. McKerrall scored 2 of East Fife's 4 goals in the replay. East Fife had a remarkably fortuitous run to the final, not having to play any of the top 5 clubs in the League. Kilmarnock, 18th in Division 1 and just one point away from relegation, had knocked out both Celtic and Rangers and were managed at the time by the great Celtic goalscorer Jimmy McGrory. It is fair to say, then, that the vagaries of the draw were as responsible for East Fife's success as anything else.

Division 2 finalists: Apart from East Fife (1927 and 1938) only Renton (1895), Dumbarton (1897) and Kilmarnock (1898) have appeared in the final while not in Division 1.

Non-League winners: When Queen's Park won the trophy in 1893, and also when they were beaten finalists in 1892 and 1900, they were not members of the League.

Relegated finalists: When Dumbarton reached the 1897 final they were bottom of Division 2 with just 6 points from 18 games and were not re-elected to the League at the end of the season. They also lost the final, 5-1 to Rangers. Albion Rovers were bottom of the sole division of the Scottish League when beaten 3-2 by Kilmarnock in 1920.

Most consecutive finals: 7 - Celtic, between 1969 and 1975. They won five.

Played outside Glasgow: Only one final has been played outside Glasgow – the 1896 game between Hearts and Hibs at Logie Green, home of Edinburgh's other League club, St Bernard's. The crowd was only 16,034 as many were said to have stayed away expecting the ground to be packed. The 1980 and 1981 League Cup finals were contested in Dundee.

Closest finish: The most remarkable comeback in a Scottish Cup final was in 1910 when Dundee were 2-0 down to Clyde with only 7 minutes left and yet equalised at 2-2 with goals by John Hunter and Johnny Langland. The clubs drew a second game 0-0 before Dundee won the third game 2-1. The other tight, and even more poignant,

finish was in 1931 when Motherwell were leading Celtic 2-0 with just 8 minutes left. Then Jimmy McGrory scored and, in the 90th minute, Motherwell centre-half Alan Craig headed a cross by Celtic winger Bertie Thomson into his own goal when there was no Celtic player anywhere near the ball. Celtic won the replay 4-2 and Motherwell had to wait another 20 years before they won the Cup for the first time.

OTHER ROUNDS

Most semi-finals: Up to and including 1983, Celtic had appeared in 51 semi-finals (and, remarkably, lost only 10) while Rangers had appeared in 50.

First ever game: The Scottish Cup began in October 1873 with a game between Renton and Kilmarnock at Queen's Club in Crosshill, Glasgow. Renton won 3-0 but were no doubt helped by the fact that Kilmarnock had previously played under rugby rules (their ground is still called Rugby Park), and kept forgetting that they could not handle the ball.

Entered every year: Dumbarton, Kilmarnock and Queen's Park have entered every year.

Cup double: Queen's Park came nearer than any other club to winning the two premier Cup competitions, the FA Cup and Scottish Cup, in 1884. They had already been awarded the Scottish Cup when Vale of Leven failed to appear for the final (*see* REPLAYS) and met Blackburn Rovers at Kennington Oval in the FA Cup final. They lost 2-1, but the game was a thoroughly contentious one. According to the Queen's Park team, referee Major Marindin visited them afterwards and told them that one Blackburn goal would have been disallowed, and one Queen's Park goal would have been given, had they only appealed. At the time referees had no theoretical authority to actually decide anything on the field. As their name implies, they were only there to be referred to by the teams in case of a dispute.

Giantkilling: Giantkilling in Scotland is relatively rare. The most celebrated example is Berwick Rangers' 1-0 defeat of Rangers on Saturday 28 January 1967, when a Sammy Reid goal took the English side through in a Scottish Cup first-round tie. As a Division C side in 1953–54, Berwick Rangers had

also defeated East Stirlingshire 7-0, Ayr United 5-1 and Dundee 3-0. However, Fraserburgh of the Highland League produced perhaps a more commendable display in beating Dundee 1-0 in the first round of the 1958–59 competition. Dundee were fourth in Division 1 at the time but it should be noted that the better Highland League sides have long been regarded as the equals if not the superiors of some Division 2 clubs. The biggest win by a non-League club over a senior side was actually Gala Fairydean's 9-1 defeat of Clydebank on 15 September 1965. This was at the beginning of Clydebank's intermediate season between playing as East Stirlingshire-Clydebank and rejoining the League as plain Clydebank. As most of the senior players had gone back to East Stirling they were, at the time, fielding only a junior side. By coincidence, Gala and Clydebank were the two candidates for election to the League that season. Gala were passed over despite their win and have never been members of the Scottish League

ABOVE: Rangers keeper Martin is not amused by Sammy Reid's giantkilling goal in the Scottish Cup. Berwick defeated the Glaswegians 1-0 on 28 January 1967.
OPPOSITE: Bob Gillespie, chairman of Queen's Park, at a 1952 club meeting. His chain of office is made up of Scottish Cup medals. Gillespie was the last amateur to appear for Scotland, in 1933.

before or since. In actual fact there have only been two defeats of Scottish First Division sides by non-League opposition since the Second World War. Apart from Fraserburgh 1 Dundee 0 mentioned above, Elgin City defeated Ayr United 1-0 in 1966–67. Ayr at the time were in the midst of a run of 31 consecutive games without a win, were firmly anchored at the bottom of the division and, in fact, won only one game that season – the worst performance in the Scottish First Division this century. Speaking of non-League Cup exploits, perhaps the oddest was that of Stirling Albion who competed in the Scottish League Cup in 1945–46 before they had ever played a game in the Scottish League!

Scottish Cup winners: Despite having been in existence for over 110 years, there have, in fact, been very few winners of the Scottish Cup. On 1 January 1984, the list was as follows:

Celtic	26
Rangers	24
Queen's Park	10
Hearts	5
Aberdeen	4
Clyde	3
Vale of Leven	3
Dunfermline, Falkirk, Hibernian, Kilmarnock, Renton, St Mirren and Third Lanark	2
Airdrie, Dumbarton, Dundee, East Fife, Morton, Motherwell, Partick Thistle and St Bernard's	1

Repeat finals: There have only been three, none between Celtic and Rangers. In 1881 and 1882 Queen's Park defeated Dumbarton after 2 games each year. In 1892 and 1893 Queen's Park and Celtic shared honours, though after one protested game each year, and it was not until 1982 and 1983 that Rangers and Aberdeen repeated the trick.

SCOTTISH FA CUP 1873-74

Quarter-finals
Queen's Park v Eastern	1-0
Renton v Dumbarton	0-0, 1-0
Alexandria Athletic v Blythwood	0-2
Clydesdale v 3rd Lanark Rifle V.	1-1, 0-0, 1-0

Semi-finals
Queen's Park v Renton	2-0
Clydesdale v Blythwood	4-0

Final
Queen's Park 2 Clydesdale 0
(First Hampden Park, 21.3.74, 3,500)
Scorers: McKinnon, Leckie

SCOTTISH FA CUP 1874-75

Quarter-finals
Queen's Park w.o. Rovers*	
Dumbarton v 3rd Lanark Rifle Volunteers	1-0
Renton v Eastern	1-0
[Clydesdale received bye]	

Semi-finals
Queen's Park v Clydesdale	0-0, 2-2, 1-0
Renton v Dumbarton	0-0, 1-0

Final
Queen's Park 3 Renton 0
(First Hampden Park, 10.4.75, 7,000)
Scorers: Weir, Highet, McKinnon
*Scratched

SCOTTISH FA CUP 1875-76

Quarter-finals
Queen's Park v Dumbreck	2-0
Vale of Leven v Rovers	2-0
3rd Lanark Rifle Volunteers v Western	5-0
[Dumbarton received bye]	

Semi-finals
Queen's Park v Vale of Leven	3-1
3rd Lanark Rifle Volunteers v Dumbarton	3-0

Final
Queen's Park 1:2 3rd Lanark Rifle Volunteers 1:0
(Hamilton Crescent, 11.3.76, 10,000 [replay 18.3.76, 6,000])
Scorers: Highet, Drinnan; Highet(2)

SCOTTISH FA CUP 1876-77

Quarter-finals
Vale of Leven v Queen's Park	2-1
Ayr Thistle v Lancefield	2-2, 1-0
Rangers v Lennox	3-0

Semi-finals
Vale of Leven v Ayr Thistle	9-0
[Rangers received bye]	

Final
Vale of Leven 1:0:3 Rangers 1:0:2
(First Hampden Park, 17.3.77, 10,000 [replays, 7.4.77, 15,000 & 7,500]) (third game 13.4.77)
Scorers: Paton, o.g.; Baird, Paton, o.g.; (Rangers) Campbell, McNiel

SCOTTISH FA CUP 1877-78

Quarter-finals
Vale of Leven v Parkgrove	5-0
Renton v Mauchline	3-1
3rd Lanark Rifle Volunteers v South Western	2-1
(after 0-1 result with crowd interference)	

Semi-finals
3rd Lanark Rifle Volunteers v Renton	1-1, 1-0
[Vale of Leven received bye]	

Final
Vale of Leven 1 3rd Lanark Rifle Volunteers 0
(First Hampden Park, 30.3.78, 5,000)
Scorer: not known

SCOTTISH FA CUP 1878-79

Quarter-finals
Vale of Leven v Dumbarton	3-1
Rangers v Queen's Park	1-0
[Helensburgh received bye]	

Semi-finals
Vale of Leven v Helensburgh	3-0
[Rangers received bye]	

Final
Vale of Leven *1 Rangers 1
(First Hampden Park, 19.4.79, 9,000)

*Vale of Leven were awarded the trophy after Rangers refused to play the replay on 26 April 1879. Rangers declined to appear after the SFA had turned down a protest that they had scored a legitimate second goal in the first game.

Scorers: Ferguson, Struthers

SCOTTISH FA CUP 1879-80

Quarter-finals
Dumbarton v Hibernian	6-0
Pollockshields Athletic v South Western	6-1
Thornliebank v Third Lanark	2-1
[Queen's Park received bye]	

Semi-finals
Queen's Park v Dumbarton	1-0
Thornliebank v Pollockshields Athletic	2-1

Final
Queen's Park 3 Thornliebank 0
(First Cathkin Park, 21.2.80, 4,000)

Scorers: not known

SCOTTISH FA CUP 1880-81

Quarter-finals
Queen's Park v Central	10-0
Vale of Leven v Arthurlie	2-0
Dumbarton v Rangers	3-1

Semi-finals
Dumbarton v Vale of Leven	2-0
[Queen's Park received bye]	

Final
Queen's Park *2:3 Dumbarton *1:1
(Kinning Park, 27.3.81, 10,000 [replay, 9.4.81, 7,000])
Scorers (final): Smith (2), Kerr; Meikleham

*Dumbarton's protest about spectators on the pitch was upheld

---

SCOTTISH FA CUP 1881-82

Quarter-finals
Queen's Park v Shotts	15-0
Kilmarnock Athletic v Arthurlie	5-2
Cartvale v West Calder	5-3
Dumbarton v Rangers	5-1

Semi-finals
Queen's Park v Kilmarnock Athletic	3-2
Dumbarton v Cartvale	11-2

Final
Queen's Park 2:4 Dumbarton 2:1
(First Cathkin Park, 18.3.82, 12,500 [replay 1.4.82, 8,000])
Scorers (replay): Richmond, Kerr, Harrower, Kay; Miller

SCOTTISH FA CUP 1882-83

Quarter-finals
Dumbarton v Queen's Park	3-1
Pollockshields Athletic v Third Lanark	1-1, 5-2
Kilmarnock Athletic v Arthurlie	†1-0
Vale of Leven v Partick Thistle	4-0

Semi-finals
Dumbarton v Pollockshields Athletic	5-0
Vale of Leven v Kilmarnock Athletic	1-1, 2-0

Final
Dumbarton 2:2 Vale of Leven 2:1
(First Hampden Park 31.3.83, 9,000 [replay 7.4.83, 12,000])
Scorers: (first game) Paton, McArthur, Johnstone, McCrae; (second game) Brown, Anderson, Friel

†after three drawn games

SCOTTISH FA CUP 1883-84

Quarter-finals
Queen's Park v Cartvale	6-1
Hibernian v Battlefield	6-1
Cambuslang v Rangers	1-5
Vale of Leven v Pollockshields Athletic	4-2

Semi-finals
Hibernian v Queen's Park	1-5
Vale of Leven v Rangers	3-0

Final
Queen's Park* awarded cup

*Vale of Leven asked for the final to be postponed because of the illness of two players and the family bereavement of another. The Scottish FA decided that was impossible due to other engagements, such as the international against England. Vale did not appear for the final and the trophy was awarded to Queen's Park

---

SCOTTISH FA CUP 1884-85

Quarter-finals
Renton v Rangers	5-3
Hibernian v Annbank	5-0
Cambuslang v Battlefield	3-1
Vale of Leven v Thornliebank	4-3

Semi-finals
Renton v Hibernian	3-2
Vale of Leven v Cambuslang	0-0, 3-1

Final
Renton 0:3 Vale of Leven 0:1
(Second Hampden Park, 2.3.85, 2,500 [replay 3,500])

SCOTTISH FA CUP 1885-86

Quarter-finals
Hibernian v Cambuslang	3-2
[Queen's Park, Renton & Third Lanark received byes]	

Semi-finals
Third Lanark v Queen's Park	0-3
Hibernian v Renton	0-2

Final
Queen's Park 3 Renton 1
(First Cathkin Park, 13.2.86, 7,000)

SCOTTISH FA CUP 1886-87

Quarter-finals
Third Lanark v Hibernian	1-2
Port Glasgow Athletic v Vale of Leven	1-3
Kilmarnock v Queen's Park	0-5
Hurlford v Dumbarton	0-0, 2-1*, 1-3

Semi-finals
Hibernian v Vale of Leven	3-1
Queen's Park v Dumbarton	1-2

Final
Hibernian 2 Dumbarton 1
(Second Hampden Park, 12,000)

*Result nullified by the Scottish FA after Hurlford had insisted on playing on a frozen pitch
Scorers: (Hibernian) Clark, Lafferty;

SCOTTISH FA CUP 1887-88

Quarter-finals
Renton v Dundee Wanderers	5-1
Queen's Park v Vale of Leven Wanderers	7-1
Abercorn v Arbroath	3-1
Cambuslang v Our Boys	6-0

Semi-finals
Renton v Queen's Park	3-1
Abercorn v Cambuslang	1-1, 1-10

Final
Renton 6 Cambuslang 1
(Second Hampden Park, 4.2.88, 11,000)

SCOTTISH FA CUP 1888-89

Quarter-final
Third Lanark v Campsie	5-1
Dumbarton Athletic v Renton	1-2
Dumbarton v St Mirren	1-1, 2-2, 2-2, 3-1
East Stirlingshire v Celtic	1-2

Semi-finals
Third Lanark v Renton	2-0
Dumbarton v Celtic	1-4

Finals
Third Lanark *3:2 Celtic *0:1
(Second Hampden Park, 2.2.89, 18,000 [replay 9.2.89, 13,000])
Scorers: Marshall, Oswald; McCallum (replay)

*The first game was declared void because of a snowstorm; Third Lanark tried to claim the trophy but the Scottish FA ordered a replay

---

SCOTTISH FA CUP 1889-90

Quarter-finals
Queen's Park v Leith Athletic	1-0
Abercorn v Hibernian	6-2
Third Lanark v Kilbirnie	4-1
Vale of Leven v East End	4-0

Semi-finals
Queen's Park v Abercorn	2-0
Vale of Leven v Third Lanark	3-0

Final
Queen's Park 1:2 Vale of Leven 1:1
(Ibrox, 15.2.90, 11,000 [replay 22.2.90, 14,000])
Scorers: Hamilton, Stewart; Bruce

SCOTTISH FA CUP 1890-91

Quarter-finals
Heart of Midlothian v East Stirlingshire	3-1
Third Lanark v Queen's Park	1-1, 2-2, 4-1
Leith Athletic v Abercorn	2-3
Dumbarton v Celtic	3-0

Semi-finals
Heart of Midlothian v Third Lanark	4-1
Dumbarton v Abercorn	3-1

Final
Heart of Midlothian 1 Dumbarton 0
(Second Hampden Park, 7.2.91, 16,000) (Mason)

SCOTTISH FA CUP   1891-92

Quarter-finals
Celtic v Cowlairs	4-1
Rangers v Annbank	2-0
Renton v Heart of Midlothian	4-4, 2-2, 3-2
Dumbarton v Queen's Park	2-2, 1-4

Semi-finals
Celtic v Rangers	5-3
Renton v Queen's Park	1-1, 0-3

Final
Celtic *1 :5 Queen's Park *0 :1
(Ibrox, 26,000) (12.3.92, 9.4.92)
Scorers (final): McMahon 3, Campbell 2; Waddell

*final replayed after first game disrupted by crowd

SCOTTISH FA CUP   1892-93

Quarter-finals
Heart of Midlothian v Queen's Park	1-1, 2-5
Broxburn Shamrock v St Mirren	4-3
St Bernard's v Rangers	3-2
Celtic v Third Lanark	5-1

Semi-finals
Queen's Park v Broxburn Shamrock	4-2
Celtic v St Bernard's	5-0

Final
Queen's Park *0 :2 Celtic *1 :1
(Ibrox, 18,000) (25.2.93, 11.3.93)
Scorers: Towie (first); Sellar (2), Blessington (second)

* final replayed after protest over frosty pitch; teams played after agreeing pitch was unfit.

SCOTTISH FA CUP   1893-94

Quarter-finals
Clyde v Rangers	0-5
Abercorn v Queen's Park	3-3, 3-3, 0-2
Third Lanark v Port Glasgow Athletic	2-1
Celtic v St Bernard's	8-1

Semi-finals
Rangers v Queen's Park	1-1, 3-1
Third Lanark v Celtic	3-5

Final
Rangers 3 Celtic 1
(Second Hampden Park, 17.2.94, 17,000)
Scorers: Barker, McCreadie, McPherson; Maley

SCOTTISH FA CUP   1894-95

Quarter-finals
St Bernard's v Clyde	2-1
Heart of Midlothian v King's Park	4-2
Dundee v Celtic	1-0
Ayr Parkhouse v Renton	2-3

Semi-finals
Heart of Midlothian v St Bernard's	0-0, 0-1
Dundee v Renton	1-1, 3-3, 0-3

Final
St Bernard's 2 Renton 1
(Ibrox, 20.4.95, 15,000)
Scorers: Clelland (2), Duncan

SCOTTISH FA CUP   1895-96

Quarter-finals
Heart of Midlothian v Arbroath	4-0
St Bernard's v Queen's Park	3-2
Renton v Third Lanark	3-3, 2-0
Hibernian v Rangers	3-2

Semi-finals
Heart of Midlothian v St Bernard's	1-0
Hibernian v Renton	2-1

Final
Heart of Midlothian 3 The Hibernians 1
(Logie Green, Edinburgh, 14.3.96, 16,034)
Scorers: Baird, King, Michael; O'Neil

SCOTTISH FA CUP   1896-97

Quarter-finals
Dundee v Rangers	0-4
Morton v Abercorn	2-2, 3-2
Kilmarnock v Third Lanark	3-1
Dumbarton v St Bernard's	2-0

Semi-finals
Morton v Rangers	2-7
Dumbarton v Kilmarnock	4-3

Final
Rangers 5 Dumbarton 1
(Second Hampden Park, 20.3.97, 14,000)

SCOTTISH FA CUP   1897-98

Quarter-finals
Queen's Park v Rangers	1-3
Third Lanark v Hibernian	2-0
Dundee v Heart of Midlothian	3-0
Ayr Parkhouse v Kilmarnock	2-7

Semi-finals
Rangers v Third Lanark	1-1, 2-2, 2-0
Kilmarnock v Dundee	3-2

Final
Rangers 2 Kilmarnock 0
(Second Hampden Park, 26.3.98, 13,000)

SCOTTISH FA CUP   1898-99

Quarter-finals
Celtic v Queen's Park	4-2*, 2-1
Port Glasgow Athletic v Partick Thistle	7-3
Kilmarnock v St Mirren	0-2
Rangers v Clyde	4-0

Semi-finals
Celtic v Port Glasgow Athletic	4-2
St Mirren v Rangers	1-2

Final
Celtic 2 Rangers 0
(Second Hampden Park, 22.4.99, 25,000)

*abandoned

SCOTTISH FA CUP 1899-1900

Quarter-finals
Celtic v Kilmarnock	4-0
Rangers v Partick Thistle	6-1
Third Lanark v Heart of Midlothian	1-2
Queen's Park v Dundee	1-0

Semi-finals
Celtic v Rangers	2-2, 4-0
Queen's Park v Heart of Midlothian	2-1

Final
Celtic 4 Queen's Park 3
(Ibrox, 14.4.1900, 15,000)

SCOTTISH FA CUP 1900-01

Quarter-finals
Port Glasgow Athletic v Heart of Midlothian	1-5
Hibernian v Morton	2-0
St Mirren v Third Lanark	0-0, 1-1, 3-3, 1-0
Dundee v Celtic	0-1

Semi-finals
Heart of Midlothian v Hibernian	1-1, 2-1
Celtic v St Mirren	1-0

Final
Heart of Midlothian 4 Celtic 3
(Ibrox, 6.4.01, 12,000)

SCOTTISH FA CUP   1901-02

Quarter-finals
Hibernian v Queen's Park	7-1
Rangers v Kilmarnock	2-0
Falkirk v St Mirren	0-1
Heart of Midlothian v Celtic	1-1, 1-2

Semi-finals
Hibernian v Rangers	2-0
Celtic v St Mirren	3-2

Final
The Hibernians 1 Celtic 0
(Celtic Park, 26.4.02, 16,000)

SCOTTISH FA CUP   1902-03

Quarter-finals
Celtic v Rangers	0-3
Stenhousemuir v Partick Thistle	3-0
Dundee v Hibernian	0-0, 0-0, 1-0
Heart of Midlothian v Third Lanark	2-1

Semi-finals
Rangers v Stenhousemuir	4-1
Dundee v Heart of Midlothian	0-0, 1-0

Final
Rangers 1 :0 :2 Heart of Midlothian 1 :0 :0
(Celtic Park, 40,000 [replay 35,000, second replay 32,000]) (11.4.03, 18.4.03, 25.4.03)

SCOTTISH FA CUP 1903-04

Quarter-finals

Celtic v Dundee	1-1, 0-0, 5-0
Third Lanark v Kilmarnock	3-0
Leith Athletic v Morton	1-3
St Mirren v Rangers	0-1

Semi-finals

Celtic v Third Lanark	2-1
Rangers v Morton	3-0

Final

Celtic 3 Rangers 2
(Hampden Park, 16.4.04, 65,000)

SCOTTISH FA CUP 1904-05

Quarter-finals

Third Lanark v Aberdeen	4-1
St Mirren v Airdrieonians	0-0, 1-3
Celtic v Partick Thistle	3-0
Rangers v Beith	5-1

Semi-finals

Airdrieonians v Third Lanark	1-2
Celtic v Rangers	0-2

Final

Third Lanark 0:3 Rangers 0:1
(Hampden Park, 8.4.05, 54,000 [replay 55,000])

SCOTTISH FA CUP 1905-06

Quarter-finals

Celtic v Heart of Midlothian	1-2
Port Glasgow Athletic v Rangers	1-0
Airdrieonians v St Mirren	0-0, 0-2
Hibernian v Third Lanark	2-3

Semi-finals

Port Glasgow Athletic v Heart of Midlothian	0-2
St Mirren v Third Lanark	1-1, 0-0, 0-1

Final

Heart of Midlothian 1 Third Lanark 0
(Ibrox, 28.4.06, 25,000)

SCOTTISH FA CUP 1906-07

Quarter-finals

Rangers v Celtic	0-3
St Mirren v Hibernian	1-1, 1-1, 0-2
Queen's Park v Renton	4-1
Heart of Midlothian v Raith Rovers	2-2, 1-0

Semi-finals

Celtic v Hibernian	0-0, 0-0, 3-0
Heart of Midlothian v Queen's Park	1-0

Final

Celtic 3 Heart of Midlothian 0
(Hampden Park, 20.4.07, 50,000)

SCOTTISH FA CUP 1907-08

Quarter-finals

Raith Rovers v Celtic	0-3
Aberdeen v Queen's Park	3-1
Hibernian v Kilmarnock	0-1
St Mirren v Heart of Midlothian	2-2, 1-0*, 3-1

Semi-finals

Aberdeen v Celtic	0-1
Kilmarnock v St Mirren	0-0, 0-2

Final

Celtic 5 St Mirren 1
(Hampden Park, 18.4.08, 55,000)

*abandoned

SCOTTISH FA CUP 1908-09

Quarter-finals

Celtic v Airdrieonians	3-1
Clyde v St Mirren	3-1
Third Lanark v Falkirk	1-2
Rangers v Queen's Park	1-0

Semi-finals

Celtic v Clyde	0-0, 2-0
Falkirk v Rangers	0-1

Final

Celtic *2:*1 Rangers *2:*1
(Hampden Park, 10.4.09, 70,000 [replay, 17.4.09, 61,000])

* The crowd rioted when, as stated in the rules, extra time was not played after the replay, and hundreds were injured. As a result both clubs refused to play a third match and the Scottish FA agreed that the trophy would not be awarded

---

SCOTTISH FA CUP 1909-10

Quarter-finals

Motherwell v Dundee	1-3
Hibernian v Heart of Midlothian	0-1* 1-0
Celtic v Aberdeen	2-1
Queen's Park v Clyde	2-2, 2-2, 1-2

Semi-finals

Hibernian v Dundee	0-0, 0-0, 0-1
Clyde v Celtic	3-1

Final

Dundee 2:0:2 Clyde 2:0:1
(Ibrox, 62,300 [replay 24,500, second replay 25,400]) (9.4.10, 16.4.10, 20.4.10)

*abandoned

SCOTTISH FA CUP 1910-11

Quarter-finals

Celtic v Clyde	1-0
Aberdeen v Forfar Athletic	6-0
Dundee v Rangers	2-1
Hamilton Academicals v Motherwell	2-1

Semi-finals

Celtic v Aberdeen	1-0
Hamilton Academicals v Dundee	3-2

Final

Celtic 0:2 Hamilton Academicals 0:0
(Ibrox, 8.4.11, 45,000 [replay, 15.4.11, 24,700])

SCOTTISH FA CUP 1911-12

Quarter-finals

Aberdeen v Celtic	2-2, 0-2
Morton v Heart of Midlothian	0-1
Third Lanark v Motherwell	3-1
Kilmarnock v Clyde	1-6

Semi-finals

Celtic v Heart of Midlothian	3-0
Clyde v Third Lanark	3-1

Final

Celtic 2 Clyde 0
(Ibrox, 6.4.12, 46,000)

SCOTTISH FA CUP 1912-13

Quarter-finals

Falkirk v Dumbarton	1-0
Celtic v Heart of Midlothian	0-1
Clyde v Dundee	1-1, 0-0, 2-1
Raith Rovers v St Mirren	2-1

Semi-finals

Falkirk v Heart of Midlothian	1-0
Raith Rovers v Clyde	1-1, 1-0

Final

Falkirk 2 Raith Rovers 0
(Celtic Park, 12.4.13, 45,000)

SCOTTISH FA CUP 1913-14

Quarter-finals

Motherwell v Celtic	1-3
Third Lanark v Stevenston United	1-1, 0-0, 1-0
St Mirren v Partick Thistle	1-0
Queen's Park v Hibernian	1-3

Semi-finals

Celtic v Third Lanark	2-0
Hibernian v St Mirren	3-1

Final

Celtic 0:4 The Hibernians 0:1
(Ibrox, 11.4.14, 56,000 [replay, 17.4.14, 30,000])

SCOTTISH FA CUP 1919-20

Quarter-finals

Armadale v Kilmarnock	1-2
Morton v Third Lanark	3-0
Rangers v Celtic	1-0
Albion Rovers v Aberdeen	2-1

Semi-finals

Kilmarnock v Morton	3-2
Albion Rovers v Rangers	0-0, 1-1, 2-0

Final

Kilmarnock 3 Albion Rovers 2
(Hampden Park, 17.4.20, 95,000)

Kilmarnock: Blair, Hamilton, Gibson, Bagan, Shortt, Neave, McNaught, M. Smith, J. Smith, Culley, McPhail
Albion: Short, Penman, Bell, Wilson, Black, Ford, Ribchester, James White, John White, Watson, Hillhouse
Scorers: Culley, Shortt, J. Smith; Watson, Hillhouse

SCOTTISH FA CUP 1920-21

Quarter-finals
Partick Thistle v Motherwell	0-0, 2-2, 2-1
Celtic v Heart of Midlothian	1-2
Dundee v Albion Rovers	0-2
Dumbarton v Rangers	0-3

Semi-finals
Partick v Heart of Midlothian	0-0, 0-0, 2-0
Rangers v Albion Rovers	4-1

Final
Partick Thistle 1 Rangers 0
(Celtic Park, 16.4.20, 28,300)

Partick: Campbell, Crichton, Bulloch, Harris, Hamilton, Borthwick, Blair, Kinloch, Johnston, McMenemy, Salisbury
Rangers: Robb, Manderson, McCandless, Meiklejohn, Dixon, Bowie, Archibald, Cunningham, Henderson, Cairns, Morton
Scorers: Blair

SCOTTISH FA CUP 1921-22

Quarter-finals
Motherwell v Morton	1-2
Hamilton Academicals v Aberdeen	0-0, 0-2
Partick Thistle v Queen of the South	1-0
Rangers v St Mirren	1-1, 2-0

Semi-finals
Morton v Aberdeen	3-1
Rangers v Partick Thistle	2-0

Final
Morton 1 Rangers 0
(Hampden Park, 15.4.22, 75,000)

Morton: Edwards, McIntyre, R. Brown, Gourlay, Wright, McGregor, McNab, McKay, Buchanan, A. Brown, McMinn
Rangers: Robb, Manderson, McCandless, Meiklejohn, Dixon, Muirhead, Archibald, Cunningham, Henderson, Cairns, Morton
Scorer: Gourlay

SCOTTISH FA CUP 1922-23

Quarter-finals
Celtic v Raith Rovers	1-0
Motherwell v Bo'ness	4-2
Dundee v Third Lanark	1-1, 0-0, 0-1
Hibernian v Aberdeen	2-0

Semi-finals
Celtic v Motherwell	2-0
Hibernian v Third Lanark	1-0

Final
Celtic 1 Hibernian 0
(Hampden Park, 31.3.23, 80,100)

Celtic: Shaw, McNair, W. McStay, J. McStay, Cringan, MacFarlane, McAtee, Gallagher, Cassidy, McLean, Connelly
Hibs: Harper, McGinnigle, Dornan, Kerr, Miller, Shaw, Ritchie, Dunn, McColl, Halligan, Walker
Scorer: Cassidy

SCOTTISH FA CUP 1923-24

Quarter-finals
Airdrieonians v Ayr United	1-1, 0-0, 1-0
Heart of Midlothian v Falkirk	1-2
Aberdeen v St Bernard's	3-0
Hibernian v Partick Thistle	2-2, 1-1, 2-1

Semi-finals
Airdrieonians v Falkirk	2-1
Aberdeen v Hibernian	0-0, 0-0, 0-1

Final
Airdrieonians 2 Hibernian 0
(Ibrox, 19.4.24, 59,218)

Airdrie: Ewart, Dick, McQueen, Preston, McDougall, Bennie, Reid, Russell, Gallacher, McPhail, Somerville
Hibs: Harper, McGinnigle, Dornan, Kerr, Miller, Shaw, Ritchie, Dunn, McColl, Halligan, Walker
Scorer: Russell 2

SCOTTISH FA CUP 1924-25

Quarter-finals
St Mirren v Celtic	0-0, 1-1, 0-1
Kilmarnock v Rangers	1-2
Aberdeen v Hamilton Academicals	0-2
Dundee v Broxburn United	1-0

Semi-finals
Celtic v Rangers	5-0
Dundee v Hamilton Academicals	1-1, 2-0

Final
Celtic 2 Dundee 1
(Hampden Park, 11.4.25, 75,137)

Celtic: Shevlin, W. McStay, Hilley, Wilson, J. McStay, McFarlane, Connolly, Gallacher, McGrory, Thomson, McLean
Dundee: Britton, Brown, Thomson, Ross, W. Rankine, Irvine, Duncan, McLean, Halliday, J. Rankin, Gilmour
Scorers: Gallagher, McGrory; McLean

SCOTTISH FA CUP 1925-26

Quarter-finals
St Mirren v Airdrieonians	2-0
Morton v Rangers	0-4
Third Lanark v Aberdeen	1-1, 0-3
Celtic v Dumbarton	6-1

Semi-finals
St Mirren v Rangers	1-0
Celtic v Aberdeen	2-1

Final
St Mirren 2 Celtic 0
(Hampden Park, 10.4.26, 98,620)

St Mirren: Bradford, Findlay, Newbiggin, Morrison, Summers, McDonald, Morgan, Gebbie, McCrae, Howieson, Thomson
Celtic: Shevlin, W. McStay, Hilley, Wilson, J. McStay, McFarlane, Connolly, Thomson, McGrory, McInally, Leitch
Scorers: McCrae, Howieson

SCOTTISH FA CUP 1926-27

Quarter-finals
Bo'ness v Celtic	2-5
Falkirk v Rangers	2-2, 2-1
Partick Thistle v Dundee United	5-0
Arthurlie v East Fife	0-3

Semi-finals
Celtic v Falkirk	1-0
East Fife v Partick Thistle	2-1

Final
Celtic 3 East Fife 1
(Hampden Park, 16.4.27, 80,070)

Celtic: J. Thomson, W. McStay, Hilley, Wilson, J. McStay, McFarlane, Connolly, A. Thomson, McInally, McMenemy, McLean
East Fife: Gilfillan, Robertson, Gillespie, Hope, Brown, Russell, Weir, Paterson, Wood, Barrett, Edgar
Scorers: McLean, Connelly, Robertson; Wood

SCOTTISH FA CUP 1927-28

Quarter-finals
Albion Rovers v Rangers	0-1
Dunfermline Athletic v Hibernian	0-4
Queen's Park v Partick Thistle	1-0
Motherwell v Celtic	0-2

Semi-finals
Rangers v Hibernian	3-0
Celtic v Queen's Park	2-1

Final
Rangers 4 Celtic 0
(Hampden Park, 14.4.28, 118,115)

Rangers: W. Hamilton, Gray, R. Hamilton, Buchanan, Meiklejohn, Craig, Archibald, Cunningham, Fleming, McPhail, Morton
Celtic: J. Thomson, W. McStay, Donaghue, Wilson, J. McStay, McFarlane, Connolly, A. Thomson, McGrory, McInally, McLean
Scorers: Meiklejohn (pen), McPhail, Archibald 2

SCOTTISH FA CUP 1928-29

Quarter-finals
Raith Rovers v Kilmarnock	2-3
Celtic v Motherwell	0-0, 2-1
St Mirren v Aberdeen	4-3
Rangers v Dundee United	3-1

Semi-finals
Celtic v Kilmarnock	0-1
Rangers v St Mirren	3-2

Final
Kilmarnock 2 Rangers 0
(Hampden Park, 6.4.29, 114,708)

Kilmarnock: Clemie, Robertson, Nibloe, Morton, McLaren, McEwan, Connell, Smith, Cunningham, Williamson, Aitken
Rangers: T. Hamilton, Gray, R. Hamilton, Buchanan, Meiklejohn, Craig, Archibald, Muirhead, Fleming, McPhail, Morton
Scorers: Aitken, Williamson

SCOTTISH FA CUP 1929-30

Quarter-finals
Rangers v Montrose	3-0
Dundee v Heart of Midlothian	2-2, 0-4
St Mirren v Hamilton Academicals	3-4
Partick Thistle v Falkirk	3-1

Semi-finals
Rangers v Heart of Midlothian	4-1
Partick Thistle v Hamilton Academicals	3-1

Final
Rangers 0:2 Partick Thistle 0:1
(Hampden Park, 16.4.30, 107,475 [replay 103,686])

Rangers: T. Hamilton, Gray, R. Hamilton, Buchanan, Meiklejohn, Craig, Archibald, Marshall, Fleming, McPhail, Nicholson
Partick: Jackson, Calderwood, Rae, Elliot, Lambie, McLeod, Ness, Grove, Boardman, Ballantyne, Torbet
Scorers: Marshall, Craig; Torbet

[no change in teams for replay]

SCOTTISH FA CUP 1930-31

Quarter-finals
Celtic v Aberdeen	4-0
Bo'ness v Kilmarnock	1-1, 0-5
Third Lanark v St Mirren	1-1, 0-3
Cowdenbeath v Motherwell	0-1

Semi-finals
Celtic v Kilmarnock	3-0
Motherwell v St Mirren	1-0

Final
Celtic 2:4 Motherwell 2:2
(Hampden Park, 11.4.31, 105,000 [replay 98,579])

Celtic: J. Thomson, Cook, McGonagle, Wilson, J. McStay, Geatons, R. Thomson, A. Thomson, McGrory, Scarff, Napier
Motherwell: McClory, Johnman, Hunter, Wales, Craig, Telfer, Murdoch, McMenemy, McFadyen, Stevenson, Ferrier
Scorers: McGrory, Craig (og); Stevenson, McMenemy; *Replay*: R. Thomson 2, McGrory 2; Murdoch, Stevenson

[no change in teams for replay]

SCOTTISH FA CUP 1931-32

Quarter-finals
Rangers v Motherwell	2-0
Clyde v Hamilton Academicals	0-2
Airdrieonians v Partick Thistle	4-1
Dunfermline Athletic v Kilmarnock	1-3

Semi-finals
Rangers v Hamilton Academicals	5-2
Kilmarnock v Airdrieonians	3-2

Final
Rangers 1:3 Kilmarnock 1:0
(Hampden Park, 16.4.32, 111,982 [replay 104,965])

Rangers: Hamilton, Gray, McAuley, Meiklejohn, Simpson, Brown, Archibald, Marshall, English, McPhail, Morton
Kilmarnock: Bell, Leslie, Nibloe, Morton, Smith, McEwan, Connell, Muir, Maxwell, Duncan, Aitken
Scorers: McPhail; Maxwell; *Replay*: Fleming, McPhail, English

[no change in teams for replay]

SCOTTISH FA CUP 1932-33

Quarter-finals
Celtic v Albion Rovers	1-1, 3-1
Heart of Midlothian v Hibernian	0-0, 2-0
Clyde v Stenhousemuir	3-2
Motherwell v Kilmarnock	3-3, 8-3

Semi-finals
Celtic v Heart of Midlothian	0-0, 2-1
Motherwell v Clyde	2-0

Final
Celtic 1 Motherwell 0
(Hampden Park, 15.4.33, 102,339)

Celtic: Kennaway, Hogg, McGonagle, Wilson, J. McStay, Geatons, R. Thomson, A. Thomson, McGrory, Napier, O'Donnell
Motherwell: McClory, Crapnell, Ellis, Wales, Blair, McKenzie, Murdoch, McMenemy, McFadyen, Stevenson, Ferrier
Scorer: McGrory

SCOTTISH FA CUP 1933-34

Quarter-finals
Rangers v Aberdeen	1-0
St Johnstone v Queen of the South	2-0
Albion Rovers v Motherwell	1-1, 0-6
St Mirren v Celtic	2-0

Semi-finals
Rangers v St Johnstone	1-0
St Mirren v Motherwell	3-1

Final
Rangers 5 St Mirren 0
(Hampden Park, 21.4.34, 113,403)

Rangers: Hamilton, Gray, McDonald, Meiklejohn, Simpson, Brown, Main, Marshall, Smith, McPhail, Nicholson
St Mirren: McCloy, Hay, Ancell, Gebbie, Wilson, Miller, Knox, Latimer, McGregor, McCabe, Phillips
Scorers: Nicholson 2, McPhail, Smith, Main

SCOTTISH FA CUP 1934-35

Quarter-finals
Motherwell v Rangers	1-4
Airdrieonians v Heart of Midlothian	2-3
Aberdeen v Celtic	3-1
Hamilton Academicals v St Johnstone	3-0

Semi-finals
Rangers v Heart of Midlothian	1-1, 2-1
Aberdeen v Hamilton Academicals	1-2

Final
Rangers 2 Hamilton Academicals 1
(Hampden Park, 20.4.35, 87,286)

Rangers: Dawson, Gray, McDonald, Kennedy, Simpson, Brown, Main, Venters, Smith, McPhail, Gillick
Hamilton: Morgan, Wallace, Bulloch, Cox, McStay, Murray, King, McLaren, Wilson, Harrison, Reid
Scorers: Smith 2; Harrison

SCOTTISH FA CUP 1935-36

Quarter-finals
Aberdeen v Rangers	0-1
Clyde v Motherwell	3-2
Falkirk v Dunfermline Athletic	5-0
Morton v Third Lanark	3-5

Semi-finals
Rangers v Clyde	3-0
Falkirk v Third Lanark	1-3

Final
Rangers 1 Third Lanark 0
(Hampden Park, 18.4.36, 88,859)

Rangers: Dawson, Gray, Cheyne, Meiklejohn, Simpson, Brown, Fiddes, Venters, Smith, McPhail, Turnbull
Third Lanark: Muir, Carabine, Hamilton, Blair, Denmark, McInnes, Howe, Gallacher, Hay, Kennedy, Kinnaird
Scorer: McPhail

SCOTTISH FA CUP 1936-37

Quarter-finals
Celtic v Motherwell	4-4, 2-1
St Mirren v Clyde	0-3
Morton v Queen of the South	4-1
Hamilton Academicals v Aberdeen	1-2

Semi-finals
Celtic v Clyde	2-0
Aberdeen v Morton	2-0

Final
Celtic 2 Aberdeen 1
(Hampden Park, 24.4.37, 147,365)

Celtic: Kennaway, Hogg, Morrison, Geatons, Lyon, Paterson, Delaney, Buchan, McGrory, Crum, Murphy
Aberdeen: Johnstone, Cooper, Temple, Dunlop, Falloon, Thomson, Beynon, McKenzie, Armstrong, Mills, Lang
Scorers: Crum, Buchan; Armstrong

SCOTTISH FA CUP 1937-38

Quarter-finals
East Fife v Raith Rovers	2-2, 3-2
St Bernard's v Motherwell	3-1
Falkirk v Rangers	1-2
Kilmarnock v Ayr United	2-2, 5-0

Semi-finals
Kilmarnock v Rangers	4-3
St Bernard's v East Fife	1-1, 1-1, 1-2

Final
East Fife 1:4 Kilmarnock 1:2
(Hampden Park, 23.4.38, 80,091 [replay 92,716])

East Fife: Milton, Lairs, Tate, Russell, Sneddon, Harvey, Adams, McLeod, McCartney, Miller, McKerrall
Kilmarnock: Hunter, Fyfe, Millot, Robertson, Stewart, Ross, Thomson, Reid, Collins, McAvoy, McGrogan
Scorers: McLeod; McAvoy; *Replay*: McKerrall 2, McLeod, Miller; Thomson (pen), McGrogan

[no change in teams for replay]

SCOTTISH FA CUP 1938-39

Quarter-finals

Clyde v Third Lanark	1-0
Hibernian v Alloa Athletic	3-1
Aberdeen v Queen of the South	2-0
Motherwell v Celtic	3-1

Semi-finals

Clyde v Hibernian	1-0
Aberdeen v Motherwell	1-1, 1-3

Final

Clyde 4 Motherwell 0
(Hampden Park, 22.4.39, 94,799)

Clyde: Brown, Kirk, Hickie, Beaton, Falloon, Weir, Robeson, Wallace, Martin, Noble, Gillies
Motherwell: Murray, Wales, Ellis, McKenzie, Blair, Telfer, Ogilvie, Bremner, Mathie, Stevenson, McCulloch
Scorers: Martin 2, Wallace, Noble

SCOTTISH FA CUP 1946-47

Quarter-finals

Dundee v Aberdeen	1-2
Arbroath v Heart of Midlothian	2-1
East Fife v Motherwell	0-2
Hibernian v Dumbarton	2-0

Semi-finals

Aberdeen v Arbroath	2-0
Hibernian v Motherwell	2-1

Final

Aberdeen 2 Hibernian 1
(Hampden Park, 19.4.47, 82,140)

Aberdeen: Johnstone, McKenna, Taylor, McLaughlin, Dunlop, Waddell, Harris, Hamilton, Williams, Baird, McCall
Hibs: Kerr, Govan, Shaw, Howie, Aird, Kean, Smith, Finnigan, Cuthbertson, Turnbull, Ormond
Scorers: Hamilton, Williams; Cuthbertson

SCOTTISH FA CUP 1947-48

Quarter-finals

Rangers v East Fife	1-0
Hibernian v St Mirren	3-1
Celtic v Montrose	4-0
Airdrieonians v Morton	0-3

Semi-finals

Rangers v Hibernian	1-0
Morton v Celtic	1-0

Final

Rangers 1:1 Morton 1:0
(Hampden Park, 17.4.48, 129,176 [replay 133,570])

Rangers: Brown, Young, Shaw, McColl, Woodburn, Cox, Rutherford, Gillick, Thornton, Findlay [replay: Williamson], Duncanson
Morton: Cowan, Mitchell, Whigham, Campbell, Miller, Whyte, Hepburn, Murphy, Cupples, Orr, Liddell
Scorers: Gillick; Whyte; Replay: Williamson

[Morton unchanged for replay]

SCOTTISH FA CUP 1948-49

Quarter-finals

Rangers v Partick Thistle	4-0
Hibernian v East Fife	0-2
Heart of Midlothian v Dundee	2-4
Stenhousemuir v Clyde	0-1

Semi-finals

Rangers v East Fife	3-0
Clyde v Dundee	2-2, 2-1

Final

Rangers 4 Clyde 1
(Hampden Park, 23.4.49, 108,435)

Rangers: Brown, Young, Shaw, McColl, Woodburn, Cox, Waddell, Duncanson, Thornton, Williamson, Rutherford
Clyde: Gullan, Gibson, Mennie, Campbell, Milligan, Long, Davies, Wright, Linwood, Galletly, Bootland
Scorers: Young (2 pens), Williamson, Duncanson; Galletly

SCOTTISH FA CUP 1949-50

Quarter-finals

Rangers v Raith Rovers	1-1, 1-1, 2-0
Queen of the South v Aberdeen	3-3, 2-1
Partick Thistle v Stirling Albion	5-1
Stenhousemuir v East Fife	0-3

Semi-finals

Rangers v Queen of the South	1-1, 3-0
East Fife v Partick Thistle	2-1

Final

Rangers 3 East Fife 0
(Hampden Park, 22.4.50, 118,262)

Rangers: Brown, Young, Shaw, McColl, Woodburn, Cox, Rutherford, Findlay, Thornton, Duncanson, Rae
East Fife: Easson, Laird, Stewart, Philp, Finlay, Aitken, Black, Fleming, Morris, Brown, Duncan
Scorers: Findlay, Thornton 2

SCOTTISH FA CUP 1950-51

Quarter-finals

Celtic v Aberdeen	3-0
Dundee v Raith Rovers	1-2
Airdrieonians v Hibernian	0-3
Ayr United v Motherwell	2-2, 1-2

Semi-finals

Celtic v Raith Rovers	3-2
Hibernian v Motherwell	1-3

Final

Celtic 1 Motherwell 0
(Hampden Park, 21.4.51, 131,943)

Celtic: Hunter, Fallon, Rollo, Evans, Boden, Baillie, Weir, Collins, McPhail, Peacock, Tully
Motherwell: Johnstone, Kilmarnock, Shaw, McLeod, Paton, Redpath, Humphries, Forrest, Kelly, Watson, Aitkenhead
Scorer: McPhail

SCOTTISH FA CUP 1951-52

Quarter-finals

Rangers v Motherwell	1-1, 1-2
Airdrieonians v Heart of Midlothian	2-2, 4-6
Third Lanark v Falkirk	1-0
Dundee v Aberdeen	4-0

Semi-finals

Motherwell v Heart of Midlothian	1-1, 1-1, 3-1
Dundee v Third Lanark	2-0

Final

Motherwell 4 Dundee 0
(Hampden Park, 19.4.52, 120,000)

Motherwell: Johnstone, Kilmarnock, Shaw, Cox, Paton, Redpath, Sloan, Humphries, Kelly, Watson, Aitkenhead
Dundee: Henderson, Fallon, Cowan, Gallagher, Cowie, Boyd, Hill, Patillo, Flavell, Steel, Christie
Scorers: Watson, Redpath, Humphries, Kelly

SCOTTISH FA CUP 1952-53

Quarter-finals

Rangers v Celtic	2-0
Heart of Midlothian v Queen of the South	2-1
Clyde v Third Lanark	1-2
Hibernian v Aberdeen	1-1, 0-2

Semi-finals

Rangers v Heart of Midlothian	2-1
Third Lanark v Aberdeen	1-1, 1-2

Final

Rangers 1:1 Aberdeen 1:0
(Hampden Park, 25.4.53, 129,681 [replay 112,619])

Rangers: Niven, Young, Little, McColl, Stanners [replay: Woodburn], Pryde, Waddell, Grierson, Paton, Prentice [replay: Simpson], Hubbard
Aberdeen: Martin, Mitchell, Shaw, Harris, Young, Allister, Rodger, Yorston, Buckley, Hamilton, Hather
Scorers: Prentice; Yorston; Replay: Simpson

[Aberdeen unchanged for replay]

SCOTTISH FA CUP 1953-54

Quarter-finals

Hamilton Academicals v Celtic	1-2
Partick Thistle v Motherwell	1-1, 1-2
Rangers v Berwick Rangers	4-0
Aberdeen v Heart of Midlothian	3-0

Semi-finals

Celtic v Motherwell	2-2, 3-1
Rangers v Aberdeen	0-6

Final

Celtic 2 Aberdeen 1
(Hampden Park, 24.4.54, 129,926)

Celtic: Bonnar, Haughney, Meechan, Evans, Stein, Peacock, Higgms, Fernie, Fallon, Tully, Mochan
Aberdeen: Martin, Mitchell, Caldwell, Allister, Young, Glen, Leggat, Hamilton, Buckley, Clunie, Hather
Scorers: Mochan, Fallon; Buckley

SCOTTISH FA CUP 1954-55

Quarter-finals
Clyde v Falkirk	5-0
Aberdeen v Heart of Midlothian	1-1, 2-0
Airdrieonians v Motherwell	4-1
Celtic v Hamilton Academicals	2-1

Semi-finals
Aberdeen v Clyde	2-2, 0-1
Airdrieonians v Celtic	2-2, 0-2

Final
Clyde 1:1 Celtic 1:0
(Hampden Park, 23.4.55, 106,111 [replay 68,735])

Clyde: Hewkins, Murphy, Haddock, Granville, Anderson, Laing, Divers, Robertson, Hill, Brown, Ring
Celtic: Bonnar, Haughney, Meechan, Evans, Stein, Peacock, Collins [*replay:* Fallon], Fernie, McPhail, Walsh, Tully
Scorers: Robertson; Walsh; *Replay:* Ring

[Clyde unchanged for replay]

SCOTTISH FA CUP 1955-56

Quarter-finals
Heart of Midlothian v Rangers	4-0
Raith Rovers v Partick Thistle	2-1
Queen of the South v Clyde	2-4
Celtic v Airdrieonians	2-1

Semi-finals
Heart of Midlothian v Raith Rovers	0-0, 3-0
Celtic v Clyde	2-1

Final
Heart of Midlothian 3 Celtic 1
(Hampden Park, 21.4.56, 133,339)

Hearts: Duff, Kirk, McKenzie, Mackay, Glidden, Cumming, Young, Conn, Bauld, Wardhaugh, Crawford
Celtic: Beattie, Meechan, Fallon, Smith, Evans, Peacock, Craig, Haughney, Mochan, Fernie, Tully
Scorers: Crawford 2, Conn; Haughney

SCOTTISH FA CUP 1956-57

Quarter-finals
Falkirk v Clyde	2-1
Dumbarton v Raith Rovers	0-4
Celtic v St Mirren	2-1
Kilmarnock v Airdrieonians	3-1

Semi-finals
Falkirk v Raith Rovers	2-2, 2-0
Celtic v Kilmarnock	1-1, 1-3

Final
Falkirk 1:2 Kilmarnock 1:1
(Hampden Park, 20.4.57, 83,000 [replay 79,785])

Falkirk: Slater, Parker, Rae, Wright, Irvine, Prentice, Murray, Grierson, Merchant, Moran, O'Hara
Kilmarnock: Brown, Collins, J. Stewart, R. Stewart, Toner, McKay, Mays, Harvey, Curlett, Black, Burns
Scorers: Prentice (pen); Curlett; *Replay:* Merchant, Moran, Curlett

[no change in teams for replay]

SCOTTISH FA CUP 1957-58

Quarter-finals
Clyde v Falkirk	2-1
Motherwell v Aberdeen	2-1
Queen of the South v Rangers	3-4
Hibernian v Third Lanark	3-2

Semi-finals
Clyde v Motherwell	3-2
Rangers v Hibernian	2-2, 1-2

Final
Clyde 1 Hibernian 0
(Hampden Park, 26.4.58, 95,124)

Clyde: McCulloch, Murphy, Haddock, Walters, Finlay, Clinton, Herd, Currie, Coyle, Robertson, Ring
Hibs: Leslie, Grant, McLelland, Turnbull, Patterson, Baxter, Fraser, Aitken, Baker, Preston, Ormond
Scorer: Coyle

SCOTTISH FA CUP 1958-59

Quarter-finals
St Mirren v Dunfermline Athletic	2-1
Stirling Albion v Celtic	1-3
Third Lanark v Hibernian	2-1
Aberdeen v Kilmarnock	3-1

Semi-finals
St Mirren v Celtic	4-0
Third Lanark v Aberdeen	1-1, 0-1

Final
St Mirren 3 Aberdeen 1
(Hampden Park, 25.4.59, 108,591)

St Mirren: Walker, Lapsley, Wilson, Neilson, McGugan, Leishman, Rodger, Bryceland, Baker, Gemmell, Miller
Aberdeen: Martin, Caldwell, Hogg, Brownlee, Clunie, Glen, Ewan, Davidson, Baird, Wishart, Hather
Scorers: Bryceland, Miller, Baker; Baird

SCOTTISH FA CUP 1959-60

Quarter-finals
Rangers v Hibernian	3-2
Celtic v Partick Thistle	2-0
Ayr United v Clyde	0-2
Eyemouth United v Kilmarnock	1-2

Semi-finals
Rangers v Celtic	1-1, 4-1
Clyde v Kilmarnock	0-2

Final
Rangers 2 Kilmarnock 0
(Hampden Park, 23.4.60, 108,017)

Rangers: Niven, Caldow, Little, McColl, Paterson, Stevenson, Scott, McMillan, Miller, Baird, Wilson
Kilmarnock: Brown, Richmond, Watson, Beattie, Toner, Kennedy, Stewart, McInally, Kerr, Black, Muir
Scorer: Millar 2

SCOTTISH FA CUP 1960-61

Quarter-finals
Dunfermline Athletic v Alloa Athletic	4-0
Heart of Midlothian v St Mirren	0-1
Motherwell v Airdrieonians	0-1
Celtic v Hibernian	1-1, 1-0

Semi-finals
Celtic v Airdrieonians	4-0
Dunfermline Athletic v St Mirren	0-0, 1-0

Final
Dunfermline Athletic 0:2 Celtic 0:0
(Hampden Park, 22.4.61, 113,618 [replay 87,866])

Dunfermline: Connaghan, Fraser, Cunningham, Mailer, Williamson [*replay:* Sweeney], Miller, Peebles, Smith, Thomson, Dickson, Melrose
Celtic: Haffey, Mackay, Kennedy [*replay:* O'Neil], Crerand, McNeill, Clark, Gallagher, Fernie, Hughes, Chalmers, Byrne
Scorers: Thomson, Dickson

SCOTTISH FA CUP 1961-62

Quarter-finals
Kilmarnock v Rangers	2-4
Stirling Albion v Motherwell	0-6
Celtic v Third Lanark	4-4, 4-0
Dunfermline Athletic v St Mirren	0-1

Semi-finals
Rangers v Motherwell	3-1
Celtic v St Mirren	1-3

Final
Rangers 2 St Mirren 0
(Hampden Park, 21.4.62, 126,930)

Rangers: Ritchie, Shearer, Caldow, Davis, McKinnon, Baxter, Henderson, McMillan, Millar, Brand, Wilson
St Mirren: Williamson, Campbell, Wilson, Stewart, Clunie, McLean, Henderson, Bryceland, Kerrigan, Fernie, Beck
Scorers: Brand, Wilson

SCOTTISH FA CUP 1962-63

Quarter-finals
Dundee v Rangers	1-1, 2-3
Dundee United v Queen o' South	1-1, 1-1, 4-0
Raith Rovers v Aberdeen	2-1
St Mirren v Celtic	0-1

Semi-finals
Rangers v Dundee United	5-2
Raith Rovers v Celtic	2-5

Final
Rangers 1:3 Celtic 1:0
(Hampden Park, 4.5.63, 129,527 [replay 120,263])

Rangers: Ritchie, Shearer, Provan, Greig, McKinnon, Baxter, Henderson, McLean [*replay:* McMillan], Millar, Brand, Wilson
Celtic: Haffey, Mackay, Kennedy, McNamee, McNeill, Price, Johnstone [*replay:* Chalmers], Murdoch, Hughes, Divers, Brogan [*replay:* Craig]
Scorers: Brand; Murdoch; *Replay:* Wilson, Brand 2

SCOTTISH FA CUP 1963-64

Quarter-finals

Rangers v Celtic	2-0
Dunfermline Athletic v Ayr United	7-0
Kilmarnock v Falkirk	2-1
Dundee v Motherwell	1-1, 4-2

Semi-finals

Rangers v Dunfermline Athletic	1-0
Kilmarnock v Dundee	0-4

Final

Rangers 3 Dundee 1
(Hampden Park, 25.4.64, 120,982)

Rangers: Ritchie, Shearer, Provan, Greig, McKinnon, Baxter, Henderson, McLean, Millar, Brand, Wilson
Dundee: Slater, Hamilton, Cox, Seith, Ryden, Stuart, Penman, Cousins, Cameron, Gilzean, Robertson
Scorers: Millar 2, Brand; Cameron

SCOTTISH FA CUP 1964-65

Quarter-finals

Celtic v Kilmarnock	3-2
Motherwell v Heart of Midlothian	1-0
Hibernian v Rangers	2-1
Dunfermline Athletic v Stirling Albion	2-0

Semi-finals

Celtic v Motherwell	2-2, 3-0
Hibernian v Dunfermline Athletic	0-2

Final

Celtic 3 Dunfermline Athletic 2
(Hampden Park, 24.4.65, 108,800)

Celtic: Fallon, Young, Gemmell, Murdoch, McNeill, Clark, Chalmers, Gallagher, Hughes, Lennox, Auld
Dunfermline: Herriot, W. Callaghan, Lunn, Thomson, McLean, T. Callaghan, Edwards, Smith, McLaughlin, Melrose, Sinclair
Scorers: Auld 2, McNeill; Melrose, McLaughlin

SCOTTISH FA CUP 1965-66

Quarter-finals

Rangers v St Johnstone	1-0
Dumbarton v Aberdeen	0-3
Dunfermline Athletic v Kilmarnock	2-1
Celtic v Heart of Midlothian	3-3, 3-1

Semi-finals

Aberdeen v Rangers	0-0, 1-2
Celtic v Dunfermline Athletic	2-0

Final

Rangers 0:1 Celtic 0:0
(Hampden Park, 23.4.66, 126,552 [replay 98,202])

Rangers: Ritchie, Johansen, Provan, Greig, McKinnon, Millar, Wilson, Watson, Forrest (*replay*: McLean), Johnston, Henderson
Celtic: Simpson, Young [*replay*: Craig], Gemmell, Murdoch, McNeill, Clark, Johnstone, McBride, Chalmers, Gallagher [*replay*: Auld], Hughes
Scorer: Johansen

SCOTTISH FA CUP 1966-67

Quarter-finals

Celtic v Queen's Park	5-3
Clyde v Hamilton Academicals	0-0, 5-1
Dundee United v Dunfermline Athletic	1-0
Hibernian v Aberdeen	1-1, 0-3

Semi-finals

Celtic v Clyde	0-0, 2-0
Dundee United v Aberdeen	0-1

Final

Celtic 2 Aberdeen 0
(Hampden Park, 29.4.67, 127,117)

Celtic: Simpson, Craig, Gemmell, Murdoch, McNeill, Clark, Johnstone, Wallace, Chalmers, Auld, Lennox
Aberdeen: Clark, Whyte, Shewan, Munro, McMillan, Peterson, Wilson, Smith, Storrie, Melrose, Johnstone
Scorer: Wallace 2

SCOTTISH FA CUP 1967-68

Quarter-finals

Dunfermline Athletic v Partick Thistle	1-0
St Johnstone v Airdrieonians	2-1
Morton v Elgin City	2-1
Rangers v Heart of Midlothian	1-1, 0-1

Semi-finals

Dunfermline Athletic v St Johnstone	1-1, 2-1
Heart of Midlothian v Morton	1-1, 2-1

Final

Dunfermline Athletic 3 Heart of Midlothian 1
(Hampden Park, 27.4.68, 56,366)

Dunfermline: Martin, W. Callaghan, Lunn, McGarty, Barry, T. Callaghan, Lister, Paton, Gardner, Robertson, Edwards, (Thomson)
Hearts: Cruickshank, Sneddon, Mann, Anderson, Thomson, Miller, Jensen, Townsend, Ford, Irvine, Traynor. (Moller)
Scorers: Gardner 2, Lister (pen); Lunn (og)

SCOTTISH FA CUP 1968-69

Quarter-finals

Celtic v St Johnstone	3-2
Dundee United v Morton	2-3
Aberdeen v Kilmarnock	0-0, 3-0
Rangers v Airdrieonians	1-0

Semi-finals

Celtic v Morton	4-1
Rangers v Aberdeen	6-1

Final

Celtic 4 Rangers 0
(Hampden Park, 26.4.69, 132,874)

Celtic: Fallon, Craig, Gemmell, Murdoch, McNeill, Brogan (Clark), Connelly, Chalmers, Wallace, Lennox, Auld
Rangers: Martin, Johansen, Mathieson, Greig, McKinnon, D. Smith, Henderson, Penman, Ferguson, Johnston, Persson
Scorers: McNeill, Lennox, Connelly, Chalmers

SCOTTISH FA CUP 1969-70

Quarter-finals

Falkirk v Aberdeen	0-1
Motherwell v Kilmarnock	0-1
East Fife v Dundee	0-1
Celtic v Rangers	3-1

Semi-finals

Aberdeen v Kilmarnock	1-0
Celtic v Dundee	2-1

Final

Aberdeen 3 Celtic 1
(Hampden Park, 11.4.70, 108,434)

Aberdeen: Clark, Boel, Murray, Hermiston, McMillan, M. Buchan, McKay, Robb, Forrest, Harper, Graham. (G. Buchan)
Celtic: Williams, Hay, Gemmell, Murdoch, McNeill, Brogan, Johnstone, Wallace, Connelly, Lennox, Hughes (Auld)
Scorers: Harper (pen), McKay 2; Lennox

SCOTTISH FA CUP 1970-71

Quarter-finals

Celtic v Raith Rovers	7-1
Kilmarnock v Airdrieonians	2-3
Hibernian v Dundee	1-0
Rangers v Aberdeen	1-0

Semi-finals

Celtic v Airdrieonians	3-3, 2-0
Hibernian v Rangers	0-0, 1-2

Final

Celtic 1:2 Rangers 1:1
(Hampden Park, 8.5.71, 120,092 [replay 12.5.71, 103,332])

Celtic: Williams, Craig, Brogan, Connelly, McNeill, Hay, Johnstone, Lennox, Wallace [*replay*: Macari], Callaghan, Hood (sub. Macari, *replay* Wallace)
Rangers: McCloy, Miller [*replay*: Denny], Mathieson, Greig, McKinnon, Jackson, Henderson, Penman (sub. D. Johnstone both matches), Stein, MacDonald, W. Johnston
Scorers: Lennox; D. Johnstone; *Replay*: Macari, Hood (pen); Craig (og)

SCOTTISH FA CUP 1971-72

Quarter-finals

Celtic v Heart of Midlothian	1-1, 1-0
Raith Rovers v Kilmarnock	1-3
Motherwell v Rangers	2-2, 2-4
Hibernian v Aberdeen	2-0

Semi-finals

Celtic v Kilmarnock	3-1
Rangers v Hibernian	1-1, 0-2

Final

Celtic 6 Hibernian 1
(Hampden Park, 6.5.72, 106,102)

Celtic: Williams, Craig, Brogan, Murdoch, McNeill, Connelly, Johnstone, Deans, Macari, Dalglish, Callaghan
Hibs: Herriot, Brownlie, Schaedler, Stanton, Black, Blackley, Edwards, Hazel, Gordon, O'Rourke, Duncan (Auld)
Scorers: Deans 3, McNeill, Macari 2; Gordon

SCOTTISH FA CUP 1972-73

Quarter-finals
Rangers v Airdrieonians	2-0
Partick Thistle v Ayr United	1-5
Montrose v Dundee	1-4
Celtic v Aberdeen	0-0, 1-0

Semi-finals
Ayr United v Rangers	0-2
Celtic v Dundee	0-0, 3-0

Final

Rangers 3 Celtic 2
(Hampden Park, 5.5.73, 122,714)

Rangers: McCloy, Jardine, Mathieson, Greig, Johnstone, MacDonald, McLean, Forsyth, Parlane, Conn, Young, (Smith)
Celtic: Hunter, McGrain, Brogan (Lennox), Murdoch, McNeill, Connelly, Johnstone, Deans, Dalglish, Hay, Callaghan
Scorers: Parlane, Conn, Forsyth; Dalglish, Connelly (pen)

SCOTTISH FA CUP 1973-74

Quarter-finals
Celtic v Motherwell	2-2, 1-0
Hibernian v Dundee	3-3, 0-3
Heart of Midlothian v Ayr United	1-1, 2-1
Dunfermline Athletic v Dundee United	1-1, 0-4

Semi-finals
Celtic v Dundee	1-0
Heart of Midlothian v Dundee United	1-1, 2-4

Final

Celtic 3 Dundee United 0
(Hampden Park, 4.5.74, 75,959)

Celtic: Connaghan, McGrain (Callaghan), Brogan, Murray, McNeill, McCluskey, Johnstone, Hood, Deans, Hay, Dalglish
Dundee United: Davie, Gardner, Kopel, Copland, D. Smith (Traynor), W. Smith, Payne (Rolland), Knox, Gray, Fleming, Houston
Scorers: Hood, Murray, Deans

SCOTTISH FA CUP 1974-75

Quarter-finals
Dumbarton v Celtic	1-2
Heart of Midlothian v Dundee	1-1, 2-3
Aberdeen v Motherwell	0-1
Arbroath v Airdrieonians	2-2, 0-3

Semi-finals
Celtic v Dundee	1-0
Airdrieonians v Motherwell	1-1, 1-0

Final

Celtic 3 Airdrieonians 1
(Hampden Park, 3.5.75, 75,457)

Celtic: Latchford, McGrain, Lynch, Murray, McNeill, McCluskey, Hood, Glavin, Dalglish, Lennox, Wilson
Airdrie: McWilliams, Jonquin, Cowan, Menzies, Black, Whiteford, McCann, Walker, McCulloch (March), Lapsley (Reynolds), Wilson
Scorers: Wilson 2, McCluskey; McCann

SCOTTISH FA CUP 1975-76

Quarter-finals
Queen of the South v Rangers	0-5
Motherwell v Hibernian	2-2, 1-1, 2-1
Dumbarton v Kilmarnock	2-1
Montrose v Heart of Midlothian	2-2, 2-2, 1-2

Semi-finals
Motherwell v Rangers	2-3
Dumbarton v Heart of Midlothian	0-0, 0-3

Final

Rangers 3 Heart of Midlothian 1
(Hampden Park, 1.5.76, 85,354)

Rangers: McCloy, Miller, Greig, Forsyth, Jackson, MacDonald, McLean, Hamilton (Jardine), Henderson, McKean, Johnstone
Hearts: Cruickshank, Brown, Burrell (Aird), Jeffries, Gallacher, May, Gibson (Park), Busby, Shaw, Callachan, Prentice
Scorers: Johnstone 2, MacDonald; Shaw

SCOTTISH FA CUP 1976-77

Quarter-finals
Celtic v Queen of the South	5-1
Arbroath v Dundee	1-3
Heart of Midlothian v East Fife	0-0, 3-2
Rangers v Motherwell	2-0

Semi-finals
Celtic v Dundee	2-0
Rangers v Heart of Midlothian	2-0

Final

Celtic 1 Rangers 0
(Hampden Park, 7.5.77, 54,252)

Celtic: Latchford, McGrain, Lynch, Stanton, McDonald, Aitken, Dalglish, Edvaldsson, Craig, Wilson, Conn. (Burns and Doyle)
Rangers: Kennedy, Jardine, Greig, Forsyth, Jackson, Watson (Robertson), McLean, Hamilton, Parlane, MacDonald, Johnstone. (Miller)
Scorer: Lynch (pen)

SCOTTISH FA CUP 1977-78

Quarter-finals
Rangers v Kilmarnock	4-1
Dundee United v Queen's Park	2-0
Partick Thistle v Dumbarton	2-1
Aberdeen v Morton	2-2, 2-1

Semi-finals
Rangers v Dundee United	2-0
Aberdeen v Partick Thistle	4-2

Final

Rangers 2 Aberdeen 1
(Hampden Park, 6.5.78, 61,563)

Rangers: McCloy, Jardine, Greig, Forsyth, Jackson, MacDonald, McLean, Russell, Johnstone, Smith, Cooper (Watson)
Aberdeen: Clark, Kennedy, Ritchie, McMaster, Garner, Miller, Sullivan, Fleming (Scanlon), Harper, Jarvie, Davidson
Scorers: MacDonald, Johnstone; Ritchie

SCOTTISH FA CUP 1978-79

Quarter-finals
Rangers v Dundee	6-3
Dumbarton v Partick Thistle	0-1
Aberdeen v Celtic	1-1, 2-1
Hibernian v Heart of Midlothian	2-1

Semi-finals
Partick Thistle v Rangers	0-0, 0-1
Aberdeen v Hibernian	1-2

Final

Rangers 0:0:3 Hibernian 0:0:2
(Hampden Park, 12.5.79, 50,610 [replay 16.5.79, 33,506, second replay 28.5.79, 30,602])

Rangers: McCloy, Jardine, Dawson, Johnstone, Jackson, MacDonald (Miller), McLean, Russell, Parlane, Smith, Cooper
Hibs: McArthur, Brazil, Duncan, Bremner, Stewart, McNamara, Hutchinson (Rae), MacLeod, Campbell, Callachan, Higgins

Replay: **Rangers:** Unchanged; Miller came on for McLean. **Hibs:** Rae for Hutchinson; Brown came on for Higgins

Second replay: **Rangers:** Watson for Smith; Miller came on for Watson, Smith for McLean **Hibs:** Unchanged from replay; Brown came on for Callachan, Hutchinson for Higgins
Scorers: Johnstone 2, Duncan (og); Higgins, MacLeod (pen)

SCOTTISH FA CUP 1979-80

Quarter-finals
Celtic v Morton	2-0
Berwick Rangers v Hibernian	0-0, 0-1
Partick Thistle v Aberdeen	1-2
Rangers v Heart of Midlothian	6-1

Semi-finals
Celtic v Hibernian	5-0
Aberdeen v Rangers	0-1

Final

Celtic 1 Rangers 0
(Hampden Park, 10.5.79, 70,303)

Celtic: Latchford, Sneddon, McGrain, Aitken, Conroy, MacLeod, Provan, Doyle (Lennox), McCluskey, Burns, McGarvey
Rangers: McCloy, Jardine, Dawson, Forsyth (Miller), Jackson, Stevens, Cooper, Russell, Johnstone, Smith, MacDonald (McLean)
Scorer: McCluskey

SCOTTISH FA CUP 1980-81

Semi-finals
Morton v Rangers	1-2
Celtic v Dundee United	0-0, 2-3

Final

Rangers 0:4 Dundee United 0:1
(Hampden Park, 9.5.81, 55,000 [*Replay:* Hampden Park, 12.5.81, 43,009])

Rangers: Stewart, Jardine, Stevens, Forsyth, Dawson, McLean, Russell, Bett, Redford, McAdam (Cooper), Johnston (MacDonald)
Dundee United: MacAlpine, Holt, Hegarty, Narey, Kopel, Kirkwood, Phillip (Stark), Bannon, Milne, Dodds, Sturrock (Pettigrew)
Replay
Rangers: Stewart, Jardine, Stevens, Forsyth, Dawson, Russell, Bett, Redford, Cooper, Johnstone, MacDonald
Dundee United: Unchanged
Scorers: Cooper, Russell, MacDonald 2; Dodds

SCOTTISH FA CUP 1981-82

Quarter-finals

Aberdeen v Kilmarnock	2-2, 4-2
Queen's Park v Forfar Athletic	1-2
Rangers v Dundee	2-0
St Mirren v Dundee United	1-0

Semi-finals

Aberdeen v St Mirren	1-1, 3-2
Forfar Athletic v Rangers	0-0, 1-3

Final

Aberdeen 4 Rangers 1 (aet)
(Hampden Park, 22.5.82, 53,788)
Aberdeen: Leighton, Kennedy, Rougvie,
McMaster (Bell), McLeish, Miller, Strachan,
Cooper, McGhee, Simpson, Hewitt (Black)
Rangers: Stewart, Jardine (McAdam), Dawson,
McClelland, Jackson, Bett, Cooper, Russell
Dalziel (McLean), Miller, MacDonald
Scorers: McLeish, McGhee, Strachan, Cooper;
MacDonald

SCOTTISH FA CUP 1982-83

Quarter-finals

Airdrieonians v St Mirren	0-5
Celtic v Hearts	4-1
Partick Thistle v Aberdeen	1-2
Queen's Park v Rangers	1-2

Semi-finals

Aberdeen v Celtic	1-0
Rangers v St Mirren	1-1, 1-0

Final

Aberdeen 1 Rangers 0 (aet)
(Hampden Park, 21.5.83, 62,979)
Aberdeen: Leighton, McMaster, Rougvie
(Watson), Cooper, McLeish, Strachan, Miller,
Simpson, McGhee, Black, Weir (Hewitt)
Rangers: McCloy, Dawson, McClelland,
McPherson, Paterson, Bett, Cooper (Davies),
McKinnon, Clark, Russell, MacDonald (Dalziel)
Scorer: Black

SCOTTISH FA CUP 1983-84

Quarter-finals

Aberdeen v Dundee U.	0-0, 1-0
Motherwell v Celtic	0-6
Dundee v Rangers	2-2, 3-2
St Mirren v Morton	4-3

Semi-finals

Aberdeen v Dundee	2-0
St Mirren v Celtic	1-2

Final

Aberdeen 2 Celtic 1 (aet)
(Hampden Park, 19.5.84, 58,900)

Aberdeen: Leighton, McKimmie, McLeish,
Miller, Rougvie (Stark), Strachan, Cooper,
Simpson, Weir (Bell), Black, McGhee.
Celtic: Bonner, McGrain, Aitken, W. McStay,
Reid (Melrose), P. McStay, Burns, MacLeod,
Provan, McGarvey, McClair (Sinclair).
Scorers: Black, McGhee; P. McStay

*TOP: Davie McCrae scores what is thought to be the quickest ever goal in a Scottish Cup final,
after 30 seconds for St Mirren against Celtic in the 1926 final. St Mirren won the game 2-0.
Because of the crush, numerous St Mirren fans were still outside the ground at the time.*
*CENTRE: Gordon Strachan scores Aberdeen's third goal in the 4-1 crushing of Rangers in the
1982 Scottish Cup final at Hampden on 22 May 1982.*
*BOTTOM: One year later in 1983 and Aberdeen and Rangers provide the first repeat Cup final this
century. Here Leighton and Miller clear from McPherson. Black scored and Aberdeen won 1-0.*

157

Scottish League

CHAMPIONSHIPS

Most: 37 – Rangers (including 1890–91 when they shared with Dumbarton) up to and including 1983–84.

Consecutive: 9 – Celtic, between 1965–66 and 1973–74. Rangers' best run is 5, from 1926–27 to 1930–31.

Non-Glasgow: The only occasion on which neither Rangers nor Celtic featured in the top three of the Scottish League at the end of the season was in 1964–65, when the order was Kilmarnock, Hearts and Dunfermline. It was another 15 years (Aberdeen in 1980) before neither won the Championship. Between 1904 (Third Lanark) and 1948 (Hibernian) only one club other than Rangers or Celtic won the Championship (Motherwell in 1932).

Division 2 Championships: Ayr United hold the record of 6 Division 2 (Division 1 since 1975–76) Championships plus 3 runners-up places.

Division 3: This ill-fated League lasted less than 3 seasons before it was abandoned. The winners were:
1923–24 Arthurlie
1924–25 Nithsdale Wanderers
1925–26 Helensburgh (season abandoned)
After the Second World War, Division 'C' was reintroduced, though largely composed of the reserve sides of League clubs. In its first three years, however, it was won by clubs who gained promotion to Division 'B'.
1946–47 Stirling Albion
1947–48 East Stirlingshire
1948–49 Forfar Athletic
The League was then divided into North-East and South-West sections and was taken over by the reserve sides, though one or two current League clubs (notably Brechin and Stranraer) played there for a while.

FIXTURES

Wartime congestion: Owing to restrictions on midweek games, several Scottish clubs had to play two matches a day during the First World War:
Celtic beat Raith 6-0 at Celtic Park and Motherwell 3-1 at Fir Park on Thursday 15 April 1915.
Motherwell had lost 3-0 to Ayr at Fir Park on the same afternoon that they had to meet Celtic in the evening (*above*).
Clyde beat St Mirren 2-1 at Shawfield on the afternoon of Saturday 14 April 1917 and lost 1-0 to Third Lanark at Cathkin Park (Second Hampden Park) in the evening.
Queen's Park beat Partick 2-0 at Firhill on the afternoon of Saturday 21 April 1917 and then lost 1-0 to Rangers in the evening.

Rangers had lost 3-1 away to Hamilton on the afternoon of 21 April 1917 before beating Queen's Park in the evening (*above*).

Rangers/Celtic players: Only 3 men are known to have played for both clubs. The first was George Livingstone, who joined Rangers in 1906 having previously played for several clubs, including Celtic. Alec Bennett joined Rangers direct from Celtic in 1908. Alfie Conn, who joined Celtic in March 1977 from Spurs, had previously played for Rangers. He had the remarkable distinction of playing in a Scottish Cup final for each side against the other (1973 and 1977) – and being on the winning side in both. Rangers are only known to have actually played one Catholic – Laurie Blyth between 1951 and 1953 – despite their protestations of non-discrimination and the controversy continues unabated.

(*continued on p. 172*)

ABOVE: Celtic's Ronnie Glavin flicks the ball past Aberdeen's McMaster (4) in a Scottish League game at Pittodrie in October 1978. The following season Aberdeen were to break a 15-year stranglehold on the Championship by the duo, only the 12th time this century that the League title had gone elsewhere.
LEFT: The Renton side which was proclaimed 'Champions of the World' after defeating West Brom in 1888. They won the Cup in 1885 and 1888 but were to leave the League 1897.

SCOTTISH LEAGUE 1890-91

1	Dumbarton‡	18	13	3	2	61:21	29
2	Rangers‡	18	13	3	2	58:25	29
3	Celtic §	18	11	3	4	48:21	21
4	Cambuslang	18	8	4	6	47:42	20
5	Third Lanark §	18	8	3	7	38:39	15
6	Hearts	18	6	2	10	31:37	14
7	Abercorn	18	5	2	11	36:47	12
8	St Mirren	18	5	1	12	39:62	11
9	Vale of Leven	18	5	1	12	27:65	11
10	Cowlairs §	18	3	4	11	24:50	6

SCOTTISH LEAGUE 1891-92

1	Dumbarton	22	18	1	3	79:28	37
2	Celtic	22	16	3	3	62:22	35
3	Hearts	22	15	4	3	65:35	34
4	Leith	22	12	1	9	51:41	25
5	Rangers	22	12	2	9	59:46	24
6	Third Lanark	22	9	4	9	44:47	22
7	Renton	22	8	5	9	38:44	21
8	Clyde	22	8	4	10	63:62	20
9	Abercorn	22	6	5	11	47:59	17
10	St Mirren	22	4	5	13	43:60	13
11	Cambuslang	22	2	6	14	22:53	10
12	Vale of Leven	22	0	5	17	24:100	5

SCOTTISH LEAGUE 1892-93

1	Celtic	18	14	1	3	54:25	29
2	Rangers	18	12	4	2	41:27	28
3	St Mirren	18	9	2	7	40:39	20
4	Third Lanark	18	9	1	8	54:40	19
5	Hearts	18	8	2	8	40:42	18
6	Leith	18	8	1	9	35:31	17
7	Dumbarton	18	8	1	9	35:35	17
8	Renton	18	5	5	8	31:44	15
9	Abercorn	18	5	1	12	35:52	11
10	Clyde	18	2	2	14	25:55	6

SCOTTISH DIVISION 1 1893-94

1	Celtic	18	14	1	3	53:32	29
2	Hearts	18	11	4	3	46:32	26
3	St Bernard's	18	11	1	6	53:41	23
4	Rangers	18	8	4	6	44:30	20
5	Dumbarton	18	7	5	6	32:35	19
6	St Mirren	18	7	3	8	50:46	17
7	Third Lanark	18	7	3	8	37:45	17
8	Dundee	18	6	3	9	43:58	15
9	Leith	18	4	2	12	36:46	10
10	Renton†	18	1	2	15	23:52	4

SCOTTISH DIVISION 2 1893-94

1	Hibernian	18	13	3	2	83:29	29
2	Cowlairs	18	13	1	4	75:32	27
3	Clyde*	18	11	2	5	51:36	24
4	Motherwell	18	11	1	6	61:46	23
5	Partick	18	10	0	8	56:58	20
6	Port Glasgow A. =	18	9	2	7	52:53	13
7	Abercorn	18	5	2	11	42:60	12
8	Morton	18	4	1	13	36:62	9
9	Northern	18	3	3	12	29:66	9
10	Thistle	18	2	3	13	31:74	7

SCOTTISH DIVISION 1 1894-95

1	Hearts	18	15	1	2	50:18	31
2	Celtic	18	11	4	3	50:29	26
3	Rangers	18	10	2	6	41:26	22
4	Third Lanark	18	10	1	7	51:39	21
5	St Mirren	18	9	1	8	34:36	19
6	St Bernard's	18	8	1	9	39:40	17
7	Clyde	18	8	0	10	40:49	16
8	Dundee	18	6	2	10	28:33	14
9	Leith†	18	3	1	14	32:64	7
10	Dumbarton	18	3	1	14	27:58	7

SCOTTISH DIVISION 2 1894-95

1	Hibernian*	18	14	2	2	92:27	30
2	Motherwell	18	10	2	6	56:39	22
3	Port Glasgow A.	18	8	4	6	62:56	20
4	Renton**	17	10	0	7	46:44	20
5	Morton	18	9	1	8	59:63	19
6	Airdrie	18	8	2	8	68:45	18
7	Partick	18	8	2	8	50:60	18
8	Abercorn	18	7	3	8	48:65	17
9	Dundee W.**	17	3	1	13	44:86	9
10	Cowlairs	18	2	3	13	37:77	7

SCOTTISH DIVISION 1 1895-96

1	Celtic	18	15	0	3	64:25	30
2	Rangers	18	11	4	3	57:39	26
3	Hibernian	18	11	2	5	58:39	24
4	Hearts	18	11	0	7	68:36	22
5	Dundee	18	7	2	9	33:42	16
6	Third Lanark	18	7	1	10	47:51	15
7	St Bernard's	18	7	1	10	36:53	15
8	St Mirren	18	5	3	10	31:51	13
9	Clyde	18	4	3	11	39:59	11
10	Dumbarton	18	4	0	14	36:74	8

SCOTTISH DIVISION 2 1895-96

1	Abercorn*	18	12	3	3	55:31	27
2	Leith	18	11	1	6	55:37	23
3	Renton	18	9	3	6	40:28	21
4	Kilmarnock	18	10	1	7	45:45	21
5	Airdrie	18	7	4	7	48:44	18
6	Partick	18	8	2	8	44:54	18
7	Port Glasgow A.	18	6	4	8	40:41	16
8	Motherwell	18	5	3	10	31:47	13
9	Morton	18	4	4	10	32:40	12
10	Linthouse	18	5	1	12	25:48	11

SCOTTISH DIVISION 1 1896-97

1	Hearts	18	13	2	3	47:22	28
2	Hibernian	18	12	2	4	50:20	26
3	Rangers	18	11	3	4	64:30	25
4	Celtic	18	10	4	4	42:18	24
5	Dundee	18	10	2	6	38:30	22
6	St Mirren	18	9	1	8	38:29	19
7	St Bernard's	18	7	0	11	32:40	14
8	Third Lanark	18	5	1	12	29:46	11
9	Clyde	18	4	0	14	27:65	8
10	Abercorn†	18	1	1	16	21:88	3

SCOTTISH DIVISION 2 1896-97

1	Partick*	18	14	3	1	61:28	31
2	Leith	18	13	1	4	54:28	27
3	Kilmarnock	18	10	1	7	44:33	21
4	Airdire	18	10	1	7	48:39	21
5	Morton	18	7	2	9	38:40	16
6	Renton	18	6	2	10	34:40	14
7	Linthouse §	18	8	2	8	44:52	14
8	Port Glasgow A.	18	4	5	9	39:50	13
9	Motherwell	18	6	1	11	40:55	13
10	Dumbarton	18	2	2	14	27:64	6

SCOTTISH DIVISION 1 1897-98

1	Celtic	18	15	3	0	56:13	33
2	Rangers	18	13	3	2	71:15	29
3	Hibernian	18	10	2	6	48:28	22
4	Hearts	18	8	4	6	54:33	20
5	Third Lanark	18	8	2	8	37:38	18
6	St Mirren	18	8	2	8	30:36	18
7	Dundee¶	18	5	3	10	29:36	13
8	Partick¶	18	6	1	11	34:64	13
9	St Bernard's	18	4	1	13	35:67	19
10	Clyde	18	1	3	14	20:84	5

SCOTTISH DIVISION 2 1897-98

1	Kilmarnock	18	14	1	3	64:29	29
2	Port Glasgow A.	18	12	1	5	66:35	25
3	Morton	18	9	4	5	47:38	22
4	Leith	18	9	2	7	39:38	20
5	Linthouse	18	6	4	8	37:39	16
6	Ayr	18	7	2	9	36:42	16
7	Abercorn	18	6	4	8	33:41	16
8	Airdrie	18	6	2	10	44:56	14
9	Hamilton††	18	5	2	11	28:51	12
10	Motherwell	18	3	4	11	31:56	10

††Hamilton took the place of Renton, who resigned after 4 matches

SCOTTISH DIVISION 1 1898-99

1	Rangers	18	18	0	0	79:18	36
2	Hearts	18	12	2	4	56:30	26
3	Celtic	18	11	2	5	51:33	24
4	Hibernian	18	10	3	5	42:43	23
5	St Mirren	18	8	4	6	46:32	20
6	Third Lanark	18	7	3	8	33:38	17
7	St Bernard's	18	4	4	10	30:37	12
8	Clyde	18	4	4	10	23:48	12
9	Partick†	18	2	2	14	19:58	6
10	Dundee	18	1	2	15	23:65	4

SCOTTISH DIVISION 2 1898-99

1	Kilmarnock*	18	14	4	0	73:24	32
2	Leith	18	12	3	3	63:38	27
3	Port Glasgow A.	18	12	1	5	75:51	25
4	Motherwell	18	7	6	5	41:40	20
5	Hamilton	18	7	1	10	48:58	15
6	Airdrie	18	6	3	9	35:46	15
7	Morton	18	6	1	11	36:41	13
8	Ayr	18	5	3	10	35:51	13
9	Linthouse	18	5	1	12	29:62	11
10	Abercorn	18	4	1	13	41:65	9

SCOTTISH DIVISION 1 1899-1900

1	Rangers	18	15	2	1	69:27	32
2	Celtic	18	9	7	2	46:27	25
3	Hibernian	18	9	6	3	43:24	24
4	Hearts	18	10	3	5	41:24	23
5	Kilmarnock	18	6	6	6	30:37	18
6	Dundee	18	4	7	7	36:39	15
7	Third Lanark	18	5	5	8	31:36	15
8	St Mirren¶	18	3	6	9	30:46	12
9	St Bernard's †¶	18	4	4	10	29:47	12
10	Clyde†	18	2	0	16	25:70	4

SCOTTISH DIVISION 2 1899-1900

1	Partick*	18	14	1	3	56:26	29
2	Morton*	18	14	0	4	66:25	28
3	Port Glasgow A.	18	10	0	8	50:41	20
4	Motherwell	18	9	1	8	38:36	19
5	Leith	18	9	1	8	32:37	19
6	Abercorn	18	7	2	9	46:39	16
7	Hamilton	18	7	1	10	33:46	15
8	Ayr	18	6	2	10	39:48	14
9	Airdrie	18	4	3	11	27:49	11
10	Linthouse	18	2	5	11	28:68	9

SCOTTISH DIVISION 1 1900-01

1	Rangers	20	17	1	2	60:25	35
2	Celtic	20	13	3	4	49:28	29
3	Hibernian	20	9	7	4	29:22	25
4	Morton	20	9	3	8	40:40	21
5	Kilmarnock	20	7	4	9	35:47	18
6	Third Lanark	20	6	6	8	20:29	18
7	Dundee	20	6	5	9	36:35	17
8	Queen's Park	20	7	3	10	33:37	17
9	St Mirren	20	5	6	9	33:43	16
10	Hearts	20	5	4	11	22:30	14
11	Partick†	20	4	2	14	28:49	10

SCOTTISH DIVISION 2 1900-01

1	St Bernard's	18	10	5	3	41:26	25
2	Airdrie	18	11	1	6	46:35	23
3	Abercorn	18	9	3	6	37:33	21
4	Clyde	18	9	2	7	43:35	20
5	Port Glasgow A.	18	9	1	8	45:44	19
6	Ayr	18	9	0	9	32:34	18
7	E. Stirlingshire	18	7	4	7	35:39	18
8	Leith	18	5	3	10	23:33	13
9	Hamilton	18	4	4	10	44:51	12
10	Motherwell	18	4	3	11	26:42	11

SCOTTISH DIVISION 1 1901-02

1	Rangers	18	13	2	3	43:29	28
2	Celtic	18	11	4	3	38:28	26
3	Hearts	18	10	2	6	32:21	22
4	Third Lanark	18	7	5	6	30:26	19
5	St Mirren	18	8	3	7	29:28	19
6	Hibernian	18	6	4	8	36:24	16
7	Kilmarnock	18	5	6	7	21:25	16
8	Queen's Park	18	5	4	9	21:32	14
9	Dundee	18	4	5	9	16:31	13
10	Morton	18	1	5	12	18:40	7

SCOTTISH DIVISION 2 1901-02

1	Port Glasgow A.*	22	14	4	4	71:31	32
2	Partick*	22	14	3	5	55:26	31
3	Motherwell	22	12	2	8	50:44	26
4	Airdrie	22	10	5	7	40:32	25
5	Hamilton	22	11	3	8	45:40	25
6	St Bernard's	22	10	2	10	30:30	22
7	Leith	22	9	3	10	34:38	21
8	Ayr	22	8	5	9	27:33	21
9	E. Stirlingshire	22	8	3	11	36:46	19
10	Arthurlie	22	6	5	11	32:42	17
11	Abercorn	22	4	5	13	27:57	13
12	Clyde	22	5	3	14	22:50	13

*promoted/elected †relegated ‡Dumbarton and Rangers declared joint champions after drawing 2-2 in a play-off §Four points deducted for infringements = Seven points deducted for fielding an ineligible player **Dundee Wanderers and Renton played only once when Renton failed to appear for the return fixture; Dundee awarded both points ¶Played off to determine which club would have to seek re-election

SCOTTISH DIVISION 1 — 1902-03

1	Hibernian	22	16	5	1	48:18	37
2	Dundee	22	13	5	4	31:12	31
3	Rangers	22	12	5	5	56:30	29
4	Hearts	22	11	6	5	46:27	28
5	Celtic	22	8	10	4	36:30	26
6	St Mirren	22	7	8	7	39:40	22
7	Third Lanark	22	8	5	9	34:27	21
8	Partick	22	6	7	9	34:50	19
9	Kilmarnock	22	6	4	12	24:43	16
10	Queen's Park	22	5	5	12	33:48	15
11	Port Glasgow A.	22	3	5	14	26:49	11
12	Morton	22	2	5	15	22:55	9

SCOTTISH DIVISION 2 — 1902-03

1	Airdrie*	22	15	5	2	43:19	35
2	Motherwell*	22	12	4	6	44:35	28
3	Ayr	22	12	3	7	34:24	27
4	Leith	22	11	5	6	43:41	27
5	St Bernard's	22	12	2	8	45:32	26
6	Hamilton	22	11	1	10	44:35	23
7	Falkirk	22	8	7	7	39:37	23
8	E. Stirlingshire	22	9	3	10	46:41	21
9	Arthurlie	22	6	8	8	34:46	20
10	Abercorn	22	5	2	15	35:58	12
11	Raith	22	3	5	14	34:55	11
12	Clyde	22	2	7	13	22:40	11

SCOTTISH DIVISION 1 — 1903-04

1	Third Lanark	26	20	3	3	61:26	43
2	Hearts	26	18	3	5	62:34	39
3	Celtic	26	18	2	6	68:27	38
4	Rangers	26	16	6	4	80:33	38
5	Dundee	26	13	2	11	54:45	28
6	St Mirren	26	11	5	10	45:38	27
7	Partick	26	10	7	9	46:41	27
8	Queen's Park	26	6	9	11	28:47	21
9	Port Glasgow A.	26	8	4	14	32:49	20
10	Hibernian	26	7	5	14	29:40	19
11	Morton	26	7	4	15	32:53	18
12	Airdrie	26	7	4	15	32:62	18
13	Motherwell	26	6	3	17	26:61	15
14	Kilmarnock	26	4	5	17	24:63	13

SCOTTISH DIVISION 2 — 1903-04

1	Hamilton	22	16	5	1	56:19	37
2	Clyde	22	12	5	5	51:36	29
3	Ayr	22	11	6	5	33:30	28
4	Falkirk	22	11	4	7	50:34	26
5	Raith	22	8	5	9	40:38	21
6	E. Stirlingshire	22	8	5	9	35:40	21
7	Leith	22	8	4	10	42:40	20
8	St Bernard's	22	9	2	11	31:43	20
9	Albion‡	22	8	5	9	47:37	19
10	Abercorn	22	6	4	12	38:55	16
11	Arthurlie	22	5	5	12	37:50	15
12	Ayr Parkhouse	22	3	4	15	23:61	10

‡two points deducted for fielding an ineligible player

SCOTTISH DIVISION 1 — 1904-05

1	Celtic §	26	18	5	3	68:31	41
2	Rangers	26	19	3	4	83:28	41
3	Third Lanark	26	14	7	5	60:28	35
4	Airdrie	26	11	5	10	38:45	27
5	Hibernian	26	9	8	9	39:39	26
6	Partick	26	12	2	12	36:56	26
7	Dundee	26	10	5	11	43:37	25
8	Hearts	26	11	3	12	46:44	25
9	Kilmarnock	26	9	5	12	29:45	23
10	St Mirren	26	9	4	13	33:36	22
11	Port Glasgow A.	26	8	5	13	30:51	21
12	Queen's Park	26	6	8	12	28:45	20
13	Morton	26	7	4	15	27:50	18
14	Motherwell	26	6	2	18	28:53	14

§Celtic won championship after play-off with Rangers

SCOTTISH DIVISION 2 — 1904-05

1	Clyde	22	13	6	3	38:22	32
2	Falkirk*	22	12	4	6	31:25	28
3	Hamilton	22	12	3	7	40:22	27
4	Leith	22	10	4	8	36:26	24
5	Ayr	22	11	1	10	46:37	23
6	Arthurlie	22	9	5	8	37:42	23
7	Aberdeen*	22	7	7	8	36:26	21
8	Albion	22	8	4	10	38:53	20
9	E. Stirlingshire	22	7	5	10	38:38	19
10	Raith	22	9	1	12	30:34	19
11	Abercorn	22	8	1	13	31:45	17
12	St Bernard's	22	3	5	14	23:54	11

SCOTTISH DIVISION 1 — 1905-06

1	Celtic	30	24	1	5	76:19	49
2	Hearts	30	18	7	5	64:27	43
3	Airdrie	30	15	8	7	53:31	38
4	Rangers	30	15	7	8	58:48	37
5	Partick	30	15	6	9	44:40	36
6	Third Lanark	30	16	2	12	62:39	34
7	Dundee	30	11	12	7	40:33	34
8	St Mirren	30	13	5	12	41:37	31
9	Motherwell	30	9	8	13	50:62	26
10	Morton	30	10	6	14	35:54	26
11	Hibernian	30	10	5	15	35:40	25
12	Aberdeen	30	8	8	14	36:48	24
13	Falkirk	30	9	5	16	52:68	23
14	Port Glasgow A.¶	30	6	8	16	38:68	20
15	Kilmarnock¶	30	8	4	18	46:68	20
16	Queen's Park	30	5	4	21	41:88	14

*Played off to determine which club would have to seek re-election

SCOTTISH DIVISION 2 — 1905-06

1	Leith	22	15	4	3	46:21	34
2	Clyde*	22	11	9	2	37:21	31
3	Albion	22	12	3	7	48:29	27
4	Hamilton*	22	12	2	8	45:34	26
5	St Bernard's	22	9	4	9	42:34	22
6	Arthurlie	22	10	2	10	42:43	22
7	Ayr	22	9	3	10	43:51	21
8	Raith	22	6	7	9	36:42	19
9	Cowdenbeath	22	7	3	12	27:39	17
10	Abercorn	22	6	5	11	29:45	17
11	Vale of Leven	22	6	4	12	34:49	16
12	E. Stirlingshire	22	1	10	11	26:47	12

SCOTTISH DIVISION 1 — 1906-07

1	Celtic	34	23	9	2	80:30	55
2	Dundee	34	18	12	4	53:26	48
3	Rangers	34	19	7	8	69:33	45
4	Airdrie	34	18	6	10	59:44	42
5	Falkirk	34	17	7	10	73:58	41
6	Third Lanark	34	15	9	10	57:48	39
7	St Mirren	34	12	13	9	50:44	37
8	Clyde	34	15	6	13	47:52	36
9	Hearts	34	11	13	10	47:43	35
10	Motherwell	34	12	9	13	45:49	33
11	Aberdeen	34	10	10	14	48:55	30
12	Hibernian	34	10	10	14	40:49	30
13	Morton	34	11	6	17	41:50	28
14	Partick	34	9	8	17	40:60	26
15	Queen's Park	34	9	6	19	51:66	24
16	Hamilton	34	8	5	21	40:64	21
17	Kilmarnock	34	8	5	21	40:72	21
18	Port Glasgow A.	34	7	7	20	30:67	21

SCOTTISH DIVISION 2 — 1906-07

1	St Bernard's	22	14	4	4	41:24	32
2	Vale of Leven	22	13	1	8	54:35	27
3	Arthurlie	22	12	3	7	50:39	27
4	Dumbarton	22	11	3	8	52:35	25
5	Leith	22	10	4	8	40:35	24
6	Albion	22	10	3	9	43:36	23
7	Cowdenbeath‡	22	10	5	7	36:39	23
8	Ayr	22	7	6	9	34:38	20
9	Abercorn	22	5	7	10	29:47	17
10	Raith¶	22	6	4	12	39:47	16
11	E. Stirlingshire¶	22	6	4	12	37:48	16
12	Ayr Parkhouse	22	5	2	15	32:64	12

¶Played off to determine which club would have to seek re-election

‡2 points deducted for fielding ineligible player

SCOTTISH DIVISION 1 — 1907-08

1	Celtic	34	24	7	3	86:27	55
2	Falkirk	34	22	7	5	102:40	51
3	Rangers	34	21	8	5	74:40	50
4	Dundee	34	20	8	6	70:27	48
5	Hibernian	34	17	9	8	55:42	42
6	Airdrie	34	18	5	11	58:41	41
7	St Mirren	34	13	10	11	50:59	36
8	Aberdeen	34	13	9	12	45:44	35
9	Third Lanark	34	13	7	14	45:50	33
10	Motherwell	34	12	7	15	61:53	31
11	Hamilton	34	10	8	16	54:65	28
12	Hearts	34	11	6	17	50:62	28
13	Morton	34	9	9	16	43:66	27
14	Kilmarnock	34	6	13	15	38:61	25
15	Partick	34	8	9	17	43:69	25
16	Queen's Park	34	7	8	19	54:84	22
17	Clyde	34	5	8	21	36:75	18
18	Port Glasgow A.	34	5	7	22	39:98	17

Jimmy McGrory (hoops) is deprived of a goal by a Motherwell defender's hand-ball during a League game at Celtic Park on Saturday 4 February 1933. Motherwell were League Champions at the time, the only occasion they have managed this feat.

SCOTTISH DIVISION 2 1907-08

1	Raith	22	14	2	6	37:23	30
2	Dumbarton‡	22	12	5	5	49:32	27
3	Ayr	22	11	5	6	40:33	27
4	Abercorn	22	9	5	8	33:30	23
5	E. Stirlingshire	22	9	5	8	30:32	23
6	Ayr Parkhouse	22	11	0	11	38:38	22
7	Leith	22	8	5	9	41:40	21
8	St Bernard's	22	8	5	9	31:32	21
9	Albion	22	7	5	10	36:48	19
10	Vale of Leven	22	5	8	9	25:31	18
11	Arthurlie	22	6	5	11	33:45	17
12	Cowdenbeath	22	5	4	13	26:35	14

‡two points deducted for fielding an ineligible player

SCOTTISH DIVISION 1 1908-09

1	Celtic	34	23	5	6	71:24	51
2	Dundee	34	22	6	6	70:32	50
3	Clyde	34	21	6	7	61:37	48
4	Rangers	34	19	7	8	91:38	45
5	Airdrie	34	16	9	9	67:46	41
6	Hibernian	34	16	7	11	40:32	39
7	St Mirren	34	15	6	13	53:45	36
8	Aberdeen	34	15	6	13	61:53	36
9	Falkirk	34	13	7	14	58:56	33
10	Kilmarnock	34	13	7	14	47:61	33
11	Third Lanark	34	11	10	13	56:49	32
12	Hearts	34	12	8	14	54:49	32
13	Port Glasgow A.	34	10	8	16	39:52	28
14	Motherwell	34	11	6	17	47:73	28
15	Queen's Park	34	6	13	15	42:65	25
16	Hamilton	34	6	12	16	42:72	24
17	Morton	34	8	7	19	39:90	23
18	Partick	34	2	4	28	38:102	8

SCOTTISH DIVISION 2 1908-09

1	Abercorn	22	13	5	4	40:18	31
2	Raith	22	11	6	5	46:22	28
3	Vale of Leven	22	12	4	6	39:25	28
4	Dumbarton	22	10	5	7	34:34	25
5	Ayr	22	10	3	9	43:36	23
6	Leith	22	10	3	9	37:33	23
7	Ayr Parkhouse	22	8	5	9	29:31	21
8	St Bernard's	22	9	3	10	34:37	21
9	E. Stirlingshire	22	9	3	10	28:34	21
10	Albion	22	9	2	11	37:48	20
11	Cowdenbeath	22	4	4	14	19:42	12
12	Arthurlie	22	5	1	16	29:55	11

SCOTTISH DIVISION 1 1909-10

1	Celtic	34	24	6	4	63:22	54
2	Falkirk	34	22	8	4	71:28	52
3	Rangers	34	20	6	8	70:35	46
4	Aberdeen	34	16	8	10	44:29	40
5	Clyde	34	14	9	11	47:40	37
6	Dundee	34	14	8	12	52:44	36
7	Third Lanark	34	13	8	13	62:44	34
8	Hibernian	34	14	6	14	33:40	34
9	Airdrie	34	12	9	13	46:57	33
10	Motherwell	34	12	8	14	59:60	32
11	Kilmarnock	34	12	8	14	53:60	32
12	Hearts	34	12	7	15	59:50	31
13	St Mirren	34	13	5	16	49:58	31
14	Queen's Park	34	12	6	16	54:74	30
15	Hamilton	34	11	6	17	50:67	28
16	Partick	34	8	10	16	47:59	26
17	Morton	34	11	3	20	38:60	25
18	Port Glasgow A.†	34	3	5	26	25:95	11

SCOTTISH DIVISION 2 1909-10

=1	Leith	22	13	7	2	44:19	33
=1	Raith*	22	14	5	3	36:21	33
3	St Bernard's	22	12	3	7	43:31	27
4	Dumbarton	22	9	5	8	44:38	23
5	Abercorn	22	7	8	7	38:40	22
6	Vale of Leven	22	8	5	9	36:38	21
7	Ayr	22	9	3	10	37:40	21
8	E. Stirlingshire	22	9	2	11	38:43	20
9	Albion	22	7	5	10	34:39	19
10	Arthurlie	22	6	5	11	34:47	17
11	Cowdenbeath	22	7	3	12	22:34	17
12	Ayr Parkhouse	22	4	3	15	27:43	11

=1 Leith and Raith were declared joint champions

SCOTTISH DIVISION 1 1910-11

1	Rangers	34	23	6	5	90:34	52
2	Aberdeen	34	19	10	5	53:28	48
3	Falkirk	34	17	10	7	65:42	44
4	Partick	34	17	8	9	50:41	42
5	Celtic	34	15	11	8	48:18	41
6	Dundee	34	18	5	11	54:42	41
7	Clyde	34	14	11	9	45:36	39
8	Third Lanark	34	16	7	11	59:53	39
9	Hibernian	34	15	6	13	44:48	36
10	Kilmarnock	34	12	10	12	43:45	34
11	Airdrie	34	12	9	13	49:53	33
12	St Mirren	34	12	7	15	46:57	31
13	Morton	34	9	11	14	49:51	29
14	Hearts	34	8	8	18	42:59	24
15	Raith	34	7	10	17	36:56	24
16	Hamilton	34	8	5	21	31:60	21
17	Motherwell	34	8	4	22	37:66	20
18	Queen's Park	34	5	4	25	28:80	14

SCOTTISH DIVISION 2 1910-11

1	Dumbarton	22	15	1	6	55:31	31
2	Ayr	22	12	3	7	52:36	27
3	Albion	22	10	5	7	27:21	25
4	Leith	22	9	6	7	42:43	24
5	Cowdenbeath	22	9	5	8	31:27	23
6	St Bernard's	22	10	2	10	36:39	22
7	E. Stirlingshire	22	7	6	9	28:35	20
8	Port Glasgow A.	22	8	3	11	27:32	19
9	Dundee Hibs	22	7	5	10	29:36	19
10	Arthurlie	22	7	5	10	26:33	19
11	Abercorn	22	9	1	12	39:50	19
12	Vale of Leven	22	4	8	10	22:31	16

SCOTTISH DIVISION 1 1911-12

1	Rangers	34	24	3	7	86:34	51
2	Celtic	34	17	11	6	58:33	45
3	Clyde	34	19	4	11	56:32	42
4	Hearts	34	16	8	10	54:40	40
5	Partick	34	16	8	10	47:40	40
6	Morton	34	14	9	11	44:44	37
7	Falkirk	34	15	6	13	46:43	36
8	Dundee	34	13	9	12	52:41	35
9	Aberdeen	34	14	7	13	44:44	35
10	Airdrie	34	12	8	14	40:41	32
11	Third Lanark	34	12	7	15	40:57	31
12	Hamilton	34	11	8	15	32:44	30
13	Hibernian	34	12	5	17	44:47	29
14	Motherwell	34	11	5	18	34:44	27
15	Raith	34	9	9	16	39:59	27
16	Kilmarnock	34	11	4	19	38:60	26
17	Queen's Park	34	8	9	17	29:53	25
18	St Mirren	34	7	10	17	32:59	24

SCOTTISH DIVISION 2 1911-12

1	Ayr*	22	16	3	3	54:24	35
2	Abercorn	22	13	4	5	43:22	30
3	Dumbarton	22	13	1	8	47:31	27
4	Cowdenbeath	22	12	2	8	39:31	26
5	Johnstone	22	10	4	8	29:27	24
6	St Bernard's	22	9	5	8	38:36	23
7	Leith	22	9	4	9	31:34	22
8	Arthurlie	22	7	5	10	26:30	19
9	E. Stirlingshire	22	7	3	12	21:31	17
10	Dundee Hibs	22	5	5	12	21:41	15
11	Vale of Leven	22	6	1	15	19:37	13
12	Albion*	22	6	1	15	26:50	13

* Both games played at Ayr

SCOTTISH DIVISION 1 1912-13

1	Rangers	34	24	5	5	76:41	53
2	Celtic	34	22	5	7	53:28	49
3	Hearts	34	17	7	10	71:43	41
4	Airdrie	34	15	11	8	64:46	41
5	Falkirk	34	14	12	8	56:38	40
6	Hibernian	34	16	5	13	63:54	37
7	Motherwell	34	12	13	9	47:39	37
8	Aberdeen	34	14	9	11	47:40	37
9	Clyde	34	13	9	12	41:44	35
10	Hamilton	34	12	8	14	44:47	32
11	Kilmarnock	34	10	11	13	37:54	31
12	St Mirren	34	10	10	14	50:60	30
13	Morton	34	11	7	16	50:59	29
14	Dundee	34	8	13	13	33:46	29
15	Third Lanark	34	8	12	14	31:41	28
16	Raith	34	8	10	16	46:60	26
17	Partick	34	10	4	20	40:55	24
18	Queen's Park	34	5	3	26	34:88	13

SCOTTISH DIVISION 2 1912-13

1	Ayr*	26	13	8	5	45:19	34
2	Dunfermline	26	13	7	6	45:27	33
3	E. Stirlingshire	26	12	8	6	43:27	32
4	Abercorn	26	12	7	7	33:31	31
5	Cowdenbeath	26	12	6	8	36:27	30
6	Dumbarton*	26	12	5	9	39:30	29
7	St Bernard's	26	12	3	11	36:34	27
8	Johnstone	26	9	6	11	31:43	24
9	Albion	26	10	3	13	38:40	23
10	Dundee Hibs	26	6	10	10	34:43	22
11	St Johnstone	26	7	7	12	29:38	21
12	Vale of Leven	26	8	5	13	28:45	21
13	Arthurlie	26	7	5	14	37:49	19
14	Leith	26	5	8	13	26:47	18

SCOTTISH DIVISION 1 1913-14

1	Celtic	38	30	5	3	81:14	65
2	Rangers	38	27	5	6	79:31	59
3	Hearts	38	23	8	7	70:29	54
4	Morton	38	26	2	10	76:51	54
5	Falkirk	38	20	9	9	69:51	49
6	Airdrie	38	18	12	8	72:43	48
7	Dundee	38	19	5	14	64:53	43
8	Third Lanark	38	13	10	15	42:51	36
9	Clyde	38	11	11	16	46:46	33
10	Ayr	38	13	7	18	58:74	33
11	Raith	38	13	6	19	56:57	32
12	Kilmarnock	38	11	9	18	48:68	31
13	Hibernian	38	12	6	20	58:75	30
14	Aberdeen	38	10	10	18	38:55	30
15	Partick	38	10	9	19	37:51	29
16	Queen's Park	38	10	9	19	52:84	29
17	Motherwell	38	11	6	21	49:66	28
18	Hamilton	38	11	6	21	46:65	28
19	Dumbarton	38	10	7	21	45:87	27
20	St Mirren	38	8	6	24	38:73	22

SCOTTISH DIVISION 2 1913-14

1	Cowdenbeath	22	13	5	4	34:17	31
2	Albion	22	10	7	5	38:33	27
3	Dunfermline	22	11	4	7	46:28	26
4	Dundee Hibs	22	11	4	7	36:31	26
5	St Johnstone	22	9	5	8	48:38	23
6	Abercorn	22	10	3	9	32:32	23
7	St Bernard's	22	8	6	8	39:31	22
8	E. Stirlingshire	22	7	8	7	40:36	22
9	Arthurlie	22	8	4	10	35:37	20
10	Leith	22	5	9	8	31:37	19
11	Vale of Leven	22	5	3	14	23:47	13
12	Johnstone	22	4	4	14	20:55	12

SCOTTISH DIVISION 1 1914-15

1	Celtic	38	30	5	3	91:25	65
2	Hearts	38	27	7	4	83:32	61
3	Rangers	38	23	4	11	74:47	50
4	Morton	38	18	12	8	74:48	48
5	Ayr	38	20	8	10	55:40	48
6	Falkirk	38	16	7	15	48:48	39
7	Hamilton	38	16	6	16	60:55	38
8	Partick	38	15	8	15	56:58	38
9	St Mirren	38	14	8	16	56:65	36
10	Airdrie	38	14	7	17	54:60	35
11	Hibernian	38	12	11	15	59:66	35
12	Kilmarnock	38	15	4	19	55:59	34
13	Dumbarton	38	13	8	17	51:66	34
14	Aberdeen	38	11	11	16	39:52	33
15	Dundee	38	12	9	17	43:61	33
16	Third Lanark	38	10	12	16	51:57	32
17	Clyde	38	12	6	20	44:59	30
18	Motherwell	38	10	10	18	49:66	30
19	Raith	38	9	10	19	53:68	28
20	Queen's Park	38	4	5	29	27:90	13

SCOTTISH DIVISION 2 1914-15

1	Cowdenbeath‡	26	16	5	5	49:17	37
2	Leith‡	26	15	7	4	54:31	37
3	St Bernard's‡	26	18	1	7	66:34	37
4	E. Stirlingshire	26	13	5	8	53:46	31
5	Clydebank	26	13	4	9	68:37	30
6	Dunfermline	26	13	2	11	49:39	28
7	Johnstone	26	11	5	10	41:52	27
8	St Johnstone	26	10	6	10	56:53	26
9	Albion	26	9	7	10	37:42	25
10	Lochgelly	26	9	3	14	44:60	21
11	Dundee Hibs	26	8	3	15	48:61	19
12	Abercorn	26	5	7	14	35:65	17
13	Arthurlie	26	6	4	16	36:66	16
14	Vale of Leven	26	4	5	17	33:66	13

‡Played each other to determine top 3 placings at end of season; Cowdenbeath declared champions

SCOTTISH LEAGUE 1915-16

1	Celtic	38	32	3	3	116:23	67
2	Rangers	38	25	6	7	87:39	56
3	Morton‡	37	22	7	8	83:35	51
4	Ayr	38	20	8	10	72:45	48
5	Partick	38	19	8	11	65:41	46
6	Hearts‡	37	20	6	11	66:45	46
7	Hamilton	38	19	3	16	68:76	41
8	Dundee	38	18	4	16	57:49	40
9	Dumbarton	38	13	11	14	53:64	37
10	Kilmarnock	38	12	11	15	46:49	35
11	Aberdeen	38	11	12	15	51:64	34
12	Falkirk	38	12	9	17	45:61	33
13	St Mirren	38	13	4	21	50:67	30
14	Motherwell	38	11	8	19	55:81	30
15	Airdrieonians	38	11	8	19	44:71	30
16	Clyde	38	11	7	20	49:71	29
17	Third Lanark	38	9	11	18	38:56	29
18	Queen's Park	38	11	6	21	53:100	28
19	Hibernian	38	9	7	22	44:70	25
20	Raith	38	9	5	24	30:65	23

‡Morton and Hearts played only once

SCOTTISH LEAGUE 1916-17

1	Celtic	38	27	10	1	79:17	64
2	Morton	38	24	6	8	72:39	54
3	Rangers	38	24	5	9	68:32	53
4	Airdrieonians	38	21	8	9	71:38	50
5	Third Lanark	38	19	11	8	53:37	49
6	Kilmarnock	38	18	7	13	69:45	43
7	St Mirren	38	15	10	13	49:43	40
8	Motherwell	38	16	6	16	57:58	38
9	Partick	38	14	7	17	44:43	35
10	Dumbarton	38	12	11	15	56:73	35
11	Hamilton	38	13	9	16	54:73	35
12	Falkirk	38	12	10	16	57:57	34
13	Clyde	38	10	14	14	41:51	34
14	Hearts	38	14	4	20	44:59	32
15	Ayr	38	12	7	19	46:59	31
16	Dundee	38	13	4	21	58:71	30
17	Hibernian	38	10	10	18	57:72	30
18	Queen's Park	38	11	7	20	56:81	29
19	Raith	38	8	7	23	42:91	23
20	Aberdeen	38	7	7	24	36:68	21

SCOTTISH LEAGUE 1917-18

1	Rangers	34	25	6	3	66:24	56
2	Celtic	34	24	7	3	66:26	55
3	Kilmarnock	34	19	5	10	69:41	43
4	Morton	34	17	9	8	53:42	43
5	Motherwell	34	16	9	9	70:51	41
6	Partick	34	14	12	8	51:37	40
7	Queen's Park	34	14	6	14	64:63	34
8	Dumbarton	34	13	8	13	48:49	34
9	Clydebank	34	14	5	15	55:56	33
10	Hearts	34	14	4	16	41:58	32
11	St Mirren	34	11	7	16	42:50	29
12	Hamilton	34	11	6	17	52:63	28
13	Third Lanark	34	10	7	17	56:62	27
14	Falkirk	34	9	9	16	38:58	27
15	Airdrieonians	34	10	6	18	46:58	26
16	Hibernian	34	8	9	17	42:57	25
17	Clyde	34	9	2	23	37:72	20
18	Ayr	34	5	9	20	32:61	19

SCOTTISH LEAGUE 1918-19

1	Celtic	34	26	6	2	71:22	58
2	Rangers	34	26	5	3	86:16	57
3	Morton	34	18	11	5	76:38	47
4	Partick	34	17	7	10	62:43	41
5	Motherwell	34	14	10	10	51:40	38
6	Hearts	34	14	9	11	59:52	37
7	Ayr	34	14	9	11	57:53	37
8	Queen's Park	34	15	5	14	59:57	35
9	Kilmarnock	34	14	7	13	61:59	35
10	Clydebank	34	12	8	14	52:65	32
11	St Mirren	34	10	12	12	43:55	32
12	Third Lanark	34	11	9	14	60:60	31
13	Airdrie	34	9	11	14	45:54	29
14	Hamilton	34	11	5	18	49:75	27
15	Dumbarton	34	7	8	19	31:57	22
16	Falkirk	34	6	8	20	46:72	20
17	Clyde	34	7	6	21	45:75	20
18	Hibernian	34	5	4	25	28:87	14

SCOTTISH LEAGUE 1919-20

1	Rangers	42	31	9	2	106:25	71
2	Celtic	42	29	10	3	89:31	68
3	Motherwell	42	23	11	8	73:53	57
4	Dundee	42	22	6	14	79:65	50
5	Clydebank	42	20	8	14	78:54	48
6	Morton	42	16	13	13	71:48	45
7	Airdrie	42	17	10	15	57:43	44
8	Third Lanark	42	16	11	15	57:62	43
9	Kilmarnock	42	20	3	19	59:74	43
10	Ayr	42	15	10	17	72:69	40
11	Dumbarton	42	13	13	16	57:65	39
12	Queen's Park	42	14	10	18	67:73	38
13	Partick	42	13	12	17	51:62	38
14	St Mirren	42	15	8	19	63:81	38
15	Clyde	42	14	9	19	64:71	37
16	Hearts	42	14	9	19	57:72	37
17	Aberdeen	42	11	13	18	46:64	35
18	Hibernian	42	13	7	22	60:79	33
19	Raith	42	11	10	21	61:82	32
20	Falkirk	42	10	11	21	45:74	31
21	Hamilton	42	11	7	24	56:86	29
22	Albion	42	10	7	25	42:77	27

SCOTTISH LEAGUE 1920-21

1	Rangers	42	35	6	1	91:24	76
2	Celtic	42	30	6	6	86:35	66
3	Hearts	42	20	10	12	74:49	50
4	Dundee	42	19	11	12	54:48	49
5	Motherwell	42	19	10	13	75:51	48
6	Partick	42	17	12	13	53:39	46
7	Clyde	42	21	3	18	63:62	45
8	Third Lanark	42	19	6	17	74:61	44
9	Morton	42	15	14	13	66:58	44
10	Airdrie	42	17	9	16	71:64	43
11	Aberdeen	42	14	14	14	53:54	42
12	Kilmarnock	42	17	8	17	62:68	42
13	Hibernian	42	16	9	17	58:57	41
14	Ayr	42	14	12	16	62:69	40
15	Hamilton	42	14	12	16	44:57	40
16	Raith	42	16	5	21	54:58	37
17	Albion	42	11	12	19	57:68	34
18	Falkirk	42	11	12	19	54:72	34
19	Queen's Park	42	11	11	20	45:80	33
20	Clydebank	42	7	14	21	47:72	28
21	Dumbarton	42	10	4	28	41:89	24
22	St Mirren	42	7	4	31	43:92	18

SCOTTISH DIVISION 1 1921-22

1	Celtic	42	27	13	2	83:20	67
2	Rangers	42	28	10	4	83:26	66
3	Raith	42	19	13	10	66:43	51
4	Dundee*	42	19	11	12	57:40	49
5	Falkirk	42	16	17	9	48:38	49
6	Partick	42	20	8	14	57:53	48
7	Hibernian	42	16	14	12	55:44	46
8	St Mirren	42	17	12	13	71:61	46
9	Third Lanark	42	17	12	13	58:52	46
10	Clyde	42	16	12	14	60:51	44
11	Albion	42	17	10	15	55:51	44
12	Morton	42	16	10	16	58:57	42
13	Motherwell	42	16	7	19	63:58	39
14	Ayr*	42	13	12	17	55:63	38
15	Aberdeen	42	13	9	20	48:54	35
16	Airdrie	42	12	11	19	46:56	35
17	Kilmarnock	42	13	9	20	56:83	35
18	Hamilton	42	9	16	17	51:62	34
19	Hearts	42	11	10	21	50:60	32
20	Dumbarton†	42	10	10	22	46:81	30
21	Queen's Park†	42	9	10	23	38:82	28
22	Clydebank†	42	6	8	28	34:103	20

* Both games played at Dundee

SCOTTISH DIVISION 2 1921-22

1	Alloa*	38	26	8	4	81:32	60
2	Cowdenbeath	38	19	9	10	56:30	47
3	Armadale	38	20	5	13	64:49	45
4	Vale of Leven	38	17	10	11	56:43	44
5	Bathgate	38	16	11	11	56:41	43
6	Bo'ness	38	16	7	15	57:49	39
7	Broxburn	38	14	11	13	43:43	39
8	Dunfermline	38	14	10	14	56:42	38
9	St Bernard's	38	15	8	15	50:49	38
10	Stenhousemuir	38	14	10	14	50:51	38
11	Johnstone	38	14	10	14	46:59	38
12	East Fife	38	15	7	16	55:54	37
13	St Johnstone	38	12	11	15	41:52	35
14	Forfar	38	11	12	15	44:53	34
15	E. Stirlingshire	38	12	10	16	43:60	34
16	Arbroath	38	11	11	16	45:56	33
17	King's Park	38	10	12	16	47:65	32
18	Lochgelly	38	11	9	18	46:56	31
19	Dundee Hibs	38	10	8	20	47:65	28
20	Clackmannan	38	10	7	21	41:75	27

SCOTTISH DIVISION 1 1922-23

1	Rangers	38	23	9	6	67:29	55
2	Airdrie	38	20	10	8	58:38	50
3	Celtic	38	19	8	11	52:39	46
4	Falkirk	38	14	17	7	44:32	45
5	Aberdeen	38	15	12	11	46:34	42
6	St Mirren	38	15	12	11	54:44	42
7	Dundee	38	17	7	14	51:45	41
8	Hibernian	38	17	7	14	45:40	41
9	Raith	38	13	13	12	31:43	39
10	Ayr	38	13	12	13	43:44	38
11	Partick	38	14	9	15	51:48	37
12	Hearts	38	11	15	12	51:50	37
13	Motherwell	38	13	10	15	59:60	36
14	Morton	38	12	11	15	44:47	35
15	Kilmarnock	38	14	7	17	57:66	35
16	Clyde	38	12	9	17	36:44	33
17	Third Lanark	38	11	8	19	40:59	30
18	Hamilton	38	11	7	20	43:59	29
19	Albion†	38	8	10	20	38:64	26
20	Alloa†	38	6	11	21	27:52	23

SCOTTISH DIVISION 2 1922-23

1	Queen's Park*	38	24	9	5	73:31	57
2	Clydebank*	38	21	10	7	69:29	52
3	St Johnstone §	38	19	12	7	60:39	48
4	Dumbarton	38	17	8	13	61:40	42
5	Bathgate	38	16	9	13	67:55	41
6	Armadale	38	15	11	12	63:52	41
7	Bo'ness	38	12	17	9	48:46	41
8	Broxburn	38	14	12	12	40:43	40
9	East Fife	38	16	7	15	48:42	39
10	Lochgelly	38	16	5	17	41:64	37
11	Cowdenbeath §	38	16	6	16	56:52	36
12	King's Park	38	14	6	18	46:60	34
13	Dunfermline	38	11	11	16	47:44	33
14	Stenhousemuir	38	13	7	18	53:67	33
15	Forfar	38	13	7	18	51:73	33
16	Johnstone	38	13	6	19	41:62	32
17	Vale of Leven	38	11	8	19	50:59	30
18	St Bernard's §	38	8	15	15	39:50	29
19	E. Stirlingshire	38	10	8	20	48:69	28
20	Arbroath	38	8	12	18	45:69	28

§two points deducted for fielding an ineligible player

SCOTTISH DIVISION 1 1923-24

1	Rangers	38	25	9	4	72:22	59
2	Airdrie	38	20	10	8	72:46	50
3	Celtic	38	17	12	9	56:33	46
4	Raith	38	18	7	13	56:38	43
5	Dundee	38	15	13	10	70:57	43
6	St Mirren	38	15	12	11	53:45	42
7	Hibernian	38	15	11	12	66:52	41
8	Partick	38	15	9	14	58:55	39
9	Hearts	38	14	10	14	61:50	38
10	Motherwell	38	15	7	16	58:63	37
11	Morton	38	16	5	17	48:54	37
12	Hamilton	38	15	6	17	52:57	36
13	Aberdeen	38	13	10	15	37:41	36
14	Ayr	38	12	10	16	38:60	34
15	Falkirk	38	13	6	19	46:53	32
16	Kilmarnock	38	12	8	18	48:65	32
17	Queen's Park	38	11	9	18	43:60	31
18	Third Lanark	38	11	8	19	54:78	30
19	Clyde†	38	10	9	19	40:70	29
20	Clydebank†	38	10	5	23	42:71	25

SCOTTISH DIVISION 2 1923-24

1	St Johnstone*	38	22	12	4	79:33	56
2	Cowdenbeath*	38	23	9	6	78:33	55
3	Bathgate	38	16	12	10	58:49	44
4	Stenhousemuir	38	16	11	11	58:45	43
5	Albion	38	15	12	11	67:53	42
6	King's Park	38	16	10	12	67:56	42
7	Dunfermline	38	14	11	13	52:45	39
8	Johnstone	38	16	7	15	60:56	39
9	Dundee United	38	12	15	11	41:41	39
10	Dumbarton	38	17	5	16	55:58	39
11	Armadale	38	16	6	16	56:63	38
12	East Fife	38	14	9	15	54:47	37
13	Bo'ness	38	13	11	14	45:52	37
14	Forfar	38	14	7	17	43:68	35
15	Broxburn	38	13	8	17	50:56	34
16	Alloa	38	14	6	18	44:53	34
17	Arbroath	38	12	8	18	49:51	32
18	St Bernard's	38	11	10	17	49:54	32
19	Vale of Leven	38	11	9	18	41:67	31
20	Lochgelly	38	4	4	30	20:86	12

SCOTTISH DIVISION 1 1924-25

1	Rangers	38	25	10	3	76:26	60
2	Airdrie	38	25	7	6	85:31	57
3	Hibernian	38	22	8	8	78:43	52
4	Celtic	38	18	8	12	77:44	44
5	Cowdenbeath	38	16	10	12	76:65	42
6	St Mirren	38	18	4	16	65:63	40
7	Partick	38	14	10	14	60:61	38
8	Dundee	38	14	8	16	48:55	36
9	Raith	38	14	8	16	52:60	36
10	Hearts	38	12	11	15	65:69	35
11	St Johnstone	38	12	11	15	56:71	35
12	Kilmarnock	38	12	9	17	53:64	33
13	Hamilton	38	15	3	20	50:63	33
14	Morton	38	12	9	17	46:69	33
15	Aberdeen	38	11	10	17	46:56	32
16	Falkirk	38	12	8	18	44:54	32
17	Queen's Park	38	12	8	18	50:71	32
18	Motherwell	38	10	10	18	55:64	30
19	Ayr†	38	11	8	19	43:65	30
20	Third Lanark†	38	11	8	19	53:84	30

SCOTTISH DIVISION 2 1924-25

1	Dundee U.*	38	20	10	8	58:44	50
2	Clydebank*	38	20	8	10	65:42	48
3	Clyde	38	20	7	11	72:39	47
4	Alloa	38	17	11	10	57:33	45
5	Arbroath	38	16	10	12	47:46	42
6	Bo'ness	38	16	9	13	71:48	41
7	Broxburn	38	16	9	13	48:54	41
8	Dumbarton	38	15	10	13	45:44	40
9	East Fife	38	17	5	16	66:58	39
10	King's Park	38	15	8	15	54:46	38
11	Stenhousemuir	38	15	7	16	51:58	37
12	Arthurlie	38	14	8	16	56:60	36
13	Dunfermline	38	14	7	17	62:57	35
14	Armadale	38	15	5	18	55:62	35
15	Albion	38	15	5	18	46:61	35
16	Bathgate	38	12	10	16	58:74	34
17	St Bernard's	38	14	4	20	52:70	32
18	E. Stirlingshire	38	11	8	19	58:72	30
19	Johnstone	38	12	4	22	53:85	28
20	Forfar	38	10	7	21	46:67	27

SCOTTISH DIVISION 1 1925-26

1	Celtic	38	25	8	5	97:40	58
2	Airdrie	38	23	4	11	95:54	50
3	Hearts	38	21	8	9	87:56	50
4	St Mirren	38	20	7	11	62:52	47
5	Motherwell	38	19	8	11	67:46	46
6	Rangers	38	19	6	13	79:55	44
7	Cowdenbeath	38	18	6	14	87:68	42
8	Falkirk	38	14	14	10	61:57	42
9	Kilmarnock	38	17	7	14	79:77	41
10	Dundee	38	14	9	15	47:59	37
11	Aberdeen	38	13	10	15	49:54	36
12	Hamilton	38	13	9	16	68:79	35
13	Queen's Park	38	15	4	19	70:81	34
14	Partick	38	10	13	15	64:73	33
15	Morton	38	12	7	19	57:84	31
16	Hibernian	38	12	6	20	72:77	30
17	Dundee	38	11	6	21	52:74	28
18	St Johnstone	38	9	10	19	43:78	28
19	Raith†	38	11	4	23	46:81	26
20	Clydebank†	38	7	8	23	55:92	22

SCOTTISH DIVISION 2 1925-26

1	Dunfermline*	38	26	7	5	109:43	59
2	Clyde*	38	24	5	9	87:51	53
3	Ayr	38	20	12	6	77:39	52
4	East Fife	38	20	9	9	98:73	49
5	Stenhousemuir	38	19	10	9	74:52	48
6	Third Lanark	38	19	8	11	72:47	46
7	Arthurlie	38	17	5	16	81:75	39
8	Bo'ness	38	17	5	16	65:70	39
9	Albion	38	16	6	16	78:71	38
10	Arbroath	38	17	4	17	80:73	38
11	Dumbarton	38	14	10	14	54:78	38
12	Nithsdale	38	15	7	16	79:82	37
13	King's Park	38	14	9	15	67:73	37
14	St Bernard's	38	15	5	18	86:82	35
15	Armadale	38	14	5	19	82:101	33
16	Alloa	38	11	8	19	54:63	30
17	Queen o' South	38	10	8	20	64:88	28
18	E. Stirlingshire	38	10	7	21	59:89	27
19	Bathgate	38	7	6	25	60:105	20
20	Broxburn	38	4	6	28	55:126	14

SCOTTISH DIVISION 1 1926-27

1	Rangers	38	23	10	5	85:41	56
2	Motherwell	38	23	5	10	81:52	51
3	Celtic	38	21	7	10	101:55	49
4	Airdrie	38	18	9	11	97:64	45
5	Dundee	38	17	9	12	77:51	43
6	Falkirk	38	16	10	12	77:60	42
7	Cowdenbeath	38	18	6	14	74:60	42
8	Aberdeen	38	13	14	11	73:72	40
9	Hibernian	38	16	7	15	62:71	39
10	St Mirren	38	16	5	17	78:76	37
11	Partick	38	15	6	17	89:74	36
12	Queen's Park	38	15	6	17	74:84	36
13	Hearts	38	12	11	15	65:64	35
14	St Johnstone	38	13	9	16	55:69	35
15	Hamilton	38	13	9	16	60:85	35
16	Kilmarnock	38	12	8	18	54:71	32
17	Clyde	38	10	9	19	54:85	29
18	Dunfermline	38	10	8	20	53:85	28
19	Morton†	38	12	4	22	56:101	28
20	Dundee U.†	38	7	8	23	56:101	22

SCOTTISH DIVISION 2 1926-27

1	Bo'ness*	38	23	10	5	86:41	56
2	Raith*	38	21	7	10	92:52	49
3	Clydebank	38	18	9	11	94:75	45
4	Third Lanark	38	17	10	11	67:48	44
5	E. Stirlingshire	38	18	8	12	93:75	44
6	East Fife	38	19	4	15	103:91	42
7	Arthurlie	38	18	5	15	90:83	41
8	Ayr	38	13	15	10	67:68	41
9	Forfar	38	15	7	16	66:79	37
10	Stenhousemuir	38	12	12	14	69:75	36
11	Queen o' South	38	16	4	18	72:80	36
12	King's Park	38	13	9	16	76:75	35
13	St Bernard's	38	14	6	18	70:77	34
14	Armadale	38	12	10	16	69:78	34
15	Alloa	38	11	11	16	70:78	33
16	Albion	38	11	11	16	74:87	33
17	Bathgate	38	13	7	18	76:98	33
18	Dumbarton	38	13	6	19	69:84	32
19	Arbroath	38	13	6	19	64:82	32
20	Nithsdale	38	7	9	22	59:100	23

SCOTTISH DIVISION 1 1927-28

1	Rangers	38	26	8	4	109:36	60
2	Celtic	38	23	9	6	93:39	55
3	Motherwell	38	23	9	6	92:46	55
4	Hearts	38	20	7	11	89:50	47
5	St Mirren	38	18	8	12	77:76	44
6	Partick	38	18	7	13	85:67	43
7	Aberdeen	38	19	5	14	71:61	43
8	Kilmarnock	38	15	10	13	68:78	40
9	Cowdenbeath	38	16	7	15	66:68	39
10	Falkirk	38	16	5	17	76:69	37
11	St Johnstone	38	14	8	16	66:67	36
12	Hibernian	38	13	9	16	73:75	35
13	Airdrie	38	12	11	15	59:69	35
14	Dundee	38	14	7	17	65:80	35
15	Clyde	38	10	11	17	46:72	31
16	Queen's Park	38	12	6	20	69:80	30
17	Raith	38	11	7	20	60:89	29
18	Hamilton	38	11	6	21	67:86	28
19	Bo'ness†	38	9	8	21	48:86	26
20	Dunfermline†	38	4	4	30	41:126	12

SCOTTISH DIVISION 2 1927-28

1	Ayr*	38	24	6	8	117:60	54
2	Third Lanark*	38	18	9	11	99:66	45
3	King's Park	38	16	12	10	84:68	44
4	East Fife	38	18	7	13	87:73	43
5	Forfar	38	18	7	13	83:73	43
6	Dundee U.	38	17	9	12	81:73	43
7	Arthurlie	38	18	4	16	84:90	40
8	Albion	38	17	4	17	79:69	38
9	E. Stirlingshire	38	14	10	14	84:76	38
10	Arbroath	38	16	4	18	84:86	36
11	Dumbarton	38	16	4	18	66:72	36
12	Queen o' South	38	15	6	17	92:106	36
13	Leith	38	13	9	16	76:71	35
14	Clydebank	38	16	3	19	78:80	35
15	Alloa	38	12	11	15	72:76	35
16	Stenhousemuir	38	15	5	18	75:81	35
17	St Bernard's	38	15	5	18	75:101	35
18	Morton	38	13	8	17	65:82	34
19	Bathgate	38	10	11	17	62:81	31
20	Armadale	38	8	8	22	53:112	24

SCOTTISH DIVISION 1 1928-29

1	Rangers	38	30	7	1	107:32	67
2	Celtic	38	22	7	9	67:44	51
3	Motherwell	38	20	10	8	85:66	50
4	Hearts	38	19	9	10	91:57	47
5	Queen's Park	38	18	7	13	100:69	43
6	Partick	38	17	7	14	91:70	41
7	Aberdeen	38	16	8	14	81:69	40
8	St Mirren	38	16	8	14	78:74	40
9	St Johnstone	38	14	10	14	57:70	38
10	Kilmarnock	38	14	8	16	79:74	36
11	Falkirk	38	14	8	16	68:86	36
12	Hamilton	38	13	9	16	58:83	35
13	Cowdenbeath	38	14	5	19	55:69	33
14	Hibernian	38	13	6	19	54:62	32
15	Airdrie	38	12	7	19	56:65	31
16	Ayr	38	12	7	19	65:84	31
17	Clyde	38	12	6	20	47:71	30
18	Dundee	38	9	11	18	58:68	29
19	Third Lanark†	38	10	6	22	71:102	26
20	Raith†	38	9	6	23	52:105	24

SCOTTISH DIVISION 2 1928-29

1	Dundee U.*	36	24	3	9	99:55	51
2	Morton*	36	21	8	7	85:49	50
3	Arbroath	36	19	9	8	90:60	47
4	Albion	36	18	8	10	95:67	44
5	Leith	36	18	7	11	78:56	43
6	St Bernard's	36	16	9	11	77:55	41
7	Forfar	35	14	10	11	69:75	38
8	East Fife	35	15	6	14	88:77	36
9	Queen o' South	36	16	4	16	86:79	36
10	Bo'ness	35	15	5	15	62:62	35
11	Dunfermline	36	13	7	16	66:72	33
12	E. Stirlingshire	36	14	4	18	71:75	32
13	Alloa	36	12	7	17	64:77	31
14	Dumbarton	36	11	9	16	59:78	31
15	King's Park	36	8	13	15	60:84	29
16	Clydebank	36	11	5	20	70:86	27
17	Arthurlie‡	32	9	7	16	51:73	25
18	Stenhousemuir	35	9	6	20	52:90	24
19	Armadale	36	8	7	21	47:99	23
20	Bathgate resigned during the season						

‡Arthurlie resigned with four games to play, leaving matches against Forfar, East Fife, Bo'ness and Stenhousemuir unplayed

SCOTTISH DIVISION 1 1929-30

1	Rangers	38	28	4	6	94:32	60
2	Motherwell	38	25	5	8	104:48	55
3	Aberdeen	38	23	7	8	85:61	53
4	Celtic	38	22	5	11	88:46	49
5	St Mirren	38	18	5	15	73:56	41
6	Partick	38	16	9	13	72:61	41
7	Falkirk	38	16	9	13	62:64	41
8	Kilmarnock	38	15	9	14	77:73	39
9	Ayr	38	16	6	16	70:92	38
10	Hearts	38	14	9	15	69:69	37
11	Clyde	38	13	11	14	64:69	37
12	Airdrie	38	16	4	18	60:66	36
13	Hamilton	38	14	7	17	76:81	35
14	Dundee	38	14	6	18	51:58	34
15	Queen's Park	38	15	4	19	67:80	34
16	Cowdenbeath	38	13	7	18	64:74	33
17	Hibernian	38	9	11	18	45:62	29
18	Morton	38	10	7	21	67:95	27
19	Dundee U.†	38	7	8	23	56:109	22
20	St Johnstone†	38	6	7	25	48:96	19

SCOTTISH DIVISION 2 1929-30

1	Leith*	38	23	11	4	92:42	57
2	East Fife*	38	26	5	7	114:58	57
3	Albion	38	24	6	8	101:60	54
4	Third Lanark	38	23	6	9	92:53	52
5	Raith	38	18	8	12	94:67	44
6	King's Park	38	17	8	13	109:80	42
7	Queen o' South	38	18	6	14	65:63	42
8	Forfar	38	18	5	15	98:95	41
9	Arbroath	38	16	7	15	83:87	39
10	Dunfermline	38	16	6	16	99:85	38
11	Montrose	38	14	10	14	79:87	38
12	E. Stirlingshire	38	16	4	18	83:75	36
13	Bo'ness	38	15	4	19	67:95	34
14	St Bernard's	38	13	6	19	65:65	32
15	Armadale	38	13	5	20	56:91	31
16	Dumbarton	38	14	2	22	77:95	30
17	Stenhousemuir	38	11	5	22	75:108	27
18	Clydebank	38	7	10	21	66:92	24
19	Alloa	38	9	6	23	55:104	24
20	Brechin	38	7	4	27	57:125	18

SCOTTISH DIVISION 1 1930-31

1	Rangers	38	27	6	5	96:29	60
2	Celtic	38	24	10	4	101:34	58
3	Motherwell	38	24	8	6	102:42	56
4	Partick	38	24	5	9	76:44	53
5	Hearts	38	19	6	13	90:63	44
6	Aberdeen	38	17	7	14	79:63	41
7	Cowdenbeath	38	17	7	14	58:65	41
8	Dundee	38	17	5	16	65:63	39
9	Airdrie	38	17	5	16	59:66	39
10	Hamilton	38	16	5	17	59:57	37
11	Kilmarnock	38	15	5	18	59:60	35
12	Clyde	38	15	4	19	60:87	34
13	Queen's Park	38	13	7	18	71:72	33
14	Falkirk	38	14	4	20	77:87	32
15	St Mirren	38	11	8	19	49:72	30
16	Morton	38	11	7	20	58:83	29
17	Leith	38	8	11	19	52:85	27
18	Ayr	38	8	11	19	53:92	27
19	Hibernian†	38	9	7	22	49:81	25
20	East Fife†	38	8	4	26	45:113	20

SCOTTISH DIVISION 2 1930-31

1	Third Lanark*	38	27	7	4	107:42	61
2	Dundee U.*	38	21	8	9	93:54	50
3	Dunfermline	38	20	7	11	83:50	47
4	Raith	38	20	6	12	93:72	46
5	Queen o' South	38	18	6	14	83:66	42
6	St Johnstone	38	18	6	14	76:64	42
7	E. Stirlingshire	38	17	7	14	85:74	41
8	Montrose	38	19	3	16	75:90	41
9	Albion	38	14	11	13	80:83	39
10	Dumbarton	38	15	8	15	73:72	38
11	St Bernard's	38	14	9	15	85:66	37
12	Forfar	38	15	6	17	78:83	36
13	Alloa	38	15	5	18	65:87	35
14	King's Park	38	14	6	18	78:70	34
15	Arbroath	38	15	4	19	83:94	34
16	Brechin	38	13	7	18	52:84	33
17	Stenhousemuir	38	13	6	19	78:98	32
18	Armadale	38	13	2	23	74:99	28
19	Clydebank	38	10	2	26	61:108	22
20	Bo'ness	38	9	4	25	54:100	22

SCOTTISH DIVISION 1 1931-32

1	Motherwell	38	30	6	2	119:31	66
2	Rangers	38	28	5	5	118:42	61
3	Celtic	38	20	8	10	94:50	48
4	Third Lanark	38	21	4	13	92:81	46
5	St Mirren	38	20	4	14	77:56	44
6	Partick	38	19	4	15	58:59	42
7	Aberdeen	38	16	9	13	57:49	41
8	Hearts	38	17	5	16	63:61	39
9	Kilmarnock	38	16	7	15	68:70	39
10	Hamilton	38	16	6	16	84:65	38
11	Dundee	38	14	10	14	61:72	38
12	Cowdenbeath	38	15	8	15	66:78	38
13	Clyde	38	13	9	16	58:70	35
14	Airdrie	38	13	6	19	74:81	32
15	Morton	38	12	7	19	78:87	31
16	Queen's Park	38	13	5	20	59:79	31
17	Ayr	38	11	7	20	70:90	29
18	Falkirk	38	11	5	22	70:76	27
19	Dundee U.†	38	6	7	25	40:118	19
20	Leith†	38	6	4	28	46:137	16

SCOTTISH DIVISION 2 1931-32

1	E. Stirlingshire*	38	26	3	9	111:55	55
2	St Johnstone*	38	24	7	7	102:52	55
3	Raith	38	20	6	12	83:65	46
4	Stenhousemuir	38	19	8	11	88:76	46
5	St Bernard's	38	19	7	12	81:62	45
6	Forfar	38	19	7	12	90:79	45
7	Hibernian	38	18	8	12	73:52	44
8	East Fife	38	18	5	15	107:77	41
9	Queen o' South	38	18	5	15	99:91	41
10	Dunfermline	38	17	6	15	78:73	40
11	Arbroath	38	17	5	16	82:78	39
12	Dumbarton	38	14	10	14	70:68	38
13	Alloa	38	14	7	17	73:74	35
14	Bo'ness	38	15	4	19	70:103	34
15	King's Park	38	14	5	19	97:93	33
16	Albion	38	13	2	23	81:104	28
17	Montrose	38	11	6	21	60:96	28
18	Armadale	38	10	5	23	68:102	25
19	Brechin	38	9	7	22	52:97	25
20	Edinburgh C.	38	5	7	26	78:146	17

SCOTTISH DIVISION 1 1932-33

1	Rangers	38	26	10	2	113:43	62
2	Motherwell	38	27	5	6	114:53	59
3	Hearts	38	21	8	9	84:51	50
4	Celtic	38	20	8	10	75:44	48
5	St Johnstone	38	17	10	11	70:57	44
6	Aberdeen	38	18	6	14	85:58	42
7	St Mirren	38	18	6	14	73:60	42
8	Hamilton	38	18	6	14	92:78	42
9	Queen's Park	38	17	7	14	78:79	41
10	Partick	38	17	6	15	75:55	40
11	Falkirk	38	15	6	17	70:70	36
12	Clyde	38	15	5	18	69:75	35
13	Third Lanark	38	14	7	17	70:80	35
14	Kilmarnock	38	13	9	16	72:86	35
15	Dundee	38	12	9	17	58:74	33
16	Ayr	38	13	4	21	62:96	30
17	Cowdenbeath	38	10	5	23	65:111	25
18	Airdrie	38	10	3	25	55:102	23
19	Morton†	38	6	9	23	49:97	21
20	E. Stirlingshire†	38	7	3	28	55:115	17

SCOTTISH DIVISION 2 1932-33

1	Hibernian*	34	25	4	5	80:29	54
2	Queen o' South*	34	20	9	5	93:59	49
3	Dunfermline	34	20	7	7	89:44	47
4	Stenhousemuir	34	18	6	10	67:58	42
5	Albion	34	19	2	13	82:57	40
6	Raith	34	16	4	14	83:67	36
7	East Fife	34	15	4	15	85:71	34
8	King's Park	34	13	8	13	85:80	34
9	Dumbarton	34	14	6	14	69:67	34
10	Arbroath	34	14	5	15	65:62	33
11	Alloa	34	14	5	15	60:58	33
12	St Bernard's	34	13	6	15	67:64	32
13	Dundee U.	34	14	4	16	65:67	32
14	Forfar	34	12	4	18	68:87	28
15	Brechin	34	11	4	19	65:95	26
16	Leith	34	10	5	19	43:81	25
17	Montrose	34	8	5	21	63:89	21
18	Edinburgh C.	34	4	4	26	39:133	12

19 Bo'ness and Armadale were expelled in Nov 1932 being unable to meet match guarantees

SCOTTISH DIVISION 1 1933-34

1	Rangers	38	30	6	2	118:41	66
2	Motherwell	38	29	4	5	97:45	62
3	Celtic	38	18	11	9	78:53	47
4	Queen o' South	38	21	3	14	75:78	45
5	Aberdeen	38	18	8	12	90:57	44
6	Hearts	38	17	10	11	86:59	44
7	Kilmarnock	38	17	9	12	73:64	43
8	Ayr	38	16	10	12	87:92	42
9	St Johnstone	38	17	6	15	74:53	40
10	Falkirk	38	16	6	16	73:68	38
11	Hamilton	38	15	8	15	65:79	38
12	Dundee	38	15	6	17	68:64	36
13	Partick	38	14	5	19	73:78	33
14	Clyde	38	10	11	17	56:70	31
15	Queen's Park	38	13	5	20	65:85	31
16	Hibernian	38	12	3	23	51:69	27
17	St Mirren	38	9	9	20	46:75	27
18	Airdrie	38	10	6	22	59:103	26
19	Third Lanark†	38	8	9	21	62:103	25
20	Cowdenbeath†	38	5	5	28	58:118	15

SCOTTISH DIVISION 2 1933-34

1	Albion*	34	20	5	9	74:47	45
2	Dunfermline*	34	20	4	10	90:52	44
3	Arbroath	34	20	4	10	83:53	44
4	Stenhousemuir	34	18	4	12	70:73	40
5	Morton	34	17	5	12	67:64	39
6	Dumbarton	34	17	3	14	67:68	37
7	King's Park	34	14	8	12	78:70	36
8	Raith	34	15	5	14	71:55	35
9	E. Stirlingshire	34	14	7	13	65:74	35
10	St Bernard's	34	15	4	15	75:56	34
11	Forfar	34	13	7	14	77:71	33
12	Leith	34	12	8	14	63:60	32
13	East Fife	34	12	8	14	71:76	32
14	Brechin	34	13	5	16	60:70	31
15	Alloa	34	11	9	14	55:68	31
16	Montrose	34	11	4	19	53:81	26
17	Dundee U.	34	10	4	20	81:88	24
18	Edinburgh C.	34	4	6	24	37:111	14

SCOTTISH DIVISION 1 1934-35

1	Rangers	38	25	5	8	96:46	55
2	Celtic	38	24	4	10	92:45	52
3	Hearts	38	20	10	8	87:51	50
4	Hamilton	38	19	10	9	87:67	48
5	St Johnstone	38	18	10	10	66:46	46
6	Aberdeen	38	17	10	11	68:54	44
7	Motherwell	38	15	10	13	83:64	40
8	Dundee	38	16	8	14	63:63	40
9	Kilmarnock	38	16	6	16	76:68	38
10	Clyde	38	14	10	14	71:69	38
11	Hibernian	38	14	8	16	59:70	36
12	Queen's Park	38	13	10	15	61:80	36
13	Partick	38	15	5	18	61:68	35
14	Airdrie	38	13	7	18	64:72	33
15	Dunfermline	38	13	5	20	56:96	31
16	Albion	38	10	9	19	62:77	29
17	Queen o' South	38	11	7	20	52:72	29
18	Ayr	38	12	5	21	61:112	29
19	St Mirren†	38	11	5	22	49:70	27
20	Falkirk†	38	9	6	23	58:82	24

SCOTTISH DIVISION 2 1934-35

1	Third Lanark*	34	23	6	5	94:43	52
2	Arbroath*	34	23	4	7	78:42	50
3	St Bernard's	34	20	7	7	103:47	47
4	Dundee U.	34	18	6	10	105:65	42
5	Stenhousemuir	34	17	5	12	86:80	39
6	Morton	34	17	4	13	88:64	38
7	King's Park	34	18	2	14	86:71	38
8	Leith	34	16	5	13	69:71	37
9	East Fife	34	16	3	15	79:73	35
10	Alloa	34	12	10	12	68:61	34
11	Forfar	34	13	8	13	77:73	34
12	Cowdenbeath	34	13	6	15	84:75	32
13	Raith	34	13	3	18	68:73	29
14	E. Stirlingshire	34	11	7	16	57:76	29
15	Brechin	34	10	6	18	51:98	26
16	Dumbarton	34	9	4	21	60:105	22
17	Montrose	34	7	6	21	58:105	20
18	Edinburgh C.	34	3	2	29	45:134	8

SCOTTISH DIVISION 1 1935-36

1	Celtic	38	32	2	4	115:33	66
2	Rangers	38	27	7	4	110:43	61
3	Aberdeen	38	26	9	3	96:50	61
4	Motherwell	38	18	12	8	77:58	48
5	Hearts	38	20	7	11	88:55	47
6	Hamilton	38	15	7	16	77:74	37
7	St Johnstone	38	15	7	16	70:81	37
8	Kilmarnock	38	14	7	17	69:64	35
9	Partick	38	12	10	16	64:72	34
10	Dunfermline	38	13	8	17	73:92	34
11	Third Lanark	38	14	5	19	63:71	33
12	Arbroath	38	11	11	16	46:69	33
13	Dundee	38	11	10	17	67:80	32
14	Queen's Park	38	11	10	17	58:75	32
15	Queen o' South	38	11	9	18	54:72	31
16	Albion	38	13	4	21	69:92	30
17	Hibernian	38	11	7	20	56:82	29
18	Clyde	38	10	8	20	63:84	28
19	Airdrie†	38	9	9	20	68:91	27
20	Ayr†	38	11	3	24	53:98	25

SCOTTISH DIVISION 2 1935-36

1	Falkirk*	34	28	3	3	132:34	59
2	St Mirren*	34	25	2	7	114:41	52
3	Morton	34	21	6	7	117:60	48
4	Alloa	34	19	6	9	65:51	44
5	St Bernard's	34	18	4	12	106:78	40
6	East Fife	34	16	6	12	86:79	38
7	Dundee U.	34	16	5	13	108:81	37
8	E. Stirlingshire	34	13	8	13	70:75	34
9	Leith	34	15	3	16	67:77	33
10	Cowdenbeath	34	13	5	16	76:77	31
11	Stenhousemuir	34	13	3	18	59:78	29
12	Montrose	34	13	3	18	58:82	29
13	Forfar	34	10	7	17	60:81	27
14	King's Park	34	11	5	18	55:109	27
15	Edinburgh C.	34	8	9	17	57:83	25
16	Brechin	34	8	6	20	57:96	22
17	Raith	34	9	3	22	60:96	21
18	Dumbarton	34	5	6	23	52:121	16

SCOTTISH DIVISION 1 1936-37

1	Rangers	38	26	9	3	88:32	61
2	Aberdeen	38	23	8	7	89:44	54
3	Celtic	38	22	8	8	89:58	52
4	Motherwell	38	22	7	9	96:54	51
5	Hearts	38	24	3	11	99:60	51
6	Third Lanark	38	20	6	12	79:61	46
7	Falkirk	38	19	6	13	98:66	44
8	Hamilton	38	18	5	15	91:96	41
9	Dundee	38	12	15	11	58:69	39
10	Clyde	38	16	6	16	59:70	38
11	Kilmarnock	38	14	9	15	60:70	37
12	St Johnstone	38	14	8	16	74:68	36
13	Partick	38	11	12	15	73:68	34
14	Arbroath	38	13	5	20	57:84	31
15	Queen's Park	38	9	12	17	51:77	30
16	St Mirren	38	11	7	20	68:81	29
17	Hibernian	38	6	13	19	54:83	25
18	Queen o' South	38	8	8	22	49:95	24
19	Dunfermline†	38	5	11	22	65:98	21
20	Albion†	38	5	6	27	53:116	16

SCOTTISH DIVISION 2 1936-37

1	Ayr*	34	25	4	5	122:49	54
2	Morton*	34	23	5	6	110:42	51
3	St Bernard's	34	22	4	8	102:51	48
4	Airdrie	34	18	8	8	85:60	44
5	East Fife	34	15	8	11	76:51	38
6	Cowdenbeath	34	14	10	10	75:59	38
7	E. Stirlingshire	34	18	2	14	81:78	38
8	Raith	34	16	4	14	72:66	36
9	Alloa	34	13	7	14	64:65	33
10	Stenhousemuir	34	14	4	16	82:86	32
11	Leith	34	13	5	16	62:65	31
12	Forfar	34	11	8	15	73:89	30
13	Montrose	34	11	6	17	65:100	28
14	Dundee U.	34	9	9	16	72:97	27
15	Dumbarton	34	11	5	18	57:83	27
16	Brechin	34	8	9	17	64:98	25
17	King's Park	34	11	3	20	61:106	25
18	Edinburgh C.	34	2	3	29	42:120	7

SCOTTISH DIVISION 1 1937-38

1	Celtic	38	27	7	4	114:42	61
2	Hearts	38	26	6	6	90:50	58
3	Rangers	38	18	13	7	75:49	49
4	Falkirk	38	19	9	10	82:52	47
5	Motherwell	38	17	10	11	78:69	44
6	Aberdeen	38	15	9	14	74:59	39
7	Partick	38	15	9	14	68:70	39
8	St Johnstone	38	16	7	15	78:81	39
9	Third Lanark	38	11	13	14	68:73	35
10	Hibernian	38	11	13	14	57:65	35
11	Arbroath	38	11	13	14	58:79	35
12	Queen's Park	38	11	12	15	59:74	34
13	Hamilton	38	13	7	18	81:76	33
14	St Mirren	38	14	5	19	58:66	33
15	Clyde	38	10	13	15	68:78	33
16	Queen o' South	38	11	11	16	58:71	33
17	Ayr	38	9	15	14	66:85	33
18	Kilmarnock	38	12	9	17	65:91	33
19	Dundee†	38	13	6	19	70:74	32
20	Morton†	38	6	3	29	64:127	15

SCOTTISH DIVISION 2 1937-38

1	Raith*	34	27	5	2	142:54	59
2	Albion*	34	20	8	6	97:50	48
3	Airdrie	34	21	5	8	100:53	47
4	St Bernard's	34	20	5	9	75:49	45
5	East Fife	34	19	5	10	104:61	43
6	Cowdenbeath	34	17	9	8	115:71	43
7	Dumbarton	34	17	5	12	85:66	39
8	Stenhousemuir	34	17	5	12	87:78	39
9	Dunfermline	34	17	5	12	82:76	39
10	Leith	34	16	5	13	71:56	37
11	Alloa	34	11	4	19	78:106	26
12	King's Park	34	11	4	19	64:96	26
13	E. Stirlingshire	34	9	7	18	55:95	25
14	Dundee U.	34	9	5	20	69:104	23
15	Forfar	34	8	6	20	67:100	22
16	Montrose	34	7	8	19	56:88	22
17	Edinburgh C.	34	7	3	24	77:135	17
18	Brechin	34	5	2	27	53:139	12

‡Division 1 was called 'A' and Division 2 was called 'B' from 1946–47 to 1955–56 inclusive

SCOTTISH DIVISION 1 1938-39

1	Rangers	38	25	9	4	112:55	59
2	Celtic	38	20	8	10	99:53	48
3	Aberdeen	38	20	6	12	91:61	46
4	Hearts	38	20	5	13	98:70	45
5	Falkirk	38	19	7	12	73:63	45
6	Queen o' South	38	17	9	12	69:64	43
7	Hamilton	38	18	5	15	67:71	41
8	St Johnstone	38	17	6	15	85:82	40
9	Clyde	38	17	5	16	78:70	39
10	Kilmarnock	38	15	9	14	73:86	39
11	Partick	38	17	4	17	74:87	38
12	Motherwell	38	16	5	17	82:86	37
13	Hibernian	38	14	7	17	68:69	35
14	Ayr	38	13	9	16	76:83	35
15	Third Lanark	38	12	8	18	80:96	32
16	Albion	38	12	6	20	65:90	30
17	Arbroath	38	11	8	19	54:75	30
18	St Mirren	38	11	7	20	57:80	29
19	Queen's Park†	38	11	5	22	57:83	27
20	Raith†	38	10	2	26	65:99	22

SCOTTISH DIVISION 2 1938-39

1	Cowdenbeath	34	28	4	2	120:45	60
2	Alloa	34	22	4	8	91:46	48
3	East Fife	34	21	6	7	99:61	48
4	Airdrie	34	21	5	8	85:57	47
5	Dunfermline	34	18	5	11	99:78	41
6	Dundee	34	15	7	12	99:63	37
7	St Bernard's	34	15	6	13	79:79	36
8	Stenhousemuir	34	15	5	14	74:69	35
9	Dundee U.	34	15	3	16	78:69	33
10	Brechin	34	11	9	14	82:106	31
11	Dumbarton	34	9	12	13	68:76	30
12	Morton	34	11	6	17	74:88	28
13	King's Park	34	12	2	20	87:92	26
14	Montrose	34	10	5	19	82:96	25
15	Forfar	34	11	3	20	74:138	25
16	Leith	34	10	4	20	57:83	24
17	E. Stirlingshire	34	9	4	21	89:130	22
18	Edinburgh C.	34	6	4	24	58:119	16

Cowdenbeath and Alloa not promoted

SCOTTISH DIVISION 1‡ 1946-47

1	Rangers	30	21	4	5	76:26	46
2	Hibernian	30	19	6	5	69:33	44
3	Aberdeen	30	16	7	7	58:41	39
4	Hearts	30	16	6	8	52:43	38
5	Partick	30	16	3	11	74:59	35
6	Morton	30	12	10	8	58:45	34
7	Celtic	30	13	6	11	53:55	32
8	Motherwell	30	12	5	13	58:54	29
9	Third Lanark	30	11	6	13	56:64	28
10	Clyde	30	9	9	12	55:65	27
11	Falkirk	30	8	10	12	62:61	26
12	Queen o' South	30	9	8	13	44:69	26
13	Queen's Park	30	8	6	16	47:60	22
14	St Mirren	30	9	4	17	47:65	22
15	Kilmarnock†	30	6	9	15	44:66	21
16	Hamilton†	30	2	7	21	38:85	11

SCOTTISH DIVISION 2‡ 1946-47

1	Dundee*	26	21	3	2	113:30	45
2	Airdrie*	26	19	4	3	78:38	42
3	East Fife	26	12	7	7	58:39	31
4	Albion	26	10	7	9	50:54	27
5	Alloa	26	11	5	10	51:57	27
6	Raith	26	10	6	10	45:52	26
7	Stenhousemuir	26	8	7	11	43:53	23
8	Dunfermline	26	10	3	13	50:72	23
9	St Johnstone	26	9	4	13	45:47	22
10	Dundee U.	26	9	4	13	53:60	22
11	Ayr	26	9	2	15	56:73	20
12	Arbroath	26	7	6	13	42:63	20
13	Dumbarton	26	7	4	15	41:54	18
14	Cowdenbeath	26	6	6	14	44:77	18

SCOTTISH DIVISION 1‡ 1947-48

1	Hibernian	30	22	4	4	86:27	48
2	Rangers	30	21	4	5	64:28	46
3	Partick	30	16	4	10	61:42	36
4	Dundee	30	15	3	12	67:51	33
5	St Mirren	30	13	5	12	54:58	31
6	Clyde	30	12	7	11	52:57	31
7	Falkirk	30	10	10	10	55:48	30
8	Motherwell	30	13	3	14	45:47	29
9	Hearts	30	10	8	12	37:42	28
10	Aberdeen	30	10	7	13	45:45	27
11	Third Lanark	30	10	6	14	56:73	26
12	Celtic	30	10	5	15	41:56	25
13	Queen o' South	30	10	5	15	49:74	25
14	Morton	30	9	6	15	47:43	24
15	Airdrie†	30	7	7	16	39:78	21
16	Queen's Park†	30	9	2	19	45:75	20

SCOTTISH DIVISION 2‡ 1947-48

1	East Fife*	30	25	3	2	103:36	53
2	Albion*	30	19	4	7	58:49	42
3	Hamilton	30	17	6	7	75:45	40
4	Raith	30	14	6	10	83:66	34
5	Cowdenbeath	30	12	8	10	56:53	32
6	Kilmarnock	30	13	4	13	72:62	30
7	Dunfermline	30	13	3	14	72:71	29
8	Stirling A.	30	11	6	13	85:66	28
9	St Johnstone	30	11	5	14	69:63	27
10	Ayr	30	9	9	12	59:61	27
11	Dumbarton	30	9	7	14	66:79	25
12	Alloa§	30	10	6	14	53:77	24
13	Arbroath	30	10	3	17	55:62	23
14	Stenhousemuir	30	6	11	13	53:83	23
15	Dundee U.	30	10	2	18	58:88	22
16	Leith	30	6	7	17	45:84	19

§two points deducted for fielding unregistered players

SCOTTISH DIVISION 1‡ 1948-49

1	Rangers	30	20	6	4	63:32	46
2	Dundee	30	20	5	5	71:48	45
3	Hibernian	30	17	5	8	75:52	39
4	East Fife	30	16	3	11	64:46	35
5	Falkirk	30	12	8	10	70:54	32
6	Celtic	30	12	7	11	48:40	31
7	Third Lanark	30	13	5	12	56:52	31
8	Hearts	30	12	6	12	64:54	30
9	St Mirren	30	13	4	13	51:47	30
10	Queen o' South	30	11	8	11	47:53	30
11	Partick	30	9	9	12	50:63	27
12	Motherwell	30	10	5	15	44:49	25
13	Aberdeen	30	7	11	12	39:48	25
14	Clyde	30	9	6	15	50:67	24
15	Morton†	30	7	8	15	39:51	22
16	Albion†	30	3	2	25	30:105	8

SCOTTISH DIVISION 2‡ 1948-49

1	Raith*	30	20	2	8	80:44	42
2	Stirling A.*	30	20	2	8	71:47	42
3	Airdrie	30	16	9	5	76:42	41
4	Dunfermline	30	16	9	5	80:58	41
5	Queen's Park	30	14	7	9	66:49	35
6	St Johnstone	30	14	4	12	58:51	32
7	Arbroath	30	12	8	10	62:56	32
8	Dundee U.	30	10	7	13	60:67	27
9	Ayr	30	10	7	13	51:70	27
10	Hamilton	30	9	8	13	48:57	26
11	Kilmarnock	30	9	7	14	58:61	25
12	Stenhousemuir	30	8	8	14	50:54	24
13	Cowdenbeath	30	9	5	16	53:58	23
14	Alloa	30	10	3	17	42:85	23
15	Dumbarton	30	8	6	16	52:79	22
16	E. Stirlingshire	30	6	6	18	38:67	18

SCOTTISH DIVISION 1‡ 1949-50

1	Rangers	30	22	6	2	58:26	50
2	Hibernian	30	22	5	3	86:34	49
3	Hearts	30	20	3	7	86:40	43
4	East Fife	30	15	7	8	58:43	37
5	Celtic	30	14	7	9	51:50	35
6	Dundee	30	12	7	11	49:46	31
7	Partick	30	13	3	14	55:45	29
8	Aberdeen	30	11	4	15	48:56	26
9	Raith	30	9	8	13	45:54	26
10	Motherwell	30	10	5	15	53:58	25
11	St Mirren	30	8	9	13	42:49	25
12	Third Lanark	30	11	3	16	44:62	25
13	Clyde	30	10	4	16	56:73	24
14	Falkirk	30	7	10	13	48:72	24
15	Queen o' South†	30	5	6	19	31:63	16
16	Stirling A.†	30	6	3	21	38:77	15

SCOTTISH DIVISION 2‡ 1949-50

1	Morton*	30	20	7	3	77:33	47
2	Airdrie*	30	19	6	5	79:40	44
3	Dunfermline	30	16	4	10	71:57	36
4	St Johnstone	30	15	6	9	64:56	36
5	Cowdenbeath	30	16	3	11	63:56	35
6	Hamilton	30	14	6	10	57:44	34
7	Dundee U.	30	14	5	11	74:56	33
8	Kilmarnock	30	14	5	11	50:43	33
9	Queen's Park	30	12	7	11	63:59	31
10	Forfar	30	11	8	11	53:56	30
11	Albion	30	10	7	13	49:61	27
12	Stenhousemuir	30	8	8	14	54:72	24
13	Ayr	30	8	6	16	53:80	22
14	Arbroath	30	5	9	16	47:69	19
15	Dumbarton	30	6	4	20	39:62	16
16	Alloa	30	5	3	22	47:96	13

SCOTTISH DIVISION 1‡ 1950-51

1	Hibernian	30	22	4	4	78:26	48
2	Rangers	30	17	4	9	64:37	38
3	Dundee	30	15	8	7	47:30	38
4	Hearts	30	16	5	9	72:45	37
5	Aberdeen	30	15	5	10	61:50	35
6	Partick	30	13	7	10	57:48	33
7	Celtic	30	12	5	13	48:46	29
8	Raith	30	13	2	15	52:52	28
9	Motherwell	30	11	6	13	58:65	28
10	East Fife	30	10	8	12	48:66	28
11	St Mirren	30	9	7	14	35:51	25
12	Morton	30	10	4	16	47:59	24
13	Third Lanark	30	11	2	17	40:51	24
14	Airdrie	30	10	4	16	52:67	24
15	Clyde†	30	8	7	15	37:57	23
16	Falkirk†	30	7	4	19	35:81	18

SCOTTISH DIVISION 2‡ 1950-51

1	Queen o' South*	30	21	3	6	69:35	45
2	Stirling A.*	30	21	3	6	78:44	45
3	Ayr	30	15	6	9	64:40	36
4	Dundee U.	30	16	4	10	78:58	36
5	St Johnstone	30	14	5	11	68:53	33
6	Queen's Park	30	13	7	10	56:53	33
7	Hamilton	30	12	8	10	65:49	32
8	Albion	30	14	4	12	56:51	32
9	Dumbarton	30	12	5	13	52:53	29
10	Dunfermline	30	12	4	14	58:73	28
11	Cowdenbeath	30	12	3	15	61:57	27
12	Kilmarnock	30	8	8	14	44:49	24
13	Arbroath	30	8	5	17	46:78	21
14	Forfar	30	9	3	18	43:76	21
15	Stenhousemuir	30	9	2	19	51:80	20
16	Alloa	30	7	4	19	58:98	18

SCOTTISH DIVISION 1‡ 1951-52

1	Hibernian	30	20	5	5	92:36	45
2	Rangers	30	16	9	5	61:31	41
3	East Fife	30	17	3	10	71:49	37
4	Hearts	30	14	7	9	69:53	35
5	Raith	30	14	5	11	43:42	33
6	Partick	30	12	7	11	48:51	31
7	Motherwell	30	12	7	11	51:57	31
8	Dundee	30	11	6	13	53:52	28
9	Celtic	30	10	8	12	52:55	28
10	Queen o' South	30	10	8	12	50:60	28
11	Aberdeen	30	10	7	13	65:58	27
12	Third Lanark	30	9	8	13	51:62	26
13	Airdrie	30	11	4	15	54:69	26
14	St Mirren	30	10	5	15	43:58	25
15	Morton†	30	9	6	15	49:56	24
16	Stirling A.†	30	5	5	20	36:99	15

SCOTTISH DIVISION 2‡ 1951-52

1	Clyde*	30	19	6	5	100:45	44
2	Falkirk*	30	18	7	5	80:34	43
3	Ayr	30	17	5	8	55:45	39
4	Dundee U.	30	16	5	9	75:60	37
5	Kilmarnock	30	16	2	12	62:48	34
6	Dunfermline	30	15	2	13	74:65	32
7	Alloa	30	13	6	11	55:49	32
8	Cowdenbeath	30	12	8	10	66:67	32
9	Hamilton	30	12	6	12	47:51	30
10	Dumbarton	30	10	8	12	51:57	28
11	St Johnstone	30	9	7	14	62:68	25
12	Forfar	30	10	4	16	59:97	24
13	Stenhousemuir	30	8	6	16	57:74	22
14	Albion	30	6	10	14	39:57	22
15	Queen's Park	30	8	4	18	40:62	20
16	Arbroath	30	6	4	20	40:83	16

SCOTTISH DIVISION 1‡ 1952-53

1	Rangers	30	18	7	5	80:39	43
2	Hibernian	30	19	5	6	93:51	43
3	East Fife	30	16	7	7	72:48	39
4	Hearts	30	12	6	12	59:50	30
5	Clyde	30	13	4	13	78:78	30
6	St Mirren	30	11	8	11	52:58	30
7	Dundee	30	9	11	8	44:37	29
8	Celtic	30	11	7	12	51:54	29
9	Partick	30	10	9	11	55:63	29
10	Queen o' South	30	10	8	12	43:61	28
11	Aberdeen	30	11	5	14	64:68	27
12	Raith Rovers	30	9	8	13	47:53	26
13	Falkirk	30	11	4	15	53:63	26
14	Airdrie	30	10	6	14	53:75	26
15	Motherwell†	30	10	5	15	57:80	25
16	Third Lanark†	30	8	4	18	52:75	20

SCOTTISH DIVISION 2‡ 1952-53

1	Stirling A.*	30	20	4	6	64:43	44
2	Hamilton*	30	20	3	7	72:40	43
3	Queen's Park	30	15	7	8	70:46	37
4	Kilmarnock	30	17	2	11	74:48	36
5	Ayr	30	17	2	11	76:56	36
6	Morton	30	15	3	12	79:57	33
7	Arbroath	30	13	7	10	52:57	33
8	Dundee U.	30	12	5	13	52:56	29
9	Alloa	30	12	5	13	63:68	29
10	Dumbarton	30	11	6	13	58:67	28
11	Dunfermline	30	9	9	12	51:58	27
12	Stenhousemuir	30	10	6	14	56:65	26
13	Cowdenbeath	30	8	7	15	37:54	23
14	St Johnstone	30	8	6	16	41:63	22
15	Forfar	30	8	4	18	54:88	20
16	Albion	30	5	4	21	44:77	14

SCOTTISH DIVISION 1‡ 1953-54

1	Celtic	30	20	3	7	72:29	43
2	Hearts	30	16	6	8	70:45	38
3	Partick	30	17	1	12	76:54	35
4	Rangers	30	13	8	9	56:35	34
5	Hibernian	30	15	4	11	72:51	34
6	East Fife	30	13	8	9	55:45	34
7	Dundee	30	14	6	10	46:47	34
8	Clyde	30	15	4	11	64:67	34
9	Aberdeen	30	15	3	12	66:51	33
10	Queen o' South	30	14	4	12	72:53	32
11	St Mirren	30	12	4	14	44:54	28
12	Raith	30	10	6	14	56:60	26
13	Falkirk	30	9	7	14	47:61	25
14	Stirling A.	30	10	4	16	39:62	24
15	Airdrie†	30	5	5	20	41:92	15
16	Hamilton†	30	4	3	23	29:94	11

SCOTTISH DIVISION 2‡ 1953-54

1	Motherwell*	30	21	3	6	109:43	45
2	Kilmarnock*	30	19	4	7	71:39	42
3	Third Lanark	30	13	10	7	78:48	36
4	Stenhousemuir	30	14	8	8	66:58	36
5	Morton	30	15	3	12	85:65	33
6	St Johnstone	30	14	3	13	80:71	31
7	Albion	30	12	7	11	55:63	31
8	Dunfermline	30	11	9	10	48:57	31
9	Ayr	30	11	8	11	50:56	30
10	Queen's Park	30	9	9	12	56:51	27
11	Alloa	30	7	10	13	50:72	24
12	Forfar	30	10	4	16	38:69	24
13	Cowdenbeath	30	9	5	16	67:81	23
14	Arbroath	30	8	7	15	53:67	23
15	Dundee U.	30	8	6	16	54:79	22
16	Dumbarton	30	7	8	15	51:92	22

SCOTTISH DIVISION 1‡ 1954-55

1	Aberdeen	30	24	1	5	73:26	49
2	Celtic	30	19	8	3	76:37	46
3	Rangers	30	19	3	8	67:33	41
4	Hearts	30	16	7	7	74:45	39
5	Hibernian	30	15	4	11	64:54	34
6	St Mirren	30	12	8	10	55:54	32
7	Clyde	30	11	9	10	59:50	31
8	Dundee	30	13	4	13	48:48	30
9	Partick	30	11	7	12	49:61	29
10	Kilmarnock	30	10	6	14	46:58	26
11	East Fife	30	9	6	15	51:62	24
12	Falkirk	30	8	8	14	42:54	24
13	Queen o' South	30	9	6	15	38:56	24
14	Raith	30	10	3	17	49:57	23
15	Motherwell†	30	9	4	17	42:62	22
16	Stirling A.†	30	2	2	26	29:105	6

SCOTTISH DIVISION 2‡ 1954-55

1	Airdrie*	30	18	10	2	103:61	46
2	Dunfermline*	30	19	4	7	72:40	42
3	Hamilton	30	17	5	8	74:51	39
4	Queen's Park	30	15	5	10	65:36	35
5	Third Lanark	30	13	7	10	63:49	33
6	Stenhousemuir	30	12	8	10	70:51	32
7	St Johnstone	30	15	2	13	60:51	32
8	Ayr	30	14	4	12	61:73	32
9	Morton	30	12	5	13	58:69	29
10	Forfar	30	11	6	13	63:80	28
11	Albion	30	8	10	12	50:69	26
12	Arbroath	30	8	8	14	55:72	24
13	Dundee U.	30	8	6	16	55:70	22
14	Cowdenbeath	30	8	5	17	55:72	21
15	Alloa	30	7	6	17	51:75	20
16	Brechin	30	8	3	19	53:89	19

SCOTTISH DIVISION 1‡ 1955-56

1	Rangers	34	22	8	4	85:27	52
2	Aberdeen	34	18	10	6	87:50	46
3	Hearts	34	19	7	8	99:47	45
4	Hibernian	34	19	7	8	86:50	45
5	Celtic	34	16	9	9	55:39	41
6	Queen o' South	34	16	5	13	69:73	37
7	Airdrie	34	14	8	12	85:96	36
8	Kilmarnock	34	12	10	12	52:45	34
9	Partick	34	13	7	14	62:60	33
10	Motherwell	34	11	11	12	53:59	33
11	Raith	34	12	9	13	58:75	33
12	East Fife	34	13	5	16	61:69	31
13	Dundee	34	12	6	16	56:65	30
14	Falkirk	34	11	6	17	58:75	28
15	St Mirren	34	10	7	17	57:70	27
16	Dunfermline	34	10	6	18	42:82	26
17	Clyde†	34	8	6	20	50:74	22
18	Stirling A.†	34	4	5	25	23:82	13

SCOTTISH DIVISION 2‡ 1955-56

1	Queen's Park*	36	23	8	5	78:28	54
2	Ayr*	36	24	3	9	103:55	51
3	St Johnstone	36	21	7	8	86:45	49
4	Dumbarton	36	21	5	10	83:62	47
5	Stenhousemuir	36	20	4	12	82:54	44
6	Brechin	36	18	6	12	60:56	42
7	Cowdenbeath	36	16	7	13	80:85	39
8	Dundee U.	36	12	14	10	78:65	38
9	Morton	36	15	6	15	71:69	36
10	Third Lanark	36	16	3	17	80:64	35
11	Hamilton	36	13	7	16	86:84	33
12	Stranraer	36	14	5	17	77:92	33
13	Alloa	36	12	7	17	67:73	31
14	Berwick	36	11	9	16	52:77	31
15	Forfar	36	10	9	17	62:75	29
16	E. Stirlingshire	36	9	10	17	66:94	28
17	Albion	36	8	11	17	58:82	27
18	Arbroath	36	10	6	20	47:67	26
19	Montrose	36	4	3	29	44:133	11

SCOTTISH DIVISION 1 1956-57

1	Rangers	34	26	3	5	96:48	55
2	Hearts	34	24	5	5	81:48	53
3	Kilmarnock	34	16	10	8	57:39	42
4	Raith	34	16	7	11	84:58	39
5	Celtic	34	15	8	11	58:43	38
6	Aberdeen	34	18	2	14	79:59	38
7	Motherwell	34	16	5	13	72:66	37
8	Partick	34	13	8	13	53:51	34
9	Hibernian	34	12	9	13	69:56	33
10	Dundee	34	13	6	15	55:61	32
11	Airdrie	34	13	4	17	77:89	30
12	St Mirren	34	12	6	16	58:72	30
13	Queen's Park	34	11	7	16	55:59	29
14	Falkirk	34	10	8	16	51:70	28
15	East Fife	34	10	6	18	59:82	26
16	Queen o' South	34	10	5	19	54:96	25
17	Dunfermline†	34	9	6	19	54:74	24
18	Ayr†	34	7	5	22	48:89	19

SCOTTISH DIVISION 2 1956-57

1	Clyde*	36	29	6	1	122:39	64
2	Third Lanark*	36	24	3	9	105:51	51
3	Cowdenbeath	36	20	5	11	87:65	45
4	Morton	36	18	7	11	81:70	43
5	Albion	36	18	6	12	98:80	42
6	Brechin	36	15	10	11	72:68	40
7	Stranraer	36	15	10	11	79:77	40
8	Stirling A.	36	17	5	14	81:64	39
9	Dumbarton	36	17	4	15	101:70	38
10	Arbroath	36	17	4	15	79:57	38
11	Hamilton	36	14	8	14	69:68	36
12	St Johnstone	36	14	6	16	79:80	34
13	Dundee U.	36	14	6	16	75:80	34
14	Stenhousemuir	36	13	6	17	71:81	32
15	Alloa	36	11	5	20	66:99	27
16	Forfar	36	9	5	22	75:100	23
17	Montrose	36	7	7	22	54:124	21
18	Berwick	36	7	6	23	58:114	20
19	E. Stirlingshire	36	5	7	24	56:121	17

SCOTTISH DIVISION 1						1957-58	
1 Hearts	34	29	4	1	132:29	62
2 Rangers	34	22	5	7	89:49	49
3 Celtic	34	19	8	7	84:47	46
4 Clyde	34	18	6	10	84:61	42
5 Kilmarnock	34	14	9	11	60:55	37
6 Partick	34	17	3	14	69:71	37
7 Raith	34	14	7	13	66:56	35
8 Motherwell	34	12	8	14	68:67	32
9 Hibernian	34	13	5	16	59:60	31
10 Falkirk	34	11	9	14	64:82	31
11 Dundee	34	13	5	16	49:65	31
12 Aberdeen	34	14	2	18	68:76	30
13 St Mirren	34	11	8	15	59:66	30
14 Third Lanark	34	13	4	17	69:88	30
15 Queen o' South	34	12	5	17	61:72	29
16 Airdrie	34	13	2	19	71:92	28
17 East Fife†	34	10	3	21	45:88	23
18 Queen's Park†	34	4	1	29	41:114	9

SCOTTISH DIVISION 2						1957-58	
1 Stirling A.*	36	25	5	6	105:48	55
2 Dunfermline*	36	24	5	7	120:42	53
3 Arbroath	36	21	5	10	89:72	47
4 Dumbarton	36	20	4	12	92:57	44
5 Ayr	36	18	6	12	98:81	42
6 Cowdenbeath	36	17	8	11	100:85	42
7 Brechin	36	16	8	12	80:81	40
8 Alloa	36	15	9	12	88:78	39
9 Dundee U.	36	12	9	15	81:77	33
10 Hamilton	36	12	9	15	70:79	33
11 St Johnstone	36	12	9	15	67:85	33
12 Forfar	36	13	6	17	70:71	32
13 Morton	36	12	8	16	77:83	32
14 Montrose	36	13	6	17	55:72	32
15 E. Stirlingshire	36	12	5	19	55:79	29
16 Stenhousemuir	36	12	5	19	68:98	29
17 Albion	36	12	5	19	53:79	29
18 Stranraer	36	9	7	20	54:83	25
19 Berwick	36	5	5	26	37:109	15

SCOTTISH DIVISION 1						1958-59	
1 Rangers	34	21	8	5	92:51	50
2 Hearts	34	21	6	7	92:51	48
3 Motherwell	34	18	8	8	83:50	44
4 Dundee	34	16	9	9	61:51	41
5 Airdrie	34	15	7	12	64:62	37
6 Celtic	34	14	8	12	70:53	36
7 St Mirren	34	14	7	13	71:74	35
8 Kilmarnock	34	13	8	13	58:51	34
9 Partick	34	14	6	14	59:66	34
10 Hibernian	34	13	6	15	68:70	32
11 Third Lanark	34	11	10	13	74:83	32
12 Stirling A.	34	11	8	15	54:64	30
13 Aberdeen	34	12	5	17	63:66	29
14 Raith	34	10	9	15	60:70	29
15 Clyde	34	12	4	18	62:66	28
16 Dunfermline	34	10	8	16	68:87	28
17 Falkirk†	34	10	7	17	58:79	27
18 Queen o' South†	34	6	6	22	38:101	18

SCOTTISH DIVISION 2						1958-59	
1 Ayr*	36	28	4	4	115:48	60
2 Arbroath*	36	23	5	8	86:59	51
3 Stenhousemuir	36	20	6	10	87:68	46
4 Dumbarton	36	19	7	10	94:61	45
5 Brechin	36	16	10	10	79:65	42
6 St Johnstone	36	15	10	11	54:44	40
7 Hamilton	36	15	8	13	76:62	38
8 East Fife	36	15	8	13	83:81	38
9 Berwick	36	16	6	14	63:66	38
10 Albion	36	14	7	15	84:79	35
11 Morton	36	13	8	15	68:85	34
12 Forfar	36	12	9	15	73:87	33
13 Alloa	36	12	7	17	76:81	31
14 Cowdenbeath	36	13	5	18	67:79	31
15 E. Stirlingshire	36	10	8	18	50:77	28
16 Stranraer	36	8	11	17	63:76	27
17 Dundee U.	36	9	7	20	62:86	25
18 Queen's Park	36	9	6	21	53:80	24
19 Montrose	36	6	6	24	49:96	18

SCOTTISH DIVISION 1						1959-60	
1 Hearts	34	23	8	3	102:51	54
2 Kilmarnock	34	24	2	8	67:45	50
3 Rangers	34	17	8	9	72:38	42
4 Dundee	34	16	10	8	70:49	42
5 Motherwell	34	16	8	10	71:61	40
6 Clyde	34	15	9	10	77:69	39
7 Hibernian	34	14	7	13	106:85	35
8 Ayr	34	14	6	14	65:73	34
9 Celtic	34	12	9	13	73:59	33
10 Partick	34	14	4	16	54:78	32
11 Raith	34	14	3	17	64:62	31
12 Third Lanark	34	13	4	17	75:83	30
13 Dunfermline	34	10	9	15	72:80	29
14 St Mirren	34	11	6	17	78:86	28
15 Aberdeen	34	11	6	17	54:72	28
16 Airdrie	34	11	6	17	56:80	28
17 Stirling A.†	34	7	8	19	55:72	22
18 Arbroath†	34	4	7	23	38:106	15

SCOTTISH DIVISION 2						1959-60	
1 St Johnstone*	36	24	5	7	87:47	53
2 Dundee U.*	36	22	6	8	90:45	50
3 Queen o' South	36	21	7	8	94:52	49
4 Hamilton	36	21	6	9	91:62	48
5 Stenhousemuir	36	20	4	12	86:67	44
6 Dumbarton	36	18	7	11	67:53	43
7 Montrose	36	19	5	12	60:52	43
8 Falkirk	36	15	9	12	77:43	39
9 Berwick	36	16	5	15	62:55	37
10 Albion	36	14	8	14	71:78	36
11 Queen's Park	36	17	2	17	65:79	36
12 Brechin	36	14	6	16	66:66	34
13 Alloa	36	13	5	18	70:85	31
14 Morton	36	10	8	18	67:79	28
15 E. Stirlingshire	36	10	8	18	68:82	28
16 Forfar	36	10	8	18	53:84	28
17 Stranraer	36	10	3	23	53:79	23
18 East Fife	36	7	6	23	50:87	20
19 Cowdenbeath	36	6	2	28	42:124	14

SCOTTISH DIVISION 1						1960-61	
1 Rangers	34	23	5	6	88:46	51
2 Kilmarnock	34	21	8	5	77:45	50
3 Third Lanark	34	20	2	12	100:80	42
4 Celtic	34	15	9	10	64:46	39
5 Motherwell	34	15	8	11	70:57	38
6 Aberdeen	34	14	8	12	72:72	36
7 Hearts	34	13	8	13	51:53	34
8 Hibernian	34	15	4	15	66:69	34
9 Dundee U.	34	13	7	14	60:58	33
10 Dundee	34	13	6	15	61:53	32
11 Partick	34	13	6	15	59:69	32
12 Dunfermline	34	12	7	15	65:81	31
13 Airdrie	34	10	10	14	61:71	30
14 St Mirren	34	11	7	16	53:58	29
15 St Johnstone	34	10	9	15	47:63	29
16 Raith	34	10	7	17	46:67	27
17 Clyde†	34	6	11	17	55:77	23
18 Ayr†	34	5	12	17	51:81	22

SCOTTISH DIVISION 2						1960-61	
1 Stirling A.*	36	24	7	5	89:37	55
2 Falkirk*	36	24	6	6	100:40	54
3 Stenhousemuir	36	24	2	10	99:69	50
4 Stranraer	36	19	6	11	83:55	44
5 Queen o' South	36	20	3	13	77:52	43
6 Hamilton	36	17	7	12	84:80	41
7 Montrose	36	19	2	15	75:65	40
8 Cowdenbeath	36	17	6	13	71:65	40
9 Berwick	36	14	9	13	62:69	37
10 Dumbarton	36	15	5	16	78:82	35
11 Alloa	36	13	7	16	78:68	33
12 Arbroath	36	13	7	16	56:76	33
13 East Fife	36	14	4	18	70:80	32
14 Brechin	36	9	9	18	60:78	27
15 Queen's Park	36	10	6	20	61:87	26
16 E. Stirlingshire	36	9	7	20	59:100	25
17 Albion	36	9	6	21	60:89	24
18 Forfar	36	10	4	22	65:98	24
19 Morton	36	5	11	20	56:93	21

SCOTTISH DIVISION 1						1961-62	
1 Dundee	34	25	4	5	80:46	54
2 Rangers	34	22	7	5	84:31	51
3 Celtic	34	19	8	7	81:37	46
4 Dunfermline	34	19	5	10	77:46	43
5 Kilmarnock	34	16	10	8	74:58	42
6 Hearts	34	16	6	12	54:49	38
7 Partick	34	16	3	15	60:55	35
8 Hibernian	34	14	5	15	58:72	33
9 Motherwell	34	13	6	15	65:62	32
10 Dundee U.	34	13	6	15	70:71	32
11 Third Lanark	34	13	5	16	59:60	31
12 Aberdeen	34	10	9	15	60:73	29
13 Raith	34	10	7	17	51:73	27
14 Falkirk	34	11	4	19	45:68	26
15 Airdrie	34	9	7	18	57:78	25
16 St Mirren	34	10	5	19	52:80	25
17 St Johnstone†	34	9	7	18	35:61	25
18 Stirling A.†	34	6	6	22	34:76	18

SCOTTISH DIVISION 2						1961-62	
1 Clyde*	36	15	4	7	108:47	54
2 Queen o' South*	36	24	5	7	78:33	53
3 Morton	36	19	6	11	78:64	44
4 Alloa	36	17	8	11	92:78	42
5 Montrose	36	15	11	10	63:50	41
6 Arbroath	36	17	7	12	66:59	41
7 Stranraer	36	14	11	11	61:62	39
8 Berwick	36	16	6	14	83:70	38
9 Ayr	36	15	8	13	71:63	38
10 East Fife	36	15	7	14	60:59	37
11 E. Stirlingshire	36	15	4	17	70:81	34
12 Queen's Park	36	12	9	15	64:62	33
13 Hamilton	36	14	5	17	78:79	33
14 Cowdenbeath	36	11	9	16	65:77	31
15 Stenhousemuir	36	13	5	18	69:86	31
16 Forfar	36	11	8	17	68:76	30
17 Dumbarton	36	9	10	17	49:66	28
18 Albion	36	10	5	21	42:74	25
19 Brechin	36	5	2	29	44:123	12

SCOTTISH DIVISION 1						1962-63	
1 Rangers	34	25	7	2	94:28	57
2 Kilmarnock	34	20	8	6	92:40	48
3 Partick	34	20	6	8	66:44	46
4 Celtic	34	19	6	9	76:44	44
5 Hearts	34	17	9	8	85:59	43
6 Aberdeen	34	17	7	10	70:47	41
7 Dundee U.	34	15	11	8	67:52	41
8 Dunfermline	34	13	8	13	50:47	34
9 Dundee	34	12	9	13	60:49	33
10 Motherwell	34	10	11	13	60:63	31
11 Airdrie	34	14	2	18	52:76	30
12 St Mirren	34	10	8	16	52:72	28
13 Falkirk	34	12	3	19	54:69	27
14 Third Lanark	34	9	8	17	56:68	26
15 Queen o' South	34	10	6	18	36:75	26
16 Hibernian	34	8	9	17	47:67	25
17 Clyde†	34	9	5	20	49:83	23
18 Raith†	34	2	5	27	35:118	9

SCOTTISH DIVISION 2						1962-63	
1 St Johnstone*	36	25	5	6	83:37	55
2 E. Stirlingshire*	36	20	9	7	80:50	49
3 Morton	36	23	2	11	100:49	48
4 Hamilton	36	18	8	10	69:56	44
5 Stranraer	36	16	10	10	81:70	42
6 Arbroath	36	18	4	14	74:51	40
7 Albion	36	18	2	16	72:79	38
8 Cowdenbeath	36	15	7	14	72:61	37
9 Alloa	36	15	6	15	57:56	36
10 Stirling A.	36	16	4	16	74:75	36
11 East Fife	36	15	6	15	60:69	36
12 Dumbarton	36	15	4	17	64:64	34
13 Ayr	36	13	6	17	68:77	32
14 Queen's Park	36	13	6	17	66:72	32
15 Montrose	36	13	5	18	57:70	31
16 Stenhousemuir	36	13	5	18	54:75	31
17 Berwick	36	11	7	18	57:77	29
18 Forfar	36	9	5	22	73:99	23
19 Brechin	36	3	3	30	39:113	9

SCOTTISH DIVISION 1 1963-64

1	Rangers	34	25	5	4	85:31	55
2	Kilmarnock	34	22	5	7	77:40	49
3	Celtic	34	19	9	6	89:34	47
4	Hearts	34	19	9	6	74:40	47
5	Dunfermline	34	18	9	7	64:33	45
6	Dundee	34	20	5	9	94:50	45
7	Partick	34	15	5	14	55:54	35
8	Dundee U.	34	13	8	13	65:49	34
9	Aberdeen	34	12	8	14	53:53	32
10	Hibernian	34	12	6	16	59:66	30
11	Motherwell	34	9	11	14	51:62	29
12	St Mirren	34	12	5	17	44:74	29
13	St Johnstone	34	11	6	17	54:70	28
14	Falkirk	34	11	6	17	54:84	28
15	Airdrie	34	11	4	19	52:97	26
16	Third Lanark	34	9	7	18	47:74	25
17	Queen o' South†	34	5	6	23	40:92	16
18	E. Stirlingshire†	34	5	2	27	37:91	12

SCOTTISH DIVISION 2 1963-64

1	Morton*	36	32	3	1	135:37	67
2	Clyde*	36	22	9	5	81:44	53
3	Arbroath	36	20	6	10	79:46	46
4	East Fife	36	16	13	7	92:57	45
5	Montrose	36	19	6	11	79:57	44
6	Dumbarton	36	16	6	14	67:59	38
7	Queen's Park	36	17	4	15	57:54	38
8	Stranraer	36	16	6	14	71:73	38
9	Albion	36	12	12	12	67:71	36
10	Raith	36	15	5	16	70:61	35
11	Stenhousemuir	36	15	5	16	83:75	35
12	Berwick	36	10	10	16	68:84	30
13	Hamilton	36	12	6	18	65:81	30
14	Ayr	36	12	5	19	58:83	29
15	Brechin	36	10	8	18	61:98	28
16	Alloa	36	11	5	20	64:92	27
17	Cowdenbeath	36	7	11	18	46:72	25
18	Forfar	36	6	8	22	57:104	20
19	Stirling A.	36	6	8	22	47:99	20

SCOTTISH DIVISION 1 1964-65

1	Kilmarnock	34	22	6	6	62:33	50
2	Hearts	34	22	6	6	90:49	50
3	Dunfermline	34	22	5	7	83:36	49
4	Hibernian	34	21	4	9	75:47	46
5	Rangers	34	18	8	8	78:35	44
6	Dundee	34	15	10	9	86:63	40
7	Clyde	34	17	6	11	64:58	40
8	Celtic	34	16	5	13	76:57	37
9	Dundee U.	34	15	6	13	59:51	36
10	Morton	34	13	7	14	54:54	33
11	Partick	34	11	10	13	57:58	32
12	Aberdeen	34	12	8	14	59:75	32
13	St Johnstone	34	9	11	14	57:62	29
14	Motherwell	34	10	8	16	45:54	28
15	St Mirren	34	9	6	19	38:70	24
16	Falkirk	34	7	7	20	43:85	21
17	Airdrie†	34	5	4	25	48:110	14
18	Third Lanark†	34	3	1	30	22:99	7

SCOTTISH DIVISION 2 1964-65

1	Stirling A.*	36	26	7	3	84:31	59
2	Hamilton*	36	21	8	7	86:53	50
3	Queen o' South	36	16	13	7	84:50	45
4	Queen's Park	36	17	9	10	57:41	43
5	ES/Clydebank	36	15	10	11	64:50	40
6	Stranraer	36	17	6	13	74:64	40
7	Arbroath	36	13	13	10	56:51	39
8	Berwick	36	15	9	12	73:70	39
9	East Fife	36	15	7	14	78:77	37
10	Alloa	36	14	8	14	71:81	36
11	Albion	36	14	5	17	56:60	33
12	Cowdenbeath	36	11	10	15	55:62	32
13	Raith	36	9	14	13	54:61	32
14	Dumbarton	36	13	6	17	55:67	32
15	Stenhousemuir	36	11	8	17	49:74	30
16	Montrose	36	10	9	17	80:91	29
17	Forfar	36	9	7	20	63:89	25
18	Ayr	36	9	6	21	49:67	24
19	Brechin	36	6	7	23	53:102	19

SCOTTISH DIVISION 1 1965-66

1	Celtic	34	27	3	4	106:30	57
2	Rangers	34	25	5	4	91:29	55
3	Kilmarnock	34	20	5	9	73:46	45
4	Dunfermline	34	19	6	9	94:55	44
5	Dundee U.	34	19	5	10	79:51	43
6	Hibernian	34	16	6	12	81:55	38
7	Hearts	34	13	12	9	56:48	38
8	Aberdeen	34	15	6	13	61:54	36
9	Dundee	34	14	6	14	61:61	34
10	Falkirk	34	15	1	18	48:72	31
11	Clyde	34	13	4	17	62:64	30
12	Partick	34	10	10	14	55:64	30
13	Motherwell	34	12	4	18	52:69	28
14	St Johnstone	34	9	8	17	58:81	26
15	Stirling A.	34	9	8	17	40:68	26
16	St Mirren	34	9	4	21	44:82	22
17	Morton†	34	8	5	21	42:84	21
18	Hamilton†	34	3	2	29	27:117	8

SCOTTISH DIVISION 2 1965-66

1	Ayr*	36	22	9	5	78:37	53
2	Airdrie*	36	22	6	8	107:56	50
3	Queen o' South	36	18	11	7	83:53	47
4	East Fife	36	20	4	12	72:55	44
5	Raith	36	16	11	9	71:43	43
6	Arbroath	36	15	13	8	72:52	43
7	Albion	36	18	7	11	58:54	43
8	Alloa	36	14	10	12	65:65	38
9	Montrose	36	15	7	14	67:63	37
10	Cowdenbeath	36	15	7	14	69:68	37
11	Berwick	36	12	11	13	69:58	35
12	Dumbarton	36	14	7	15	63:61	35
13	Queen's Park	36	13	7	16	62:65	33
14	Third Lanark	36	12	8	16	55:65	32
15	Stranraer	36	9	10	17	64:83	28
16	Brechin	36	10	7	19	52:92	27
17	E. Stirlingshire	36	9	5	22	59:91	23
18	Stenhousemuir	36	6	7	23	47:93	19
19	Forfar	36	7	3	26	61:120	17

SCOTTISH DIVISION 1 1966-67

1	Celtic	34	26	6	2	111:33	58
2	Rangers	34	24	7	3	92:31	55
3	Clyde	34	20	6	8	64:48	46
4	Aberdeen	34	17	8	9	72:38	42
5	Hibernian	34	19	4	11	72:49	42
6	Dundee	34	16	9	9	74:51	41
7	Kilmarnock	34	16	8	10	59:46	40
8	Dunfermline	34	14	10	10	72:52	38
9	Dundee U.	34	14	9	11	68:62	37
10	Motherwell	34	10	11	13	59:60	31
11	Hearts	34	11	8	15	39:48	30
12	Partick	34	9	12	13	49:68	30
13	Airdrie	34	11	6	17	41:53	28
14	Falkirk	34	11	4	19	33:70	26
15	St Johnstone	34	10	5	19	53:73	25
16	Stirling A.	34	5	9	20	31:85	19
17	St Mirren†	34	4	7	23	25:81	15
18	Ayr†	34	1	7	26	20:86	9

SCOTTISH DIVISION 2 1966-67

1	Morton*	38	33	3	2	113:20	69
2	Raith*	38	27	4	7	95:44	58
3	Arbroath	38	25	7	6	75:32	57
4	Hamilton	38	18	8	12	74:60	44
5	East Fife	38	19	4	15	70:63	42
6	Cowdenbeath	38	16	8	14	70:55	40
7	Queen's Park	38	15	10	13	78:68	40
8	Albion	38	17	6	15	66:62	40
9	Queen o' South	38	15	9	14	84:76	39
10	Berwick	38	16	6	16	63:55	38
11	Third Lanark	38	13	8	17	67:78	34
12	Montrose	38	13	8	17	63:77	34
13	Alloa	38	15	4	19	55:74	34
14	Dumbarton	38	12	9	17	56:64	33
15	Stranraer	38	13	7	18	57:73	33
16	Forfar	38	12	3	23	74:106	27
17	Stenhousemuir	38	9	9	20	62:104	27
18	Clydebank	38	8	8	22	59:92	24
19	E. Stirlingshire	38	7	10	21	44:87	24
20	Brechin	38	8	7	23	58:93	23

SCOTTISH DIVISION 1 1967-68

1	Celtic	34	30	3	1	106:24	63
2	Rangers	34	28	5	1	93:34	61
3	Hibernian	34	20	5	9	67:49	45
4	Dunfermline	34	17	5	12	64:41	39
5	Aberdeen	34	16	5	13	63:48	37
6	Morton	34	15	6	13	57:53	36
7	Kilmarnock	34	13	8	13	59:57	34
8	Clyde	34	15	4	15	55:55	34
9	Dundee	34	13	7	14	62:59	33
10	Partick	34	12	7	15	51:67	31
11	Dundee U.	34	10	11	13	53:72	31
12	Hearts	34	13	4	17	56:61	30
13	Airdrie	34	10	9	15	45:58	29
14	St Johnstone	34	10	7	17	43:52	27
15	Falkirk	34	7	12	15	36:50	26
16	Raith	34	9	7	18	58:86	25
17	Motherwell†	34	6	7	21	40:66	19
18	Stirling A.†	34	4	4	26	29:105	12

SCOTTISH DIVISION 2 1967-68

1	St Mirren*	36	27	8	1	100:23	62
2	Arbroath*	36	24	5	7	87:34	53
3	East Fife	36	21	7	8	71:47	49
4	Queen's Park	36	20	8	8	76:47	48
5	Ayr	36	18	6	12	69:48	42
6	Queen o' South	36	16	6	14	73:57	38
7	Forfar	36	14	10	12	57:63	38
8	Albion	36	14	9	13	62:55	37
9	Clydebank	36	13	8	15	62:73	34
10	Dumbarton	36	11	11	14	63:74	33
11	Hamilton	36	13	7	16	49:58	33
12	Cowdenbeath	36	12	8	16	57:62	32
13	Montrose	36	10	11	15	54:64	31
14	Berwick	36	13	4	19	34:54	30
15	E. Stirlingshire	36	9	10	17	61:74	28
16	Brechin	36	8	12	16	45:62	28
17	Alloa	36	11	6	19	42:69	28
18	Stranraer	36	8	4	24	41:80	20
19	Stenhousemuir	36	7	6	23	34:93	20

SCOTTISH DIVISION 1 1968-69

1	Celtic	34	23	8	3	89:32	54
2	Rangers	34	21	7	6	81:32	49
3	Dunfermline	34	19	7	8	63:45	45
4	Kilmarnock	34	15	14	5	50:32	44
5	Dundee U.	34	17	9	8	61:49	43
6	St Johnstone	34	16	5	13	66:59	37
7	Airdrie	34	13	11	10	46:44	37
8	Hearts	34	14	8	12	52:54	36
9	Dundee	34	10	12	12	47:48	32
10	Morton	34	12	8	14	58:68	32
11	St Mirren	34	11	10	13	40:54	32
12	Hibernian	34	12	7	15	60:59	31
13	Clyde	34	9	13	12	35:50	31
14	Partick	34	9	10	15	39:53	28
15	Aberdeen	34	9	8	17	50:59	26
16	Raith	34	8	5	21	45:67	21
17	Falkirk†	34	5	8	21	33:69	18
18	Arbroath†	34	5	6	23	41:82	16

SCOTTISH DIVISION 2 1968-69

1	Motherwell*	36	30	4	2	112:23	64
2	Ayr*	36	23	7	6	82:31	53
3	East Fife	36	21	6	9	82:45	48
4	Stirling A.	36	21	6	9	67:40	48
5	Queen o' South	36	20	7	9	75:41	47
6	Forfar	36	18	7	11	71:56	47
7	Albion	36	19	5	12	60:56	43
8	Stranraer	36	17	7	12	57:45	41
9	E. Stirlingshire	36	17	5	14	70:62	39
10	Montrose	36	15	4	17	59:71	34
11	Queen's Park	36	13	7	16	50:59	33
12	Cowdenbeath	36	12	5	19	54:67	29
13	Clydebank	36	6	15	15	52:67	27
14	Dumbarton	36	11	5	20	46:69	27
15	Hamilton	36	8	8	20	37:72	24
16	Berwick	36	7	9	20	42:70	23
17	Brechin	36	8	6	22	40:78	22
18	Alloa	36	7	7	22	45:79	21
19	Stenhousemuir	36	6	6	24	55:125	18

SCOTTISH DIVISION 1 — 1969-70

		P	W	D	L	F:A	Pts
1	Celtic	34	27	3	4	96:33	57
2	Rangers	34	19	7	8	67:40	45
3	Hibernian	34	19	6	9	65:40	44
4	Hearts	34	13	12	9	50:36	38
5	Dundee U.	34	16	6	12	62:64	38
6	Dundee	34	15	6	13	49:44	36
7	Kilmarnock	34	13	10	11	62:57	36
8	Aberdeen	34	14	7	13	55:45	35
=9	Dunfermline	34	15	5	14	45:45	35
=9	Morton	34	13	9	12	52:52	35
11	Motherwell	34	11	10	13	49:51	32
12	Airdrie	34	12	8	14	59:64	32
13	St Johnstone	34	11	9	14	50:62	31
14	Ayr	34	12	6	16	37:52	30
15	St Mirren	34	8	9	17	39:54	25
16	Clyde	34	9	7	18	34:56	25
17	Raith†	34	5	11	18	32:67	21
18	Partick†	34	5	7	22	41:82	17

SCOTTISH DIVISION 1 — 1971-72

		P	W	D	L	F:A	Pts
1	Celtic	34	28	4	2	96:28	60
2	Aberdeen	34	21	8	5	80:26	50
3	Rangers	34	21	2	11	71:38	44
4	Hibernian	34	19	6	9	62:34	44
5	Dundee	34	14	13	7	59:38	41
6	Hearts	34	13	13	8	53:49	39
7	Partick	34	12	10	12	53:54	34
8	St Johnstone	34	12	8	14	52:58	32
9	Dundee U.	34	12	7	15	55:70	31
10	Motherwell	34	11	7	16	49:69	29
11	Kilmarnock	34	11	6	17	49:64	28
12	Ayr	34	9	10	15	40:58	28
13	Morton	34	10	7	17	46:52	27
14	Falkirk	34	10	7	17	44:60	27
15	Airdrie	34	7	12	15	44:76	26
16	East Fife	34	5	15	14	34:61	25
17	Clyde†	34	7	10	17	33:66	24
18	Dunfermline†	34	7	9	18	31:50	23

SCOTTISH DIVISION 1 — 1973-74

		P	W	D	L	F:A	Pts
1	Celtic	34	23	7	4	82:27	53
2	Hibernian	34	20	9	5	75:42	49
3	Rangers	34	21	6	7	67:34	48
4	Aberdeen	34	13	16	5	46:26	42
5	Dundee	34	16	7	11	67:48	39
6	Hearts	34	14	10	10	54:43	38
7	Ayr	34	15	8	11	44:40	38
8	Dundee U.	34	15	7	12	55:51	37
9	Motherwell	34	14	7	13	45:40	35
10	Dumbarton	34	11	7	16	43:58	29
11	Partick	34	9	10	15	33:46	28
12	St Johnstone	34	9	10	15	41:60	28
13	Arbroath	34	10	7	17	52:69	27
14	Morton	34	8	10	16	37:49	26
15	Clyde	34	8	9	17	29:65	25
16	Dunfermline	34	8	8	18	43:65	24
17	East Fife†	34	9	6	19	26:51	24
18	Falkirk†	34	4	14	16	33:58	22

SCOTTISH DIVISION 2 — 1969-70

		P	W	D	L	F:A	Pts
1	Falkirk*	36	25	6	5	94:34	56
2	Cowdenbeath*	36	24	7	5	81:35	55
3	Queen o' South	36	22	6	8	72:49	50
4	Stirling A.	36	18	10	8	70:40	46
5	Arbroath	36	20	4	12	76:39	44
6	Alloa	36	19	5	12	62:41	43
7	Dumbarton	36	17	6	13	55:46	40
8	Montrose	36	15	7	14	57:55	37
9	Berwick	36	15	5	16	67:55	35
10	East Fife	36	15	4	17	59:63	34
11	Albion	36	14	5	17	53:64	33
12	E. Stirlingshire	36	14	5	17	58:75	33
13	Clydebank	36	10	10	16	47:65	30
14	Brechin	36	11	6	19	47:74	28
15	Queen's Park	36	10	6	20	38:62	26
16	Stenhousemuir	36	10	6	20	47:89	26
17	Stranraer	36	9	7	20	56:75	25
18	Forfar	36	11	1	24	55:83	23
19	Hamilton	36	8	4	24	42:92	20

SCOTTISH DIVISION 2 — 1971-72

		P	W	D	L	F:A	Pts
1	Dumbarton*	36	24	4	8	89:51	52
2	Arbroath*	36	22	8	6	71:41	52
3	Stirling A.	36	21	8	7	75:37	50
4	St Mirren	36	24	2	10	84:47	50
5	Cowdenbeath	36	19	10	7	69:28	48
6	Stranraer	36	18	8	10	70:62	44
7	Queen o' South	36	17	9	10	56:38	43
8	E. Stirlingshire	36	17	7	12	60:58	41
9	Clydebank	36	14	11	11	60:52	39
10	Montrose	36	15	6	15	73:54	36
11	Raith	36	13	8	15	56:65	34
12	Queen's Park	36	12	9	15	47:61	33
13	Berwick	36	14	4	18	53:50	32
14	Stenhousemuir	36	10	8	18	41:58	28
15	Brechin	36	8	7	21	41:79	23
16	Alloa	36	9	4	23	41:75	22
17	Forfar	36	6	9	21	32:84	21
18	Albion	33	7	6	23	36:61	20
19	Hamilton	36	4	8	24	31:93	16

SCOTTISH DIVISION 2 — 1973-74

		P	W	D	L	F:A	Pts
1	Airdrie*	36	28	4	4	102:25	60
2	Kilmarnock*	36	26	6	4	96:44	58
3	Hamilton	36	24	7	5	68:38	55
4	Queen o' South	36	20	7	9	73:41	47
5	Raith	36	18	9	9	69:48	45
6	Berwick	36	16	13	7	53:35	45
7	Stirling A.	36	17	6	13	76:50	40
8	Montrose	36	15	7	14	71:64	37
9	Stranraer	36	14	8	14	64:70	36
10	Clydebank	36	13	8	15	47:48	34
11	St Mirren	36	12	10	14	62:66	34
12	Alloa	36	15	4	17	47:58	34
13	Cowdenbeath	36	11	9	16	59:85	31
14	Queen's Park	36	12	4	20	42:64	28
15	Stenhousemuir	36	11	5	20	44:59	27
16	E. Stirlingshire	36	9	5	22	47:73	23
17	Albion	36	7	6	23	38:72	20
18	Forfar	36	5	6	25	42:94	16
19	Brechin	36	5	4	27	33:99	14

SCOTTISH DIVISION 1 — 1970-71

		P	W	D	L	F:A	Pts
1	Celtic	34	25	6	3	89:23	56
2	Aberdeen	34	24	6	4	68:18	54
3	St Johnstone	34	19	6	9	59:44	44
4	Rangers	34	16	9	9	58:34	41
5	Dundee	34	14	10	10	53:45	38
6	Dundee U.	34	14	8	12	53:54	36
7	Falkirk	34	13	9	12	46:53	35
8	Morton	34	13	8	13	44:44	34
9	Airdrie	34	13	8	13	60:65	34
10	Motherwell	34	13	8	13	43:47	34
11	Hearts	34	13	7	14	41:40	33
12	Hibernian	34	10	10	14	47:53	30
13	Kilmarnock	34	10	8	16	43:67	28
14	Ayr	34	9	8	17	37:54	26
15	Clyde	34	8	10	16	33:59	26
16	Dunfermline	34	6	11	17	44:56	23
17	St Mirren†	34	7	9	18	38:56	23
18	Cowdenbeath†	34	7	3	24	33:77	17

SCOTTISH DIVISION 1 — 1972-73

		P	W	D	L	F:A	Pts
1	Celtic	34	26	5	3	93:28	57
2	Rangers	34	26	4	4	74:30	56
3	Hibernian	34	19	7	8	74:33	45
4	Aberdeen	34	16	11	7	61:34	43
5	Dundee	34	17	9	8	68:43	43
6	Ayr	34	16	8	10	50:51	40
7	Dundee U.	34	17	5	12	56:51	39
8	Motherwell	34	11	9	14	38:48	31
9	East Fife	34	11	8	15	46:54	30
10	Hearts	34	12	6	16	39:50	30
11	St Johnstone	34	10	9	15	52:67	29
12	Morton	34	10	8	16	47:53	28
13	Partick	34	10	8	16	40:53	28
14	Falkirk	34	7	12	15	38:56	26
15	Arbroath	34	9	8	17	39:63	26
16	Dumbarton	34	6	11	17	43:72	23
17	Kilmarnock†	34	7	8	19	40:71	22
18	Airdrie†	34	4	8	22	34:75	16

SCOTTISH DIVISION 1‡ — 1974-75

		P	W	D	L	F:A	Pts
1	Rangers	34	25	6	3	86:33	56
2	Hibernian	34	20	9	5	69:37	49
3	Celtic	34	20	5	9	81:41	45
4	Dundee U.	34	19	7	8	72:43	45
5	Aberdeen	34	16	9	9	66:43	41
6	Dundee	34	16	6	12	48:42	38
7	Ayr	34	14	8	12	50:61	36
8	Hearts	34	11	13	10	47:52	35
9	St Johnstone	34	11	12	11	41:44	34
10	Motherwell	34	14	5	15	52:57	33
11	Airdrie	34	11	9	14	43:55	31
12	Kilmarnock	34	8	15	11	52:68	31
13	Partick	34	10	10	14	48:62	30
14	Dumbarton	34	7	10	17	44:55	24
15	Dunfermline	34	7	9	18	46:66	23
16	Clyde	34	6	10	18	40:63	22
17	Morton	34	6	10	18	31:62	22
18	Arbroath	34	5	7	22	34:66	17

‡First 10 clubs formed new Premier Division; bottom 8 clubs plus top 6 from Division 2 formed new Division 1

SCOTTISH DIVISION 2‡ — 1974-75

		P	W	D	L	F:A	Pts
1	Falkirk	38	26	2	10	76:29	54
2	Queen o' South	38	23	7	8	77:33	53
3	Montrose	38	23	7	8	70:37	53
4	Hamilton	38	21	7	10	69:30	49
5	East Fife	38	20	7	11	57:42	47
6	St Mirren	38	19	8	11	74:52	46
7	Clydebank	38	18	8	12	50:40	44
8	Stirling A.	38	17	9	12	67:55	43
9	E. Stirlingshire	38	16	8	14	56:52	40
10	Berwick	38	17	6	15	53:49	40
11	Stenhousemuir	38	14	11	13	52:42	39
12	Albion	38	16	7	15	72:64	39
13	Raith	38	14	9	15	48:44	37
14	Stranraer	38	12	11	15	47:65	35
15	Alloa	38	11	11	16	49:56	33
16	Queen's Park	38	10	10	18	41:54	30
17	Brechin	38	9	7	22	44:85	25
18	Meadowbank	38	9	5	24	26:87	23
19	Cowdenbeath	38	5	12	22	39:76	21
20	Forfar	38	1	7	30	27:102	9

SCOTTISH PREMIER DIVISION 1975-76

1	Rangers	36	23	8	5	60:24	54
2	Celtic	36	21	6	9	71:42	48
3	Hibernian	36	18	7	11	55:43	43
4	Motherwell	36	16	8	12	56:48	40
5	Hearts	36	13	9	14	39:45	35
6	Ayr	36	14	5	17	46:59	33
7	Aberdeen	36	11	10	15	49:50	32
8	Dundee U.	36	12	8	16	46:48	32
9	Dundee†	36	11	10	15	49:62	32
10	St Johnstone†	36	3	5	28	29:79	11

SCOTTISH DIVISION 1 1975-76

1	Partick*	26	17	7	2	47:19	41
2	Kilmarnock*	26	16	3	7	44:29	35
3	Montrose	26	12	6	8	53:43	30
4	Dumbarton	26	12	4	10	35:46	28
5	Arbroath	26	11	4	11	41:39	26
6	St Mirren	26	9	8	9	37:37	26
7	Airdrie	26	7	11	8	44:41	25
8	Falkirk	26	10	5	11	38:35	25
9	Hamilton	26	7	10	9	37:37	24
10	Queen o' South	26	9	6	11	41:47	24
11	Morton	26	7	9	10	31:40	23
12	East Fife	26	8	7	11	39:53	23
13	Dunfermline†	26	5	10	11	30:51	20
14	Clyde†	26	5	4	17	34:52	14

SCOTTISH DIVISION 2 1975-76

1	Clydebank*	26	17	6	3	44:13	40
2	Raith*	26	15	10	1	45:22	40
3	Alloa	26	14	7	5	44:28	35
4	Queen's Park	26	10	9	7	41:33	29
5	Cowdenbeath	26	11	7	8	44:43	29
6	Stirling A.	26	9	7	10	41:33	25
7	Stranraer	26	11	3	12	49:43	25
8	East Stirlingshire	26	8	8	10	33:33	24
9	Albion	26	7	10	9	35:38	24
10	Stenhousemuir	26	9	5	12	39:44	23
11	Berwick	26	7	5	14	32:44	19
12	Forfar	26	4	10	12	28:48	18
13	Brechin	26	6	5	15	28:52	17
14	Meadowbank	26	5	6	15	24:53	16

SCOTTISH PREMIER DIVISION 1976-77

1	Celtic	36	23	9	4	79:39	55
2	Rangers	36	18	10	8	62:37	46
3	Aberdeen	36	16	11	9	56:42	43
4	Dundee U.	36	16	9	11	54:45	41
5	Partick	36	11	13	12	40:44	35
6	Hibernian	36	8	18	10	34:35	34
7	Motherwell	36	10	12	14	57:60	32
8	Ayr	36	11	8	17	44:68	30
9	Hearts†	36	7	13	16	49:66	27
10	Kilmarnock†	36	4	9	23	32:71	17

SCOTTISH DIVISION 1 1976-77

1	St Mirren*	39	25	12	2	91:38	62
2	Clydebank*	39	24	10	5	89:38	58
3	Dundee	39	21	9	9	90:55	51
4	Morton	39	20	10	9	77:52	50
5	Montrose	39	16	9	14	61:62	41
6	Airdrie	39	13	12	14	63:58	38
7	Dumbarton	39	14	9	16	63:68	37
8	Arbroath	39	17	3	19	46:62	37
9	Queen o' South	39	11	13	15	58:65	35
10	Hamilton	39	11	10	18	44:59	32
11	St Johnstone	39	8	13	18	42:64	29
12	East Fife	39	8	13	18	40:71	29
13	Raith†	39	8	11	20	45:68	27
14	Falkirk†	39	6	8	25	36:85	20

SCOTTISH DIVISION 2 1976-77

1	Stirling A.*	39	22	11	6	59:29	55
2	Alloa*	39	19	13	7	73:45	51
3	Dunfermline	39	20	10	9	52:36	50
4	Stranraer	39	20	6	13	74:53	46
5	Queens Park	39	17	11	11	65:51	45
6	Albion	39	15	12	12	74:61	42
7	Clyde	39	15	11	13	68:64	41
8	Berwick	39	13	10	16	37:51	36
9	Stenhousemuir	39	15	5	19	38:49	35
10	E. Stirlingshire	39	12	8	19	47:63	32
11	Meadowbank	39	8	16	15	41:57	32
12	Cowdenbeath	39	13	5	21	46:64	31
13	Brechin	39	7	12	20	51:77	26
14	Forfar	39	7	10	22	43:68	24

SCOTTISH PREMIER DIVISION 1977-78

1	Rangers	36	24	7	5	76:39	55
2	Aberdeen	36	22	9	5	68:29	53
3	Dundee U.	36	16	8	12	42:32	40
4	Hibernian	36	15	7	14	51:43	37
5	Celtic	36	15	6	15	63:54	36
6	Motherwell	36	13	7	16	45:52	33
7	Partick	36	14	5	17	52:64	33
8	St Mirren	36	11	8	17	52:63	30
9	Ayr†	36	9	6	21	36:68	24
10	Clydebank†	36	6	7	23	23:64	19

SCOTTISH DIVISION 1 1977-78

1	Morton*	39	25	8	6	85:42	58
2	Hearts*	39	24	10	5	77:42	58
3	Dundee	39	25	7	7	91:44	57
4	Dumbarton	39	16	17	6	65:48	49
5	Stirling A.	39	15	12	12	60:52	42
6	Kilmarnock	39	14	12	13	52:46	40
7	Hamilton	39	12	12	15	54:56	36
8	St Johnstone	39	15	6	18	52:64	36
9	Arbroath	39	11	13	15	42:55	35
10	Airdrie	39	12	10	17	50:64	34
11	Montrose	39	10	9	20	55:71	29
12	Queen o' South	39	8	13	18	44:68	29
13	Alloa†	39	8	8	23	44:84	24
14	East Fife†	39	4	11	24	39:74	19

SCOTTISH DIVISION 2 1977-78

1	Clyde*	39	21	11	7	71:32	53
2	Raith*	39	19	15	5	63:34	53
3	Dunfermline	39	18	12	9	64:41	48
4	Berwick	39	16	16	7	68:51	48
5	Falkirk	39	15	14	10	51:46	44
6	Forfar	39	17	8	14	61:55	42
7	Queen's Park	39	13	15	11	52:51	41
8	Albion	39	16	8	15	68:68	40
9	East Stirlingshire	39	15	8	16	55:65	38
10	Cowdenbeath	39	13	8	18	75:78	34
11	Stranraer	39	13	7	19	54:63	33
12	Stenhousemuir	39	10	10	19	43:67	30
13	Meadowbank	39	6	10	23	43:89	22
14	Brechin	39	7	6	26	45:73	20

SCOTTISH PREMIER DIVISION 1978-79

1	Celtic	36	21	6	9	61:37	48
2	Rangers	36	18	9	9	52:35	45
3	Dundee U.	36	18	8	10	56:37	44
4	Aberdeen	36	13	14	9	59:36	40
5	Hibernian	36	12	13	11	44:48	37
6	St Mirren	36	15	6	15	45:41	36
7	Morton	36	12	12	12	52:53	36
8	Partick	36	13	8	15	42:39	34
9	Hearts†	36	8	7	21	49:71	23
10	Motherwell†	36	5	7	24	33:86	17

SCOTTISH DIVISION 1 1978-79

1	Dundee*	39	24	7	8	68:36	55
2	Kilmarnock*	39	22	10	7	72:35	54
3	Clydebank	39	24	6	9	78:50	54
4	Ayr	39	21	5	13	71:52	47
5	Hamilton	39	17	9	13	62:60	43
6	Airdrie	39	16	8	15	72:61	40
7	Dumbarton	39	14	11	14	58:49	39
8	Stirling A.	39	13	9	17	43:55	35
9	Clyde	39	13	8	18	54:65	34
10	Arbroath	39	11	11	17	50:61	33
11	Raith	39	12	8	19	47:55	32
12	St Johnstone	39	10	11	18	57:66	31
13	Montrose†	39	8	9	22	55:92	25
14	Queen o' South†	39	8	8	23	43:93	24

SCOTTISH DIVISION 2 1978-79

1	Berwick*	39	22	10	7	82:44	54
2	Dunfermline*	39	19	14	6	66:40	52
3	Falkirk	39	19	12	8	66:37	50
4	East Fife	39	17	9	13	64:53	43
5	Cowdenbeath	39	16	10	13	63:58	42
6	Alloa	39	16	9	14	57:62	41
7	Albion	39	15	10	14	57:56	40
8	Forfar	39	13	12	14	55:52	38
9	Stranraer	39	18	2	19	52:66	38
10	Stenhousemuir	39	12	8	19	54:58	32
11	Brechin	39	9	14	16	49:65	32
12	E. Stirlingshire	39	12	8	19	61:87	32
13	Queen's Park	39	8	12	19	46:57	28
14	Meadowbank	39	8	8	23	37:74	24

SCOTTISH PREMIER DIVISION 1979-80

1	Aberdeen	36	19	10	7	68:36	48
2	Celtic	36	18	11	7	61:38	47
3	St Mirren	36	15	12	9	56:49	42
4	Dundee U.	36	12	13	11	43:30	37
5	Rangers	36	15	7	14	50:46	37
6	Morton	36	14	8	14	51:46	36
7	Partick	36	11	14	11	43:47	36
8	Kilmarnock	36	11	11	14	36:52	33
9	Dundee†	36	10	6	20	47:73	26
10	Hibernian†	36	6	6	24	29:67	18

SCOTTISH DIVISION 1 1979-80

1	Hearts*	39	20	13	6	58:39	53
2	Airdrie*	39	21	9	9	78:47	51
3	Ayr	39	16	12	11	64:51	44
4	Dumbarton	39	19	6	14	59:51	44
5	Raith	39	14	15	10	59:46	43
6	Motherwell	39	16	11	12	59:48	43
7	Hamilton	39	15	10	14	60:59	40
8	Stirling A.	39	13	13	13	40:40	39
9	Clydebank	39	14	8	17	58:57	36
10	Dunfermline	39	11	13	15	39:57	35
11	St Johnstone	39	12	10	17	57:74	34
12	Berwick	39	8	15	16	57:64	31
13	Arbroath†	39	9	10	20	50:79	28
14	Clyde†	39	6	13	20	43:69	25

SCOTTISH DIVISION 2 1979-80

1	Falkirk*	39	19	12	8	65:35	50
2	E. Stirlingshire*	39	21	7	11	55:40	49
3	Forfar	39	19	8	12	63:51	46
4	Albion	39	16	12	11	73:56	44
5	Queen's Park	39	16	9	14	59:47	41
6	Stenhousemuir	39	16	9	14	56:51	41
7	Brechin	39	15	10	14	61:59	40
8	Cowdenbeath	39	14	12	13	54:52	40
9	Montrose	39	14	10	15	60:63	38
10	East Fife	39	12	9	18	45:57	33
11	Stranraer	39	12	8	19	51:65	32
12	Meadowbank	39	12	8	19	42:70	32
13	Queen o' South	39	11	9	19	51:69	31
14	Alloa	39	11	7	21	44:64	29

SCOTTISH PREMIER DIV 1980-81

1	Celtic	36	26	4	6	84:37	56
2	Aberdeen	36	19	11	6	61:26	49
3	Rangers	36	16	12	8	60:32	44
4	St Mirren	36	18	8	10	56:47	44
5	Dundee U.	36	17	9	10	66:42	43
6	Partick	36	10	10	16	32:48	30
7	Airdrie	36	10	9	17	36:55	29
8	Morton	36	10	8	18	36:58	28
9	Kilmarnock†	36	5	9	22	23:65	19
10	Hearts†	36	6	6	24	27:71	18

SCOTTISH DIVISION 1 1980-81

1	Hibernian*	39	24	9	6	67:24	57
2	Dundee*	39	22	8	9	64:40	52
3	St Johnstone	39	20	11	8	64:45	51
4	Raith	39	20	10	9	49:32	50
5	Motherwell	39	19	11	9	65:51	49
6	Ayr	39	17	11	11	59:42	45
7	Hamilton	39	15	7	17	61:57	37
8	Dumbarton	39	13	11	15	49:50	37
9	Falkirk	39	13	8	18	39:52	34
10	Clydebank	39	10	13	16	48:59	33
11	E. Stirlingshire	39	6	17	16	41:56	29
12	Dunfermline	39	10	7	22	41:58	27
13	Stirling†	39	6	11	22	18:48	23
14	Berwick†	39	5	12	22	31:82	22

SCOTTISH DIVISION 2 1980-81

1	Queen's Park*	39	16	18	5	62:43	50
2	Queen o' South*	39	16	14	9	66:53	46
3	Cowdenbeath	39	18	9	12	63:48	45
4	Brechin	39	15	14	10	52:46	44
5	Forfar	39	17	9	13	63:57	43
6	Alloa	39	15	12	12	61:54	42
7	Montrose	39	16	8	15	66:55	40
8	Clyde	39	14	12	13	68:63	40
9	Arbroath	39	13	12	14	58:54	38
10	Stenhousemuir	39	13	11	15	63:58	37
11	East Fife	39	10	15	14	44:53	35
12	Albion	39	13	9	17	59:72	34
13	Meadowbank	39	11	7	21	42:64	29
14	Stranraer	39	7	8	24	36:83	22

SCOTTISH PREMIER DIVISION 1981-82

1	Celtic	36	24	7	5	79:33 55
2	Aberdeen	36	23	7	6	71:29 53
3	Rangers	36	16	11	9	57:45 43
4	Dundee United	36	15	10	11	61:38 40
5	St Mirren	36	14	9	13	49:52 37
6	Hibernian	36	11	14	11	48:40 36
7	Morton	36	9	12	15	31:54 30
8	Dundee	36	11	4	21	46:72 26
9	Partick†	36	6	10	20	35:59 22
10	Airdrieonians†	36	5	8	23	31:76 18

SCOTTISH DIVISION 1 1981-82

1	Motherwell*	39	26	9	4	92:36 61
2	Kilmarnock*	39	17	17	5	60:29 51
3	Hearts	39	21	8	10	65:37 50
4	Clydebank	39	19	8	12	61:53 46
5	St Johnstone	39	17	8	14	69:60 42
6	Ayr	39	15	12	12	56:50 42
7	Hamilton	39	16	8	15	52:49 40
8	Queen's Park	39	13	10	16	41:41 36
9	Falkirk	39	11	14	14	49:52 36
10	Dunfermline	39	11	14	14	46:56 36
11	Dumbarton	39	13	9	17	49:61 35
12	Raith	39	11	7	21	31:59 29
13	E Stirlingshire†	39	7	10	22	38:77 24
14	Queen o'South†	39	4	10	25	44:93 18

SCOTTISH DIVISION 2 1981-82

1	Clyde*	39	24	11	4	79:38 59
2	Alloa*	39	19	12	8	66:42 50
3	Arbroath	39	20	10	9	62:50 50
4	Berwick	39	20	8	11	66:38 48
5	Brechin	39	18	10	11	61:43 46
6	Forfar	39	15	15	9	59:35 45
7	East Fife	39	14	9	16	48:51 37
8	Stirling	39	12	11	16	39:44 35
9	Cowdenbeath	39	11	13	15	51:57 35
10	Montrose	39	12	8	19	49:74 32
11	Albion	39	13	5	21	52:74 31
12	Meadowbank	39	10	10	19	49:62 30
13	Stenhousemuir	39	11	6	22	41:65 28
14	Stranraer	39	7	6	26	36:85 20

SCOTTISH PREMIER DIVISION 1982-83

1	Dundee United	36	24	8	4	90:35 56
2	Celtic	36	25	5	6	90:36 55
3	Aberdeen	36	25	5	6	76:24 55
4	Rangers	36	13	12	11	52:41 38
5	St Mirren	36	11	12	13	47:51 34
6	Dundee	36	9	11	16	42:53 29
7	Hibernian	36	11	7	18	35:51 29
8	Motherwell	36	11	5	20	39:73 27
9	Morton†	36	6	8	22	30:74 20
10	Kilmarnock†	36	3	11	22	28:91 17

SCOTTISH DIVISION 1 1982-83

1	St Johnstone*	39	25	5	9	59:37 55
2	Hearts*	39	22	10	7	79:38 54
3	Clydebank	39	20	10	9	72:49 50
4	Partick	39	20	9	10	66:45 49
5	Airdrie	39	16	7	16	62:46 39
6	Alloa	39	14	11	14	52:52 39
7	Kalkirk	39	15	6	18	45:55 36
8	Dumbarton	39	13	10	16	50:59 36
9	Hamilton	39	11	12	16	54:66 34
10	Raith	39	13	8	18	64:63 34
11	Clyde	39	14	6	19	55:66 34
12	Ayr	39	12	8	19	45:61 32
13	Dunfermline†	39	7	17	15	39:69 31
14	Queen's Park†	39	16	11	22	44:80 23

SCOTTISH DIVISION 2 1982-83

1	Brechin*	39	21	3	5	77:38 55
2	Meadowbank*	39	23	8	8	64:45 54
3	Arbroath	39	21	7	11	78:51 49
4	Forfar	39	18	12	9	58:37 48
5	Stirling A	39	18	10	11	57:41 46
6	East Fife	39	16	11	12	68:43 43
7	Queen o' South	39	17	7	15	75:56 42
8	Cowdenbeath	39	13	12	14	55:53 38
9	Berwick	39	13	10	16	47:60 36
10	Albion	39	14	6	19	55:66 34
11	Stenhousemuir	39	7	14	18	43:66 29
12	Stranraer	39	10	6	23	46:79 27
13	E Stirling	39	7	9	23	43:79 23
14	Montrose	39	8	6	25	37:86 22

SCOTTISH PREMIER DIVISION 1983-84

1	Aberdeen	36	25	7	4	78:21 57
2	Celtic	36	21	8	7	80:41 50
3	Dundee U.	36	18	11	7	67:39 47
4	Rangers	36	15	12	9	53:41 42
5	Hearts	36	10	16	10	38:47 36
6	St Mirren	36	9	14	13	55:59 32
7	Hibernian	36	12	7	17	45:55 31
8	Dundee	36	11	5	20	50:74 27
9	St Johnstone†	36	10	3	23	36:81 23
10	Motherwell†	36	4	7	25	31:75 15

SCOTTISH DIVISION 1 1983-84

1	Morton*	39	21	12	6	75:46 54
2	Dumbarton*	39	20	11	8	66:44 51
3	Partick	39	19	8	12	67:50 46
4	Clydebank	39	16	13	10	62:50 45
5	Brechin	39	14	14	11	56:58 42
6	Kilmarnock	39	16	6	17	57:53 38
7	Falkirk	39	16	6	17	46:54 38
8	Clyde	39	12	13	14	53:50 37
9	Hamilton	39	11	14	14	43:46 36
10	Airdrie	39	13	10	16	45:53 36
11	Meadowbank	39	12	10	17	49:69 34
12	Ayr	39	10	12	17	56:70 32
13	Raith†	39	10	11	18	53:62 31
14	Alloa†	39	8	10	21	41:64 26

SCOTTISH DIVISION 2 1983-84

1	Forfar*	39	27	9	3	73:31 63
2	East Fife*	39	20	7	12	57:42 47
3	Berwick	39	16	11	12	60:38 43
4	Stirling A.	39	14	14	11	51:42 42
5	Arbroath	39	18	6	15	51:46 42
6	Queen O' South	39	16	10	13	51:46 42
7	Stenhousemuir	39	14	11	14	47:57 39
8	Stranraer	39	13	12	14	47:47 38
9	Dunfermline	39	13	10	16	44:45 36
10	Queens Park	39	14	8	17	58:63 36
11	E. Stirlingshire	39	10	11	18	51:66 31
12	Montrose	39	12	7	20	36:59 31
13	Cowdenbeath	39	10	9	20	44:58 29
14	Albion	39	8	11	20	46:76 27

SCOTTISH DIVISION 3 — 1923-24

1	Arthurlie	30	21	5	4	59:24	47
2	E. Stirlingshire	30	17	8	5	63:36	42
3	Queen o' South	30	14	10	6	64:31	38
4	Montrose	30	15	6	9	60:48	36
5	Dykehead	30	16	1	13	55:41	33
6	Nithsdale W.	30	13	7	10	42:35	33
7	Beith	30	14	4	12	49:41	32
8	Mid-Annandale	30	13	5	12	59:48	31
9	Royal Albert	30	12	4	14	44:53	28
10	Dumbarton Harp	30	10	8	12	40:51	28
11	Solway Star	30	9	9	12	42:48	27
12	Clackmannan	30	10	7	13	37:54	27
13	Galston	30	11	3	16	53:70	25
14	Peebles	30	7	8	15	43:56	22
15	Helensburgh	30	5	7	18	46:72	17
16	Brechin City	30	4	6	20	28:76	14

SCOTTISH DIVISION 3 — 1924-25

1	Nithsdale W.	30	18	7	5	81:40	43
2	Queen o' South	30	17	6	7	67:32	40
3	Solway Star	30	15	10	5	41:28	40
4	Vale of Leven	30	17	4	9	61:43	38
5	Lochgelly	30	15	4	11	59:41	34
6	Leith Athletic	30	13	5	12	48:42	31
7	Helensburgh	30	12	7	11	68:60	31
8	Peebles	30	12	7	11	64:57	31
9	Royal Albert	30	9	8	13	48:61	26
10	Clackmannan	30	10	6	14	35:48	26
11	Galston	30	10	6	14	39:70	26
12	Dykehead*	29	7	11	11	30:47	25
13	Beith	30	9	6	15	62:74	24
14	Brechin City*	29	9	4	16	51:61	24
15	Mid-Annandale	30	7	7	16	47:70	21
16	Montrose	30	8	4	18	39:66	20
17	Dumbarton Harp†	17	5	3	9	25:47	13

* Only played each other once
† Withdrew half-way through season. Fixtures expunged.

SCOTTISH DIVISION 3 — 1925-26

1	Helensburgh	30	16	6	8	66:47	38
2	Leith Athletic	29	16	5	8	73:41	37
3	Forfar Athletic	28	16	3	9	61:42	35
4	Dykehead	28	14	5	9	62:47	33
5	Royal Albert	28	16	1	11	75:61	33
6	Mid-Annandale	29	14	3	12	50:54	31
7	Vale of Leven	26	14	2	10	78:55	30
8	Montrose	26	12	3	11	56:58	28
9	Brechin City	28	12	3	13	67:73	27
10	Lochgelly	29	9	9	11	58:63	27
11	Solway Star	29	9	6	14	50:62	24
12	Beith	27	9	4	14	58:68	22
13	Johnstone	29	7	6	16	55:74	20
14	Clackmannan	25	5	8	12	42:74	18
15	Peebles	26	9	0	17	52:76	18
16	Galston	15	4	4	7	38:46	12

SCOTTISH DIVISION C — 1946-47

1	Stirling Albion	18	13	4	1	66:22	30
2	Dundee Res.	18	12	2	4	60:37	26
3	Leith Athletic	18	11	3	4	57:33	25
4	East Stirling	18	10	2	6	54:40	22
5	St Johnstone Res.	18	8	5	5	52:37	21
6	Forfar	18	6	2	10	32:46	14
7	Montrose	18	5	2	11	39:53	12
8	Brechin	18	4	4	10	42:77	12
9	Dundee United Res.	18	3	3	12	42:77	9
10	Edinburgh City	18	3	3	12	36:75	9

SCOTTISH DIVISION C — 1947-48

1	East Stirling	22	18	3	1	72:26	39
2	East Fife Res.	22	16	3	3	63:38	35
3	Forfar	22	14	4	4	69:40	32
4	Kilmarnock Res.	22	10	3	9	52:41	23
5	St Johnstone Res.	22	9	4	9	44:51	22
6	Dundee United Res.	22	9	2	11	56:57	20
7	Montrose	22	7	5	10	43:70	19
8	Arbroath Res.	22	7	4	11	45:57	18
9	Leith Athletic Res.	22	7	3	12	44:60	17
10	Brechin	22	6	4	12	43:54	16
11	Edinburgh City	22	6	3	13	54:60	15
12	Raith Rovers Res.	22	3	2	17	36:67	8

SCOTTISH DIVISION C — 1948-49

1	Forfar	22	17	1	4	80:37	35
2	Leith Athletic	22	15	3	4	76:29	33
3	Brechin	22	13	4	5	67:38	30
4	Montrose	22	10	5	7	59:50	25
5	Queens Pk Strollers	22	9	6	7	52:52	24
6	Airdrie Res.	22	9	4	9	66:66	22
7	St Johnstone Res.	22	9	4	9	42:44	22
8	Dundee United Res.	22	10	2	10	58:67	22
9	Raith Rovers Res.	22	6	7	9	56:60	19
10	Kilmarnock Res.	22	5	3	14	41:54	13
11	Dunfermline Res.	22	4	3	15	43:84	11
12	Edinburgh City	22	2	4	16	26:85	8

Division 3: The 1925–26 season was abandoned as incomplete, though most of the teams had played almost all their fixtures. Though Helensburgh were technically League Champions, Leith Athletic are generally regarded as the winners because of their better points per game record.

Division C: After the 1948–49 Division C season, further reserve sides were added to the League and it ceased to act as an independent entity. The League was further sub-divided into North East and South West sections until 1955, when the remaining teams were taken into the Second Division (Montrose, East Stirling, Berwick Rangers, Stranraer and Dumbarton). Brechin City had managed to win the North East section in 1953–54.

Winners: A complete list is as follows:
1923–24 Arthurlie
1924–25 Nithsdale Wanderers
1925–26 Helensburgh/Leith Athletic
1946–47 Stirling Albion
1947–48 East Stirlingshire
1948–49 Forfar Athletic
1949–50 Hibs Reserves/Clyde Reserves
1950–51 Hearts Reserves/Clyde Reserves
1951–52 Dundee Reserves/Rangers Reserves
1952–53 Aberdeen Reserves/Rangers Reserves
1953–54 Brechin City/Rangers Reserves
1954–55 Aberdeen Reserves/Partick Reserves

BELOW: Eamonn Bannon scores the most important goal in the 74 year history of Dundee United, their second against rivals Dundee at Dens Park on 14 April 1983. United won the game 2-1, the other goal coming from Ralph Milne, and United therefore pipped both Aberdeen and Celtic by a single point to win their first ever Scottish League Championship. United's 56 points was also a Scottish Premier Division record.

Scottish League Cup

This new competition was founded in 1946–47 to continue the popular Scottish Southern League Cup (*see* WARTIME FOOTBALL) which had existed through the war. It also allowed the minor clubs more fixtures. Originally it was played on the basis of 8 or 9 groups, with the winners going through to the quarter-finals, but from 1977 to 1980 it was a straight knock-out tournament.

Most wins: 12 – Rangers (up to 1 Sept 1984).

Consecutive appearances: 14 – Celtic appeared in the final every season from 1964–65 to 1977–78. They lost 7 of their last 8 appearances.

Most semi-final appearances: 25 – Rangers.

Division 2 winners: East Fife are the only side to win the trophy while playing in Division 2 (or Division 1 since 1975–76). They beat Falkirk after a replay in 1947–48.

Biggest final win: Celtic 7 Rangers 1 on 19 October 1957. This is also the biggest win in any British first-class final, and Rangers' record defeat.

Scottish Southern League Cup: For the record, the actual finals in that wartime competition which was the forerunner of the League Cup, were as follows. All the games were played at Hampden Park.

Saturday 17 May 1941 Rangers 4 Hearts 2 (after 1-1 draw)

Saturday 9 May 1942 Rangers 1 Morton 0

Saturday 8 May 1943 Rangers 1 Falkirk 1 (Rangers won on corners)

Saturday 20 May 1944 Hibernian 0 Rangers 0 (Hibernian won on corners)

Saturday 12 May 1945 Rangers 2 Motherwell 1

Saturday 11 May 1946 Aberdeen 3 Rangers 2

The last of these included all the top clubs and is generally regarded as the first true Scottish League Cup.

TOP: Aberdeen's Harry Yorston puts away one of the record 160 goals he scored for the club in the 1950s, against Queen of the South at Palmerston Park in March 1956. Harry's father Benny helped establish a unique family double by setting Aberdeen's single season record with 38 in 1929-30.

ABOVE: Colin Jackson's winning goal for Rangers v Aberdeen in the League Cup final on 31 March 1979. Aberdeen had beaten Rangers 3-2 on 11 April 1946 in the very first Scottish League Cup final.

LEFT: Ayr's Jerry Christie sees his shot saved by Clydebank keeper Jim Gallacher at Somerset Park in a November 1979 Division 1 game. Ayr have won the Scottish secondary division a record 6 times and also recorded the biggest score in a League Cup game – 11-1 v Dumbarton in 1952.

SCOTTISH LG CUP* 1945-46

Quarter-finals (neutral grounds)
Aberdeen v Ayr United	2-0
Airdrieonians v Clyde	1-0
Heart of Midlothian v East Fife	3-0
Rangers v Dundee	3-1

Semi-finals
Aberdeen v Airdrieonians	2-2, 5-3
Heart of Midlothian	2-1

Final

Aberdeen 3 Rangers 2 (11.5.46)

Aberdeen: Johnstone, Cooper, McKenna, Cowie, Dunlop, Taylor, Kiddie, Hamilton, Williams, Baird, McCall
Rangers: John Shaw, Gray, Jock Shaw, Watkins, Young, Symon, Waddell, Thornton, Arnison, Duncanson, Caskie
Scorers: Baird, Williamson, Taylor; Duncanson, Thornton

*Scottish Southern League Cup

SCOTTISH LG CUP 1946-47

Quarter-finals
Rangers v Dundee United (2-1, 1-1)	3-2
Airdrieonians v Hibernian (4-4, 0-1)	4-5
Heart of Midlothian v East Fife (0-1, 5-2)	5-3
Dundee v Aberdeen (0-1, 2-3)	2-4

Semi-finals
Rangers v Hibernian	3-1
Aberdeen v Heart of Midlothian	6-2

Final

Rangers 4 Aberdeen 0 (5.4.47)

Rangers: Brown, Young, Jock Shaw, McColl, Woodburn, Rae, Rutherford, Gillick, Williamson, Thornton, Duncanson
Aberdeen: Johnstone, Cooper, McKenna, McLaughlin, Dunlop, Taylor, Harris, Hamilton, Williams, Baird, McCall
Scorers: Duncanson 2, Williamson, Gillick

SCOTTISH LG CUP 1947-48

Quarter-finals
Heart of Midlothian v East Fife	3-4
Aberdeen v Leith Athletic	8-2
Rangers v Stenhousemuir	2-0
Falkirk v Hamilton Academicals	3-1

Semi-finals
Aberdeen v East Fife	0-1
Falkirk v Rangers	1-0

Final

East Fife 4 Falkirk 1 (1.11.48)
[after 0-0 draw]

East Fife: Niven, Laird, Stewart, Philip, Finlay, Aitken, Adams, D. Davidson, Morris, 'J. Davidson, Duncan
Falkirk: J. Dawson, White, McPhie, Bolt, R. Henderson, Gallagher, Fiddes, Alison, Aikman, J. Henderson, K. Dawson [Whitelaw and Fleck played first final for Gallagher and Alison]
Scorers: Duncan 3, Adams; Aikman

SCOTTISH LG CUP 1948-49

Quarter-finals
Rangers v St Mirren	1-0
Alloa Athletic v Dundee	1-1, 1-3
Hamilton A. v Airdrieonians	1-1, 1-1, 1-0
Raith Rovers v East Fife	5-3

Semi-finals
Rangers v Dundee	4-1
Raith Rovers v Hamilton Academicals	2-0

Final

Rangers 2 Raith Rovers 0 (12.3.49)

Rangers: Brown, Young, Jock Shaw, McColl, Woodburn, Cox, Gillick, Paton, Thornton, Duncanson, Rutherford
Raith: Westland, McLure, McNaught, Young, Colville, Leigh, Maule, Collins, Penman, Brady, Joyner
Scorers: Gillick, Paton

SCOTTISH LG CUP 1949-50

Quarter-finals
Forfar Athletic v East Fife (1-3, 1-5)	2-8
Rangers v Cowdenbeath (2-3, 3-1)	5-4
Partick Thistle v Hibernian (4-2, 0-4)	4-6
Airdrieonians v Dunfermline A. (3-4, 0-0)	3-4

Semi-finals
East Fife v Rangers	2-1
Dunfermline Athletic v Hibernian	2-1

Final

East Fife 3 Dunfermline Athletic 0
(29.10.49)

East Fife: McGarrity, Laird, Stewart, Philip, Finlay, Aitken, Black, Fleming, Morris, Brown, Duncan
Dunfermline: Johnstone, Kirk, McLean, McCall, Clarkson, Whyte, Mayes, Cannon, Henderson, McGairy, Smith
Scorers: Fleming, Duncan, Morris

SCOTTISH LG CUP 1950-51

Quarter-finals
Celtic v Motherwell (1-4, 0-1)	1-5
Ayr United v Dundee United (3-0, 2-1)	5-1
Queen of the South v Alloa (1-0, 2-2)	3-2
Aberdeen v Hibernian (4-1, 1-4, 1-1, 1-5)	7-11

Semi-finals
Motherwell v Ayr United	4-3
Hibernian v Queen of the South	3-1

Final

Motherwell 3 Hibernian 0 (28.10.50)

Motherwell: Johnstone, Kilmarnock, Shaw, McLeod, Paton, Redpath, Watters, Forrest, Kelly, Watson, Aitkenhead
Hibs: Younger, Govan, Ogilvie, Buchanan, Paterson, Combe, Smith, Johnstone, Reilly, Ormond, Bradley
Scorers: Kelly, Forrest, Watters

SCOTTISH LG CUP 1951-52

Quarter-finals
Falkirk v Dundee (0-0, 1-2)	1-2
St Johnstone v Motherwell (0-4, 0-3)	0-7
Celtic v Forfar Athletic (4-1, 1-1)	5-2
Dunfermline Ath. v Rangers (1-0, 1-3)	2-3

Semi-finals
Dundee v Motherwell	5-1
Rangers v Celtic	3-0

Final

Dundee 3 Rangers 2 (27.10.51)

Dundee: Brown, Fallon, Cowan, Gallacher, Cowie, Boyd, Toner, Pattillo, Flavell, Steel, Christie
Rangers: Brown, Young, Little, McColl, Woodburn, Cox, Waddell, Findlay, Thornton, Johnson, Rutherford
Scorers: Flavell, Pattillo, Boyd; Findlay, Thornton

SCOTTISH LG CUP 1952-53

Quarter-finals
Stirling Albion v Dundee (3-1, 0-5)	3-6
Morton v Hibernian (0-6, 3-6)	3-12
Rangers v Third Lanark (0-0, 2-0)	2-0
St Johnstone v Kilmarnock (1-3, 1-4)	2-7

Semi-finals
Dundee v Hibernian	2-1
Kilmarnock v Rangers	1-0

Final

Dundee 2 Kilmarnock 0 (25.10.52)

Dundee: R. Henderson, Fallon, Frew, Ziesing, Boyd, Cowie, Toner, A. Henderson, Flavell, Steel, Christie
Kilmarnock: Niven, Collins, Hood, Russell, Thyne, Middlemass, Henaughan, Harvey, Mayes, Jack, Murray
Scorer: Flavell 2

SCOTTISH LG CUP 1953-54

Quarter-finals
East Fife v Dunfermline Athletic (6-2, 3-2)	9-4
Third Lanark v Hibernian (0-4, 0-4)	0-8
Rangers v Ayr United (4-2, 2-3)	6-5
Kilmarnock v Partick Thistle (4-3, 0-4)	4-7

Semi-finals
East Fife v Hibernian	3-2
Partick Thistle v Rangers	2-0

Final

East Fife 3 Partick Thistle 2 (24.10.53)

East Fife: Curran, Emery, S. Stewart, Christie, Finlay, McLennan, J. Stewart, Fleming, Bonthrone, Gardiner, Matthew
Partick: Ledgerwood, McGowan, Gibb, Crawford, Davidson, Kerr, McKenzie, Howitt, Sharpe, Wright, Walker
Scorers: Gardiner, Fleming, Christie; Walker, McKenzie

SCOTTISH LG CUP 1954-55

Quarter-finals

St Johnstone v Hearts (0-5, 0-2)	0-7
Ayr United v Airdrieonians (2-1, 1-6)	3-7
Morton v East Fife (2-2, 0-2)	2-4
Motherwell v Rangers (2-1, 1-1)	3-2

Semi-finals

Airdrieonians v Heart of Midlothian	1-4
East Fife v Motherwell	1-2

Final

Heart of Midlothian 4 Motherwell 2
(23.10.54)

Hearts: Duff, Parker, McKenzie, Mackay, Glidden, Cumming, Souness, Conn, Bauld, Wardhaugh, Urquhart.
Motherwell: Weir, Kilmarnock, McSeveney, Cox, Paton, Redpath, Hunter, Aitken, Bain, Humphries, Williams
Scorers: Bauld 3, Wardhaugh; Redpath (pen), Bain

SCOTTISH LG CUP 1955-56

Quarter-finals

Aberdeen v Heart of Midlothian (5-3, 4-2)	9-5
Hamilton A. v Rangers (1-2, 0-8)	1-10
St Johnstone v Motherwell (1-2, 1-0, 0-2)	2-4
St Mirren v Dumbarton (5-1, 1-1)	6-2

Semi-finals

Rangers v Aberdeen	1-2
Motherwell v St Mirren	3-3, 0-2

Final

Aberdeen 2 St Mirren 1 (22.10.55)

Aberdeen: Martin, Mitchell, Caldwell, Wilson, Clunie, Glen, Leggat, Yorston, Buckley, Wishart, Hather
St Mirren: Lorney, Lapsley, Mallan, Neilson, Telfer, Holmes, Rodger, Laird, Brown, Gemmell, Callan
Scorers: Mallan (og), Leggat; Holmes

SCOTTISH LG CUP 1956-57

Quarter-finals

Celtic v Dunfermline Athletic (6-0, 0-3)	6-3
Brechin City v Clyde (3-2, 1-3)	4-5
Dundee v Dundee United (7-3, 1-2)	8-5
Cowdenbeath v Partick Thistle (1-2, 1-2)	2-4

Semi-finals

Celtic v Clyde	2-0
Partick Thistle v Dundee	0-0, 3-2

Final

Celtic 3 Partick Thistle 0
(31.10.56 [after 0-0 draw, 27.10.56])

Celtic: Beattie, Haughney, Fallon, Evans, Jack, Peacock, Walsh, Collins, McPhail, Tully, Fernie (Mochan replaced Walsh in the second game)
Patrick: Ledgerwood, Kerr, Gibb, Collins, Davidson, Mathers, McKenzie, Smith, Hogan, Wright, Ewing (Crawford and McParland replaced Davidson and Smith in the second game)
Scorers: McPhail 2, Collins

SCOTTISH LG CUP 1957-58

Quarter-finals

Celtic v Third Lanark (6-1, 3-0)	9-1
Aberdeen v Clyde (1-2, 2-4)	3-7
Hamilton A. v Brechin City (2-4, 0-1)	2-5
Kilmarnock v Rangers (2-1, 1-3)	3-4

Semi-finals

Clyde v Celtic	2-4
Rangers v Brechin City	4-0

Final

Celtic 7 Rangers 1 (19.10.57)

Celtic: Beattie, Donnelly, Fallon, Fernie, Evans, Peacock, Tully, Collins, McPhail, Wilson, Mochan
Rangers: Niven, Shearer, Caldow, McColl, Valentine, Davis, Scott, Simpson, Murray, Baird, Hubbard
Scorers: Mochan 2, Wilson, McPhail 3, Fernie (pen); Simpson

SCOTTISH LG CUP 1958-59

Quarter-finals

Ayr United v Heart of Midlothian (1-5, 1-3)	2-8
Kilmarnock v Dunfermline Ath. (4-1, 3-3)	7-4
Celtic v Cowdenbeath (2-0, 8-1)	10-1
Partick Thistle v Arbroath (2-1, 1-1)	3-2

Semi-finals

Heart of Midlothian v Kilmarnock	3-0
Celtic v Partick Thistle	1-2

Final

Heart of Midlothian 5 Partick Thistle 1
(25.10.58)

Hearts: Marshall, Kirk, Thomson, Mackay, Glidden, Cumming, Hamilton, Murray, Bauld, Wardhaugh, Crawford
Partick: Ledgerwood, Hogan, Donlevy, Matters, Davidson, Wright, McKenzie, Thomson, Smith, McParland, Ewing
Scorers: Bauld 2, Murray 2, Hamilton; Smith

SCOTTISH LG CUP 1959-60

Quarter-finals

Motherwell v Heart of Midlothian (1-1, 2-6)	3-7
Cowdenbeath v East Fife (3-1, 2-1)	5-2
Raith Rovers v Arbroath (2-2, 1-2)	3-4
Third Lanark v Falkirk (2-1, 3-0)	5-1

Semi-finals

Heart of Midlothian v Cowdenbeath	9-3
Third Lanark v Arbroath	3-0

Final

Heart of Midlothian 2 Third Lanark 1
(24.10.59)

Hearts: Marshall, Kirk, Thomson, Bowman, Cumming, Higgins, Smith, Crawford, Young, Blackwood, Hamilton
Third Lanark: Robertson, Lewis, Brown, Reilly, McCallum, Cunningham, McInnes, Craig, D. Hilley, Gray, I. Hilley
Scorers: Hamilton, Young; Gray

SCOTTISH LG CUP 1960-61

Quarter-finals

Rangers v Dundee (1-0, 4-3)	5-3
Queen of the South v Dumbarton (2-0, 1-2)	3-2
Hamilton A. v Stenhousemuir (4-0, 4-5)	8-5
Clyde v Kilmarnock (1-2, 1-3)	2-5

Semi-finals

Rangers v Queen of the South	7-0
Kilmarnock v Hamilton Academicals	5-1

Final

Rangers 2 Kilmarnock 0
(29.10.60, 82, 063)

Rangers: Niven, Shearer, Caldow, Davis, Paterson, Baxter, Scott, McMillan, Millar, Brand, Wilson
Kilmarnock: J. Brown, Richmond, Watson, Beattie, Toner, Kennedy, H. Brown, McInally, Kerr, Black, Muir
Scorers: Brand, Scott

SCOTTISH LG CUP 1961-62

Quarter-finals

Rangers v East Fife (3-1, 3-1)	6-2
Motherwell v St Johnstone (2-3, 1-1)	3-4
Ayr United v Stirling Albion (4-2, 0-3)	4-5
Hamilton A. v Heart of Midlothian (1-2, 0-2)	1-4

Semi-finals

Rangers v St Johnstone	3-2
Heart of Midlothian v Stirling Albion	2-1

Final

Rangers 3 Heart of Midlothian 1
[after 1-1 draw; 28.10.61, 88, 635]

Rangers: Ritchie, Shearer, Caldow, Davis, Baillie, Baxter, Scott, McMillan, Millar, Brand, Wilson [Paterson played first final for Baillie]
Hearts: Cruickshank, Kirk, Holt, Cumming, Polland, Higgins, Ferguson, Davidson, Bauld, Blackwood, Hamilton [Marshall, Elliot, Wallace and Gordon played first final for Cruickshank, Davidson, Bauld and Blackwood]
Scorers: Millar, Brand, McMillan; Davidson
Scorers first game: Millar (pen); Cumming (pen)

SCOTTISH LG CUP 1962-63

Quarter-finals

Morton v Heart of Midlothian (0-3, 1-3)	1-6
Queen o' South v St Johnstone (1-0, 1-4)	2-4
Dumbarton v Rangers (1-3, 1-1)	2-4
Partick Thistle v Kilmarnock (1-2, 1-3)	2-5

Semi-finals

St Johnstone v Heart of Midlothian	0-4
Rangers v Kilmarnock	2-3

Final

Heart of Midlothian 1 Kilmarnock 0
(27.10.62, 51, 280)

Hearts: Marshall, Polland, Holt, Cumming, Barry, Higgins, Wallace, Paton, Davidson, W. Hamilton, J. Hamilton
Kilmarnock: McLaughlan, Richmond, Watson, O'Connor, McGrory, Beattie, Brown, Black, Kerr, McInally, McIlroy
Scorer: Davidson

SCOTTISH LG CUP 1963-64

Quarter-finals

East Fife v Rangers (1-1, 0-2)	1-3
Stirling Albion v Berwick Rangers (2-2, 3-4)	5-6
Dundee v Hibernian (3-3, 0-2)	3-5
Motherwell v Morton (0-0, 0-2)	0-2

Semi-finals

Rangers v Berwick Rangers	3-1
Morton v Hibernian	1-1, 1-0

Final

Rangers 5 Morton 0 (26.10.63, 105, 907)

Rangers: Ritchie, Shearer, Provan, Greig, McKinnon, Baxter, Henderson, Willoughby, Forrest, Brand, Watson
Morton: Brown, Boyd, Mallan, Reilly, Kiernan, Strachan, Adamson, Campbell, Stevenson, McGraw, Wilson
Scorers: Forrest 4, Willoughby

SCOTTISH LG CUP 1964-65

Quarter-finals

Dunfermline Athletic v Rangers (0-3, 2-2)	2-5
Dundee United v Hamilton A. (8-0, 2-1)	10-1
Clyde v Morton (0-3, 2-0)	2-3
East Fife v Celtic (2-0, 0-6)	2-6

Semi-finals

Dundee United v Rangers	1-2
Celtic v Morton	2-0

Final

Rangers 2 Celtic 1 (24.10.64, 91, 000)

Rangers: Ritchie, Provan, Caldow, Greig, McKinnon, Wood, Brand, Millar, Forrest, Baxter, W. Johnston
Celtic: Fallon, Young, Gemmell, Clark, Cushley, Kennedy, Johnstone, Murdoch, Chalmers, Divers, Hughes
Scorers: Forrest 2; Johnstone

SCOTTISH LG CUP 1965-66

Quarter-finals

Raith Rovers v Celtic (1-8, 0-4)	1-12
Alloa Athletic v Hibernian (0-2, 2-11)	2-13
Kilmarnock v Ayr United (2-0, 2-2)	4-2
Airdrieonians v Rangers (1-5, 0-4)	1-9

Semi-finals

Celtic v Hibernian	2-2, 4-0
Rangers v Kilmarnock	6-4

Final

Celtic 2 Rangers 1 (23.10.65, 107, 609)

Celtic: Simpson, Young, Gemmell, Murdoch, McNeill, Clark, Johnstone, Gallagher, McBride, Lennox, Hughes
Rangers: Ritchie, Johansen, Provan, Wood, McKinnon, Greig, Henderson, Willoughby, Forrest, Wilson, W. Johnston
Scorers: Hughes (2 pens); Young (og)

SCOTTISH LG CUP 1966-67

Quarter-finals

Celtic v Dunfermline Athletic (6-3, 3-1)	9-4
Montrose v Airdrieonians (3-3, 1-5)	4-8
Morton v Aberdeen (3-1, 0-3)	3-4
Ayr United v Rangers (1-1, 0-3)	1-4

Semi-finals

Celtic v Airdrieonians	2-0
Rangers v Aberdeen	2-2, 2-0

Final

Celtic 1 Rangers 0 (29.10.66, 94,532)

Celtic: Simpson, Gemmell, O'Neill, Murdoch, McNeill, Clark, Johnstone, Lennox, McBride, Auld, Hughes (Chalmers)
Rangers: Martin, Johansen, Provan, Greig, McKinnon, D. Smith, Henderson, Watson, McLean, A. Smith, W. Johnson. (Wilson)
Scorer: Lennox

SCOTTISH LG CUP 1967-68

Quarter-finals

Celtic v Ayr United (6-2, 2-0)	8-2
Morton v Kilmarnock (3-2, 2-1)	5-3
Queen's Park v St Johnstone (0-5, 1-3)	1-8
East Fife v Dundee (0-1, 0-4)	0-5

Semi-finals

Celtic v Morton	7-1
Dundee v St Johnstone	3-1

Final

Celtic 5 Dundee 3 (28.10.67, 66, 660)

Celtic: Simpson, Craig, Gemmell, Murdoch, McNeill, Clark, Chalmers, Lennox, Wallace, Auld (O'Neill), Hughes
Dundee: Arroll, R. Wilson, Houston, Murray, G. Stewart, A. Stuart, Campbell, J. McLean, S. Wilson, G. McLean, Bryce
Scorers: Chalmers 2, Wallace, Lennox, Hughes; G. McLean 2, J. McLean

SCOTTISH LG CUP 1968-69

Quarter-finals

Celtic v Hamilton Academicals (10-0, 4-2)	14-2
Ayr United v Clyde (0-1, 0-2)	0-3
Stranraer v Dundee (0-4, 0-6)	0-10
East Fife v Hibernian (1-4, 1-2)	2-6

Semi-finals

Celtic v Clyde	1-0
Dundee v Hibernian	1-2

Final

Celtic 6 Hibernian 2 (5.4.69, 74, 000)

Celtic: Fallon, Craig, Gemmell (Clark), Murdoch, McNeill, Brogan, Johnstone, Wallace, Chalmers, Auld, Lennox
Hibs: Allan, Shevlane, Davis, Stanton, Madsen, Blackley, Marinello, Quinn, Cormack, O'Rourke, Stevenson
Scorers: Lennox 3, Wallace, Auld, Craig; O'Rourke, Stevenson

SCOTTISH LG CUP 1969-70

Quarter-finals

Aberdeen v Celtic (0-0, 1-2)	1-2
Dumbarton v Ayr United (1-4, 0-1)	1-5
Morton v Motherwell (3-0, 0-3, 0-1)	3-4
St Johnstone v Falkirk (5-1, 6-2)	11-3

Semi-finals

Ayr United v Celtic	3-3, 1-2
Motherwell v St Johnstone	0-2

Final

Celtic 1 St Johnstone 0
(Hampden Park, 25.10.69, 73,067)

Celtic: Fallon, Craig, Hay, Murdoch, McNeill, Brogan, Callaghan, Hood, Hughes, Chalmers (Johnstone), Auld
St Johnstone: Donaldson, Lambie, Coburn, Gordon, Rooney, McPhie, Aird, Hall, McCarry (Whitelaw), Connolly, Aitken
Scorer: Auld

SCOTTISH LG CUP 1970-71

Quarter-finals

Hibernian v Rangers (1-3, 1-3)	2-6
Falkirk v Cowdenbeath (0-1, 0-0)	0-1
Partick Thistle v Dumbarton (3-3, 2-3)	5-6
Dundee v Celtic (2-2, 1-5)	3-7

Semi-finals

Cowdenbeath v Rangers	0-2
Celtic v Dumbarton	0-0, 4-3

Final

Rangers 1 Celtic 0
(Hampden Park, 24.10.70, 105,000)

Rangers: McCloy, Jardine, Miller, Conn, McKinnon, Jackson, Henderson, A. MacDonald, D. Johnstone, Stein, W. Johnston
Celtic: Williams, Craig, Quinn, Murdoch, McNeill, Hay, Johnstone, Connelly, Wallace, Hood (Lennox), Macari
Scorer: D. Johnstone

SCOTTISH LG CUP 1971-72

Quarter-finals

St Johnstone v Partick Thistle (2-0, 1-5)	3-5
Falkirk v Hibernian (2-0, 0-1)	2-1
St Mirren v Stirling Albion (2-0, 3-0)	5-0
Clydebank v Celtic (0-5, 2-6)	2-11

Semi-finals

Falkirk v Partick Thistle	0-2
Celtic v St Mirren	3-0

Final

Partick Thistle 4 Celtic 1
(Hampden Park, 23.10.71, 62,740)

Partick: Rough, Hansen, Forsyth, Glavin (Gibson), Campbell, Strachan, McQuade, Coulston, Bone, Rae, Lawrie
Celtic: Williams, Hay, Gemmell, Murdoch, Connelly, Brogan, Johnstone (Craig), Dalglish, Hood, Callaghan, Macari
Scorers: Rae, Lawrie, McQuade, Bone; Dalglish

SCOTTISH LG CUP   1972-73

Quarter-finals

Hibernian v Airdrieonians (6-2, 4-1)	10-3
Rangers v St Johnstone (1-1, 2-0)	3-1
Aberdeen v East Fife (3-0, 4-1)	7-1
Dundee v Celtic (1-0, 2-3, 4-1*)	7-4

Semi-finals

Hibernian v Rangers	1-0
Aberdeen v Celtic	2-3

Final

Hibernian 2 Celtic 1
(Hampden Park, 9.12.72, 71,696)

Hibs: Herriot, Brownlie, Schaedler, Stanton, Black, Blackley, Edwards, O'Rourke, Gordon, Cropley, Duncan
Celtic: Williams, McGrain, Brogan, McCluskey, McNeill, Hay, Johnstone (Callaghan), Connelly, Dalglish, Hood, Macari
Scorers: Stanton, O'Rourke; Dalglish

*play off at Hampden Park

SCOTTISH LG CUP   1973-74

Quarter-finals

Dundee v Clyde (1-0, 2-2)	3-2
Albion Rovers v Kilmarnock (2-0, 2-5)	4-5
Rangers v Hibernian (2-0, 0-0)	2-0
Celtic v Aberdeen (3-2, 0-0)	3-2

Semi-finals

Dundee v Kilmarnock	1-0
Celtic v Rangers	3-1

Final

Dundee 1 Celtic 0
(Hampden Park, 15.12.73, 27,974)

Dundee: Allan, R. Wilson, Gemmell, Ford, Stewart, Phillip, Duncan, Robinson, Wallace, J. Scott, Lambie
Celtic: Hunter, McGrain, Brogan, McCluskey, McNeill, Murray, Hood (Johnstone), Hay (Connelly), P. Wilson, Callaghan, Dalglish
Scorer: Wallace

SCOTTISH LG CUP   1974-75

Quarter-finals

Celtic v Hamilton Academicals (2-0, 4-2)	6-2
Partick Thistle v Airdrieonians (2-5, 1-1)	3-6
Heart of Midlothian v Falkirk (0-0, 0-1)	0-1
Kilmarnock v Hibernian (3-3, 1-4)	4-7

Semi-finals

Celtic v Airdrieonians	1-0
Falkirk v Hibernian	0-1

Final

Celtic 6 Hibernian 3
(Hampden Park, 26.10.74, 53,848)

Celtic: Hunter, McGrain, Brogan, Murray, McNeill, McCluskey, Johnstone, Dalglish, Deans, Hood, Wilson
Hibs: McArthur, Brownlie (Smith), Bremner, Stanton, Spalding, Blackley, Edwards, Cropley, Harper, Munro, Duncan (Murray)
Scorers: Johnstone, Deans 3, Wilson, Murray; Harper 3

SCOTTISH LG CUP   1975-76

Quarter-finals

Rangers v Queen of the South (1-0, 2-2)	3-2
Hibernian v Montrose (1-0, 1-3)	2-3
Partick Thistle v Clydebank (4-0, 0-1)	4-1
Stenhousemuir v Celtic (0-2, 0-1)	0-3

Semi-finals

Montrose v Rangers	1-5
Celtic v Partick Thistle	1-0

Final

Rangers 1 Celtic 0
(Hampden Park, 25.10.75, 58,806)

Rangers: Kennedy, Jardine, Greig, Forsyth, Jackson, MacDonald, McLean, Stein, Parlane, Johnstone, Young
Celtic: Latchford, McGrain, Lynch, McCluskey, McDonald, Edvaldsson, Hood (McNamara), Dalglish, Wilson (Glavin), Callaghan, Lennox
Scorer: MacDonald

SCOTTISH LG CUP   1976-77

Quarter-finals

Aberdeen v Stirling Albion (1-0, 0-1, 0-2*)	1-3
Rangers v Clydebank (3-3, 1-1, 0-0†, 2-1†)	6-5
Heart of Midlothian v Falkirk (4-1, 3-4)	7-5
Albion Rovers v Celtic (0-1, 0-5)	0-6

Semi-finals

Aberdeen v Rangers	5-1
Celtic v Heart of Midlothian	2-1

Final

Aberdeen 2 Celtic 1
(Hampden Park, 6.11.76, 69,707)

Aberdeen: Clark, Kennedy, Williamson, Smith, Garner, Miller, Sullivan, Scott, Harper, Jarvie (Robb), Graham
Celtic: Latchford, McGrain, Lynch, Edvaldsson, McDonald, Aitken, Doyle, Glavin, Dalglish, Burns (Lennox), Wilson
Scorers: Jarvie, Robb; Dalglish (pen)

*at Dens Park   †at Firhill

SCOTTISH LG CUP   1977-78

Quarter-finals

Rangers v Dunfermline Athletic (3-1, 3-1)	6-2
Queen of the South v Forfar A. (3-3, 0-1)	3-4
Dundee United v Hearts (3-1, 0-2)	*3-3
St Mirren v Celtic (1-3, 0-2)	1-5

Semi-finals

Forfar Athletic v Rangers	2-5
Celtic v Heart of Midlothian	2-0

Final

Rangers 2 Celtic 1
(Hampden Park, 18.3.78, 60,168)

Rangers: Kennedy, Jardine, Greig, Forsyth, Jackson, MacDonald, McLean, Hamilton (Miller), Johnstone, Smith, Cooper (Parlane)
Celtic: Latchford, Sneddon, Lynch (Wilson), Munro, McDonald, Dowie, Glavin (Doyle), Edvaldsson, McCluskey, Aitken, Burns
Scorers: Cooper, Smith; Edvaldsson

*Hearts won 4-2 on penalties

SCOTTISH LG CUP   1978-79

Quarter-finals

Rangers v Arbroath (1-0, 2-1)	3-1
Montrose v Celtic (1-1, 1-3)	2-4
Morton v Hibernian (1-0, 0-2)	1-2
Ayr United v Aberdeen (3-3, 1-3)	4-6

Semi-finals

Celtic v Rangers	2-3
Aberdeen v Hibernian	1-0

Final

Rangers 2 Aberdeen 1
(Hampden Park, 31.3.79, 54,000)

Rangers: McCloy, Jardine, Dawson, Johnstone, Jackson, MacDonald, McLean, Russell, Urquhart (Miller), Smith (Parlane), Cooper
Aberdeen: Clark, Kennedy, McLelland, McMaster, Rougvie, Miller, Strachan, Archibald, Harper, Jarvie (McLeish), Davidson
Scorers: MacDonald, Jackson; Davidson

SCOTTISH LG CUP   1979-80

Quarter-finals

Dundee United v Raith Rovers (0-0, 1-0)	1-0
Hamilton A. v Dundee (3-1, 0-1)	3-2
Morton v Kilmarnock (3-2, 2-3)	*5-5
Aberdeen v Celtic (3-2, 1-0)	4-2

Semi-finals

Dundee United v Hamilton Academicals	6-2
Aberdeen v Morton	2-1

Final

Dundee United 0 Aberdeen 0
(Hampden Park, 8.12.79, 27,173)

United: McAlpine, Stark, Kopel, Phillip (Fleming), Hegarty, Narey, Bannon, Sturrock, Pettigrew, Holt, Payne (Murray)
Aberdeen: Clark, Kennedy, Rougvie, McLeish, Garner, Miller, Strachan, Archibald, McGhee (Jarvie), McMaster (Hamilton), Scanlon

Replay
Dundee United 3 Aberdeen 0
(Dens Park, Dundee, 12.12.79, 28,933)

United: Fleming for Phillip, Kirkwood for Payne
Aberdeen: Unchanged; Jarvie substituted McGhee, Hamilton substituted Scanlon
Scorers: Pettigrew 2, Sturrock

*Morton won on penalties

SCOTTISH LG CUP   1980-81

Quarter-finals

Celtic v Partick Thistle (1-0, 2-1)	3-1
Aberdeen v Dundee (0-0, 0-1)	0-1
Clydebank v Dundee United (2-1, 1-4)	3-5
Hibernian v Ayr United (2-2, 0-2)	2-4

Semi-finals

Dundee United v Celtic (1-1, 3-0)	4-1
Ayr United v Dundee (1-1, 2-3)	3-4

Final

Dundee 0 Dundee United 3
(Dens Park, Dundee, 6.12.80, 24,456)

Dundee United: McAlpine, Holt, Kopel, Phillip, Hegarty, Narey, Bannon, Payne, Pettigrew, Dodds, Sturrock
Dundee: D. Geddes, Barr, Schaedler, Fraser, Glennie, McGheachie (Scrimgour), Mackie, Stephen, Sinclair, Williamson (Shirra), A. Geddes
Scorers: Dodds, Sturrock 2

SCOTTISH LG CUP 1981-82

Quarter-finals

Aberdeen v Berwick (5-0, 3-0)	8-0
Brechin City v Rangers (0-4, 0-1)	0-5
Hamilton v Dundee United (0-4, 0-5)	0-9
Forfar Athletic v St Mirren (1-1, 0-6)	1-7

Semi-finals

Dundee United v Aberdeen (0-1, 3-0)	3-1
St Mirren v Rangers (2-2, 1-2)	3-4

Final

Rangers 2 Dundee United 1
(Hampden Park, 28.11.81, 53,777)
Rangers: Stewart, Jardine, Miller, Stevens, Jackson, Bett, Cooper, Johnstone, Russell, MacDonald, Dalziel (Redford).
Dundee United: McAlpine, Holt, Stark, Narey, Hegarty, Phillip, Bannon, Milne, Kirkwood, Sturrock, Dodds
Scorers: Cooper, Redford; Milne

SCOTTISH LG CUP 1982-83

Quarter-finals

Celtic v Partick Thistle (4-0, 3-0)	7-0
St Mirren v Hearts (1-1, 1-2)	2-3
Aberdeen v Dundee United (1-3, 0-1)	1-4
Kilmarnock v Rangers (1-6, 0-6)	1-12

Semi-finals

Celtic v Dundee United (2-0, 1-2)	3-2
Rangers v Hearts (2-0, 2-1)	4-1

Final

Celtic 2 Rangers 1
(Hampden Park, 2.12.82, 55,372)
Celtic: Bonner, McGrain, Sinclair, Aitken, McAdam, MacLeod, Provan, McStay (Reid), McGarvey, Burns, Nicholas.
Rangers: Stewart, McKinnon, Redford, McClelland, Paterson, Bett, Cooper, Prytz (Dawson), Johnstone, Russell (MacDonald), Smith
Scorers: Nicholas, MacLeod; Bett

SCOTTISH LG CUP 1983-84

Quarter-finals

Played as 4 groups of 4; qualifiers: Aberdeen, Airdrie, Alloa, Celtic, Clydebank, Dundee, Dundee United, Hearts, Hibs, Kilmarnock, Meadowbank, Morton, Motherwell, Rangers, St Johnstone, St Mirren

Semi-finals

Dundee United v Rangers (1-1, 0-2)	1-3
Aberdeen v Celtic (0-0, 0-1)	0-1

Final

Rangers 3 Celtic 2 (aet)
(Hampden Park, 25.3.84, 66,369)
Rangers: McCloy, Nicholl, Dawson, McClelland, Paterson, McPherson, Russell, McCoist, MacDonald, Cooper
Celtic: Boner, McGrain, Reid, Aitken, McAdam, MacLeod, Provan, McStay, McGarvey, Burns, McClair
Scorers: McCoist (inc 2 pens); McClair, Reid

Davie Cooper (far right) scores Rangers first goal in the 1981–82 Scottish League Cup final in which Rangers defeated Dundee United 2-1 on 28 November 1981. United thus missed out on a hat-trick of successes for they had won the trophy in 1979–80 and 1980–81, on both occasions in their home city. These two finals, at Dens Park, are the only ones held outside Glasgow this century.

Sendings Off & Suspensions

SENDINGS OFF

Fastest: This is thought to be Wrexham's Ambrose Brown after 20 seconds of a Division 3N game at Hull on Friday 25 December 1936. John Ritchie of Stoke City was sent off within 30 seconds of appearing as a substitute at Kaiserslautern (West Germany) in the UEFA Cup in 1972. Stoke lost 4-0.

Debuts: Five players are known to have been sent off on their debuts:
John Burns of Rochdale v Stockport in Division 3N on Saturday 29 October 1921;
Gerry Casey of Tranmere v Torquay in Division 3 on Saturday 19 August 1967;
Brian Myton of Middlesbrough v Cardiff in Division 2 on Saturday 7 September 1968;
Kevin Tully of Blackpool v Burnley in Division 2 on Monday 27 December 1971;
Nigel Crouch of Colchester v Gillingham in the League Cup first round on Saturday 9 August 1980.

Successive matches: Jimmy Turnbull, the Manchester United centre-forward, was sent off against Aston Villa at Old Trafford on 16 October 1909 (United won 2-0) and against Sheffield United at Bramall Lane on 23 October 1909 (Manchester won 1-0).

Cup finals: No player has ever been sent off in an FA Cup final or League Cup final.

Scottish Cup finals: Jock Buchanan of Rangers was sent off in the 1929 final, which Kilmarnock won 2-0. Doug Rougvie of Aberdeen was sent off in the 1978–79 Scottish League Cup final.

FA Cup semi-finals: Only two players have been sent off since the Second World War –

Mick Martin of West Bromwich v Ipswich at Highbury on 8 April 1978 and Brian Kidd of Everton v West Ham at Villa Park on 12 April 1980. Arthur Childs of Hull City was sent off v Arsenal at Villa Park in a 1930 semi-final replay on 26 March 1930.

First red card was shown to David Wagstaffe of Blackburn at Orient on 2 October 1976. The last red cards were also given at Brisbane Road, where on 17 January 1981 Nigel Gray and Cardiff's Gary Stevens had only five minutes to go before abolition but were sent off for fighting.

Career: Willie Johnston holds the record with 15 dismissals between January 1969 and March 1983 – 7 with Rangers, 4 with WBA, 2 with Hearts, 1 with Vancouver Whitecaps and 1 for Scotland (Argentina).

In a single match: On two occasions there have been 4 players sent off in a single game. The first was during a Division 3N match between Crewe and Bradford PA on 8 January 1955 and all 4 were sent off in the space of 5 minutes. The second occasion was during the Rotherham v Wrexham Division 3 game on 15 February 1977. All four teams lost 2 players.

From one side: There have been three occasions on which a side has had three players dismissed. The first was on 10 April 1968 when Clydebank had Stan King, Tony Moy and Dennis Ruddy sent off against East Fife at Methil. East Fife won 6-0. Plymouth had Davey, Provan and Saxton sent off at Port Vale in Division 3 on Sunday 10 March 1974 (Plymouth lost 2-1) and Oxford also had Shuker, Tait and Houseman sent off in a Division 2 game at Blackpool on 21 February 1976. Oxford lost 2-0.

Best disciplinary record: Tottenham hold the record for the longest period without a sending off – 35 years. Cecil Poynton, later club trainer, was sent off against Stoke in a

Brian Kidd (centre, being restrained by linesman) in process of becoming only the third man to be sent off in an FA Cup semi-final – at Villa Park for Everton against West Ham on 12 April 1980.

Division 2 match on 27 October 1928. No first-team player was to receive his marching orders until 24 April 1963 when the highly unlikely Jimmy Greaves was dismissed during a European Cup Winners Cup semi-final against OFK in Belgrade.

Most in a day: 9 players were sent off in Football League matches on both 25 Sept 1982 and 28 April 1984 (7 in Division 1).

Most in a season: 157 players were sent off in first-class English football in 1981–82 (132 League, 20 League Cup, 5 FA Cup). This compares with a low of 12 sent off in Football League matches in 1946–47.

INTERNATIONALS

England: Alan Mullery was the first player to be sent off while respresenting England – against Yugoslavia in Florence during the European Championship on 5 June 1968.

Scotland: Billy Steel was the first Scotsman to be sent off, against Austria in Vienna on 27 May 1951.

Wales: Trevor Hockey became the first Welshman to be sent off, during the World Cup qualifying game against Poland in Katowice on 26 September 1973. Oddly Alan Ball had just become the second Englishman sent off in the same country in the same World Cup – against Poland at Chorzow on 6 June 1973.

Ireland: Billy Ferguson became the first man to be sent off in an Irish shirt as well as the first ever to be sent off in a Home International when England beat Northern Ireland 2-0 in Belfast on 22 October 1966.

Wembley: Despite the commonly held belief that Antonio Rattin was the first player to be sent off at Wembley, that honour actually went to Boris Stankovic, captain of Yugoslavia in the 1948 Olympics, who was sent off against Sweden on Friday 13 August 1948. The referee was Mr Ling, of England, and the Swedes won 3-1. Since 1948, Rattin, Billy Bremner and Kevin Keegan (in the 1974 Charity Shield) and Gilbert Dresch of Luxembourg (during an international on 30 March 1977) have been sent off there.

SUSPENSIONS

Longest: Enoch West was one of the players who was responsible for fixing the result of a Manchester United v Liverpool game on Friday 2 April 1915. United won 2-0 but the result was allowed to stand. West later sued the *Athletic News* for libel when they printed this story, but he eventually had to admit that it was true. His life suspension was not lifted until 1945 – when he was 62 – and hence lasted 30 years. The other players

involved in the scandal had their suspensions lifted after the First World War in recognition of war service. West's name is also to be found in the record books for two other reasons – with Nottingham Forest he was Division 1's leading scorer in 1907–08 with 27 goals and he was, with Hooper and Spouncer, one of three men to each score a hat-trick for the same team in a single game (v Leicester Fosse in 1909).

For on-field misconduct: One player has received a 12 month suspension for on-field misconduct. William Cook of Oldham was suspended for refusing to leave the field on 3 April 1915 (oddly, just a day after the game which lead to West's suspension) after the referee had sent him off v Middlesbrough.

Most often: Frank Barson, who played for Barnsley, Aston Villa, Manchester United, Watford, Hartlepools and Wigan Borough, was almost certainly suspended more often than any other player – though contemporaries stopped counting at 12.

Billy Bremner leaves the field after he and Kevin Keegan had become the first British players to be sent off at Wembley, in the Charity Shield on 10 August 1974.

SOUTHERN LEAGUE

1895	Millwall A.	1940*	Lovell's Ath.
1896	Millwall A.	1941	*Not contested*
1897	Southampton	1942	*Not contested*
1898	Southampton	1943	*Not contested*
1899	Southampton	1944	*Not contested*
1900	Tottenham H.	1945	*Not contested*
1901	Southampton	1946	Chelmsford C.
1902	Portsmouth	1947	Gillingham
1903	Southampton	1948	Merthyr
1904	Southampton	1949	Gillingham
1905	Bristol R.	1950	Merthyr
1906	Fulham	1951	Merthyr
1907	Fulham	1952	Merthyr
1908	QPR	1953	Headington U.
1909	Northampton T.	1954	Merthyr
1910	Brighton	1955	Yeovil T.
1911	Swindon T.	1956	Guildford C.
1912	QPR	1957	Kettering T.
1913	Plymouth A.	1958	Gravesend & N.
1914	Swindon T.	1959	Bedford T.
1915	Watford	1960	Bath C.
1916	*Not contested*	1961	Oxford U.
1917	*Not contested*	1962	Oxford U.
1918	*Not contested*	1963	Cambridge C.
1919	*Not contested*	1964	Yeovil T.
1920	Portsmouth	1965	Weymouth
1921	Brighton Res.	1966	Weymouth
1922	Plymouth Res.	1967	Romford
1923	Ebbw Vale	1968	Chelmsford C.
1924	Peterborough	1969	Cambridge U.
1925	South'ton Res.	1970	Cambridge U.
1926	Plymouth Res.	1971	Yeovil T.
1927	Brighton Res.	1972	Chelmsford C.
1928	Kettering T.	1973	Kettering T.
1929	Plymouth Res.	1974	Dartford
1930	Aldershot	1975	Wimbledon
1931	Dartford	1976	Wimbledon
1932	Dartford	1977	Wimbledon
1933	Norwich Res.	1978	Bath C.
1934	Plymouth Res.	1979	Worcester C.
1935	Norwich Res.	1980†	Bridgend T.
1936	Margate	1981†	Alvechurch
1937	Ipswich T.	1982†	Wealdstone
1938	Guildford C.	1983	A.P. Leamington
1939	Colchester U.		

*emergency competition
† winners of play-off between Midland and Southern Divisions

Southern League

The Southern League was formed on Friday, 12 January 1894, largely due to Millwall's initiative at a time when the London FA would not countenance professionalism. Arsenal had previously tried to arrange a League for southern clubs but, with many sides scared of being ostracised by the London FA, Arsenal eventually gave up and joined the Football League instead. The original members of the Southern League were Millwall, Ilford, Luton, Clapton, 2nd Scots Guards, Reading, Swindon, Chatham and Royal Ordnance Factories. Southampton St Mary's, later Southampton, came in soon afterwards.

Highest points: 71, by Merthyr and Colchester in 1949–50.

FA Cup winners: Tottenham were a Southern League club when they won the FA Cup in 1901, though finishing only fifth in the table that season. Southampton reached the final in both 1900 and 1902.

Semi-finalists: The Southern League produced 2 semi-finalists in 1899–1900. Unfortunately Southampton and Millwall were drawn against each other, with Southampton winning 3-0 at Reading after a 0-0 draw at Crystal Palace.

Organisation: Between 1920 and 1940, in season 1958–59 and from 1979 onwards, the League was conducted on the basis of two or three leagues of theoretical equal standing. This was to avoid excessive travelling costs. Teams in these Leagues did not necessarily play the same number of matches or play all other teams an equal number of times. As a result, the number of games in each division varied enormously and several teams played in more than one of the leagues at the same time. In 1935–36, for instance, there were only 21 sides in the 3 separate sections (Eastern, Central and Western) but 9 teams played in two of the three. The sections were variously called English/Welsh, East/West, Central, Midweek, and even South–East/North–West. The League winners given in the table (*left*) are the winners of the annual Championship match, played in the inter-war period between the winners of the two senior sections.

Sponsored Tournaments

EXHIBITION SERIES

Until the sudden proliferation of Cups in the early 1970s, there had been only three tournaments which had brought together English and Scottish clubs for a single prize since the Scottish clubs had ceased to compete in the FA Cup in 1887.

SPONSORED TOURNAMENTS

WATNEY CUP FINALS

Year	Winners		Runners-up	
1970	Derby County	4	Manchester United	1
1971	Colchester United	*4	West Bromwich	*4
1972	Bristol Rovers	†0	Sheffield United	†0
1973	Stoke City	2	Hull City	0

*Colchester won 4-3 on penalties †Bristol Rovers won 7-6 on penalties

TEXACO CUP FINALS

Season	Winners		Runners-up	
1970–71	Wolverhampton W.	4	Heart of Midlothian	1
1971–72	Derby County	2	Airdrieonians	1
1972–73	Ipswich Town	4	Norwich City	2
1973–74	Newcastle United	*2	Burnley	*1
1974–75	Newcastle United	3	Southampton	1

*Single game result: the other finals were two legged, with aggregate scores given

DRYBROUGH CUP FINALS

Year	Winners		Runners-up	
1971	Aberdeen	2	Celtic	1
1972	Hibernian	5	Celtic	3
1973	Hibernian	1	Celtic	0
1974	Celtic	*2	Rangers	*2
1975	Not contested			
1976	Not contested			
1977	Not contested			
1978	Not contested			
1979	Rangers	3	Celtic	1
1980	Aberdeen	2	St Mirren	1
1981	Competition abandoned			

*Celtic won 4-2 on penalties

BLAXNIT CUP

Season	Winners
1971–72	Cork Hibernians
1972–73	Cork Hibernians
1973–74	Ards
1974–75	Not contested
1975–76	Not contested
1976–77	Abandoned

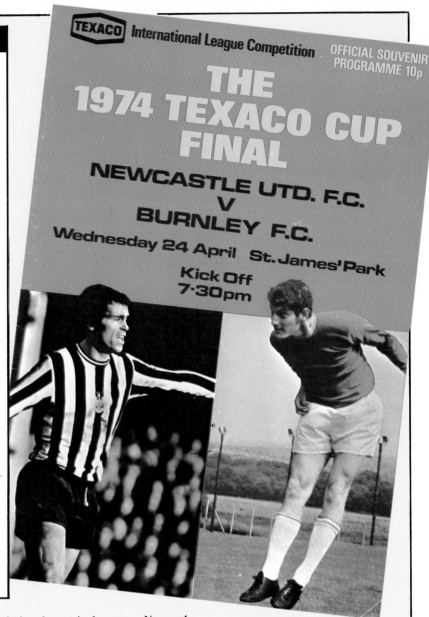

TEXACO International League Competition OFFICIAL SOUVENIR PROGRAMME 10p

THE 1974 TEXACO CUP FINAL

NEWCASTLE UTD. F.C. V BURNLEY F.C.

Wednesday 24 April   St. James' Park

Kick Off 7·30pm

RIGHT: The programme from the only Texaco Cup final played as a single game – Newcastle v Burnley in 1974. By this stage the short honeymoon of the sponsored and extra tournaments was over. The Watney Cup had gone, the Texaco was to last just one more season, and the Anglo-Italian was virtually defunct.

British League Cup 1902: This was organised for the victims of the Ibrox disaster and was contested by Celtic, Rangers, Everton and Sunderland. Celtic won the tournament, beating Rangers 3-2 in the final. Originally the trophy had been the Glasgow Exhibition Cup, won by Rangers and then donated by them for the new competition.

Exhibition Cup 1938: This was organised to coincide with a major exhibition being held in Glasgow at the time and was contested by Aberdeen, Celtic, Hearts, Rangers, Brentford, Chelsea, Everton and Sunderland. Celtic won again, beating Everton 1-0 in the final.

Coronation Cup 1953: This competition, to mark Elizabeth's accession, contained a remarkably strong field – Arsenal, Manchester United, Tottenham, Newcastle, Celtic, Aberdeen, Hibernian and Rangers. Remarkably, Celtic won their third trophy, beating Hibernian 2-0 in the final. So Celtic remain the only club ever to have won a genuinely first-class supernumary tournament.

OTHER SPONSORSHIP

Watney Cup: Sponsored by the brewery, this was a pre-season competition organised among the sides which scored most goals in each of the four English divisions. It was a short-lived experiment which, apart from some innovative ideas over scoring, did little to promote the game.

Texaco Cup: Sponsored by the petrol company, this was arranged among some of the many clubs in the Football and Scottish Leagues which had no other commitments. Always a second-class event, it eventually became the Anglo-Scottish Cup.

Drybrough Cup: The Scottish equivalent of the Watney Cup, it has been more successful in attracting crowds.

Blaxnit Cup: A more useful scheme which brought together leading clubs from both Northern Ireland and the Republic.

Ford Sporting League: Sponsored by the motor company, this lasted for only one season – 1970-71 – and was based on points for good behaviour and goals scored. Oldham won it easily and received £70,000 for their trouble. The rules of the competition said they had to spend the money on ground improvements, which they did, while at the same time they had to approach the local council for financial help in running the team and club.

Hennessey Gold Cup: A Northern Irish competition sponsored by the brandy manufacturers, the Gold Cup had been in existence before Hennessey's sponsorship began. In recent years existing competitions, in particular the Isthmian League, have been sponsored by commercial concerns such as Rothmans and Berger, and these are covered under the usual name of the competition if at all.

181

Substitutes

FIRST

First ever substitute allowed in a first-class match was almost certainly the Welsh goalkeeper A. Pugh, who played for Rhostyllen. He replaced the Welsh keeper S.G. Gillam (of Wrexham) during the Wales v Scotland game at Wrexham on Monday 15 April 1889. He obviously did well, with the game ending 0-0 – the first time ever that Wales had prevented Scotland scoring. In 13 previous games the Scots had scored 59 goals and it was the first time Wales had even drawn with them. Strangely, this was Pugh's only international.

Wales were also allowed to substitute goalkeeper Leigh Richmond Roose with Bolton's Dai Davies at Wrexham on Monday 16 March 1908. Their opponents were England (who won 7-1) and, after Roose's injury, the keeper was initially replaced by full-back Chas Morris. When Morris was also injured, Davies was allowed to come on. Davies had also created another record by becoming the only joint soccer/rugby league international ever.

League game: A player named Morgan is thought to have replaced one called Morrison for Partick Thistle in a Scottish League game against Rangers at Firhill on Saturday 20 January 1917.

Football League game: The first day on which substitutes were allowed by the FA and League was Saturday 21 August 1965. The first man to come on as a substitute was Keith Peacock of Charlton, against Bolton at Burnden Park in Division 2.

Scottish first-class game: Other than the Partick Thistle oddity above, Archie Gemmill was the first substitute to come on in a Scottish first-class match – for St Mirren against Clyde on Saturday 13 August 1966 in a League Cup game.

FA Cup final: Dennis Clarke came on as a substitute for West Bromwich v Everton on 18 May 1968, replacing John Kaye.

For other side: Stan Mortensen made his first international appearance as a substitute for Wales on Saturday 25 September 1943. He was on the England bench but Wales had no substitute in this wartime international and, when Ivor Powell was injured, Mortensen took his place in the second half. England won 8-3.

GOALSCORERS

First-class game: The first British player to score a goal after coming on as a substitute in any first-class game was Jimmy Mullen (of Wolves) for England. He came on for Jackie Milburn against Belgium in Brussels on Thursday 18 May 1950, when England won 4-1. Mortensen, Mannion and Bentley scored the other goals.

Football League game: Bobby Knox of Barrow scored against Wrexham in Division 4 on 21 August 1965, the first day that substitutes were allowed.

Scottish game: Gus Moffat of Motherwell scored against Dunfermline in a Scottish League Cup game on 13 August 1966, the first day that substitutes were allowed north of the border. Two substitutes were allowed in first-class Scottish games from the start of the 1972–73 season.

FA Cup final: Eddie Kelly became the first (and so far only) substitute to score in a Cup final, for Arsenal v Liverpool on 8 May 1971.

Quickest goal: Brendan O'Callaghan scored within 10 seconds of appearing as a substitute (for Viv Busby) for Stoke v Hull City in Division 2 on Wednesday 8 March 1978. It was O'Callaghan's first appearance for Stoke and the only goal of the game.

Test Matches

ENGLAND

Test matches were used to determine the promotion and relegation places between Divisions 1 and 2 from 1892–93 to 1897–98. From 1892–93 to 1894–95 the bottom three and top three had to play off in a simple knockout format, but from 1895–96 to 1897–98 the bottom and top two played all 3 other clubs in a mini-league. The oddest conclusion resulting from this was in 1892–93. Notts County and Accrington, 14th and 15th in Division 1, were relegated while Manchester United, who finished 16th and bottom, stayed up. At the same time, Sheffield United and Darwen, 2nd and 3rd in Division 2, were promoted, while Birmingham, who finished top, had to remain in that Division. The system was finally abandoned in 1898 after a game between Stoke and Burnley on Saturday 30 April. Before the game was played, it was clear to both sides that a draw would ensure a Division 1 place for both clubs next season. The game ended, too suspiciously for comfort, at 0-0.

SCOTLAND

Automatic promotion and relegation was not introduced until 1921–22, but teams at the bottom of Division 1 before that date

Eddie Kelly (second left, partly hidden) scores Arsenal's first goal in the 1971 FA Cup final v Liverpool. He remains the only substitute to score in an FA Cup final. Despite appearances, George Graham (centre) never touched the ball. Arsenal won 2-1 in extra time.

1892–93

Sheffield United 1 Accrington 0 *(at Trent Bridge)*
Darwen 3 Notts County 0 *(at Ardwick)*
Small Heath 1 Newton Heath 1 *(at Stoke)*
Small Heath 2 Newton Heath 5 *(at Bramall L.)*
[As a result, Sheffield United and Darwen, who had finished 2nd and 3rd in Division 2, were promoted and Notts County (14th in Division 1) were relegated, while Newton Heath, 5 points adrift at the bottom, stayed up. Accrington also lost their Division 1 place and were then unable to continue in Division 2 because of heavy debts and went out of existence]

1893–94

Small Heath 3 Darwen 1 *(at Stoke)*
Liverpool 2 Newton Heath 0 *(at Blackburn)*
Preston North End 4 Notts County 0 *(at Bramall Lane)*
[Liverpool and Small Heath (1st and 2nd in Division 2) were promoted; Darwen and Newton Heath (15th and 16th, the bottom two in Division 1) were relegated]

1894–95

Bury 1 Liverpool 0 *(at Blackburn)*
Stoke 3 Newton Heath 0 *(at Vale Park)*
Derby County 2 Notts County 1 *(at Leicester)*
[Bury (top of Division 2) were promoted in place of Liverpool (bottom of Division 1)]

1895–96

Manchester City 1 West Bromwich Albion 1
West Bromwich Albion 6 Manchester City 1
Liverpool 4 Small Heath 0
Small Heath 0 Liverpool 0
Liverpool 2 West Bromwich Albion 0
West Bromwich Albion 2 Liverpool 0
Manchester City 3 Small Heath 0
Small Heath 8 Manchester City 0
[From this season onwards games were played on a home and away basis between the bottom two clubs in Division 1 and the top two clubs in Division 2. Liverpool and WBA headed a theoretical League table after these matches, with 5 points each. They were thus given Division 1 places and, in effect, Liverpool replaced Small Heath in Division 1]

1896–97

Notts County 1 Sunderland 0
Sunderland 0 Notts County 0
Newton Heath 2 Burnley 0
Burnley 2 Newton Heath 0
Burnley 0 Notts County 1
Notts County 1 Burnley 1
Sunderland 2 Newton Heath 0
Newton Heath 1 Sunderland 0
[Notts County headed the table with 6 points, Sunderland second with 4. Hence Notts County, top of Division 2, replaced Burnley, bottom of Division 1]

1897–98

Newcastle United 2 Stoke City 1
Stoke City 1 Newcastle United 0
Burnley 2 Blackburn Rovers 0
Blackburn Rovers 1 Burnley 0
Newcastle United 4 Blackburn Rovers 0
Blackburn Rovers 4 Newcastle United 3
Burnley 0 Stoke City 2
Stoke City 0 Burnley 0
[Stoke and Burnley, who had been bottom of Division 1 and top of Division 2 respectively, led the table after these games with 5 points each, and both were awarded Division 1 places. The League decided to increase the number of Division 1 clubs from 16 to 18 so Blackburn and Newcastle (who had come second in Division 2) were also offered Division 1 places—hence rendering the whole series pointless. The test matches were abandoned in favour of two-up and two-down after this season]

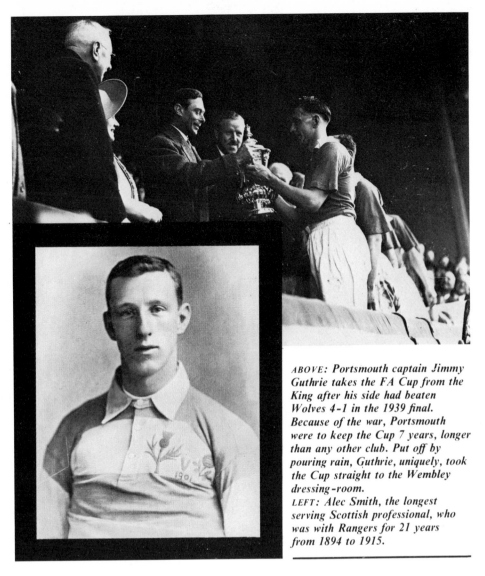

ABOVE: Portsmouth captain Jimmy Guthrie takes the FA Cup from the King after his side had beaten Wolves 4-1 in the 1939 final. Because of the war, Portsmouth were to keep the Cup 7 years, longer than any other club. Put off by pouring rain, Guthrie, uniquely, took the Cup straight to the Wembley dressing-room.

LEFT: Alec Smith, the longest serving Scottish professional, who was with Rangers for 21 years from 1894 to 1915.

had to seek re-election. As a result, there were several test matches played:

1897–98: Dundee beat Partick Thistle 2-0 to decide which club would have to seek re-election.

1899–1900: St Mirren beat St Bernard's 2-1 to decide which of the two would have to seek re-election.

1905–06: Port Glasgow beat Kilmarnock 6-0 in a re-election play-off.

1906–07: Raith Rovers beat East Stirlingshire 3-2 in a re-election play-off.

1914–15: Cowdenbeath, Leith Athletic and St Bernard's played a series of test matches at the end of season 1914-15 to decide the Championship of Division 2, eventually won by Cowdenbeath. None of the sides were actually promoted (*see* GOAL AVERAGE).

Time Spans

UNDEFEATED

Overall: 8½ years – Queen's Park were undefeated from their formation on Tuesday 9 July 1867 until Wanderers beat them in London on Saturday 5 February 1876. As they did not actually play a real game for a year after their formation (a 2-0 defeat of Thistle on 1 August 1868) and as the quality of the opposition was hardly of the highest at the time, this record is not comparable with later ones. Their second game was not until 29 May 1869, when they beat Hamilton Gymnasium by 4 goals and 9 touch-downs to 0. A more realistic record is Celtic's 17 months from 13 November 1915 to 21 April 1917 in 62 consecutive games, all in the Scottish League.

England: 18 months – Blackburn Rovers were undefeated from December 1880 to April 1882, when they lost the FA Cup final to Old Etonians.

Since League formation: 1 year 13 days – Preston won their first League game, 5-2 against Burnley on Saturday 8 September 1888, and were not defeated in *any* first-class game until Saturday 21 September 1889, when they lost 5-3 at Villa Park. They won both League and FA Cup in 1888–89.

League games only: 1 year 13 days – Nottingham Forest matched Preston's record exactly to the day some 90 years later. On 26 November 1977 they drew 0-0 at home with West Bromwich Albion and were not defeated in a League game until 9 December 1978, when Liverpool beat them 2-0 at Anfield. This astonishing run covered 42 games and is the only instance of a League club completing a whole 'season' of League games undefeated since the divisions were extended in 1919.

It could be argued that Forest's run was technically 1 year 20 days, as their previous defeat had been at Leeds on 19 November 1978 – but it is impossible to make a comparison with Preston as the latter's run started from the beginning of the Football League. Preston's record covered both League and Cup games, of course, (though rather fewer matches than Forest's) and Celtic's Scottish League run (*above*) was longer, though in the rather different conditions of wartime football.

All Scottish fixtures: 1 year 10 days – since Celtic's run in the First World War, Rangers completed the longest undefeated run of first-class games on Wednesday 27 March 1929, when they lost 3-1 at Douglas Park, Hamilton. Their previous defeat had been 45 games (39 League, 6 Scottish Cup) before, on 17 March 1928.

Since entering League: 1 year 6 days – Liverpool gained election to the Football League (Division 2) in 1893, where they played their first competitive match, away to Middlesbrough Ironopolis, on 2 September. They won 2-0. They then completed 27 more Division 2 games that season, won a test match against Newton Heath to enter Division 1, and then drew away at Blackburn and Burnley on 1 and 3 September 1894 respectively before suffering their first League defeat 2-1 at home to Aston Villa on Saturday 8 September 1894. They had lost 3 Lancashire League games the previous season.

FA Cup: 3 years 11 months – Blackburn Rovers did not lose an FA Cup game between 18 November 1882 (when Darwen beat them 1-0 in the second round) and Saturday 30 October 1886 (when Renton beat them 2-0 in the first round). They played 24 games in all during that run.

Holders of FA Cup: 7 years – Portsmouth retained the FA Cup from 1939 to 1946 because of the intervention of the war.

League Cup: 3 years 6 months – Nottingham Forest did not lose a League Cup tie *or* game between Monday 20 September 1976, when Coventry beat them 3-0 at home in the third round, and Saturday 15 March 1980, when they lost the final 1-0 to Wolves.

Scottish Cup competitions: 3 years 357 days – Celtic did not lose a Scottish League Cup tie between 21 August 1965 and 13 August 1969, when Rangers beat them 2-1 at Ibrox. They did, however, lose the 1966 Scottish Cup final and were beaten in the first round of the 1967-68 Scottish Cup during this period.

At home, all competitions: 8¼ years – Rotherham United did not lose a home game between Saturday 1 April 1939 (when they lost 2-0 in Division 3N to Hull City) and Monday 15 September 1947, when they lost 2-0 to Southport in the same division. In the meantime they had played 35 first-class games, 29 in the League (including 2 in the abandoned 1939-40 season) and 6 in the Cup. Only 4 of those games had been drawn

and Rotherham went right through the 1946-47 season winning 22 consecutive games and then drawing their very last one, on Saturday 7 June against Rochdale. In normal times the record is by Airdrie, who were unbeaten at home for 3 years and 73 days between 23 September 1922 and 5 December 1925. The span involved 61 League games and 6 Cup matches. In normal times in England the record is held by Liverpool, unbeaten at Anfield in all competitions between a defeat by Birmingham on 21 January 1978 and another by Leicester, then bottom of Division 1, on 31 January 1981.

WITHOUT A WIN

Overall: 1 year & 1 month – Vale of Leven did not win a Scottish League or Cup game between 25 April 1891 and May 1892, when they were voted out of the League. Forfar

surpassed this between 25 September 1974 and 4 October 1975 when they went 36 games without a win covering 1 year and 9 days. The longest run in England is thought to be one of 301 days by Rochdale between 7 November 1931 and 3 September 1932, when they broke their duck with an amazing 6-2 win away at York.

FA Cup: 18 years – Rochdale won in the first round of the 1927-28 competition and then did not win again until the first round in 1945-46. Remarkably they only managed one draw in this period – on 27 November 1937 v Lincoln. On 25 November 1933 Rochdale were 2-1 down at amateurs Sutton United when with just a few seconds left, the Rochdale centre-forward appeared to score from close in. The referee disallowed the goal, however, claiming that he had blown for full-time just as the ball crossed the

ABOVE: *Trevor Francis, scorer of the only goal of the 1979 European Cup final, his first European game. Francis's transfer to Forest from Birmingham in February 1979 was the first £1,000,000 deal and the first time that the transfer ceiling had been doubled in one move.*

LEFT: *Andy Gray evades Steve Walford to score at Highbury in 1979. Gray became Britain's most expensive player when he moved from Villa to Wolves for £1,475,000.*

line. The only other time that a similar decision has actually affected the final result of an FA Cup tie was three years earlier, in the 1929–30 semi-final between Huddersfield and Sheffield Wednesday at Old Trafford. A Wednesday shot entered the net just as the whistle blew, was disallowed, and Huddersfield, leading 2-1 at the time, won the game.

GOALSCORING

None conceded: 7½ years – Queen's Park did not concede a goal between their formation in 1867 and 16 January 1875, when Vale of Leven scored against them in a friendly. Immediately afterwards, they drew 2-2 with Clydesdale in a Scottish Cup semi-final replay.

None scored: 19 hours 53 minutes – Stirling Albion did not score a goal in nearly 20 hours of first-class football between 31 January 1981 and 8 August 1981, when Torrance scored in a Scottish League Cup match at Falkirk. The run encompassed 13 complete scoreless games. Mansfield Town did not score at home for the first 833 minutes of the 1971–72 Division 3 season. They broke their duck against Plymouth on 18 December 1971 having gone 10 home games without scoring.

None scored away: 10 months – Exeter City did not score an away goal in any first-class match between Thursday 12 April 1923 and Saturday 16 February 1924.

PLAYERS

Ever-present international: 7½ years – Billy Wright did not miss an England international between Wednesday 3 October 1951 (when England drew 2-2 with France at Highbury) and Saturday 17 October 1959, when he was dropped before the game against Wales at Cardiff. His last game in the sequence had been on 28 May 1959 v USA in Los Angeles. This run is also a world record for any player.

League career: 24 years 1 month – Ted Sagar joined Everton on 26 March 1929 and stayed with the club as a goalkeeper until May 1953. The Scottish record is one of 21 years by Alec Smith, an outside-left with Rangers between 1894 and 1915 (his first game was against Notts County on 30 April 1894), Alex McNair, who was a half-back with Celtic between 1904 and 1925 and Bobby Evans (Celtic, Chelsea and Raith) 1946–67.

See also: CONSECUTIVE SEQUENCES, PLAYERS, REPLAYS

Transfers

FIRST AND HIGHEST

First £500: Alf Common, from Sheffield United to Sunderland in 1902.

First £1,000: Alf Common, from Sunderland to Middlesbrough in February 1905. On 25 February Common scored the only goal of a game at Bramall Lane to give Middlesbrough their first away win for 2 years.

First £2,000: Danny O'Shea, from West Ham United to Blackburn Rovers in December 1912.

First £2,500: Horace Barnes, from Derby County to Manchester City in May 1914.

First £3,000: Joseph Lane, from Blackpool to Birmingham in 1920. He received £1,000 of the fee and the FA shortly afterwards banned players from taking a cut to discourage their 'shopping around'. The actual fee was £3,600.

First £5,000: Syd Puddefoot, from West Ham United to Falkirk in February 1922. The actual fee was £5,500. The first £5,000 transfer between English clubs was also in 1922, by Sunderland to Hull City for Mick Gilhooley.

First £7,500: James Gibson, from Partick Thistle to Aston Villa in 1927.

First £8,000: Jack Hill, from Burnley to Newcastle United in October 1928.

First £10,000: David Jack, from Bolton Wanderers to Arsenal, also in October 1928. The fee was given as £10,340 but is sometimes quoted as £10,670 or £10,890.

First £14,000: Bryn Jones, from Wolves to Arsenal in August 1938. This remained the pre-War record.

First £15,000: Billy Steel, from Morton to Derby in 1947. The actual fee was £15,500.

First £20,000: Tommy Lawton, from Chelsea to Notts County in November 1947.

First £25,000: Johnny Morris, from Manchester United to Derby County in March 1949.

First £30,000: Trevor Ford, from Aston Villa to Sunderland in October 1950.

Worth weight in gold: Jackie Sewell was accorded that literal title in 1951 when he was transferred from Notts County to Sheffield Wednesday for £34,500. At the time the price of gold was fixed at $35 an ounce, so the comparison was more meaningful than it would be today. Interestingly, since then, the price of players has inflated at about twice the rate of the price of gold. Gold, however, lasts longer.

First £40,000 between British clubs: Albert Quixall, from Sheffield Wednesday to Manchester United in September 1958. The actual fee was £45,000.

First £50,000 between British clubs: Denis Law, from Huddersfield Town to Manchester City in March 1960. The actual fee was £55,000.

First £60,000 involving a British club: John Charles, from Leeds United to Juventus, in June 1957. The actual fee was £65,000.

First £60,000 between British clubs: Tony Kay, from Sheffield Wednesday to Everton in December 1962.

First £100,000 involving a British club: Denis Law, from Manchester City to Torino in July 1961. Law was also the first player for whom a British club paid £100,000 when Manchester United gave £115,000 to Torino for him in July 1962. When Tottenham bought Jimmy Greaves from AC Milan in November 1961, they claimed to have paid £99,999.

First £100,000 between British clubs: Alan Ball, who moved from Blackpool to Everton for £110,000 in August 1966.

First £150,000: Allan Clarke, from Fulham to Leicester City in June 1968.

First £200,000: Martin Peters, from West Ham to Tottenham in March 1970. Jimmy Greaves was also traded in the deal, so the fee for Peters is only an estimate.

First £300,000: Bob Latchford, from Birmingham City to Everton in February 1974. The fee, including player exchanges, was given as £350,000.

First £400,000: Kenny Dalglish, from Celtic to Liverpool, on Wednesday 10 August 1977. The actual fee was £440,000. Two months earlier Liverpool had transferred Kevin Keegan to SV Hamburg for £500,000 in the first £½ million deal involving a British club.

First £500,000 between British clubs: David Mills, from Middlesbrough to West Bromwich Albion on Wednesday 10 January

1979. The actual fee was quoted as £512,000.

First £1,000,000: Trevor Francis, from Birmingham City to Nottingham Forest on Wednesday 14 February 1979. The actual fee to Birmingham was £975,000 which, with VAT, the player's percentage, the League levy and other sundries, added up to around £1,150,000.

Current highest: Bryan Robson moved from West Bromwich to Manchester United for around £1,500,000 in October 1981. When commissions, VAT etc were taken into account, the transfer was estimated to have cost United £1,800,000.

TRANSFER MISCELLANY

First transfer limit: The League set a limit of £350 in January 1908, but it lasted only until April that year. Clubs were able to get round it by throwing in makeweight reserves for a further £350 each.

Most transfers: 15 – Leslie Roberts played for 16 different Football League clubs between 1921 and 1936.

Most transfer requests: 34 – Stan Bowles reputedly made 34 separate transfer requests between joining QPR in September 1972 and leaving them for Nottingham Forest in 1979, a rate of one every two or three months. Ironically, he had not recently made a request when he was eventually sold.

Open choice: On Saturday 16 April 1932 Stoke City played Bristol City in a Division 2 fixture at Ashton Gate. Bristol, bottom of the table, were so hard up that they offered Stoke any player in their side for £250 cash. Stoke snapped up winger Joe Johnson, who played for England five years later. Stoke and Bristol drew 0-0, but Stoke finished third and Bristol bottom.

Quickest return: The fastest instance of paying off a transfer fee was probably Stoke City's purchase of the veteran Stanley Matthews in October 1961. On Saturday 14 October they drew 1-1 at home with Preston in Division 2 and attracted a crowd of 8,409; two weeks later they beat Huddersfield 3-0 in another Division 2 game before 35,974. In the interim they had signed Matthews and the extra receipts at his first home game more than repaid his £2,500 transfer fee from Blackpool.

Played for both sides: There are three instances which are commonly given of intervening transfers causing players to appear for both sides in the same match, though only one is anything like correct. That was James Oakes, who played for Port Vale in a Division 2 game against Charlton at The Valley on Monday 26 December 1932. The game was abandoned and, when it was replayed on Wednesday 26 April 1933, he had been transferred to Charlton and played left-back for them. Charlton won 2-1.

The other two instances involve players appearing for one side when their names had been printed in the match programme for the other. On Saturday 7 February 1925 Albert Pape had travelled with Clapton Orient to Old Trafford for a Division 2 game. Before it began, he was transferred

to United and played for them in their 4-2 win. A similar thing happened to Bert Sproston, who was transferred to Manchester City just before their Division 2 game with Tottenham on Saturday 5 November 1938. City won 2-0.

Trebles

All three domestic competitions: Rangers won all 3 Scottish trophies in 1948–49, 1963–64, 1975–76 and 1977–78. Celtic did the same in 1966–67 (when they also won the Glasgow and European Cups) and 1968–69. No English club has ever come even reasonably near that treble.

Three FA Cup wins: Wanderers 1876–78 and Blackburn Rovers 1884–86.

Three Scottish Cup wins: Queen's Park 1874–76 & 1880–82, Vale of Leven 1877–79, and Rangers 1934–36, 1948–50 & 1962–64.

TOP: *A view of the first few minutes of the Tottenham v Aston Villa second round FA Cup tie on Saturday 20 February 1904. Spurs fans invaded the pitch after Villa took a 1-0 lead (the first time supporters had been known to do this deliberately in England) and the match was abandoned. It was replayed the following Thursday at Villa Park, where Tottenham won 1-0.*

LEFT ABOVE: *Manchester City players leave the Old Trafford pitch after the referee had abandoned a Manchester derby after 85 minutes on 27 April 1974. City won 1-0 and United were consequently relegated.*

ABOVE: *John Charles Clegg, chairman of the FA Council and referee of a contentious Division 1 game between Burnley and Blackburn on 12 December 1891. Ten of the Blackburn players finally left the pitch in protest over Clegg's decisions.*

LEFT: *Police attempt to regain control of the crowd after Newcastle fans had invaded the pitch when the home side went 3-1 down to Forest in an FA Cup quarter-final on 9 March 1974. Though Newcastle won 4-3, the FA uniquely ordered the game replayed, which it was twice at neutral Goodison Park.*

Unfinished Games

ENGLISH FIRST CLASS MATCHES

There are only six known instances of an English first-class game having been left incomplete:

Burnley v Blackburn in Division 1 on Saturday 12 December 1891. Blackburn were losing 3-0 when one man from each side was sent off for fighting. The Blackburn team protested at referee J.C. Clegg's decision and the whole side, with the exception of goalkeeper Herbert Arthur, left the pitch. Burnley kicked off, 'scored' again (with Arthur appealing for offside) and the referee abandoned the game. There was some confusion as to whether the game had actually ended, but the League insisted that the result stood as 3-0. Clegg became President of the FA on Lord Kinnaird's death in 1923.

Walsall Town Swifts v Newcastle in Division 2 on Saturday 29 December 1894. The Walsall players refused to take the field because they had not been paid. They finally did, but so late that the game was eventually abandoned through bad light with Newcastle leading 3-2. The League decided that it would be unfair to ask Newcastle to replay and the result stood.

Middlesbrough v Oldham in Division 1 on Saturday 3 April 1915. This game, the most celebrated incident of its kind, was abandoned after 56 minutes when Oldham left-back William Cook refused to accept the referee's decision to dismiss him. Oldham had gone to Middlesbrough needing a win to effectively secure the League Championship. When Cook was sent off, Oldham were 4-1 down and, as he refused to leave the field, the referee abandoned the game. The League ordered the result to stand and Cook was banned for a year – no great hardship as by then the League had been abandoned for the duration of the war.

Barrow v Gillingham in Division 4 on Monday 9 October 1961. Gillingham had missed their train, hired a plane and still arrived too late for the kick-off. The game was abandoned due to bad light after 75 minutes with Barrow leading 7-0, and the result was allowed to stand.

Manchester United v Manchester City in Division 1 on Saturday 27 April 1974. After 85 minutes Denis Law, who had spent most of his career at Old Trafford, back-heeled the ball into the net to give his new club, Manchester City, a 1-0 lead and condemn Manchester United to Division 2. The crowd invaded the pitch and the game was abandoned, but the result stood and United were relegated. It was the last goal Denis Law ever scored in first-class football.

Derby County v Fulham in Division 2 on Saturday 14 May 1983 ended 78 seconds early after the crowd invaded the pitch. Derby were winning 1-0 at the time and Fulham protested that there had been fans on the pitch for at least the last 15 minutes. While a commission accepted Fulham's arguments as being valid, they did not order a replay because of the peculiar circumstances of the match, which was played on the last day of the season. When the game began, Derby needed to win to be sure of avoiding relegation, while Fulham needed to win to gain promotion to Division 1. Because of the way other results fell, Derby were safe whether the game was replayed or not and it was felt that it would be unfair to Leicester, who had taken the third promotion spot, to give Fulham a second chance on the possibility that they might have scored twice in the last few minutes. What was peculiar about this game was that it is the only instance of a game remaining unfinished because of disruption by the *winning* side or its supporters.

SCOTTISH FIRST-CLASS MATCHES

There have been seven instances of matches or ties being left incomplete in the history of Scottish first-class football:

Dumbarton v Vale of Leven at Boghead on Saturday 12 December 1891, which was abandoned with Dumbarton leading 8-0 and several Vale players having already left the pitch exhausted. Dumbarton were declared winners. Coincidentally, this was on the same day as the Burnley v Blackburn game above.

Dumbarton v Clyde in a Scottish Cup first round replay on Saturday 17 December 1892; Dumbarton were leading 6-1 when Clyde supporters invaded the pitch and the game was abandoned. The Glaswegians were understandably annoyed as their side had won the first game 4-1 on November 26 only to have a replay ordered when Dumbarton protested the eligibilty of one of their players.

Rangers v Celtic at Celtic Park on Saturday 25 March 1905 when Celtic's Jimmy Quinn was ordered off after 78 minutes and the crowd invaded the pitch. The game was abandoned and Celtic conceded the game to Rangers 2-0.

Rangers v Celtic 1909: The 1908–09 Scottish Cup is the only major competition contested outside war-time in the British Isles which was never completed. The final, played in April 1909, was drawn 1-1. There had been some press comment about the high number of drawn games in the Scottish Cup, and there had even been suggestions that the draws were fixed to gain more entrance money for the clubs. Celtic equalised in the 88th minute when Rangers goalkeeper Harry Rennie stepped over his own line and the referee awarded Celtic a goal. This caused some debate, though no trouble, but when the game was replayed the following Saturday and Jimmy Quinn again gave Celtic a late equaliser for the game to finish 1-1 the crowd invaded the pitch shouting for extra time. Scottish FA rules at the time only allowed extra time after 2 replays (the English FA allowed it after one) so the players did not emerge. In the ensuing riots playboxes were burned to the ground and the goalposts disappeared. The following week Celtic and Rangers met and decided they would not replay the tie, and the Scottish FA eventually had no option but to accept their decision.

Clyde v Rangers on Saturday 10 February 1912 was abandoned after 73 minutes when the crowd invaded the pitch at Shawfield. Rangers fans were held responsible and the game was awarded to Clyde 3-1.

Celtic v Dundee on Monday 26 April 1920 was abandoned after 85 minutes when the crowd invaded the pitch and the result was allowed to stand at 1-1.

Hibernian v Dundee on 28 August 1950 in the Scottish League Cup was abandoned at half-time because of a waterlogged pitch and never completed because Hibs had already won the qualifying group.

REMAINING TIME COMPLETED

The Wednesday v Aston Villa: On Saturday 26 November 1898 the Division 1 game between The Wednesday and Aston Villa at Owlerton was abandoned because of bad light after 79 minutes, with Wednesday winning 3-1. The League ordered that the extra 11 minutes had to be played on Monday 13 March 1899; they were, with Villa travelling to Sheffield to concede one more goal for a final result of 4-1.

West Ham v Millwall Athletic: While there is no comparable instance in first-class football to the Wednesday v Villa game above, West Ham and Millwall's Southern League game at Canning Town on 23 December 1899 was abandoned in the fog after 70 minutes. Rather than replay the match, the Southern League ordered the remaining 20 minutes completed on 28 April at Millwall, where the teams were due to meet in the return fixture. Millwall had been leading 2-0 in the original fixture and the score remained at that as the 20 minutes were played out. The teams then commenced their second game, which West Ham won 1-0. This game is therefore unique in two ways. Firstly it is the only occasion when both teams could claim a victory in the same match on the same day; secondly it is usually referred to as the only match to have begun in one century (1899) and finished in the next (1900). The latter point is not strictly accurate as the 20th century actually began on 1 January 1901.

RIGHT ABOVE: Forest's Neil Martin and Newcastle's Frank Clark can only watch as Newcastle fans invade the pitch during the famous quarter-final tie of 9 March 1974. The game, won by Newcastle, was declared void (a unique occurence this century) and replayed twice at Goodison Park before United eventually won 1-0. This meant that Forest had played three consecutive ties in the same round away from home, another unique feature (excluding semi-finals) of this tie.
RIGHT: A brief midfield respite for Australia during the international at Sydney Cricket Ground on 30 June 1951. England won 17-0.

Victories

SINGLE GAMES

All-time record: Arbroath 36 Bon Accord 0 in the first round of the Scottish Cup on Saturday 12 September 1885. On the same day Dundee Harp defeated Aberdeen Rovers 35-0, easily the second highest victory in any British first-class match.

English record: Preston 26 Hyde 0 in the FA Cup first round on Saturday 15 October 1887. The referee is reputed to have lost his watch and the match lasted 2 hours.

League record: Airdrieonians 15 Dundee Wanderers 1 in Scottish Division 2 on Saturday 1 December 1894.

Football League record: Three clubs have scored 13 goals in an English League game: Stockport County 13 Halifax Town 0 in Division 3N on Saturday 6 January 1934; Tranmere Rovers 13 Oldham Athletic 4 in Division 3N on Thursday 26 December 1935; Newcastle United 13 Newport County 0 in Division 2 on Saturday 5 October 1946.

British away record: Redding Athletic 0 Camelon 17 in the Scottish Cup 2nd round on Saturday 24 September 1887. The game was played at Meadow Park, Polmont (near Falkirk) and both clubs came from villages in the area.

English away record: Clapton 0 Nottingham Forest 14 in the first round of the FA Cup on Saturday 17 January 1891.

Division 1: Three clubs have scored 12 goals in a Division 1 game:

Aston Villa 12 Accrington 2 on Saturday 12 March 1892;

West Bromwich Albion 12 Darwen 0 on Monday 4 April 1892;

RECORD VICTORIES OF CURRENT LEAGUE CLUBS

Football League

Aldershot	8-1 v Gateshead, Division 4, 13.9.58
Arsenal	12-0 v Loughborough Town, Division 2, 12.3.1900
Aston Villa	13-0 v Wednesbury Old Alliance, FA Cup 1st round, 30.10.86
Barnsley	9-0 v Loughborough Town, Division 2, 28.1.99 & v *Accrington Stanley, Division 3N, 3.2.34
Birmingham City	12-0 v Walsall Town Swifts, Division 2, 17.12.1892 & v Doncaster Rovers, Division 2, 11.4.03
Blackburn Rovers	11-0 v Rossendale United, FA Cup 1st rd, 25.10.1884
Blackpool	10-0 v Lanerossi Vicenza, Anglo-Italian Cup, 10.6.72
Bolton Wanderers	13-0 v Sheffield United, FA Cup 2nd round, 1.2.90
Bournemouth	11-0 v Margate, FA Cup 1st round, 20.11.71
Bradford City	11-1 v Rotherham United, Division 3N, 25.8.28
Brentford	9-0 v Wrexham, Division 3, 15.10.63
Brighton	10-1 v Wisbech, FA Cup 1st round, 13.11.65
Bristol City	11-0 v Chichester, FA Cup 1st round, 5.11.60
Bristol Rovers	15-1 v Weymouth, FA Cup preliminary rd, 17.11.1900
Burnley	9-0 v Darwen, Division 1, 9.1.92 & v Crystal Palace, FA Cup 2nd rd. replay, 27.1.09 & v New Brighton, FA Cup 4th round, 26.1.57
Bury	12-1 v Stockton, FA Cup 1st round replay, 2.2.1897
Cambridge United	6-0 v Darlington, Division 4, 18.9.71
Cardiff City	9-2 v Thames, Division 3S, 6.2.32
Carlisle United	8-0 v Hartlepools United, Division 3N, 1.9.28 & v Scunthorpe United, Division 3N, 25.12.52
Charlton Athletic	8-1 v Middlesbrough, Division 1, 12.9.53
Chelsea	13-0 v Jeunesse Hautcharage, E. Cup Winners Cup 1st round, 29.9.71
Chester	12-0 v York City, Division 3N, 1.2.36
Chesterfield	10-0 v Glossop North End, Division 2, 17.1.03
Colchester United	9-1 v Bradford City, Division 4, 30.12.61
Coventry City	9-0 v Bristol City, Division 3S, 28.4.34
Crewe Alexandra	8-0 v Rotherham United, Division 3N, 1.10.32 11-1 v Birmingham St George's, F. Alliance, 12.3.1892
Crystal Palace	9-0 v Barrow, Division 4, 10.10.59
Darlington	9-2 v Lincoln City, Division 3N, 7.1.28
Derby County	12-0 v Finn Harps, UEFA Cup 3rd round, 15.9.76
Doncaster Rovers	10-0 v Darlington, Division 4, 25.1.64
Everton	11-2 v Derby County, FA Cup 1st round, 18.1.90
Exeter City	8-1 v Coventry City, Division 3S, 4.12.26 & v Aldershot, Division 3S, 4.5.35
Fulham	10-1 v Ipswich Town, Division 1, 26.12.63
Gillingham	10-1 v Gorleston, FA Cup 1st round, 16.11.57
Grimsby Town	9-2 v Darwen, Division 2, 15.4.99
Halifax Town	7-0 v Bishop Auckland, FA Cup 2nd round replay, 10.1.67
Hartlepool United	10-1 v Barrow, Division 4, 4.4.59
Hereford United	11-0 v Thynnes, FA Cup qualifying round, 13.9.47
Huddersfield Town	10-1 v Blackpool, Division 1, 13.12.30
Hull City	11-1 v Carlisle United, Division 3N, 14.1.39
Ipswich Town	10-0 v Floriana, European Cup 1st round, 25.9.62
Leeds United	10-0 v Lyn Oslo, European Cup 1st round, 17.9.69
Leicester City	13-0 v Notts Olympic, FA Cup 1st qual. rd., 13.10.1894
Lincoln City	11-1 v Crewe Alexandra, Division 3N, 29.9.51
Liverpool	11-0 v Stromsgodset Drammen, European Cup Winners Cup 1st round, 17.9.74
Luton Town	12-0 v Bristol Rovers, Division 3S, 13.4.36
Manchester City	11-3 v Lincoln City, Division 2, 23.3.95
Manchester United	10-0 v Anderlecht, European Cup pr. round, 26.9.56†
Mansfield Town	9-2 v Rotherham United, Division 3N, 27.12.32 & v Hounslow Town, FA Cup 1st rd. replay, 5.11.62
Middlesbrough	10-3 v Sheffield United, Division 1, 18.11.33
Millwall	9-1 v Torquay United, Division 3S, 29.8.27 & v Coventry City, Division 3S, 19.11.27
Newcastle United	13-0 v Newport County, Division 2, 5.10.46
Newport County	10-0 v Merthyr Town, Division 3S, 10.4.30
Northampton Town	11-1 v Southend, Southern League, 12.12.09
Norwich City	10-2 v Coventry City, Division 3S, 15.3.30
Nottingham Forest	14-0 v *Clapton, FA Cup 1st round, 17.1.91
Notts County	15-0 v Rotherham Town, FA Cup 1st round, 24.10.1885
Oldham Athletic	11-0 v Southport, Division 4, 26.12.62
Orient	9-2 v Aldershot, Division 3S, 10.2.34 & v Chester, League Cup 3rd round, 17.10.62
Oxford United	7-0 v Barrow, Division 4, 19.12.64
Peterborough United	8-1 v Oldham Athletic, Division 4, 26.11.69
Plymouth Argyle	8-1 v Millwall, Division 2, 16.1.32
Portsmouth	9-1 v Notts County, Division 2, 9.4.27
Port Vale	9-1 v Chesterfield, Division 2, 24.9.32
Preston North End	26-0 v Hyde, FA Cup 1st series 1st round, 15.10.87

Football League

Queen's Park Rangers	9-2 v Tranmere Rovers, Division 3, 3.12.60
Reading	10-2 v Crystal Palace, Division 3S, 4.9.46
Rochdale	8-1 v Chesterfield, Division 3N, 18.12.26
Rotherham United	8-0 v Oldham Athletic, Division 3N, 26.5.47
Scunthorpe United	9-0 v Boston United, FA Cup 1st round, 21.11.53
Sheffield United	11-2 v Cardiff City, Division 1, 1.1.26
Sheffield Wednesday	12-0 v Halliwell, FA Cup 1st round, 17.1.91
Shrewsbury Town	7-0 v Swindon Town, Division 3S, 6.5.55
Southampton	14-0 v Newbury, FA Cup 1st qual. round, 13.9.1894
Southend United	10-1 v Golders Green, FA Cup 1st round, 24.11.34 & v Brentwood, FA Cup 2nd round, 7.12.68
Stockport County	13-0 v Halifax Town, Division 3N, 6.1.34
Stoke City	10-3 v West Bromwich Albion, Division 1, 4.2.37
Sunderland	11-1 v Fairfield, FA Cup 1st round, 2.2.95
Swansea City	12-0 v Sliema Wanderers, ECWC 1st rd, 15.9.82
Swindon Town	10-1 v Farnham United Breweries, FA Cup 1st round, 28.11.25
Torquay United	9-0 v Swindon Town, Division 3S, 8.3.52
Tottenham Hotspur	13-2 v Crewe Alexandra, FA Cup 4th round replay, 3.2.60
Tranmere Rovers	13-4 v Oldham Athletic, Division 3N, 26.12.35
Walsall	10-0 v Darwen, Division 2, 4.3.99
Watford	10-1 v Lowestoft Town, FA Cup 1st round, 27.11.26
West Bromwich Albion	12-0 v Darwen, Division 1, 4.4.92
West Ham United	10-0 v Bury, Milk Cup 2nd rd, 2nd leg, 24.10.83
Wigan Athletic	7-2 v *Scunthorpe United, Division 4, 12.3.82
Wimbledon	7-2 v Windsor & Eton, FA Cup 1st round, 22.11.80
Wolverhampton W.	14-0 v Crosswell's Brewery, FA Cup 2nd rd, 13.11.86
Wrexham	10-1 v Hartlepools United, Division 4, 3.3.62
York City	9-1 v Southport, Division 3N, 2.2.57

Scottish League

Aberdeen	13-0 v Peterhead, Scottish Cup 3rd round, 10.2.23
Airdrieonians	15-1 v Dundee Wanderers, Division 2, 1.12.94
Albion Rovers	12-0 v Airdriehill, Scottish Cup 1st round, 3.9.87
Alloa Athletic	9-2 v Forfar Athletic, Division 2, 18.3.33
Arbroath	36-0 v Bon Accord, Scottish Cup 1st round, 12.9.85
Ayr United	11-1 v Dumbarton, League Cup, 13.8.52
Berwick Rangers	8-1 v Forfar Athletic, Division 2, 25.12.65 & v Vale of Leithen, Scottish Cup pr. round, 30.9.67
Brechin City	12-1 v Thornhill, Scottish Cup 1st round, 28.1.26
Celtic	11-0 v Dundee, Division 1, 26.10.95
Clyde	11-1 v Cowdenbeath, Division 2, 6.10.51
Clydebank	8-1 v Arbroath, Division 1, 3.1.77
Cowdenbeath	12-0 v Johnstone, Scottish Cup 1st round, 21.1.28
Dumbarton	13-1 v Kirkintilloch Central, Scottish Cup 1st rd. 1.9.88
Dundee	10-0 v *Alloa, Division 2, 8.3.47 & v Dunfermline Athletic, Division 2, 22.3.47
Dundee United	14-0 v Nithsdale Wanderers, Scottish Cup 1st round, 17.1.31
Dunfermline Athletic	11-2 v Stenhousemuir, Division 2, 27.9.30
East Fife	13-2 v Edinburgh City, Division 2, 11.12.37
East Stirlingshire	10-1 v Stenhousemuir, Scottish Cup 1st round, 1.9.88
Falkirk	12-1 v Laurieston, Scottish Cup 2nd round, 23.3.93
Forfar Athletic	14-1 v Lindertis, Scottish Cup 1st round, 1.9.88
Hamilton Academicals	10-2 v Cowdenbeath, Division 1, 15.10.32
Heart of Midlothian	15-0 v King's Park, Scottish Cup 2nd round, 13.2.37
Hibernian	15-1 v Peebles Rovers, Scottish Cup 2nd rd. 11.2.61
Kilmarnock	13-2 v Saltcoats Victoria, Scottish Cup 2nd rd., 12.9.96
Meadowbank Thistle	6-1 v Stenhousemuir, Division 2, 6.2.82
Montrose	12-0 v *Vale of Leithen, Scottish Cup 2nd rd., 4.1.75
Morton	11-0 v Carfin Shamrock, Scottish Cup 1st rd., 13.11.86
Motherwell	12-1 v Dundee United, Division 2, 23.1.54
Partick Thistle	16-0 v Royal Albert, Scottisn Cup 1st round, 17.1.31
Queen of the South	11-1 v Stranraer, Scottish Cup 1st round, 16.1.32
Queen's Park	16-0 v St Peter's, Scottish Cup 1st round, 12.9.85
Raith Rovers	10-1 v Coldstream, Scottish Cup 2nd round, 13.2.54
Rangers	14-2 v Whitehill, Scottish Cup 2nd round, 22.9.1883 & v Blairgowrie, Scottish Cup 1st round, 20.1.34
St Johnstone	8-1 v *Partick Thistle, League Cup, 16.8.69
St Mirren	15-0 v Glasgow University, Scottish Cup 1st rd., 30.1.60
Stenhousemuir	9-2 v Dundee United, Division 2, 17.4.37
Stirling Albion	7-0 v Albion Rovers, Division 2, 19.11.47, v Montrose, Division 2, 28.9.57, v *St Mirren, Division 1, 5.3.60 & v Arbroath, Division 2, 11.3.61
Stranraer	7-0 v Brechin City, Division 2, 6.2.65

*home club †played at Maine Road

189

Nottingham Forest 12 Leicester Fosse 0 on Wednesday 21 April 1909.
Division 2: Newcastle v Newport (*above*).
Division 3: Stockport v Halifax and Tranmere v Oldham (*above*).
Division 4: Oldham Athletic 11 Southport 0 on Wednesday 26 December 1962.
FA Cup: Preston v Hyde (*above*).
Football League Cup/Milk Cup: West Ham 10 Bury 0 in the second round second leg game at Upton Park on 24 October 1983. The Football League Cup record was a remarkable oddity for it involved two teams who were no longer members of the League. Workington beat Barrow 9-1 in the first round on Wednesday 2 September 1964 and would, in fact, have won 10-1 if the referee had been a little more generous as Dave Carr's 90th minute shot was crossing the line as the final whistle went.
Scottish League: Airdrieonians 15 Dundee Wanderers 1 (*above*) in Division 2.
Scottish Premier/Division 1: On only one occasion has there been an 11-goal margin in a Scottish senior division game, Celtic 11 Dundee 0 on Saturday 26 October 1895.
Scottish League Cup: Ayr United 11 Dumbarton 1, in a group game on Wednesday 13 August 1952.
Scottish away record: Redding Athletic 0 Camelon 17 (*above*).
Internationals: Although England beat Australia 17-0 in Sydney on Saturday 30 June 1951, this is not recognised by the FA as an official international; nor is the English amateur side's defeat of a French national side (not amateur in the English meaning of the term) in Paris on Thursday 1 November 1906, when England won 15-0. The biggest recognised win by any of the home countries is therefore England's 13-0 defeat of Ireland in Belfast on Saturday 18 February 1882. It is, of course, debatable whether the Irish team that day was any more an 'official' or competent team than the Australian or French sides mentioned previously.
Against other opposition: Chelsea defeated Jeunesse Hautcharage 13-0 in the European Cup Winners Cup at Stamford Bridge on 29 September 1971. Their aggregate victory in this tie (21-0) is also a record for a British club in any first-class fixture.
Semi-finals: Dumbarton 11 Cartvale 2 (Scottish Cup, 1882) and Cambuslang 10 Abercorn 1 (Scottish Cup, 1888 replay). In England, three sides have scored 6 goals in an FA Cup single-game semi-final: Newcastle defeated Fulham 6-0 at Anfield in 1908, West Bromwich defeated Nottingham Forest 6-2 at Derby in a second replay in 1892, and Manchester City defeated Aston Villa 6-1 at Huddersfield in 1934.
Without scoring a goal: QPR and Derby drew 0-0 in both legs of a League Cup second round tie in 1980 and QPR won on penalties. This is the only occasion on which a team has won a first class domestic fixture without scoring a goal though Inter-Milan defeated Celtic on penalties in the 1971–72 European Cup semi-final after two goalless draws. With penalty deciders now accepted, it will become more common.

INTERNATIONALS
England: England 13 Ireland 0 in Belfast on Saturday 18 February 1882.
Scotland: Scotland 11 Ireland 0 on Saturday 23 February 1901 at the Second Hampden Park.
Wales: Wales 11 Ireland 0 on Saturday 3 March 1888 at Wrexham.
Ireland/Northern Ireland: Northern Ireland 7 Wales 0 at Celtic Park on Saturday 1 February 1930.
Eire: Eire 8 Malta 0 on 16 November 1983 at Lansdowne Road, Dublin.

10 GOALS OR MORE
First-class games when one team or other reaches double figures are more common than one would imagine. There have been 61 examples in the Football League alone, though only one of these was away from home (Burslem Port Vale 0 Sheffield United 10 on 10 December 1892). There are also well over 100 occasions when one side or other has scored 12 goals or more in a major competitive fixture, though nearly all were in nineteenth-century Scottish Cup or FA Cup matches between ill-matched opponents. In recent years there has also been a spate of high scoring in European games against Maltese or Luxembourgoise opposition and it is difficult to take these records seriously. The last time a First Division fixture saw double figures was on Thursday 26 December 1963 when Fulham beat Ipswich 10-1. The last time that a Football League club scored 10 goals was on Saturday 25 January 1964, when Doncaster beat Darlington 10-0 in Division 4.

20 GOALS OR MORE
For the record, there are only six occasions when a side has scored more than 19 goals in a first-class fixture:
● Arbroath 36 Bon Accord 0, Scottish Cup 1st round, Saturday 12 September 1885. The Arbroath scorers were Petrie 13, Munro 7, Robertson 6, Crawford 6, Mar-

shall 2, Tickett 2. Arbroath were leading 15-0 at half-time and it was reported that the score should have been 42-0 but that referee David Stormont had disallowed 6 goals to try and keep the figure respectable. It has recently emerged that Arbroath's opposition were not a football club at all but a cricket team who received the invitation by mistake.
● Dundee Harp 35 Aberdeen Rovers 0, Scottish Cup 1st round, Saturday 12 September 1885. The game was played at East Dock Street Dundee, and the teams were actually called simply Harp and Rovers. Harp were leading 16-0 at half-time and their scorers were D'Arcy 10, McGirl 6, Murphy 5, Murray 4, Rock 3, Lees 3, Neill 3 and D'Arcy Senior 1.
● Preston North End 26 Hyde 0, FA Cup 1st round, Saturday 15 October 1887.
● Cowlairs 21 Victoria 1, Scottish Cup 1st round, Saturday 7 September 1889.
● Arbroath 20 Orion 0, Scottish Cup 1st round, Saturday 3 September 1887.
● Johnstone 20 Greenock Abstainers 0, Scottish Cup 1st round, Saturday 5 September 1891.

12 AGAINST LEAGUE OPPOSITION
There have only been 20 occasions on which a club side has scored 12 goals or more while playing against first-class (i.e. League status) opposition:
● Aston Villa 12 Accrington 2, Division 1, Saturday 12 March 1892;
● West Bromwich Albion 12 Darwen 0 on Monday 4 April 1892;
● Small Heath 12 Walsall Town Swifts 0, Division 2, Saturday 17 December 1892;
● Airdrieonians 15 Dundee Wanderers 1, Scottish Division 2, Saturday 1 December 1894;
● Darwen 12 Walsall 0, Division 2, Saturday 26 December 1896;
● Woolwich Arsenal 12 Loughborough Town 0, Division 2, Monday 12 March 1900;

- Small Heath 12 Doncaster Rovers 0, Division 2, Saturday 11 April 1903;
- Nottingham Forest 12 Leicester Fosse 0, Division 1, Wednesday 21 April 1909;
- King's Park 12 Forfar Athletic 2, Scottish Division 2, Thursday 2 January 1930;
- Stockport County 13 Halifax Town 0, Division 3N, Saturday 6 January 1934;
- Barrow 12 Gateshead 1, Division 3N, Saturday 5 May 1934;
- Tranmere Rovers 13 Oldham Athletic 4, Division 3N, Thursday 26 December 1935;
- Chester 12 York City 0, Division 3N, Saturday 1 February 1936;
- Luton Town 12 Bristol Rovers 0, Division 3S, Monday 13 April 1936;
- Dundee United 12 East Stirlingshire 1, Scottish Division 2, Monday 13 April 1936;
- Heart of Midlothian 15 King's Park 0, Scottish Cup 2nd round, Saturday 13 March 1937;
- East Fife 13 Edinburgh City 2, Scottish Division 2, Saturday 11 December 1937;
- Newcastle United 13 Newport County 0, Division 2, Saturday 5 October 1946;
- Motherwell 12 Dundee United 1, Scottish Division 2, Saturday 23 January 1954;
- Tottenham Hotspur 13 Crewe Alexandra 2, FA Cup 4th round, Wednesday 3 February 1960.

Since Spurs defeat of Crewe there have been several instances of British clubs scoring 12 goals in European matches (eg Swansea v Sliema, Derby v Finn Harps, Chelsea v Jeunesse) but these can hardly be regarded as comparable.

LEFT: Mick Robinson (11) turns away after scoring one of Eire's 6 goals against Cyprus on 19 November 1980. This was then Eire's record victory, achieved in a World Cup qualifier. Robinson has another claim to the record books: born in Leicester, he plays for Eire by virtue of one of his great-grandmothers being Irish. This is the most obscure relationship yet used to justify an international selection.

LEFT CENTRE: The programme from the 1890 FA Cup final, played at Kennington Oval on 29 March 1890. There are only two older programmes in existence. Blackburn won the game 6-1 to establish the highest aggregate in an FA Cup final and their six goals have never been surpassed, though Bury beat Derby 6-0 in 1903. Blackburn's goals were scored by Lofthouse, Walton, John Southworth and three from William Townley, the first ever hat-trick in an FA Cup final. A particular oddity of the final was that Wednesday had been beaten 3-2 in a quarter-final replay by Notts County. The Sheffielders protested that County had played an ineligible man and the game was played a third time with Wednesday winning 2-1. The first time the match had been played, Wednesday won 5-0 in a blizzard but then County's protests about the pitch were upheld. Only one other side, Charlton in 1946, has reached a final after losing a match on the way.

BOTTOM: The Arbroath team photographed just after their remarkable 36-0 defeat of Bon Accord, still the biggest victory in a first-class match anywhere in the world. On the floor, left, is outside-right John Petrie, who established another unbeaten record with 13 goals. Centre standing is keeper Ned Doig, the only Arbroath player ever to be capped. It has recently been suggested that Arbroath had actually been drawn against Orion FC of Aberdeen in this Scottish Cup first round game, but that the invitation went to Orion Cricket Club by mistake. The latter decided to play the game anyway and changed their name to Bon Accord for the occasion. This explains why Bon Accord arrived with neither kit nor shirts. The referee, David Stormont, apparently disallowed at least six other perfectly legitimate goals in an attempt to give the score some respectability. Two seasons later Arbroath were, by coincidence, drawn against the real Orion and beat them almost as handsomely. On Saturday 3 September 1887 Arbroath won 20-0, and their two wins against the two Orions are among the six biggest wins in first-class British football history.

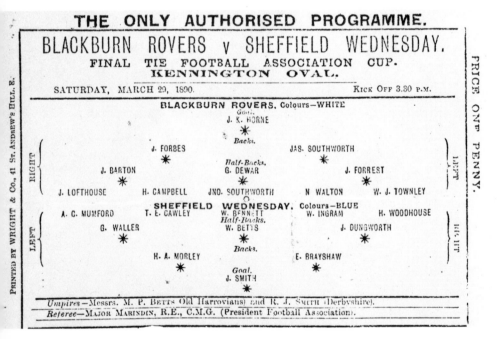

WARTIME FOOTBALL

FIRST WORLD WAR 1915-16

Midland Regional Tournament: **Nottingham F.**
Midland Tournament (South): **Nottingham F.**
Midland Tournament (North): **Leeds City**
Midland Tournament (Central): **Grimsby Town**
Lancashire Regional Tournament: **Manchester C.**
Lancashire Tournament (South): **Manchester C.**
Lancashire Tournament (North): **Burnley**
London Combination: **Chelsea**
London Supplementary Tournaments:
   Chelsea & West Ham
South-Western Combination: **Portsmouth**
Scottish League: **Celtic**

FIRST WORLD WAR 1916-17

Midland Regional Tournament: **Leeds City**
Midland Subsidiary Tournament: **Bradford P.A.**
Lancashire Regional Tournament: **Liverpool**
Lancashire Subsidary Tournament: **Rochdale**
London Combination: **West Ham United**
Scottish League: **Celtic**

FIRST WORLD WAR 1917-18

Midland Regional Tournament: **Leeds City**
Midland Subsidiary Tournament: **Grimsby**
Lancashire Regional Tournament: **Stoke**
Lancashire Subsidiary Tournament: **Liverpool**
League Championship play-off: **Leeds City**
London Combination: **Chelsea**
Scottish League: **Rangers**

FIRST WORLD WAR 1918-19

League Championship play-off: **Nottingham F.**
Midland Regional Tournament: **Nottingham F.**
Midland Subsidiary Tournament 'A': **Sheffield U.**
Midland Subsidiary Tournament 'B': **Birmingham**
Midland Subsidiary Tournament 'C': **Bradford P.A.**
Midland Subsidiary Tournament 'D': **Hull City**
Lancashire Regional Tournament: **Everton**
Lancashire Sub. Tournament 'A': **Blackpool**
Lancashire Sub. Tournament 'B': **Oldham A.**
Lancashire Sub. Tournament 'C': **Manchester C.**
Lancashire Subsidiary Tournament 'D': **Liverpool**
London Combination: **Brentford**
Scottish Victory Cup: **St Mirren**
Scottish League: **Celtic**

SECOND WORLD WAR 1939-40

League Cup: **West Ham United**
Midland League: **Wolverhampton Wanderers**
West League: **Stoke City**
North-East League: **Huddersfield Town**
North-West League: **Bury**
South League 'A': **Arsenal**
South League 'B': **Queen's Park Rangers**
South League 'C': **Tottenham Hotspur**
South League 'D': **Crystal Palace**
South-West League: **Plymouth Argyle**
East Midland League: **Chesterfield**
Scottish Championship play-off: **Rangers**
Scottish League (West & South): **Rangers**
Scottish League (East & North): **Falkirk**
Scottish Emergency Cup: **Rangers**

SECOND WORLD WAR 1940-41

League Cup: **Preston North End**
Northern Regional League: **Preston North End**
Southern Regional League: **Crystal Palace**
Western Regional Cup: **Bristol City**
London Cup: **Reading**
Lancashire Cup: **Manchester United**
Midland Cup: **Leicester City**
Combined Cities Cup: **Middlesbrough**
Scottish Southern League: **Rangers**
Scottish Southern League Cup: **Rangers**
Scottish Summer Cup: **Hibernian**

SECOND WORLD WAR 1941-42

League Cup: **Wolverhampton Wanderers**
League North: **Blackpool**
League South: **Leicester City**
London League: **Arsenal**
London Cup: **Brentford**
Scottish Southern League: **Rangers**
Scot. North-East League (Autumn): **Rangers**
Scot. North-East League (Spring): **Aberdeen**
Scottish Southern League Cup: **Rangers**
Scot. North-East Autumn League Cup: **Aberdeen**
Scot. North-East Spring League Cup: **Aberdeen**
Scottish Summer Cup: **Rangers**

SECOND WORLD WAR 1942-43

League North: **Blackpool**
League South: **Arsenal**
League West: **Lovells Athletic**
League North Cup: **Blackpool**
League South Cup: **Arsenal**
League West Cup: **Swansea Town**
Scottish Southern League: **Rangers**
Scot. North-East League (Autumn): **Aberdeen**
Scot. North-East League (Spring): **Aberdeen**
Scottish Southern League Cup: **Rangers**
Scot. North-East Autumn League Cup: **Aberdeen**
Scot. North-East Spring League Cup: **Aberdeen**
Scottish Summer Cup: **St Mirren**

SECOND WORLD WAR 1943-44

League North: **Blackpool**
League South: **Tottenham Hotspur**
League West: **Lovells Athletic**
League North Cup: **Aston Villa**
League South Cup: **Charlton Athletic**
League West Cup: **Bath City**
Scottish Southern League: **Rangers**
Scot. North-East League (Autumn): **Raith R.**
Scot. North-East League (Spring): **Aberdeen**
Scottish Southern League Cup: **Hibernian**
Scot. North-East Autumn League Cup: **Rangers**
Scot. North-East Spring League Cup: **Rangers**
Scottish Summer Cup: **Motherwell**

SECOND WORLD WAR 1944-45

League North: **Huddersfield Town**
League South: **Tottenham Hotspur**
League West: **Cardiff City**
League North Cup: **Bolton Wanderers**
League South Cup: **Chelsea**
Scottish Southern League: **Rangers**
Scot. North-East League (Autumn): **Dundee**
Scot. North-East League (Spring): **Aberdeen**
Scottish Southern League Cup: **Rangers**
Scot. North-East Autumn League Cup: **Aberdeen**
Scot. North-East Spring League Cup: **Aberdeen**
Scottish Summer Cup: **Partick Thistle**
Victory in Europe Cup: **Celtic**

SECOND WORLD WAR 1945-46

League North: **Sheffield United**
League South: **Birmingham City**
League 3 North (West): **Accrington Stanley**
League 3 North (East): **Rotherham United**
League 3 South (North): **QPR**
League 3 South (South): **Crystal Palace**
League 3 North Cup: **Rotherham United**
League 3 South Cup: **Bournemouth**
Scottish Southern League 'A': **Rangers**
Scottish Southern League 'B': **Dundee**
Scottish Victory Cup: **Rangers** . .
FA Cup: **Derby County**
Scottish Southern League Cup: **Aberdeen**

Wartime & Victory Football

Football League 1939: Most League clubs completed three fixtures before the League was abandoned in September 1939. For the record, Blackpool were leading the First Division with 6 points, Luton the Second, Accrington Division 3N and Reading Division 3S. With 5 games played Rangers led the Scottish Division 1 and Dundee the Scottish Division 2.

The Scottish League continued throughout the First World War. The Football League was contested in 1914–15. For records of that season see the tabular section of FOOTBALL LEAGUE.

Champions: The Football League was disrupted by the two world wars for as many as 11 seasons. In two of these seasons, there was an unofficial champion. At the end of the 1917–18 season, Lancashire Section champions Stoke played off against Midland Section champions Leeds City. Leeds won 2-0 at home, lost 1-0 at Stoke, and became League Champions on aggregate. In 1919 they were thrown out of the League for financial irregularities which occured during their wartime successes – when they were still only a Division 2 club.

In 1918–19 Midland Section winners Nottingham Forest could only draw with Lancashire Section winners Everton 0-0 at home, but then won 1-0 at Goodison to become League Champions. Forest had to wait nearly 60 years before their first ever official League Championship.

Few of the wartime tournaments were played to first-class standard and players could 'guest' for any club. Tommy Lawton, among others, occasionally played in two games on the same day for different clubs.

International appearances: England's Stanley Matthews recorded most, with 29. Tommy Walker appeared most times for Scotland (11), and Dai Pearson for Wales (15). Northern Ireland played only 3 wartime or victory internationals.

TOP: *Raich Carter charges Welsh keeper Sidlow during the wartime international in Cardiff on 6 May 1944.*
CENTRE: *Stanley Matthews played in more wartime and victory internationals than any other professional. Here he is tackled by Scotland left-back Jim Stephen in the game at Wembley on 19 February 1944.*
BOTTOM: *Matthews again, playing for the RAF against the Civil Defence on 6 March 1943 at 'a ground somewhere in England' according to the wary caption.*

193

Year	Winners		Runners-up		Year	Winners		Runners-up	
1878	Wrexham	1	Druids	0	1929	Connah's Quay	3	Cardiff City	0
1879	Newtown	1	Wrexham	0	1930	Cardiff City	0:4	Rhyl	0:2
1880	Druids	2	Ruthin	1	1931	Wrexham	7	Shrewsbury Town	0
1881	Druids	2	Newtown White Stars	0	1932	Swansea Town	1:2	Wrexham	1:0
1882	Druids	2	Northwich Victoria	1	1933	Chester	2	Wrexham	0
1883	Wrexham	1	Druids	0	1934	Bristol City	1:3	Tranmere Rovers	1:0
1884	Oswestry Town	3	Druids	0	1935	Tranmere Rovers	1	Chester	0
1885	Druids	2	Oswestry Town	0	1936	Crewe Alexandra	2	Chester	0
1886	Druids	5	Newtown	2	1937	Crewe Alexandra	1:3	Rhyl	1:1
1887	Chirk	4	Davenham	2	1938	Shrewsbury Town	2:2	Swansea Town	2:1
1888	Chirk	5	Newtown	0	1939	South Liverpool	2	Cardiff City	1
1889	Bangor	2	Northwich Victoria	1	1940	Wellington Town	4	Swansea Town	0
1890	Chirk	1	Wrexham	0	1941–46	*Not contested*			
1891	Shrewsbury Town	5	Wrexham	2	1947	Chester	0:5	Merthyr Tydfil	0:1
1892	Chirk	2	Westminster Rovers	1	1948	Lovells Athletic	3	Shrewsbury Town	0
1893	Wrexham	2	Chirk	1	1949	Merthyr Tydfil	2	Swansea Town	0
1894	Chirk	2	Westminster Rovers	0	1950	Swansea Town	4	Wrexham	1
1895	Newtown	3	Wrexham	2	1951	Merthyr Tydfil	1:3	Cardiff City	1:2
1896	Bangor	3	Wrexham	1	1952	Rhyl	4	Merthyr Tydfil	3
1897	Wrexham	2	Newtown	0	1953	Rhyl	2	Chester	1
1898	Druids	1:2	Wrexham	1:1	1954	Flint Town United	2	Chester	0
1899	Druids	2:1	Wrexham	2:0	1955	Barry Town	1:4	Chester	1:3
1900	Aberystwyth	3	Druids	0	1956	Cardiff City	3	Swansea Town	2
1901	Oswestry Town	1	Druids	0	1957	Wrexham	2	Swansea Town	1
1902	Wellington	1	Wrexham	0	1958	Wrexham	1:2	Chester	1:0
1903	Wrexham	8	Aberaman	0	1959	Cardiff City	2	Lovells Athletic	0
1904	Druids	3	Aberdare Athletic	2	1960	Wrexham	0:1	Cardiff City	0:0
1905	Wrexham	3	Aberdare Athletic	0	1961	Swansea Town	3	Bangor City	1
1906	Wellington	3	Whitchurch	2	1962†	Bangor City	*5	Wrexham	*4
1907	Oswestry	2	Whitchurch	0	1963	Borough United	*2	Newport County	*1
1908	Chester	3	Connah's Quay	1	1964†	Cardiff City	*5	Bangor City	*3
1909	Wrexham	1	Chester	0	1965†	Cardiff City	*8	Wrexham	*2
1910	Wrexham	2	Chester	1	1966†	Swansea Town	*5	Chester	*2
1911	Wrexham	6	Connah's Quay	1	1967	Cardiff City	*4	Wrexham	*3
1912	Cardiff City	0:3	Pontypridd	0:0	1968	Cardiff City	*6	Hereford United	*1
1913	Swansea Town	0:1	Pontypridd	0:0	1969	Cardiff City	*5	Swansea Town	*1
1914	Wrexham	1:1	Llanelli	1:0	1970	Cardiff City	*5	Chester	*0
1915	Wrexham	1:1	Swansea Town	1:0	1971	Cardiff City	*4	Wrexham	*1
1916–19	*Not contested*				1972	Wrexham	*3	Cardiff City	*2
1920	Cardiff City	2	Wrexham	1	1973	Cardiff City	*5	Bangor City	*1
1921	Wrexham	1:3	Pontypridd	1:1	1974	Cardiff City	*2	Stourbridge	*0
1922	Cardiff City	2	Ton Pentre	0	1975	Wrexham	*5	Cardiff City	*2
1923	Cardiff City	3	Aberdare Athletic	2	1976	Cardiff City	*6	Hereford United	*5
1924	Wrexham	2:1	Merthyr Town	2:0	1977	Shrewsbury Town	*4	Cardiff City	*2
1925	Wrexham	3	Flint	1	1978	Wrexham	*3	Bangor City	*1
1926	Ebbw Vale	3	Swansea Town	2	1979	Shrewsbury Town	*2	Wrexham	*1
1927	Cardiff City	2	Rhyl	0	1980	Newport County	*5	Shrewsbury Town	*1
1928	Cardiff City	2	Bangor	0	1981	Swansea City	*2	Hereford	*1
					1982	Swansea City	*2	Cardiff City	*1
					1983	Swansea City	*4	Wrexham	*1

*aggregate scores   †3 games required; home and away but not aggregate basis

Welsh Cup

Oldest clubs in Wales were founded around Wrexham in 1870. The oldest are Druids, who played in Plasmadoc Park, Ruabon. In 1875–76 Wrexham, Chirk and Oswestry (then regarded as a Welsh club – the town housed, for instance, the headquarters of the Cambrian Railway) were all formed.

Welsh FA: First meeting at Wynnstay Arms, Wrexham on Wednesday 2 February 1876 after G.A. Clay-Thomas had published a letter in 'The Field'. For a few days the association was known as the Cambrian FA.

First international: The only resolution passed by the embryonic association on 2 February 1876 was to play Scotland on Saturday 25 March 1876. The Welsh did so and lost, respectably, 4-0.

First Welsh Cup tie: Tuesday 30 October 1877 between Druids and Newtown (at Newtown). Druids won and went on to the final.

First Welsh Cup final: Saturday 30 March 1878 when Wrexham beat Druids 1-0. Their goal was scored by James Davies. They had to wait until February 1879 for their Cup and medals as the FA had no money.

Most Welsh Cup wins: 21 – Wrexham (up to 1 January 1984).

No Welsh involvement: In 1933–34 Bristol City beat Tranmere Rovers at Chester in a Welsh Cup final replay (after a 1-1 draw at Wrexham). Hence neither club, nor the ground, had any Welsh association. In fact, the trophy was not regained by a Welsh club until 1948.

Biggest attendance: 39,000 people saw the 1956 final at Ninian Park, when Cardiff City defeated Swansea Town 3-2.

Welsh League: Cardiff City Reserves hold the record for most points in a season with 72 in the southern section in 1922–23. That year also saw Llanelli awarded second place with 61 points though Swansea had 62, the reason being Llanelli had played one game less after Abertillery could not continue.

See also: INTERNATIONALS

RIGHT TOP: Newport County's Kevin Moore evades the attentions of a Shrewsbury defender during the home leg of the 1980 Welsh Cup final. Newport won 2-1 at home and 3-0 away for only their second honour – they had won Division 3S in 1938-39.

RIGHT CENTRE: Cardiff keeper Bobby Wilson saves during the first leg of the 1965 Welsh Cup final at Ninian Park. Cardiff beat Wrexham 5-1 but then lost 1-0 at the Racecourse. Under the odd system then in operation, the teams had to play-off – with Cardiff winning a third game 3-0.

RIGHT BOTTOM: The Welsh League split into North and South sections, with 5 separate divisions in all, during the 1920s, largely to save on travelling costs.

FAR RIGHT: The Western League is the major tournament in the West Country. In earlier years, however, even London clubs regularly competed. In 1903-04 Tottenham played their first team in both Southern and Western Leagues, winning the latter and coming second in the former. Portsmouth had won both competitions in 1901-02.

J.C. YOUNG

The Welsh National Football League.
(SOUTHERN SECTION).

Season 1923-24.

Handbook.

Price : 1/-.

R. GUY & SON, Printers, 56 Portmanmoor Road, Splott. CARDIFF: 1923

Wins

MOST IN A SEASON

Overall record: 35 – Rangers in Scottish Division 1 in 1920–21 (42 games).

English record: 33 – Doncaster Rovers in Division 3N in 1946–47 (42).

Division 1: 31 – Tottenham in 1960–61 (42).

Division 2: 32 – Tottenham in 1919–20 (42).

Division 3: 33 – Doncaster Rovers (*above*).

Division 4: 32 – Lincoln in 1975–76 (46).

Scottish non-Division 1/Premier: 33 – Morton in Division 2 in 1966–67 (38).

Percentage: Morton's record is the best if taken as a percentage of games played – they won 87% of their games in 1966–67 compared with Rangers' 83% in 1920–21. In a season of far fewer games, Rangers have achieved 100% (*below*).

Every game in a season: No team has ever won every first-class game they have contested in a season, but Rangers came closest in 1898–99 when they had a 100% record in the League (winning all 18 games) and won 4 Scottish Cup games in a row before losing their very last (and 23rd) game of the season, the Scottish Cup final, 2-0 to Celtic.

LEAST IN A SEASON

Overall record: 0 – Vale of Leven in the Scottish League in 1891–92. They played 18 games, of which they drew 5 and lost 13. This is the only occasion when a British first-class club has failed to record a single win in a League season.

One win only: Eight other Scottish clubs have obtained just one League win in a season:

Renton, 1893–94, Division 1 (18 games);
Abercorn, 1896–97, Division 1 (18);
Clyde, 1897–98, Division 1 (18);
Dundee, 1898–99, Division 1 (18);
Morton, 1901–02, Division 1 (18);
East Stirling, 1905–06, Division 2 (22);
Ayr United, 1966–67, Division 1 (34);
Forfar, 1974–75, Division 2 (38).

Forfar's performance is clearly the worst in recent years and is arguably worse than Vale of Leven's overall record. They achieved only 9 points. Only one English club has ever managed to record only 1 win in a League season – Loughborough Town, out of 34 games in Division 2 in 1899–1900.

English record: 1 – Loughborough (*above*).

Division 1: 3 – Stoke in 1889–90 (22 games), and Woolwich Arsenal in 1912–13 (38).

Division 2: 1 – Loughborough Town (*above*).

Division 3: 2 – Rochdale in 1973–74 (46 games). No club ever recorded so few Division 3 wins, even in the days of Division 3N and 3S. Rochdale themselves, in their record-breaking season (in every other sense) of 1931–32, managed to win 4 games. In 1973–74, however, they drew 17.

Division 4: 3 – Southport in 1976–77 (46).

Scottish Division 1/Premier: 0 – Vale of Leven (*above*). In recent times, the worst record was by Stirling Albion in 1954–55, with just 2 wins from 30 games.

Scottish non-Division 1/Premier: 1 – Forfar

Athletic (*above*).

At home: Five English clubs have managed just one home win in a season; Arsenal in 1912–13 (Division 1), Blackpool in 1966–67 (Division 1), Notts County in 1904–05 (Division 1), Loughborough in 1899–1900 (Division 2) and Rochdale in 1931–32 (Division 3N).

TROPHIES

If all six major trophies now available to English clubs are taken into account (FA Cup, Football League, Football League Cup, European Cup, European Cup Winners' Cup, UEFA Cup) then Liverpool have the best record over the years, having won 24 of these trophies since their foundation in 1892. The list of leading English trophy winners in all six competitions is as follows (up to 1 January 1984):

Liverpool 24, Aston Villa 18, Arsenal 14, Manchester United and Tottenham Hotspur 13, Newcastle United 11, Everton 10, Manchester City and Wolverhampton Wanderers 9, Blackburn Rovers and Sunderland 8, Nottingham Forest, Sheffield Wednesday and West Bromwich 7, Leeds United 6. In the three domestic trophies, Liverpool lead the way with 19 successes by 1 January 1984. In terms of *different* first-class competitions won, Nottingham Forest have more honours than any other with 8 – the League, the FA Cup, the League Cup, the European Cup, the European Super Cup, the Anglo-Scottish Cup, the Second Division and the Third Division South.

Youngest Players

APPEARANCES AND GOALS

Senior fixtures: Campbell Buchanan was still only 14 when he played for Wolves against WBA on Saturday 26 September 1942 in a Wartime League game. He later played in the Football League for Bournemouth and Norwich before retiring in 1961.

First-class fixture: As Buchanan's appearance cannot be regarded as a first-class game, the youngest player to appear in a first-class fixture might be said to be goalkeeper Ronnie Simpson, who appeared for Queen's Park against Kilmarnock in the Scottish Southern League Cup on Saturday 11 August 1945, three days before the end of the war. He was 14 years 304 days old. He was 15 years 310 days old when he appeared in his first Scottish League game, against Hibernian on Saturday 17 August 1946, and was still playing 25 years later. Remarkably, Simpson became the *oldest* player to make a Scottish international debut 22 years later, against England at Wembley on Saturday 15 April 1967, when he was aged 36 years 196 days. Scotland inflicted the first defeat on the hosts since they had won the World Cup. Simpson was Celtic's goalkeeper the following month

YOUTH FOOTBALL

FA YOUTH CHALLENGE CUP

Yr	Winners	Yr	Winners	Yr	Winners
1953	Manchester U.	1963	West Ham U.	1973	Ipswich T.
1954	Manchester U.	1964	Manchester U.	1974	Tottenham H.
1955	Manchester U.	1965	Everton	1975	Ipswich T.
1956	Manchester U.	1966	Arsenal	1976	WBA
1957	Manchester U.	1967	Sunderland	1977	Crystal Palace
1958	Wolves	1968	Burnley	1978	Crystal Palace
1959	Blackburn R.	1969	Sunderland	1979	Millwall
1960	Chelsea	1970	Tottenham H.	1980	Aston Villa
1961	Chelsea	1971	Arsenal	1981	West Ham
1962	Newcastle U.	1972	Aston Villa	1982	Watford
				1983	Norwich City

FA COUNTY YOUTH CHALLENGE CUP

Yr	Winners	Yr	Winners	Yr	Winners
1945	Staffordshire	1958	Staffordshire	1971	Lancashire
1946	Berks & Bucks	1959	Birmingham	1972	Middlesex
1947	Durham	1960	London	1973	Hertfordshire
1948	Essex	1961	Lancashire	1974	Nottinghamshire
1949	Liverpool	1962	Middlesex	1975	Durham
1950	Essex	1963	Durham	1976	Northamptonshire
1951	Middlesex	1964	Sheffield & H.	1977	Liverpool
1952	Sussex	1965	Northumberland	1978	Liverpool
1953	Sheffield & H.	1966	Leics & Rutland	1979	Hertfordshire
1954	Liverpool	1967	Northamptonshire	1980	Liverpool
1955	Bedfordshire	1968	North Riding	1981	Lancashire
1956	Middlesex	1969	Northumberland	1982	Devon
1957	Hampshire	1970	Hertfordshire	1983	London

FA SCHOOLS TROPHY

Yr	Winners	Yr	Winners	Yr	Winners
1905	London	1933	Sunderland	1959	*Brierley Hill, Sedgeley & T'tn
1906	Sheffield	1934	Manchester		*Doncaster
1907	West Ham	1935	Manchester	1960	Manchester
1908	Derby	1936	*Preston	1961	Barnsley
1909	Sheffield		*West Ham	1962	Stoke
1910	Sunderland	1937	Liverpool	1963	Stoke
1911	Chester-le-St.	1938	Manchester	1964	Erdington & S.
1912	West Ham	1939	Swansea	1965	*Leicester
1913	Watford	1940	*Not contested*		*Swansea
1914	Sheffield	1941	*Not contested*	1966	East London
1915	Carddiff	1942	*Not contested*	1967	Liverpool
1916	Bradford	1943	*Not contested*	1968	*Manchester
1917	West Ham	1944	*Not contested*		*Waltham Forest
1918	Liverpool	1945	*Not contested*	1969	Liverpool
1919	Grimsby	1946	Leicester	1970	Liverpool
1920	Reading	1947	Salford	1971	Huyton
1921	Liverpool	1948	*Leicester	1972	Chelmsford
1922	South London		*Stockport	1973	Liverpool
1923	Sheffield	1949	Barnsley	1974	Manchester
1924	North Staffs	1950	Swansea	1975	Barking
1925	Sheffield	1951	Liverpool	1976	Liverpool
1926	Grimsby	1952	Ilford	1977	South London
1927	E. N'berland	1953	Swansea	1978	Newham
1928	North Staffs	1954	Liverpool	1979	Bristol
1929	S. N'berland	1955	Swansea	1980	Gr. Manchester
1930	Newcastle	1956	Liverpool	1981	High Wycombe
1931	Islington	1957	*Barnsley	1982	Sheffield
1932	*Manchester		*Southampton	1983	*Middlesbrough
	*Southampton	1958	Bristol		*Sunderland
					*shared trophy

ABOVE LEFT: Paul Allen and goalscorer Trevor Brooking during the 1980 FA Cup final, which West Ham won 1–0. At 17 years and 245 days, Allen was the youngest player ever to appear in an FA Cup final.

LEFT: The Newcastle Schoolboys line up at White Hart Lane before their FA Schools Trophy semi-final against West Ham on Saturday 2 May 1914. West Ham won, but lost to Sheffield in the final. The Newcastle team appears to have mislaid one member; note also that the goalkeeper is wearing a different jersey as well as the traditional cap. Separate jerseys for keepers were only introduced in 1909. The English Schools FA also organises an annual County Schools knockout tournament, which should not be confused with the FA County Youth Challenge Cup.

when they become the first British club to win the European Cup.

English first-class club: Eamonn Collins was 14 years and 322 days old when he came on as substitute for Blackpool against Kilmarnock in an Anglo-Scottish Cup fixture on Tuesday 9 September 1980.

Football League: Albert Geldard was 15 years 158 days old when he played for Bradford P.A. against Millwall in Division 2 on Monday 16 September 1929. Ken Roberts was the same age to the day when he made his debut for Wrexham, against Bradford, in Division 3N on Saturday 1 September 1951.

League scorer: Ronnie Dix was 15 years 180 days old when he scored for Bristol Rovers against Norwich in Division 3S on Saturday 3 March 1928. He had made his debut a week earlier.

Scottish League: Sam McMillan of Ayr United was 15 years and 212 days when he played against Queen's Park on 14 March 1953 but he did not actually register as an Ayr player until 1955. The youngest *registered* player was Neil McNab of Morton, who played against Partick Thistle on 14 April 1973 aged 15 years and 314 days.

Cup final: Paul Allen was 17 years 245 days old when he appeared for West Ham against Arsenal on 10 May 1980.

100 goals: Jimmy Greaves was 20 years 261 days old when he scored his 100th League goal on Saturday 19 November 1960 for Chelsea against Manchester City at Stamford Bridge. Chelsea won 6-3.

Youngest sides: On Monday 4 April 1966, Port Vale played a side against Bradford City with an average age of under 18. Oddly, their manager, Stanley Matthews, was the oldest man ever to appear in Division 1 (*see* OLDEST PLAYERS).

ABOVE: Scotland keeper Ronnie Simpson saves on the line during his debut game at Wembley on 15 April 1967. He was then aged 36, the oldest Scottish debutant ever. Nearly 22 years before on 11 August 1945, aged 14 years 304 days, he had become the youngest player ever to appear in a fixture still recognised as first-class, for Queen's Park.
RIGHT: Denis Law, Scotland's second youngest, scores for Manchester United against Everton.

INTERNATIONALS

Overall: Norman Whiteside of Manchester United was just 17 years and 42 days when he appeared in his first international for Northern Ireland against Yugoslavia in Zaragoza on 17 June 1982. He was also the youngest player ever to appear in the World Cup finals. Another Irishman, Norman Kernaghan, of Belfast Celtic, was only 16 years 277 days when he played for the Irish League against the Football League on Wednesday 25 September 1935. He did not make a full international appearance, however, until he was 17 years and 80 days old. It is thought possible that W.K. Gibson of Cliftonville was younger than either when he appeared for Ireland against Wales on Saturday 24 February 1894.

England: Duncan Edwards was 18 years 183 days old when he appeared against Scotland on Saturday 2 April 1955.

Scotland: John Lambie was 17 years and 92 days old when he appeared against Ireland on 20 March 1886. Denis Law, who is usually quoted as Scotland's youngest, was in fact 18 years 236 days old when he appeared against Wales on Saturday 18 October 1958 but Law also scored on his debut.

Youth Football

Biggest win: The largest win in a single competitive youth game was in 1953, when Manchester United beat Nantwich Youth 23-0 in the FA Youth Challenge Cup.

Biggest reversal: In the 1958 final of the FA Youth Challenge Cup Chelsea beat Wolves 5-1 in the first leg and then lost the second 6-1 for Wolves to take the trophy.

Most successful: Over the years, the most successful youth teams have been Liverpool Schools, winning the English Schools Trophy 11 times, and Manchester United, winning the FA Youth Challenge Cup 6 times.

TOP RIGHT: Aged just 17 years and 42 days, Norman Whiteside of Manchester United and Northern Ireland became the youngest player ever to appear in the finals of the World Cup and the youngest ever to appear in a full international for one of the home countries. The game was against Yugoslavia in Zaragoza in the 1982 World Cup and Whiteside (left) is seen being closed down by the Yugoslav number 4, Velmid Zajec. The game ended 0-0. Whiteside was not the youngest international ever, however, for Pele had made his debut for Brazil when four months younger.

CENTRE RIGHT: It was a record breaking spell for Whiteside. On 26 March 1983 he scored in the Milk Cup final against Liverpool and is seen being congratulated. Then, on 26 May (BOTTOM RIGHT) he scored in the FA Cup final replay against Brighton. He therefore became the only player ever to score in both major domestic English finals in the same season.

Index